HARDCORE
VISUAL BASIC®

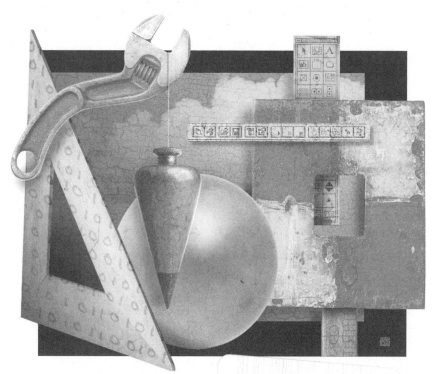

BRUCE MCKINNEY

PUBLISHED BY
Microsoft Press
A Division of Microsoft Corporation
One Microsoft Way
Redmond, Washington 98052-6399

Library of Congress Cataloging-in-Publication Data
McKinney, Bruce, 1953–
    Hardcore Visual BASIC / Bruce McKinney.
        p.   cm.
    Includes index.
    ISBN 1-55615-667-7
    1. Microsoft Visual Basic.   2. BASIC (Computer program language)
    I. Title.
    QA76.73.B3M398   1995
    005.265--dc20   95-38791
                                                                   CIP

Printed and bound in the United States of America.

1 2 3 4 5 6 7 8 9   MLML   0 9 8 7 6 5

Distributed to the book trade in Canada by Macmillan of Canada, a division of Canada Publishing
Corporation.

A CIP catalogue record for this book is available from the British Library.

Microsoft Press books are available through booksellers and distributors worldwide. For further
information about international editions, contact your local Microsoft Corporation office. Or contact
Microsoft Press International directly at fax (206) 936-7329.

Acquisitions Editor: Eric Stroo
Project Editor: Mary Renaud
Technical Editor: Dail Magee Jr.

To J. Laufer, whoever he or she is.

The first manual I ever wrote for Microsoft (Macro Assembler 3.1416, if you must know) went out with a postage-paid feedback card requesting a rating for the manual's usability, completeness, and readability. On the overall scale of 5 for excellent and 1 for poor, Laufer checked all the 1 boxes and drew an arrow to the bottom of the page, where the following words (toned down a little) were scrawled in unmistakable outrage: "Examples!!!!! Damn it."

OK, J. Laufer. You got 'em.

C ONTENTS

FOREWORD

It's late on a workday evening when the phone rings. The name *BruceM* on my phone's LCD display, combined with his latest posting on the internal Visual Basic users' e-mail alias, implies an upcoming 45-minute discussion about a deficiency in the latest beta version of Visual Basic 4. I suppress the fleeting temptation to let the call ring through. Too often the warts, holes, and bugs Bruce finds as he delves through the code while researching his book must be fixed—and the sooner the changes are made, the better. I lean back and pick up: "Hi, Bruce. Let me guess...." Within Microsoft, Bruce McKinney is one of the main advocates for advanced users of Visual Basic—and certainly the most persistent. Every product needs an internal critic, and Visual Basic is lucky to have Bruce as its dedicated gadfly.

Career paths at Microsoft weave a fractal tapestry of relationships with attractors that, if not truly strange, are at least somewhat odd. One recurring pattern seems to be that past work on Microsoft FORTRAN predisposes one toward a later association with Visual Basic. Bruce McKinney and I first met when he became the FORTRAN run-time developer while I was the support lead. His strong opinions about what constituted usable development tools were immediately apparent, and he drove forward the implementation of many long-requested run-time features. Bruce writes code that does things; and when the tools he uses don't allow him to do what he wants, he fixes them.

One obvious thread joining FORTRAN and Visual Basic is that the architecture of both is designed to avoid the direct use of pointers. This results in some distinct limitations with respect to the C-centric design of operating systems, among other things. Both languages thus tend to attract the type of people who see these restrictions as a challenge—an underdesigned overpass disguised as a roadblock. There is a strange thrill in discovering that, despite all documentation to the contrary, you really *can* find a way to implement some proscribed functionality; it's both the satisfaction of getting a task done and the glee of defying all the rules to do it. The book you have in hand is inspired by this iconoclastic intolerance for barriers and by a distinctive philosophy of software design that accepts no bounds. The code, tricks, and tips herein are a result of many hours of research into the new features presented by Visual Basic 4.

As a program manager of Visual Basic, I should address some implicit questions: "Well, why should anything be difficult to implement using Visual Basic? Why shouldn't you be able to do anything you want?" Most how-to customer service calls regarding Visual Basic don't focus on being unable to create recursive data structures in the absence of pointers or on other language-specific limitations, but instead are related to the inability to access all operating-system functionality in a transparent manner. Visual Basic is specifically designed to abstract out the low-level details of creating an application for Windows; this implies encapsulating specific functionality into higher-level constructs. Since the goal of encapsulation is organization, and successful organization sometimes requires simplification, we must often make decisions about what functionality is or is not interesting and important enough to support—otherwise, we'd end up with a confusing, overdetermined implementation. That the benefits of simplification hugely outweigh the imposed limitations is indicated by the enormous success of Visual Basic as a development tool for Windows.

Alongside Visual Basic's built-in functionality, advanced users have always had the vast majority of Windows APIs at their disposal. This has allowed a two-tier approach: core Visual Basic functionality, supplemented by direct access to the operating-system interfaces. Very large, sophisticated applications have been successfully developed and deployed with only these two tiers. This strategy comes up short, however, in its inability to provide function pointers that can register Visual Basic procedures as callback functions; its lack of generic Windows message handling; its inability to dereference function pointers for the API calls so implemented; and its lack of support for direct pointer dereferencing, which restricts dealing with C structures that contain nested pointers.

The historical design perspective has been that if key functionality is to be exposed, it should be exposed as a built-in, encapsulated feature that all Visual Basic customers can benefit from—a better option than exposing unprocessed facets of the base operating system that only a more restricted set of experts can use. The most common proposal for reaching this third tier of difficulty is to use C/C++ in combination with Visual Basic, rather than turning Visual Basic into a limited edition of C. This book offers a useful alternative approach: a core set of utilities combined with sufficient information to allow the advanced user to achieve just about any functionality desired.

Visual Basic 4 transports the philosophy of facilitating and simplifying the creation of Windows-based programs into the heart of new operating-system territory: OLE Automation. Visual Basic has evolved from a rapid application-development environment, strong on quick user-interface creation, to become the fastest way to create a fully functional database application and now to become a premier tool for creating OLE Automation servers and clients. To perform this feat, we redesigned Visual Basic itself from the ground up to consume and use OLE Automation for all its own communication with its components, most notably the Visual Basic for Applications language engine, the Jet and Data Access Objects database engine, and OLE custom controls. During the development of Visual Basic 4, Microsoft completed two major 32-bit operating systems, Windows 95 and Windows NT 3.51. Visual Basic raised the quality bar on the OLE and OLE Automation support in these releases through its extreme exercise of the technology. C++ OLE Automation developers now turn to Visual Basic as an object prototyper or a client test engine development tool.

An interesting thing occurred as a result of supporting OLE Automation: the Visual Basic language made a major paradigm shift to object support. This came about because of a confluence of necessities: Visual Basic needed to become more object-oriented, and it needed to support OLE Automation more completely. The result is that Visual Basic 4 classes create objects that are always OLE Automation objects, eliminating the distinction found in C++ between generic class objects and OLE objects. With the simple switch of a property, an internal class model can provide OLE components for public consumption. Bruce analyzes the potential and the implications of this implementation throughout this book as he puts Visual Basic objects to practical use. He also includes tools that make it easier to create object code, and he offers valuable observations on object coding styles and pitfalls.

This book is part advanced user manual, part utility toolkit, and part personal exploration of the joys and frustrations of coding with Visual Basic. Bruce has no shortage of opinions, based on his years of software development using a wide variety of tools. That's just as well. All information that presumes to impart knowledge passes through a prism of opinion. And for technical information, I find that an overt opinion is always preferable; it frees you from the task of reading between the lines and expedites the process of sharpening your own personal perspective. I'm sure that advanced Visual Basic developers will find this book not only useful but interesting and provocative as well.

John Norwood
Program Manager
Visual Basic Product Group

ACKNOWLEDGMENTS

I feel like an Oscar winner. Of course, nobody's given me any awards, but I still get an opportunity to drop a few names, make a political statement, credit my kids and pets, and reminisce about old times. So let's start at the top.

Hi, Mom. Hi, Dad. Hi, Chuck and Kandace.

To the people who put up with me when I was writing this book, or when I was learning how to write it: Thanks, Rhonda. Thanks, Sarah. Thanks, Sam. Thanks, Peggy.

I've had some writing mentors. Thanks to Linda Jaech and Stewart Konzen for hiring me when I had little or no qualifications—at least not on paper. Thanks to Bill Johnston for making me a journalist, albeit a bad one. And thanks to Strunk and White.

As for programming mentors, I'd have to go back to Cleon White, the best teacher I ever had. Mr. White crammed as much math as possible into my stubborn head until my junior year, when I decided to become a famous writer instead of an engineer. I'm sorry, Mr. White; every day, I'm sorry.

Then there's Rich Gillman, who believed I was a programmer when hardly anyone else did, and Gene Apperson, who actually uttered the words falsely attributed later in this book to Joe Hacker: "It doesn't matter how fast your code is if it doesn't work." Thanks to José Oglesby who kept pushing me when I wanted to give up on FORTRAN. On second thought... No, let it stand. Thanks to my two favorite programming authors, Steve Maguire and Michael Abrash.

I want to dedicate the Basic part of this book (all the rest of it) to everyone on a certain e-mail alias whose name I've been asked not to mention. Microsoft maintains this internal alias for discussion of Visual Basic issues. Most people on the alias are Microsoft employees, many of them working on Microsoft internal tools. Some work for other companies but are on Microsoft e-mail because of contract work or other connections. On this alias, questions come from everyone, but answers tend to come from the same people. Some of the regulars are experts because they wrote parts of Visual Basic or its manuals. Others became experts in the same way you will be an expert if you get the spirit of this book—because they wouldn't take no for an answer.

To name a few and mention some of their contributions: Adam Overton; Antonio Maraglino; Benjamin Bourderon (splitter bars); Bob Guy (killing modules); Bruce Ramsey; Bryce Ferguson (help with splitter bars); Chris St. Valentine; Curt Carpenter; David McCauley; Dennis Quinn; Ed Staffin (Basic guru and author of Message Blaster); Eric Ledoux; Francis Gan; Fred Freeland; Gary Lemmon; Geoff Bauman; Hai Nguyen; Hubert Daubmeier; Jeff Webb; Jim Cash (module suggestions and lots more); Jim Collins (saved my bits by identifying key bugs); Joe Kennebec; John Schwabacher; Josh Kaplan; Karl Garand (fade); Keith Pleas (lots of cool tricks); Kenneth Lassesen (lots of ideas and a few good arguments); Lewis Chapman (saved me from nonrandom shuffling); Mark Buettemeier; Nick Baker; Patrick Dengler; Randall Kern; Rhy Mednick; Rob Purser; Robert Scheffler; Roman Lutz (screen capture); Ron West; Rutherford Le Blang; Scott Butler; Scott Ferguson (help going back to before Visual Basic); Sonja Al-Kass; Stephen Weatherford (identified a critical bug in Notify); Steve Anonsen; Steve Glenner (Is Nothing); Steve Hayr; Steven Mitchell; Ted Keith; Tim Brown; Troy Strain; Vernon Lee; Wayne Radinsky (subclassing help, but for naught); and Wayne Torman.

On the Visual Basic team, several people put up with my "negative attitude" and helped me understand the strengths and limitations of object-oriented programming in Basic. Thanks especially to Craig Symonds of the Visual Basic for Applications team and John Norwood and Joe Robison of the Visual Basic team. Matt Curland, graphics and OLE wizard extraordinaire, is responsible for many of the hardest of the hardcore techniques in this book. Thanks also to Arman Gharib; Betty Chin (configuration expert); Brent Aliverti (help with toolbar buttons, bitmaps, and icons); Brian Lewis (p-code and memory allocation); Chris Dias; Dirk Haworth (add-ins); Doug Franklin (type-library expert); Glenn Hackney (object and OLE server guru); my old buddy John Burke (error handling); Lauren Feaux; Mark Roberts (collections); Michael Bond (UDTs ByVal); Peter Golde (add-ins, DoEvents, and initialization sequence); Philippe Nicolle (icons); Prashant Ramanathan (settings); Steven Lees (LastDllError); Tim Patterson (bytes and VarPtr); and Todd Apley.

Francis Hogle of the Windows 95 team helped me understand the true faith of shell programming. I apologize for departing from it to do what you have to do in Visual Basic. I also learned a lot from *Programming the Windows 95 User Interface*, by Nancy Winnick Cluts (Microsoft Press, 1995). I was fortunate to be able to borrow code from this book before it was published.

At Microsoft Press, thanks to my editor, Mary Renaud, for protecting me from myself. It wasn't as painful as I feared. Often she left work even later than I did. Thanks to Dail Magee Jr., my technical editor, and to Eric Stroo, my boss during most of the project and acquisitions editor during the rest of it. Thank you, Jim Fuchs, for setup and for being around to chat about techie stuff even though it seldom had anything do with Basic. Thanks to Peggy McCauley for stir-fry and other ideas. Marc Young, thanks for the pig tail. And thanks to many others: artists David Holter and Michael Victor; proofreaders Jennifer Harris, Sally Anderson, Lisa Theobald, and Stephanie Marr; typesetting and production experts Barb Runyan, Jim Kramer, David Mighell, and especially Sybil Ihrig of VersaTech Associates and Tara Fort of Aardvark Word Processing; editor Janna Hecker Clark; and indexer Lynn Armstrong.

And thanks to all you imaginary end-users in Swinen and Cathistan for the opportunity to serve you, however indirectly.

INTRODUCTION

If you study your 10 favorite Windows-based applications as models for your own programs, you'll probably come up with a wish list: "I want one of those. That's nice, but I want mine to be a little different. What if I combined one of these and one of those and then added something else?" But when you try to figure out how to implement these features with Visual Basic, you sometimes come up short.

Microsoft Visual Basic makes it easy to write 90 percent of your application, but when you reach that last 10 percent, it seems to be fighting you every step of the way. There's no way to do a seemingly simple task like modifying the Control menu. The language provides little support for sorting, searching, or parsing. Simple animation takes up hours of research and experimentation, with marginal results.

Let's face it. Visual Basic is a language with limits. Eventually you'll want to do something that Visual Basic won't do, or you'll want to do something fast that Visual Basic does slowly. You can understand why a language this easy has to make some compromises in flexibility and power—but you don't want to accept it. There must be a way.

Visual Basic Without Limits

Hardcore Visual Basic is a book for people who like Basic but don't like limits. It's for people who won't take no for an answer. If you're willing to go the extra mile for better performance and more functionality, you'll have fun with this book.

Beyond the Windows API Limits

Back in the old days before Microsoft Windows, there was MS-DOS. It was easy to start programming under MS-DOS, especially with Basic. You could go a long way without really understanding what you were doing. But if you wanted to program without limits, you had to learn about low memory, ports, and MS-DOS and BIOS interrupts. Visual Basic is the same way, but more so. If you're serious, you have to get under the hood.

In Windows programming, getting under the hood means learning about messages, windows, processes, and all the other elements of the Windows application programming interface (API). Unfortunately for Basic programmers, you have to learn most of this stuff in another language—C. It was different in the MS-DOS days. You could do almost anything in Basic, and if you did need to use another language, you could pick the one you wanted. Many Basic programmers chose assembler, not C.

OLE object technology complicates matters further. Although it's possible to write OLE code in C, sane programmers use C++. Visual Basic programmers who know just enough C to get by might be in for a rude surprise. A little C isn't enough to enable you to write the OLE controls and OLE servers that are required for serious enhancement of Visual Basic version 4. Despite the big differences between the two, I generally use the term *C* as a code word for both C and C++ when I talk about those other languages.

This book tries to minimize the C (and C++) requirements. A lot of you chose Visual Basic specifically because you didn't know C, didn't like C, or didn't like the C Windows SDK programming model (or its C++ MFC cousin). Therefore, C and its relatives are optional here. You don't need a C compiler, although this book and its companion CD-ROM contain some C code. All the tools written in C are also provided as DLLs or executables so that you can use them as is. One premise of this book is that, using the tools provided, you can do anything in Visual Basic. Well, almost anything. But that doesn't mean you can do everything fast. Visual Basic runs p-code, not the executable code you can produce with C. There's no way around that.

Beyond the Object Limits

Visual Basic has finally become an object-oriented language, although nobody understands exactly what that means. No one had ever written object-oriented code in Basic before Visual Basic 4 entered its beta stages. Documenters didn't understand it. Developers didn't understand it. I certainly didn't understand it. Object-oriented Basic was an adventure. Still is.

Object-oriented code in this book goes far beyond anything you'll see in Visual Basic manuals, but it doesn't even approach the limits. I learned how to program Visual Basic classes largely by experimenting, based on my knowledge of other object-oriented languages. After playing with this for almost a year, I still keep running across neat tricks and falling into unexpected traps.

Just as it took several years for programmers to explore the limits of Visual Basic version 1, it will take some time before people really start to appreciate the wonders of object-oriented Basic. *Hardcore Visual Basic* gives object-oriented pioneers a head start.

Beyond the Basic Limits

If you don't mind using C++ (or C, or Pascal, or even FORTRAN), you can combine the best of both worlds. You can use Visual Basic for what it does best—creating user interfaces quickly, using the most efficient development and debugging environment available. You can use C for the meat of your program, the parts where no sacrifice of performance or functionality is acceptable, no matter what the cost. You will pay a price in programming time and ease of debugging for the parts you write in C, just as you pay a performance penalty for the parts you write in Basic. But you'll be able to get full-function programs up and running faster than developers who limit themselves to one language.

Unfortunately, you'll need a different book to learn how to do this. I plan to write that book when I get done with this one. Look for it soon from Microsoft Press. In the meantime, the companion CD provides some hints of what you can do.

What This Book Is About

Hardcore Visual Basic is targeted at intermediate and advanced programmers who use Visual Basic Professional Edition version 4 to develop applications for Microsoft Windows 3.1, Microsoft Windows NT, and Microsoft Windows 95. That's the short mission. In fact, the book may prove useful to others as well.

The most important new feature of Visual Basic version 4 is that it's a different language—Visual Basic for Applications. VBA was introduced in 1993 in Microsoft Excel and Microsoft Project, was added to Microsoft Access in 1994, and will eventually appear in many other Microsoft applications. Visual Basic is now just another client of Visual Basic for Applications (although a very important one), in the same way that Microsoft Excel and Project are clients. The language engine is technically separate from the environment. You can see this in the separate entries for Visual Basic and Visual Basic for Applications in the Object Browser.

What does this difference mean to you? It means that if you know Visual Basic, you know Visual Basic for Applications and, to a lesser extent, vice versa. The version of Visual Basic for Applications found in Visual Basic is the same one that will appear in Microsoft Access for Windows 95. Therefore, you can use almost all the Visual Basic for Applications techniques shown in this book (but not the Visual Basic techniques) without change in Access. But which techniques are for which? Only the Shadow knows. You'll have to experiment. I haven't tested the code under Access, but most of it should work. The internal objects—App, Screen, Printer, and Debug—are specific to Visual Basic and aren't guaranteed to work in other Visual Basic for Applications environments. The controls provided with Visual Basic are general controls that should work in any VBA application, even if they aren't shipped with that application.

At publication time, the version of Visual Basic for Applications that is used by Microsoft Excel and Project is not the same as the version used by Visual Basic and Access. General code (not spreadsheet-oriented or project-oriented) written for the older versions should work fine under Visual Basic, but Visual Basic code might not work in older VBA applications. For example, Microsoft Excel and Project don't support controls. Also at publication time, Microsoft Word for Windows used WordBasic rather than Visual Basic for Applications. This language is similar to but incompatible with Visual Basic for Applications. During the lifetime of this book, versions of Microsoft Word, Excel, Project, and possibly other Microsoft applications will be released with the current (or later) versions of Visual Basic for Applications. When that happens, the code in this book will be applicable to those environments.

Although I've written *Hardcore Visual Basic* primarily for users of Visual Basic Professional Edition, owners of two other Visual Basic products can also use the book. The first, Visual Basic Standard Edition, is a 32-bit product designed specifically for the Windows 95 operating system. Most of my code is written for dual environments, using conditional compilation (a new feature of Visual Basic) to make code work in either a 16-bit or a 32-bit environment. All that is wasted if you use the standard edition because it limits you to 32-bit mode. You'll also get less Windows API documentation and fewer controls. I didn't test with the standard edition, so you'll have to work out any problems for yourself. The second product, Visual Basic Enterprise Edition, is a more expensive client/server superset of Visual Basic. Everything I say about Visual Basic should also apply to this new product, but the enterprise edition has many additional features that I don't discuss.

Visual Basic version 4 contains major changes from earlier versions, and this book pushes them to the limit. Some of the code, however, was developed under Visual Basic 3 before the first beta versions of Visual Basic 4 became available. (Many of the Windows API techniques described here would work even under version 1.) The signature for Visual Basic 4 modules differs from that used in earlier versions, so you won't be able to use the code on the companion CD without modification, but you can copy it into old modules. Why would you want to continue using Visual Basic version 3? Because it's the cheapest Basic still targeted specifically at Windows 3.1. If your clients don't need 32-bit programs, you might want to keep it around. But sifting through and converting my code from version 4 to version 3 will be your problem.

You'll need access to current Windows API documentation to take full advantage of this book. That's no problem for most Visual Basic users because the CDs for Visual Basic Professional and Enterprise Editions include the Microsoft

Developer Network/Visual Basic starter kit. The MSDN/VB starter kit has all the 16-bit and 32-bit Windows API information you need and more. It's intended to be a teaser for the complete Microsoft Developer Network Development Library CD, and it may indeed persuade you to buy the full product. But it also contains information that is critical for hardcore Basic programmers. You won't get far in this book without the starter kit or equivalent Windows API documentation. The MSDN/VB starter kit doesn't come with Visual Basic Standard Edition or with the disk version of the professional edition. If you have one of these or Visual Basic for Applications, you'll need to find separate Windows API documentation.

Microsoft's Windows API documentation, whether in help files or in books, is oriented toward the C language. Figuring out how to use C documentation for Basic programming is one of the topics of this book, but you might want additional help. I'm a great admirer of Daniel Appleman's _Visual Basic Programmer's Guide to the Windows API_ (Ziff-Davis Press, 1993). Perhaps he (or someone else) will do a Win32 version soon.

I wrote _Hardcore Visual Basic_ using several different operating environments. In the early stages, I used Microsoft Windows for Workgroups as my main environment, occasionally booting under Windows NT (although some of the low-level operations don't work well in the 16-bit emulation layer of Windows NT). When beta versions of Visual Basic 4 became available, I started using Windows NT on my primary machine and Windows for Workgroups on my secondary machine. When I obtained beta versions of Windows 95, I switched my secondary machine to that operating system. I still had to boot into Windows for Workgroups occasionally to make sure that all the new features still worked there.

I probably spent more time developing in 32-bit mode under Windows NT than in other environments, but I gave the code a workout under Windows 95 late in the project. Using multiple environments is a difficult business, and if there are bugs in my code (incredible as it may seem), that's the area where I'd expect to find them.

One more point: this book assumes knowledge of Visual Basic 4 features—classes, collections, properties, optional arguments, OLE servers, add-ins...the list goes on. Version 4 is a major update, and you'll see a lot of new features (starting with the one everyone has been begging for since version 1 rolled off the assembly line—a line continuation character). I'm going to be talking about these features as if you already know the basics. If you buy my book immediately after version 4 is released, you might feel a little lost. But you can read the product documentation and the online help to get up to speed. Just because something is new doesn't mean that it's hardcore.

What This Book Is Not About

What is this book *not* about? Hard to say, exactly. It's about advanced programming techniques, but lots of advanced topics aren't mentioned. It's about professional programming, but again, that's a wide topic whose surface we will barely scratch. It's about taking advantage of new features in Visual Basic 4, but a lot of the code would work just fine in version 1.

Here are some specific topics that *Hardcore Visual Basic* won't cover:

- Database programming. Programming databases is a very hot topic, and somebody should definitely write a book about it. (Some people already have.) This isn't such a book. A chapter or two on databases wouldn't be enough, and, besides, I'm not qualified.

- Controls. There are tricks aplenty to using complex controls such as grids. I touch on list boxes and text boxes, but only to demonstrate general principles that you can apply to more complex controls. Documenting controls is the business of control vendors, and, in any case, there are too many controls to cover here.

- MDI forms and menus. I must confess to an irrational dislike of the MDI interface. I like my programs to be single document with lots of buttons and no menus. I don't defend this prejudice, but neither do I think that MDI and menus are really advanced topics that should be included here. Read the product documentation.

- Help authoring and the Setup Toolkit. These are worthy topics, and, in some cases, advanced topics—but for the most part they are not programming topics and therefore are not in this book.

- APIs to the max. I'd love to spend a few months writing code for MAPI or WINSOCK or multimedia. Networks and telephony sound really interesting, and I wish that I had time for enhanced graphics APIs such as WinG, OpenGL, or WinToon. These are all great topics—for other books.

- Project management, interface design, team programming, testing, feedback evaluation, system analysis, caffeine procurement, sponge basketball, and most of the other elements that make up successful software development. This book is about code only. My user interfaces are nothing to write home about. My programs are small and manageable. I wrote and designed them myself without having to coordinate with others. In other words, my job as a software developer isn't quite as real as yours. (My other job as an author is just as real as anybody's, with its own version of deadline hell.) Nevertheless, I did have time to explore some programming problems that you might have put off until "real soon now." Being a hardcore code jockey isn't all there is to software development, but it is worth something.

The Companion CD-ROM

Hardcore Visual Basic offers many specific examples at various levels of difficulty. Most programmers will find something of value to plug into their own programs, perhaps with minor modifications. But code that you can use is a side benefit. The real goal is to give you the confidence to do anything you want with Visual Basic.

The code you see in the book is the tip of an iceberg. For every line shown, probably 10 more appear on the CD. It's true that some of the sample code on the CD isn't very interesting. You already know how to fill list boxes, open files, and respond to button clicks. But you'll also find a lot of hardcore code that wasn't quite interesting enough to get into the book.

In addition, the companion CD contains several non-Basic tools that you can use from Basic:

- The Windows API type library replaces most of your Windows Declare and Const statements with simpler, more efficient alternatives.

- The VBUTIL dynamic-link library contains the functions Basic forgot.

I wrote these tools, and I'm responsible for them. They're required for most of the samples in the book. In addition, I include two utilities from other authors. These are provided as a courtesy; take 'em or leave 'em, as is. I endorse them, but you'll have to talk to the authors for support. These utilities are used in the book but aren't essential to it.

- Message Blaster is a shareware utility for capturing Windows messages. Many Basic programmers are familiar with the 16-bit VBX version. The 32-bit OLE control version has a few new tricks up its sleeve. (I discuss Message Blaster in Chapter 5.) The version supplied will work for you, but it won't work for your customers. You'll have to purchase the full version from WareWithAll, Inc.

- The callback server is another utility for capturing Windows messages and handling Windows callbacks (also discussed in Chapter 5). This one is free, and it has the same warranty you get on most free software—none. The author, Matt Curland, would probably be interested in your problem reports, but no guarantees.

You might find a few other non-Basic goodies on the CD as well.

The Windows API Type Library

I wish I could tell you that the Windows API type library will eliminate the need to ever write another Declare statement. Chapter 2 explains why this worthy goal can be approached but not quite reached. We'll talk more about type libraries, especially in Chapters 2 and 10. Basically, they provide an efficient alternative to Declare and Const statements. The Object Browser shows the standard type libraries Visual Basic provides to connect your code with Basic DLLs and controls. The Windows API type library connects your code to Windows system DLLs in the same way. Table A is a brief summary of what you'll find in the library.

Module	Description
Kernel and KernelConst	Functions and constants from the kernel library
User and UserConst	Functions and constants from the user (window management) library
GDI and GDIConst	Functions and constants from the Graphics Device Interface library
WinBase and WinBaseConst	Base functions and constants from the 32-bit kernel library
Multimedia	Functions and constants from the multimedia library
WinMessage	Message constants and SendMessage function aliases
Shell	Constants and messages from the shell library
CommonControl	Functions for common controls such as ImageList
OleAuto	OLE type conversion functions
Registry	Registry functions and constants
Network	Network functions and constants
ErrorConst	Win32 API error constants
CommonConst	Control characters and other useful constants

Table A. *Summary of the Windows API type library.*

The last module, CommonConst, needs a little more explanation. When I first discovered type libraries, while working with the Visual Basic beta, I defined my own character constants for the constants that Basic won't let you define. The most useful lives in my type library as *sCrLf*—a carriage return/linefeed combination. You'll see it used frequently throughout this book. But Visual Basic offers *vbCrLf*. Why not use the one provided instead of defining my own? Actually, the question should be posed the other way: Why are they using my constants?

I became so attached to my constants that I decided all Basic programmers should be entitled to the same, whether they bought my book or not. So I entered a bug report (suggestions at Microsoft are sent on the same form as bugs) requesting that similar constants be added to Visual Basic. At the end of the report, I gave the type-library source code implementing my constants. You can see similar code in WIN.ODL. Type-library constants aren't difficult to implement, but I sent my suggestion so late in the beta cycle that I didn't really expect to see it accepted for Visual Basic 4. But it was, as you can see if you check the Constants module in the VBA section of the Object Browser.

Adding a feature, even a simple one, is not a simple matter in a product as large as Visual Basic. By the time the constants were added and documented, my book was pretty far along, and changing every *sCrLf* in every sample to *vbCrLf* didn't seem like a good use of my time. Besides, I had added some new constants Visual Basic didn't have. So I kept using my own. You must load my type library specifically in order to use my constants, whereas theirs are always loaded by default. Table B presents a side-by-side list of their constants and mine, along with some similar constants you might easily confuse.

Theirs	Mine	Description
vbNullChar	sNullChr	Null character, Chr$(0)
—	sEmpty	Empty string ("")
vbEmpty	—	Uninitialized variant
Empty	—	Uninitialized variant (slower when used as an empty string)
vbNull	—	Variant with no valid data
vbNullString	sNullStr	Null pointer with String type (pass to API functions)
—	pNull	Null pointer with Long type (pass to API functions)
—	hNull	Null (0) handle
vbCrLf	sCrLf	Carriage return/linefeed combination
—	sCrLfCrLf	Two of them
vbCr	sCr	Carriage return
vbLf	sLf	Linefeed
—	sBell	Bell character (ASCII 7)
vbTab	sTab	Tab character (ASCII 9)
vbVerticalTab	sVerticalTab	Vertical tab (ASCII 11)
vbFormFeed	sFormFeed	Formfeed character (ASCII 12)
vbBack	sBack	Backspace character (ASCII 8)
—	cMaxPath	Maximum length of a file path
—	cMaxName	Maximum length of a filename
—	sQuote1	Single quote
—	sQuote2	Double quote

Table B. *Common constants.*

The VBUTIL Library

Basic sports a very flexible and powerful library, but like most language libraries, it has a few annoying limitations. The VBUTIL library fills a few holes I just couldn't tolerate. Here's a summary of the general functions available for both 16-bit and 32-bit modes:

GetFullPath	Converts relative paths to full paths, and breaks full paths into their parts
SearchDirs	Searches directory lists (such as the PATH environment variable)
GetTempDir, GetTempFile	Creates temporary files in a temporary directory
ExistFile	Checks for the existence of a file
Interrupt	Calls system interrupts (16-bit only)
LoByte, HiByte, and friends	Extracts Bytes from Words, and Words from DWords
MakeWord, MakeDWord	Compresses Bytes into Words, and Words into DWords
LShiftWord and friends	Shifts bits left or right

The library also contains 16-bit emulations of useful functions available only in the 32-bit kernel library:

GetDiskFreeSpace	Gets the size and free space of a disk drive
GetDriveType	Gets the type of a disk drive (floppy, hard, network, and so on)
GetLogicalDrives	Determines what drives are available
GetTempPath, GetTempPathName	Creates temporary files in a temporary directory (wrapped by GetTempDir and GetTempFile)
GetFullPathName	Gets the full path of a file (wrapped by GetFullPath)
SearchPath	Searches a directory path for a file (wrapped by SearchDirs)
FlushFileBuffers	Flushes the contents of a system file handle to disk
GetLastError, SetLastError	Gets or sets error codes

You'll find more details on the VBUTIL functions in Chapter 3.

Sample Programs

Table C summarizes the sample programs provided on the companion CD and indicates the chapters in which the programs are discussed.

Project	Chapter(s)	Description
TimeIt	1	Time It tests various performance problems throughout the book. You can add your own problems.
BugWiz	1 and 9	Debug Wizard maintains Assert and Profile procedures and illustrates polymorphism with the CBugFilter class.
AllAbout	1 and 9	All About illustrates an About box with all the trimmings (including a hidden animation command) and also gets system information.
RegTlb	2	This program registers a type library.
PropShop	1 and 8	The Property Shop is a wizard that creates property procedures and pastes them in your code windows.
WinWatch	5 and 7	WinWatch tells you everything you ever wanted to know about all your windows.
KillMod	5	This 16-bit program kills unwanted DLLs (the shortest useful program ever).
FunNGame	6	Fun 'n Games demonstrates various drawing and painting techniques.
BitBlast	6	Bit Blast illustrates blitting with PaintPicture, BitBlt, and StretchBlt.
Edward	8	Edward the editor demonstrates ways to write modular code, including turning a text box into an editor.
Edwina	8 and 11	Edward the editor's more sophisticated cousin.
RunMenu	9	This program runs the menus of other programs.
SieveSrv	10	The Sieve Server sample serves prime numbers on an OLE platter.
SieveCli	10	The Sieve Client takes prime numbers from various OLE servers including the Sieve Server.
BTools	10	This sample add-in gives the Visual Basic IDE new commands.
Columbus	11	A Windows 95 Explorer that never reaches his destination.
AppPath	11	AppPath makes programs available from any directory under Windows 95.
Browse	11	Browse Picture Files uses a file notification server to update views of icons, bitmaps, cursors, and metafiles (32-bit only).
T programs	All	These short test programs illustrate specific techniques.

Table C. *Hardcore sample program summary.*

More important than the samples themselves are the modules containing code shared by many samples. This code is ready to plop into your programs. Some of the modules are interrelated, so you might have to include several of them. Table D lists the modules.

Module	Description
Utility	The granddaddy module used in every sample; contains all the generic helper functions that didn't fit anywhere else
Debug	Debugging and profile procedures that disappear from your EXEs (used by Utility and most other modules)
Better, Better32	Improved versions of Visual Basic procedures
Bytes	Tools for accessing byte arrays (blobs)
WinTool	Tools for manipulating windows
WinType	User-defined types used by WinTool, GDITool, and others
InstTool	Tools for manipulating instances and processes
ExeType	Tools for determining the target environment of an executable file
GDITool	Tools for graphics
MenuTool	Tools for manipulating menus
PicTool	Tools for manipulating Picture objects
ComCtl	Tools for manipulating ImageList controls and other common controls (32-bit only)
ComDlg	Common dialog tools (without the CommonDialog control)
FindFile	Tools for finding files or directories
Sort	Tools for sorting, searching, and shuffling
AdInTool	Tools for add-ins
Cards	Declare statements for the CARDS library used in games for Windows
Parse	Tools for parsing strings
Registry	Tools for manipulating the Registry
Settings	Tools for making windows, forms, and controls persistent
FileInfo	Tools for getting Windows 95 shell information on files (32-bit only)

Table D. *Hardcore functional modules.*

Last but not least, you can reuse some of my classes and forms in your programs. Some classes actually represent collections or controls. In many cases, the object-oriented way is better than the functional way of wrapping related groups of functions. Table E lists the classes and forms.

Module	Type	Description
Drive	Class	CDrive represents a single disk drive.
Drives	Collection	NDrives is a collection of all the drives on the system.
Stack	Collection	CStack is a first-in, last-out data storage mechanism.
Window	Class	CWindow represents a window.
GetColor	Control	CGetColor represents a picture box containing a color palette.
GetColor	Form	FGetColor represents a form dialog containing a color palette.
KeyState	Class	CKeystate represents the keyboard.
MenuItem	Class	CMenuItem represents a menu item.
MenuList	Class	CMenuList represents all the items on a menu (including other menus).
PicGlass	Class	CPictureGlass creates a movable, transparent bitmap (an icon).
Editor	Control	CEditor turns a TextBox or RichTextBox control into an editor.
Search	Form	FSearch creates Find and Replace dialog boxes.
OpenPic	Form	FOpenPicture creates an Open dialog box that previews pictures (icons, bitmaps, cursors, and metafiles).
Point, Rect	Classes	CPoint and CRect represent points and rectangles (alternatives to TPoint and TRect types).
Sieve	Class	CSieve returns all the prime numbers up to a given maximum.
SListBox	Control	CSortedListBox represents a ListBox control sorted in an order specified by properties.
System	Class object	The System object (the only instance of CSystem) provides all the information known about the host computer.
Version	Class	CVersion represents the version information of an executable file.
Video	Class	CVideo represents all the information known about the video system.
About	Form	FAbout creates an About dialog box.
BugFilt	Class	CBugFilter is "inherited" from the imaginary virtual CFilter class.

Table E. *Hardcore object-oriented modules.* *(continued)*

Table E. *continued*

Module	Type	Description
SortHelp	Class	CSortHelp provides swap and compare methods for polymorphic sorting.
FileInfo	Class	CFileInfo provides Windows 95 document information about a file or a special folder (32-bit only).
VSplit, HSplit	Controls	CVSplit and CHSplit represent two controls joined by a vertical splitter bar.
TrayIcon	Class	CTrayIcon lets you put your own status icons on the Taskbar (Windows 95 only).
✓ Notify	OLE Server	CFileNotify sends file change notifications to clients (Win32 only).
ShareStr	Class	CSharedString represents a shared memory location through a memory-mapped file (Win32 only).

Don't Take It Too Seriously

This book has been an endless project, following the Visual Basic beta cycle through many unexpected turns and switchbacks. Hard disks have crashed. Deadlines have been missed. Operating systems have appeared. Lies have been told. Files have been trashed. Love has been lost. Mail has flamed. Tools have failed. Networks have crawled. Pockets have been picked. Midnight oil has burned. Hair has fallen out or turned purple. Managers have departed. Bugs have entered bug-free programs with absolutely no programmer assistance. The original Chapter 10 has disappeared into the ozone.

Despite all that, I'm not complaining. You'll see a few flames and criticisms about limitations of the language later in the book, but make no mistake: Visual Basic version 4 is an amazing product, with many radical innovations inside a framework of compatibility. Its shortcomings result from trying to accomplish too much in one update. Basic has always been fun, but this version offers a lot of new toys, and I had a good time playing with them. No other language gives the instant gratification you get from Visual Basic. I think you'll be entertained and enlightened. I was.

1

The Spirit of Basic

Every computer language has its own feel, its own atmosphere, its own spirit. You can't really define this spirit, but you know what it is when you see it. I think of Basic as the antithesis of a statement attributed to Albert Einstein:

Make things as simple as possible—but no simpler.

Had that quote been written by the original designers of Basic, John Kemeny and Thomas Kurtz, it would have been simplified further:

Make things simpler than possible.

That is the contradiction hardcore Visual Basic programmers live with. We want things to be simple, elegant, and intuitive—but they aren't. We want our programs to model reality—but they don't. We want our language to work the way we think, not the way computers or operating systems want us to think—but we're not willing to pay the price.

The nebulous Spirit of Basic exists only in our minds. Real implementations of Basic, including Microsoft Visual Basic, have to compromise. Sacrilege keeps creeping in. There's an inherent conflict between the desire to keep it simple and the desire to do what needs to be done, whatever the cost. I use the term *un-Basic* to describe these compromises, whether they are built into the language or built into our code.

This book tries to maintain the Spirit of Basic, against all odds. Sometimes it's tough. First, the book deals at length with the Microsoft Windows API, which was written in C and is permeated with the Spirit of C. Second, the book's philosophy is to accept no limits, although Visual Basic has built-in limits that can be overcome only with great effort. Third, Basic is slowly becoming an object-oriented language, but it remains to be seen how well objects can be realized in the Spirit of Basic. We won't know the full answer until the next major revision of Visual Basic, although version 4 makes a good opening argument.

Despite the inclusion of techniques that can only be described as un-Basic, this book is not about how to write C in Basic. I'll try to keep things Basic and to wrap un-Basic code in wrapper routines so that you can use it without constantly thinking about the heresies involved.

Language Purification

Basic is an old language—developed in 1964—and it still carries a lot of baggage from the past. During its 30 years, Basic picked up a lot of bad habits, which it has only recently begun to shed. Over the years, Microsoft has played a large role in both the good and the bad developments in Basic.

If you'd like to know the history of the language you're programming in, try to find a copy of the book *Back to BASIC: The History, Corruption, and Future of the Language* (Addison-Wesley, 1985), by Basic inventors Kemeny and Kurtz. The book is largely a diatribe against unnamed "Street Basics" that poisoned the language with line numbers, unnecessary data types, and Gotos. The book mentions no names, but anyone who programmed in the 1980s knows that Microsoft's GW-BASIC and IBM's version of the same program, called BASICA, are the worst of the Street Basics being attacked. As a self-taught programmer who wrote his first programs with GW-BASIC, I can confirm that these were indeed wretched languages, richly deserving all the opprobrium piled on them by defenders of the true faith.

Back to BASIC was also propaganda for True BASIC, a compiler designed to restore Basic as a structured language. By the time it hit the streets, however, True BASIC was too late. QuickBASIC from Microsoft and Turbo BASIC from Borland were already attempting to undo the damage caused by GW-BASIC. In fact, Microsoft had started the atonement earlier with both interpreted and compiled versions of MacBASIC. True BASIC was destined to lose the battle, but in a larger sense it won the war. Visual Basic has become almost as structured as C, almost as flexible as Pascal, almost as good for scientific work as FORTRAN, better for business work than COBOL, more powerful for manipulating data than Xbase, and, in a few more iterations, it might even become as object-oriented as Smalltalk and as good at list processing as LISP.

Because Visual Basic ran in the Microsoft Windows environment and had a completely new programming model, it didn't need to be compatible with earlier Basics. It was a time for purification. For example, you won't find the following abominations in the Visual Basic documentation: PEEK, POKE, DEF SEG, CALL ABSOLUTE, DEF FN, BLOAD, BSAVE, FRE, SADD, VARPTR, and VARSEG—not to mention debugging statements such as the infamous TRON (which inspired a movie) and TROFF. Nevertheless, some language purists are still not satisfied.

Here is my personal list of features that you should cross out of your Basic language reference. If Microsoft won't clean up the language, you should do it on your own. You don't have to agree with my version of Basic (although you'll need to get used to it for the duration of this book), but I hope that it will get you started defining your own subset of the language.

While/Wend

There's nothing terribly wrong with the While/Wend looping structure of Basic, other than the ugliness of the pseudoword Wend. But why waste your coding energy on a vague feature when Basic offers a clear, concise one? The Do Loop control structure of Basic is a thing of elegance compared to the crude looping of C and Pascal. You can test at the beginning or at the end for true or false conditions in a natural, English-like way. Perpetual loops can be coded clearly instead of requiring an ugly hack such as Pascal's *While (True)* or C's *for (;;)*. The Exit Loop statement allows you to escape a loop cleanly. I hate to see beautiful code ruined with While/Wend, even though I admit that this is an aesthetic preference with no connection to efficiency or correctness.

Gosub/Return

Gosub was useful in the bad old days when all variables were global and Select Case didn't exist. But why Gosub, Return, and On Gosub remain in Visual Basic is beyond me. Perhaps they were left in for compatibility of some kind, although I find it hard to imagine a procedure using these statements that one could port from an earlier Basic.

I've heard it argued that it's more efficient to use Gosub and Return than to use subs and functions. Well, yes, but technically you could write all your code using only If, Then, and Goto—that would be more efficient still, if you ever got it debugged. If Gosub is what it takes to write efficient code in Basic, I'll take C. Fortunately, it's not.

Goto

You're probably expecting an anti-Goto diatribe, but I don't mind Goto at all. It has its uses, primarily with error traps. Because error handling is inherently unstructured, an unstructured feature like Goto fits right in. If you use Goto for any other purpose, however, chances are you're writing bad code. The C version of goto actually makes some code easier to read as well as more efficient, but that's because C's switch statement is less powerful than Basic's Select Case. Old versions of Pascal needed Goto because they lacked Basic's complete syntax for early exit from loops and procedures. Basic provides the tools for structured programming.

Nevertheless, a procedure containing Goto is hidden in at least one example in this book. I'm so ashamed of myself for not devising a clearer way to write this code that I'm not going to point it out. A free bucket of bits to the first person who finds it and tells me how I should have written the procedure.

The Continue Statement That Isn't

Basic does have one small hole in its structured looping: unlike C, it has no Continue statement. You can get out of a loop early with Exit For or Exit Do, but you can't skip to the next iteration. Here's an example:

```
Do While fFun
    If fUncommon Then
        DoUncommon
    Else
        DoCommon
        AndSoOnFor20Lines
    End If
Loop
```

This code violates one of the principles of structured code: indent the exceptions, not the rules. If you want to get out of the loop on the uncommon condition, you can use Exit Do, but you don't have a Basic statement to continue the loop. What you want is this:

```
Do While fFun
    If fUncommon Then
        DoCommon
        Continue Do  ' Or maybe call it Next Do
    End If
    DoCommon
    AndSoOnFor20Lines
Loop
```

You can fake the nonexistent Continue Do and Continue For statements if you use Goto:

```
Do While fFun
    If fUncommon Then
        DoCommon
        Goto ContinueDo
    End If
    DoCommon
    AndSoOnFor20Lines
ContinueDo:
Loop
```

Let

According to Kemeny and Kurtz, omitting Let on any assignment is a sign of bad programming practice, and only Street Basics allow such horrible habits. The reason: Let distinguishes use of the equal sign (=) for assignment from its use for tests of equality. It's true that Basic is the only popular modern language that overloads the equal sign to mean both assignment and equality. C uses = for assignment and == for equality. Pascal uses the symbol := for assignment and = for equality. In FORTRAN, = means assignment, and .EQ. means equality.

If you think about it, *Let a = 1* is technically accurate. It also allows compilers to optimize more efficiently. In other words, this pedantic nonsense makes perfect sense. Fortunately, Microsoft didn't buy this argument, and neither should you.

Rem

I used to think that no one had actually used Rem for comments since 1985. Recently, however, I encountered a long piece of complex Basic code that looked strangely like an MS-DOS batch file. All the comments were preceded by Rem. Please don't do this. Basic is probably the only computer language ever invented that has a keyword to initiate comments. If everyone pretends that Rem doesn't exist, maybe Microsoft will remove it in the next version.

Option Base and Zero-Based Arrays

Programmers start counting at 0. The rest of the world starts counting at 1. Kemeny and Kurtz tell the story of how they dealt with this difference of opinion. Originally, the first dimension of a Basic array was 1 because that's how normal people count and Basic was designed for normal people. But Basic also needed to work for mathematicians, who usually think of matrices as starting at 0, so Basic changed to start the first element at 0.

This wasn't so great either. Common sense tells you that in the statement *Dim ai(10)*, the array *ai* contains 10 elements—but in fact it contains 11. That might be OK in C, where common sense is not a high priority, but it rubs Basic programmers the wrong way. So the Option Base statement was added, which lets you specify whether you want your arrays to make sense (start at 1) or be mathematically correct (start at 0).

Of course, as Pascal programmers knew all along, 1 and 0 aren't the only places you might want to start counting. Kemeny and Kurtz finally figured this out and changed Basic to let you specify the starting and ending points of arrays:

```
Dim ai(1 To 10) As Integer
Dim ad(0 To 49) As Double
Dim as(-10 To 10) As String
```

Kemeny and Kurtz didn't add this modification to Basic until 1979. ANSI Basic didn't get it until 1983. Microsoft Basic got it several years later. And I didn't figure it out until I started writing this book. But now I'm a convert. I always use To when declaring arrays. There's nothing wrong with zero-based arrays, but you should declare the starting point specifically:

```
Dim asTitle(0 To 29) As String
```

Consider the extra five keystrokes cheap insurance against off-by-one errors.

Of course, that technique doesn't save you from needing to know that the default starting point is 0 in Basic-created arrays such as the controls array.

> **WARNING** If you buy my argument about always using To in array definitions, you must also stop making assumptions about the use of array elements. In other words, you can't assume that *aBears(0)* is the first bear in the array. An alternative rule used by many programmers is to completely avoid both To and Option Base 1. That's OK with me (although you won't see it in this book). Just be sure that you don't mix the two approaches.

For Next Loops

Basic lets you do the following:

```
For x = 1 To 10
    For y = 1 To 10
        For z = 1 To 10
            ' Do something
Next x, y, z
```

Don't do it. Type out each Next at the appropriate indent level. Some programmers always put the variable name after Next. In fact, many programmers do this with comments even in languages that don't support it, and they do it for all ending statements, not only Next. For example:

```
End Function ' GetStuff
End Sub ' DoStuff
End Select ' iChoice
Loop ' Do While x
End If ' I < 10
End With ' oftFirst
```

I salute this careful coding style, and I wish that I had the self-discipline to follow it myself.

For Ever

Everyone knows how a For loop works. Well, maybe. Consider this loop:

```
For i = 1 To Len(s)
    ' Do something with characters of string s
Next
```

This For loop is a shortcut for a Do loop like the following:

```
i = 1
Do While i <= Len(s)
    ' Do something with characters of string s
    i = i + 1
Loop
```

The comparison is not exact, however. What if the statements in the loop change the length of the string *s* by deleting or adding characters? In fact, something very different is happening. In the Do loop, the length of the string is checked every time through; in the For loop, it's checked only once. So the Do loop equivalent of the For loop is actually this:

```
i = 1
iTemp = Len(s)
Do While i <= iTemp
    ' Do something with characters of string s
    i = i + 1
Loop
```

There are two morals to this story:

- To write efficient Do loops, try to keep While and Until tests simple. Don't test the length of a string every time through the loop if you know that the length won't change. Consider reorganizing simple Do loops into For loops.

- If you're changing what's being tested inside the loop, consider changing a For loop to a Do loop. Another trick that sometimes works is to process a For loop backward, changing only items that have already been counted. The following loop, which removes selected items from a list box, works as written, but it would fail if you counted forward, because deleting items changes the list count and the current item:

```
For i = lstData.ListCount - 1 To 0 Step -1
    If lstData.Selected(i) Then lstData.RemoveItem i
Next
```

Data Types

Basic started as a language with only two data types: numbers and strings. It might seem as though the language has come a long way, to user-defined types, forms, and classes in the current version, but you could make a case that Basic has actually gone the other way, becoming a language with only one type—which essentially means a typeless language. To state it more accurately, Basic has become a language with two modes: typed and typeless.

As you'll see in Chapter 4, typeless mode (using Variant for all variables) is increasingly important. New features such as optional arguments, parameter arrays, and collections work only in typeless mode, and that throws some confusion into what I'm about to propose. Nevertheless, full steam ahead.

Visual Basic allows a variety of programming styles for handling variable declarations (or the lack of same). No other language offers such flexibility. In Pascal or C, you declare the type of each variable at the top of the procedure, and that's that. In Basic, you don't need to declare any variables except arrays, but if you choose you can make Basic as strict about variable declarations as Pascal. Let's look back at the history of Basic to understand where this confusion came from.

A Short History of Basic Types

Kemeny and Kurtz designed Basic with numbers and strings as its two data types. A variable was always a number unless it ended with a dollar sign, in which case it was a string. A number was actually a floating-point number, although users didn't need to know this. There was no such thing as an integer. Kemeny and Kurtz claimed that this was a feature. For example, in comparing Basic to Pascal, their book *Back to BASIC* had this to say:

> Incidentally, Pascal requires that the user know about two kinds of numbers—integer and real. Reals are used for general computation, while integers must be used in for-loops and as array subscripts. Pascal thus permanently burdens the user with matters that are temporary peculiarities of the ways computers do arithmetic. (page 96)

Is the difference between integers and floating-point numbers simply a relic of computer technology? I think not. In any case, performance was obviously not a priority. Developers of Basic compilers and interpreters never bought this line. The compilers and particularly the interpreters castigated by Kemeny and Kurtz as "Street Basic" added types for integers, long integers, and various sizes of real numbers. User-defined types and fixed-length strings crept into the language. Basic acquired the types of Pascal without the discipline of enforced data declarations. You could simply add a type-declaration character ($, &, %, !, #, or @) to a variable to specify its type. Or you could use the DEF statement (borrowed from a similar feature in FORTRAN) to specify that variables with a certain initial character would have a particular type.

Then Microsoft shook things up again, returning to the roots of Basic with the introduction of the Variant type, which can contain any native type. You need only this one type; the computer, not the programmer, chooses which type goes into a variant. You pay a price for this convenience (refer to the "Performance" sidebar on page 42), but in many cases it's worth the cost. Variants contain not only the variable data but also information about the variable. This enables Basic to do automatic type conversion and lets you do your own type checking. Variants can also include special values such as Null, Nothing, Empty, and Error. I'll be talking about variants and the trade-offs involved in using them throughout this book.

The introduction of Option Explicit in Visual Basic 2 was another milestone in the history of Basic data types. By setting Option Explicit, you force yourself to declare every variable, just as you do in Pascal. This feature prevents one of the most common and annoying Basic bugs, the misspelling error. If you misspell the name of a variable, Basic creates a new variable with the new spelling and the default data type (formerly Single, now Variant). You think that you're assigning a value to or calculating with the original variable, but you're actually using the new one. You don't need to hit this bug very often to decide that declaring every variable is not too high a price to pay to avoid it.

Dollar Signs in Basic Functions

Visual Basic is moving away from type-declaration characters. Version 4 offers two new simple types—Byte and Boolean—but it does not provide a type-declaration character for either of them. Nor does it provide type-declaration characters for complex types such as Object, Form, Control, and Variant. There just aren't enough characters to go around.

Despite this trend, the dollar-sign character for strings still rules in one important context. Basic functions that return strings come in two styles: naked and dressed to kill. The naked version of Mid takes a variant argument and returns a variant. The dressed-up version (Mid$) takes a string argument and returns a string. Basic manuals no longer note this difference, but it exists just the same. (The Time It program described later in this chapter demonstrates the surprisingly big difference between calling Mid and Mid$ in different contexts.)

I really don't like the looks of those dollar signs. I'd much rather use the naked version. But I'm not willing to take a major speed hit for cosmetic reasons. Therefore, you'll see the dressed-up version in samples that use strings (common) and the naked version in samples that use variants (rare).

Choosing a Data Style

In deciding your personal style for handling variables, you need to consider several factors:

- Do you want to declare a specific type for every variable? Or do you want to use default types?

- Do you want the convenience (and the risk) of automatic variable allocations? Or are you willing to declare every variable in order to make your code more reliable?

- How do you feel about Basic shortcuts such as the DefInt statement or the type-declaration characters?

Let's look at several popular data declaration styles.

Joseph

He's been programming in Basic since the first IBM PC rolled off the assembly line. Back in the days of BASICA, he learned to start all programs with *DefInt A-Z*. He still does. Most of his variables are integers, and he can simply make them up and use them on the fly. Same with strings and real numbers, except that he has to add $, !, and other type-declaration characters. Joseph never declares simple variables before use. He thinks that Dim is for arrays. It annoys him to have to use Dim for user-defined types, but he's gotten used to that as just one more Basic anomaly. He finds it particularly useful to make up variables in the Debug window.

Joseph is a disciplined coder with a complicated naming convention for variables. He doesn't run into the misspelled-variable problem very often, and when he does, he has enough experience to track down the problem quickly. Joseph writes so much good code so quickly that many of the younger programmers try to imitate his style. Somehow it doesn't work as well for them. They spend a lot of time debugging.

Susan

She came to Visual Basic from C. She thought that Basic was a toy language, and she wasn't happy about being assigned to work with it. She still makes disparaging comments about Basic's lack of pointers and its other limitations. Nevertheless, although she hates to admit it, she's hooked. She gets more work done in Visual Basic than she ever imagined doing in C. But old habits die hard.

She programs in Basic as if it were C. She always uses Option Explicit and declares every variable with an explicit data type. She never uses Variant. Susan thinks that type-declaration characters are an abomination and uses them only when absolutely necessary in constants. She doesn't even know that DefInt is a legal statement.

Karin

She got hooked on programming while writing Lotus 1-2-3 macros. Later she added WordBasic macros to her repertoire. From there it was an easy step to Visual Basic for Applications in the latest version of Microsoft Excel. Recently someone told her that if she knew Visual Basic for Applications, she automatically knew Visual Basic 4. She tried it; she likes it.

Karin is writing a front-end application that puts a friendly interface on Microsoft Word for Windows, Microsoft Excel, and Visio. Most of the Excel samples use Variant, so she acquired that habit. She declares every variable with Dim, but she doesn't give a data type, relying on the default Variant type. Last week she spent two late nights debugging a program that was getting random values in one of the variables. As it turned out, she had misspelled a variable name. Karin was surprised that Basic would let her do that. One of her colleagues explained Option Explicit. The whole idea sounded kind of weird, but she hasn't had any trouble since she started using it.

Her colleague is trying to persuade her to use Integers rather than Variants as loop counters. She understands the concept, but it seems like a lot of trouble, and she doubts it would make a noticeable difference in her programs.

Bruce

He's writing a book about Visual Basic. He wants to use a consistent coding style throughout the book and to recommend this style to others without being dogmatic. He's written code in Basic, FORTRAN, Pascal, C, and C++. He liked them all (except FORTRAN) and wishes he had a language that combined the best of each.

One of his first programs with the old GW-BASIC was an accounting program. After several weeks of work and hundreds of lines of code, the accounts didn't balance because he had created all the variables with the default Single data type instead of Integer. In the spirit of Kemeny and Kurtz, he hadn't known the difference. He's been leery of default data types ever since.

He uses Option Explicit religiously and declares every variable with Dim and an explicit data type. He likes Variants and uses them for variables that will need a lot of data conversions. But he has a great deal of experience with coding in assembly language, and he hates to write code that is less than optimally efficient, even when he knows the extra efficiency isn't critical. Therefore, he uses specific simple data types whenever he can.

From Pascal and C programming, Bruce learned the habit of declaring all variables at the top of the block. But when he discovered that C++ allows you to declare variables wherever you first need them, he was an instant convert and adapted his Basic style accordingly. Unlike most Basic coders, he puts Dim statements next to the first use and when possible initializes the variable on the next line. One of his pet peeves about Basic is that it doesn't allow him to combine the Dim and the initialization statements, but he fakes it the best he can.

Bruce is tempted by the convenience of type-declaration characters, but he's decided not to use them because they're available only for some types but not for others. Besides, they're ugly. He thinks that the Def*type* statement is a ridiculous feature, but he uses it reluctantly for reasons described in Chapter 2.

Visibility and Lifetime of Variables

Every language has rules for defining the visibility and the lifetime of variables and procedures. Basic is no exception, although unfortunately the rules seem to change with each version. Throughout the twisted history of the language, attempts to add new features without breaking old ones have created a mess. The Basic landscape is dotted with abandoned scope and visibility modifiers such as Shared, Common, and now Global. In the current version, even the best intentions have not made matters any clearer. Consider the following.

The Dim keyword (the least mnemonic name in the language) creates a variable with local visibility and temporary lifetime when used within a procedure (except that the lifetime is permanent if the procedure is declared to be static), but when used outside a procedure, Dim creates a variable with private visibility and permanent lifetime (despite the fact that lifetime is meaningless in a standard module, although it is important in a class or form module). Private and Public are declarators for variables, but they are modifiers for constants, declarations, types, and procedures.

If you can understand that and if you always use Dim correctly, you don't need this book. For the rest of us, it might help to create a myth and pretend to believe it. Here are the "commandments" that are embodied in my Basic data myth:

- The word *Dim* actually means *Local* in the native tongue of the Basic ethnic group of northeastern Cathistan. Therefore, you should use Dim only for local variables. Basic might pretend to let you use Dim in other contexts, but your code will be haunted by evil spirits.

- Use Static for local variables with permanent lifetime. Never declare functions static because doing so changes the meaning of Dim and causes warts.

- Use Private for variables with module visibility. Resist the temptation to use Dim in this context even though it might seem to work for a time.

- Use Public for variables with global visibility. In the distant past (one version ago, according to some sources), Global meant public. Some corrupters of the true faith claim that it still works as a form of homage to the evil god Compatibility. Ignore this rumor.

- Always declare dynamic (resizable) arrays with empty parentheses and the proper variable keyword. (See the four previous commandments.) The claim that Redim can be used on local variables without a prior declaration leads to madness.

- Always specify Public or Private for user-defined types and Declare statements. Basic will enforce this for class and form modules, but it provides a default for standard modules, although you will never remember it. Some experts believe that you should also follow this rule for constants and procedures, although I have used the defaults and lived to tell the tale.

For those literal-minded readers who want facts rather than opinions, Table 1-1 lists the default visibility for the various elements you can declare in your programs.

	Standard Module	Form and Class Modules
Constants	Default private	Default private
	Private OK	Private OK
	Public OK	Public illegal
User-defined types	Default public	Default illegal
	Private OK	Private required
	Public OK	Public illegal
Declare statements	Default public	Default illegal
	Private OK	Private required
	Public OK	Public illegal
Variables	Default private*	Default private*
	Private OK	Private OK
	Public OK	Public creates property
Functions and subs	Default public	Default creates method
	Private OK	Private OK
	Public OK	Public creates method
Properties	Default public	Default public
	Private OK	Private OK
	Public OK	Public OK

*Default means declaring with Dim rather than with Public or Private.

Table 1-1. *Public and private defaults.*

Watch Your Types

One of the most dangerous errors in Visual Basic occurs when you try to put several declarations on one line. For example:

```
Dim c, i, h As Integer
```

You believe that you've defined three integers, but you haven't. Instead, you have two variants (the default type for the first two) and one specifically declared integer. Here's another variation:

```
Dim c As Integer, i, h
```

Pascal programmers might be more likely to write the first line, whereas C programmers might tend to write the second. In either case, the problem is particularly dangerous because the code will work correctly 90 percent of the time, although perhaps not efficiently.

I've made a similar error in Declare statements, thinking that because I put ByVal with the first parameter I didn't need it with the second:

```
Declare Sub Line Lib "MyDll" (ByVal x As Integer, y As Integer)
```

Some programmers avoid this problem by declaring every variable on a separate line:

```
Dim c As Integer
Dim i As Integer
Dim h As Long
```

That's a little too extreme for me, but I salute the intention.

Naming Conventions

The most important thing about a naming convention is that you should have one. If you name each variable according to the whim of the moment, you'll not only end up with strange names that you won't remember later, but you'll also spend your mental energy dreaming up clever variable names instead of clever algorithms. A naming convention should be automatic. Two people using the same convention should come up with the same variable names a high percentage of the time. That might be unrealistic in practice, but it's a worthy goal.

In reading working code and programming books over the years, I've seen a lot of styles, many of them well thought out and helpful to the development process. I've also seen bad variable names make some good code hard to read.

Frequently, however, wretched naming conventions go hand in hand with wretched code. And one of the most wretched conventions is offered to you free by the Visual Basic environment.

When the environment offers default names such as Form1, Control2, and Text3, just say no! I first encountered this bizarre behavior when I was invited to participate in a usability test of Visual Basic 1 several months before its release. For my first button, Visual Basic helpfully provided the caption Command1 and the variable name *Command1*. I didn't understand the difference. How could anyone imagine that I would ever want a button with the caption Command1? And the idea that I would want a variable named *Command1* seemed only slightly less ridiculous.

I still find the default variable names mildly annoying and wish that Visual Basic had options to always leave the Caption, Text, and Name properties blank. I'd like a pop-up dialog box where I can enter a name as soon as I create a new form or control. Now when I insert a control, I immediately set the Caption (or Text) property and then give the control a reasonable name. It's tempting to leave the default name on static labels that will never be accessed by name, but I resist even that. Instead, I put my static labels in a control array. This saves a little memory, and if I copy and paste an existing label, Basic automatically names it and adds it to the array.

FLAME

In writing this book, I read a lot of Basic code from many programmers. I'm tempted to publicly curse all those who post code (including large programs) to the public domain using the write-only naming convention provided by Visual Basic. Folks, it is *very* difficult to interpret your code. But I suspect that my curse is unnecessary. If you haven't already paid the price, you will when you try to go back and modify your own code a year from now. The convenience of whipping out code this way is not worth the pain of trying to maintain it.

Basic Hungarian

Hungarian works for me. No doubt you've seen this convention used sometimes, sort of, in some code contained in Visual Basic samples and documentation. I don't claim that this convention is better than other naming conventions or that it doesn't have problems. But I've used Hungarian in various languages (including, believe it or not, FORTRAN), and it applies well to Visual Basic.

I'm not trying to evangelize Hungarian. Everyone I know who uses it (including me) hated it at first. It just grows on you. Maybe it will grow on you enough to make you a convert during the course of this book—or maybe it won't. In any case, being able to read Hungarian is a skill you won't regret acquiring. If you haven't really understood the point of the snippets of Hungarian code you have seen in various Microsoft manuals, here's a brief introduction that will make reading the sample code easier.

Long-time Microsoft developer Charles Simonyi, who happens to be Hungarian by birth, developed the convention. That—along with the fact that C code written in this style looks like foreign gibberish to the uninitiated—prompted the name. The idea (simplified to a point that would probably horrify Simonyi) is that variables should consist of two parts: a lowercase base type indicating the kind of variable, and an initial-cap qualifier that distinguishes this variable from others of the same kind.

For example, an integer that keeps track of the file position would have the base type *i* and the qualifier *Pos* to form the variable *iPos*. If you must keep track of both a file position and a line position in the same context, you need to qualify further: *iFilePos* and *iLinePos*. If you were creating a Project Save As dialog box, you might call it FProjectSaveAs and fill it with controls such as cboFiles, cbo-Dirs, lstFileTypes, lstDrives, cmdOk, cmdCancel, and cmdNetwork. If you had an array of buttons to activate different windows, the base type *cmd* wouldn't be enough, so you could modify it with the array prefix *a*, as in *acmdWindow*. To access this array, you might need a count variable showing the number of windows, *cWindow*, and an index to the current window, *iWindowCur*. In a small function using only one local index variable, you don't need a qualifier—just call it *i*.

This doesn't begin to touch on the complexity of the original Hungarian convention. In addition, the whole idea has been bastardized. At least three incompatible official dialects of Hungarian are used at Microsoft, with many smaller variations used by different departments and individuals and with different programming languages. Unfortunately, the crudest of these is the one used in the Windows Software Development Kit and now spreading confusion to the world. In a few short years, the Hungarian coding convention has evolved as much as natural languages evolve in a thousand years.

Compare, for example, the naming convention in the Windows SDK Help file with the ones in the Visual Basic API Help file shipped with Visual Basic 3. (If you don't have version 3, never mind.) Both files are aimed at C programmers—the first at those writing Windows-based programs in C, and the second at those writing VBX controls in C. You'd expect both files to use the same convention, but the names for similar variables are in fact very different, although both systems are vaguely recognizable as Hungarian.

In the SDK, for example, a Boolean variable has the prefix *b* for Boolean. In the Visual Basic API, a Boolean variable has the prefix *f* for flag. In the SDK, a variable used as a bit flag has the prefix *w* or *dw* for Word or DWord, indicating its type—or at least the Windows include file version of its type. In the Visual Basic API, a similar variable has the prefix *fs* or *fl* for flag of short or flag of long, respectively, indicating both its use and its type. This goes on. Windows SDK names sometimes indicate the use of the variable, but more often they simply indicate the data type, and even then in an artificial form that has no relation to Basic (or to C, for that matter).

Much of the confusion in current Hungarian variations comes from trying to make the prefix do too many conflicting things. At various times, I've seen the prefix used to indicate several different concepts. Even if you don't buy Hungarian, any naming convention must deal with some of the following elements:

- The purpose of the variable. Is the variable used as a handle, a Boolean flag, a bit flag (an array of bits), an index, a count, an ordinal, a string, or an ID? Generally, this is the most useful piece of information you can provide, and it's language independent. A handle is a handle, regardless of the language.

- The data type of the variable. This information is usually irrelevant because the data type is implied by the purpose. Furthermore, the data type is language specific. If you design your naming convention for a language that supports signed and unsigned types (C and most variations of Pascal), the convention becomes irrelevant for languages that have only signed integers (Basic and FORTRAN). And if you use specific features of your language to define your own type names, those names will be irrelevant in languages that don't let you name your own types (most languages). If you're familiar with the Windows API, you're sensing that I don't think much of its naming conventions. Right you are. A good deal of Chapter 2 will be spent telling you how to translate these names into something intelligible to Basic. The naming conventions proposed here ignore the data type.

- The context of the variable. Generally, this means using a modifier indicating that the variable is in an array or a collection. Languages that support pointers require a modifier to distinguish a pointer to a variable from the variable itself. You can use a count modifier to indicate a count of variables. For example, if the modifier *h* is for a handle, *a* is for an array, *p* is for a pointer, and *c* is for a count, then you could have an *ah* (an array of handles), a *ph* (a pointer to a handle), or a *ch* (a count of handles).

- The scope of the variable. Some conventions clearly distinguish variables that are local, global, or somewhere in between (module-level in Visual Basic). Usually, local is assumed to be the default, requiring no modifier, and *g* is used as a prefix modifier for globals. By extension, you could use *m* as a prefix modifier for module-level variables. This isn't a bad idea in principle, but in practice I don't find it very useful in Basic. I don't use globals often, and the distinction between local and module-level variables is usually clear from the context. Also, it would be easy to get carried away with distinguishing between static and normal locals or between fixed and dynamic arrays.

■ The modifiability of the variable. Many conventions distinguish constants from variables, usually by making constants all uppercase. I don't find this distinction very useful. A constant can be identified when necessary by its name and the context. If *clr* is the prefix for a color, it's pretty clear that *clrTitle* is a variable and *clrRed* is a constant. In addition, if you want to make the title red by assigning *clrRed* to *clrTitle*, it doesn't make much difference whether *clrRed* is a variable or a constant.

What I'm creating here is a more portable Hungarian that works for Basic. I don't often care what type a variable has when I use it; I care only what it is for. Some handles are 16-bit, some are 32-bit—but I'm much more interested in whether it's a handle to a window, a file, or a GDI object. I use integers for different purposes: counts, indexes, handles, ordinals, and bit fields. Whether they are Longs or Integers usually doesn't matter after the declaration. If I need to know, I can go back to the declaration and check.

The point of Hungarian is not to be an absolute standard for everyone, but to be standard across a given department, project, program, or, in this case, book. I've used the conventions defined in Table 1-2 throughout (consistently, I hope).

Some prefixes modify other prefixes. For example, *acmd* is an array of buttons, *ccmd* is a count of buttons, and *ncmd* is a collection of buttons. Strict Hungarian always uses *c* as a modifier. You could use *ciWindow* as a count of indexes to windows or *chWindow* as a count of handles to windows, but I often find that I can make the meaning clearer by omitting the second part of the prefix. If I'm counting windows, *cWindow* is sufficient.

I'll introduce and explain some additional conventions later in the book. In particular, some of the new object-oriented features of Visual Basic require further discussion and variations.

Variable naming conventions are one thing; type naming conventions are another. You can define several kinds of types in Basic, including forms, classes, collection-like classes, and user-defined types. Like other types, they are essentially templates that define the features of the type. I start my type names with the letter *T, C, N,* or *F* (for Type, Class, Collection, or Form) in order to clearly distinguish the kind of types and to distinguish types from variables and procedures. For example, I use the names TPoint, CPictureGlass, NDrives, and FGetColor.

Prefix	Variable or Object
i	integer index (type Integer or Long)
h	handle
ord	ordinal (a numeric identification code used when the specific value is unimportant except to distinguish the variable from others)
x, y	x and y coordinates of points
dx, dy	delta (or distance) in terms of x and y coordinates (dx is width, dy is height)
f	Boolean
af	bit flag (an array of Booleans represented by bits)
r	real number (either Single or Double)
b	byte
v	variant
cur	currency
time	time (in variant format)
date	date (in variant format)
dt	date and time combined in variant
s	string
p	pointer (Long variable from or for an API function)
cmd	button
chk	check box
txt	text box
pb	picture box
pic	picture
lst	list box
cbo	combo box
lbl	label
mnu	menu
tmr	timer
opt	option button (radio button)
c	count
a	array
n	collection
r	reference to object

Table 1-2. *Hardcore Hungarian.*

User-defined type must be the worst name ever given to a major language feature. Why couldn't the QuickBasic developers who added this feature have given it a one-word name? If you borrow features from other languages, why not borrow the names (*structure* or *record*) of those features? Language is a living thing that doesn't accept bad terminology without a fight. On the Visual Basic programming team, user-defined types have become known as UDTs. Think of them as Unified Data Templates or whatever seems to fit the acronym. In any case, this book calls them UDTs from here on out.

Every UDT, class, form, or collection needs a prefix for the variables associated with it. Sometimes the variable prefix just jumps out at me. For instance, *drive* and *drives* were the obvious choices for CDrive and NDrives, discussed in Chapter 4. These might be long prefixes, but generally you'll have only one variable of each type, so it works out. The main point is to choose prefixes you can remember.

Stir It Up

The trouble with naming conventions is that you'll have a hard time sticking to just one. Let's say that you buy my arguments and adopt my Basic dialect of Hungarian. But you also use a lot of Windows API calls, so you need to be familiar with Windows Hungarian as used in the Windows SDK. You also want to be portable to 32 bits, and you'll soon see that Win32 Hungarian is subtly different from Win16 Hungarian. In addition, you read a lot of sample code from the Basic manuals, which use a slightly different version of Hungarian (when they use it at all). The code you paste from Visual Basic Help usually doesn't use Hungarian. Visual Basic for Applications is gradually developing its own conventions for dealing with OLE servers that are used by or created with Basic. The OLE server manual suggests some guidelines. And of course you probably have several other third-party books in your Basic library, each with a different convention. Some of them might even use the dreaded default Command1 convention.

And that's just Basic. If you write the occasional OLE control in C++, you'll have to deal with conflicting conventions from Windows, the Microsoft Foundation Class (MFC) Library, and OLE.

It's a hard life. All you can do is choose the naming convention that makes the most sense to you and then stick with it, no matter what other folks (me included) might say.

Efficient Code

Critics of Visual Basic will tell you that efficient Basic code is an oxymoron. Visual Basic executes p-code, so it can never be as efficient as C or assembly language, both of which execute native code. That's true, sort of, sometimes, but it doesn't mean that you shouldn't try to make your code efficient. In fact, there's all the more reason not to contribute to the inefficiency by writing sloppy code.

If you can write a procedure in either of two ways, both of which take about the same time to write and both of which have about the same chance of being buggy, choose the one that executes faster. But what's faster? You can guess how Basic works and try to think through which techniques might be faster, but how can you know for sure?

The bottom line is that you can't. You don't know what Visual Basic is doing, and it's not easy to find out. To understand why, let's review the concept of p-code.

P-Code Summary

When you write a line of code, Visual Basic breaks it down into expressions and encodes the expressions into a shorthand form known as p-code instructions. In other words, each line is compiled as it is written. Some lines contain shared information that cannot be compiled independently (mainly Dim statements and procedure definitions). This is why you have to restart if you change certain lines in break mode.

At run time, the p-code interpreter works through your program, decoding and executing instructions. These p-code instructions are smaller than the equivalent native code, thus dramatically reducing the size of the executable program. But the system must load the p-code interpreter into memory in addition to the code, and it must decode each instruction.

Furthermore, the translation process affects the efficiency of the code. Because encoding is done line by line, Visual Basic never optimizes across lines. Many compiler optimization techniques work by analyzing blocks of code and finding ways to eliminate inefficiency and duplication. The compiler philosophy is that, since you compile only once, you can take as long as you want to analyze as much code as necessary to generate the best results possible. Not only is Visual Basic unable to look at multiple lines, but it must also look at each subexpression separately and usually can't even optimize on individual lines. It must translate each expression instantly and independently.

Although this sounds terrible for efficiency, many Basic programs appear to run just as fast and efficiently as if they had been written in C. This is because most of the code being executed in a Windows-based program is not your code; it's Windows DLL code that was written in C or assembler. Also, much of the Basic code you execute consists of functions written in C or assembler and located in the Basic run-time library. In addition, most of the statements you write in Visual Basic are user-interface statements that execute fast enough. You can't see the difference even if they are slow.

> **NOTE** Another reason Basic code is slower than the compiled code of many other languages is that Basic always does run-time error checking. You can't expect a language that validates every statement to offer the same performance as a language that leaves you at the mercy of your own error checking. Of course, if you were to write a C program that does all the run-time error checking Basic does, you not only would pay the same performance penalty but also would have to write the error handlers.

To sum up, p-code offers significant advantages:

- Your executable code is much smaller than native code, which reduces program size on disk and in memory.

- In virtual-memory operating systems (Windows 3.1 enhanced mode and all 32-bit versions of Windows), smaller code often means less disk swapping.

- Because each line is encoded independently when you write it, you don't have to recompile after each change. Although technically Visual Basic is a compiler, it runs like an interpreter. You can edit lines at run time and keep executing without a restart.

In exchange for these benefits, you pay a price:

- Decoding and executing p-code instructions take a lot longer than executing native code. Native code is executed directly by the processor. P-code is executed indirectly by the p-code interpreter.

- You don't know what's going on. Visual Basic translates some of your code into p-code. It translates other parts of your code into calls to native code in DLLs and in the Basic run-time library. But you don't know which code is translated into what.

For example, consider this line:

```
sChar = Mid$(sTxt, 3, 1)
```

In C, that line translates into something like this:

```
sChar = sTxt[2];
```

This in turn translates into three or four assembly language instructions. But what will Visual Basic do with it? Will it recognize that the second and third arguments are constants and that all it must do is get the third character of the string and stuff it into the destination string? Or will it call a native-code Mid$ function somewhere in the Basic library? If it simply stuffs the character, will the overhead of doing so in p-code be greater than the cost of executing a native-code Mid$ function plus the overhead of making the call into a DLL? You don't know.

In C or other high-level languages, you can usually get an assembly language listing or step through your code in an assembly-level debugger to see exactly what's going on. Even if you do this with Basic (the following section tells you how), you'll have difficulty interpreting the p-code.

Examining P-Code

If you're the adventurous type, and if disassembled machine code doesn't scare you, you can examine Basic p-code. You'll need a low-level debugger that disassembles code. Source-line debuggers such as the one in 16-bit Visual C++ won't work (unless you happen to have the source for VB.EXE). I use CodeView for Windows, but you can probably adjust for Multiscope or others, including 32-bit debuggers.

The key to breaking into Visual Basic code is the DebugBreak API routine. In case you're curious, its assembly language implementation might look like this:

```
DebugBreak PROC
    int 3
    ret
DebugBreak ENDP
```

The INT 3 instruction signals any active debugger to break out of execution. That's how debuggers work—by temporarily putting an INT 3 wherever they want a breakpoint. Now load VB.EXE into the debugger. I do this by creating a CodeView for Windows icon that executes this command line:

```
c:\msvc\bin\cvw.exe c:\vb\vb.exe
```

When you click the icon, CodeView warns that you don't have debugging information for VB.EXE. That's OK. Press F5 or click Go. CodeView steps back, and Visual Basic takes over, running normally.

Put a DebugBreak statement in your Basic source just before the line you want to examine. You probably want to start with something simple but recognizable:

```
DebugBreak
i = &HABCD
```

Now run the program. When you hit the breakpoint, you'll pop up in the debugger on the INT 3 instruction, followed by a RET instruction. Step through them. When you step past RET, you'll be in the strange world of p-code.

Let's just say that this code doesn't look like any C or assembler code I've disassembled before. If you want to know more, the MSDN/VB starter kit has an article on p-code, and the Visual C++ manuals discuss the p-code generated by Microsoft's compiler. The main point here is how many instructions it takes to do a simple task. In disassembled C code, the example statement would translate to something like this:

```
mov WORD PTR i, 0ABDCh
```

You'll be sobered to see how many instructions it takes to do the same thing in p-code.

What You Don't Know Hurts You

Even if you knew exactly what code was executing, timing code in a multitasking operating system is difficult and inconsistent. Let's summarize what you don't know about Visual Basic timing:

- Code in Windows DLLs is written in C or assembler and is thus native code, but you don't know exactly when you're running Windows code and when you're running Basic code.

- A lot of code for Basic statements and functions is native code in the Basic run-time library, but you can't be sure when you're running Basic native code and when you're running p-code.

- Windows 3.1 is a non-preemptive operating system, which means that you can make educated guesses about when other programs will interrupt your code, but you can't tell for sure. If you test a piece of code several times, chances are good that other operations in the system will cause you to get different results each time.

- Windows NT and Windows 95 are preemptive operating systems, which means that you haven't a clue about when other programs will interrupt your code. If you test a piece of code several times, you will get different results each time.

- Anything you do to time your Windows code will itself take time, thus changing your results. You need to time the code while timing it and then time it while not timing it, and compare the results to see how timing it affects the timing. But you can't.

A lot of variables come into play, but one thing is clear: to find the most efficient way of performing an operation, you need to test multiple times.

The Time It Application

The Time It program is designed to answer performance questions. Its interface is simple, as you can see in Figure 1-1. You select a performance problem from a list box. Time It displays a description of the problem and the default number of iterations needed to run the test. You can modify the number of iterations. Click the Time It button (or double-click the item) to run the test. Nothing fancy. The goal of the Time It design is simply to make it easy to add new problems to the list box. (That turns out to be unexpectedly difficult in Basic, but for now let's look only at the mechanics of timing operations in Basic and Windows.)

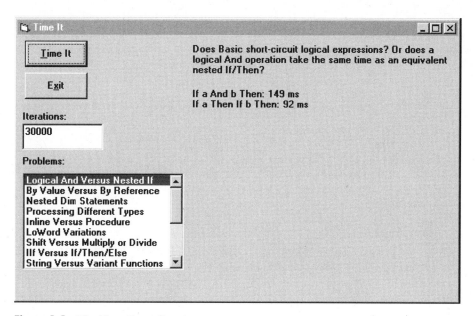

Figure 1-1. *The Time It application.*

Timing in Basic

Timing should be easy in Basic. You get the start time from the Timer function, carry out the operation, and get the ending time. Subtract the start time from the ending time, and you have the operation time. But in what units of time?

According to the Basic documentation, Timer returns the number of seconds since midnight. You'd need a lot of iterations to get meaningful timing results if Timer actually returned whole seconds, but fortunately it returns seconds as a real number, nominally accurate to hundredths of a second. Actually, the Timer code (in 16-bit mode, at least) seems to be based on the execrable MS-DOS time functions, which are accurate only to about a tenth of a second. If that's close enough for you, go ahead.

I prefer to use the multimedia timeGetTime function (multimedia procedures introduce one more weird naming convention), which returns milliseconds. In case, like me, you can never remember the difference between milliseconds, microseconds, and maxiseconds, I looked it up for you: milliseconds are thousandths of a second, microseconds are millionths of a second, and maxiseconds are how long I wasted trying different timing functions before I settled on timeGetTime. Don't be sidetracked, for example, by the TimerCount API function. It's more difficult to use, and it doesn't exist in 32-bit Windows.

I use a set of profile procedures to time operations, keeping them in DEBUG.BAS along with my debug procedures. As I do with the debug procedures, I use conditional compilation and various other debugging techniques so that the profile procedures can disappear in the release version of my program. ("Assert Yourself," page 29, discusses issues of writing debugging code in more detail.) The design of the routines is simple and not very interesting, so I'll concentrate on how to use them.

Before timing an operation, you need two Long integers to contain the result:

```
Dim ms As Long, msOut As Long
```

I invented the Hungarian prefix *ms* to represent milliseconds. You pass one of these expressions to ProfileStart:

```
ProfileStart ms
```

ProfileStart gets the start time from the system and stores it in the argument variable. You do the operation and then pass the start time to ProfileStop, which calculates the duration and returns it in the second variable:

```
ProfileStop ms, msOut
```

You can use the result—*msOut*, in this case—in an expression or wherever you need it.

You're probably thinking that it would be more convenient to have ProfileStart and ProfileStop as functions rather than returning values through parameters. Maybe so, but I specifically designed them as subs to discourage calling them in expressions where they might cause side effects. "An Assertion Implementation," page 30, describes other reasons for writing debug procedures as subs.

The Visual Basic Code Profiler, which comes with the Professional and Enterprise editions, works a lot like ProfileStart and ProfileStop. But the Code Profiler takes a shotgun approach, while I use a scalpel. The Code Profiler add-in automatically inserts (and later removes) profile statements before and after every line of code in your program. When you run the program, the data from each profile measurement is stored in a database so that you can spend the next two weeks analyzing it. This is a little more profile data than I need, but maybe it will work for you.

Short-Circuiting Logical Expressions: A Timing Example

As an example, consider the problem of short-circuiting logical expressions. Assume the following code:

```
If i <= 20 And i >= 10 Then i = i + 1
```

Looking at this logically, you can see that if *i* is greater than 20, it's pointless to check whether it's also less than 10. Some compilers and interpreters know this and skip the second condition (*short-circuiting* is the technical term) if the first condition settles the matter. But is Visual Basic among them? Consider an alternative but equivalent statement:

```
If i <= 20 Then If i >= 10 Then i = i + 1
```

In this case, I'm not trusting Visual Basic to optimize. I tell it to always check the first condition and to check the second only if the first is true. If Basic can optimize the first example, these two pieces of code should run at about the same speed. There's only one way to find out:

```
Function LogicalAndVsNestedIf(cIter As Long) As String
    Dim ms As Long, msOut As Long
    Dim sMsg As String, i As Integer, iIter As Long

    i = 21
    ProfileStart ms
    For iIter = 1 To cIter
        If i <= 20 And i >= 10 Then i = i + 1
    Next
    ProfileStop ms, msOut
    sMsg = "If a And b Then: " & msOut & " ms" & sCrLf
```

(continued)

```
    i = 21
    ProfileStart ms
    For iIter = 1 To cIter
        If i <= 20 Then If i >= 10 Then i = i + 1
    Next
    ProfileStop ms, msOut
    sMsg = sMsg & "If a Then If b Then: " & msOut & " ms" & sCrLf

    LogicalAndVsNestedIf = sMsg

End Function
```

The results will vary, depending on the computer and the operating system used, on what other programs are running at the same time, on whether the program runs under 16-bit or 32-bit Visual Basic, and on whether the moon is full. I ran all the timing tests in this book on a 66-MHz Pentium-based computer. The "Performance" sidebar on page 29 indicates the results: no short-circuit.

Just so you don't think that Basic is unsophisticated and unnecessarily inefficient, you should understand that it has its reasons. In Basic, the And and Or operators double as logical operators and bitwise operators. You would have a different situation with the following line:

```
If a Or b Or c = &HEACC Then Exit Sub
```

In this case, you're combining the bits of *a*, *b*, and *c* and then testing to see whether the result has a specific value. A short-circuit would be inappropriate. But for Basic to know that, it would need to look at the entire expression and make some assumptions (possibly erroneous) about your intentions. For example, Basic could assume that an expression with an equal sign is always bitwise, but that an expression without an equal sign is always logical. That's an iffy assumption, and Basic doesn't make it.

WARNING Visual Basic's failure to short-circuit logical expressions can cause problems other than performance. Consider the following expression:

```
If (iStart > 1) And Mid$(s, iStart - 1, 1) = " " Then
```

The first condition attempts to protect against an illegal condition in the second. If *iStart* is 1, the second argument of Mid$ is 0, which causes an illegal function call. You might hope that since the first condition is false, the second illegal statement won't be executed and you won't get that obnoxious error. Wrong!

PERFORMANCE

Problem: Does Basic short-circuit logical expressions? Or does a logical And operation take the same time as an equivalent nested If/Then?

Problem	16-Bit Mode	32-Bit Mode
If a And b Then	76 ms	96 ms
If a Then If b Then	52 ms	61 ms

Conclusion: This is the first of many timing notes. Don't take the numbers too seriously; they're for rough comparison only. For real results, run the Time It program yourself on machines like the ones you expect your customers to use. In this case, however, the difference is dramatic enough to justify a conclusion: Basic does not short-circuit logical expressions. You can write faster code by not combining expressions with the And or Or operator. Use this knowledge judiciously. Most of the time, logical expressions are easier to read and maintain, and the extra time won't make any difference. But if you're coding a really tight loop...

Assert Yourself

Basic programmers have been too long deprived of one of the common tools of debugging—the assertion procedure. Assertion deals with the concept of proof. If you write a piece of code, how can you prove that it works? If it crashes, you've proved that it doesn't work. But if it runs successfully, you've proved only that it ran successfully this time, not that it will run next time, with different input.

The way to approach proof in programming is to rule out all invalid inputs, call the procedure, and then verify that its output is valid. Although you can't always determine which inputs are invalid, and you can't always figure out a way to validate output, it's nevertheless worth trying. You often rule out many invalid inputs and at least partially validate output by using assertion procedures. An assertion procedure simply evaluates an expression, terminating the program with an appropriate message if the asserted expression is false.

For example, the following sub insists that users call it according to internal rules not enforced by the language:

```
Sub InsertChar(sTarget As String, sChar As String, iPos As Integer)
    BugAssert Len(sChar) = 1        ' Accept characters only
    BugAssert iPos <= Len(sTarget)  ' Don't insert beyond end
    Mid$(sTarget, iPos, 1) = sChar  ' Do work
End Sub
```

The secret of successful assertion is to assert every possible condition that might go wrong. Of course, you won't feel comfortable asserting aggressively if you know that each assertion increases the size and decreases the speed of your finished application. For that reason, assertion procedures are traditionally coded conditionally so that they exist during a debugging phase but disappear when the finished product is shipped. Conditional compilation makes this possible. Starting with version 4, Visual Basic offers conditional compilation, although in a much less flexible implementation than C programmers might expect.

Assert the Basic Way

If you assert a lie (for instance, that 2 and 2 is 5) in an MS-DOS C program, your program will terminate, and you'll see output such as this on the command line:

```
Assertion failed: 2 + 2 == 5, file c:\lies.c, line 6
```

You'd have a hard time doing the same thing in Visual Basic. The C compiler knows the file and the line number where the error occurred, but Basic has no means of providing that information. The C compiler knows that the text *2 + 2 == 5* was passed to assert as an argument. Basic knows only that the value of *2 + 2 = 5* (false) was passed to an assertion procedure. So Basic can output only the result *Assertion failed*, with no information about why or where the failure occurred.

Although Visual Basic can't match the output of a C compiler, it does have one big advantage: the Stop statement. If you put a Stop directly after the assertion failure, you're in a perfect position to step into the code that caused the failure and fix it on the spot, assuming that you're working in the environment. If your program is an EXE, Stop simply terminates the program, and you won't have a clue where the offending code is located. In theory, any program that works in the environment should also work in an EXE, but in reality that's not always the case, especially when you start playing tricks with the Windows API.

An Assertion Implementation

Here's one way to code an assertion procedure in Visual Basic:

```
Sub BugAssert(ByVal fExpression As Variant, _
              Optional sExpression As Variant)
#If afDebug Then
    If fExpression Then Exit Sub
    If IsMissing(sExpression) Then sExpression = sEmpty
    BugMessage "BugAssert failed: " & sExpression
    Stop
#End If
End Sub
```

Conditional Compilation for Blockheads

Conditional compilation is a familiar feature in many languages, but it might be new to Basic programmers (although old-timers may remember metacommands from MS-DOS and Macintosh Basic compilers). Basic conditional statements (like their metacommand ancestors) give instructions to the compiler (or interpreter) about how to create the program. The results of the commands live on at run time, but the commands themselves are long gone.

Another way to think of this is that conditional compilation is an easy way of commenting out blocks of code. Let's say you want to try out different destroy algorithms. In previous versions of Basic, you might have written this:

```
SafeSlowDestroy earth
'FastRiskyDestroy earth
```

After running the safe, slow version a few times to ensure that it works, you would have commented out the first line and removed the comment from the second to test it. Of course, in reality, each block would probably have more than one line, and affected code might be scattered in several places. Changing these calls by hand is a major inconvenience with great potential for bugs. Conditional compilation makes it easy to switch back and forth:

```
#Const fSafeSlow = 1
#If fSafeSlow Then
    SafeSlowDestroy earth
#Else
    FastRiskyDestroy earth
#End If
```

To try the fast, risky version, simply change the definition of the *fSafeSlow* constant to 0. Notice that the syntax for compile-time tests and constants is exactly the same as for run-time tests and constants except that the compile-time lines start with a pound sign (#). If you don't define an *fSafeSlow* constant in this example, it is assumed to be 0. This default enables you to fake the C language #ifdef and #ifndef statements even though Basic doesn't directly support them.

In Basic, there's no relation or communication between compile-time and run-time statements. You can't use a constant created with #Const in an If statement, and you can't use a constant created with Const in an #If statement. Despite syntax similarities, compile-time Basic and run-time Basic are different languages handled by different language interpreters at different times.

The short assertion procedure on page 30 packs in some interesting twists. First is the optional argument. The intention is to fill the argument with a string containing the same information you would get from the C compiler. You could fill in both arguments yourself when writing code, but normally you would just use the simple version at design time:

```
BugAssert 2 + 2 = 5
```

I wrote a text-processing program that scans through source code and automatically fills in the second argument:

```
BugAssert 2 + 2 = 5, "2 + 2 = 5, file TEST.FRM, line 325"
```

Visual Basic might not know the expression, file, and line, but it's easy enough to write a program that does. Microsoft refers to programs that modify source code as *wizards* and includes several of them in Visual C++. The Visual Basic environment has built-in wizards (although they are not called by that name) that generate event procedures and other code. The Debug Wizard (BUGWIZ.EXE) shown in Figure 1-2 is the first of several wizards used in this book. For now, we're interested only in the program; we'll return to the code in Chapter 9.

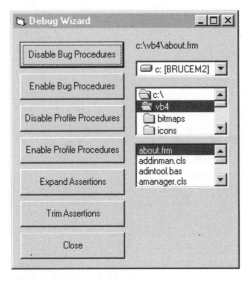

Figure 1-2. *The Debug Wizard.*

Of course, the line number is of limited use when you edit with the Visual Basic editor since, unlike most programmer's editors, it doesn't indicate the current line number, and it gives you no way to go to a specific line number. I provide the line number in case you occasionally cheat and use a real programmer's editor on Basic source code, as I do.

The next interesting thing about the code is the Exit Sub statement in the first unconditional line. For readability of structured code, I normally use an If/End If block. In this case, however, the important thing is not readability, but that the Stop statement is the last executable statement of the routine. This makes it more convenient to step back through the assertion procedure and come out in the calling procedure ready to debug.

Now consider the call to BugMessage. You might wonder why I call the procedure BugAssert instead of Assert. I put all my debug routines in the DEBUG.BAS module and start each name with *Bug*. Then I can easily search for all words that start with *Bug* and replace them with *'Bug*, thus commenting out all debug calls before I ship my program. Debug Wizard performs this operation automatically. (Incidentally, that's another reason all my Bug routines are subs, not functions. You can't comment out functions mechanically.)

You might well ask what the point is. Isn't conditional compilation supposed to take care of that? Yes, and this trick would be unnecessary in C or any other language that uses a preprocessor. In C, the preprocessor that handles #if and related statements is simply a text-processing program, not unlike my Debug Wizard. It converts the C statement

```
assert(2 + 2 == 5)
```

to a statement roughly equivalent to this when debugging is on:

```
if !(2 + 2 == 5)
    printf("Assertion failed: %s, file %s, %d\n", "2 + 2 == 5",
            "lies.c", "666");
```

If debugging is off, the preprocessor will produce a blank—absolutely no code. If you look back at BugAssert, you'll see that if debugging is off, it will produce something—an empty procedure.

Think about calling an empty procedure hundreds of times in the code you ship to customers. Think about doing it in p-code. It might even be worthwhile to step through the p-code of an empty procedure. (See "Examining P-Code," page 23.) An empty procedure might be cheap comparatively. But the motto of the defensive programmer is "When in doubt, assert." Personally, I can't follow this advice comfortably if I know that every assertion costs a call, a return, and many worthless bytes of code. I wrote Debug Wizard to eliminate all that code. I need to run it only occasionally during the life of a project.

NOTE Debug Wizard wouldn't need to remove empty BugAssert subs if you had a tool that eliminated dead code from Visual Basic executables. At least one third-party tool claims to do this. I'm not naming or endorsing products I haven't tried, but it's something to consider.

Other Debug Messages

Assertions aren't the only kind of debug message you might want to see. In a previous life, I worked on a FORTRAN run-time library containing an extremely complex system of debug outputs. By setting various command-line options during a library build, you could dump different parts of the library entrails for easy run-time divination. Nothing (except good sense) prevents you from enhancing my debug code to something just as complex.

That's up to you. I'm simply going to show you BugMessage. You can call it directly to display messages about your status and location, or you can write routines that call it the way BugAssert does. My debug module (DEBUG.BAS) also contains a BugProfileStop sub that calls BugMessage to write profile information to the output destination.

BugMessage uses the following compile-time constants:

```
#Const afLogfile = 1
#Const afMsgBox = 2
#Const afDebugWin = 4
```

These identify the output destination for the message. Because your program is running under Windows, you have no command line to write to. You must send the message somewhere that won't interfere with your program screen.

You can write to a dialog box, although dialog assertions can get annoying. If you're running in the Visual Basic environment, you can write to the Debug window. Finally, you can write debugging output to a log file for later inspection. A log file usually works best in addition to (not instead of) one of the other output destinations. In theory you could set all these bits at once, but in reality you'll usually pick one of the first three and then consider adding the log file as a secondary destination. Here's the code to handle different destinations:

```
Sub BugMessage(sMsg As String)
#If afDebug And afLogfile Then
    If hLogfile = 0 Then
        hLogfile = FreeFile
        ' Warning: multiple instances can overwrite log file
        Open App.EXEName & ".DBG" For Output Shared As hLogfile
        ' Challenge: rewrite to give each instance its own log file
    End If
```

```
      Print #hLogfile, sMsg
#End If
#If afDebug And afMsgBox Then
      MsgBox sMsg
#End If
#If afDebug And afDebugWin Then
      Debug.Print sMsg
#End If
End Sub
```

Debug.Print

If you open a log file for debug information, who's going to close it? Well, DEBUG.BAS contains a BugTerm sub that you can call in the Unload event of your main form to close the file. If you don't bother, however, you'll probably still be OK because Visual Basic closes all open files when it terminates. Notice that log files have the project executable name and the extension DBG. You might want to clean up once in a while so that your disk doesn't fill up with obsolete DBG files.

CHALLENGE   The traditional Windows output destination is a debugging terminal. You hook up a dumb terminal to your serial port and send debugging output to the port. Assertions and other debug messages scroll past on this neanderthal device without interfering with the operation of your program. The Windows API provides the OutputDebugString function to send output to a debugging terminal, but I had trouble getting this to work satisfactorily under Windows 3, and I never got it to work with Basic under 32-bit Windows. You could enhance the BugMessage sub by adding an option that opens a COM port and writes output to it.

Setting Debug Constants

BugAssert and other debug procedures expect a constant named *afDebug* to indicate not only whether debugging is on but also where to send debug output. You can set the constant in several ways.

The easiest way to set *afDebug* is to ignore it, which has the effect of setting it to 0 (False). Your code will work, but your assertions won't. You might find the default 0 value useful for other situations, however.

You can also set the constant in the DEBUG.BAS source module. You might think that it would be handy to set the *afDebug* constant in each source file so that you could debug some modules and not others. Unfortunately, that doesn't work. Constants defined in source modules are module-level variables. BugAssert and other routines that test the *afDebug* constant are located in DEBUG.BAS. They don't know or care about constants defined in other modules. Since you'll use the DEBUG.BAS module in various projects, you don't want the value of the *afDebug* constant to change every time you modify it in the source file. Instead, you want a project-wide way of setting the constant.

You can set project constants on the Advanced tab of the Options dialog box (as shown in Figure 1-3), or you can set them on the VB.EXE command line. If you spend all of your time working on one project, the command-line method might work for you. I switch projects constantly, so I find the Options dialog box more convenient. This puts the constant entry into the project, as you can see by examining the VBP file.

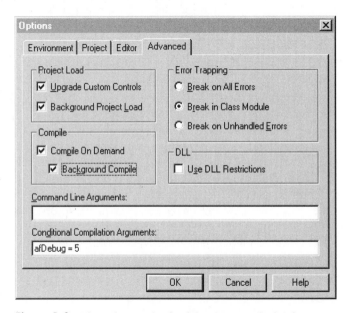

Figure 1-3. *The Advanced tab of the Options dialog box.*

The Options dialog box and the command line don't know Basic. You can't enter True or False, constants that are defined in the source file, hexadecimal numbers, or Basic operators. If you need to combine bit constants, you can't use an expression such as *afDebugWin And afLogFile*. Instead, you have to figure out that this means *&H1 And &H4*, calculate, convert to decimal, and enter *afDebug = 5* in the dialog box field.

Because my standard configuration is to send debugging output to the Debug window and create a log file, I put these settings in both the AUTO32LD and AUTO16LD projects so that they are automatically added to all new projects. You might prefer other settings, particularly when debugging EXE programs.

What to Assert

Asserting is an art form. Languages have been specifically designed—Eiffel comes to mind—to encourage it. Books have been written about it. Steve Maguire's *Writing Solid Code* (Microsoft Press, 1993) is an excellent book on asserting and other debugging topics, although you'll have to translate from C to Basic as you read it. I can only touch on the subject here, but you'll see examples throughout the sample code.

The most important thing to know about debug code is when to assert and when to validate. Validating means checking the input at run time and taking appropriate action. If you ask the user for a number between 1 and 10, you have to recognize when the user enters 11 and ask again politely (or handle 11 anyway, or round down to 10, or delete everything on the idiot's hard disk, or whatever). But you can't assert.

Here's an example. Lots of Windows API functions return error values, but errors don't always mean the same thing. A common Windows sequence (as you'll see in future chapters) is to create, use, and delete. It works like this:

```
hSomething = CreateSomething(x, y, clr, AND_SO_ON)
' Do something with hSomething
f = DeleteSomething(hSomething)
```

In this case, CreateSomething either returns a handle to a Something or returns a 0 handle (the constant *hNull*) indicating failure. DeleteSomething returns True or False, depending on whether you can delete the object.

If you get *hNull* back from CreateSomething, it's not your fault. There's probably not enough memory, or Windows has used up all the Somethings. It's your responsibility to politely tell the user to choose some other action. If Delete-Something fails, however, it probably *is* your fault. You passed *hSomething* to the wrong procedure, or you traded an *hSomething* for an *hAnything* and forgot to swap it back. For whatever reason, the *hSomething* variable no longer contains a Something handle. There's no point telling the user. What could you say? You must do some soul-searching to fix the bug. But an assertion such as this one catches the mistake:

```
hSomething = CreateSomething(x, y, clr, AND_SO_ON)
If hSomething = hNull Then
    BackWayOut
    Exit Sub
End If
' Do something with Something
f = DeleteSomething(hSomething)
BugAssert f
```

WARNING Resist the temptation to combine assertions with other statements. The line

```
BugAssert DeleteSomething(hSomething)
```

seems to work, but if you replace *BugAssert* with ' *BugAssert*, you'll get an unpleasant surprise when DeleteSomething disappears along with the assertion.

Incidentally, if you notice more assertions in the examples in early chapters of this book than in late ones, well...that's no excuse for you to do the same. Never let tight deadlines compromise your efforts to write correct code. It takes longer to debug than to write it right the first time.

2

The Second Level of Basic Enlightenment

Visual Basic doesn't do pointers. Windows does. That's the contradiction you must resolve in order to achieve the second level of enlightenment.

You've already mastered the first level—designing forms and using Basic statements. The second level—calling the Windows API—requires a different kind of understanding. Even if you have experienced moments of clarity and truth with previous versions of Visual Basic, you must now learn again as a little child, because the gods have changed the rules.

Although on the surface this chapter appears to be about how to write Declare statements for Windows API functions, it is actually a meditation on the mysteries of pointers. Although it takes you step by step through the syntax of passing integers, user-defined types, arrays, and strings to DLL functions, below the surface its theme is addresses and how to become one with them. And just when you think you've reached a higher plane, it unveils a type library that makes much of what you've learned irrelevant.

So let's start at the beginning—with *addresses,* locations in memory containing data or instructions. Everything a running program does consists of manipulating addresses and their contents. As designed by Kemeny and Kurtz, however, Basic shielded you from addresses. You could have programmed for years without knowing that memory even existed, much less that locations within it were called addresses.

Meanwhile, Brian Kernighan and Dennis Ritchie designed C, a language that not only allowed you to get addresses but also let you put them in variables called pointers, manipulate those variables to point at different addresses, and do almost anything that you could previously do only in assembly language. The C philosophy is pretty much the opposite of the Basic philosophy in every way. And C is the language in which—and seemingly for which—Microsoft wrote Windows.

Basic is abstract; C is specific. Basic is high-level; C is low-level. Basic is protective; C is undisciplined. Basic is basic; C is un-Basic. A good C programmer can write a Basic interpreter. A good Basic programmer can write a C pretty printer while the C programmer is still declaring variables.

Fortunately, you don't have to learn C to be a Windows programmer. But you do need to know some of the things C programmers know—things that Basic programmers aren't supposed to worry their pretty little heads with. Nevertheless, this chapter won't wander too far from the Basic Way. It will show you some tricks for keeping your un-Basic excursions short and wrapping up the results so that they look Basic.

Writing Portable Code

Before discussing the practical problems of writing Declare statements, we need a short detour to talk about something that's been a long time coming. Windows and Basic are finally entering the world of 32-bit programming. It seems strange that the most popular operating systems—MS-DOS and Windows—are the last to adopt a technology long common in UNIX, Macintosh, Amiga, and nearly every other modern operating system. But better late than never, and better that Basic comes along, bringing easy 32-bit programming to the masses.

The fact is that 16 bits are just not enough to hold all the data that computers need to work on at the lowest level. It's a minor miracle that Windows works at all under this handicap. I'd like to tell you that the segment nightmare is finally over, the 64-KB roadblock is down, the resource jam has been blown to bits. I wish I could tell you to convert all your 16-bit programs to 32 bits, move all the old programs to one directory, and type *del *.*.* Unfortunately, we live in the real world. Those old programs and operating systems won't be gone when you wake up tomorrow morning. Most of us will have to deal with the problems of portability during the transition.

Portability Strategies

In the interim, here are some strategies to consider:

It's a whole new ball game. Buy Windows NT or Windows 95, and tell your customers to do the same. Copy VB32.EXE over your VB.EXE. Convert all your programs to 32 bits, and ship them. Customers who insist on old operating systems can use old programs. A lot of us would like to follow this strategy, but we dare not. Too many customers out there with Windows 3.1; too many questions about 32-bit versions of Windows. But if you're one of the lucky few with a guaranteed customer base of 32-bit users, the world just got simpler. (If you're thinking that the Win32s extension might make this strategy possible even under 16-bit Windows, forget it. You'll get nothing but rude error messages.)

I'll believe it when I see it. Stick with what works until your customers tell you differently. This strategy is risky because your customers can change their minds faster than you can change your software. But if you like, you can ignore the portability issues and keep on trucking. Just don't say I didn't warn you.

Move forward, but cover your behind. Develop your programs under 32-bit Windows, but make them portable to (and test them on) Windows 3.1. This strategy is more difficult, especially for hardcore Visual Basic programmers, who tend to use Windows API calls frequently. Visual Basic version 4 provides conditional compilation to make the dual-mode strategy possible, but, frankly, conditional compilation is still a little rough around the edges; you'll encounter a lot of gotchas and inconveniences. Porting code is never as easy as you hope it will be, as the Visual Basic development team learned. In addition, marketing two versions of your program raises more questions: do you sell the versions separately, or do you put them both in the box? Despite the problems, this book assumes that most Visual Basic programmers will choose this strategy.

Integer Size

The 32-bit world differs from its 16-bit counterpart in many ways, but the one that matters most is the register size. A lot happens between a register on the processor and a variable in Basic p-code, but the register size indirectly affects the variable. Let's talk about assembly language for a moment, since that's what goes on beneath the surface, even in Basic code.

In 16-bit mode, registers are 16 bits (2 bytes) wide. In order to do arithmetic with values larger than 16 bits, you must put them into multiple registers and, in most cases, use multiple instructions to process them. For example, when passing arguments on the stack, it takes two pushes to store a 32-bit value but only one for a 16-bit value. The two-register approach also applies to pointers—variables containing addresses—except that the operations required are more complex and slower (in ways that need not concern us here). This difference filters down to Basic p-code, which takes significantly more time to deal with Longs than with Integers in 16-bit mode.

In 32-bit mode, registers are 32 bits (4 bytes) wide. You can do arithmetic with 32-bit values directly in registers—one operation, one instruction. It takes one push to put a 32-bit value on the stack and one pop to take it off. Pointers fit into registers, and, generally, pointer operations are as simple and fast as arithmetic operations. In fact, it's the 16-bit values that don't fit and could take longer to process. Of course, 16-bit values are a subset of 32-bit values, so you can simply zero the top 2 bytes and still do 16-bit operations in registers. You must check for overflow, however, which could require extra operations and extra time. Fortunately, Intel processors have subset 16-bit and 8-bit registers that enable the processor to check overflow with no noticeable performance penalty. (Most 32-bit processors don't share this advantage, and if Visual Basic ever reaches the Macintosh and other platforms, you will pay a penalty.) In theory, 32-bit operations should be as fast as—or even slightly faster than—16-bit operations.

Visual Basic and the Windows API take different approaches to the new system integer size of 32-bit mode. Basic wants to pretend that nothing has happened, that old code should work on the new system with no changes. An integer used to be 16 bits wide, so it still is. As a high-level language, Basic will shield you from changes going on in the system, even at the cost of performance. But things aren't really the same now, especially not to the hardcore Visual Basic programmer.

C, like most low-level languages, supports three types of integers: short, long, and int. The short type is 16 bits; the long type is 32 bits; and the int type is the system word size. In other words, int is 16 bits under MS-DOS and Windows 3.1, but 32 bits under most other microprocessor environments, including Windows NT and Windows 95. On a few supercomputers, int is 64 bits.

PERFORMANCE

Problem: Compare counting with various Basic types: Integer, Long, Single, Double, Currency, and Variant.

Problem	16-Bit Mode	32-Bit Mode
Integer	486 ms	662 ms
Long	776 ms	731 ms
Single	1623 ms	929 ms
Double	1621 ms	962 ms
Currency	1678 ms	1279 ms
Variant	2392 ms	1978 ms

Conclusion: Contrary to my prediction, Integers are faster than Longs, even in 32-bit mode. I can only speculate that in p-code it's faster to validate Integers than Longs. Remember that Basic does run-time overflow validation beyond what is done by the processor.

C programmers normally use int for everything they can, not really caring whether most loop counters are short or long, only that they are as fast as possible. In compiled languages, the system word size is always the fastest and most efficient. Also, using the system word size makes it easier to achieve another of C's primary goals: portability among different processors. The Windows API supports the C philosophy, which means that almost every integer in every API call that used to be 16-bit is now 32-bit. Even Booleans are 32 bits wide, although only one of those bits matters.

The Basic philosophy of pretending that nothing happened starts to break down with handles. Basic passes through the system values for the hWnd and hDC properties, and the values passed through have grown to 32 bits. Of course, the only thing you can do with an hWnd or an hDC is pass it to an API function, which expects the larger size anyway. Basic never documented the types of hWnd and hDC, so the change in type isn't usually a problem, but Basic's lack of a type for system integers does cause difficulties, as you'll see soon.

Calling the Windows API from Basic

The vague concept we usually call the Windows API is, in practical terms, a growing collection of dynamic-link libraries. Basic programmers can simply think of DLLs as libraries of procedures. You don't really need to know that DLLs are loaded at run time, that multiple programs can use the same DLL at the same time, or that the procedures in DLLs must be carefully written to allow this to happen safely.

As a Basic programmer, the key fact you need to know about DLLs is that they are written in another language—it doesn't really matter that it's usually C. That other language has a different idea than Basic does about the best way to use addresses. This difference extends to all the fundamental questions of life:

- What is a string?

- What is an array?

- How big is an integer?

- What is an argument, and how should it be passed?

- What is a type, and how can it be ignored?

- What can a procedure return, and how?

These are closed questions with simple answers in Basic, but when you start calling DLLs, everything you know is, if not wrong, at least incomplete. To reach a deeper understanding of DLL functions, you have to go to that mysterious place where Basic parameters and variables meet C pointers and references: the stack.

No Pointers in Basic

Every now and then, somebody suggests to the powers that be at Microsoft that maybe the next version of Basic ought to support pointers. It won't happen. I've heard rumors that the no-pointers directive comes from the highest source— a certain top-level executive who once implemented an important version of Basic. I don't often lunch with this individual, so I can't verify the source, but I'm sure Basic isn't going to become C with a different syntax.

Low-level Basic has already been tried and found wanting. During the 1980s, many versions of Basic had keywords like PEEK, POKE, DEF SEG, BLOAD, BSAVE, and SADDR that let you manipulate addresses behind the scenes. In BASICA or GW-BASIC, you could create an assembly language routine by poking hex numbers representing machine code into an array and then using GOTO to jump to the array and execute the code. In other words, you could write Basic code more twisted than any C code.

Microsoft purged these horrors when it developed Visual Basic. If you write entirely in Basic, you cannot get at an address. Believe me, I've tried.

Anatomy of a Basic Procedure Call

To pass by value or not by value: that is the question. To answer it, you need to go to the stack, farther down than Basic programmers normally go. Programming languages from Basic to C use the stack to pass arguments from caller code to a callee procedure. We'll first examine how this works for calls to Basic procedures and later expand our knowledge to cover calls to API procedures.

Basic programmers can afford to have a simplified view of the stack as an area of memory used for temporary one-way communication. The caller puts arguments on the stack and then calls a procedure. The callee can examine or modify the information. As soon as the callee returns, the portion of the stack used by the callee disappears. (Actually, it is reused.) In other words, the stack is write-only to the caller and effectively read-only to the callee (since no one will be around to see the results of stack writes). The purpose of this mechanism is protection: caller and callee can't access each other's data without permission.

There are as many ways to pass data on a stack as there are languages and data types. When a caller in one language (say, Basic) tries to pass data to another (say, C), the connection works only if both languages agree on a convention. The caller must put the data on the stack in the exact place and format expected by the receiver. For now, we're concerned with only one aspect of calling conventions: whether the caller and the receiver agree to pass by value or by reference. Left to their own devices, Basic will pass by reference, and C will receive by value.

As an example, take the ZapemByRef and ZapemByVal procedures defined in the ZAPI library. This new dynamic-link library (ZAPI.DLL) makes it easy for Windows-based programs to zap space aliens in a consistent and portable manner, regardless of what Zap hardware and Zap device driver happen to be attached to the computer. If the ZapemByRef procedure were written in Basic, it might look something like this:

```
Sub ZapemByRef(ordAlien As Integer)
    If ordAlien = ordMartian Then
        ' Do whatever it takes; then set 0 for successful zap
        ordAlien = 0
    End If
    ' Handle other aliens
End Sub
```

Now assume that this procedure is called with the following lines:

```
Const ordMartian = 7
    ⋮
Dim ordCur As Integer
ordCur = ordMartian
ZapemByRef ordCur
If ordCur = 0 Then BuryEm
```

Figure 2-1 shows what the stack looks like to the caller and to the callee. The caller passes its argument using the default Basic convention of calling by reference. It puts the address of the variable being passed on the stack.

Caller's View

```
ordCur = ordMartian   ' 7
ZapemByRef ordCur
If ordCur = 0 Then
    ⋮
```

Callee's View

```
Sub ZapemByRef(ordAlien As Integer)
    If ordAlien = ordMartian Then   ' Read
        ⋮
        ordAlien = 0                ' Write
        ⋮
    End Sub
```

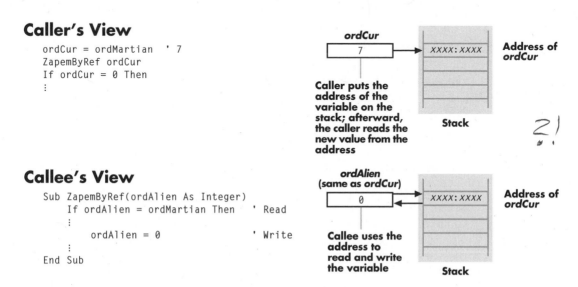

Figure 2-1. *Passing by reference.*

Giving another procedure an address is an act of trust. You've given away the key to modifying whatever is located at that address (and, incidentally, any adjacent addresses). In this case, the ZapemByRef procedure can read or write the parameter (which it calls *ordAlien*, even though the address is actually the same as *ordCur*). Technically, reads and writes are done indirectly through a pointer, an operation that takes a little more processing than modifying a variable directly. Basic hides this, however, and makes writing to a by-reference parameter look the same as writing to any other variable.

ZapemByRef is a textbook example of bad design. To mention only one of its problems, what if a user passed the *ordMartian* constant directly instead of assigning it to a variable? Would the caller really pass the address of a constant? How constant would that constant be if you were passing its address around? What if the user passed the number 7 instead of *ordMartian*? It turns out that passing a constant by reference is perfectly legal, but Basic implements this feature by creating a temporary variable and passing the address of that variable. ZapemByRef could then write to that variable (using the *ordAlien* alias), but the caller wouldn't be able to check the results because it wouldn't have a name for the temporary variable.

Let's move on to ZapemByVal. This procedure is a function that returns a Boolean value to indicate success or failure:

```
Function ZapemByVal(ByVal ordAlien As Integer) As Boolean
    If ordAlien = ordMartian Then
        ' Do whatever it takes; then set True for successful zap
        ZapemByVal = True
        Exit Function
    End If
    ' Handle other aliens
End Sub
```

Now assume that this function is called with the following lines:

```
Const ordMartian = 7
    ⋮
If ZapemByVal(ordMartian) Then DoWhatNeedsToBeDone
```

This looks better. The call takes fewer lines of code because the constant is passed directly. Success or failure comes back through the return value.

Under the hood, caller and callee treat the argument in completely different ways. Instead of copying the address of the argument onto the stack, the caller copies the value. Figure 2-2 shows the stack from the viewpoint of both caller and callee. If ZapemByVal were to modify the *ordMartian* variable, the stack value would change, but this value will disappear into the sunset as soon as Zapem-ByVal returns. So if the function happens to need a scratch variable, there's no

Caller's View

```
If ZapemByVal(ordMartian) Then
    ⋮
```

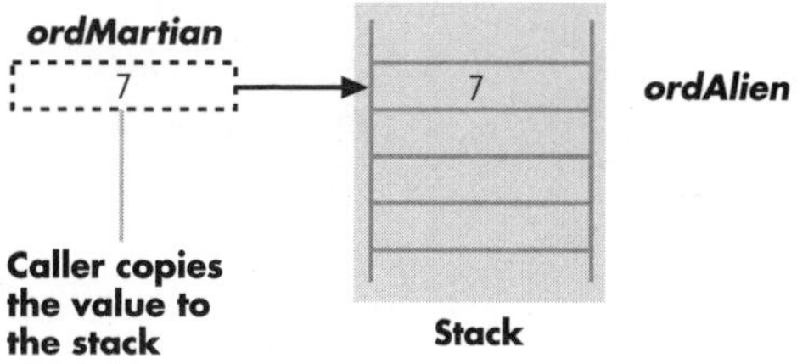

ordMartian

7

Caller copies
the value to
the stack

7   *ordAlien*

Stack

Callee's View

```
Function ZapemByVal(ByVal ordAlien As Integer) As Boolean
    If ordAlien = ordMartian Then        ' Read
    ⋮                                    ' Don't write
End Function
```

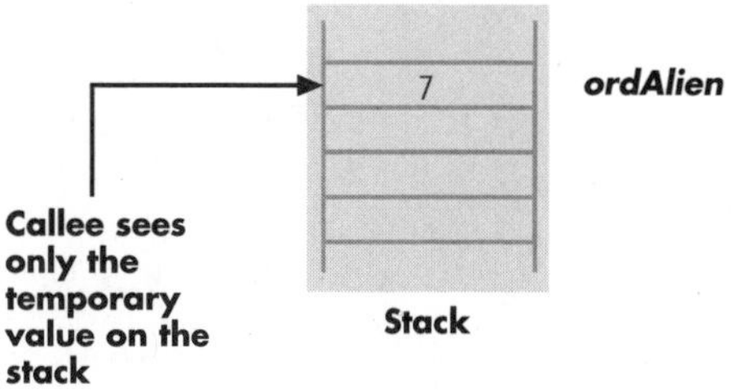

Callee sees
only the
temporary
value on the
stack

7   *ordAlien*

Stack

Figure 2-2. *Passing by value.*

technical reason not to use *ordMartian* for this purpose after it has been read. (In practice, however, using a variable for anything other than what its name implies is a good way to write unmaintainable code.)

Which parameter passing method should you choose? Since passing by reference is the default, the temptation is to accept it without thinking for Basic procedures. And if you compare the timing of the two methods, as I did in the "Performance" sidebar on page 50, you'll see that this isn't a bad strategy. Results vary depending on the arguments, but the difference isn't great enough to justify changing code. Other factors, many of which we will discuss later, are more important. When you are dealing with Windows API calls, however, the primary factor is what Windows tells you to do. Why Windows chooses one method or another in different circumstances should tell you something about choices in your Basic code.

Anatomy of a DLL Procedure Call

We've been pretending that the ZAPI functions are written in Basic to be called by Basic, but in reality they are written as a C DLL to be called from C, Pascal, Logo, Scheme, and the current language of the month. The ZAPI library needs to be in native code not only for speed but also because many callers won't have the Visual Basic run-time DLL on their disks. The last thing the author of ZAPI had in mind was making it easy to call API functions from Basic. Internally, ZAPI uses whatever conventions are most efficient (usually taken from C, but sometimes from Pascal).

In order to call a procedure in a DLL, you must write a Declare statement for it. (We'll talk about the type-library alternative to Declare statements later.) The Zapem API function, shown in Figure 2-3, serves as a preliminary model of how to write and use Declare statements.

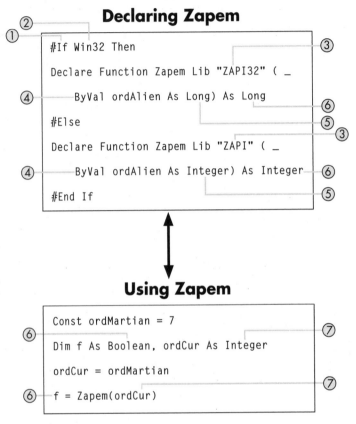

Figure 2-3. *Both sides of a DLL call.*

A lot is packed into this short bit of code. Take a look at the labeled sections in Figure 2-3, which correspond to the numbered sections here:

1. Notice how the code begins. I have yet to see a Declare statement that you could use for both 16-bit and 32-bit modes. It's theoretically possible, but generally you have to use conditional compilation to create different versions.

2. You can test conditionally for the predefined constant *Win32*. Visual Basic defines this constant as 0 in the 16-bit version or −1 in the 32-bit version. A *Win16* constant is defined with the opposite values, but as long as Visual Basic supports only two environments, you need only one of these constants.

3. You must include the name of the DLL containing the procedure. The name of the 32-bit version usually contains the digits *32*, although you can use the same name for both DLLs as long as they are in different locations. If you're calling your own DLL, you probably know the name. If you're calling the Windows API, you sometimes have to guess. C programmers don't need to put the DLL name in their declarations, and since most API documentation is designed for C programmers, you might have trouble figuring it out. Microsoft Visual C++ (32-bit version) comes with a file named WIN32API.CSV that tells all for Win32, but there seems to be no comparable information for Win16. C compilers usually come with tools for dumping executables; try EXEHDR for 16-bit and DUMPBIN for 32-bit. If that doesn't work, use the trial-and-error method, starting with the DLLs shown in Table 2-1 on the next page.

4. The big question is whether to pass by value or by reference. Most arguments should be passed by value, but you'll hear a lot about the exceptions later in this chapter.

5. Most integer values have Integer type in 16-bit mode and Long type in 32-bit mode. Values that are too big for 16 bits are Long in both modes. Integer arguments in 32-bit mode are as common as spotted zebras.

6. The original Basic version of Zapem returned a Boolean value, but the Windows BOOL type isn't the same as a Basic Boolean. BOOL is 16 bits in 16-bit mode and 32 bits in 32-bit mode, whereas Boolean is always 16 bits. Although you should declare what Windows calls BOOL as Long in 32-bit mode, you can assign the result to Boolean. Basic automatically performs the type conversion from Long or Integer to Boolean on return values.

7. What size argument do you pass to a parameter that expects a Long in one mode and an Integer in another? If the values you are passing will always be within Integer range (as these alien ordinals always will be), you can pass an Integer. Basic will do automatic type conversion. But if the value will overflow the Integer range in 32-bit mode, you'd better make it a Long on both sides. (We'll look at specific examples and exceptions later.)

Services	16-Bit DLL	32-Bit DLL
Common controls	COMMCTRL	COMCTL32
Common dialogs	COMMDLG	COMDLG32
DDE	DDEML	USER32
Drag and drop, icon extraction, Windows 95 shell	SHELL	SHELL32
Graphics Device Interface	GDI.EXE	GDI32
Graphics (3-D lines and surfaces)	None	OPENGL32
Graphics (games and animation)	WING	WING32
Memory, disks, processes, resources, tasks, modules	KERNEL.EXE	KERNEL32
Modules, tasks, timing, advanced heap and memory	TOOLHELP	None
Multimedia, sound, MIDI, joysticks, timing	MMSYSTEM	WINMM
Networks (WNet)	USER.EXE	MPR
Networks (LanMan)	NETAPI	NETAPI32
NT Security and other advanced services	None	ADVAPI32
OLE	OLE2	OLE32
OLE Automation and type conversion	OLE2DISP	OLEAUT32
Registry	SHELL	ADVAPI32
Version checking	VER	VERSION
Windows, menus, strings, messages	USER.EXE	USER32

Table 2-1. *Windows system DLLs.*

PERFORMANCE

Problem: How does the timing of arguments passed by value compare to the timing of arguments passed by reference (the default)?

Problem	16-Bit Mode	32-Bit Mode
Variable Integer by value	200 ms	182 ms
Variable Integer by reference	206 ms	184 ms
Variable Double by value	227 ms	193 ms
Variable Double by reference	229 ms	192 ms
Variable String by value	1623 ms	1653 ms
Variable String by reference	768 ms	443 ms

Conclusion: For most types, not enough difference to spit at.

That's the quick introduction to API calls. When you get down to actual coding, though, things get complicated. Every type of argument has its own quirks and patterns, and you must look at each type specifically. Fortunately, the Windows API never uses the Variant, Currency, Single, or Double type. The remaining types fall into patterns that we can discuss one by one.

> **NOTE** The OLE API does use Variant and other Visual Basic data types. Theoretically, you could use them in declarations for the OLE system DLLs or for OLE-compatible DLLs that you write. You can even use the Optional and ParamArray attributes in Declare statements. This chapter, however, concentrates on the integer and string types used by the Windows API. Chapter 3 says a little more about Basic types used in C DLLs, but for the most part this topic deserves an in-depth treatment in another book.

Why Roll Your Own?

Visual Basic comes with text files containing Declare statements for most of the Windows API functions you might want to use. You even get a little wizard program that cuts declarations out of those files and pastes them into your application. So why bother learning how to write your own?

Well, here's a little story of heartbreak, despair, and wasted effort. WritePrivateProfileString used to be one of the most popular functions in the Windows API because it allowed you to save data between sessions—functionality that Basic should have provided long ago but didn't until this version. Everyone wanted to use this function. Everyone pasted the declaration from the Help file or the text file. Everyone had trouble using it. Everyone then called Microsoft Product Support or, if they worked at Microsoft, sent e-mail to the internal Visual Basic programming alias. I used to see at least one such query a month about WritePrivateProfileString.

The problem was that the declaration shipped with Visual Basic was, to put it charitably, strange. It wasn't wrong. In fact, a note in the text file (which no one seemed to read) explained how to use the declaration. I would say, however, that of the four or five alternatives for writing this declaration, the one chosen was the worst and the most likely to cause problems. Fortunately, the new GetSetting, SaveSetting, DeleteSetting, and GetAllSettings functions make this problem irrelevant.

The point is, don't trust anyone's declarations—especially not mine. If you roll your own (or at least know how), you won't suffer because of someone else's bad choices. You have a lot of options, many of which I'll show you later in this chapter.

The API Contract

You can think of the interface between Basic and the Windows API as a legal contract. On the one side, Basic wishes to acquire certain services and resources. On the other side, the Windows API is in the business of providing those services and resources. However, since each party is providing information that could be dangerous to the other, and since the parties don't speak the same language, both feel the need for a legal contract spelling out the terms and limits of the transaction.

The Windows API provides its side of the contract as part of the specifications of its DLLs. These are spelled out in the API documentation and are partially enforced by the actual DLL interfaces. Visual Basic submits a legal request in the form of a Declare statement. It checks the declaration against the DLL interface and rejects anything incompatible.

Ignore at Your Own Risk

C programmers are not like us. When Brian Kernighan (or Dennis Ritchie) writes a function, he makes it return something whether most callers need to receive anything or not. For example, that most popular of C functions, printf, returns the number of characters it prints—information that is totally worthless 95 percent of the time and that is ignored by C programmers 99 percent of the time. No problem. C programmers can use the return value:

```
c = printf("Four");
```

Or they can ignore it:

```
printf("Four");
```

In previous versions of Visual Basic, Basic programmers (like Pascal and FORTRAN programmers) had to think very carefully about whether to make each procedure a sub or a function. It was rude to return something users didn't need; they had to declare a junk variable just to receive it. But you didn't want to leave out something that was critical to a few users just because it was worthless to most. Visual Basic version 4 eliminates this dilemma. Callers can ignore the return value of functions. The statement

```
Call TakeStuffAndGiveJunk("Stuff")
```

or the statement

```
TakeStuffAndGiveJunk "Stuff"
```

As any lawyer can tell you, it's impossible to fully specify the terms of a transaction in a legal contract. You try to define everything you can think of and handle the rest on an ad hoc basis. If something goes wrong, you can sue after the fact. Unfortunately, "lawsuits" in the Windows world often end up as unhandled exceptions, general protection faults, unrecoverable application errors, and cold boots. The next sections explain how far the API contract goes and how to avoid conflicts in areas the law doesn't cover.

Integer Parameters

Most parameters in the Windows API are integers of one kind or another. C makes a distinction between signed and unsigned integers, but to Basic they're all signed. You can assign all integers—signed and unsigned—to Integers and Longs. "Hammering Bits," page 113, discusses some of the problems you might have dealing with integers when you think they are unsigned but Basic thinks they are signed.

is equivalent to the following:

```
Dim iJunk As Integer
iJunk = TakeStuffAndGiveJunk("Stuff")
```

I discovered this by accident and didn't believe it at first, but it's true. If you use the Sub syntax on a function, the return is automatically deposited in that great bit bucket in the sky, which is exactly the same place *iJunk* goes if you never use it again.

Because the Windows API is written in and for C, lots of API routines return dubious information, which you can ignore. For example, many API Set functions return the previous value so that you can restore it later if necessary. This is great if you need to restore the old setting, but if your change is permanent, you can use the Call syntax to throw away the return value.

A word of warning: the ability to call functions the same way you call subs does not authorize you to ignore error return values, no matter how inconvenient. Assume that every function comes with one of those little mattress tags that says, "Do not ignore under penalty of law. Violators will be prosecuted." Never assume that an error can't happen in your program. (Do what I say, not what I do.)

Although you can drop the Call keyword and the parentheses surrounding arguments, I prefer to keep them so that I can tell at a glance that this really is a function. The Call syntax reminds me that I threw away the return value on purpose, not out of ignorance or absentmindedness.

In the Windows API, you usually pass integers by value using the ByVal attribute. Table 2-2 lists the kinds of integers you'll see in the API documentation and shows how to handle them in Declare statements.

Windows API	16-Bit Basic	32-Bit Basic
int, INT	ByVal Integer	ByVal Long
UINT	ByVal Integer	ByVal Long
BOOL	ByVal Integer	ByVal Long
WORD	ByVal Integer	ByVal Integer
DWORD	ByVal Long	ByVal Long
WPARAM	ByVal Integer	ByVal Long
LPARAM, LRESULT	ByVal Long	ByVal Long
COLORREF	ByVal Long	ByVal Long
ATOM	ByVal Integer	ByVal Integer
HANDLE and friends	ByVal Integer	ByVal Long
BYTE	ByVal Byte	ByVal Byte
char	ByVal Byte	ByVal Byte

Table 2-2. *Integers in the Windows API.*

NOTE In previous versions of Visual Basic, you had to use the Integer type to represent the few Windows API calls that take char or BYTE arguments. Version 4 adds the Byte type, which represents an 8-bit integer.

For passing integers, the API contract is simple. Basic agrees to put integer values on the stack and never see them again. Windows can do whatever it wants with those values. All that can go wrong here is that you could pass an integer too large for an Integer type or a Long type. Basic will catch this error before it gets anywhere near Windows. Of course, you could always pass a value that a particular API function doesn't understand, but Windows promises to politely fail and return an error code in these cases.

Here's a simple integer example. The 16-bit API documentation shows FloodFill as follows:

```
BOOL FloodFill(hdc, nXStart, nYStart, clrref)
HDC hdc;           // Handle of device context
int nXStart;       // X-coordinate of starting position
int nYStart;       // Y-coordinate of starting position
COLORREF clrref;   // Color of fill boundary
```

You declare it this way in Basic:

```
# If Win32 Then
Declare Function FloodFill Lib "GDI32" (ByVal hdc As Long, _
    ByVal x As Long, ByVal y As Long, _
    ByVal clrref As Long) As Long
# Else
Declare Function FloodFill Lib "GDI" (ByVal hdc As Integer, _
    ByVal x As Integer, ByVal y As Integer, _
    ByVal clrref As Long) As Long
# End If
```

You don't have much choice about how to declare this function, but you can choose how to declare any variables you plan to pass to it.

A color is always type Long, whatever the mode, but you do have choices about the x and y values. The question is whether either value will ever be higher than 32,767 or lower than −32,768. You'd need an awfully big monitor to exceed those values if you're measuring in pixels. I hope to have such a monitor on my desk someday, but for now I consider it fairly safe to use Integer variables. Keep in mind that Windows can measure screen real estate in many modes. (Basic uses twips by default.) You can choose to keep the default Single type, or you might want to use Long. If the values fit, Basic will convert these values to Long or Integer as appropriate. Generally it's not a problem.

NOTE   Under Windows NT, screen coordinates can be 32-bit values. Under Windows 95, screen coordinates are 16-bit values even though they fit in 32-bit variables. This still makes them larger than screen coordinates under Windows 3.x. The largest 16-bit signed number (the only kind Basic understands) that can fit in an Integer is 32,767. The largest 16-bit signed number that can fit in a Long is 65,535.

The hDC (handle to a device context) presents a different problem. Handles always (or almost always) contain 16-bit values in 16-bit mode. They always contain 32-bit values in 32-bit mode. So what can you do? Well, you can declare the handle variable in conditional blocks:

```
# If Win32 Then
Private hImage As Long
# Else
Private hImage As Integer
# End If
```

This might be the most efficient solution, but your code will end up unreadable and impossible to maintain. Instead you could declare all handles as Long:

```
Private hImage As Long
```

Yes, this wastes a few bytes, and, yes, the code is slightly less efficient in 16-bit mode. But the extra bytes and cycles are worth the cost to make the code maintainable. Besides, the 16-bit version will be headed for the dustbin of history real soon now.

Although Basic doesn't provide a built-in type for system integers, there is a way to declare them. I find this technique distasteful because it requires one of my least favorite Basic language features. Back in the days of BASICA, every program with any pretensions of efficiency had to start with the following line:

```
DefInt A-Z
```

Many programmers still use this technique to make Integer (rather than Variant) the default type for all their variables. Normally, I don't like default types and never use them. My programming mentor, Joe Hacker (whom you'll meet in Chapter 3), says, "If you have a choice of saying what you mean or accepting a default, always say what you mean."

I hate to abandon that good advice, but think for a minute what it would mean if you had the following lines at the start of each module:

```
#If Win32 Then
DefLng A-Z
#Else
DefInt A-Z
#End If
```

You'd have a system integer type. If you ask me (nobody did, but I told them anyway), the language ought to have a built-in system integer type—call it SysInt. It would certainly make portable programming easier. No such type exists, so I add my own.

Since this fake type violates my standard of declaring the type of every variable, I use an extra comment to declare the type by convention:

```
Dim hWnd ' As SysInt
```

I don't always use the SysInt type. Usually Long works just as well, and the tiny size and performance difference in 16-bit mode is negligible. But I often use SysInt for graphics, an area where I don't care to make any sacrifices.

NOTE I use the Windows version of Hungarian in sample declarations, although I don't like it. "Basic Hungarian," page 15, explains what I don't like and how my version of Hungarian differs. Apologies for any confusion this causes. The parameter names in declarations are ignored anyway, and I thought it would be better for my declarations to match the API documentation. Besides, I created a lot of my Declare statements by cutting, pasting, and modifying C prototypes, and I was too lazy to change the names.

Pointers to Integers

Basic programmers can pass by reference by default without really knowing how or why, but C programmers don't have this luxury. The C language doesn't have an automatic way to specify that a variable should be passed by reference instead of by value (although C++ and Pascal do). Instead, C programmers pass by reference by explicitly passing a pointer to the variable. In other words, C programmers do on purpose what Basic programmers do by accident. But when you mix the two approaches by accessing the Windows API, Basic must defer to C.

The only reason the Windows API uses pointers to integers is to return them. You can put only one value in the function return, so if you need to return more than one value, you have to use reference parameters. For a few procedures, you put a meaningful value into the variable before passing it and then get a modified version back. More commonly, you simply pass an empty variable; the return is all that matters.

Documentation for the 16-bit API shows pointers to integers as FAR *DWORD, FAR *HWND, or something similar. The asterisk indicates that the variable is a pointer to a DWORD (Long in Basic). *FAR* means…well, trust me, if you don't already know, you don't want to. It doesn't matter because every address is far in Basic. C allows such complex pointer declarations that it offers an aliasing feature to give them readable names. The 32-bit documentation shows pointers with equivalent defined pointer types such as LPDWORD and LPHWND. Table 2-3 on the next page shows values commonly seen in API documentation.

The GetScrollRange function illustrates how to pass integers by reference. It needs to return two integers—the top and bottom of the scroll range—so it uses pointers to integers to return them. The 16-bit C documentation shows this:

```
void GetScrollRange(hwnd, fnBar, lpnMinPos, lpnMaxPos)
HWND hwnd;              // Handle of window with scroll bar
int fnBar;             // Scroll bar flags
int FAR* lpnMinPos;    // Receives minimum position
int FAR* lpnMaxPos;    // Receives maximum position
```

Windows API	16-Bit Basic	32-Bit Basic
LPINT, int FAR*	Integer	Long
LPUINT, UINT FAR*	Integer	Long
LPBOOL, BOOL FAR*	Integer	Long
LPBYTE, BYTE FAR*	Byte	Byte
LPWORD, WORD FAR*	Integer	Integer
LPDWORD, DWORD FAR*	Long	Long
LPHANDLE, HANDLE FAR*, and friends	Integer	Long

Table 2-3. *Pointers to integers in the Windows API.*

The 32-bit version looks the same except for the last two lines:

```
LPINT lpMinPos;        // Receives minimum position
LPINT lpMaxPos;        // Receives maximum position
```

The Basic declaration looks like this:

```
# If Win32 Then
Declare Function GetScrollRange Lib "User32" ( _
    ByVal hWnd As Long, ByVal nBar As Long, _
    lpMin As Long, lpMax As Long) As Long
# Else
Declare Function GetScrollRange Lib "USER" ( _
    ByVal hWnd As Integer, ByVal nBar As Integer, _
    lpMin As Integer, lpMax As Integer) As Integer
# End If
```

Calling the function is another matter, however. It seems simple enough—just declare the variables to be received as Long so that they'll work for either 16-bit or 32-bit mode:

```
Dim iMin As Long, iMax As Long
f = GetScrollRange(txtTest.hWnd, SB_HORZ, iMin, iMax)
```

This works in 32-bit mode, but if you call it in 16-bit mode, you'll see the message *ByRef argument type mismatch*. Try declaring the variable another way:

```
Dim iMin As Integer, iMax As Integer
```

Now 16-bit mode works, but 32-bit mode fails with the same error.

To understand why, consider what would happen if Basic allowed you to pass Integer variables to GetScrollRange in 32-bit mode. Once Basic passes the address of the variable to Windows, it has no control over what Windows does to that variable. If Windows writes the value 100,000 into the variable, whatever happens to be next to it in memory will be trashed. To prevent this, the API contract insists that all arguments passed by reference must be the exact size specified in the declaration. (In fact, the rule goes beyond the API contract and applies to procedures written in Basic, for the same reasons. Use ByVal if a numeric parameter of a sub or a function will be used as input only and if you also want Basic to automatically perform type conversions of arguments.)

The bottom line is that to receive variables by reference through the Windows API, you must use conditional compilation:

```
# If Win32 Then
    Dim iMin As Long, iMax As Long
# Else
    Dim iMin As Integer, iMax As Integer
# End If
    f = GetScrollRange(txtTest.hWnd, SB_HORZ, iMin, iMax)
    txtTest.Text = "Scroll range: Min = " & iMin & ", Max = " & iMax
```

Better yet, use the SysInt shortcut described earlier:

```
Dim iMin ' As SysInt
Dim iMax ' As SysInt
```

Fortunately, you'll rarely see integers returned through pointers in the 16-bit Windows API, but this is not uncommon in procedures specific to the 32-bit API. Of course, if you're using only 32-bit procedures, you needn't worry about this conflict.

User-Defined Types

In Basic, you pass UDTs (*structures* in C) to Windows API functions by reference for three possible reasons. The first is the same reason you pass integers by reference—so that you can get something back. The second is that most UDT variables are too large to pass efficiently by value. The third and deciding reason is that Basic won't let you pass them by value even if you want to. You'll see an example in Chapter 5 ("Window position and size," page 211) in which the first two reasons don't apply and you have to jump through hoops to get around the third.

The window placement functions illustrate. The GetWindowPlacement function returns window position values through a TWindowPlacement type (a WINDOWPLACEMENT structure in C), and the SetWindowPlacement function saves values in the same structure. As with most examples in this chapter, it's not important what these functions do; we're concerned only with the syntax and what is passed at the lowest level.

The C documentation for the placement functions looks like this:

```
BOOL GetWindowPlacement(hwnd, lpwndpl)
HWND hhwnd;                          // Handle of window
WINDOWPLACEMENT FAR* lpwndpl;        // Address for position data

BOOL SetWindowPlacement(hwnd, lpwndpl)
HWND hhwnd;                          // Handle of window
const WINDOWPLACEMENT FAR* lpwndpl; // Address of position data
```

The only difference between the two functions, other than the name, is that SetWindowPlacement has *const* in the WINDOWPLACEMENT type. I'll explain that difference shortly.

The Basic user-defined type looks like this:

```
#If Win32 Then
Private Type TWindowPlacement
    length As Long
    Flags As Long
    showCmd As Long
    ptMinPosition As TPoint
    ptMaxPosition As TPoint
    rcNormalPosition As TRect
End Type
#Else
Private Type TWindowPlacement
    length As Integer
    Flags As Integer
    showCmd As Integer
    ptMinPosition As TPoint
    ptMaxPosition As TPoint
    rcNormalPosition As TRect
End Type
#End If
```

It would be nice if you could use the fake SysInt type to create just one UDT that works for both environments:

```
Private Type TWindowPlacement
    length ' As SysInt
    Flags  ' As SysInt
    ⋮
```

Unfortunately, Basic requires a specific As Type clause for each UDT field.

NOTE

As you've probably noticed, the difference between 16-bit mode and 32-bit mode is largely mechanical. The 32-bit library has a different name, and all Integers come out as Longs. To save space, I'll show only the 16-bit versions from now on, except when a difference other than word size arises. I chose 16-bit versions for examples so that you can see the difference between types that have the default word size and those that are always 32-bit.

The 16-bit Basic Declare statements look like this:

```
Declare Function SetWindowPlacement Lib "User" ( _
    ByVal hWnd As Integer, lpwndpl As TWindowPlacement) As Integer
Declare Function GetWindowPlacement Lib "User" ( _
    ByVal hWnd As Integer, lpwndpl As TWindowPlacement) As Integer
```

You simply pass GetWindowPlacement an empty *TWindowPlacement* variable and read the result out of the variable afterward:

```
Dim wp As TWindowPlacement
' First set type length for Windows
wp.length = Len(wp)
' Get coordinates and other data about the window
f = GetWindowPlacement(hWnd, wp)
' Read and use the data
sValue = wp.showCmd & ","
sValue = sValue & wp.Flags & ","
```

Notice how the length field is set to the length of the structure before the call. This is called planning ahead. If Microsoft designs a new version of Windows that has more fields in the TWindowPlacement type, your old code won't necessarily be broken. Windows will be able to tell from the length field whether you have the new and improved structure or the old standby. You'll see length fields in a few of the original Windows structures—and a lot more of them in newer structures such as those in TOOLHELP and Win32.

WARNING

While writing this book, I forgot to set the length field and wasted several hours in fruitless debugging so that you won't have to. Don't let my suffering be in vain.

The SetWindowPlacement function looks almost the same, but it works in the opposite way. You put values into the variable first and then call the function to pass them to the system:

```
' Remember to set length
wp.length = Len(wp)
' Send all your settings to the system
f = SetWindowPlacement(hWnd, wp)
```

If you look back at the declarations, you can see that the *TWindowPlacement* variable is passed by reference in both the Set and Get functions. In the Get function, it must be passed by reference so that Windows can fill in the new value. In the Set function, it's passed by reference only to avoid wasting stack space. That's where the const keyword in the C parameter definition comes in.

C allows you to specify that a variable is being passed by reference for convenience, not for modification. When you pass the address of a variable, you give the receiver the right to modify it. The const keyword revokes that right. It would be nice if this protection were written into the Basic side of the API contract. Just imagine being able to put a ReadOnly attribute on Basic by-reference parameters so that an error is generated if the callee changes the value. Fortunately, it's unnecessary for the Basic-to-Windows interface because Windows enforces the const attribute. You can rest assured that if the documentation for an API parameter says that it's const, anything passed to it will come back untouched.

Arrays

Like UDTs, arrays must be passed by reference, and for the same reasons. The big difference is that Windows knows the size of a UDT used by an API procedure, but it doesn't know how many elements an array contains. In fact, that's usually the reason you pass arrays to Windows—so that you can give varying numbers of elements. This means, however, that the API procedure needs to ask for the length in a separate parameter.

This requirement highlights another difference between C and Basic. Basic always knows how many elements an array contains (just as it knows the size of a string). C doesn't, forcing the C programmer to keep track. Windows, in the C tradition, has the same requirement. This isn't true of OLE, however. From its interface, you might almost think that OLE was written in Basic. It wasn't, but Visual Basic types had a strong influence on its design. OLE supports a type called the *safe array* that just happens to have exactly the same format as a Basic array. Or perhaps it's the other way around. In any case, arrays passed to OLE procedures are more intuitive than those passed to Windows procedures.

For example, the Polygon API function (discussed in Chapter 6) passes an array of TPoint variables along with the number of points in the array. Polygon connects the dots. The function looks like this on the C side:

```
BOOL Polygon(hdc, lppt, cPoints)
HDC hdc;                    // Handle of device context
const POINT FAR* lppt;  // Address of array with points for vertices
int cPoints;                // Number of points in array
```

The Basic UDT and declaration look like this:

```
Type TPoint
    x As Integer
    y As Integer
End Type
Declare Function Polygon Lib "GDI" (ByVal hdc As Integer, _
    lppt As TPoint, ByVal cPoints As Integer) As Integer
```

Notice that the *lppt* parameter is passed by reference. You might think this is because TPoint is a user-defined type, and UDTs are always passed by reference. Not so. The reason *lppt* is passed by reference is that in C an array is actually the address of the first element. If you pass a variable by reference, you're actually passing its address, which is just what C (and Windows) thinks an array is. Another way to see this is to think of a variable as an array with one element. That's why the Polygon declaration looks exactly as it would if the function took one TPoint variable instead of an array of them.

To pass an array, you pass the first element. Here's an example:

```
Dim ptPoly(1 To 5) As TPoint
For i = 1 To 5
    ' Calculate each point
    ⋮
Next i
Call Polygon(hDC, ptPoly(1), 5)
```

This gives you lots of rope—enough to hang yourself. For example, you don't have to pass the start of the array or all the elements in it. The call

```
Call Polygon(hDC, ptPoly(2), 3)
```

passes the second through fourth elements of the array.

If you look at arrays in legal terms, the contract isn't worth the polish on the shoes of the lawyer who wrote it. Windows wants an array, but Basic can't be sure that's what you're giving. Windows wants the number of elements in the array, but Basic isn't going to count them. It's up to you to tell the truth. If you claim that the array contains 10 elements when it really has 5, Windows will happily use those last 5 elements whether they exist or not. Your machine might head south in a hurry.

When you look up the syntax for declarations, you'll see that it's possible to put empty parentheses on a parameter to indicate that you're passing an array. Don't try it with API functions. This feature is used for calling OLE DLLs that know about Basic-style safe arrays with an encoded size. If OLE had a GDI library, the OlePolygon function might look like this:

```
Declare Function OlePolygon Lib "OLEGDI" (ByVal hdc As Integer, _
    lppt() As TPoint) As Boolean
⋮
Call OlePolygon(hDC, ptPoly)
```

You'll get errors if you try to pass an entire array to a C-style procedure that expects the first element of an array, or if you try to pass the first element of an array to an OLE-style function that expects the entire array.

Typeless Variables

The Windows API frequently requires typeless parameters. The idea is to pass different types of data to the same function. For example, the GetObject function handles pens, brushes, fonts, bitmaps, and palettes through the same parameter. This works fine in weakly typed languages such as C. It doesn't work so well in Basic, a schizophrenic language that can't make up its mind whether to be strongly typed or weakly typed. The Declare statement, at any rate, is strongly typed, most of the time. (Basic is also a typeless language, through its Variant type; but just as Basic doesn't do pointers, Windows doesn't do variants.)

Every variable has a type, explicit or assumed, regardless of the host language. When you pass a variable to a function, that function must figure out the type so that it knows what to do with the variable. The type can be embedded in the data (as in Basic Variants), or it can be supplied as a separate parameter to the function. That's the easy part. The tricky part is getting Basic to turn off its data typing so that you can pass different kinds of data. The Alias attribute of the Declare statement and the Any type of parameters enable you to lie, cheat, steal, and have your way with data.

The GetObject API function illustrates several points about untyped parameters. The C version looks like this:

```
int GetObject(hgdiobj, cbBuffer, lpvObject)
HGDIOBJ hgdiobj;        // Handle of object
int cbBuffer;           // Size of buffer for object information
void FAR* lpvObject;    // Address of buffer for object information
```

To use GetObject, you pass it the handle of a logical pen, a brush, a font, a bitmap, or a palette. You pass the length of the data you want to get back and the address of the variable where you want the data placed. This variable will have type LOGPEN, LOGBRUSH, LOGFONT, BITMAP, or int, depending on the data. Windows will use the handle to find the data and will then copy it to the variable.

The Basic prototype presents several problems. First, GetObject is the name of a Visual Basic function. In previous versions of Visual Basic, you got an error if you tried to declare a function with an existing function name, but version 4 offers no objections if you redefine GetObject with either a Declare statement or a Basic function. Nevertheless, don't do it. You should rename this function. I call mine VBGetObject.

> **NOTE** You can redefine a function to replace the built-in version with a new version. For example, you could write your own InStr with the appropriate optional arguments. Any code you wrote earlier that uses the built-in InStr will work with your new version. This is how you use the renaming feature. You abuse it by giving your function the same name as the built-in version but different behavior.

You'll encounter the name problem in several cases in the Windows API, and it's likely to come up any time you try to use a DLL written for another language. For example, the Windows API includes the _lopen, _lread, _lwrite, and _lclose functions, but you can't write declarations for them because a Basic name can't start with an underscore. Basic provides the Alias attribute to let you specify that a name recognized in one way by the DLL can have a different Basic name.

The second problem is to turn off Basic's type checking. In other words, you need a type that corresponds to a C void pointer. The Any type passed by reference is a rough equivalent. When you declare a parameter with As Any, you cancel the contract. Basic no longer promises the Windows API anything in particular. Windows promises to write no more than the specified number of bytes to the specified variable, whether they fit or not. It's up to you to pass a variable that can accept the data. If you're the kind of programmer who doesn't mind working without a net, you might be getting bright ideas about using As Any in your own procedures. Forget it. Basic accepts As Any only in Declare statements. Use Variant, not As Any, to write typeless functions in Basic.

The declaration for VBGetObject looks like this:

```
Declare Function VBGetObject Lib "GDI" Alias "GetObject" ( _
    ByVal hObject As Integer, ByVal nCount As Integer, _
    lpvObject As Any) As Integer
```

The Basic version of C's BITMAP type looks like this:

```
Type TBitmap
    Type As Integer
    Width As Integer
    Height As Integer
    WidthBytes As Integer
    Planes As Byte
    BitsPixel As Byte
    Bits As Long
End Type
```

You can pass a TBitmap variable to VBGetObject:

```
Dim bmp As TBitmap
    ⋮
c = VBGetObject(pbBitmap.Picture, Len(bmp), bmp)
```

That's easy enough if you happen to know that the Picture property of a picture box containing a bitmap is actually a bitmap handle. (Chapter 6 explains this and related issues.) But you'd better be sure that whatever gets passed to the function is what you say it is. If you pass a bitmap handle in parameter 1, the length of a TLogPen in parameter 2, and a TLogBrush variable in parameter 3, you won't like the results.

If you ignore the safety net that Basic offers, you must be ready to accept the consequences. Or, better yet, use the safety net. You can alias as many functions as you want to the same API function, so why not do a type-safe version for each data type?

```
Declare Function GetObjectBrush Lib "GDI" Alias "GetObject" ( _
    ByVal hObject As Integer, ByVal nCount As Integer, _
    lplbObject As TLogBrush) As Integer
Declare Function GetObjectPen Lib "GDI" Alias "GetObject" ( _
    ByVal hObject As Integer, ByVal nCount As Integer, _
    lplbObject As TLogPen) As Integer
Declare Function GetObjectBitmap Lib "GDI" Alias "GetObject" ( _
    ByVal hObject As Integer, ByVal nCount As Integer, _
    lplbObject As TBitmap) As Integer
```

Don't let the increased safety make you overconfident. If you pass a TLogPen variable to GetObjectBrush, you get the error *ByRef argument type mismatch*. But if you pass a Pen handle to GetObjectBrush, neither Basic nor Windows complains. Windows gets the data type and the data from the handle, but it can't tell whether you passed the matching length and destination variable.

Dealing with Strings

An integer is an integer is an integer in any language, but every language has its own ideas about strings. In Basic, a string is supposed to be a black box. You put things in through Basic statements; the system allocates, moves, and resizes the data without your knowledge or interference; you get things back in the expected format. In C, in contrast, you must understand exactly how strings are stored in memory to process them correctly and efficiently. Nothing is allocated, moved, or resized unless you do it.

This fundamental difference between C strings and Basic strings is probably the biggest problem you face in dealing with the Windows API. Essentially, you have to get un-Basic with strings—you have to know what Basic programmers aren't supposed to know.

Strings Inside Out

The C string format, known in API jargon as LPSTR, is a sequence of characters terminated by the null character (ASCII value 0), as shown in Figure 2-4 on the next page. Notice that the length of the string isn't stored. C programmers must either keep track of the length themselves or call a function that calculates the length by looping through each character until it finds a terminating null.

Supposedly, the implementation of Basic strings isn't documented because it might change in a later version of Basic. In fact, the format of Basic strings is well known and changed little from QuickBasic to Visual Basic 3. These strings were at least partially documented in the VBX custom control documentation, where they went by the name HLSTR (high-level string). Figure 2-4 illustrates the format.

However, if you ignored Microsoft's advice and wrote C DLLs that took advantage of your knowledge of Basic strings, you are now officially up the creek. Visual Basic 4 has changed the rules. Basic now uses the BSTR format, officially described in the OLE Automation documentation. Figure 2-4 points out the difference. BSTRs are better than HLSTRs for two reasons. First, they have one less pointer. Second, they are already null terminated, so Basic doesn't have to null-terminate before passing them on to C.

As a Basic programmer, you must make an unnatural distinction when passing strings to the Windows API: you have to separate input strings from output strings and handle each case in a completely different fashion. This takes some getting used to.

Sending Strings to the Windows API

Sending input strings to the Windows API is simple and direct. Your API calls look pretty much the same as calls to Basic procedures. The trick is in defining the declarations.

LPSTR (What Windows wants)

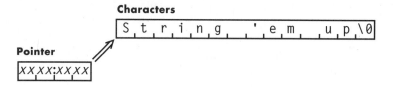

HLSTR (What Visual Basic 3 has)

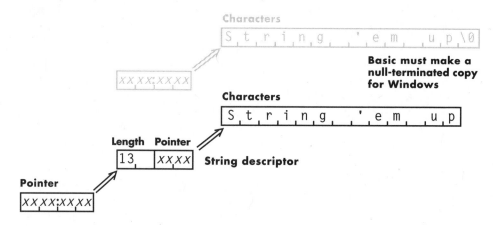

BSTR (What Visual Basic 4 has)

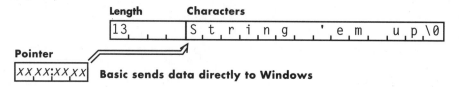

Figure 2-4. *Three kinds of strings.*

The designers of Visual Basic enabled Basic-to-C conversion by overloading the ByVal attribute to mean something other than what its name implies—that is, they lied. Passing a string by value doesn't actually pass it by value. Doing so would imply that all the bytes of the string are placed on the stack. Instead, Basic simply passes by value a pointer to the string. In Visual Basic 3, Basic also needed to ensure that the HLSTR was null terminated, which sometimes meant that the string had to be copied to a temporary string for processing by C and then copied back to the real Basic version afterward in case C modified the string copy. Those days are over now because BSTRs are already null terminated.

In the Windows API documentation, C string parameters have the type LPCSTR if the string is to be used only as input. (The *C* in the name indicates a constant.) Parameters have the type LPSTR if the string is to be used as an output buffer filled by the function. (In 32-bit code, the type is sometimes LPCTSTR or LPTSTR, but this is a Unicode difference that you can ignore. To Basic, LPCTSTR is the same as LPCSTR, and LPTSTR is the same as LPSTR.)

For example, the FindWindow documentation looks like this:

```
HWND FindWindow(lpszClassName, lpszWindow)
LPCSTR lpszClassName;    // Address of class-name string
LPCSTR lpszWindow;       // Address of window-name string
```

A Word to the Wise

Figure 2-4 demonstrates how BSTRs work, but given what happened to those who wrote DLLs using HLSTRs, do you dare take advantage of this knowledge in your DLLs? Well, not directly. But you'll find a significant difference between Microsoft's level of commitment to HLSTRs and its commitment to BSTRs.

The BSTR format is officially part of OLE, not just part of a specific language. Microsoft is committed to creating public standards based on OLE. Fire would fall from heaven if Microsoft announced a year from now that current OLE servers and controls would not work in future versions of Windows and Visual Basic for Applications.

Microsoft has not committed to the internal BSTR format. In fact, the OLE documentation specifically states that you should manipulate BSTRs only through the OLE string functions—SysAllocString, SysAllocStringLen, SysReAllocString, SysReAllocStringLen, SysFreeString, and SysStringLen—which are located in the 16-bit OLE2DISP.DLL or the 32-bit OLEAUT32.DLL. If you follow the rules, Microsoft promises that your functions will still work even if the internal BSTR format changes.

Cynics might point out that Microsoft provided similar routines for HLSTRs in the control development tools. But Microsoft never promised that these would work anywhere other than in VBXs, and in fact they do still work in VBXs. The moral of this story is to use the SysString functions in the OLE DLLs. Visual Basic and Visual Basic programs require these DLLs, so don't worry about availability.

If you ignore this warning and manipulate string data directly based on my diagrams, don't forget your paddle.

You can declare the function as follows:

```
Declare Function FindWindow Lib "USER" ( _
    ByVal lpClassName As String, _
    ByVal lpWindowName As String) As Integer
```

Notice that both strings are passed by value. Now assume that you want to call FindWindow to find the window handle of the Project window in the Visual Basic environment and that the current project is APITEST.MAK. You could write the following code:

```
hProject = FindWindow("PROJECT", "APITEST.MAK")
```

PROJECT is the class name of the Project window, and APITEST.MAK is the title. (Chapter 5 explains window classes and titles; for now, we're concerned only with the syntax.)

What's really going on here? The string *"PROJECT"* appears to be 7 characters long, but because it includes a terminating null character—Chr$(0)—the real length is 8 characters. Internally, the string also includes a preceding Long containing the length. Therefore, the string uses 12 bytes of memory, although the stored length is what Basic would expect: 7. Basic needs to know the length of the string at all times. The Basic Len function probably grabs the length out of the preceding byte without checking the characters. When you pass the string to the Windows API, however, the length is lost. C doesn't know or care how long a string is.

If you look at this exchange as a contract, Basic promises that when it passes a string with the ByVal attribute, the string will be null terminated and the address of the first character will be passed on the stack. The Windows API promises that if the string is constant (LPCSTR or LPCTSTR), it will not modify the string or assume anything about the characters after the terminating null.

But this contract is less than bulletproof. Windows expects that the string will contain only one null character, the last. Basic makes no such promise. A passed string could have multiple null characters, which are perfectly legal in a Basic string. You as the programmer must ensure that the strings you pass don't have inappropriate embedded nulls. As a practical matter, however, this usually isn't a problem because few Basic programmers embed nulls in strings intended for Windows functions.

Passing Null Pointers

If C were a type-safe language like Basic, passing input strings to the Windows API would always be simple, but many Windows API functions accept a null pointer when the type is String. When you pass a normal string, you are actually passing a pointer to the characters of the string—in other words, the address of the first character. But the C language and the Windows API recognize one special pointer that represents no address. The value of this pointer is 0, but it doesn't represent address 0 even if that address is valid in the current environment. The null pointer is used as a signal to ignore a given parameter.

Passing a null pointer to a string procedure was a major hassle in previous versions of Visual Basic. A null pointer was a Long constant zero (0&), which you couldn't pass to a String parameter. You had to write special versions of Declare statements to accommodate parameters that might take null pointers, using one of the choices described earlier. (See "Typeless Variables," page 64.) You could either throw away type safety with As Any, or you could write multiple aliases to accommodate all the possible combinations of strings and null pointers. In today's modern Basic, those hacks are just a bad memory—like those throw-away pop-can tabs that used to litter the highways before many readers of this book were born. Now you can simply pass the predefined constant *vbNullString* as a string argument.

The previous section assumed that you pass the FindWindow API function a window title and a window class, but in reality you can pass a string for one of these and pass a null pointer in the other to signal that you don't care about it.

For example, assume that you know the title of the window but not the class. You might think that you could pass an empty string for the class:

```
hProject = FindWindow("", "APITEST.MAK")
```

This searches for the window with title *TEST.MAK* and class nothing—but you're unlikely to find a window without a class. To search by title only, you must pass a null pointer rather than an empty string. If you've done this in previous versions, you might try the following:

```
hProject = FindWindow(0&, "APITEST.MAK")
```

Because Basic sees that FindWindow wants a string, it politely converts *0&* to *"0"*. You don't get an error (as you would have in Visual Basic version 3), but neither do you find the window unless you happen to have a window with class 0. ("What Happened to Type Checking?" page 126, discusses other side effects of Basic's new ability to convert integers to strings and vice versa.)

Here's the correct way to solve this problem in Basic:

```
hProject = FindWindow(vbNullString, "APITEST")
hProject = FindWindow("PROJECT", vbNullString)
hProject = FindWindow("PROJECT", "APITEST")
```

This might seem obvious to some of you, but it looks like a miracle to old hands who remember the hacks of yesteryear.

Wrapping String Functions

Although passing *vbNullString* as a string argument is a vast improvement, it's still un-Basic. The Basic Way to signal that a string should be ignored is to use optional arguments, a technique you can see in Basic string functions such as Mid$ and InStr. Up to now, Basic was a little rude about this. It used optional arguments but wouldn't let you do the same, although you could fake them by using an empty string (rather than a null pointer) as a signal to ignore the argument. For example, you could write a wrapper function that worked as follows:

```
hProject = VB3FindWindow("", "APITEST")
hProject = VB3FindWindow("PROJECT", "")
hProject = VB3FindWindow("PROJECT", "APITEST")
```

The new version of Visual Basic not only allows optional arguments but also lets you assign them by name. You can now write a function that can be called as shown here:

```
hProject = VBFindWindow(, "APITEST")
hProject = VBFindWindow("PROJECT")
hProject = VBFindWindow("PROJECT", "APITEST")
hProject = VBFindWindow(vTitle:="APITEST")
hProject = VBFindWindow(vClass:="PROJECT")
```

The code for this function is simple:

```
Function VBFindWindow(Optional vClass As Variant, _
                      Optional vTitle As Variant) ' As SysInt
    If IsMissing(vClass) Then vClass = vbNullString
    If IsMissing(vTitle) Then vTitle = vbNullString
    VBFindWindow = FindWindow(vClass, vTitle)
End Function
```

You'll see more optional arguments throughout this book, although I won't specifically explain the technique. It's in the manual. You'll also see more wrappers around API functions. I use a convention to identify such wrappers: the letters *VB* followed by the name of the Windows API function.

Unicode Versus Basic

You have to jump through one more hoop to write 32-bit declarations for API procedures that deal with strings. I'll show you the hoop first and then explain why it's necessary.

Here's the 32-bit declaration for FindWindow:

```
Declare Function FindWindow Lib "USER32" Alias "FindWindowA" ( _
    ByVal lpClassName As Any, ByVal lpWindowName As Any) As Integer
```

Notice the alias to FindWindowA. It turns out that USER32.DLL contains two different FindWindow functions, neither of which is named FindWindow. FindWindowA handles the 8-bit ANSI character strings that you're used to and that Visual Basic supports. FindWindowW handles 16-bit Unicode strings.

Null and Empty

Don't let the various definitions of *null* and *empty* confuse you:

- The *null character* is ASCII character 0. You can represent this string as Chr$(0), but it's more efficient to use the constant *sNullChr*.

- The term *null string* is commonly used to describe what this book calls an *empty string,* that is, a string with no characters. You can represent this string with empty quotes (""), but it's more efficient to use the constant *sEmpty*. The Basic keyword Empty is a Variant constant representing an empty string for string Variants or 0 for numeric Variants. You can use it anywhere you use *sEmpty*, but it's significantly less efficient for string operations.

- A *null pointer* is a 32-bit integer with value 0 representing address 0. You will normally pass a null pointer to a string parameter with the constant *vbNullString* (or its equivalent in my type library, *sNullStr*). In a few Windows API situations, you might need to pass a null pointer to a numeric parameter. You can use the constant *pNull* for these cases. Incidentally, the *vbNullString* constant also works as an empty string, although you can't use *sEmpty* as a null pointer.

- Another null you'll run into frequently (especially in Chapter 5) is a *null handle*. You can use the constant *hNull*.

- The Null keyword represents a Variant containing no valid data. It's commonly used for databases and gives an error if used in a string context.

- The Nothing keyword also has nothing to do with strings, but I include it here for completeness. It represents an object variable that hasn't yet been set to an object. (See Chapter 4.)

The constants *sNullChr, sEmpty, pNull,* and *hNull* are not part of Basic, but they are provided as part of the Windows API type library described in the Introduction and later in this chapter.

Use constants whenever you can. If you use empty quotes ("") in your program 5000 times, you'll end up with 5000 empty strings, each taking up at least 5 bytes. If you use *sEmpty* 5000 times, you'll get one empty string.

Programmers in C, C++, and some other languages can use either function under Windows NT, but not under Window 95. Visual Basic programmers who aren't masochists should use the ANSI version regardless of the operating system.

All you need to do is alias your 32-bit API declarations to the proper ANSI function name. You can usually identify the ones that need this treatment by their string parameters. Occasionally, you'll encounter a procedure with no string parameters that has both Unicode and ANSI versions. The GetWindowTextLength function, for example, has no string parameters, but it needs two versions so that you can get the length of either the ANSI title or the Unicode title of a window. The Unicode issue is already handled in the functions supported by the Windows API type library, discussed at the end of this chapter.

Unicode exists because many human languages have more than 256 symbols (characters), and 8-bit characters aren't large enough to store them all. The current version of Basic handles this universal problem with double-byte character strings (DBCS). The DBCS system works by recognizing certain 8-bit characters whose role is to signal that the next character is not a standard character—perhaps it's a Chinese ideogram or a Sumerian hieroglyphic. Unicode works by extending characters to 16 bits so that instead of having 256 characters you can have 65,535—enough to handle all the characters of almost all the world's languages.

In this version of Visual Basic, Unicode is an obstacle that you must overcome. In the next version (or maybe the version after that), it will be a feature you can use. Maybe you'll be able to specify individual strings as ANSI or Unicode, or maybe you'll have to specify ANSI or Unicode for the whole program. In the long run, Unicode will completely replace ANSI and DBCS as the standard way of representing characters, and Visual Basic will send only Unicode strings to the outside world. In the short run, 32-bit Visual Basic already stores all characters internally as Unicode, although it translates them back to ANSI strings whenever it sends them to API functions or writes them to disk. This internal architecture was chosen for performance reasons related to the fact that Visual Basic is OLE inside and out (as Chapter 10 will pound into your head). I don't understand all the reasons, but I do know that the Basic architects were well aware of the trade-offs and chose the lesser of two evils after testing both.

If you think about Unicode, it seems like a whole lot of zeros going nowhere. All the text characters employed by those of us who use English fit in the first 128 bytes, meaning that half of each 16-bit Unicode character is zero. If you do a hex dump of a 32-bit Visual Basic program, you'll see all those zeros lined up in neat little columns in the part of the file where string constants are stored. Every zero must be filtered out when you send a string to the API and then reinserted when you get the string back. But the Unicode conversion is more than just converting to and from zeros. Try the following to find out which characters use more than 8 bits:

```
For i = 0 To 255
    Debug.Print Hex$(AscW(Chr$(i)))
Next
```

For the most part, you don't need to worry about Unicode conversion. Once you've set up your Declare statements (or loaded the Windows API type library), everything happens automatically. But just when you think you've got Unicode under control, something turns up that doesn't work quite the way you expected. For example, Win32 supports both Unicode and ANSI versions of all functions, but 32-bit OLE supports only Unicode. If you want to call 32-bit OLE functions from Visual Basic, you'll have to pass Unicode strings (even in Windows 95, which doesn't support Unicode in any other context). Normally, you don't call OLE functions, because Basic does OLE for you—and what it doesn't do, you can't do in Basic anyway. But I do call the LoadTypeLib and RegisterTypeLib functions in the REGTLB program (which you'll see later).

When Basic sees that you want to pass a string to an outside function, it conveniently squishes the internal Unicode strings into ANSI strings. But if the function expects Unicode, you must find a way to make Basic leave your 16-bit characters alone. The new Byte type was added specifically for those cases in which you don't want the languages messing with data behind your back. We'll be looking at more examples of this in "Reading and Writing Blobs," page 119. For now, let's look at some Unicode basics that will set the stage for calling Unicode API functions.

Basic allows you to assign strings to byte arrays and byte arrays to strings:

```
Dim ab() As Byte, s As String
s = "ABC"
ab = s
s = ab
```

What would you expect these statements to do? If you guessed that the first byte of *ab* will contain "A", the second "B", and the third "C", you guessed wrong (for 32-bit mode, at least). If you didn't guess, but typed it in and tried to watch *ab* in the Debug window, you're also wrong. All you'll see is *Can't evaluate watches on arrays*. It's a little tricky to figure out exactly what a byte array or a string really contains. If you're in doubt, call one of my HexDump functions (in UTILITY.BAS). HexDump works on Byte arrays, and HexDumpS works on strings. HexDumpB, too, works on strings, but it dumps them as bytes rather than as characters. Here's what you get if you dump the variables shown earlier in the Debug window:

```
? HexDump(ab, vTwoColumn:=False)
41 00 42 00 43 00         A.B.C.
```

(continued)

```
? HexDumpB(s, vTwoColumn:=False)
41 00 42 00 43 00        A.B.C.
? HexDumpS(s, vTwoColumn:=False)
41 42 43                 ABC
```

Of course, that's in 32-bit mode; in 16-bit mode, all three dumps come out the same.

But what if you want to put the 8-bit ANSI characters of a string into a byte array without the zeros? Basic lets you force Unicode conversion by using the StrConv function:

```
ab = StrConv(s, vbFromUnicode)
```

A hex dump shows the bytes without zeros:

```
41 42 43                 ABC
```

Now let's assign the byte array back to the string:

```
s = ab
```

If you look at *s* in the Debug window at this point, you may be surprised to see the string *"?C"*. What is this?

Well, what you have in the first 16-bit character is "AB" (&H4241). The Unicode character &H4241 represents the *sacatai* hieroglyphic in the Basic dialect of northeastern Cathistan. In the second character, you have "C\0" (&H0043). The Unicode character &H0043 represents the *C* character we all know and love. Visual Basic doesn't know anything about the *sacatai* hieroglyphic or any other Unicode characters above 255, so it just displays them as question marks. To convert the byte array back to a recognizable string, undo the previous StrConv function:

```
s = StrConv(ab, vbUnicode)
```

The string now looks "right" in the debugger and "wrong" in the hex dump.

Unfortunately, the StrConv function with vbUnicode fails in 16-bit Visual Basic. You must do conditional compilation for portable conversions. Here's a wrapper that hides the details:

```
Function StrToStrB(ByVal s As String) As String
#If Win32 Then
    StrToStrB = StrConv(s, vbFromUnicode)
#Else
    StrToStrB = s
#End If
End Function
```

You can guess StrBToStr.

Back to the problem of passing OLE Unicode strings. The solution is simply to assign the string argument to a byte array and pass the array as if it were a string. Byte arrays aren't automatically null terminated, so you have to do it yourself.

```
Function RegTypelib(sLib As String) As Long
    Dim suLib() As Byte, errOK As Long, objTLib As Object
    suLib = sLib & vbNullChar
    errOK = LoadTypeLib(suLib(0), objTLib)
    If errOK = 0 Then errOK = RegisterTypeLib(objTLib, suLib(0), 0&)
    Set objTLib = Nothing
    RegTypelib = errOK
End Function
```

Notice how you pass the first character of the byte array, as described earlier. Of course, if you're going to claim in the code that you're passing an array of bytes, you must tell the same story in the Declare statement:

```
#If Win32 Then
Private Declare Function LoadTypeLib Lib "oleaut32.dll" ( _
    pFileName As Byte, pobjTLib As Object) As Long
#Else
Private Declare Function LoadTypeLib Lib "typelib.dll" ( _
    pFileName As Byte, pobjTLib As Object) As Long
#End If
```

If you're a masochist running under Windows NT, you can call all your API functions this way. It's theoretically possible to write a Visual Basic application that maintains all strings as Unicode, writes Unicode strings to files, and calls only Unicode API functions. Possible, but I'd have to say no, thanks. I'll wait.

Getting Strings from the Windows API

Now let's look at the other reason for passing strings—to get a string back from Windows. In Basic, if you want a procedure to return a string, you can simply make the procedure a function with String return type. This doesn't work well in C and many other languages, for reasons I won't examine. Suffice it to say that you could never get two language designers to agree on a format for string returns. The safe, portable way to get a string back from a procedure is to pass the address where the string is to be placed along with the maximum length of the string. For example, the C version of the GetWindowText function looks like this:

```
int GetWindowText(hwnd, lpsz, cbMax)
HWND hwnd;      // Handle of window
LPSTR lpsz;     // Address of buffer for text
int cbMax;      // Maximum number of bytes to copy
```

The Basic version looks like this:

```
Declare Function GetWindowText Lib "USER" (ByVal hwnd As Integer, _
    ByVal lpsz As String, ByVal cbMax As Integer) As Integer
```

The following fragment uses this function the long way. (We'll consider short-cuts later.)

```
Dim sTemp As String, sTitle As String, c As Integer
sTemp = String$(255, 0)
c = GetWindowText(hProject, sTemp, 256)
sTitle = Left$(sTemp, c)
```

Let's look carefully again at this call as a contract. Basic promises that it will null-terminate a string and pass its address (although null-terminating the string is wasted in this case because Windows doesn't care about nulls in output strings). Windows promises that it will not write more than the maximum character count passed to it into the address it receives, that it will append a null to whatever it writes (the null is included in the maximum number written), and that it will return the actual number of non-null characters written in the return value.

Neither side promises enough room in memory for the characters to be written. That part is up to you. If you pass a 10-byte string but claim that the size is 255, Windows might cheerfully write 245 bytes of data into whatever resides next to your string in memory. You will be in for a rude surprise, possibly much later in your program, when you try to use whatever used to be in that memory before you overwrote it.

The example ensures that the string is long enough by changing *sTemp* to a string of 255 null characters, using the String$ function. (You actually get 256 nulls because Basic always appends a null.) You can use the Space$ function to create a space-padded string in the same way. Another way to ensure that you never overwrite anything useful is to pass the actual length of the string as the maximum:

```
c = GetWindowText(hProject, sTemp, Len(sTemp) + 1)
```

If you do this when the actual length of *sTemp* is 0, you won't overwrite anything, but you will get a truncated version of the window title that might give the mistaken impression that the window has no title when in fact you simply didn't allow space for the title.

Let's assume that you provide a 255-character string and that the title of the window is *Hello*. You get back from the function the 5 characters of the string, followed by a null, followed by 249 nulls. GetWindowText returns 5. When a C program sees this string, it assumes from the placement of the null character that the string is 5 characters long. Basic assumes that the string is 255 characters long. If you really want a Basic string of 5 characters, you must assign it. The return value gives you the information you need to do this politely with the Left$ function. Incidentally, you could use just one string for both the temporary and the permanent versions:

```
sTitle = String$(255, 0)
c = GetWindowText(hProject, sTitle, 256)
sTitle = Left(sTitle, c)
```

You might expect that it would be more efficient to pass a fixed-length string than to use the String$ function to pad a string, but that turns out to be a bad idea. Because fixed-length strings are not BSTRs and don't have a terminating null, Basic must make a copy of the string, append a null, and pass the copy when you pass them to Windows. When the procedure returns, Basic must copy the copy back to the original—wasted effort all around. If the string is an output string, there's no need to copy the results back to the original because they haven't changed. If the string is an input string, there's no need to make a null-terminated copy. But Basic knows none of that and must cover all bases.

BSTRs were designed to avoid this kind of inefficiency. So do yourself a favor, and don't use fixed-length strings. Period. They are always inefficient. (Well, OK, you can use them in user-defined types, as described later in this chapter. That's why they were added to Basic.)

You can avoid padding a string every time you need to pass one to Basic. Define the string at the module level, and pad it out only once—in Form_Load, Form_Initialize, or Class_Initialize. Just make sure that this string is really temporary. Never change its size, and always copy the relevant portion to a permanent string immediately after use. That way, later calls won't be able to overwrite useful data.

Wrap It Up

Face it. Passing empty string buffers with lengths is un-Basic; the Basic Way is to simply return the string. You can choose to put up with the C style of strings every time you call GetWindowText or a similar function, or you can decide to deal with it once by wrapping the Windows API function in a Basic function. Here's how to do this for GetWindowText:

```
Function VBGetWindowText(ByVal hWnd) As String
    Dim c As Integer, s As String
    c = GetWindowTextLength(hWnd)
    If c <= 0 Then Exit Function
    s = String$(c, 0)
    c = GetWindowText(hWnd, s, c + 1)
    VBGetWindowText = s
End Function
```

The trick in this type of function is to decide the length of the string to allocate. GetWindowTextLength and GetWindowText are the only function pair in the Windows API in which one returns the length expected by the other. Even in this case, it might be more efficient to assume that no window title will be larger than 255 bytes and to allocate that size without checking the actual size. The string will just be thrown away when the function returns, so no harm is done if you allocate too much space. Worst case is that someone will use a window title 300 bytes long, and you'll truncate it to 255. Serves them right.

The Windows API offers many variations on this theme. When the string is informational, the function usually truncates if you don't provide a large enough buffer. If the string is a filename, the function copies nothing but returns the actual size of the data. A truncated filename would be worse than no name at all. If you get back more than you put in, you need to allocate a bigger string and call again. Sometimes, the Windows API documentation clearly states the maximum size you need to pass in; other times, you can guess. For example, if a function returns a full file specification, you can safely pass the maximum path size for the operating system—64 bytes in Win16 and 260 in Win32.

Dealing with Pointers

Some Windows API functions return pointers. Sometimes the pointer comes back in the return value, sometimes in a reference argument. And sometimes it comes back in a field of a UDT. Regardless of how you get it, you can do only one thing with a pointer: pass it on. In Basic, you should treat pointers the same way you treat handles. A handle is a sacred object passed to you for safekeeping, and modifying it will incur the wrath of the gods. As far as Basic is concerned, pointers should be treated with the same reverence.

You'll see pointers in the Windows API documentation as either a type followed by *FAR* * (often *void FAR* *) or a defined type starting with *LP* (such as LPVOID). The *LP* in LPVOID stands for *long pointer,* for reasons lost in the ancient history of Windows. Everyone except the designers of Windows calls this a *far pointer*. Technically, there is also such a thing as a *near pointer* (NP), but you should never use one in Basic. In C, when you declare a pointer, you must specify what it points to. You can't do that in Basic; instead, you have to lie to force Basic to accept pointers at all. You claim that the pointer is a Long. Once you get the pointer, you never (well, you almost never) do anything with it except pass it to another Windows API. Generally, you deal with pointers as pointers only when allocating memory. Chapter 7 discusses the specific tips and tricks that are involved.

Fixed-Length Strings in UDTs

A few Windows functions use structures (UDTs to Basic programmers) containing strings. This creates a problem because a Basic string in a Basic UDT differs somewhat from a C string in a C structure. I once made the foolish mistake of asserting on a Microsoft e-mail alias where Visual Basic is discussed that you cannot use Windows structures containing strings in Basic. Take my word for it: don't try to tell hardcore Basic programmers what they can and cannot do.

In C, as in Basic, a structure can contain two types of strings. In Basic, the first type is called a fixed-length string; in C, it is called an array of characters. The TModuleEntry type illustrates. It looks like this in C:

```c
typedef struct tagMODULEENTRY
{
    DWORD dwSize;
    char szModule[10];
    HMODULE hModule;
    WORD wcUsage;
    char szExePath[256];
    WORD wNext;
} MODULEENTRY;
```

In Basic, it looks like this:

```
Type TModuleEntry
    dwSize As Long
    szModule As String * 10
    hModule As Integer
    wcUsage As Integer
    szExePath As String * 256
    wNext As Integer
End Type
```

No problem. The *szModule* and *szExePath* fields look the same internally in both C and Basic. Everything is cool when you pass the Basic variable to the ModuleFirst function in TOOLHELP.DLL. Of course, some additional work goes on in the background. In 32-bit mode, fixed-length strings are stored as Unicode, but they must be converted to ANSI when passed to API functions.

If you pass a UDT with a fixed-length string to a Unicode API function (such as an OLE function), you'll need to code the string as an array of bytes and handle the Unicode conversion yourself.

Variable-Length Strings in UDTs

The other type of string is relatively rare in Windows API functions, although it shows up all the time in the common dialog functions in COMMDLG.DLL and in COMDLG32.DLL. It appears, for example, in the OPENFILENAME structure used by the GetOpenFileName function:

```
typedef struct tagOFN
{
    DWORD       lStructSize;
    HWND        hwndOwner;
    HINSTANCE   hInstance;
    LPCSTR      lpstrFilter;
    ⋮
}   OPENFILENAME;
```

In this structure, *lpstrFilter* is not a string, but a pointer to a string whose data is located somewhere else. Previous versions of Visual Basic offered only one choice. You had to implement the corresponding UDT this way:

```
Private Type TOpenFileNameOld
    lStructSize As Long
    hwndOwner As Integer
    hInstance As Integer
    lpstrFilter As Long
    ⋮
End Type
```

Notice that *lpstrFilter* is given type Long so that it can hold a pointer to a string. But how to get that pointer? There were various hacks to do this in previous versions of Visual Basic, and those hacks still work in 16-bit mode. One used VarPtr, which you'll see in another context, and another used a side effect of the lstrcpy API function. I'll say no more because neither hack works under 32-bit Visual Basic. A pointer to a 32-bit Basic string is either a pointer to the internal Unicode version, which ANSI API functions wouldn't know what to do with, or it's a pointer to the temporary version used in ANSI conversion, which would be gone by the time you called the function that needed the UDT.

The only portable solution is to code the UDT the obvious way:

```
Private Type TOpenFileName
    lStructSize As Long
    hwndOwner As Integer
    hInstance As Integer
    lpstrFilter As String
    ⋮
End Type
```

With your type defined this way, you can simply assign the string:

```
opendlg.lpstrFilter = sFilter
```

This might seem obvious to new Basic programmers, but it's a minor miracle to old hands. Refer back to Figure 2-4, page 68, to see why this technique would never have worked in version 3. The old HLSTR format was a pointer to a pointer to characters, but the new BSTR format is a direct pointer to characters. The only difference between an LPSTR and a BSTR is that the BSTR has a prefix. In other words, BSTR type is a superset of LPSTR type, and the common subset is the only thing Windows cares about.

Don't forget that a string used as an input buffer must be large enough to receive the data. Frequently, structures containing buffers to receive strings have an accompanying field containing the maximum length. Be sure to set the maximum-length field and pad your strings before assigning them to the string field. When you get them back, you'll usually want to truncate after the first null. Use the StrZToStr function from UTILITY.BAS. If you need to assign a null pointer to a string field, use *vbNullString* or *sNullStr*. "The Windows/Basic Way of Implementing Common Dialogs," page 376, has examples of these techniques, and you can see other examples in COMDLG.BAS.

Other Pointers in UDTs

Once in a while, you might need to load a pointer to something other than a string into a UDT field. For example, the CHOOSEFONT structure used by the ChooseFont function has a field for a pointer to a LogFont structure. This is an obscure problem, so I'll be brief here. You can see the whole solution in COMDLG.BAS.

The Basic TChooseFont structure looks like this:

```
Private Type TChooseFont
    lStructSize As Long
    hwndOwner As Long               ' Caller's window handle
    hDC As Long                     ' Printer DC/IC or NULL
    lpLogFont As Long               ' Pointer to TLogFont
    ⋮
```

You need to fill the *lpLogFont* field with a TLogFont variable, but how? Assume that you have the following:

```
Dim fnt As TChooseFont, lfnt As TLogFontB
```

The code on the next page shows two ways to make the assignment.

```
#Const HalfDozen = 1
#If Six Then
    fnt.lpLogFont = VarPtr(lfnt)
#ElseIf HalfDozen Then
    fnt.lpLogFont = GetRefPtr(lfnt)
#End If
```

If you remember VarPtr, you're a real Basic old-timer. VarPtr was a function in QuickBasic, Basic Professional Development System, Macintosh Basic, GW-BASIC, and BASICA. You pass VarPtr a variable; it returns a pointer to that variable. Street Basic squared. Obviously, Visual Basic can have no trace of this abomination. Or can it? Some hardcore programmers will even dump DLLs to uncover dirty secrets. Here's the 32-bit version:

```
Declare Function VarPtr Lib "VB40032" (lpVoid As Any) As Long
```

Notice that the DLL name in the Declare statement is version-specific. You'll have to change it for every version of Visual Basic, and the next version might not even have this undocumented feature.

If VarPtr seems like a maintenance nightmare, you can use GetRefPtr from the VBUTIL DLL. I can't resist showing the C code:

```
DWORD DLLAPI GetRefPtr( LPVOID lpVoid )
{
    return (DWORD)lpVoid;
}
```

For those of you who aren't C-literate, this function simply uses C type conversion to get around Basic's strong typing. Here's the 32-bit Declare statement from UTILITY.BAS:

```
Declare Function GetRefPtr Lib "VBUTIL32" (lpVoid As Any) As Long
```

One other problem. When you pass a UDT variable directly to an API function, Basic knows what you've done and will convert any fixed-length strings in the UDT to ANSI. But when you assign a pointer to a TLogFont variable to the *lpLogFont* field of a TChooseFont variable, Basic has no idea what the pointer points to, and it will do no conversion on the UDT field. Normally, TLogFont would use the following field to hold the font name:

```
FaceName As String*32
```

But in this case you have to define FaceName as an array of bytes:

```
FaceName(0 To 31) As Byte
```

You must handle Unicode conversion yourself. You can check out the details in COMDLG.BAS.

Forget Everything You Just Learned

If writing Declare statements seems complicated and tedious, don't worry about it. You don't have to write many of the Declare statements shown in this chapter. Instead, you can use the type libraries WIN16.TLB and WIN32.TLB. These type libraries contain the declarations and constants for most of the Windows API, so you don't need to write them in Basic.

Has everything up to now in this chapter been unnecessary? Not exactly. To master the Windows API, you still need to understand what's going on. You won't regret anything you've learned here even if you never use it again. But you will have to use part of it, because type libraries have limits.

Type Libraries

A type library is a binary file containing all the type information you need to use procedures or classes in DLLs. Forget about classes for the moment; we are interested only in procedures and any constants those procedures use as arguments.

You get several type libraries with Visual Basic. You can examine them in the Object Browser by clicking the Object Browser toolbar button or by pressing F2. If you click in the Libraries/Projects drop-down list box, you'll see the type library for the current project plus standard libraries marked *VB - Visual Basic objects and procedures* and *VBA - Visual Basic For Applications*. You might also see type libraries for the Data Access Object and any custom controls used by your current project.

If you open any of the sample projects provided with this book, you'll also see a type library marked *Win - Windows API Functions*. When you select it, you'll see the Windows API functions and constants broken out into categories, as shown in Figure 2-5 on the next page. In other words, using this type library is roughly equivalent to including WIN31API.TXT and WINMMSYS.TXT in your 16-bit projects and WIN32API.TXT in your 32-bit projects.

To include this feature in every project you create from now on, simply load the appropriate type library into AUTO16LD.VBP or AUTO32LD.VBP. You might also want to load it into existing projects to replace existing Declare and

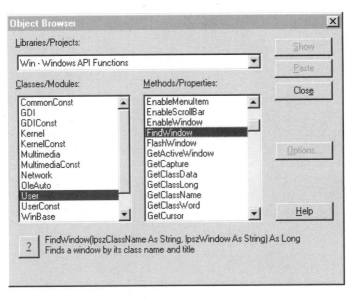

Figure 2-5. *Browsing in the Windows API type library.*

Const statements. Figure 2-6 shows the References dialog box, where you load type libraries. The checked references are the type libraries used by your current project. The unchecked references are others that have been registered in the Windows Registry.

If a type library has already been registered, you'll see it in the References dialog box. Chapter 10 explains more about what registering means. The long and short of it is that if you ran the setup program provided on the companion CD, the Windows API type library is already registered on your machine. That's because setup runs a program called REGTLB16.EXE or REGTLB32.EXE to register the appropriate type library. You can run this program yourself if you ever have any problem registering a type library. (Run it once without arguments to get a syntax screen.) You can also register a type library by using the Browse button in the References dialog box, but using REGTLB is better because it attempts to register both 16-bit and 32-bit versions of the type library. The Browse button will register only the 16-bit type library from 16-bit Visual Basic or the 32-bit version from 32-bit Visual Basic. You can see code for this program in REGTLB.BAS.

Your customers don't need the Windows API type library to run programs that you develop using the type library. The exception to this rule is if you sell programming tools containing Visual Basic source code that uses the type library. In that case, customers should also buy this book. But it's up to them. You can build a setup that copies the type library files to the customer's disk and calls REGTLB to register them (as the setup program on the companion CD does).

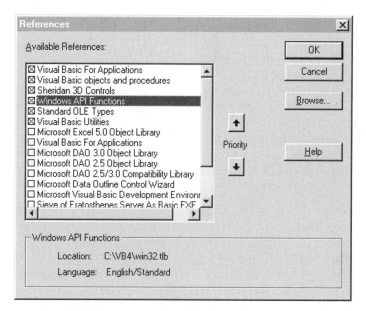

Figure 2-6. *The References dialog box.*

The situation is similar for VBUTIL16.DLL and VBUTIL32.DLL. These DLLs contain an embedded type library that must be registered and loaded in order to use the DLL function from the Visual Basic environment. You need to register the type library, but your customers don't (unless they are programmers).

Of course, using the Windows API type library isn't exactly the same as using Basic files containing Declare and Const statements. There's good news, and there's bad news.

The good news is that type libraries are free. If you include WIN31API.TXT in a project, you pay for the overhead of the hundreds of Declare statements in the file, although you might use only two or three. In previous versions of Visual Basic, you couldn't even load this file because it would have used up all the available memory. I've been told it's possible now, but I haven't tried because doing so would be a stupid waste of resources; nobody uses all the Windows API functions in a single program. If you load WIN16.TLB, however, you pay only for the declarations you use. In theory, you should never have to write a Declare statement again.

The bad news is that you can't put some kinds of declarations in type libraries. The problem lies with limitations of the Object Description Language (ODL) used to create type libraries. This language was designed primarily to describe the interfaces of OLE objects. The ability to describe non-OLE DLLs such as those in the Windows API appears to have been an afterthought. Compatibility with features unique to Visual Basic was definitely not a priority.

If you're curious about Object Description Language, you can see an example on the companion CD. WIN.ODL is the source file from which WIN16.TLB and WIN32.TLB were created. ODL declarations look like a cross between C prototypes and Basic Declare statements, with a few features from the Ada language thrown in. To build a type library from an ODL source file, you need a program named MKTYPLIB. The batch files that compile WIN.ODL are provided on the companion CD, but you will need MKTYPLIB.EXE to run them. Since this program isn't supplied with Visual Basic, you're on your own if you want to modify my type libraries or create new ones. The tools and documentation you need are supplied with Microsoft Visual C++. Further discussion of type-library creation belongs in another book.

The main things you won't find in WIN.ODL are UDTs and functions that use them. ODL supports C structures and C++ classes through its typedef statement, but Basic UDTs have a different and incompatible internal format. You can't define the equivalent of UDTs. That's a pretty big hole in the Windows API. I counted more than 60 structures in the 16-bit Windows API, although most of these are specialized types used by only two or three functions. Unfortunately, a few structures such as RECT, POINT, and SIZE pop up throughout the API, and doing without them is a major inconvenience.

If your mind works like mine, you're probably thinking that although it would be annoying to have to write all those UDTs in Basic rather than including them in the type library, that doesn't mean you can't use the functions. Maybe you could have a BAS file containing only the types and still put the declarations in the type library with the ODL equivalent of As Any on the UDT parameters. Unfortunately, ODL doesn't have an equivalent for As Any. C programmers might expect *void* * to work in this context, but no such luck.

Chapter 6 will have more to say about this subject, but the bottom line is that you normally write UDTs, and Declare statements for procedures that use them, in Basic. Furthermore, As Any has other uses. You might remember an earlier discussion of the two ways to write Declare statements with typeless parameters. One is to use As Any, and the other is to write Declare statements with different names aliased to the same DLL function. Fortunately, ODL supports aliases, and you'll find many of them in the Windows API type library.

For example, the SendMessage function is the ultimate typeless procedure. You can't do much without adding aliases such as SendMessageAsLong, SendMessageAsString, SendMessageForLong, and SendMessageForInt. You'll find these and others in the type library, but when you need to use SendMessage to pass or receive a UDT variable, you'll have to use the generic SendMessage declaration in UTILITY.BAS. (SendMessage is described in "Sending Messages," page 236.)

Inside Declarations

You don't need to understand how Visual Basic implements Declare statements and type-library declarations in order to use them, but you can never know too much. This summary should give you a feel for the overhead of Declare statements. (My summary is based not on inside information, but on my experience writing code to emulate the LoadLibrary function in a previous job.)

When you write a Declare statement in a source file, Basic encodes it as binary data consisting of all the information Basic will need later to call the API procedure. This includes strings representing the procedure name, the library name, and the alias (if any). Basic must also save the type of each argument, the return value (for functions), and a pointer (empty at this point) for the address of the procedure. All this information is saved whether or not the procedure is ever called.

The overhead of declarations from a type library is similar except that Basic saves only the information for procedures called by the program. Of course, you also get declaration information for procedures in dead code or for procedures that are called only during some execution paths, but at least you don't pay for the whole Windows API even though most of it is in the type library.

When you first encounter the API procedure at run time, Basic looks up the encoded declaration data and checks the library name. If the library (DLL) is already loaded into memory—Windows libraries such as KERNEL, USER, and GDI always will be—Basic gets the handle of the library. If the DLL has not been loaded, Basic uses the LoadLibrary function to load it into memory and get the library handle.

Basic then calls the GetProcAddress function, passing it the name of the procedure and the library handle, to get the address of the procedure code in the DLL. Basic checks the type information provided by the declaration against the type information in the DLL. If it finds a conflict, you'll see a run-time error. If not, Basic uses the type information for each argument and the address of the procedure to make the procedure call.

Organizing Declarations

If you throw out the hundred or more API functions that use structures, the Windows API type library can still provide declarations for hundreds more. I haven't counted, but probably 80 percent of the Windows API uses only integers and strings. You'll need to write the others in Basic, and you'll have to find a way to organize them.

Declare statements take time and memory to process, so it's important to organize them carefully to reduce overhead. Previous versions of Visual Basic didn't support the Private attribute in Declare statements, and thus you didn't have much choice about how you organized them. The current version gives you the same flexibility for declarations as for procedures, types, and variables— and forces you to make the same trade-offs.

To understand the trade-offs, let's look at the extremes. On the one hand, you could write one big module containing public declarations for every API routine you'll ever need and include this module in every project. Visual Basic even comes with several such modules, but they're not intended to be included in projects as is. That would be too wasteful.

At the other extreme, you could insert a private declaration for each API function called in each code, form, or class module that needs them. Visual Basic has an API Viewer program that makes it easy to paste copies of the appropriate Declare statements into your code. This is the most efficient alternative if each API function is used only within one module. If several modules use the declaration, each gets its own copy with the associated overhead. In addition, if you change one of the declarations, you should hunt down and modify all the others. This can be a maintenance nightmare.

A reasonable compromise is to create modules containing related Declare statements. For example, I have a COMDLG.BAS module containing all the Declare, Const, and Type statements I need for common dialogs. Other modules I use frequently include WINTOOL.BAS (window handling) and GDITOOL.BAS (graphics). These modules usually also contain related Basic procedures, including wrappers for un-Basic API functions.

I also use private declarations in small modules that won't need related declarations. When possible, I make classes self-contained, including any Declare, Type, and Const statements that are needed. VERSION.CLS, for example, includes everything necessary to process version resources, and SYSTEM.CLS contains everything needed to get system information. I end up with a few duplicate declarations and a few that never get used, but it seems like a reasonable trade-off.

3

Basic Tools the Old-Fashioned Way

A tennis buddy recently complained about how I get ready for a set. "You don't know the meaning of the word 'warm-up.' You come out here and hit the first ball as hard as any you'll hit in a game," he said.

I had to think about that for a minute. "Well, I don't need any practice hitting soft ones."

This chapter is intended to let you warm up while also writing some Basic tools that might come in handy later. You'll see examples of the philosophy and techniques described in earlier chapters as well as a preview of techniques to come. That doesn't mean the code will be simple, however; as a hardcore programmer, you don't need practice coding soft ones.

This chapter, like the two preceding, concentrates on functional programming. Chapter 4 introduces object-oriented programming, Basic style, and we'll continue largely in object mode for the rest of the book. So enjoy the old-fashioned programming while it lasts.

Code Review

In many programming departments, code review comes with the territory. The author of a piece of code offers it up for group consumption. Participants sit down together to read the code line by line, looking for inefficiencies, wrong assumptions, unchecked errors, and better algorithms.

In theory, code review takes place in a positive atmosphere of camaraderie, with the implicit assumption that no one writes perfect code every time. But you can surely imagine situations in which comments might get brutal. In practice, most programmers host code review with fear and trembling.

So let's do some code review. Let's pick an innocent, naive rookie and rip his pitiful efforts to shreds. Let's examine some code that has been seen by millions and see if it's really up to snuff. Let's review REMLINE, the program that wouldn't die. To introduce the code, I'll turn the floor over to the owner of the code, Bruce McKinney, circa 1987. The reviewers are Joe Hacker, Jane Sensible, and their manager, Mary Hardhead.

The Program That Wouldn't Die

Bruce: As you know, this is my first work as a professional programmer—although at this point I'm only a sample programmer. This is also my introduction to parsing. I was assigned to fix REMLINE.BAS as a sample program for QuickBasic.

Joe: What the heck is a sample programmer?

Bruce: Well, there are real programmers, and there are sample programmers. I'm just a sample.

Mary: Bruce has been hired by the documentation department as a programmer. In the past, all the sample programs in the manuals and on the disk have been just thrown together by whoever happened to have time. Coding style and quality varied a lot. Bruce's job is to make all the samples use a consistent style and have consistent quality.

Joe: Well, if he works for documentation, why don't documenters review his code?

Mary: We thought it'd be good experience for him to have his code reviewed by programmers from Basic development. A sort of baptism by fire.

Jane: It might also be nice for C programmers writing the Basic language to see what it's like in the trenches. How long has it been since you tried to write serious code in Basic?

Joe: Serious code in Basic? Hmph! Can't be done.

Bruce: We'll see. Back to REMLINE. I didn't write it, and I don't know the original author. The version I got was lightly commented, had a clumsy user interface, didn't take full advantage of new Basic features, and had undocumented limitations that some people might call design bugs. My job was to clean up this private code for public consumption.

Joe: So this isn't even your code?

Bruce: Well, what we're going to talk about today is mine. I revised it heavily, and I take responsibility for it. Now, the purpose of REMLINE is to remove all unnecessary line numbers from GW-BASIC and BASICA programs so that they will look semistructured. In theory, you can then go through and change the remaining line numbers to labels as a first step toward making the code readable by humans as well as by modern versions of Basic.

Joe: You're better off just throwing away your BASICA code and starting over from scratch.

Jane: Oh, sure! That's a good marketing line. Put that on the box. "QuickBasic: Now you can rewrite all your old code."

Bruce: When I started on REMLINE, I thought it was a pretty cool program, and I had all kinds of ideas for making it even cooler. Now I tend to agree with Joe. Dump your BASICA code in the trash. In any case, we're not reviewing REMLINE; we're reviewing the parsing code in it.

REMLINE is a very simple compiler that tokenizes a source file. It recognizes certain Basic keywords associated with line numbers—Goto, Gosub, Then, Else—and indexes each one with its target line number. When it's finished indexing, it strips out all the line numbers that haven't been targeted by a keyword. A good portion of the code deals with tokenizing keywords, variables, and line numbers. REMLINE does this with imitations of the C parsing functions strtok, strspn, and strcspn.

Joe: This is crazy. I don't have time to review sample code that no one will see. Even if you ship this crap, no one will pay any attention to it, and you won't bother to ship it with the next version.

Mary: You don't have to like this assignment, but you do have to do it. Try to have a positive attitude.

Archaeologist's Note: REMLINE went on to become the most widely distributed program in the history of the planet. It shipped not only with various versions of Microsoft Basic but also with MS-DOS 5, and it still ships with every copy of Windows NT version 3.51. For reasons unknown, the problems discovered in the code review described here were never fixed. Fortunately, most of the millions of people who saw this code didn't look at it.

StrBreak and StrSpan

Bruce: In C, the basic building blocks of parsing are strspn and strcspn. My Basic names for them are StrBreak and StrSpan. To use StrBreak, you pass it the string you want to parse and a list of separator characters—space, tab, and comma, and line-break characters if the string can span multiple lines. StrBreak returns the position of the first character that is not a separator. You pass StrSpan the same arguments, and it returns the position of the first character that is a separator.

You can probably guess how to use these functions. Find the start of a token with StrBreak, find the end of the token with StrSpan, cut out the token, find the start of a token with StrBreak, find the end of the token with StrSpan...and so on to the end of the string. That's pretty much what GetToken does, but first let's take a look at StrSpan:

```
Function StrSpan1(sTarget As String, sSeps As String) As Integer

    Dim cTarget As Integer, iStart As Integer
    cTarget = Len(sTarget)
    iStart = 1
    ' Look for start of token (character that isn't a separator)
    Do While InStr(sSeps, Mid$(sTarget, iStart, 1))
        If iStart > cTarget Then
            StrSpan1 = 0
            Exit Function
        Else
            iStart = iStart + 1
        End If
    Loop
    StrSpan1 = iStart

End Function
```

StrBreak is identical except that the loop test is reversed:

```
' Look for end of token (first character that is a separator)
Do While InStr(sSeps, Mid$(sTarget, iStart, 1)) = 0
```

Archaeologist's Note: Names of functions and variables have been changed to protect the guilty. Joe Hacker's diatribes against the stupid naming conventions of the original have been edited out of this text, along with other rude remarks deemed irrelevant. The code has been updated to reflect the Visual Basic language, ignoring QuickBasic syntax differences. Different versions of the procedures are numbered. Interested historians can find the original code in most versions of QuickBasic, the Basic Professional Development System, MS-DOS 5, and Windows NT.

Joe: If they're identical except for one line, why have two functions? Why not have one function—say, StrScan—with a flag argument that can be either Span or Break? Put the loop test in a conditional. That should save some code.

Jane: Yeah, but at what cost? You might loop through these functions hundreds of times if you're parsing a big file. Is the size cost of duplicating tiny functions worth the cost of adding an extra test in a loop that will be called in a loop? Besides, the interface feels better with separate functions.

Joe: I don't care what "feels" better, but I guess I'll buy your performance argument. Let's stick with two functions.

The Parsing Problem

Complete languages have been designed to deal with the problem of parsing strings into chunks of characters (usually called *tokens*). Yacc, Lex, and Awk come to mind. Some languages have parsing statements or functions. Visual Basic has none of these, although it does have a strong set of string functions from which to build them.

Visual Basic isn't the language of choice for complicated parsing tasks such as building compilers. Needless to say, the Visual Basic language interpreter is not written in Visual Basic. In fact, parsing isn't a particularly common task in Windows programming. In MS-DOS programs, you often parse complex command lines. Under Windows, however, the command lines are usually simple enough that you might be tempted to process them with program-specific code, but once you get used to a good set of parsing routines, you won't go back.

Mary: Any other comments?

Jane: The length *cTarget* is calculated just once, outside the loop. That's good. The body of the loop looks pretty clean. The loop test with Mid$ called inside InStr looks messy.

Joe: It's taking one character at a time off the test string and searching for it in the separator list. Kind of an unusual use of InStr. You don't care where you find the character, only *whether* you find it. I can't think of a better way to do it, short of rewriting it in a real language, like C.

Bruce: Well, if StrSpan is OK, StrBreak is also OK because it's the same except backward. Let's move on to GetToken.

GetToken

Bruce: The original GetToken in REMLINE worked exactly like the C strtok function. It follows a classic design for iteration functions that have to be called repeatedly until they report no more items to iterate. In this type of function, you call it with one set of arguments the first time, and then you call it with another set of arguments each subsequent time.

GetToken works the same way. The first time, you pass the string to be parsed; after that, you pass an empty string. It goes like this:

```
sSeparator = ", " & sTab & sCrLf
sToken = GetToken(sCommand, sSeparator)
Do While sToken <> sEmpty
    ' Do something with sToken
    sToken = GetToken(sEmpty, sSeparator)
Loop
```

That's the philosophy. Here's the code:

```
Function GetToken1(sTarget As String, sSeps As String) As String

    ' Note that sSave and iStart must be static from call to call
    ' If first call, make copy of string
    Static sSave As String, iStart As Integer
    If sTarget <> sEmpty Then
        iStart = 1
        sSave = sTarget
    End If

    ' Find start of next token
    Dim iNew As Integer
    iNew = StrSpan1(Mid$(sSave, iStart, Len(sSave)), sSeps)
    If iNew Then
        ' Set position to start of token
        iStart = iNew + iStart - 1
    Else
        ' If no new token, return empty string
        GetToken1 = sEmpty
        Exit Function
    End If

    ' Find end of token
    iNew = StrBreak1(Mid$(sSave, iStart, Len(sSave)), sSeps)
    If iNew Then
        ' Set position to end of token
        iNew = iStart + iNew - 1
    Else
        ' If no end of token, set to end of string
        iNew = Len(sSave) + 1
    End If
    ' Cut token out of sTarget string
    GetToken1 = Mid$(sSave, iStart, iNew - iStart)
    ' Set new starting position
    iStart = iNew

End Function
```

Trouble in Paradise

Bruce: This function always works on the same string. Notice how the first block of code saves the *sTarget* argument in the static *sSave* variable for later iterations. The rest of the code uses *sSave* and ignores *sTarget*. The next block of code uses StrSpan to get the start of the token, and then the next block uses StrBreak to get the end. Once you have the start and the end, you cut out the token and return it.

Joe: What the heck are you doing with that Mid$ in your StrSpan call? And there it is again in StrBreak. Why are you passing the string length?

Bruce: Well, the first argument is the string, the second argument is the starting position—it's a static that gets updated each time through—and the last argument is the string length....

Joe: And the string length never changes. You're calculating it again and again. Furthermore, it's wrong. If you're halfway through the string, you're giving the whole length of the string. I'm surprised this works at all.

Jane: It's legal. If you give a length that goes past the end of the string, it just takes the characters to the end. But it is kind of ugly. You can drop that whole argument:

```
iNew = StrSpan1(Mid$(sSave, iStart), sSeps)
```

Bruce: Will that make it any faster?

Joe: I don't remember the Mid$ code exactly, but I doubt that it will make much difference. The main point is that it will be right instead of working by accident.

Bruce: Embarrassing. I knew better than that.

Joe: You should be embarrassed.

Jane: Oh, come on. It's the kind of mistake anybody might make.

Joe: I wouldn't make it.

Mary: Joe, we don't need this kind of negative attitude.

Joe: All right. So maybe anybody could make a slip. But the real problem with this code is deeper. It comes from coding C in Basic.

Coding C in Basic

Bruce: What do you mean?

Joe: Look what you're doing every time you call StrSpan or StrBreak. You're cutting off the remaining part of the string and passing it as an argument. That would work fine in C because C just passes pointers to strings. The whole string stays put in memory, but you're pointing only to the end of it. But in Basic, when you pass the result of Mid$ to a function, you create a new temporary string. It's a separate string that has to be created for the function it's passed to and then destroyed when the function leaves. You don't want to create any more new strings than you need.

Bruce: Well, OK, but how do I keep from creating new strings?

Joe: You just pass one string—*sSave*—but you also pass the current position.

Jane: But that means changing the design of StrSpan and StrBreak.

Joe: Yeah. So the call changes from

```
iNew = StrSpan1(Mid$(sSave, iStart), sSeps)
```

to

```
iNew = StrSpan2(sSave, iStart, sSeps)
```

Then your StrSpan implementation changes to this:

```
Function StrSpan2(sTarget As String, ByVal iStart As Integer, _
             sSeps As String) As Integer

    Dim cTarget As Integer
    cTarget = Len(sTarget)
    ' Look for start of token (character that isn't a separator)
    Do While InStr(sSeps, Mid$(sTarget, iStart, 1))
        If iStart > cTarget Then
            StrSpan2 = 0
            Exit Function
        Else
            iStart = iStart + 1
        End If
    Loop
    StrSpan2 = iStart

End Function
```

Jane: But you're making StrSpan and StrBreak harder to use. They get a confusing extra argument. I mean, who'd guess how to use these things from the arguments?

Joe: That's just how Basic works. Nothing but GetToken will call them anyway. If anybody else did use them, they'd have to deal with the same efficiency problem. If you don't like Basic, use C.

Mary: Joe, sometimes I wonder why a guy who hates Basic so much chooses to work on it. You just like to criticize, and Basic is an easy target.

Jane: He's not as tough as he acts. Actually, he has a soft spot for Basic.

Bruce: Instead of criticizing the language, you ought to fix it. Look how I have to use this stupid Mid$ function just to get a character out of a string:

```
Do While InStr(sSeps, Mid$(sTarget, iStart, 1))
```

In most languages, you access a character in a string the same way you access an element in an array of bytes—maybe something like this:

```
Do While InStr(sSeps, sTarget(iStart))
```

I hope that internally you're at least optimizing the special case of extracting a single character.

Joe: Well, I'm not sure…There might not be anything we could do. A one-character string is no different from any other string in Basic.

Mary: Maybe you should make sure. Check the code.

Archaeologist's Note: We have no record of whether the changes Joe suggested resulted in any performance benefit in the ancient Basic language of the day, but the same changes in modern Visual Basic provide a 15 percent performance improvement (in 32-bit mode) even after improving the error checking. However, you still have to use Mid$ to extract a single character.

Fastest Versus Safest

Bruce: OK, so we've optimized this code, and we're going to get a giant performance benefit. Anything else?

Jane: What happens if you pass GetToken an empty string?

Bruce: Why would you do that?

Joe: Maybe just out of orneriness.

Jane: Or maybe you're parsing a file a line at a time, and some lines are blank. I just want to know whether you're handling boundaries.

Bruce: I guess I'm not sure what would happen. I suppose a user might also pass an empty string for the separators. What else could go wrong?

Archaeologist's Note: An interminable discussion about error handling has been edited out. Here is the end of that discussion.

Bruce: OK, so we end up with this:

```
Function GetToken5(sTarget As String, sSeps As String) As String

    ' Note that sSave and iStart must be static from call to call
    ' If first call, make copy of string
    Static sSave As String, iStart As Integer, cSave As Integer

    ' Assume failure
    GetToken5 = sEmpty
```

(continued)

Better Basic Through Subclassing

"If I had designed Visual Basic, I could have made that procedure better."

Well, quit complaining and do something about it. You don't have to accept the Visual Basic run-time library. You can replace procedures with your own versions, or you can enhance procedures by subclassing them. The BETTER.BAS module fixes some of the Visual Basic procedures I didn't like. For example, the Timer function isn't accurate enough for my taste, so I replaced it:

```
Function Timer() As Single
    Timer = timeGetTime / 1000!
End Function
```

The Basic version is apparently based on the system time and date features. Like them, it is nominally accurate to a hundredth of a second, but in fact it is usually accurate only to about a tenth of a second. The timeGetTime API function is accurate to a millisecond.

To create a new version of a library procedure, you simply create a new function with the same name and parameters in your project. If you look at the Libraries/Projects drop-down list in the Object Browser dialog box, you will see that your project is always first, followed by the VBA and VB libraries. This means that any procedure you define will be called first, thus overriding anything with the same name (such as Timer) in the VBA and VB libraries.

The only problem with the better version of Timer is that it returns what most Basic programmers want (an accurate time count) rather than what the documentation says (seconds since midnight). Normally, you use Timer to measure the difference between two times. You don't care whether the time returned is seconds since midnight, seconds since the last boot, or seconds since the first MITS Altair was switched on. If for some reason you really need to know the number of seconds since midnight, you can specify the original Timer:

```
iSecondsToday = VBA.Timer
```

Does this give you an idea of how to enhance rather than replace library functions? Here's how I enhanced the Hex function to add leading zeros:

```
Function Hex(ByVal i As Long, Optional vWidth As Variant) As String
    If IsMissing(vWidth) Then
        Hex = VBA.Hex$(i)
    Else
        Hex = Right$(String$(vWidth, "0") & VBA.Hex$(i), vWidth)
    End If
End Function
```

```
        If sTarget <> sEmpty Then
            iStart = 1
            sSave = sTarget
            cSave = Len(sSave)
    Else
            If sSave = sEmpty Then Exit Function
    End If

    ' Find start of next token
    Dim iNew As Integer
    iNew = StrSpan2(sSave, iStart, sSeps)
    If iNew Then
        ' Set position to start of token
        iStart = iNew
    Else
        ' If no new token, return empty string
        Exit Function
    End If

    ' Find end of token
    iNew = StrBreak2(sSave, iStart, sSeps)
    If iNew = 0 Then
        ' If no end of token, set to end of string
        iNew = cSave + 1
    End If

    ' Cut token out of sTarget string
    GetToken5 = Mid$(sSave, iStart, iNew - iStart)
    ' Set new starting position
    iStart = iNew

End Function
```

You can see more of my improved procedures in BETTER.BAS. Most of them follow the same pattern. Use optional arguments to add new features to an existing procedure. If the user doesn't provide the argument, use the original procedure. Otherwise, call the original procedure for base functionality, and add your own embellishments.

The general term for this technique is *subclassing*. It means replacing a system feature by defining your own outer version that uses the original feature internally. There are many forms of subclassing. This version of Visual Basic does not support object-oriented subclassing through inheritance, but you'll see techniques that look a lot like subclassing throughout this book.

Bruce: But isn't this error-handling code going to slow us down?

Joe: So what?

Jane: I never thought I'd hear you say that.

Joe: Well, speed is important, but it isn't everything. If all I wanted was speed, I could write GetToken like this:

```
Function GetToken(sTarget As String, sSeps As String) As String
    GetToken = sEmpty
End Function
```

That would really be fast. I could parse huge files in no time at all.

Bruce: But it doesn't work.

Joe: It works as well as the original if you pass it invalid arguments—better, in some cases.

Mary: OK, OK. We get the point.

Joe: It doesn't matter how fast your code is if it doesn't work.

Archaeologist's Note: At this point, the code review broke down into arguments about language features and proposals for enhancements. Suffice it to say that the discussion resulted in at least one variation of GetToken, called GetQToken, which recognized each quoted string as a single token. Another version, called GetOptToken, was discussed but not implemented. It would have recognized command-line options initiated with the forward slash or the hyphen character, skipped the option characters, and returned the value of the argument. You can find modern translations of the parsing routines (including GetQToken) in PARSE.BAS; they're used in several samples, including HARDCORE.VBP and RUNMENU.VBP.

The Win32 API for Win16

At some point, you're bound to run into limitations that have no solution in Basic. If you need low-level information that Basic doesn't provide, you must go to the operating system. But if you're programming under 16-bit Windows, is the operating system Windows or MS-DOS? From Basic, you can get to Windows through the API, but if you need an MS-DOS service, you're in trouble.

The Windows 3.1 API functions—which this discussion calls the Win16 API— were designed to supplement MS-DOS. The Windows API took care of Windows; the MS-DOS API (if you could call the Int 21h and BIOS interfaces by such a fancy name) took care of lower-level operating-system and hardware functionality. But the designers of the Win32 API had a different goal. Under Windows NT and Windows 95, Win32 is the operating system. There is no MS-DOS underneath. Therefore, Win32 must provide not only all the Windows functionality but also all access to the operating system.

As a result, the Win32 API performs all the Windows tasks of the Win16 API, plus all the advanced jobs (multithreading and so on) that Win16 can't do, plus all the operating-system and device services of MS-DOS and the BIOS. For example, Win32 has a ReadFile and a WriteFile corresponding to MS-DOS Int 21h, functions 3Fh and 40h. This doesn't matter to Basic programmers because the Basic Input and Print statements hide all the details, no matter what operating system you run. But Win32 also provides functions that Basic doesn't provide.

For example, Win32 has GetDiskFreeSpace, which tells you the size of a disk and how much of it is used. Basic won't give you this information. If you want the disk size under 32-bit Visual Basic, you simply write a Declare statement for GetDiskFreeSpace and call it. But if you want similar information under 16-bit Visual Basic, you have to create your own DLL in a language that supports writing DLLs.

This isn't difficult. Microsoft C already has _dos_getdiskfree, Borland C has getdfree, and Borland Pascal has DiskFree and DiskSize, all with slightly different interfaces. The C function returns the number of bytes per sector, the sectors per cluster, the total clusters, and the free clusters in a structure. Pascal correctly assumes that you don't care about the sectors and clusters and simply provides DiskSize to tell you the size in bytes and DiskFree to tell you the number of bytes free. You can easily use one of these interfaces to implement a DLL that can be called by Basic. Or you can modify them slightly with optional arguments, for a more Basic-like interface.

Portability, however, is worth more than any minor advantage of one interface over another. What if you implemented your 16-bit disk function with the same interface as the Win32 GetDiskFreeSpace API? Then you could write equivalent Declare statements for both and use the same Basic code for either one.

I implemented some of the other Win32 functions for Win16, choosing them according to two criteria: Did they fill holes in the Basic language? Were they easy to implement? The next sections describe some of these handy functions. The declarations are in type libraries VBUTIL16.TLB or VBUTIL32.TLB, already referenced from sample programs. I'll discuss the declarations and give examples of their use. Because this is a Basic book, not a C or C++ book, I won't say much about the implementation, although all the source code is available (with comments) on the companion CD.

Most of the code in this book fits into sample programs that do something, though not necessarily something useful. The Hardcore program (HARDCORE.VBP) covers the rest of the code that doesn't fit into polite programs with friendly user interfaces. Essentially, Hardcore is just my testing code with the thinnest possible interface wrapper.

Usually, the code simply creates a string with some output and writes it to a text box. For example, most of the Win32 functions described in this chapter are buried in one sample or another on the companion CD. They're all used systematically with various input arguments in the Hardcore program. The program output might be boring, but chances are good that you can find some code to paste when you want to use one of the functions in your own program.

GetDiskFreeSpace

Let's look at what's involved in writing the GetDiskFreeSpace function. The C prototype for GetDiskFreeSpace looks like this:

```
BOOL GetDiskFreeSpace(
    LPCTSTR lpszRootPathName,
    LPDWORD lpSectorsPerCluster,
    LPDWORD lpBytesPerSector,
    LPDWORD lpFreeClusters,
    LPDWORD lpClusters);
```

The first argument is the root name, which can be either a lettered drive string (*C:*) or a UNC network drive name (*server**share*\). That's nice for 32-bit programs, but I couldn't figure out a network-independent way to get the size of network drives. No great loss, really; by the time people start commonly using UNC names instead of drive letters, they'll have stopped using 16-bit Windows. But if you can figure out a portable way to check remote disks, go ahead and modify the C code. Your enhancements shouldn't break the Basic code that uses GetDiskFreeSpace.

The rest of the arguments—what C calls pointers and Basic calls by-reference parameters—return the disk size. Here's a 16-bit Declare statement:

```
Declare Function GetDiskFreeSpace Lib "VBUTIL16" ( _
    ByVal lpRoot As String, dwSectors As Long, dwBytes As Long, _
    dwFreeClusters As Long, dwTotalClusters As Long) As Long
```

The 32-bit version of the Declare statement is the same except that the library is KERNEL32.DLL and that it uses an alias to its internal name, GetDiskFree-SpaceA (to distinguish it from the Unicode version, GetDiskFreeSpaceW). You don't actually need these Declare statements because they're included in the Windows API type library.

You can look up the C code on the companion CD if you're interested in how this works. This particular call is trivial. It simply calls the C _dos_getdiskfree function, which does nearly the same thing as GetDiskFreeSpace except that it identifies the disk by number rather than by string and returns the information in a structure rather than in arguments. Despite the internal differences, you call both the 16-bit and the 32-bit versions the same way:

```
f = GetDiskFreeSpace(sName, iSectors, iBytes, iFree, iTotal)
rFree = iSectors * iBytes * CDbl(iFree)
rTotal = iSectors * iBytes * CDbl(iTotal)
If f Then
    s = s & " with " & Format$(rFree, "#,###,###,##0")
    s = s & " free from " & Format$(rTotal, "#,###,###,##0") & sCrLf
```

Of course, most users care about bytes, not about sectors and clusters. In the long run, this entire problem is better solved with object-oriented programming. Once you have the API to do the ugly work, writing a friendly class wrapper is an easy job. (Check out the CDrive class and the NDrives collection, which are discussed in Chapter 4.)

NOTE   Under Visual Basic version 3, many programmers discovered a secret tool for getting the free space on a disk. The following Declare statement gave you a function that returned the free bytes on the current drive:

```
Declare Function DiskSpaceFree _
    Lib "SETUPKIT.DLL" () As Long
```

This doesn't work in version 4 because the function has moved to STKIT416.DLL and STKIT432.DLL. You could change the Declare statements, but I suggest that you pass. What are the chances that 4 in the filename will change to 5 in the next version? Besides, this function reports only the free disk space, not the total disk space. Furthermore, there's no guarantee that the DLL will be on every user's disk.

GetDriveType

This function tells you the drive type: a hard disk, a floppy disk, a remote disk, a RAM disk, or a CD-ROM. You pass a root name, just as you do for Get-DiskFreeSpace:

```
c = GetDriveType(sName)
s = s & "Disk " & sVal & " type: "
s = s & Choose(c + 1, "Unknown", "Invalid", "Floppy ", _
                      "Hard    ", "Network", "CD-ROM ", "RAM     ")
```

The CDrive class in Chapter 4 uses this function.

GetFullPathName

When you are given a filename or a relative path, you'll often need a full path. You could write the code to find the pathname in Basic, but the operating system can provide the information more reliably. That way, your code will work even if the rules defining paths and filenames change (as they did for Windows NT and Windows 95). Win32 provides the GetFullPathName function, and the VBUTIL DLL lets you perform the same task under Win16.

Use GetFullPathName as shown here:

```
Dim sBase As String, pBase As Long
sFullName = String$(cMaxPath, 0)
sName = txtInput.Text
c = GetFullPathName(sName, cMaxPath, sFullName, pBase)
sFullName = Left$(sFullName, c)
If c Then
    s = s & "Full name: " & sFullName & sCrLf
```

Notice the last argument passed to GetFullPathName. The function returns a pointer to the filename portion of the full pathname. That's handy in C, but it's not much use in Basic. (If you think about this, you can come up with a way to use that pointer. Hint: Use the lstrcpy function, as the code in HARDCORE.FRM does.) The Basic Way is to return the position of the filename string within the full path string. Then you can use Mid$ to cut out the filename.

The only way to get back the position instead of the pointer is to provide a wrapper function written in C. GetFullPathName was written for 16-bit mode only, but the wrapper function needs to be written for both 16-bit and 32-bit, since a pointer is equally inconvenient in either environment. The wrapper functions in Chapter 2 were written in Basic to make them look and work like Basic functions, but it doesn't make sense to write one wrapper function in C and then put it in another Basic wrapper. Therefore, I wrote this wrapper in C to return a real Basic string (a BSTR instead of an LPSTR).

First, however, do you notice anything missing from GetFullPathName? It returns the file part of the pathname but not the extension or the directory. Many languages provide a function to split a full filename into its parts. For example, Microsoft C provides _splitpath, and Borland Pascal provides FSplit. You could have a similar tool by making the wrapper return the directory and extension positions. The user could then cut out any desired piece.

If you change the interface, this becomes a different function, deserving a new name rather than a *VB* prefix, so let's call it GetFullPath:

```
s = s & sCrLf & "Test GetFullPath" & sCrLf & sCrLf
sFullName = GetFullPath(sName, iDir, iBase, iExt)
If sFullName <> sEmpty Then
    s = s & "Relative file: " & sName & sCrLf
    s = s & "Full name: " & sFullName & sCrLf
    s = s & "File: " & Mid$(sFullName, iBase) & sCrLf
    s = s & "Extension: " & Mid$(sFullName, iExt) & sCrLf
    s = s & "Base name: " & Mid$(sFullName, iBase, _
                                iExt - iBase) & sCrLf
    s = s & "Drive: " & Left$(sFullName, iDir - 1) & sCrLf
    s = s & "Directory: " & Mid$(sFullName, iDir, _
                                iBase - iDir) & sCrLf
    s = s & "Path: " & Left$(sFullName, iBase - 1) & sCrLf
Else
    s = s & "Invalid name: " & sName
End If
```

CHALLENGE   The position arguments for the directory, the base, and the extension for GetFullPath ought to be optional arguments so that you can ignore some or all of them when you need only the full pathname. But it's a lot more difficult to use variants and optional arguments in C than it is in Basic. I leave this as an exercise for those OLE and C experts among you.

If you look up the C code on the companion CD, you'll see that the big difference between the code for this Basic-like function and the code for the C-like Win32 functions is use of the OLE string functions. GetFullPath uses SysAllocString to allocate the Basic string to be returned. SysAllocString resides with its friends SysReAllocString, SysFreeString, SysStringLen, and others in the 16-bit OLE2DISP DLL or the 32-bit OLEAUT32 DLL. The C definitions can be found in DISPATCH.H. They are also declared in the Windows API type library for those braver than I who want to manage their own strings from Basic.

SearchPath

Another common file task is to find out where a file is located, if anywhere, in a path list (usually the one in the PATH environment variable). Most language libraries provide a function for this purpose: Pascal has FSearch, and Microsoft C has _searchenv. But Basic has zip. Actually, you could do this task in Basic. It's simply a matter of parsing the directory list, appending the filename, and checking to see whether the file exists. But do you really want to do this task in p-code? Furthermore, in Windows you frequently need to check other places such as the Windows directory and the executable directory (which might not be the same as the current directory).

Win32 provides the mother of all path-searching functions: SearchPath. Some of its many features, like those of GetFullPathName, don't work well for Basic. The SearchDirs function can remedy some of these problems. It works a lot like GetFullPath except that you provide one additional argument in which you can specify a directory list to search. Like GetFullPath, SearchDirs returns a real Basic string. While the Win32 SearchPath requires null pointers for arguments that signal defaults, SearchDirs recognizes empty strings, in the Basic tradition. For example:

```
sName = "vb.hlp"
sFullName = SearchDirs(sEmpty, sName, sEmpty, iDir, iBase, iExt)
If sFullName <> sEmpty Then
    s = s & "Found file " & sName
    s = s & " in " & sFullName & sCrLf
    s = s & "File: " & Mid$(sFullName, iBase) & sCrLf
    s = s & "Extension: " & Mid$(sFullName, iExt) & sCrLf
    s = s & "Base name: " & Mid$(sFullName, iBase, _
                                iExt - iBase) & sCrLf
    s = s & "Drive: " & Left$(sFullName, iDir - 1) & sCrLf
    s = s & "Directory: " & Mid$(sFullName, iDir, _
                                iBase - iDir) & sCrLf
    s = s & "Path: " & Left$(sFullName, iBase - 1) & sCrLf
Else
    s = s & "File " & sName & " not found" & sCrLf
End If
```

The first argument is the directory list to be searched. An empty string signals a search of the default Windows search path. The second argument is the file to be searched for. The third is the extension of the file (which is blank in this example because the extension is already included in the filename). The remaining arguments hold the variables in which the function will return the directory, name, and extension positions—just as GetFullPath does.

The 16-bit Windows search path differs from its 32-bit counterpart, and therefore SearchPath and SearchDirs might find different files in different environments. The 16-bit search path is the following:

1. The current directory

2. The Windows directory

3. The Windows system directory

4. The executable directory

5. The directory list in the PATH environment variable

Here is the 32-bit search path:

1. The executable directory

2. The current directory

3. The Windows system directory

4. The Windows directory

5. The directory list in the PATH environment variable

As a practical matter, users won't notice this difference unless they have too many duplicate files hanging around.

The preceding example searches for VB.HLP, which is normally in the Visual Basic directory. If you're running your program from the Visual Basic environment, the executing program is VB.EXE or VB32.EXE, and it was launched from the directory containing VB.HLP—match. If you have built an EXE program, chances are you won't run it from the Visual Basic executable directory, and VB.HLP won't be found—no match. Watch out for this gotcha when testing.

SearchDirs has other uses. It can search an environment variable:

```
sName = Environ("INCLUDE")
sFullName = SearchDirs(sName, "WINDOWS.H", sEmpty, iDir, iBase, iExt)
```

It can test for the existence of a file in the current directory:

```
sFullName = SearchDirs(".", "DEBUG.BAS", sEmpty, iDir, iBase, iExt)
```

That statement looks a lot like this one:

```
sFullName = GetFullPath("DEBUG.BAS", iDir, iExt, iBase)
```

But there's a subtle difference: GetFullPath gives a valid filename whether or not the file exists. You can use it to get the full path of a file you're about to create. SearchDirs confirms that a file with that name already exists.

Testing for the existence of a file is one of the most annoying problems in Visual Basic. Don't count on simple solutions like this:

```
fExist = (Dir$(sFullPath) <> sEmpty)
```

This works fine until you specify a file in a directory that doesn't exist. Then you're stuck in a message box. I could give you a Basic error-trapping example that always works, but you've already seen that you can do the job with SearchDirs. Fortunately, you don't have to declare those extra position variables just to check for file existence. The VBUTIL DLL provides an ExistFile function that works just the way you'd expect:

```
fExist = ExistFile(sFullPath)
```

This is one of those rare functions that is easier to write in C than in Basic.

You can also use SearchDirs to search for a file when you're not sure of the extension:

```
Dim asExts(1 To 4) As String
asExts(1) = ".EXE": asExts(2) = ".COM"
asExts(3) = ".BAT": asExts(4) = ".PIF"
For i = 1 To 4
    sFullName = SearchDirs(sEmpty, "EDIT", asExts(i), _
                           iDir, iBase, iExt)
    If sFullName <> sEmpty Then Exit For
Next
```

GetTempPath and GetTempFileName

Visual Basic doesn't give you much help with the common task of generating temporary files. Win16, however, gives you help you don't need, in the form of the GetTempDrive and GetTempFileName functions. GetTempDrive is a handy function for programmers on some other planet using some other operating system. On planet Earth, you don't need a temporary drive; you need a temporary directory. The Win16 GetTempFileName function is designed for the same aliens. (To be fair, these functions were designed in olden days, when RAM drives walked the earth.)

Win32 fixed the problem by providing GetTempPath and GetTempFileName. Although the Win32 version of GetTempFileName bears the same name as the Win16 version, it has different arguments. My Win32 for Win16 version replaces the native Win16 function. Both GetTempPath and GetTempFileName suffer from C interfaces and need Basic wrappers. Here's the raw GetTempFileName:

```
sFullName = String$(cMaxPath, 0)
Call GetTempFileName(".", "VB", 0, sFullName)
sFullName = Left$(sFullName, InStr(sFullName, sNullChr) - 1)
```

The first argument is the directory for the temporary file, and the second is a prefix for this file. For the third argument, you can supply a number yourself, or you can use 0 as a signal to let Windows choose a random hexadecimal number for the last part of the filename. I can't think of a reason to pass anything other than 0. The final argument is the buffer to receive the name. You should pass a buffer with the maximum file length for your operating system; you have no protection if you pass one that is too short. The return value is the number used for the last part of the name. I can't imagine why you would need this. Unlike most API functions, this one doesn't return the length of the string, so you have to find the length yourself by searching for the terminating null.

In short, this is an inconvenient and somewhat dangerous function that takes one useless argument and returns garbage. The Basic wrapper GetTempFile cleans it up:

```
' Get temp file for current directory
sFullName = GetTempFile(".", "MYAP")
```

For the GetTempPath function, my GetTempDir wrapper simply returns the temporary directory. It is particularly handy when used with GetTempFile:

```
' Get temp file for TEMP directory
sFullName = GetTempFile(GetTempDir(), "VB")
```

The first GetTempFile call might generate *C:\CURDIR\~MYA0633.TMP*, and the second might generate *C:\TEMP\~VB0C1.TMP*. The filenames could be a little different on different operating systems and file systems. The only guarantee is that the generated file doesn't currently exist. Windows will keep incrementing the number and trying the file until it finds a unique name. It's up to you to open the file, process it, and—unless you want to be considered the crudest and most illiterate of programmers—delete it when you have finished.

Historically, some programs have considered the environment variable specifying the temporary directory to be TEMP, while others have considered it to be TMP. TEMP is the official Windows name, and GetTempPath looks for it first. If it does not find a TEMP directory, it then looks for TMP. If that fails, it uses the current directory.

GetLogicalDrives

The GetLogicalDrives function returns a bit flag in which the first 26 bits indicate which of the 26 lettered drives are connected to disks. "Shifting Bits," page 118, shows an example of how you can use this information.

FlushFileBuffers and CommitFile

When you open a file, the operating system handles buffering of the file data behind the scenes. Most operating systems provide a back door that allows you to make sure all buffered file data is written to disk at your command. It's a good idea to flush the file buffers after writing to disk information that would be difficult to reconstruct.

Win32 provides the FlushFileBuffers function, and MS-DOS provides an equivalent function—interrupt 21h, function 68h. The C language wraps these in its _commit function. Of course, every Basic file number corresponds to an internal file handle, and the FileAttr function provides a way to convert between them. Once you have the handle, a CommitFile function is a simple matter:

```
#If Win32 = False Then
Function CommitFile(nFile As Integer) As Boolean
    Dim hFile As Integer
    hFile = FileAttr(nFile, 2)    ' Convert file number to file handle
    ' Commit file to disk
    CommitFile = FlushFileBuffers(hFile)
End Function
#End If
```

But there's a catch. As a result of a change late in Visual Basic 4's beta cycle, the FileAttr function converts file numbers to handles in 16-bit mode only. FileAttr, like all Basic file procedures, is based on the C library. In 16-bit mode, it uses low-level C run-time functions that use operating-system file handles. In 32-bit mode, those same functions work at a higher level, maintaining their own file handles. If FileAttr returns the operating-system handle, writing to the handle through the API could knock the file out of sync with the C handle. If FileAttr returns the C handle, you can't pass it to API functions. So FileAttr simply fails with a run-time error. You'll end up with an unusual spectacle: an emulated Win32 function, FlushFileBuffers, that works fine (by calling C's _commit function), while the real Win32 FlushFileBuffers doesn't work because you can't get a handle for it.

GetLastError and SetLastError

When Win32 API functions fail, they rarely return an error code indicating what went wrong. Instead, they usually return 0 or a null pointer in a return value that is normally used for some other purpose. To find the reason for the failure, you need to call the GetLastError function—and you need to call it immediately, before some other function fails and overwrites the information. This is a little like using the Basic Err function. The Win16 functions presented here follow this system. You can look in the Win32 documentation (or in the VBUTIL source files) to see the error codes that can be returned by the functions described in this chapter.

You normally don't need the SetLastError function, but if you wrote some additional Win32 emulation routines in Basic, you could use SetLastError to set the appropriate error codes.

Hammering Bits

Basic was never designed to mess with bits. Sure, it has Xor, And, Or, and Not operators. In fact, it even has Eqv and Imp logical operators that you won't find (or need) in most other languages. But it lacks unsigned integers, and its numeric type conversion facilities are extremely safe—excessively so for bit operations. As a result, the simplest operations turn out to be unexpectedly messy.

At the risk of boring some readers, let's review what a 16-bit integer is to a computer, what it is to Basic, and what it is to the Windows API. To a computer, a 16-bit integer is simply a stream of 16 bits of data. A computer language can look at this stream of bits as a signed integer with a value in the range −32,768 through 32,767, as an unsigned integer ranging from 0 through 65,535, or as 16 independent bits. (In a signed integer, the high bit signals negative numbers; in an unsigned integer, the high bit is just more numeric data.)

The Basic language simplifies matters by recognizing integers only as signed integers and, to a certain extent, as bit flags. As long as you stick with 16 bits, this is sufficient. When you mix 16-bit and 32-bit numbers, however, you get into trouble. The problem: Basic claims that 32,768 is always a 32-bit number, although any assembly language programmer will assure you that it's a perfectly valid 16-bit unsigned number. When you specify a number in hexadecimal (&HFFFF), as you tend to do when working with bits, it's easy to forget that the high bit (&H8000) represents the negative sign.

Visual Basic 4 adds one more spice to this stew. The new Byte type is actually an unsigned type representing values from 0 through 255. You can't assign −25 to a Byte variable.

To clarify this discussion, we can use the low-level terminology of debuggers (which also happens to be the high-level terminology of Windows). An unsigned character is a Byte. An unsigned 2-byte integer is a Word. An unsigned 4-byte integer is a DWord. The two most common bitwise operations are cramming Bytes into Words and Words into DWords, and ripping Bytes out of Words and Words out of Dwords.

Five Low Words

Consider the simple LoWord function, which extracts the low word of a DWord. What could be simpler? Just mask out the high byte of the argument and return the result:

```
Private Function LoWord1(dw As Long) As Integer
    LoWord1 = dw And &HFFFF&
End Function
```

This works fine as long as the low word is less than or equal to 32,767. But now try this:

```
w = LoWord1(32768)
```

You get an overflow because 32,768 is out of the integer range (−32,768 through 32,767). If you're accustomed to another language, you might expect that you could use a conversion function to force the assignment to an integer. Basic conversion functions such as CInt, however, don't force anything. They request politely. If you change the guts of LoWord as shown here, you get the same overflow error:

```
LoWord1 = CInt(dw And &HFFFF&)
```

In most languages, type conversion or casting means "force by wrapping, truncation, or whatever it takes." In Basic, it means "Mother, may I?" And in this case, the answer is always "No." You might argue that any Long from −32,767 through 65,535 can legitimately be converted to an Integer, and I'll agree with you. But we lose.

In order to do the right thing for all integers, you must specifically check for the sign bit:

```
Private Function LoWord2(dw As Long) As Integer
    If (dw And &H8000&) = 0 Then
        LoWord2 = dw And &HFFFF&
    Else
        LoWord2 = &H8000 Or (dw And &H7FFF&)
    End If
End Function
```

Checking for the sign bit takes a long time. This version of LoWord is about 24 percent slower than the previous one when the result is positive and 30 percent slower when the result is negative (32-bit timings). But remember Joe Hacker's motto: "It doesn't matter how fast your code is if it doesn't work."

There's more than one way to get a DWord in Basic. You could simply copy the bits of the low word to the result. Basic provides a roundabout method of doing this with the LSet statement. You have to set up two structures that split the data in different ways:

```
Private Type TLoHiLong
    lo As Integer
    hi As Integer
End Type

Private Type TAllLong
    all As Long
End Type
```

Then you write the data into one structure and read it out of the other:

```
Private Function LoWord3(dw As Long) As Integer
    Static lohi As TLoHiLong
    Static all  As TAllLong
    all.all = dw
    LSet lohi = all
    LoWord3 = lohi.lo
End Function
```

PERFORMANCE

Problem: Compare several methods of stripping the low word of a DWord.

Problem	16-Bit Mode	32-Bit Mode
AND positive Long	40 ms	37 ms
AND positive Long after sign check	53 ms	46 ms
AND negative Long after sign check	54 ms	48 ms
Copy low word with LSet	62 ms	54 ms
Copy low word with CopyMemory	65 ms	65 ms
AND unsigned long in C DLL	23 ms	18 ms

Conclusion: Use Basic for what Basic does well, but let C do your bit bashing.

The code on page 115 looks pretty complicated, but internally it's not doing a lot. This version is also slower than the base version. It has the advantage of always working at the same speed, regardless of the number passed to it.

There's another way to copy bits using the Windows API CopyMemory function (better known to 16-bit programmers as hmemcpy). See the sidebar below for the bizarre story of how to make this procedure portable. Here's the code to simply copy the contents of the low word to a separate word-sized variable:

```
Private Function LoWord4(dw As Long) As Integer
    Static w As Integer
    CopyMemory w, dw, 2
    LoWord4 = w
End Function
```

CopyMemory: A Strange and Terrible Saga

Experienced Visual Basic API programmers have come to know, if not love, the hmemcpy function. When C's weak data typing and Basic's strong data typing meet in the Windows API, hmemcpy is frequently called on to mediate. The *h* in the function name indicates that hmemcpy is capable of handling huge memory (greater than 64 KB), though Basic programmers rarely need it for such large chunks of memory. Unfortunately, if you look for hmemcpy in the Win32 API documentation, you'll come up with nothing—not even a note that the function is obsolete. But...

You might happen to run across the Win32 CopyMemory function, which has exactly the same arguments and in fact looks like the same procedure. The *h* has disappeared because all memory in 32-bit mode is huge. If you write a Declare statement for CopyMemory, however, giving KERNEL32.DLL as the most likely library, you'll get nothing but an error indicating that no such function exists. In fact, if you search all the 32-bit DLLs with the DumpBin utility, you won't find any containing CopyMemory. But...

If you search carefully through the Win32 C include files, you'll turn up the following in WINBASE.H:

```
#define CopyMemory RtlCopyMemory
#define MoveMemory RtlMoveMemory
#define ZeroMemory RtlZeroMemory
```

This C equivalent of an alias indicates that CopyMemory is another name for a function called RtlCopyMemory. Don't ask why; just check for RtlCopyMemory

I expected this code to beat the LSet version, but it usually came out a little slower. Besides, while LoWord was short and sweet, HiWord would have been difficult.

The plain truth is that bit bashing isn't Basic's strong point. The same function takes only one line of code in C:

```
WORD DLLAPI LoWord(DWORD dw)
{
    return (WORD) ( dw & 0xFFFF );
}
```

Not only is the C version easier to write, it's also faster. Realistically, of course, that extra speed is seldom noticeable except in the most deeply nested loops. Nevertheless, my C toolkit, provided on the companion CD in the VBUTIL DLL,

---

in KERNEL32.DLL. Again, nothing. More sleuthing in the Win32 include files reveals the reason. WINNT.H contains something like this:

```
#define RtlCopyMemory(dst, src, len) memcpy(dst, src, len)
```

In other words, RtlCopyMemory is an alias for the C memcpy function, but you can't use memcpy or any other C library function from Basic. If it's not exported from a DLL, you can't call it. But...

KERNEL32.DLL does contain an entry for RtlMoveMemory. If you check the Win32 documentation, you'll see that MoveMemory does the same thing as CopyMemory except that it handles overlapped memory in a different fashion. I can't imagine a situation in which a Basic programmer would be copying overlapped memory. No reason not to use MoveMemory instead. Since Copy-Memory is more intelligible than hmemcpy, I alias this name for both 16-bit and 32-bit versions:

```
#If Win32 Then
Declare Sub CopyMemory Lib "KERNEL32" Alias "RtlMoveMemory" ( _
    lpvDest As Any, lpvSource As Any, ByVal cbCopy As Long)
#Else
Declare Sub CopyMemory Lib "KERNEL" Alias "hmemcpy" ( _
    lpvDest As Any, lpvSource As Any, ByVal cbCopy As Long)
#End If
```

This generic Declare statement resides in UTILITY.BAS. The Windows API type library contains CopyMemory with various aliases for calling with different argument types.

includes a group of functions for splitting values and putting them back together again—LoWord, HiWord, LoByte, HiByte, MakeWord, and MakeDWord. To use these functions, include the VBUTIL type library in your project.

Shifting Bits

Occasionally you need to shift bits. This bit operation doesn't come up that often in Basic, but when you need to get a certain bit into a certain position, nothing else will do.

Shifting left 1 bit means multiplying by 2; shifting left 2 bits means multiplying by 4; and so on. Similarly, shifting right 1 bit means dividing by 2, and so on. In Basic terms, the operation starts out looking simple:

```
Function LShiftWord(w As Integer, c As Integer) As Integer
    LShiftWord = w * (2 ^ c)
End Function

Function RShiftWord(w As Integer, c As Integer) As Integer
    RShiftWord = w \ (2 ^ c)
End Function
```

> **NOTE** Since shifting is faster than the equivalent multiplication and division operations in assembly language, hardcore programmers in other languages often shift bits to optimize multiplication and division by multiples of 2. But you can see why the functions I just mentioned are useless for optimization: it doesn't do any good to fake division by shifting if your shift function fakes shifting by dividing.

These functions work as long as you feed them positive integers and the results come out as positive integers. Otherwise, things go wrong. I wasted a lot of time figuring out how to do 16-bit shifts in Basic, and even more time failing to figure out how to do 32-bit shifts. Rather than go into the sordid tale, let's just skip to the C version:

```
// Shift bits of DWord right
DWORD DLLAPI RShiftDWord( DWORD dw, unsigned c )
{
    return dw >> c;
}
```

That's it. Even if you're not a C programmer, you can probably guess the code for LShiftDWord, RShiftWord, and LShiftWord. If not, check VBUTIL.C.

The C functions even give you a chance to optimize. If you ever need to divide by 256 in a very tight loop, you might want to try *ShiftRWord(i, 8)* instead of *i / 256*. (Don't call me if your program doesn't seem to run any faster.)

A more realistic example uses the GetLogicalDrives function found in the Win32 API and in the VBUTIL DLL discussed earlier. This function returns a Long in which the corresponding bit is set for each existing drive. As you can imagine, the easiest way to check those drives is to loop through all 26 bits, shifting them one at a time into the rightmost position and then testing. Here's a function that translates bits into a more Basic-like string of pluses and minuses:

```
Function VBGetLogicalDrives() As String

    Dim f32  As Long, i As Integer, s As String
    f32 = GetLogicalDrives()
    For i = 0 To 25
        s = s & IIf(f32 And 1, "+", "-")
        f32 = RShiftDWord(f32, 1)
    Next
    VBGetLogicalDrives = s

End Function
```

Reading and Writing Blobs

One of the more tedious tasks in programming is reading arbitrary binary data from files. If you're lucky, the data is logically arranged as records, and you can simply read it into UDTs. But sometimes you have to read the data blob from hell. "Reading Resources," page 332, describes one such problem.

In previous versions of Visual Basic, you had to read and write binary data as strings. Basic provides a complete set of string functions that neither know nor care whether the data is a string of characters or a sequence of binary bytes. String functions don't work reliably in 32-bit Visual Basic, however, because strings are stored internally as Unicode characters, although they are read from and written to disks as ANSI characters. Unicode conversion can change binary data—specifically, many of the ANSI characters between 130 and 159 that have Unicode values with no numeric relation to the ANSI values. In Visual Basic 4, however, the Byte type allows you to store binary data in a stable format that won't be modified by Unicode conversion. You may want to review "Unicode Versus Basic," page 72, where this problem was introduced.

Basic provides two versions of each string function. I'll refer to the Byte versions—MidB, InStrB, LeftB, and so on—as the B versions. The recommended way to handle binary data goes something like this:

```
nBinFile = FreeFile
Open sBinFile For Binary Access Read Write Lock Write As #nBinFile
ReDim abBin(LOF(nBinFile))
Get #nBinFile, 1, abBin
sBin = abBin
' Process file with MidB$ InStrB$ LeftB$, and friends
abBin = sBin
Put #nBinFile, 1, abBin
Close #nBinFile
```

Notice that you copy the array of bytes into a string and work on that rather than on the original array. The B functions work directly on byte arrays, but they do so through type conversion—meaning that a temporary string is created for each string parameter that receives a byte array argument. It's much more efficient to create a single temporary string yourself than to let Basic create one for every call to a B function.

> **NOTE** In previous versions of Visual Basic, you couldn't read arrays of any type from a file with the Get statement or write them back with the Put statement. Now you can. Blobs in byte arrays wouldn't be worth much if you couldn't read them from files.

This is fine as far as it goes, but generally you'll be extracting numbers (and occasionally strings) from various locations in the blob. This isn't as easy as you might expect. You end up running smack into the nemesis of Basic data conversion: unsigned integers where Basic expects signed integers. Here's what the code to read a Word from a byte string looks like:

```
Function WordFromStrB(sBuf As String, iOffset As Long) As Integer
    BugAssert (iOffset + 2) <= LenB(sBuf) - 1
    Dim dw As Long
    dw = AscB(MidB$(sBuf, iOffset + 2, 1)) * 256&
    dw = dw + AscB(MidB$(sBuf, iOffset + 1, 1))
    If dw And &H8000& Then
        WordFromStrB = &H8000 Or (dw And &H7FFF&)
    Else
        WordFromStrB = dw And &HFFFF&
    End If
End Function
```

You must adjust the offset from a zero-based buffer offset to a one-based string offset. You also need to do significant work with AscB and MidB$ to extract the byte. Finally, you have to do data conversion tricks to turn the unsigned character into a signed Basic integer. If this looks ugly, try doing the same for a DWord.

The BYTES.BAS module contains a group of functions that work directly on byte arrays, efficiently converting bytes directly to numeric or string data usable in your program. BytesToWord and BytesToDWord read numeric data from blobs. BytesFromWord and BytesFromDWord write numeric data. You could add similar functions to read and write Double, Single, and other types.

Let's start with BytesToWord, since it is equivalent to the WordFromStrB function shown on the previous page:

```
Function BytesToWord(abBuf() As Byte, iOffset As Long) As Integer
    BugAssert iOffset <= UBound(abBuf) - 1
    Dim w As Integer
    CopyMemory w, abBuf(iOffset), 2
    BytesToWord = w
End Function
```

That's one way to avoid data conversion problems—just blast the data directly into memory. BytesFromWord looks the same except that the first two arguments to CopyMemory are reversed. You can guess the implementation of BytesTo-DWord and BytesFromDWord.

Converting byte arrays to strings (and vice versa) is a different matter. The strings you extract from byte arrays must look like strings to the outside, which means that you must do Unicode conversion. Here's a function that converts a byte array to a string:

```
Function BytesToStr(ab() As Byte) As String
#If Win32 Then
    BytesToStr = StrConv(ab(), vbUnicode)
#Else
    BytesToStr = ab()
#End If
End Function
```

Generally, you won't be looking at a blob as one big string, but this function is useful for converting arrays of bytes in UDTs. Normally, you'll use fixed-length strings rather than byte arrays in UDTs, but BytesToStr comes in handy if you need to pass a UDT variable to a Unicode API function (such as an OLE function). "Unicode Versus Basic," page 72, and "Other Pointers in UDTs," page 83, discuss this issue. BytesToString is also a handy way to watch a byte array that represents an ANSI string; simply put the expression *"BytesToStr(ab)"* in the Watch pane of the Debug window.

StrToBytes goes the other way, but its implementation is very different. First, a function can't return an array of bytes, so you must modify the array by reference. Second, if the array already has a size, you might need to truncate or null-pad the string. Here's the code:

```
Sub StrToBytes(ab() As Byte, s As String)
    If IsArrayEmpty(ab) Then
        ' Just assign to empty array
#If Win32 Then
        ab = StrConv(s, vbFromUnicode)
#Else
        ab = s
#End If
    Else
        Dim cab ' As SysInt
        ' Copy to existing array, padding or truncating if needed
        cab = UBound(ab) - LBound(ab) + 1
        If Len(s) < cab Then s = s & String(cab - Len(s), 0)
        CopyMemory ab(LBound(ab)), ByVal s, cab
    End If
End Sub
```

The first part of the conditional handles unsized arrays like this one:

```
Dim ab() As Byte
```

Unfortunately, Basic provides no way to distinguish such an empty array from a sized array, so I had to write the IsArrayEmpty function. The error trapping in this function is too obscene to show in this family-oriented book, but you can look it up in UTILITY.BAS.

The second part of the conditional handles sized arrays. First you calculate the target size and null-pad the source string if necessary. Then you blast the string into the array. The string that comes into this function is Unicode, but notice that there's no explicit Unicode conversion. It's not necessary because Basic does implicit Unicode conversion whenever you pass a string to an API function such as CopyMemory.

StrToBytes and BytesToStr have a very specific use for converting complete arrays of bytes, but when working with blobs you'll more often need to extract or insert fixed-length strings at an arbitrary location in memory. What you want is a Mid function and a Mid statement that work directly on arrays of bytes. The techniques shown in BytesToStr can be enhanced slightly to create a MidBytes function that works directly on byte arrays. For example, here's how you extract a string from a 5-byte field:

```
sTest = MidBytes(abTest, &H3C, 5)
```

Unfortunately, you can't implement a similar MidBytes statement in Basic because the Mid$ statement isn't a procedure. Look closely at this code:

```
Mid$(sTest, 1, 6) = "NOWAY"
```

How would you write a function that takes an assignment on the right side of an expression? You can't. Basic cheats to do this. The Basic parser translates this code into a hidden internal call that probably looks like this:

```
Ins$ "WAY", sTest, 1, 6
```

You can do the same with an InsBytes function that inserts a string at an arbitrary location in a byte array:

```
InsBytes "WAYOUT", abTest, 0, 6
```

Note that both MidBytes and InsBytes take zero-based offsets rather than one-based offsets. I'll let you look up the implementation of MidByte and InsByte in BYTES.BAS. They're essentially just BytesToStr and StrToBytes with optional arguments. You'll also find LeftBytes, RightBytes, and FillBytes. These compare roughly to Left$, Right$, and String$, but, like MidBytes and InsBytes, they have syntactical differences to accommodate the normal use of byte arrays.

For good examples of blob processing in action, check out the ExeType function in EXETYPE.BAS and the GetResources function in WINWATCH.FRM.

When All Else Fails

When your language runs out of features, you can always fall back on your operating system. Traditionally, high-level languages have provided some fall-through feature for those once-in-a-blue-moon tasks that didn't warrant building code into the language. In Basic, the Declare statement is the fall-through feature that lets you access all those little features the language designers forgot. If it's not in the language, it has to be in a DLL somewhere.

In 32-bit Basic programming, DLLs are the end of the road. If you can't do what you need with the DLLs or controls at your disposal, you'll have to use some other language to write your own DLL (and possibly a device driver to go with it). If you're lucky enough to live in a 32-bit-only world, you can skip the rest of this section. But in 16-bit programming, there's one more trick in the bag: if Windows won't do it, maybe MS-DOS or the BIOS will.

The standard way to get to this level is with an interrupt routine. Most C libraries provide interrupt functions called int86, int86x, intdos, and intdosx. Borland Pascal offers similar functions, called Intr and MsDos. QuickBasic and its relatives have CALL INTERRUPT. Until now, Visual Basic had zip.

The lack of an interrupt function in Visual Basic isn't a major shortcoming. In fact, I can't think of many instances in which you might need one. I've already plugged most of the holes I find in Basic with the functions discussed earlier in this chapter. But those are my holes. You might find others, and if you don't program in C, Pascal, or another language that can create Windows DLLs, you'll be up a creek. So here's my Interrupt function for VBUTIL16.DLL.

Interrupting the 80x86

The C DLL code for Interrupt is almost trivial: it simply calls the C int86x function. All the interrupt functions mentioned earlier work by passing structure arguments with fields representing registers—AX, BX, CX, DX, and so on. You place your input registers into the structure, call the function, and then remove the output register values.

My version is different because it assumes that, since the 80x86 processors have only six general-purpose registers, register arguments passed by reference are more convenient than a user-defined type full of registers. Using the function should be as easy as baking cookies. Put some registers in the oven. Take them out when they're done. If it weren't for segments, you wouldn't need to understand anything about 80x86 interrupts or pointers or assembly language in order to use the Interrupt function—you could just follow the directions in an interrupt recipe book.

Unfortunately, segments exist. I hate to keep talking about them when Win32 is upon us, and I swear this is absolutely the last time I'll have anything to do with a book that even has segments in the index. In the meantime, if you have no idea what a segment register is or how it works, this discussion might be tough going. I don't have space to explain a concept that will soon be as charmingly quaint as calculating with a slide rule. Bear with me if you know about segments. If you don't, skip the Interrupt function and consider yourself lucky.

If you can't guess the C implementation from the following description, you can check out the C code on the companion CD. For now, we'll just focus on how to use the Interrupt function. Here's the Declare statement:

```
Declare Function Interrupt Lib "VBUTIL16" (ByVal iInt As Integer, _
    ax As Any, bx As Any, cx As Any, dx As Any, _
    si As Any, di As Any) As Integer
```

Despite declaring them with As Any, you should think of these parameters as having type Long. Pass integer constants and variables as Longs. The purpose of the As Any type here is to allow you to pass strings. So why use Long parameters rather than Integer parameters even though registers are, predictably, 16 bits wide in 16-bit operating systems? You frequently need to fill registers with hex numbers such as &HCF01, but numbers with the high bit set won't fit. Long integers, however, can hold unsigned integers. In addition, some of the register arguments actually need to hold a segment:offset pair—a pointer.

My Interrupt function deals with segments the best it can based on the traditional register conventions used in interrupt service routines. MS-DOS functions take pointers to input strings, buffers, or structures in the DS:DX register pair. If they need a second pointer, they put it in the ES:BX register pair. Occasionally, the DS:SI and ES:DI pairs are also used for pointers. Therefore, I deal with the BX, DX, SI, and DI arguments as special-case situations that might include a segment. Since 0 is never a valid segment (at least not when calling interrupt services), the function recognizes a 0 in the high word as a signal that the argument contains only a general-purpose register. For example, if DX has a value of &H13C00FF, the Interrupt function recognizes that DS is &H13C and that DX is &HFF.

This works fine on input. On output, something is always in the segment registers, and Interrupt doesn't know whether the processor intended to return only the register or the segment and the register. But you, the user, know because the interrupt recipe book tells you what registers you'll get back. If you need the segment register pair for BX, DX, SI, or DI, it will be in the register parameter. If you need only the 16-bit register value, strip it out with the LoWord function. You'll be using LoWord, HiWord, LoByte, and HiByte often anyway, to split out the different pieces.

You won't be able to specify a register pair in which the segment value has its high bit set. An interrupt call that returns a segment value with the high bit set causes an overflow error. Although this is theoretically possible, I give you my word that it will never happen in any Interrupt call you make from a Windows-based program. Why not? You don't want to know.

Many MS-DOS functions return an error indicator in the carry flag. If the carry flag is set, the AX register usually contains an error number. The Interrupt function returns the value of the carry flag.

Machine Name Example

You can use MS-DOS function &H5E00 to get the network machine name of your computer if the computer is part of a network that passes this information to MS-DOS. I don't guarantee the accuracy of this information on all networks,

What Happened to Type Checking?

Without fanfare, the Basic language has made a major turn in Visual Basic version 4. In one sense, the change is subtle; if you never write code that contains a certain type of bug, you might not even notice. But in another sense, it's a startling break with Basic tradition that is bound to provoke lively debate among Basic language lawyers.

Imagine writing the following code:

```
Dim i As Integer, s As String, i2 As Integer, s2 As String
s = 3
i = "12345"
i2 = Mid$(i, s)
```

You know what this code will do—generate type errors. You can't assign an integer to a string, assign a string to an integer, pass an integer argument to a string parameter, pass a string argument to an integer parameter, or assign the result of a string function to an integer variable.

Oh, yes, you can. This code assigns the value 12345 to *i2* without complaint. When you look at the variables in the Watch pane of the Debug window, you'll see that the integer 3 is converted to the string *3* and the string *12345* is converted to the integer 12345. Then they are converted back when passed as arguments, and the string result is converted to an integer. These types of conversions used to work with variants, but they never worked with strings and integers.

Let's take a more realistic example:

```
i = 3
s = "12345"
s2 = Mid$(i, s)
```

I've assigned values to *i* and *s*, but imagine that these are actually calculated values—*s*, for example, is the first token in a file I'm parsing, and it happens to be numeric. I accidentally code the Mid$ function with the arguments reversed. In previous versions of Basic, I'd get an error, immediately see what was wrong, and fix it. In the current version, I get garbage. There's nothing at position 12345 of the string *3*, so the result is an empty string. If I parse a file that has a non-numeric string as its first token, I'll instantly get an invalid function call, but I might spend hours debugging before I figure this out.

Basic used to be a strongly typed language, with an optional typeless mode through the Variant type. You could choose the better performance and better error facilities of strong type checking, or you could choose the greater flexibility of typelessness. (That's not to say Basic no longer has type checking. It and I'm not arguing that you should get the machine name from MS-DOS rather than from the ComputerName entry of the *[network]* section of your SYSTEM.INI file. This is simply an example of how to pass strings to the Interrupt function.

Here's the code:

```
Private Function GetMachineName(sMachine As String) As Integer

    Dim iAx As Long, iCx As Long, f As Integer
    sMachine = String$(16, 0)
    iAx = &H5E00&
    f = Interrupt(&H21, iAx, 0&, iCx, sMachine, 0&, 0&)
    If f Then
        sMachine = sEmpty
        If iCx = 0 Then
            GetMachineName = -1    ' Network not running
        Else
            GetMachineName = -2    ' Network not installed
        End If
    Else
        ' Strip nulls off string
        sMachine = StrZToStr(sMachine)
        GetMachineName = iCx And &HFF&
    End If

End Function
```

This code is a little messy because, typically, the MS-DOS interrupt itself is a little messy. Return values less than 0 indicate failure, whereas positive values indicate the NETBIOS number. You can test this code (and another Interrupt example) by running the Hardcore program.

still won't assign the value 60000 to an integer variable, no matter how much you might want it to.)

So why the change? Believe it or not, for compatibility. The Text property of TextBox controls used to be type Variant. You could assign an Integer to this property, which was both convenient and important. The developers of Visual Basic 4 didn't want to break this feature, but they needed the better performance of a String variable. So they added type conversion of Integers to Strings. If you go that far, why not convert Strings to Integers?

I respect the motivation, but loss of type safety seems like a significant price to pay. I must admit, however, that I haven't been hitting as many debugging problems related to the change as I expected.

Sorting, Shuffling, and Searching

Entire books have been written about the art of sorting. More specifically, sorting has been explored in the granddaddy of all Microsoft demo programs, SORTDEMO, which was written for QuickBasic by former Microsoft documentation author Michael Morrow. In a previous life as a sample programmer for the Microsoft languages department, I inherited the Basic version and presided over various enhancements and translations to C, Pascal, and FORTRAN. I later saw translations by others to COBOL (believe it or not) and to C++ with MFC.

If you own older versions of Microsoft C, FORTRAN, Pascal, Basic, or COBOL, you've probably seen this program. It randomizes colored bars on the screen and then presents a menu of sorting algorithms: bubble, shell, exchange, heap, and quick. You can see how the different algorithms compare elements and exchange them, and you can compare timings. More annoying, you can *hear* the difference, as each bar plays a different tone based on its length. I can still hear the difference between a QuickSort and a HeapSort.

Unfortunately, SORTDEMO has never been translated to Visual Basic. I was tempted, but this section is about sorting as a practical task, not sorting as a science. Therefore I'll present only the sorting algorithm that SORTDEMO shows to be the most efficient—QuickSort. Computer scientists might argue that QuickSort isn't always the fastest. The efficiency of sorting algorithms varies, depending on the number of elements, how random they are, how long it takes to compare elements, how long it takes to swap them, and so on. But QuickSort is more than adequate for the tasks in this book.

QuickSort

The following QuickSort algorithm for sorting arrays is taken directly from the SORTDEMO program, with only slight modifications to make it more modular:

```
' QuickSort algorithm
Sub SortArray(aTarget() As Variant, _
            iFirst As Integer, iLast As Integer)
    Dim vSplit As Variant

    If iFirst < iLast Then

        ' Only two elements in this subdivision; exchange if
        ' they are out of order, and end recursive calls
        If iLast - iFirst = 1 Then
            If SortCompare(aTarget(iFirst), aTarget(iLast)) > 0 Then
                SortSwap aTarget(iFirst), aTarget(iLast)
            End If
        Else
```

```
Dim i As Integer, j As Integer, iRand As Integer

' Pick pivot element at random and move to end
' (consider calling Randomize before sorting)
iRand = GetRandom(iFirst, iLast)
SortSwap aTarget(iLast), aTarget(iRand)
vSplit = aTarget(iLast)
Do

    ' Move in from both sides toward pivot element
    i = iFirst: j = iLast
    Do While (i < j) And _
            SortCompare(aTarget(i), vSplit) <= 0
        i = i + 1
    Loop
    Do While (j > i) And _
            SortCompare(aTarget(j), vSplit) >= 0
        j = j - 1
    Loop

    ' If you haven't reached pivot element, it means
    ' that the two elements on either side are out of
    ' order, so swap them
    If i < j Then
        SortSwap aTarget(i), aTarget(j)
    End If
Loop While i < j

' Move pivot element back to its proper place
SortSwap aTarget(i), aTarget(iLast)

' Recursively call SortArray (pass smaller
' subdivision first to use less stack space)
If (i - iFirst) < (iLast - i) Then
    SortArray aTarget(), iFirst, i - 1
    SortArray aTarget(), i + 1, iLast
Else
    SortArray aTarget(), i + 1, iLast
    SortArray aTarget(), iFirst, i - 1
End If
        End If
    End If

End Sub
```

QuickSort works on the divide-and-conquer principle. It splits the array into two groups and then sorts both the top and the bottom. It does this by calling itself to sort each group. Recursion makes QuickSort fast but also subjects it to stack limitations. A recursive algorithm has the potential to run out of stack space as it pushes more arguments and local variables onto the stack each time it calls itself. For every recursive algorithm, there is an iterative algorithm, although the recursive version is often simpler and easier to understand. Your assignment, should you decide to accept it, is to translate my SortArray procedure into an iterative version.

The SortArray sub is used to sort arrays containing strings and integers in the Test Sort program (TSORT.VBP), shown in Figure 3-1. This program sorts arrays, collections, and list boxes. For now, we're interested only in arrays. ("The CSortedListBox Class," page 421, talks about sorting collections and list boxes.)

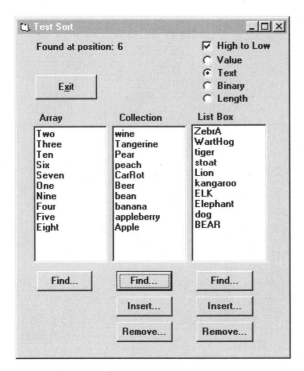

Figure 3-1. *The Test Sort program.*

SortArray is also used to sort an array of playing cards in the Fun 'n Games program (FUNNGAME.VBP) described in Chapter 6. To understand the QuickSort algorithm thoroughly, load one of these programs and step through the code. Then let's see how to make the code reusable from different projects.

Sorting Different Types

My version of SortArray sorts arrays of Variants. This is the most flexible way to define the procedure, but it won't help if you have an array of Integers or Strings to sort. You can pass an Integer argument to a Variant parameter, but you can't pass an array of Integers to a Variant array parameter. All those elements must be lined up in a row, and Basic must know the distance between them, which will be different for Integers than for Variants.

One solution is to put anything you want to sort in a Variant array. You can stuff the array with strings, integers, or real numbers, and SortArray will do the right thing with them. But it won't necessarily be fast. You probably won't see any difference if you're sorting 150 integers or 50 strings. But if you're doing the Mondo Double Sort From Down Under, you'll want to write a separate Sort-ArrayDouble for it. This process is so mechanical that you might be tempted to do it with conditional compilation:

```
# If SortArrayType = 0 Then
Sub SortArray(aTarget() As Variant, _
              iFirst As Integer, iLast As Integer)
    Dim vSplit As Variant
# ElseIf SortArrayType = 1 Then
Sub SortArray(aTarget() As Integer, _
              iFirst As Integer, iLast As Integer)
    Dim vSplit As Integer
# ElseIf SortArrayType = 2 Then
Sub SortArray(aTarget() As Long, _
              iFirst As Integer, iLast As Integer)
    Dim vSplit As Long
# ElseIf SortArrayType = 3 Then
Sub SortArray(aTarget() As String, _
              iFirst As Integer, iLast As Integer)
    Dim vSplit As String
# ElseIf SortArrayType = 4 Then
Sub SortArray(aTarget() As Single, _
              iFirst As Integer, iLast As Integer)
    Dim vSplit As Single
# ElseIf SortArrayType = 5 Then
Sub SortArray(aTarget() As Double, _
              iFirst As Integer, iLast As Integer)
    Dim vSplit As Double
# End If
    ⋮
End Sub
```

This trick is so ugly and fraught with potential for error that I hesitate to include it. Still, it's interesting to see how you can change the internal operation of a procedure simply by changing parameter and variable types. Because the default value for a conditional constant is 0, you will get the Variant version of SortArray by doing nothing. You need to define a value for SortArrayType in the Options dialog box to get any other type. One disadvantage of this hack is that you can have only one type of SortArray per project. That's one reason I recommend the cut-and-paste method of getting different SortArray routines over the conditional compilation method.

Comparing and Swapping

Sorting is essentially a simple operation. You compare the elements and swap the ones that are out of order until all are in order. A QuickSort does this differently than a Heap sort or an Insertion sort does, but all that matters to a user is how you compare and swap. Both these operations can vary greatly, depending on what you're sorting and how you want to sort it.

By changing the comparison routine, you can control whether data is sorted in ascending or descending order and other aspects of sorting. You can sort integers by value only, but you can sort strings by case-sensitive value, by case-insensitive value, by length, by the sums of the Roman numeral values of the characters, or whatever you choose. To sort objects, you'll probably want to compare based on a property such as size, color, name, position, or type.

The sort algorithm always works the same no matter what you're sorting, but the compare operation varies. You need a way to combine a generic sort routine with a specific compare routine. "Jury-Rigged Procedure Variables," page 134, describes a trick for doing this in Visual Basic; for now, let's just look at comparison code. Here's a very simple comparison routine that sorts numeric data in descending order:

```
' Define fSortCompareDef to use default SortCompare
#If fSortCompareDef Then
Private Function SortCompare(ByVal v1 As Variant, _
                             ByVal v2 As Variant) As Integer
    If v1 < v2 Then
        SortCompare = -1
    ElseIf v1 = v2 Then
        SortCompare = 0
    Else
        SortCompare = 1
    End If
End Function
#End If
```

Ignore the conditional compilation for a minute, and concentrate on the code. You can compare numeric values (and non-case-sensitive strings) with relational operators. You return −1, 0, or 1, depending on whether the first value is less than, equal to, or greater than the second value. No matter how complex your comparison, only these three results are valid. (Ignore errors for now.) Incidentally, the Basic StrComp function works the same way, for the same reasons.

The SortArray sub uses SortCompare this way:

```
If SortCompare(aTarget(iFirst), aTarget(iLast)) > 0 Then
    SortSwap aTarget(iFirst), aTarget(iLast)
End If
```

Because this code simply checks to see whether the value is greater than 0, SortCompare could still work if it returned only 1 and 0. Comparison routines are also used by search routines, however (as you'll see in "Binary Search," page 138), and these routines must be able to distinguish all three values.

Here's a very specific SortCompare:

```
Public Function SortCompare(v1 As Variant, v2 As Variant) As Integer
    ' Use string comparisons only on strings
    If TypeName(v1) <> "String" Then ordMode = ordSortVal

    Dim i As Integer
    Select Case ordMode
    ' Sort by value (same as ordSortBin for strings)
    Case ordSortVal
        If v1 < v2 Then
            i = -1
        ElseIf v1 = v2 Then
            i = 0
        Else
            i = 1
        End If
    ' Sort case-insensitive
    Case ordSortText
        i = StrComp(v1, v2, 1)
    ' Sort case-sensitive
    Case ordSortBin
        i = StrComp(v1, v2, 0)
    ' Sort by string length
    Case ordSortLen
        If Len(v1) = Len(v2) Then
            If v1 = v2 Then
                i = 0
            ElseIf v1 < v2 Then
                i = -1
```

(continued)

```
            Else
                i = 1
            End If
        ElseIf Len(v1) < Len(v2) Then
            i = -1
        Else
            i = 1
        End If
    End Select
    If fSortHiToLo Then i = -i
    SortCompare = i
End Function
```

This code tests the internal variables *ordSortMode* and *fSortHiToLo*, which are local to the program doing the sorting.

Swapping presents similar problems. To swap data, you simply assign the first element to a temporary variable, assign the second element to the first, and assign the temporary variable to the second. Here's the default swap routine for SortArray:

```
' Define fSortSwapNoDef if you provide your own swap routine
#If fSortSwapNoDef = 0 Then
Sub SortSwap(v1 As Variant, v2 As Variant)
    Dim vT As Variant
    vT = v1
    v1 = v2
    v2 = vT
End Sub
#End If
```

This works well for simple types. But if you're swapping objects, files, or some other data, you might need a different swap routine. For example, you would normally swap objects using the Set statement rather than a simple assignment operator. If you were swapping files, you might want to simply swap the names rather than actually exchanging all the data.

Jury-Rigged Procedure Variables

In most languages, you can implement user-defined compare and swap routines using a feature called *procedure variables* in Pascal, *function pointers* in C, or, more generically, *callbacks* in the SDK documentation. A procedure variable contains the address of a procedure. You can change the procedure by changing the address value. You can call the procedure by calling the variable. You can pass a procedure variable to a second procedure, thereby modifying what procedure the second procedure calls to do its job.

If Basic supported procedure variables, the SortArray sub might look like this:

```
Sub SortArray(aTarget() As Variant, _
            iFirst As Integer, iLast As Integer, _
            procCompare As SortCompareProc, _
            procSwap As SortSwapProc)
    ⋮
    If procCompare(aTarget(iFirst), aTarget(iLast)) > 0 Then
        procSwap aTarget(iFirst), aTarget(iLast)
    End If
    ⋮
```

You might then call the routine with one of these statements:

```
SortArray aFloats(), -37.2, 48.6, FloatCompare, FloatSwap
SortArray aStrings(), 1, 100, StringCompare, StringSwap
SortArray aAliens(), 0, 32, AlienCompare, AlienSwap
```

But the gods of Basic haven't seen fit to give us this simple feature, which even the lowly FORTRAN peons take for granted. In my opinion, lack of procedure variables is one of two faults that keep Basic from playing with the big kids. (The other is Basic's weakness in initializing variables.) Maybe we'll see procedure variables in the next version.

In the meantime, new visibility rules in Visual Basic 4 let you hack in a crude equivalent. In previous versions, all procedures were either global (what we now call public) or private. You could have only one public procedure with a given name. Under the new rules, procedure names have module visibility—each module can reuse the same name, and Basic decides which version to use based on visibility rules. You see an error only if you define multiple procedures with the same name and Basic can't figure out which one to use.

Figure 3-2 on the next page illustrates. Both the Card Game project and the Adventure Game project want to use the SortArray procedure in SORT.BAS. Card Game wants to sort scores and cards, both of which are coded as integers. No problem. Just define a SortSwap and a SortCompare for integers in a code module. Call SortArray in SORT.BAS from any module, and SortArray will in turn call SortSwap. Everything works because you're sorting only integers.

The Adventure Game project wants to sort player strings and monster objects. You define a SortSwap that swaps strings in the PLAYER.BAS module called by the SortArray in PLAYER.CLS. But if you try to define a MONSTER.BAS containing a SortSwap that swaps monsters, you'll have two SortSwaps at the same level in the project, and SortArray won't know which to call. You might expect the Players class and the Monster form to simply define their own SortSwap procedures instead of depending on a separate code module. But that doesn't work because any public procedure in a class or in a form has to be qualified—as FMonster.SortSwap or CPlayers.SortSwap. But the generic SortArray routine is designed to be used in various modules, and it can't know how to qualify the different sort routines. SortSwap or other procedures that fake procedure variables can be defined only in code modules.

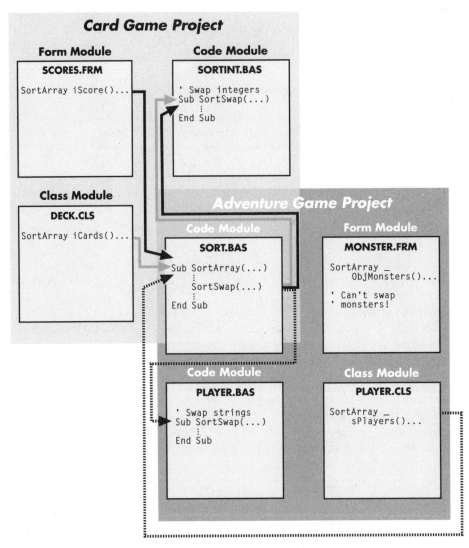

Figure 3-2. *Reusing the Sort module in different projects.*

Undoubtedly you could figure out a hack to get around this, with a global variable that indicates whether SortSwap should swap monsters or players. At some point, however, a hack becomes too confusing to be worth the risk of bugs. You'll have to decide this for your own projects.

I use a simpler scheme of default procedures based on conditional compilation. I assume that the user will most often want the default SortSwap procedure in SORT.BAS, which works for most values most people will sort. You get this procedure if you include the SORT.BAS module and do nothing. If you want to define your own swap procedure, give the *fSortSwapNoDef* constant a nonzero value in the Options dialog box. The default is the opposite for SortCompare. Most projects will need their own comparison procedures. If you want to sort numeric data only, give the *fSortCompareDef* constant a nonzero value in the Options dialog box to get the simple value version of SortCompare.

This hack depends on peculiarities of the Basic name space. In languages that support real procedure variables, you can name your procedures whatever you want—SortCompareStrings and SortCompareMonsters, for instance—rather than naming all your comparison procedures SortCompare regardless of what they compare. Remember that you can have only one SortSwap and one SortCompare per project and that you must define them in a code module.

Shuffling

The opposite of sorting is shuffling, a common task in games. Shuffling means randomizing each element in an array. The trick is that each element must appear in the array once and only once, but in a random position. You can't go through the array randomizing wildly, because you would end up with duplicate elements.

The ShuffleArray sub uses the same fake-procedure-variable technique and the same SortSwap sub as the SortArray procedure:

```
Sub ShuffleArray(a() As Variant)
    Dim iFirst As Integer, iLast As Integer
    iFirst = LBound(a): iLast = UBound(a)

    ' Randomize array
    Dim i As Integer, v As Variant, iRnd As Integer
    For i = iLast To iFirst + 1 Step -1
        ' Swap random element with last element
        iRnd = GetRandom(iFirst, i)
        SortSwap a(i), a(iRnd)
    Next
End Sub
```

Make sure that your program uses the Randomize statement (usually in Form_Load) if you want your arrays to be properly shuffled. I didn't use it in the ShuffleArray sub because in a few rare cases, you might want to shuffle the array using the same random number sequence. The statement *Rnd -1* before each call to ShuffleArray will give you the same shuffle order each time. That's all the information you need to cheat at cards—as long as you write the card games.

If you're not sure why this works, look up Randomize and Rnd and read carefully between the lines. Basic's randomizing features are more rich, complicated, and...uh, random than those of any language I know.

The algorithm works by choosing any random element between the first and last elements and exchanging it with the last element, which then is random. Next it finds a random element between the first and the next-to-last element and exchanges it with the next-to-last element. This process continues until the shuffling is finished.

The Fun 'n Games program, which is discussed in Chapter 6, uses the Shuffle sub to shuffle a deck of cards.

Binary Search

Once you sort a list of items, you can search it quickly with a binary search. A binary search splits the list into two parts, determines which one contains the search item, and then searches only that part by splitting that list into two parts. It continues in this fashion until the item is found. You can also use a binary search to insert an item into a sorted list. Instead of inserting the item at the beginning or the end and then re-sorting, you search the list for the appropriate place to insert the item.

The following BSearchArray function uses the fake-procedure-variable technique you saw in SortArray and ShuffleArray. It also reuses the SortCompare function.

```
Function BSearchArray(av() As Variant, vKey As Variant, _
                      iPos As Integer) As Boolean
    Dim iLo As Integer, iHi As Integer
    Dim iComp As Integer, iMid As Integer
    iLo = LBound(av): iHi = UBound(av)
    Do
        iMid = iLo + ((iHi - iLo) \ 2)
        iComp = SortCompare(av(iMid), vKey)
        Select Case iComp
        Case 0
```

```
            ' Item found
            iPos = iMid
            BSearchArray = True
            Exit Function
        Case Is > 0
            ' Item is in upper half
            iHi = iMid
            If iLo = iHi Then Exit Do
        Case Is < 0
            ' Item is in lower half
            iLo = iMid + 1
            If iLo > iHi Then Exit Do
        End Select
    Loop
    ' Item not found, but return position to insert
    iPos = iMid - (iComp < 0)
    BSearchArray = False

End Function
```

For an interesting example of binary search, check out the sorted list box class discussed in Chapter 9 ("The CSortedListBox Class," page 421). This class uses a binary search procedure to insert new list items at the correct location in a sorted list box.

In addition to procedures for sorting, shuffling, and searching arrays, SORT.BAS contains similar procedures for collections. We'll discuss collections in detail in Chapter 4. Sorting arrays and sorting collections are different enough to require separate procedures, but not different enough to justify separate discussions. Both versions depend on SortCompare, but swapping works differently in collections.

4

An Object Way of Basic

On the Microsoft campus, you sometimes see employees sporting T-shirts that advertise a mythical product called Object Basic. Not every Microsoft product that reaches the T-shirt stage reaches the product stage, at least not under the same name; just ask a Microsoft old-timer about Cirrus or Opus or Cashmere. In a larger sense, however, Visual Basic 4 is Object Basic, regardless of the name the marketing department puts on the box.

Object Basic has been on the horizon for a long time, and it still has a way to go. But, starting in this version, objects are now more than an afterthought. Form modules provide a way to create visual objects with properties and methods, and class modules provide a way to create your own nonvisual objects. Controls, forms, classes, OLE objects, the Data Access Object—all can be created with Dim, assigned with Set, manipulated with properties and methods, and grouped in collections.

Objects are more than a new feature; they're a way of thinking. Objects can help to make your code more modular, and you can make your objects available to any program that understands OLE Automation. In other words, your objects can be used by programs written in Visual Basic, by programs written in most versions of C and C++, and by macros in many applications, including Microsoft Word, Microsoft Excel, and the Visual Basic environment itself.

This chapter (and the rest of the book) preaches the object religion. From here on out, we'll be talking about Object Basic not as a product but as an attitude, a state of mind. By the time you finish, you'll be telling your children to change their methods and properties or face Punishment events. You'll go into a restaurant and ask your waitperson to set a Hamburger object with its Tomato and Onion properties True but with the Mustard property False. You'll write your representatives letters demanding fewer Tax events and more Service methods.

For Each friend in your Friends collection, the friend will call the Wish method with the named argument *NeverSeenThisBook : =True*.

While following the object religion, you don't need to abandon the functional philosophy. The old Basic mindset you've developed over the years isn't bad, and in any case you can't give it up entirely because Basic isn't yet sufficiently object-oriented. But functional Basic is fading, and it might even be completely optional next time around if enough programmers get the object spirit.

Object-Oriented Programming, Basic Style

Basic has its own style for doing object-oriented programming, just as it has its own style for doing most everything else. Let's look briefly at how Basic both resembles and differs from other object-oriented languages.

Encapsulation, Inheritance, and Polymorphism

Purists will no doubt argue that Visual Basic isn't an object-oriented language at all because it supports only one and a half of the three pillars of object-oriented languages—encapsulation, inheritance, and polymorphism.

Encapsulation means bringing data to life. Instead of you, the outsider, manipulating data by calling functions that act on it, you create objects that take on lives of their own, calling each other's methods, setting each other's properties, sending messages to each other, and generally interacting in ways that better model the way objects interact in real life. Previous versions of Visual Basic allowed you to use objects created in other languages; this version allows you to create your own.

Inheritance means reusing code in a hierarchical structure. For instance, a Basic programmer is a programmer is a worker is a person is an animal. All animals have heads, and therefore the Head property of a Basic programmer should inherit all the general features of animal heads plus all the features of people heads plus all the features of worker heads plus all the features of programmer heads. When creating a Head property for a BasicProgrammer object, you should need to write only the head code unique to Basic programmers. But, alas, Basic doesn't yet support inheritance in any way. Maybe next time. In the meantime, you can fake some of the advantages of inheritance through a process called *delegation*, which I'll demonstrate later, starting with the CPictureGlass class in "The Glass Picture Box," page 292.

Polymorphism means that any object will be able to do the right thing if you send it a message it understands. If I call the Hack method of a Programmer object, a Woodcutter object, and a Butcher object, each object should be able to Hack in its own special way without knowing who sent the message. Visual Basic supports this, sort of. In most object-oriented languages, however, polymorphism is filtered through inheritance. If Woodcutter and Butcher both inherit from Cutter, but Programmer inherits from Thinker, then Programmer.Hack will fail in contexts that expect Cutter.Hack. Any Hack method works in Visual Basic as long as the caller uses compatible arguments and return types. In other words, Basic has dumb polymorphism instead of the smart polymorphism that is found in languages with inheritance.

Procedures Versus Methods

Object-oriented programming turns traditional structured programming on its ear. In structured programming, you call a routine indicating what you want to do and then pass arguments specifying what to do it to, and how:

```
DoThis ToThat, WithThese
```

In object-oriented programming, you indicate what you want to work on and then specify methods to indicate what you want to do:

```
ToThis.DoThat WithThese
```

In traditional functional programming, you can pass two kinds of arguments: one indicates what you want to work on, and the other provides additional information about how to do the work. Sometimes you don't need to indicate what you want to work on, because a default object is understood. In Visual Basic terms, the statement

```
DoThis WithThese
```

really means

```
Me.DoThis WithThese
```

At other times, you don't need to specify how to work on something because you have only one possibility:

```
Me.DoThis     ' WithDefaultThese
```

Internally, the processor doesn't know anything about object-oriented programming; assembly language is always functional by nature. You'll have to fake object-oriented programming. Object-oriented languages do this internally by passing a hidden argument. When you write the code

```
ToThis.DoThat WithThese
```

in Basic (or any object-oriented language), what the processor really sees, in simplified terms, is this:

```
DoThat ToThis, WithThese
```

So how do you attach the ToThis to the DoThat in Basic? You create a template called a class (a form is a specific type of class) for CThis objects, of which the ToThis will be an instance. Within the class, you create a public DoThat sub and give it a *These* parameter. Then when you create a new ToThis instance of the CThis class, you can call it in object-oriented syntax:

```
Dim ToThis As New CThis
ToThis.DoThat WithThese
```

Simple? We'll see.

Properties: Get, Set, and Let

Visual Basic is unusual among object-oriented languages in the way it supports the concept of properties. In most object-oriented languages, setting a property means calling a Let method, and reading a property means calling a Get method. (Most languages use the word *Set* rather than *Let* in this context, but I follow the Basic tradition. Basic has another meaning for Set that we'll discuss later.) In this hypothetical, non-Basic, object-oriented language, you would see statements such as these:

```
iLine = txtNote.GetLine()
txtNote.LetLine(iLine + 1)
```

This is not the Basic Way. Properties should look like variables; you change or read them with assignment statements:

```
iLine = txtNote.Line
txtNote.Line = iLine + 1
```

Visual Basic version 4 adds Property Let, Property Get, and Property Set procedures to define properties that work with this syntax but actually consist of behind-the-scenes procedures that enable you to validate and manipulate the values being assigned or read. (Later in this chapter, "The Property Shop," page 156, tells you how to make this happen for your objects.)

The Basic Way is to create classes with lots of properties and few methods. We'll try to follow this style.

Designing Objects

The best way to design classes (including forms) is to use them before you create them. Write some code using the class as if it existed. Declare object variables with your new class type. If the class has a Create method, call it in different ways to create different kinds of objects. Set some object reference variables to refer to existing objects. Pass objects as arguments to subs and functions. Assign values to or read values from the properties of the objects. Call the methods of the objects.

It's easy and fun. You never get design-time or run-time errors. And imaginary objects of imaginary classes can acquire new methods and properties as fast as you can think them up.

We all know that air code doesn't work. Chances are that your imaginary class will never work the way you imagined it. Once you start implementing methods and properties, you'll find some of them more difficult than you expected. You might have to cut features or change the design. As you do so, revise your user code to keep it in sync.

Think of it as a client-server situation. Your class implementation is the server, and the routines that use your objects are the clients. You might want to implement features one at a time. Comment out most of the client code, and then implement some key properties and methods in the server code. Uncomment the appropriate client code, and see whether it works. If it doesn't, change it. Design is an iterative process. When you actually try to use your implementation, you'll often find that it's clumsy. Or you'll find that your client code wants to do something that can't be done. On the other hand, the process of implementing might give you new ideas for features that users would appreciate.

On major projects, you don't always have the luxury of designing by trial and error. A designer might write a specification describing all the interface elements in detail. The spec is handed to an implementor, who makes it happen. Interface changes can have major repercussions for everyone involved. Even in this situation, however, the designer follows the same process, if only in his or her imagination. Any design-implementation process that depends on the infallibility of the designer is bound to fall short. I've seen specs aplenty with sample code that never worked and never could have worked—or, worse yet, specs with no sample code.

This chapter (and to some extent the rest of the book) follows the use-first-implement-later strategy. I'll show you the objects before I show you the class. Of course, I get to cheat; you won't see all my stupid ideas that got weeded out during implementation.

NOTE   The trial-and-error process of designing classes and objects isn't a bad way to design functions and subs. The concept of testing your ideas before investing too much work in them didn't start with object-oriented programming.

Designing Classes

If you were describing a chair to someone from another planet, you might do it in several ways. You could point out some chairs and explain what they had in common. You could list all the features of chairs. But to really understand chairs inside out, you'd have to build a chair. We'll define objects and classes the same way.

Round Up the Usual Suspects

Visual Basic has always had objects, but in previous versions it wasn't obvious that each object had a class behind it. This list of the types of Basic objects gives you some hints about their classes, and it should give you a better sense of what classes are so that you'll be ready for a more formal definition later.

- Forms were the first objects in Visual Basic (before anyone started calling them objects). In previous versions, forms had the properties and methods you've come to know, but you had to take them pretty much as they came. In version 4, you can customize forms by adding your own properties and methods. "The Form Class," page 164, later in this chapter, explains how this feature can change your life. The generic class name for all forms is Form, but for each form you create you also assign a specific class name in the Name property.

- Control objects remain at the heart of Visual Basic programming. You still can't create controls with Basic, but you can create objects that work a lot like controls, as you'll see in Chapter 8 with the CEditor class. The generic class name for controls is Control, but each kind of control has its own class name: ListBox, TextBox, Image, Label, and so on.

- The Data Access Object introduced in version 3 has lots of new features, but that's about all this book will say about it. The DAO deserves its own book, and, rather than throw in an inadequate chapter or two, I'll leave the subject to more qualified authors.

- System objects include App, Clipboard, Debug, Printer, Screen, and Err. The new Err object wraps the functionality of the old Err and Error procedures in a clever way that lets you continue to use the old functional syntax while also getting additional features with a new object syntax. The Printer and App objects offer some new features, but other system objects are more or less unchanged. Each system object has a class name that is the same as its object name: App, Clipboard, and so on.

- Collection objects are a kind of smart, safe array that resizes itself dynamically and has properties and methods to access and control its data. Previous versions of Visual Basic included predefined Controls and Forms collections, and version 4 adds the Printers collection. More important, you can create your own collection objects. The class names of most predefined collections are the plural of their object names: Controls, Forms, and Printers. User-defined collections have the class name Collection.

■ OLE server objects were introduced in Visual Basic 3, and they work pretty much the same now except that there are more of them. And you can look forward to even more because Visual Basic 4 makes it easy to roll your own. It's relatively simple to modify your existing Basic programs to make them into objects understood by other programs. The class name for a server object is determined by its creator—you, if you wish to create your own.

■ User-defined classes are the means of defining OLE server objects in Basic. You'll see this feature extolled in the marketing literature for Visual Basic, and it is indeed a major enhancement. But I'd argue that the ability to write private user-defined classes within your own project is the most significant new feature in version 4. You can take almost any code module of related procedures and turn it into a class of equivalent but better-behaved methods and properties. This chapter tells you how.

■ Generic objects include all of the above. The only reason to list them separately is that they have their own class name: Object.

Objects by Feature

What makes an object an object?

■ Objects contain data. You access object data through properties that work in much the same way as the fields of UDTs. When you see the statement *dinoRex.Ferocity = 5*, you can't tell whether *dinoRex* is an object of a class type or a variable of a UDT. The two are similar in some ways. But…

■ Objects can contain methods. Methods are functions or subs that act on the object. If you see the statement *dinoRex.Eat("Raptor")*, you know that *dinoRex* isn't a variable of a UDT because variables can't eat or do anything else. But *dinoRex* might be a control or a form. Controls and forms have methods. But…

■ Although objects of the Form or Control type can produce events, objects of user-defined classes can't. Unfortunately, from a Basic programmer's standpoint, events remain acts of God. You take what you get from the objects you're given, and you like it. You can't create events for your own classes. (Well, actually, you can define cooperating classes that create events for each other, but let's ignore that for now.) Much as you might like to, you can't define your own CDinosaur class to have a dinoRex_Resize event. Not only do forms and controls come with act-of-God events, but their whole structure (in other words, their class) is predefined, and you can't do much to change it. But…

You are God when defining your own classes. Let's do it.

First Class: CProblem

You can analyze objects until your tongue turns purple, but you'll never really get the idea until you write your own. Let's start with the CProblem class, as simple a class as you'll ever see. It's a real class, used in the Time It program described in Chapter 1. You can find the class in PROBLEM.CLS on the companion CD. Each timing problem the program evaluates has a description, a title, and a number of iterations. You need a class to group these items together.

You might ask why you can't simply put the three pieces of information in a UDT and declare variables of that type:

```
Public Type TProblem
    Description As String
    Title As String
    Iterations As Long
End Type
Dim prob As TProblem
prob.Title = "The Class Problem"
```

But this doesn't work for the Time It program because the problems are going into a collection (wait for "Collecting Objects," page 174), and collections don't like UDTs. In fact, few of the new features of Visual Basic 4 are compatible with UDTs. The Basic user-defined type is passé, kept around for compatibility but out of sync with the object-oriented model.

Because a class is a kind of type, you might expect to be able to define a class this way:

```
Public Class CProblem
    Description As String
    Title As String
    Iterations As Long
End Class
```

That looks Basic, but it isn't. Many languages define classes with a similar syntax, but in Basic user-defined classes are more like forms. One form, one file; one class, one file.

The file for CProblem, PROBLEM.CLS, looks like this when you load it into the Visual Basic environment:

```
Public Description As String
Public Title As String
Public Iterations As Long
```

Fields of a class must be declared public and are called properties. If they are not public, they are simply internal variables, unknown to the outside world.

You must also name the class in the Name field of the Properties window. The class settings for CProblem are shown in Figure 4-1. In this case (and throughout this chapter), we're concerned only with private classes, and therefore the Public property is set to False. (Chapter 10 describes how to make your classes public and creatable as OLE objects.) I always use the default setting, Creatable MultiUse, for the Instancing property. In fact, all private classes are creatable, regardless of the setting.

Figure 4-1. *Properties for a class.*

So that's CProblem—a real class that serves a real purpose. But not quite the magical feature you were hoping for. This class is equivalent to the user-defined TProblem shown earlier, except that it is a class and thus creating an instance of it results in an object, not a variable. The syntax for creating a new object differs from the syntax for creating a new variable:

```
Dim prob As TProblem
Dim prob As New CProblem
```

If you omit the word *New*, you've created a reference object rather than an object:

```
Dim rprob As CProblem
```

Assigning values to the properties of an object is the same as assigning values to the fields of a UDT variable:

```
prob.Title = "Field of Dreams"
prob.Title = "Property of Dreams"
```

But you can't just assign values to properties of reference objects:

```
rprob.Title = "Property of Nightmares"   ' Error! Object not set
```

This statement causes an error unless you have already set the property. For example, you could set the reference object to the object:

```
Set rprob = prob
rprob.Title = "Property of Dreams"
```

This illustrates the syntax—but not the reason—for using reference variables. You'll see some practical examples later.

Objects are more flexible than variables, but they are also more complex and in some cases less efficient. You can put objects into variants, and you can use variants in collections, parameter arrays, and optional arguments.

C Pointers and Basic Objects

For those of you who know C or C++, it might help to think of objects as pointers and the Set statement as pointer indirection. If you're not a C person, try to follow along anyway. For this discussion, assume that you already have a Thing type. This might be a typedef to a structure in C or a class in C++. In Basic, the Thing type might be a form or a class. Doesn't matter.

In C, you can create a reference variable (a pointer, in C talk) this way:

```
Thing *pthg;           // Declare object reference variable
```

(C++ programmers should forget for the moment about the difference between pointers and references.) In Basic, you create a reference variable this way:

```
Dim rthg As Thing      ' Declare object reference variable
```

Each statement creates a reference to a theoretical object, but neither variable is initialized to an actual object. The big difference is that accessing the uninitialized variable will fail rudely in C, but politely in Basic.

In order to use a reference variable, you must have a real one, not just a reference to one. In Basic, you can frequently use pre-existing objects—controls, forms, OLE objects, system objects, and others. In C, if you want a real object, you must declare it:

```
Thing thg;             // Declare object variable
```

The syntax for creating an object in Basic looks like this:

```
Dim thg As New Thing   ' Declare object variable
```

This syntax fails for object types that aren't creatable. You can use the Instancing property to control whether your public OLE classes are creatable, but for other object types you must take what Basic gives you. For example, forms and non-OLE classes are creatable, but system objects such as Screen, App, and Printer already exist and thus are not creatable. You can create controls by placing them on a form, but you can't create them with code.

Simply creating a new Thing object doesn't mean that you can use it meaningfully. Depending on the definition of Thing, its default internal data might be meaningless. In C, you might need to initialize each field specifically. In C++, you can initialize data through a constructor routine and clean it up through a destructor. You can provide initialization data to the constructor as part of the declaration:

```
Thing thg(1, "Big", TRUE);    // Declare and initialize object
```

Basic allows you to initialize a class or a form with the Initialize event and clean it up with the Terminate event. But you have no way to provide initialization data as part of the declaration. Instead, if you want to pass initialization data to your class or form, you must do so by convention and hope that your users will follow the rules. The traditional name for initialization methods is Create:

```
Dim thg As New Thing       ' Declare object
thg.Create 1, "Big", True  ' Initialize object
```

In C, you can assign a reference variable with the address operator:

```
pthg = &thg               // Initialize object reference to object
```

In Basic, you use the Set statement:

```
Set rthg = thg            ' Initialize object reference to object
```

Once the connection is made, you can use the object reference variable in the same contexts in which you use the object variable, with the same effect.

The analogy between C and Basic starts to break down when you use object variables and object reference variables. In C, you use the -> operator to access object reference variables and the dot (.) operator to access object variables:

```
pthg->Velocity = 50;    // Object reference expression equivalent to
thg.Velocity = 50;      // object expression
```

In Basic, you use the dot operator whether or not the variable is a reference:

```
rthg.Velocity = 50     ' Object reference expression equivalent to
thg.Velocity = 50      ' object expression
```

If you need to keep track of whether a variable is a reference in Basic, you should do so with a naming convention. This book uses the letter *r* as the first letter of all reference variables.

Finally, objects and object references can have methods in Basic and C++, but not in C:

```
pthg->DoIt(cppIt);      // C++ good, C bad
thg.DoIt(cppIt);
```

Here they are in Basic:

```
rthg.DoIt(vbIt)         ' Basic excellent
thg.DoIt(vbIt)
```

Second Class: CDrive

The CProblem class is an oddity. You won't find many classes without methods or property procedures, just as you wouldn't expect to see many controls without methods or events. In fact, that's generally what distinguishes an object from a variable—an object acts. Procedures also act, but not on their own and not with their own data. You must call them and pass them variables and constants. You could say that an object is a variable that acts.

The drive functions GetDriveType and GetDiskFreeSpace discussed in Chapter 3 are traditional functions that accept data arguments and return data values. Let's turn them into objects. These drive objects won't simply *get* information about drives—they will *be* drives, telling the user everything about the physical drives the objects represent.

Test drive

When I write a new class, I start by creating a test form that exercises the class. I put a command button and a large label or a TextBox control on the form. Before I start writing the class itself, I declare an object of the proposed class in the Button event procedure and write some code that uses the properties and methods of the class, outputting any status information to the label or the text box. Normally, I name the test program using the name preceded by a *T*—FTestDrive in TDRIVE.FRM to test CDrive in DRIVE.CLS. In this case, however, I combined drive testing with testing of other information classes and forms, including an About form. The actual name of the test project is ALLABOUT.FRM in ALLABOUT.VBP. You can see it, with output from CDrive, in Figure 4-2. You might want to load this project now so that you can review the code as you read.

You can start by declaring three object variables:

```
Dim driveDat As New CDrive
Dim driveCur As New CDrive
Dim driveNet As New CDrive
```

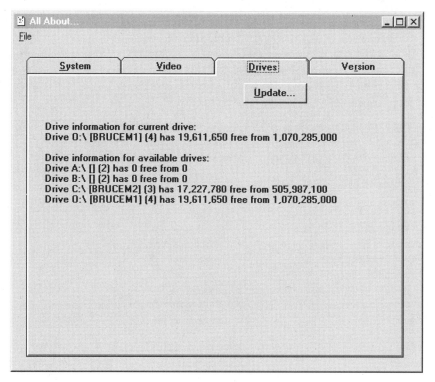

Figure 4-2. *The Drives tab of the All About program.*

At this point, the drive objects have no meaning; they aren't yet connected with any physical disk drive. You must somehow connect each Basic drive object to a real-world drive object. One way to do this is by number.

When you are programming for MS-DOS, drives are sometimes represented by the numbers 0 through 26 (with 0 representing the current drive) and sometimes by the numbers 0 through 25 (with 0 representing drive A). You need to read the documentation carefully to see which system to use for any MS-DOS function call. One of the reasons to use a class is to eliminate such inconsistent nonsense. In this case, you can magically give the CDrive class a Number property that always uses 0 through 26. As an input value, 0 represents the current drive. As an output value, 0 represents an unnumbered network drive.

You can initialize a drive as follows:

```
driveDat.Number = 1        ' Set to A:
driveCur.Number = 0        ' Set to current drive
```

Of course, to initialize a network drive, you need the more flexible root path naming system introduced in the Win32 API. Lettered drives have root paths in the form *D:*, and network drives that are not associated with letters have root paths in the form *\\server\share*. Notice that root paths always end in a backslash. When you provide a Root property as an alternative way to set or get the drive, you can set a drive as shown here:

```
driveDat.Root = "a:\"                ' Set to lettered drive
driveCur.Root = sEmpty               ' Set to current drive
driveNet.Root = "\\brucem1\root\"    ' Set to network drive
```

Once the drive is set by the Number property or the Root property, you can read either property:

```
' Assume that current drive is C:
Debug.Print driveDat.Number          ' Should print 1
Debug.Print driveCur.Number          ' Should print 3
Debug.Print driveNet.Number          ' Should print 0
Debug.Print driveDat.Root            ' Should print "A:\"
Debug.Print driveCur.Root            ' Should print "C:\"
Debug.Print driveNet.Root            ' Should print "\\BRUCEM2\ROOT\"
```

Of course, what you really want is the drive data in the form of read-only properties FreeBytes, TotalBytes, Label, and Kind. You could use them this way:

```
Const sBFormat = "#,###,###,##0"
With driveCur
    s = s & "Drive " & .Root & " [" & .Label & "] (" & .Kind & _
            ") has " & Format$(.FreeBytes, sBFormat) & _
            " free from " & Format$(.TotalBytes, sBFormat) & sCrLf
End With
```

This code would output information similar to this:

Drive C:\ [BRUCEM] (Hard) has 87,031,808 bytes free from 505,987,072

If you like, you could provide properties for other drive features such as a serial number and creation date.

Class diagrams

This is a good time to introduce the class notation that I'll use throughout the rest of this book. Class notations are a dime a dozen in object-oriented programming books, and I don't claim that mine has any special advantages. It does address the specific features of Basic classes in a way that can either show off the methods and properties of a specific class or, at a higher level, indicate relationships between classes. Figure 4-3 shows the diagram for the CDrive class.

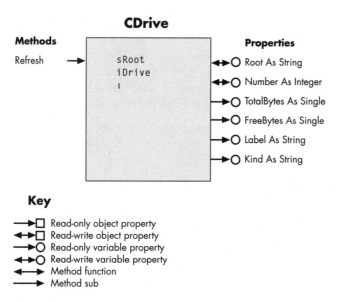

CDrive

Methods		Properties
Refresh →	sRoot iDrive ⋮	←●○ Root As String
		←●○ Number As Integer
		→○ TotalBytes As Single
		→○ FreeBytes As Single
		→○ Label As String
		→○ Kind As String

Key

→□ Read-only object property
←●□ Read-write object property
→○ Read-only variable property
←●○ Read-write variable property
←→ Method function
→ Method sub

Figure 4-3. *The CDrive class.*

For most simple classes, methods will appear on the left of the object and properties on the right. This is a convenience, not a fundamental part of the notation. Everything will appear on the right when we look at crowded object hierarchies. If it's useful to show private members of a class, they'll go inside the object box. (This is seldom necessary, however; normally, the public interface is all that matters.) The CDrive class uses only a few of the elements shown in the diagram key. I'll introduce more of these elements later, when we discuss the more complex classes that require them.

Implementing CDrive

Now that you know exactly what you want, you can start to create the CDrive class. With your test project loaded, choose Class Module from the Insert menu. (For reasons unknown, the toolbar contains Module and Form buttons but no Class button.) In the Properties window, set the Name property to CDrive. Set the Public property to False to indicate that the class is for internal use, not a public OLE server. Leave the Instancing property alone, since it doesn't affect private classes. Finally, save the class as DRIVE.CLS.

You might remember from the CProblem discussion that a property can be defined in this fashion:

```
Public Root As String
```

But if you define the Root property this way, you lose all control of it. The user can set or read it at any time without your knowledge. In CDrive, you need to do a lot of work whenever anyone sets the Root property. First you must confirm that the user has passed an actual root path. Next you calculate and store all the size and type data about the drive as soon as it is initialized. Then, when the user asks for the information later, you return the precalculated values.

The mechanism that makes this possible is the property procedure. Property Get, Property Let, and Property Set enable you to write procedures that look like variables.

The Property Shop

Let's ignore Property Set for the moment and concentrate on Get and Let property pairs. This code illustrates a classic Get/Let pair:

```
Private iStuff As Integer
    ⋮
Property Get Stuff() As Integer
    ' Do any calculations or validations here
    Stuff = iStuff
End Property

Property Let Stuff(iStuffA As Integer)
    ' Do any calculations or validations here
    iStuff = iStuffA
End Property
```

You store the data internally in a private variable, and then you define property procedures that intercept and monitor any user access to the data. You can have many variations on this theme, but the Basic operation is so mechanical that I designed a wizard program to handle the tedious paperwork. Figure 4-4 shows the Property Shop in action. Try loading and running this application.

To define a variable property with the Property Shop, type the name in the Property Name box. Select a type from the Type combo box, and be sure that the Get/Let Variable option button is selected. When you choose the Append or the New button, your Property Get and Property Let procedures appear in the text box, where you can edit them. When you're satisfied, choose the Send button. The first time you do this, a message box tells you to click the window to which you want to send the properties. Normally, you click a Visual Basic code window, and the Property Shop pastes your property procedures into that window, where you can do further editing. After you've designated a window once, the Property Shop remembers it. You can, however, choose a new target window with the Target button.

We'll discuss some other features of the Property Shop later on, particularly in Chapter 8. For now, try creating integer Get/Let properties named Stuff. You'll see results very similar to the generic properties shown earlier. Of course, the Property Shop can't handle every situation. Furthermore, it is specifically tied to my naming convention. You can modify and enhance it to better fit your coding style, but you'll hit limits and encounter situations in which it's easier to write the properties yourself.

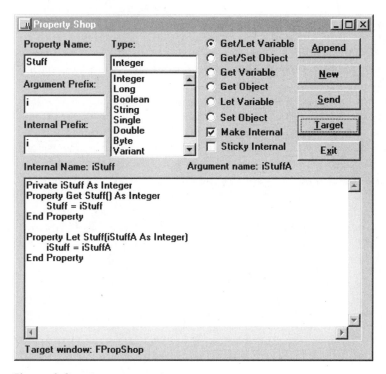

Figure 4-4. *The Property Shop.*

Try one more exercise with the Property Shop. First select the Get/Set Object option. The Type list changes to display various types of objects rather than variables. Select Collection from the list, type *Items* in the Property Name box, and choose Append or New. The Property Shop creates the Get and Set procedures to expose an internal collection to the world:

```
Private nItems As Collection
Property Get Items() As Collection
    Set Items = nItems
End Property

Property Set Items(nItemsA As Collection)
    Set nItems = nItemsA
End Property
```

Notice that although you can use Property Get to access either variables or objects, you must use Property Set for objects and Property Let for variables.

Enough property busywork. The interesting part is writing the calculation and validation code.

Naming Private Data

No matter what object-oriented language you use, you will probably run into a common naming problem. Often you must assign different names to variables that represent the same value. For example, assume that you are defining a FileName property. The program using the property might have a variable containing a filename that it wants to assign to the FileName property. A user following the Hungarian naming convention described in Chapter 1 ("Basic Hungarian," page 15) might name the variable *sFileName*. When a user assigns that value to the property, the value is actually passed as an argument to the Property Let procedure. You need a name for the filename parameter; *sFileName* springs to mind. Now you need to store the same value internally. Again, *sFileName* is the obvious choice for the name of the internal version. And what about the property name itself? From the outside, the property looks like a variable, smells like a variable, and tastes like a variable. Why shouldn't it have a variable name? How about *sFileName*?

In practical terms, using the same name for the external and internal variables is not a problem. The external variable has a different scope than all the others and might be written by a different programmer years later; therefore, similar names are no problem.

Nevertheless, following the Hungarian naming convention for properties is usually a bad idea. Your code ends up as gobbledygook: *thgMyThing.nMyCollection.iProperty*. Besides, your code will then be using a convention very different from the one used in controls, forms, and other predefined objects. Generally, it's bad manners to impose your own naming conventions on the outside world.

A conflict still exists between the parameter name in the Property Let procedure and the name in the internal version. You must make these arbitrarily different, even though they represent the same thing. You can mangle the internal version in one of two ways. The MFC class library for Visual C++, for instance, always prefixes the internal member variables in a similar situation with *m_* (as in *m_sFileName*). But I have an irrational prejudice against underscores in variable names, particularly in front of Hungarian prefixes; I'd much rather use a postfix. I considered using *I* (for internal) for all my internal variables, but I eventually switched to using *A* (for argument) with all parameter variables in Property Let statements. That way the modified name doesn't affect Property Get procedures.

Drive properties

CDrive follows a common class strategy of doing all the initialization and calculation up front—in other words, the Property Let procedures do all the work, and the Property Get procedures simply return precalculated internal data. You can also do it the other way around: assign internal variables in the Lets, and do all the calculation and validation in the Gets. The second strategy might be more effective if you are updating data frequently.

Here are the private variables of CDrive:

```
Private sRoot As String
Private iDrive As Integer
Private ordType As Integer
Private iTotalClusters As Long
Private iFreeClusters As Long
Private iSectors As Long
Private iBytes As Long
Private sLabel As String
```

And here are the property procedures to get the root path and the number:

```
Public Property Get Root() As String
    Root = sRoot
End Property

Public Property Get Number() As Integer
    If sRoot = sEmpty Then
        Number = -1
    Else
        Number = iDrive
    End If
End Property
```

Notice the check for *sRoot = sEmpty* in the Property Get Number procedure. The *sRoot* variable can be empty only if the user created a new CDrive object but didn't initialize it to a drive. You could handle this case by assuming that the user wants the current drive, but that tactic lets callers get too sloppy. Instead, you return a special value indicating an error. You can handle errors in classes in many ways. Returning an error value through a Property Get procedure is the simplest, although usually not the best. You'll see other ways of handling errors in other classes later in the book.

The key procedure in CDrive is the Root Property Let procedure:

```
Public Property Let Root(sRootA As String)
    ' Assume failure
```

(continued)

```
    sRoot = sEmpty: sLabel = sEmpty
    iSectors = 0: iBytes = 0
    iFreeClusters = 0: iTotalClusters = 0
    ' Empty means get current drive
    If sRootA = sEmpty Then sRootA = Left$(CurDir$, 3)
    ' Get drive type ordinal
    ordType = GetDriveType(sRootA)
    Select Case ordType
    Case 1
        ' Invalid root, ignore (set root to sEmpty)
    Case 0
        ' No such drive, ignore (set root to sEmpty)
    Case 2 To 6 ' Unknown, removable, fixed, remote, CD-ROM, RAM
        ' If you got here, drive is valid
        sRoot = UCase$(sRootA)
        iDrive = Asc(sRoot) - iAscA + 1
        ' Network drives have no number
        If ordType = 4 Then iDrive = 0
        ' Get disk size
        If GetDiskFreeSpace(sRoot, iSectors, iBytes, _
                            iFreeClusters, iTotalClusters) Then
            ' Failure might simply indicate empty floppy or CD drive
            ' or network drive that can't be sized under Win16;
            ' either way, you can't get label
            sLabel = GetLabel(sRoot)
        End If
    Case Else ' Shouldn't happen
        BugAssert True
    End Select
End Property
```

That might look like a lot of work, but this procedure essentially is the CDrive class. It calculates everything necessary to allow the Property Get procedures to simply read internal variables. GetDriveType, GetDiskFreeSpace, and GetLabel do the real work. We talked about the first two in Chapter 3; GetLabel is a general utility function that uses the Dir$ function to get the volume label. Check it out in UTILITY.BAS.

The Number property is much simpler:

```
Public Property Let Number(iDriveA As Integer)
    Select Case iDriveA
    Case 1 To 26
        ' Create root
        Root = Chr$(iDriveA + iAscA - 1) & ":\"
    Case 0
        ' Get current drive and create root
        Root = Left$(CurDir$, 3)
```

```
        Case Else
            ' Invalid root, set root to sEmpty
            sRoot = sEmpty
    End Select
End Property
```

This procedure calculates the root path and passes it on to the Root Property Let procedure. With everything precalculated, the TotalBytes, FreeBytes, Label, Kind, and KindStr Property Get procedures are simple:

```
Public Property Get TotalBytes() As Single
    If sRoot = sEmpty Then
        TotalBytes = -1
    Else
        TotalBytes = CSng(iTotalClusters) * iSectors * iBytes
    End If
End Property

Public Property Get FreeBytes() As Single
    If sRoot = sEmpty Then
        FreeBytes = -1
    Else
        FreeBytes = CSng(iFreeClusters) * iSectors * iBytes
    End If
End Property

Public Property Get Label() As String
    If sRoot <> sEmpty Then Label = sLabel
    ' Else Label = sEmpty
End Property

Public Property Get Kind() As Integer
    Kind = ordType
End Property

Public Property Get KindStr() As String
    If sRoot = sEmpty Then Exit Property
    KindStr = Choose(ordType + 1, "Unknown", "Invalid", "Floppy", _
                    "Hard", "Network", "CD-ROM", "RAM")
    ' Floppy or CD-ROM of size 0 means disk is missing
    If (ordType = 2 Or ordType = 5) And iTotalClusters = 0 Then
        KindStr = Kind & " Missing"
    End If
End Property
```

Notice that TotalBytes and FreeBytes return Single rather than Long (as I originally coded them). I wouldn't mind owning a disk larger than 2,147,483,648 bytes, but I didn't really expect to encounter one. When I started testing the class, I found out that a drive larger than 2 gigabytes is not uncommon on network servers. That still doesn't explain the use of the CSng function. You might expect that if you're assigning a value to a variable of one type, the language would attempt to convert any expression to the type of the target variable. This works in some languages, but not in Basic. Try the following:

```
Dim iTest As Long
iTest = 10000 * 4
```

You'll get an overflow even though the expression obviously results in a valid Long. You must convert one of the operands to a Long:

```
iTest = 10000& * 4
```

Or:

```
iTest = CLng(10000) * 4
```

The first version is more efficient if one operand is a constant, but you'll have to use the second version if all operands are variables, as they are in the examples.

TotalBytes, FreeBytes, Label, Kind, and KindStr have no Property Let statements because you can't set the size or the kind for a disk. In theory, you could set the label, but Basic won't help you—and in this case neither will I. (If you like, you can add a label-setting function to the VBUTIL DLL.) To make a property read-only, you define the Property Get procedure but not Property Let.

Drive methods

A method is simply a public sub or function inside a class (or form) module. CDrive has only one method, Refresh:

```
Public Sub Refresh()
    Root = sRoot
End Sub
```

This method forces the current drive object to reinitialize itself. When you create a drive object, it gets all the necessary information about itself. That information might change, however. If the user deletes some files, the FreeBytes property changes. If the user inserts or removes a floppy disk or a CD-ROM, several properties might change. Frequently, you declare a drive object locally, read the information you need, and let it go out of scope. But if you define a drive object at the module level, you need to refresh it before rereading values.

Here's another operation you might want:

```
Public Sub Format()
    Shell Environ$("COMMSPEC") & " /c FORMAT "  sRoot, vbHide
End Sub
```

No! Wait! It's a joke. It's not in the sample program. Look, it even has a syntax error; it won't work even if you type it in yourself. I'm not trying to reformat your hard disk.

PERFORMANCE

Problem: If you choose a class solution over an equivalent functional solution, what performance penalty, if any, must you accept? There's no easy one-to-one comparison, but the following information might give you a clue about the relative performance of methods, procedures, properties, and variables. As a bonus, you get a comparison of objects versus reference objects.

Problem	16-Bit Mode	32-Bit Mode
Call method function on object	225 ms	147 ms
Call method function on reference object	216 ms	143 ms
Call private function	99 ms	96 ms
Pass variable to method sub on object	211 ms	125 ms
Pass variable to method sub on reference object	200 ms	122 ms
Pass variable to private sub	99 ms	96 ms
Assign through Property Let on object	217 ms	131 ms
Assign through Property Let on reference object	212 ms	127 ms
Assign through private Property Let	110 ms	95 ms
Assign from Property Get on object	230 ms	143 ms
Assign from Property Get on reference object	221 ms	140 ms
Assign from private Property Get	105 ms	94 ms
Assign to public property on object	35 ms	29 ms
Assign to public property on reference object	23 ms	21 ms
Assign to private variable	24 ms	22 ms
Assign from public property on object	36 ms	30 ms
Assign from public property on reference object	25 ms	22 ms
Assign from private variable	25 ms	21 ms

Conclusion: Hard to say. Using classes and objects definitely has a performance cost. Classes that wrap very simple operations might cost more than they are worth, but for most classes, the overhead is tiny compared to the total cost of what the class actually does.

The Form Class

Forms are just classes with windows. Think of it this way: somewhere in the heart of the source code for the Basic run-time library lives a module named FORM.CLS.

You didn't know that Visual Basic is written in Visual Basic? Well, I have inside information (incorrect, like most inside information) that Visual Basic 4 is actually written in Visual Basic 5. The FORM.CLS module contains Property Let and Property Get statements for AutoRedraw, BackColor, BorderStyle, Caption, and all the other properties you see in the Properties window. It has public subs for the Circle and Line methods and public functions for the Point method. Furthermore, it defines events using a syntax that…well, I could tell you, but then I'd have to shoot you.

The FORM.CLS module didn't change much in Visual Basic versions 1 through 3—a few new properties here, a few new methods there. But for version 4, somebody got the bright idea that if a form is just a class, users should be able to add their own properties and methods. You might be thinking, "Well, that's nice, but I don't see how it affects me." That was my first impression, but as I thought more about it and experimented, the feature began to look like a major enhancement. Let's examine both the obvious and the subtle implications.

Form Classes Versus Form Objects

Although a form is like a class in most ways, it has one very unusual feature that makes it different from any other kind of Basic class—and, in fact, different from classes in all other languages I know about. This feature is so fundamental to the Visual Basic programming model that you've probably used it hundreds of times without understanding what you were doing.

Whenever you create a form class, Visual Basic automatically provides an object of that class with the same name. So when you create a new project, it comes with a form named Form1. If you take my advice, you'll immediately rename the form to something intelligible—say, FMyApp. You now have a class named FMyApp and an object named FMyApp. You can use the class name to perform class operations such as creating new form objects of the FMyApp class:

```
Dim frm As New FMyApp
```

This creates a form object with an object name that differs from its class name, but you can also use the class name as an object name:

```
FMyApp.Show vbModal
```

It's as if whenever you start a new project, click the Form toolbar button, or choose Form from the Insert menu, Visual Basic generates this internal statement:

```
Dim Form1 As New Form1
```

When you change the Name property of the form, Basic changes the internal statement to the following:

```
Dim FMyApp As New FMyApp
```

The Visual Basic documentation calls this feature *implicit form variable declaration*. I call it confusing.

You don't have to use this feature if you don't like it. I never use implicit form variables, partly because they conflict with my naming convention and partly because I think explicit features are always better than implicit ones. I always give forms a class name starting with *F*—FAllAbout, FAnimate, FFileOpen— and I almost never use the name as an object name. This requires a change in how you think about and use forms. Let's look first at startup forms.

The purpose of the startup form is quite different from the purpose of other forms. Windows calls the startup form the *top-level window:* it has no parent except the desktop. Most other forms that you declare are what Windows calls *dialog boxes*. They have a top-level form or another dialog box as their parent. So if you give the startup form a class name, where do you define the object name? You don't. In theory, you might have to refer to a startup form by its object name from some other form; but in practice, I've rarely needed to. You can refer to the startup form as Me from its own code, as in *Unload Me* or *Me.Refresh*.

A dialog form, in contrast, always needs an object name, but I never use the implicit one. Instead, I explicitly declare form objects whenever I need them:

```
Dim opfile As New FFileOpen
```

Notice that I create a Hungarian prefix by shortening and lowercasing the class name. If I need several File Open dialog boxes, I qualify them in the names:

```
Dim opfileExecutables As New FFileOpen
Dim opfileData As New FFileOpen
Dim opfileBitmap As New FFileOpen
```

Declaring your own form object variables instead of using the implicit ones has one other advantage: you can declare local form variables. The implicit variable always has module visibility.

A Better Picture File Dialog Box

Creating generic dialog boxes that are usable from various projects should be easy, and it is in most languages. Unfortunately, this seemingly simple task was quite daunting in previous versions of Visual Basic and required ugly hacks, dirty tricks, and—boo, hiss—global variables. As a result, most Visual Basic projects ended up with dialog boxes specific to the application. If you wanted a similar dialog box in another application, you cloned the first one and then modified it to work with the new application.

In most languages, using dialog boxes follows a pattern. You initialize the dialog box by setting various properties, you call the dialog box, and then you read the results from properties. This presented a major problem in previous versions of Visual Basic because you couldn't call functions in the form module from outside the form. Furthermore, you couldn't access variables in the form module. Essentially, the form was an independent entity. You sent it off to get information from the user, but you couldn't easily access the information it found. You had to write a separate code module containing procedures and global variables that both the caller and the dialog box could access. And that was just the beginning—in addition, it wasn't always clear to the caller when the dialog box had started and ended.

If I were an archaeologist, I could explain some of the workaround hacks that were developed using hidden controls, the bang operator, and the Tag property, but at this point I might as well talk about Etruscan art or Communist economics. Properties and methods now provide a clean way to communicate with forms, although you might need to do some unlearning to use them.

Let's take a practical example. When you click the ellipsis in the Picture property in the Visual Basic Properties window, you get a handy little dialog box that allows you to select the file for a metafile, an icon, a bitmap, or a cursor. The only problem is that you see the filename but not the picture, so you don't know what you're selecting. Wouldn't it be nice to display the picture somewhere in the dialog box?

You can't modify Visual Basic's Load Picture dialog box, but you can provide a better version in your own applications. Of course, you give up the efficiency and portability of the common dialog, but in this case defining your own is worth the price. My FOpenPicFile dialog box is shown in Figure 4-5.

Most of the work involved in creating this dialog box was straightforward form drawing. I drew the form to look like Visual Basic's own Load Picture dialog box, which appears to be an Open common dialog initialized for picture files. I then wrote the event code to make the code for the file system controls work like a common dialog. Nothing tricky—just steal the file system code from the Visual Basic documentation. Finally, I wrote the code to put the contents of the selected picture file in the corner of the dialog box.

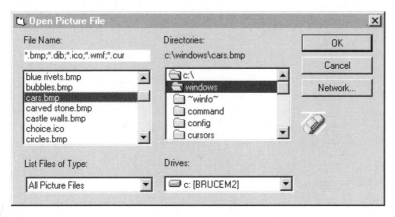

Figure 4-5. *The new and improved Picture File dialog box.*

The picture code is interesting, particularly the part that resizes the picture to fit the space if necessary; take a look at it in OPENPIC.FRM. I use the dialog box in the FUNNGAME.VBP project. Chapter 6 discusses the Fun 'n Games project in detail, but you might want to load it now and check out the code behind the Set Bitmap File button. You can also see it in HARDCORE.VBP.

> **NOTE** Coding your own emulations of common dialogs is not only expensive but also risky. I designed the Picture File dialog box under Windows 3.1 and Windows NT, but the dialog box I was emulating looks completely different under Windows 95. (And by the time you read this, it might look different under Windows NT.) You could redesign the dialog box to match the Windows 95 format, but then you'd be stuck again for Windows 97 or whatever version changes the format next. Besides, heretical as it may sound, I prefer the old format. It might lack the file icons of the Windows 95 version, but it has a nice open space in the bottom right corner for the picture.

Using the Picture File dialog box

Let's start out, as usual, by testing FOpenPicFile before writing it. To use FOpen-PicFile, you put the initial directory into the form before you load it and then get the name of the selected picture file after the form is unloaded. With the right properties, the whole thing looks easy:

```
Dim opfile As New FOpenPicFile
With opfile
    .InitDir = "c:\windows"
    .Show vbModal
```

(continued)

```
    If .FileName <> sEmpty Then
        pbBitmap.Picture = LoadPicture(.FileName)
    End If
End With
Set opfile = Nothing
```

If the properties shown for FOpenPicFile look familiar, it's because they follow the existing model set by the CommonDialog control. In fact, the code to use the CommonDialog control to load a picture file looks similar:

```
With dlgOpenPic
    .InitDir = "c:\windows"
    .Flags = cdlOFNFileMustExist Or cdlOFNHideReadOnly
    .Filter = sFilter ' *.bmp;*.dib;*.ico;*.wmf;*.cur
    .ShowOpen
    If .FileName <> sEmpty Then
        pbBitmap.Picture = LoadPicture(.FileName)
    End If
End With
```

The CommonDialog code is longer because it must handle all kinds of files in various situations, not only picture files. When you design FOpenPicFile, you can start with the CommonDialog documentation as your spec, but feature cutting proceeds rapidly. You don't need the Filter and FilterIndex properties because the purpose of the form already defines the file types. The Flags property defines various features of the dialog box, but, again, you decide the behavior. You could provide a Help button and support the various help properties (although we won't do that here). When the cutting is done, all you have left are the FileName, FileTitle, and InitDir properties.

This raises an interesting design problem. The trouble is that the FileName and FileTitle properties of CommonDialog are misnamed. Wouldn't you expect FileName to refer to the base filename and the extension? I wouldn't know what to expect from FileTitle, but I know that as a user I'd sure like to get my hands on a FullPathName property. Well, it turns out that FileName actually means the full pathname, and FileTitle means the filename. When someone else sets a bad standard, do you follow it? Or do you set your own, more logical standard? That's a tough one—and you might make a different call in each case. This time, I held my nose and followed the existing standard. (You'll see one more way to write common dialog code using the same standard in Chapter 8.)

Picture File dialog box properties

Once you know what properties (and methods) you want, all that's left is to write them. Form properties are defined in the same way as class properties.

Get With It

The With statement—stolen from Pascal and modified to fit Basic—is a fancy form of Set. The primary purpose is to make it easier and more efficient to access nested objects. For example, consider this With block:

```
With Country.State.City.Street.Houses("My")
    .Siding = ordAluminum
    .Paint clrHotPink
    .LawnOrnament = "Flamingo"
End With
```

This is equivalent to the following:

```
Dim rhouse As CHouse
Set rhouse = Country.State.City.Street.Houses("My")
rhouse.Siding = ordAluminum
rhouse.Paint clrHotPink
rhouse.LawnOrnament = "Flamingo"
```

The With version is more readable, and you don't have to declare the reference variable. Instead, a hidden one is created for you. Of course, you don't absolutely need With or Set. You can do the same thing this way:

```
Country.State.City.Street.Houses("My").Siding = ordAluminum
Country.State.City.Street.Houses("My").Paint clrHotPink
Country.State.City.Street.Houses("My").LawnOrnament = "Flamingo"
```

This code is not only harder to read but also much less efficient. Internally, Basic must look up every nested object for every access.

When you're not using nested objects (and we're not, in this chapter), the With statement is just syntactical sugar. It might save you some line wrapping, particularly if you need to access an object more than once in a line:

```
With lstHouses
    .ItemData(.ListIndex) = Len(.List(.ListIndex))
End With
```

You might find that more readable than this:

```
lstHouses.ItemData(lstHouses.ListIndex) = _
    Len(lstHouses.List(lstHouses.ListIndex))
```

But you won't see any noticeable difference in performance. If you doubt it, check the Object Access Using With item in the Time It program.

Properties usually have internal data behind them. Here are internal variables for the three FOpenPicFile properties:

```
Private sInitDir As String
Private sFilePath As String      ' d:\path\
Private sFileName As String      ' base.ext
' Full file spec is sFilePath & sFileName
```

Note that the *sFileName* variable is not the same as the FileName property. You might choose to use dumb names for compatible properties, but you should draw the line at private variables. Give them names that make sense to you, and document any resulting conflicts with comments.

Here's the FileTitle property:

```
' FileTitle is read-only
Public Property Get FileTitle() As String
    FileTitle = sFileName  ' FileTitle is actually filename
End Property
```

And here's FileName:

```
Public Property Get FileName() As String
    If sFileName <> sEmpty Then
        FileName = sFilePath & sFileName
    ' Else (commented out because strings are empty by default)
    '     FileName = sEmpty
    End If
End Property
```

```
Public Property Let FileName(sFilePathA As String)
    sFilePath = sFilePathA
End Property
```

How are *sFilePath* and *sFileName* set? The file system controls that change them set the internal variables. For example, here's how *sFilePath* is set:

```
Private Sub filPic_PathChange()
    sFilePath = NormalizePath(filPic.Path)
    If filPic.ListCount > 0 Then filPic.ListIndex = 0
End Sub
```

Here's where *sFileName* gets set and used:

```
Private Sub filPic_Click()
    sFileName = filPic.FileName
    UpdateFile sFilePath & sFileName
End Sub
```

NormalizePath (located in UTILITY.BAS) fixes a design flaw—sometimes known as a bug—that appeared in Visual Basic 1 and has been kept around ever since for compatibility: the value of the Path property ends in a backslash only for a root path, not for other paths. Don't pass this mistake on to your users.

More important, learn from Visual Basic's mistake. If you design your public interface incorrectly, you'll have to keep it incorrect forever to avoid breaking user code. Now that Visual Basic lets you write public OLE servers, this advice is more important than ever.

UpdateFile is the procedure that actually draws the picture. Check it out.

Normally, you can only write to the InitDir property, but the CommonDialog control provides a read property. Here's the code:

```
Public Property Get InitDir() As String
    InitDir = sInitDir
End Property

Public Property Let InitDir(sInitDirA As String)
    sInitDir = sInitDirA
End Property
```

This might seem too simple. The initial directory must be set in the Path property of the DirListBox control (dirPic) on the form. So why not set *dirPic.Path* in the Property Let and read from it in the Property Get?

Well, you can't read from it in Property Get because the Path property will change if the user selects a new directory. You want the initial directory, not the current or final directory. The reason for not setting *dirPic.Path* in the Property Let is more subtle. Setting a control property of a form automatically loads the form, thus activating the Form_Load event. But you don't want to load the form yet; first you need to set all preload properties so that Form_Load can use all the data for initialization.

You can safely initialize *sInitDir* in Form_Load as follows:

```
Private Sub Form_Load()
    BugMessage "Load"
    If sInitDir <> sEmpty Then
        dirPic.Path = NormalizePath(sInitDir)
    Else
        sInitDir = NormalizePath(dirPic.Path)
    End If
    ⋮
```

The Form Dance: Initialize, Load, Unload, Terminate

Visual Basic 4 adds two important form events: Initialize and Terminate. These events are what most object-oriented languages call *constructors* and *destructors*. They add flexibility and fix some longstanding problems. To see exactly how they work, try putting a BugMessage statement such as this in the Form_Initialize, Form_Load, Form_Unload, and Form_Terminate events of any form:

```
Private Sub Form_Initialize()
    BugMessage "Initialize"
End Sub
```

The BugMessage procedure (defined in DEBUG.BAS) sends a message to the Debug window, a message box, or a log file, depending on the constants set in the Options dialog box. It's useful to print the statement's important construction and destruction events if you have any doubt about what's happening.

Before you look at the next few statements, you might want to load the project FUNNGAME.VBP and set a breakpoint on the first statement in the FillPicture function in FUN.FRM. Press F8 or click the Step Over toolbar button to step through the code one statement at a time as we discuss each statement.

This code creates FOpenPicFile as a local variable:

```
Dim opf As New FOpenPicFile
```

You might expect that this statement would trigger the Initialize event, but Dim statements aren't executable. As you step through the code, you won't step on this line because it is read at compile time, not at run time.

The With statement is the first reference to the opfile object:

```
With opfile
```

The Form_Initialize event occurs when this first reference is executed. This is an important change from previous versions, in which loading and initializing were both performed in the Form_Load event. In the old days, Form_Load was called at first reference, and the form was created before you had a chance to initialize anything. In today's Basic, you have a place to put code that you want to execute before any properties or methods are called. FOpenPicFile doesn't have any such code, so its Form_Initialize event procedure is empty. Because Form_Load is no longer called here, however, the user has a chance to set internal data that couldn't have been easily set without side effects in earlier versions.

You can assign properties and call methods before loading the form. In this case, you assign the InitDir property:

```
.InitDir = "c:\windows"
```

You might remember from the preceding section that InitDir simply assigns to an internal variable. It's particularly important to avoid doing anything during initialization that might trigger a Form_Load event, which could invalidate other preload properties.

A Show statement is the way to intentionally initiate a Form_Load event:

```
.Show vbModal
```

Accessing a control on the form loads the form as a side effect, just as accessing a control inside a form method or property does. Statements like this were common when you loaded a form in previous versions of Visual Basic:

```
frmDialog!txtParty.Text = "Party On!"
```

Don't do it. Instead, provide a form property that initializes a variable, and then transfer the variable value to the control in Form_Load.

Since the opfile form object is loaded modally, you lose control when you step over the Show statement, and you don't hit the next statement in the code until the user closes the dialog box by clicking OK or Cancel.

Here's the OK button code:

```
Private Sub cmdOK_Click()
    Unload Me
End Sub
```

The Cancel button code is the same except that it also sets the *sFileName* variable to Empty. This code triggers the Form_Unload event. In previous versions of Visual Basic, Form_Unload terminated the form, wiping out all its internal variables and controls. To get around this problem, a programmer might have coded the Click event procedure this way:

```
Private Sub cmdOK_Click()
    Hide
End Sub
```

The calling code would have tried to read any required data from controls or from global variables set in the Unload event. Basic fought all your attempts to communicate with forms, but you could win if you were stubborn and clever.

Now it's easy to do. For example, the FileName property supplies the data that FOpenPicFile was designed to get:

```
    If .FileName <> sEmpty Then
        pic.Picture = LoadPicture(.FileName)
    End If
End With
```

After you get everything you want from a form, you should destroy it so that its data won't hang around in memory:

```
Set opfile = Nothing
```

The Form_Terminate event is called at this point. Actually, this statement is redundant in our example because the opfile form variable is local and will be destroyed as soon as you step to the end of the procedure. You should set forms to Nothing if you declare them at the module level or if you use the implicit variable name of the form.

NOTE   The Form_Terminate and Form_Initialize events, like all event procedures, are automatically assigned private visibility when you create them or when you convert a project from an earlier version to Visual Basic 4. All those Private attributes for event procedures might seem like bothersome noise at first, but you can see why it was done. By default, procedures in code modules have public visibility. To keep the default visibility for form and class modules the same as that for code modules, Microsoft made all procedures public. But any public procedure in a form or a class automatically becomes a public method. This is a change from previous versions, in which all form procedures were private. You certainly don't want event procedures to be public—imagine the confusion if callers could create events just by calling event methods. Nor do you want procedures from old forms suddenly becoming public. Thus the conversion.

Collecting Objects

"Visual Basic isn't a real language because it doesn't have pointers, and without pointers you can't do data structures." Ever heard that one? You might believe it if you've ever taken a computer science course on data structures. People spend whole careers figuring out new ways to write linked lists, trees, hash tables, stacks, queues, and other data abstractions, all of which are implemented with pointers. Meanwhile, Basic is stuck with only one data structure—the humble array—all because, as we've noted before, Basic doesn't do pointers.

I've seen Basic code that implements linked lists using parallel arrays of data and indexes, with the indexes used to fake pointers. It's not a pretty sight. But the point of data structures is to benefit from their functionality, not to show off fancy diagrams with nodes and branches, elegant as they may be. Collections are the first step in providing that functionality. You can fake many different data structures in Visual Basic by creating collection-like classes in Basic; we'll do one later. If you're not satisfied with the performance, you can write collections as servers in C++.

You'll see a lot of the Collection class in this book and in Visual Basic in general. We'll examine collections the same way we analyzed objects—first look at some familiar collections, then analyze what defines a collection, and finally use collections in code.

Familiar Collections

Visual Basic has always included collections and collection-like controls. This time, however, you can create your own. Let's start by looking at some internal collections.

The Forms collection contains all available forms:

```
Dim obj As Object
For Each obj In Forms
    Debug.Print obj.Name
Next
```

The Controls collection contains all the controls on a form:

```
Dim ctl As Control
For Each ctl In Controls
    Debug.Print ctl.Name
Next
```

The Printers collection contains all the printers available to the current machine:

```
Dim prt As Printer
For Each prt In Printers
    Debug.Print prt.DriverName
    ' Do something with each prt
Next
```

Technically, collection indexes are supposed to be one-based. But the internal collections were zero-based before collections were officially collections, and they remain so—even the new Printers collection is zero-based. Internal collections don't have Add and Remove methods, or, to be more accurate, their Add and Remove methods aren't public.

Collections Defined

If it doesn't have Add, Remove, and Item methods, it's not a collection. If the Item method isn't the default member, it's not a collection. If it doesn't have a Count property, it's not a collection. If it doesn't work with the For Each statement, it's not a collection. So if you want to validate that an object is officially a collection, you could do it with this code:

```
Private Function CertifyCollection(obj As Object) As Boolean
    Dim v As Variant
    With obj
        On Error Resume Next
        .Add .Count          ' Test Add and Count by adding
        v = .Item(.Count)    ' Test Item by accessing
        For Each v In obj    ' Test iteration
        Next
        .Remove .Count       ' Test Remove by removing
        CertifyCollection = (Err = 0)
    End With
End Function
```

Basic has several other features that resemble collections. Perhaps the most familiar is the ListBox control (and related controls). ListBox controls feel like collections, smell like collections, and usually act like collections—but, unfortunately, they aren't collections. They have an AddItem method instead of Add, a RemoveItem method instead of Remove, a List property instead of Item, and a ListCount property instead of Count. Worse, the For Each statement doesn't work for iterating through ListBox items.

FLAME   Perhaps I'm being picky, but I'd argue that since all the standard controls had to be rewritten as OLE controls anyway, it would've been sensible to also make them more compatible with collections. For ListBox-type controls, you could keep old method names but alias them with the new collection names. The interface to make For Each work could have been provided. Maybe next time.

Arrays are like collections in one way: you can use For Each to iterate through them. The statement

```
For Each i In ai
```

is equivalent to

```
For i = LBound(ai) To UBound (ai)
```

except that the second statement is much faster. The only reason to use For Each on an array is if you don't know the number of elements in the array—but of course you always know the number of elements in a Basic array because the LBound and UBound statements tell you. A "Performance" sidebar later in this chapter (page 182) shows the significant cost of using For Each on arrays (and the cost of using For with an index on collections). Nevertheless, I use For Each on two kinds of arrays: control arrays and parameter arrays. If you can type enough arguments or add enough controls to make performance an issue, you have my admiration—and sympathy.

A parameter array is a new feature that allows you to write procedures with a varying number of arguments. For example, here's a new and improved version of the Kill statement:

```
Kill "junk.txt", "trash.*", "bugs.bas"
Kill "enemies.1st"
```

The implementation is in BETTER.BAS:

```
Function Kill(ParamArray vFiles() As Variant) As Boolean
    Dim v As Variant
    On Error Resume Next     ' One failure shouldn't stop all
    For Each v In vFiles
        VBA.Kill v
    Next
    Kill = (Err = 0)         ' Something failed, but can't say what
End Function
```

Collection Features

A Basic collection is what some computer science books refer to as a *dictionary*— that is, a table of items in which you can look up an item by using a key. All collections have an index key, and some have string keys. Here are the features you'll find in a collection:

■ A collection grows and shrinks automatically. It's like an array that you never have to redimension. When you add an item, you never get an out-of-bounds error; and when you remove an item from the middle, you don't have to slide all the other items over or fill the empty slot with a blank marker.

■ You can access an item by its index, just as you can in an array. But you must be careful because the index can change whenever you add or remove an item. You can also access an item by its key, which is usually a string uniquely identifying the item. Using the key enables you to find the item regardless of its position.

■ Collections are unordered. New items are added at the end unless you specify a location. You can sort a collection (and we will), but don't assume anything about the order unless you control it.

■ You can use a normal For loop to iterate through a collection by its index, but it's preferable to use the For Each syntax. Your For Each loop can delete and add items without the risk of missing a new item or encountering problems because an item that existed when you started iterating has disappeared when you finish.

What's the alternative to collections? The Data Access Object, for one. If you need this kind of super-collection, you know who you are. Realistically, the competition is between collections and arrays.

The advantage of arrays is their fixed size. If you put an element in a certain position in an array, you can be sure that it will stay there until you come back. You can access an element easily and efficiently as long as you remember its location. But the disadvantage of arrays is also their fixed size. If you don't know how many items you have, you don't know how big to make the array. If you remove or add items, you have to jump through hoops to change the size.

Basic programmers can get around the conflict by resizing arrays in chunks. The code looks something like this:

```
Const iChunk = 10
Dim aItems() As Integer, iMax As Integer, i As Integer
iMax = iChunk
Redim aItems(iMax)
.
.                               ' Do some stuff that might add elements
.
If i > iMax Then                ' Make sure that index i is in bounds
    iMax = i + iChunk
    Redim aItems(iMax)
End If
aItems(i) = 6                   ' Use index i only after validating
```

In other words, you must check the index every time you use it, reallocating when the index goes out of bounds. As you can imagine, this gets expensive. Arrays also present problems when you remove items. You can remove an item from an array by moving all the later items up one slot and then adjusting the indexes of later items (if possible). Alternatively, you can mark deleted items with a special value indicating a blank.

No matter which of the dozens of possible implementations of dynamic arrays you choose, are you really sure that you want all these validations and reallocations running in p-code? You don't. Instead, you want them running in native code, and that's where they'll run if you use collections instead of arrays.

Of course, there's no free lunch. Collections can contain only Variants, and that's bound to have a cost, particularly if you're really collecting Integers. Some collection features (string keys) require objects rather than variables. Collections can have only one dimension. And so on. Obviously, arrays aren't going away, but you'll no longer need to force them to do things they're not good at.

Collections 101 (Variables)

User-defined collections start out simple, but they can quickly become complicated. Let's start at the beginning with a straightforward collection of strings:

```
Dim nAnimals As New Collection
```

What you have after this declaration is an empty collection, which is not much use until you put something in it. Here's the code to load a simple collection with strings. Actually, these strings become variants as they are stored in the collection:

```
' Create collection
With nAnimals
    .Add "Lion"
    .Add "Tiger"
    .Add "Bear"
    .Add "Shrew", , 1
    .Add "Weasel", , , 1
End With
```

The first three Add methods put *Lion*, *Tiger*, and *Bear* in the collection in that order, as items 1, 2, and 3. User-defined collections are one-based, and new items go at the end unless you specify otherwise.

Now look at the fourth Add method, which inserts *Shrew*. The second optional argument of the Add method is the Mystery Argument, to be explained in next week's episode. The third argument specifies which existing item the new item will precede. Putting the new item before item 1 means that *Shrew* will precede *Lion* and will become item 1. The fourth argument (used in the last call to the Add method) specifies which existing item the new item will follow. Putting the new item after item 1 means that *Weasel* will follow *Shrew* but precede *Lion*.

Once you have a collection, you'll want to access its members. You can use indexes, just as you do for an array:

```
Debug.Print nAnimals(3) & " " & nAnimals.Item(2)
```

Notice that *nAnimals(3)* is a shortcut for *nAnimals.Item(3)*. This works because Item is the default member for a collection and can therefore be omitted.

You might also want to replace one item of a collection with another. If you think this should work with a simple assignment, think again. The statement

```
nAnimals(2) = "Wolverine"
```

fails at run time with an *Object not set* error indicating that the items of a collection are actually objects and can't simply be assigned. But the statement

```
Set nAnimals(2) = "Wolverine"
```

fails at compile time with a *Procedure type mismatch* error because *Wolverine* isn't an object. To replace a nonobject item, you must delete the old item and insert the new one in its place:

```
nAnimals.Remove 2
nAnimals.Add "Wolverine", , 2
```

You've already seen the standard way to iterate through a collection:

```
Dim vAnimal As Variant
For Each vAnimal In nAnimals
    Debug.Print vAnimal
Next
```

Of course, you can still iterate through a collection by index:

```
Dim i As Integer
For i = 1 To nAnimals.Count
    Debug.Print nAnimals(i)
Next
```

This technique is risky, however. It's easy to confuse the indexing system because user-defined collections are one-based, while many of the predefined Visual Basic collections (Forms and Controls) are zero-based for compatibility with previous versions. Furthermore, as you might have discovered with ListBox controls, you can't delete members from or add members to a collection while iterating because this changes the index and the count, often causing the loop to fail. Yet this is one of the most frequent reasons to iterate. You can sometimes get around the limitation by iterating backward, but For Each is a more reliable looping technique.

Collections of variants are fun, but half the power of collections doesn't come into play until you start adding objects with keys. We'll get to that after a brief detour into data structures.

Data Structures in Basic

Remember how Basic can't do data structures such as stacks, queues, and trees? Well, check out this stack class. It illustrates how to store the items of a data structure in a private collection, organize the items however you want, and expose access only through the safe methods and properties you define.

A stack is a data structure in which you can add items only to the top of the stack and likewise remove them only from the top. The technical term is *LIFO*—last in, first out—but anyone who has ever stacked plates or books knows this concept. You might find it convenient for stacking forms, controls, or files. The idea is that you can't get anything out of a stack in the wrong order because the stack allows only one order.

As usual, let's start by using the class before designing it:

```
Dim beasts As New CStack, s As String
With beasts
    .Push "Lion"
    .Push "Tiger"
    .Push "Bear"
    .Push "Shrew"
    .Push "Weasel"
    Do
        Debug.Print .Pop
    Loop While .Count
End With
```

Traditionally, you "push" things onto a stack and "pop" them off. All you need to do is create a CStack class (in STACK.CLS) and define Push and Pop methods and a Count property. The code is short and sweet:

```
Private nStack As New Collection

Public Sub Push(vArg As Variant)
    nStack.Add vArg
End Sub

Public Function Pop() As Variant
    With nStack
        If .Count Then
            Pop = nStack(.Count)
            .Remove (.Count)
        End If
    End With
End Function

Property Get Count() As Variant
    Count = nStack.Count
End Property
```

The Push method simply adds items in the default position (the end of the collection). The Pop method removes them from the end of the collection. The

Count property passes on the size of the internal collection, which this example uses to check for an empty stack. Users have no other access to the collection. They can't iterate through the collection or access members by index because either action violates the definition of a stack.

CHALLENGE You can easily write other data structure classes. You might start with a queue or a circular queue. I've always wanted to write a program that illustrates various data structures graphically. In this program, you could click an option button to select a stack, a queue, a tree, or whatever. Buttons and other controls would appear, to represent the methods and properties of the data structure. As you manipulate the controls, you could add, remove, or find items represented by boxes or other graphical elements. I've pushed this problem onto your challenge stack. Pop it.

PERFORMANCE

Problem: Compare iterating through various collections with For Each to iterating through collections and arrays with For and an index variable.

Problem	16-Bit Mode	32-Bit Mode
For I on integer array	9 ms	8 ms
For Each on integer array	33 ms	13 ms
For Each on integer collection	68 ms	36 ms
For I on integer collection	160 ms	67 ms
For I on string array	42 ms	24 ms
For Each on string array	132 ms	119 ms
For Each on string collection	169 ms	143 ms
For I on string collection	203 ms	86 ms
For I on object array	53 ms	37 ms
For Each on object array	1738 ms	1436 ms
For Each on object collection	225 ms	102 ms
For I on object collection	1935 ms	1565 ms

Conclusion: Wow! Check out the cost of using collections. Of course, if an array doesn't do what you need, it doesn't matter how fast it is. When you're using collections, For Each is a big winner for iterating through collections of objects, but it doesn't make much difference on collections of variables.

Collections 201 (Objects)

Collections of variables are handy, but they tell only half the story. Collections of objects can have string keys as well as integer keys (indexes). A key is a unique value that identifies the item. Obviously, an integer index is unique, but it does not necessarily identify a particular item. In fact, the index of an item changes any time you add or delete an item with a lower index.

A string key, which you specify in the second argument of the Add method, can uniquely identify an item regardless of its position. Visual Basic documentation defines such a key as a string you can use instead of an index to access an item in a collection. But that's an incomplete description. A string key is not just any string, but a string property of the object being added to the collection.

To see how this works, you can go back to the CProblem class discussed earlier in this chapter and used in the Time It program (TIMEIT.VBP), introduced in Chapter 1. The program appears throughout this book to illustrate timing problems, but it happens to store information about those problems in a collection of problem objects. As you might recall, CProblem consists of three properties declared as public variables and no methods.

Before you start loading CProblem objects into a collection, you must define the collection:

```
Private nProblems As New Collection
```

You also need a temporary reference object where you can create each problem before you store it in the collection:

```
Private rprob As CProblem
```

Here's the code to load a problem object into a collection:

```
Set rprob = New CProblem
rprob.Title = sLogicalAndVsNestedIf
rprob.Description = _
    "Does Basic short-circuit logical expressions? " & _
    "Or does a logical And operation take the " & _
    "same time as an equivalent nested If/Then?"
rprob.Iterations = 30000&
nProblems.Add rprob, rprob.Title

Set rprob = New CProblem
rprob.Title = sByValVsByRef
⋮
```

First you create a new object in the *rprob* reference object, using Set with the New syntax. Next you initialize each property. The value *sLogicalAndVsNestedIf* assigned to the Title field is a constant initialized earlier and named so that it can be easily accessed from several locations:

```
Const sLogicalAndVsNestedIf = "Logical And Versus Nested If"
Const sByValVsByRef = "By Value Versus By Reference"
    ⋮
```

Finally you add the problem to the collection, passing the Title field as the lookup key. At this point, the problem is stored in the collection, and you can safely reuse the *rprob* object for the next problem.

The idea of using a collection here is that you can keep adding problems just by setting new properties at the bottom of the problem initialization code. You don't want to use an array because you don't know how many problems you're going to have.

After you've put a problem in the collection, you can look it up by its index:

```
Debug.Print nProblems(3).Description
```

Or you can look it up by its title:

```
Debug.Print nProblems(sLogicalAndVsNestedIf).Description
```

When you specify a string key, Basic uses a secret internal mechanism to look up the item quickly. Perhaps Basic collections use a hash table or a binary tree underneath. You don't need to know or care; it makes no difference to your code as long as the collection methods and properties don't change.

Now you can see why we ignored this argument in the preceding discussion of adding variables to collections. In the *nAnimals* collection, you were adding variant strings to the collection. Variants don't have string properties. Even if you had a way to look up *Weasel* by its string name in the *nAnimals* collection, you wouldn't need to look it up because you already know it.

Naturally, you pay a price to get the search capabilities of collections. For instance, you can't add items with duplicate keys; every item in the collection must be unique. If you add keys dynamically at run time based on user entries, you'll have to trap the duplicate-entry error and display a message warning the user to choose a unique key. You can also bet on a performance cost, although it will be small indeed compared to what you'd have to do to implement the same capability using Basic arrays.

In the Time It program, after each problem is initialized, the titles are read from the collection into a list box:

```
For Each rprob In nProblems
    lstProblems.AddItem rprob.Title
Next
lstProblems.ListIndex = 0
```

When the user clicks to select a problem, the list box returns the title, which is used to look up the problem in the collection:

```
s = lstProblems.List(lstProblems.ListIndex)
Set rprob = nProblems(s)
lblDescription.Caption = rprob.Description
txtIteration.Text = rprob.Iterations
```

The current problem is set based on the lookup, and the program uses the Description and Iterations properties to update the screen. You can look up the rest of the details of how the current problem is solved and the results displayed in the Time It program (TIMEIT.VBP).

The NDrives Collection

You can write internal collections that work the same way the Controls, Forms, and Printers collections work. For example, you can use the CDrive class to create an NDrives collection class. Notice the naming convention: although NDrives is actually a class, it has the interface of a collection, and so I use *N* in the class name. Figure 4-6 on the next page shows the NDrives collection and its relationship to the CDrive class.

Iteration through an NDrives object works as shown here:

```
Dim drives As New NDrives
Dim rdrive As CDrive
'For Each rdrive In drives
For Each rdrive In drives.Items
    With driveCur
        s = s & "Drive " & .Root & " [" & .Label & "] (" & _
                .KindStr & ") has " & _
                Format$(.FreeBytes, sBFormat) & " free from " & _
                Format$(.TotalBytes, sBFormat) & sCrLf
    End With
Next
```

The commented-out line shows how you'd like to iterate through the collection (and how you would iterate through it if Basic fully implemented collection features). But as you can see in the code, Visual Basic 4 forces you to make a compromise. More on this later.

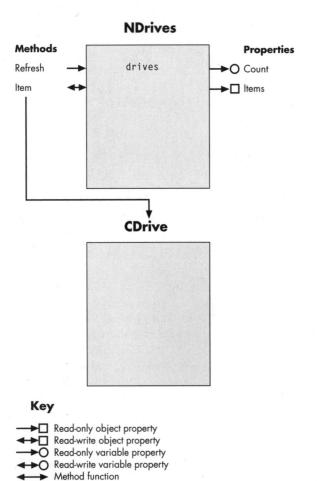

NDrives

Methods

Refresh

Item

drives

Properties

○ Count

☐ Items

CDrive

Key

→☐ Read-only object property
↔☐ Read-write object property
→○ Read-only variable property
↔○ Read-write variable property
↔ Method function
→ Method sub

Figure 4-6. *The NDrives collection.*

Looking up a specific drive in the collection works as follows:

```
'Set rdrive = drives("C:\")
Set rdrive = drives.Item("C:\")
If Not rdrive Is Nothing Then
    With rdrive
        s = s & "Drive " & .Root & " [" & .Label & "] (" & .Kind & _
                ") has " & Format$(.FreeBytes, sBFormat) & _
                " free from " & Format$(.TotalBytes, sBFormat)
    End With
End If
```

PERFORMANCE

Problem: What are collections? You know their user interface, but you don't really know what internal data structure makes them work. Normally, this isn't a concern. Who cares how they work as long as they work? But, on second thought, the internal implementation is bound to affect the efficiency of operations. If some operations are less efficient than others, it might be nice to avoid the slow ones. While writing the collection sort procedures in Chapter 9, I began to suspect that inserting elements into the middle of a collection might be an operation to avoid.

I theorized that it would be faster to insert elements at the end of a collection than at the beginning or in the middle and that insertion would get slower as you added more elements. To test this idea, I tried inserting a whole lot of elements (8000) into different parts of a collection. The results weren't quite what I expected.

Problem	16-Bit Mode	32-Bit Mode
Add first half to end of collection	103 ms	77 ms
Add last half to end of collection	127 ms	76 ms
Add first half to start of collection	163 ms	110 ms
Add last half to start of collection	162 ms	102 ms
Add first half to middle of collection	4101 ms	2044 ms
Add last half to middle of collection	12916 ms	7592 ms

Conclusion: What kind of data structure allows fast insertion at the beginning and at the end but not in the middle? This stumped me for a while, but here's a theory. If collections were implemented internally as doubly-linked lists, insertion would always cost the same. But finding a particular position (with the *before* or *after* parameter of the Add method or the *index* parameter of the Remove method) would involve iterating from the start or the end until you reached the given point. To find a position near the middle, you'd have to start at the beginning or the end, whichever was closest, and iterate almost halfway through. The more elements in the array, the farther you'd have to go. This would explain the results shown.

Of course, anything you think you know about the implementation of collections might be wrong for this version, and probably will be wrong for the next version. Still, you might want to think carefully about whether you really need to insert elements in the middle of a large collection.

Again, you must compromise a little in the implementation. In this case, looking up a drive in the collection is redundant, since you could simply use a CDrive object to get the information directly. But it illustrates a technique that might be useful in your own internal collections.

Most of the work in a class representing an internal collection is done in the Class_Initialize event procedure. Here's how it works in NDrives:

```
Private drives As New Collection
Const iAscA = 65

Private Sub Class_Initialize()
    BugMessage "Initialize NDrives collection"
    Dim i As Integer, af As Long, sRoot As String
    Dim rdrive As CDrive
    af = GetLogicalDrives()
    For i = 0 To 25
        If RShiftDWord(af, i) And 1 Then
            Set rdrive = New CDrive
            rdrive.Root = Chr$(i + iAscA) & ":\"
            drives.Add rdrive, rdrive.Root
        End If
    Next
End Sub
```

This code uses the GetLogicalDrives function and the RShiftDWord function from Chapter 3 to calculate which drives actually exist in the system. The drives are then initialized and added to the internal collection.

With the internal collection in place, it's easy to implement the standard properties and methods of a collection. You expose the Count property and the Item method by passing through the Count and Item of the internal collection:

```
Public Property Get Count() As Integer
    Count = drives.Count
End Property

Public Function Item(v As Variant) As CDrive
    On Error Resume Next
    Set Item = drives(v)
    If Err <> 0 Then
        Set Item = Nothing
    End If
End Function
```

Item is the default member of collections, enabling you to write *drives(v)* instead of *drives.Item(v)*. To make NDrives objects accessible in the same way, you simply make Item the default member of NDrives. It's too bad that Visual

Basic 4 provides no way to specify a default member for a class. This limitation can be very annoying, but at least it's only cosmetic.

User-defined classes have another serious limitation that is more than cosmetic: you cannot expose the internal enumeration property that allows For Each to iterate through the collection. This property is called _NewEnum. Your collections will work with For Each if you write them as OLE servers in C++ and make the _NewEnum property public. But that doesn't do you any good in Basic. The only workaround I've found is the risky one shown by the Items property:

```
Public Property Get Items() As Collection
    Set Items = drives
End Property
```

This property exposes your internal collection to a cruel and dangerous world. Yes, it allows your users to iterate through drives with For Each:

```
For Each rdrive In drives.Items
```

But it also allows them to add and remove items and otherwise have their way with your secret data. Your only protection is to avoid telling them that you've given away the key. If you spell out the rules and people violate them, they hurt only themselves, but it's always better to prevent data violations than to forbid them.

CHALLENGE At first glance, you might think it impossible to implement the Add and Remove properties. If I could add a new drive to my system just by calling the Add method, I'd never run out of disk space. But even the new Plug and Play standard can't promise that. On the other hand, it's easy enough to use Add to connect to a network drive and Remove to disconnect one. Check out the WNetAddConnection and WNetCancelConnection API functions. Unfortunately, 16-bit Windows makes it difficult to get network drives that are connected but are not associated with a drive letter. WNetOpenEnum lets you do this under Win32. I'll leave it to you to enhance the NDrives collection to make it fully network-aware.

Finally, NDrives has a Refresh method so that you can reinitialize the collection, just in case network drives were added or floppy disks inserted after the caller's NDrives object was created:

```
Public Sub Refresh()
    Set drives = Nothing
    Class_Initialize
End Sub
```

Property Arrays

Basic is the only language I know that uses parentheses for array subscripts. (Most languages use square brackets.) This practice leads to ambiguity in the language. Does

```
i = Zap(4)
```

assign element 4 of the *Zap* array to *i*, or does it call the Zap function with argument 4 and assign the result to *i*? I used to think this was a flaw in the language, but it's handy when you create properties that act and look like arrays.

For example, assume that you are creating a CParanoia class, whose objects have an EnemyList property. You want to use it as follows:

```
scared.EnemyList(i) = "Jones"
Calumniate scared.Enemy(i)
```

EnemyList looks like an array and acts like an array, but you must implement it as a property, and properties can't be arrays. You might expect that if you declare an array public in a form or a class, it would become a property array:

```
Public EnemyList(1 To 10) As String
```

Basic throws this statement out at compile time with a message telling you that arrays can't be public. You can usually create more reliable properties with Property Get and Property Let anyway, but it's not immediately clear how. The answer is that you fake subscripts with property parameters.

Behind your properties, you must have a private array or collection. Let's use an array here:

```
Private aEnemies(1 To 10) As String
```

Property Get procedures normally don't have parameters, but when faking subscripts, you need one argument for every array dimension. Since you're faking a one-dimensional array, you need only one argument:

```
Property Get EnemyList(i As Integer) As String
    If i >= 1 And i <= 10 Then EnemyList = aEnemies(i)
End Property
```

Property Let procedures normally have one argument, but you'll need an extra argument for each array dimension. The normal assignment parameter must be the last parameter:

```
Property Let EnemyList(i As Integer, sEnemyA As String)
    If i >= 1 And i <= 10 Then aEnemies(i) = sEnemyA
End Property
```

Expanding on this technique, you can easily design properties that represent multidimensional arrays:

```
iHiCard = deck.Cards(iClubs, iJack)
```

You can even have array properties with string or real number indexes:

```
iHiCard = deck.Cards("Clubs", "Jack")
patient.Temperature(98.6)
```

This syntax would obviously be impossible with real arrays, so you must make up what your array syntaxes mean to the data hidden in your class.

5

Taking Control of Windows

Visual Basic brings Windows programming to the masses by hiding and re-defining the details. Most Visual Basic programmers are content to accept this new, simplified model, since forms, controls, and events are easier to program than windows, dialog boxes, and messages. Why put up with the hassle of programming bare-bones Windows?

Because it is there.

What better reason does a hardcore programmer need? But if general masochism and the need to prove yourself don't go down well with your boss (or with your checkbook, if you don't have a boss), Visual Basic itself provides plenty of good reasons to learn Windows inside and out.

It seems that every Visual Basic program ever written needs just one feature that the designers of the language didn't anticipate. Furthermore, none of those missing features overlap. The Visual Basic bug database is crammed with great ideas, feature requests, and design improvements marked "Postponed." Many of those ideas are mine.

But I'm not waiting for my favorite features to appear in some future version of Visual Basic. I want them now, even if I have to cheat. Unfortunately, the solutions to my problems probably aren't the solutions to your problems. Chances are this chapter won't tell you directly how to implement that one little feature that's been driving you batty for the past few weeks. But perhaps I can help you figure it out on your own by telling you everything you never really wanted to know about processes, modules, instances, classes, messages, resources, and, of course, windows.

WinWatch

The WinWatch program monitors Windows in action. In essence, WinWatch is a teaching tool. It's not useful for much except borrowing resources, making screen shots, and learning about window titles and classes. Still, you can pick up ideas and information that you can use in more practical programs.

We'll first take the quick-and-dirty WinWatch tour and then come back for a more detailed look at the code that makes it work. You might want to load WINWATCH.VBP now. If you have a choice of operating systems, WinWatch will work better if you run the 16-bit version of Visual Basic under a 16-bit version of Windows. Otherwise, run the 16-bit WinWatch under 32-bit Windows.

Elements of WinWatch

WinWatch is a complicated program with lots of features, many of them marginal. Figure 5-1 shows WinWatch on a busy day.

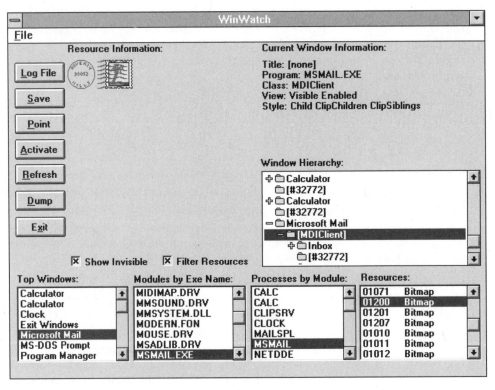

Figure 5-1. *WinWatch under 16-bit Windows.*

Beginning with the list boxes at the bottom of the interface, let's examine the elements of WinWatch:

- The Top Windows list box displays the names of all the visible top windows of programs currently running in Windows. Selecting an item in this box updates the next two list boxes to its right and the Window Hierarchy box; conversely, selecting an item in any one of those three boxes updates the Top Windows list.

- The Modules By Exe Name list box shows all the executable files—both programs and DLLs. The modules are listed not by their module names but by their executable names, which are not the same thing. You won't see any duplicates in this list. If you select a DLL or a driver, you also won't see a top window, a current window, or a process, but you'll see DLL information and possibly resources.

- The Processes By Module list box shows all the processes that are currently running—usually called *tasks* in 16-bit Windows—including invisible ones. If you run two instances of a program, you'll see them both, listed as separate entries. Each process is listed by its module name, which is usually, but not always, the base name of the executable filename.

- The Resources list box indicates the resources of the program or DLL selected in the boxes to its left. Chapter 7 covers resources in detail.

- The Current Window Information area (labeled *Current DLL Information* if you select a DLL) summarizes what you know about the currently selected item. We'll see later how you get this information.

- The Window Hierarchy box shows all the windows in the system in outline form. You can expand a window to see its child windows. When you select a different window in this box, various screen elements (the lists of top windows, modules, and processes as well as the Current Window Information area) change.

- The Resource Information area displays the currently selected resource, if one is selected. You'll see a graphical display for visual resources such as bitmaps and icons (see the postage stamp bitmap in Figure 5-1); other resources are described with text. When you select a new module in the Modules By Exe Name list box, WinWatch finds any available version resources and displays them in the Resource Information area.

- Normally, the File menu duplicates the commands found on the WinWatch buttons. But when you select a menu resource for another program, the contents of the WinWatch menu bar change to match the menu of the selected program. You can even choose that program's commands from WinWatch's menu. Chapter 7 describes how this works.

- Choosing the Log File button saves a log file named WINLIST.TXT, which contains the current window hierarchy. The log file is a text version of the information shown in the Window Hierarchy box.

- Choosing the Save button saves the current resource if it is a bitmap or an icon. You can copy pictures embedded in various programs to files. Chapter 7 explains how WinWatch steals pictures. Don't call me with hard-luck stories about lawsuits.

- The Point button puts WinWatch in point mode. When you click a window, WinWatch selects it and updates the display appropriately.

- The Activate button activates the current program, if any. (A double-click in the Top Windows list box does the same thing.)

- Choosing the Refresh button forces WinWatch to refresh the list boxes and the window hierarchy outline. Use this button if you load new programs or activate new windows while WinWatch is running.

- The Show Invisible check box determines whether invisible windows are displayed in the Window Hierarchy box. You might find the display more attractive and less confusing (although incomplete) with this setting turned off. The Filter Resources check box serves a similar purpose for resource lists.

Only 16 Bits

Although you can run WinWatch under 32-bit Windows, the results aren't particularly instructive. Figure 5-2 shows the crippled 32-bit version, which fails to display most of the information you see in the 16-bit version. In theory, the Win16 and Win32 APIs are close enough that you should be able to write any program to run in either mode. WinWatch shatters that theory. The problem is that Win32 has very different ideas about processes, modules, and instances.

When you work with 16-bit Windows, the TOOLHELP module makes it at least possible—if not easy—to monitor just about anything of interest that goes on in Windows. The TOOLHELP DLL was originally provided with the Windows SDK and included as part of Windows 3.1. But Windows NT contains no 32-bit TOOLHELP. Windows 95 does have TOOLHELP functions, but they work differently than the 16-bit versions because 32-bit Windows works differently. This version of WinWatch doesn't use them.

In 16-bit Windows, every instance of a program shares the same code but has its own data. In 32-bit Windows, every instance of a program runs in a completely different memory space. This has a lot of implications, some of which we'll examine.

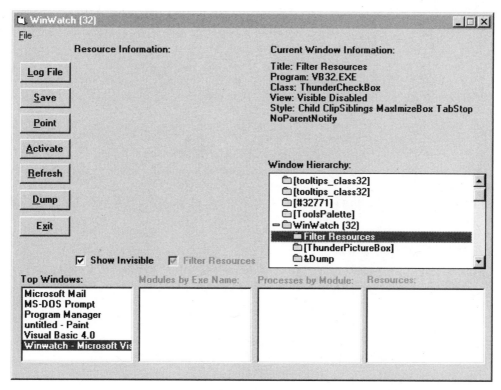

Figure 5-2. *The 32-bit version of WinWatch under Windows 95.*

You can split WinWatch code into two categories. The Top Windows list, the Current Window Information display, and the Window Hierarchy box work fine in 32-bit Windows. Managing windows is mostly the same in either environment. Of course, you'll find differences even in window code; for example, compare the Program heading in the Current Window Information area in Figures 5-1 and 5-2. We'll discuss this and other differences as we go.

The code that deals with processes, modules, and instances depends on the 16-bit TOOLHELP DLL. Because there are no portable 32-bit functions to list the processes and modules, I used conditional code to disable the controls and the functions they use. The Resources list box is empty for a different reason: lack of time on my part. Your challenge will be to fill it after reading Chapter 7.

All About Windows

All you need to know to undermine Windows, generate chaos, and muck up the system is the handle of any window you want to trash. Normally, of course, you want to enhance Windows, not subvert it. You'll discover lots of legitimate uses for window handles inside and outside your program.

In the Windows environment, almost any distinct element that you see on the screen is a window. Basic programmers might think of forms as windows, but in fact most controls—buttons, list boxes, scroll bars, option buttons, and check boxes—are also windows. Any object that has an hWnd property is a window at heart. The hWnd property is the link between the Basic world of forms and controls and the SDK world of windows, dialogs, and the pitiful version of controls known to C programmers.

WinWatch provides several features for exploring windows. At any point, the Current Window Information area tells you more than you need to know about the current window. You can change the current window by clicking an item in any of the list boxes except Resources, by navigating the window hierarchy outline, or by clicking the Point button and pointing to a window. This section looks at the code that makes these features work.

The Window Class

Imagine for a moment that Windows is written in Visual Basic and that every window you see on the screen is actually a window object of type CWindow. You might create a new window this way:

```
Dim wndMy As New CWindow
wndMy.Create("MyClass", "My Window", _
             afEnabled Or afVisible Or afOtherStyle, _
             x, y, dx, dy, hwndParent, hMenu, hInst, objOther)
```

After creating the window, you could access its properties as shown here:

```
With wndMy
    .Caption = "My New Window Title"
    afStyle = .Style
    x = .Point.x
End With
```

You could also call window methods such as these:

```
With wndMy
    .Move xNew, yNew
    If .Enabled Then .MakeActive
End With
```

Does this look at all familiar? Doesn't it look like initializing a form? In fact, this imaginary code is a very simplified view of what Visual Basic asks Windows to do when you ask Visual Basic to load a form. It's also what Visual Basic does when it loads most controls.

Inside CWindow

Let's take an inside look at CWindow. This class is undocumented, but it exists, and Windows explorers have mapped out its contents. In their flat-earth ignorance, these pioneers believe that Windows was written in C, and so they call this hidden data the WND structure. Our more enlightened view is that this block of data is nothing less than the private variables of the CWindow class.

And now, revealed for the first time, the secret heart of every window (or at least every 16-bit window):

```
Private hwndNext As Integer        ' Next sibling window
Private hwndChild As Integer       ' First child window
Private hwndParent As Integer      ' Parent window
Private hwndOwner As Integer       ' Owning window
Private rectWindow As TRect        ' Rectangle of entire window
Private rectClient As TRect        ' Rectangle of client area
Private hQueue As Integer          ' Application message queue
Private hrgnUpdate As Integer      ' Region needing update
Private ctClass As TClass          ' Window class
Private lplfnWndProc As Long       ' Window procedure
Private afStyle As Long            ' Style flags
Private afStyleExt As Long         ' Extended style flags
Private lplfnWndProc As Long       ' Window procedure
Private hMenu As Integer           ' Menu used by window
Private hBuffer As Integer         ' Buffer for title
Private scrollBar As Integer       ' Scroll bar word
Private hProperties As Integer     ' First window property
Private hwndLastActive As Integer  ' Last active popup window
Private hMenuSystem As Integer     ' System menu
```

What can you do with this information? As a practical matter, absolutely nothing. The only way you can change these private variables is through properties and methods of the public interface. In a more abstract sense, however, knowing what's inside helps you understand what the public methods and properties must work with and, thus, what they can and cannot do.

Although Windows is object-oriented in the philosophical sense of hiding data, inheriting attributes, and allowing polymorphic access to objects, its public interface is completely functional. Thus, instead of providing window objects with properties and methods, Windows provides functions that take a window handle argument.

You might like to do things the object-oriented way:

```
wndMy.Enabled = True
f = wndMy.Enabled
f = wndMy.Flash(True)
```

But in fact you have to call functions:

```
fOld = EnableWindow(hWnd, True)
f = IsWindowEnabled(hWnd)
f = FlashWindow(hWnd, True)
```

Of course, if you're dealing with Basic windows, the Enable functions don't matter because the form or control representing the window has an Enabled property. If you want to flash the window, however, you'll have to do it the Windows Way because flashing a window is an obscure feature not deemed worthy of inclusion in Visual Basic. No problem. All you need is a declaration for FlashWindow so that you can call it like this:

```
f = FlashWindow(Me.hWnd, True)
```

A Basic CWindow class

WinWatch looks at windows from the outside and must do things the Windows Way, not the Basic Way. But this was a choice, not a requirement. It's not impossible to access window features in an object-oriented way; all you need is a CWindow class written in Basic. I actually wrote this class, but WinWatch doesn't use it. Sometimes the functional philosophy is more convenient than the object religion.

You might find it amusing to check out CWindow on the companion CD, in the TWINDOW.VBP project. This class might even work for some of your projects. I'll describe the design, but frankly, I wrote CWindow more to show that it could be done than as a practical tool. It simply wraps the more common API functions related to windows in a thin layer.

CWindow has only one private member variable, *hWnd*. You initialize this internal variable using the Handle property:

```
Dim wnd As New CWindow
wnd.Handle = Me.hWnd
```

You can also initialize the object with one of a variety of Create methods:

```
wnd.CreateFromPoint x, y                 ' WindowFromPoint
wnd.CreateFromFind "MyClass", "My Title" ' FindWindow
wnd.CreateFromActive                     ' GetActiveWindow
```

Once you initialize the object, you can get and read properties or call methods:

```
wnd.Caption = "My Title"                 ' GetWindowText
wnd.Capture True                         ' SetCapture
wnd.Capture False                        ' ReleaseCapture
sClass = wnd.ClassName                   ' GetClassName
```

Most of these methods and properties have one-line implementations. Here are a couple to give you the idea:

```
Private hWnd As Long
⋮

Public Property Get Handle() As Long
    Handle = hWnd
End Property

Public Property Let Handle(ByVal hWndA As Long)
    If IsWindow(hWndA) Then hWnd = hWndA Else hWnd = hNull
End Property
```

I started writing new methods and properties as fast as I could type them, but I gave up after a while because I could see that the class wasn't going to be much use. Feel free to finish the implementation. You can see my first cut in Figure 5-3 on the next page.

The problem with CWindow is that it adds a layer of complication and inefficiency without offering much advantage. For example, imagine that the user of WinWatch selects a new window in the Window Hierarchy box. Because this outline control stores a window handle in its *ItemData* array, you can get the data you want simply by using that handle.

Which of the following is easier? Here's one example:

```
With wnd
    .Handle = outWin.ItemData(outWin.ListIndex)
    fVisible = .Visible
    sTitle = .Caption
    hInst = .Instance
End With
```

And here's an alternative:

```
hWnd = outWin.ItemData(outWin.ListIndex)
fVisible = IsWindowVisible(hWnd)
sTitle = VBGetWindowText(hWnd)
hInst = GetInstance(hWnd)
```

Either way, you must write the declarations for the Windows API functions and wrap un-Basic functions in Basic wrappers (as you'll see later). But you're still doing the same work, just packaging it differently.

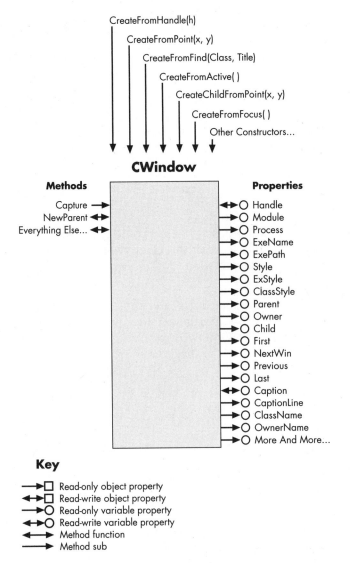

Figure 5-3. *First draft of the CWindow class.*

The Windows Way of properties

Windows stores attributes that define every window. For a Basic window, you can usually get at the attributes through properties. For a non-Basic window, you have to use a function. Sometimes access is through an orthogonal pair of Get/Set functions. Sometimes the interface is more obscure.

Table 5-1 compares the Windows Way and the Basic Way of dealing with properties. (Some of the properties that you might expect to see listed here—color, for example—are actually properties of the device context, not the window, and are therefore discussed in Chapter 6.)

Attribute	Windows Way	Basic Way
Active window	GetActiveWindow, possibly combined with GetParent	ActiveForm and ActiveControl properties
Style bits	GetWindowWord/Long with GWW/L_STYLE or GWW/L_EXSTYLE	BorderStyle, Enabled, Visible, WindowState, ControlBox, MaxButton, and MinButton properties
Window title	GetWindowText and SetWindowText	Caption property
Enabled, visible	WS_VISIBLE, WS_DISABLED style bits; IsEnabled, IsWindowVisible, EnableWindow, and ShowWindow	Enabled and Visible properties
Tab position	WS_TABSTOP style bit; GetNextDlgTabItem	TabStop and TabIndex properties
Window dimensions	GetWindowRect and SetWindowPos	Left, Top, Width, and Height properties; indirectly, Alignment and AutoSize properties
Client dimensions	GetClientRect	ScaleLeft, ScaleTop, ScaleWidth, and ScaleHeight properties
Property list	GetProp, SetProp, and RemoveProp	Minimal version in Tag property
Device context	GetDC and ReleaseDC	hDC property
Relative windows	GetWindow with GW_ constants, GetNextWindow, and GetParent	Parent property for controls, but otherwise no way
Instance handle	GetWindowWord/Long with GWW/L_HINSTANCE	App.hInstance
Task handle or process ID	GetWindowTask in 16-bit mode, GetWindowThread-ProcessID in 32-bit mode	No way
Class name	GetClassName	No way

Table 5-1. *Window properties.*

The Windows Way of methods

If you can think of something to do to a window, there's probably an API function to do it. Visual Basic provides corresponding methods for many of these operations. In some cases, properties perform operations rather than simply providing access to attributes. Table 5-2 compares the Windows Way and the Basic Way of getting things done.

As Tables 5-1 and 5-2 show, it's a mixed-up world. You won't always find an obvious comparison between the Basic Way and the Windows Way. But if you are like most hardcore programmers, your eye keeps wandering to those items that show up in the Windows Way column but not in the Basic Way column. That's the challenge the rest of this chapter attempts to meet.

Basic Wrappers for Windows Functions

Although most of the internal Windows data can be read or modified by Windows functions, few of those functions have obvious names and operations. If Windows has widgets, that doesn't mean you'll find GetWidget and SetWidget functions in the Windows API.

The next sections describe the workarounds for performing Windows operations in Basic as well as some of the reasons you might want to take the Windows Way even in Basic.

Getting Windows string data

You're already familiar not only with the Windows Way of getting string data but also with the Basic Way of getting around the Windows Way (explained in "Dealing with Strings," page 67). Remember that you can get the class name of a window with GetClassName; to make this look Basic, wrap the access in VBGetClassName:

```
Function VBGetClassName(ByVal hWnd) As String
    Dim sName As String, cName As Integer
    BugAssert hWnd <> hNull
    sName = String$(41, 0)
    cName = GetClassName(hWnd, sName, 41)
    VBGetClassName = Left$(sName, cName)
End Function
```

The window class indicates the kind of window. The main use for the class name is passing it to FindWindow to find other windows of the same class. (The VBFindWindow function was discussed in "Wrapping String Functions," page 72, as an example of how to pass strings to Windows functions.) You can also pass the class name to GetClassInfo to obtain detailed class information that you aren't likely to use in Basic.

Operation	Windows Way	Basic Way
Show in different states	ShowWindow, OpenIcon, CloseWindow, IsIconic, and IsZoomed	Show and Hide methods; WindowState property
Change position, size, or z-order	SetWindowPos, DeferWindowPos, BeginDeferWindowPos, EndDeferWindowPos, BringWindowToTop, and MoveWindow	Move and ZOrder methods; Left, Top, Width, and Height properties
Set active window	SetForegroundWindow, SetActiveWindow, and SetFocus	SetFocus method; AppActivate statement
Create	CreateWindow, RegisterClass, and so on	Mostly automatic, but Load statement starts the process
Change window placement	GetWindowPlacement and SetWindowPlacement	Left, Top, Width, and Height properties
Capture mouse	SetCapture, GetCapture, and ReleaseCapture	No way
Make system modal	SetSysModalWindow in 16-bit only	No way
Destroy	DestroyWindow	Unload statement
Update window	UpdateWindow, InvalidateRect, BeginPaint, and a slew of others	Don't worry about it (or turn off AutoRedraw property and handle in Paint event)
Iterate through window hierarchy	EnumChildWindow, EnumWindow, and GetWindow	No way
Find window	FindWindow, GetActiveWindow, and WindowFromPoint	No way
Text output	TextOut, ExtTextOut, GrayString, and others	Print method
Text sizing	GetTextExtent	TextWidth and TextHeight methods
Text alignment	SetTextAlign, SetTextJustification, and SetTextCharacterExtra functions	No direct comparison

Table 5-2. *Window methods.*

When studying the WinWatch display, you'll probably come across windows with the informative class names #32768, #32769, #32770, #32771, and #32772. These are the class names for menus, the desktop window, dialog boxes, the task window, and icon titles, respectively. Come on, folks. If you can't come up with a good class name, you can always use a foreign word like the Task List class name, TakoHachi.

In Chapter 2, you saw an example of the technique for getting strings, VBGetWindowText. Actually, WinWatch uses a slightly different version of this function, named VBGetWindowTextLine:

```
Function VBGetWindowTextLine(ByVal hWnd) As String

    Dim sTitle As String, cTitle As Integer
    sTitle = VBGetWindowText(hWnd)
    ' Chop off end of multiline captions
    cTitle = InStr(sTitle, sCr)
    VBGetWindowTextLine = IIf(cTitle, Left$(sTitle, cTitle), sTitle)

End Function
```

I originally used the VBGetWindowText function rather than VBGetWindowTextLine in WinWatch, but I wasn't counting on windows that use the window text as the content of the window. The WinWatch display needs to truncate multiline window text, but other applications might need to display the entire text, breaks and all.

The window title is useful not only as information but also to pass to the AppActivate statement. This is the Basic Way to set the focus to a particular window. The Windows Way is to pass the window handle to SetActiveWindow in 16-bit Windows or to SetForegroundWindow in 32-bit Windows. Check out the new and improved AppActivate procedure in BETTER.BAS, and look at how it is used in lstTopWin_DblClick and cmdActivate_Click.

The Windows Word and the Windows Long
Some of the juiciest chunks of window data are accessed through a somewhat bizarre system of functions and constants. If the data you need is 16 bits in size, you call GetWindowWord with a constant indicating the data you want. If the data is 32 bits, you call GetWindowLong with a constant. Similarly, you can use SetWindowWord and SetWindowLong to modify the data.

FLAME Why aren't these names Word and DWord? Or Short and Long? Why doesn't Windows provide functions to get and set each chunk of data? Why have Set functions to modify data (such as the instance handle) that no one in their right mind would modify? What happens if you pass a constant other than the ones provided in WINDOWS.H? Why didn't it occur to the designers of the first version of Windows that GetWindowWord would be obsolete if Windows ever became 32-bit? Don't ask.

The problem in Basic is that a lot of the data consists of handles. Handles are Integer in 16-bit mode, but Long in 32-bit mode. If you want to get the instance handle (don't worry about what it is yet), you could do it this way:

```
#If Win32 Then
hInst = GetWindowLong (hWnd, GWL_HINSTANCE)
#Else
hInst = GetWindowWord(hWnd, GWW_HINSTANCE)
#End If
```

I prefer to use conditionals in my declarations rather than in code. Therefore, I specify an alias to create a portable GetWindowData. The function and related constants are defined in the Windows API type library, but I'll show them here as if they were written in Basic:

```
#If Win32 Then
Declare Function GetWindowData Lib "USER32" Alias "GetWindowLongA" _
    (ByVal hWnd As Long, ByVal nIndex As Long) As Long
#Else
Declare Function GetWindowData Lib "USER" Alias "GetWindowWord" ( _
    ByVal hWnd As Integer, ByVal nIndex As Integer) As Integer
#End If
```

You also need constants:

```
Public Const GWL_WNDPROC = (-4)        ' Can't use in Basic
Public Const GWD_HINSTANCE = (-6)      ' Instance handle
Public Const GWD_HWNDPARENT = (-8)     ' Use GetParent instead
Public Const GWD_ID = (-12)            ' No idea what this is
Public Const GWL_STYLE = (-16)         ' Window style
Public Const GWL_EXSTYLE = (-20)       ' Extended window style
```

In the C include files, constants that start with *GWD* here start with *GWW* in 16-bit mode or *GWL* in 32-bit mode. But since they have the same value, you can rename them with no harm done. Note that the style and the extended style are 32-bit values in either system, so you can use GetWindowLong regardless. I do a comparable trick with the similar Get/SetClassWord/Long functions and constants (which aren't of much use to Basic programmers).

Excluding the window procedure address (which you can't use in Basic), the parent window (which has a better access function), and the ID (for which I haven't found a purpose), here are statements to retrieve the useful data:

```
Dim afStyle As Long, afExStyle As Long, hInst  ' As SysInt
hInst = GetWindowData(hWnd, GWD_HINSTANCE)
afStyle = GetWindowLong(hWnd, GWL_STYLE)
afExStyle = GetWindowLong(hWnd, GWL_EXSTYLE)
```

You can also set these values with SetWindowData and SetWindowLong, but usually you shouldn't. Later in this chapter, you'll see why changing instance handles isn't a good idea. You could, however, read in style or extended style bits, add or remove bits, and then write the results back. This is seldom necessary because Windows provides functions to modify the style bits you would be most likely to modify.

Style bits

If you were writing programs for Windows in C, you'd need to specify style bit flags in the CreateWindow function every time you wanted a new window. C doesn't have a form properties window. You'll recognize some of the style bits because they correspond directly to form properties.

WinWatch gets the style bits for each window and displays them in the Current Window Information area under the Style heading. GetWndStyle converts the bit flags to a string:

```
Private Function GetWndStyle(hWnd) As String
    Dim af As Long, s As String
    BugAssert hWnd <> hNull

    ' Get normal style
    af = GetWindowLong(hWnd, GWL_STYLE)
    If af And WS_BORDER Then s = s & "Border "
    If af And WS_CAPTION Then s = s & "Caption "
    If af And WS_CHILD Then s = s & "Child "
    ⋮
```

Windows provides shortcut functions to get style information about the current view state of the window. GetWndView uses these functions to create the View heading:

```
Public Function GetWndView(hWnd) As String
    Dim s As String
    BugAssert hWnd <> hNull
    s = IIf(IsWindowVisible(hWnd), "Visible ", "Invisible ")
    s = s & IIf(IsWindowEnabled(hWnd), "Enabled", "Disabled ")
    s = s & IIf(IsZoomed(hWnd), "Zoomed ", Empty)
    s = s & IIf(IsIconic(hWnd), "Iconic ", Empty)
    GetWndView = s
End Function
```

You can learn a lot about how forms really work by studying the WinWatch display. Run a compiled version of WinWatch and a test form with test controls in the Visual Basic environment. Change various properties and see how they affect the Current Window Information display (after you choose the Refresh button). You can probably guess most of the effects, but some might surprise you. For example, the ClipChildren style bit corresponds to the form's Clip-Controls property.

You can also change style bits, but it's not as easy as you might expect. Changing the state of the bits doesn't necessarily change the state of the window; it just knocks the bits and the state out of sync. But there is a way.

The Fun 'n Games project in Chapter 6 has a Clip Controls check box that determines whether the graphics drawn by the program write over or under the controls on the form. In theory you should be able to toggle the ClipControls property, but in reality Visual Basic lets you change the ClipControls property only at design time. It turns out, though, that ClipControls is nothing more than the WS_CLIPCHILDREN style bit. To change the ClipControls functionality (but not the property), you simply call this procedure:

```
Sub ChangeStyleBit(hWnd, f As Boolean, afNew As Long)
    Dim af As Long
    af = GetWindowLong(hWnd, GWL_STYLE)
    If f Then
        af = af Or afNew
    Else
        af = af And (Not afNew)
    End If
    Call SetWindowLong(hWnd, GWL_STYLE, af)
    ' Redraw so that change will "take"
    Call SetWindowPos(hWnd, HWND_NOTOPMOST, 0, 0, 0, 0, _
                    SWP_NOZORDER Or SWP_NOSIZE Or _
                    SWP_NOMOVE Or SWP_DRAWFRAME)
End Sub
```

The first part of the code is straightforward, but what the heck is that call at the end? The SetWindowPos API function sets the window position and, as a side effect, renews all of the style bits. The trick to this hack is getting the function to perform the side effect without performing the primary effect. The second through sixth parameters of SetWindowPos change the z-order, location, or size of a window, and the final parameter tells how to interpret the earlier parameters. In this case, you pass three NO flags telling the function to ignore it all. By themselves, these flags would simply disable the function, so you must

Thunder Classes

If you are familiar with programming for Windows in C or Pascal, you might notice that this chapter doesn't stress window classes. In fact, window classes—so important to most Windows programmers—are almost irrelevant to Basic programmers.

When programming Windows in C, you first define the classes for your windows by filling in the fields of a WNDCLASS structure and then passing this structure to RegisterClass. Windows provides default classes for control windows (such as the Edit and ComboBox classes), but there is no default class for "normal" windows. You must create and register your own class before you can call CreateWindow to create your windows. As a result, almost every application has a different name for the classes of its windows, even though those classes often contain the same attributes. Program Manager has the Progman class, Notepad has the Notepad class, Calculator has the SciCalc class, and so on.

Visual Basic programmers usually don't need to worry about classes because Basic creates and registers its own and then uses them to create its own windows, all behind the scenes. Once you start calling API functions to play with windows, however, you might want to manipulate windows through their class names occasionally.

All the names of the predefined Basic classes start with the word *Thunder*, which was the prerelease code name of Visual Basic 1. (Internally, the Basic folks were distributing a stunning bitmap showing the night sky of Seattle split by lightning and the slogan "The power to crack Windows.") Each Basic program has a main window with class ThunderMain and one or more forms with class ThunderForm. Controls have class names such as ThunderCommand-Button, ThunderListBox, and so on. In some cases, Thunder classes are made up of standard Windows control classes. For example, the ThunderComboBox class consists of what Windows calls an Edit control and a ComboBox control.

Although you don't have to worry about classes in your applications, the downside is that you can't use classes to find Basic programs as you can with other programs. Classwise, if you've seen one Visual Basic application, you've seen them all.

add the SWP_DRAWFRAME flag to ensure that the window gets updated. Pretty slimy, huh? I haven't experimented much with this function, so don't blame me if it doesn't always work for all style bits or for windows without frames.

NOTE   I got this hack from an article called "Slimy Windows Hacks" in the February 1995 issue of *Visual Basic Programmer's Journal*. The masked author identified himself only as Escher. I can't reveal his identity, but I will note that the Acknowledgments section of this book gives proper credit to all contributors.

Window position and size

Windows knows everything that you need to know about every window's position—both the rectangle of the window and the rectangle of its client area. A rectangle includes the screen coordinates of the left, right, top, and bottom, thus describing both the size and the position of the window. Various Windows API functions use the rectangle coordinates to control the size and the position of a window.

Of course, you usually won't need these functions in Basic. When working on forms and controls, it's easier to read or modify the Left, Top, Width, and Height attributes or to use the Move method. If you're interested only in the client area, you can use the ScaleLeft, ScaleTop, ScaleWidth, and ScaleHeight properties.

Occasionally, however, you'll need to perform operations that Visual Basic does not support. When you convert Basic rectangles to Windows rectangles, the following utility functions can make your code shorter:

```
Function XRight(obj As Object) As Single
    XRight = obj.Left + obj.Width
End Function

Function YBottom(obj As Object) As Single
    YBottom = obj.Top + obj.Height
End Function
```

Just be sure that anything you pass to these functions really has Left, Top, Width, and Height properties.

WinWatch has to solve a window coordinate problem. It must find the window located at a given position—specifically, the position the user points to. The cmdPoint_Click event toggles point mode on and off, the Form_MouseMove event displays information for the window to which the user is currently pointing, and the Form_MouseDown event selects the window being pointed to as the current window, forcing an update in various list boxes. Let's look at the code that makes this happen, starting with cmdPoint_Click:

```
Private Sub cmdPoint_Click()
    If cmdPoint.Caption = "&Point" Then
        fCapture = True
        cmdPoint.Caption = "End &Point"
        Call SetCapture(Me.hWnd)
        lblMsg.Caption = "Move mouse for window information"
    Else
        fCapture = False
        cmdPoint.Caption = "&Point"
        ReleaseCapture
        lblMsg.Caption = sMsg
    End If
End Sub
```

This sub toggles the form-level flag *fCapture*, changes messages and captions, and, most important, sets the form to capture all mouse movements anywhere on the screen. Normally, each window captures only its own mouse events; but with SetCapture on, you get everything.

The Form_MouseMove sub illustrates some of the problems involved in converting Windows screen coordinates to Basic form coordinates:

```
Private Sub Form_MouseMove(Button As Integer, Shift As Integer, _
                    X As Single, Y As Single)
    If fCapture Then
        Dim pt As TPoint, hWnd ' As SysInt
        Static hWndLast ' As SysInt
        ' Set point and convert it to screen coordinates
        pt.X = X / Screen.TwipsPerPixelX
        pt.Y = Y / Screen.TwipsPerPixelY
        ClientToScreen Me.hWnd, pt
        ' Find window under it
        hWnd = VBWindowFromPoint(pt.X, pt.Y)
        ' Update display only if window has changed
        If hWnd <> hWndLast Then
            Debug.Print "New Window"
            lblWin.Caption = GetWndInfo(hWnd)
            hWndLast = hWnd
        End If
    End If
End Sub
```

This code does nothing unless capture mode is on (as indicated by *fCapture*). If it is on, the mouse position that is received by the form is specified in twips, so you must multiply by Screen.TwipsPerPixelX to get *x* in pixels. The same is true for *y*. These adjusted values are put in a TPoint variable and passed to ClientToScreen to make them relative to the screen rather than to WinWatch. The adjusted values can then be passed to VBWindowFromPoint, which will return the window under the mouse pointer.

VBWindowFromPoint is one of the ugliest hacks in this book. To understand how it works, look carefully at the C prototypes for both ClientToScreen and WindowFromPoint:

```
void ClientToScreen(HWND hwnd, POINT FAR* lppt);
HWND WindowFromPoint(POINT pt);
```

In ClientToScreen, the POINT variable is passed as a pointer (by reference, in Basic terms). Every function in the Windows API passes structures this way—except two. WindowFromPoint and its cousin ChildWindowFromPoint break the rules by passing a POINT variable by value. You might remember from Chapter 2 that structures (UDTs in Basic) are always passed by reference in order to save stack space. But take a look at the size of a TPoint variable:

```
#If Win32 Then
Public Type TPoint
    x As Long
    y As Long
End Type
#Else
Public Type TPoint
    x As Integer
    y As Integer
End Type
#End If
```

In 16-bit mode, a TPoint is two Integers, which equal one Long. A pointer is also a Long. You would gain nothing if you passed by reference. Apparently, a performance-conscious designer of the first version of Windows decided to save a few clock cycles by passing by value, never anticipating that Windows might someday be ported to 32 bits. Well, it turns out that in 32-bit C you can pass a 64-bit TPoint variable by value. It might not be efficient, but at least it's portable. In Basic, however, you can't pass a UDT variable by value, period—not 32-bit, not 64-bit. Basic could have supported this for small UDTs, but the Basic designers must have assumed that no one would ever want to do it.

In 16-bit mode, you could simply lie in the Declare statement, claiming that you were passing a Long variable:

```
Declare Function WindowFromPoint(ByVal pt As Long) As Integer
```

Of course, you'd then need to pack the two parts of TPoint into a Long, using MakeDWord or a similar function. But how would you get two 32-bit values into a 64-bit variable? I suppose you might manage it with some horrifying hack that uses the LSet statement to pack two Longs into a Double and pass that by value. I chose a less obvious but more efficient solution.

Passing a TPoint variable by value means pushing two Integers onto the stack in 16-bit mode or pushing two Longs in 32-bit mode. If you can access the two parts separately, why not push them separately? Pushing two parts is equivalent to pushing the whole. The problem is what order you push them in. You have to understand the calling convention in detail to figure this out.

To make a long story short (or a Long story Integer), 16-bit Windows uses the Pascal calling convention, which passes right to left. In other words, you must pass the y coordinate first, as shown in this Declare statement:

```
Declare Function WindowFromPointYX Lib "User" _
    Alias "WindowFromPoint" (ByVal yPoint As Integer, _
    ByVal xPoint As Integer) As Integer
```

However, 32-bit Windows uses the StdCall convention, which passes left to right. You pass the x coordinate first, as shown here:

```
Declare Function WindowFromPointXY Lib "USER32" _
    Alias "WindowFromPoint" (ByVal xPoint As Long, _
    ByVal yPoint As Long) As Long
```

VBWindowFromPoint hides the crime in a wrapper function:

```
Function VBWindowFromPoint(ByVal X, ByVal Y) ' As SysInt
#If Win32 Then
    VBWindowFromPoint = WindowFromPointXY(X, Y)
#Else
    VBWindowFromPoint = WindowFromPointYX(Y, X)
#End If
End Function
```

On your own, examine the Form_MouseDown event procedure to figure out how it identifies the window being clicked and makes it the current window.

Iterating Through Windows

You can learn a lot about Windows by iterating through each window in the system and writing down its attributes. The window hierarchy is usually described as a tree, although it's diagrammed as something more like a root system. I'm told that programmers in many countries draw their trees growing upward, as the name implies. Figure 5-4 shows a tree upside down, the American way. At the top is the desktop window. Below are the top-level windows, the main windows of running programs. Below each top-level window is its own set of child windows—dialog boxes, MDI windows, buttons, and so on.

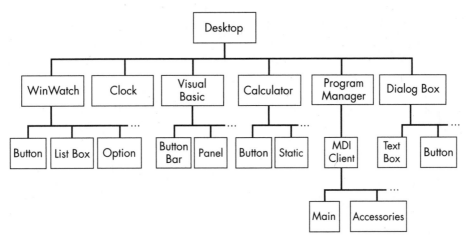

Figure 5-4. *A window tree.*

The approved way to traverse the window tree is to use EnumChildWindows to traverse each window and its children, starting at an arbitrary window. If you want to traverse all windows in the system, you start at the desktop window. Unfortunately, you can't use the Enum functions from Visual Basic because they require procedure variables (callbacks, in SDK jargon). I've already flamed about Basic's missing procedure variables back in Chapter 3. "The callback server," page 246, describes a tool that makes Enum functions possible in Basic.

Iterating the hard way

For now, let's traverse the window tree the hard way. Instead of accepting a procedure argument, my function (named IterateChildWindows) uses the fake-procedure-variable trick described in "Jury-Rigged Procedure Variables," page 134. It iterates through windows in the same way for any caller, but it calls an application-specific DoWindow routine to do whatever you want to each window it finds. Crude it may be, but at least IterateChildWindows gives you an inside look at how the window hierarchy works.

One caveat: the Windows API documentation warns that a window loop like this one risks getting caught in an infinite loop or accessing the handle of a window that no longer exists. EnumChildWindows, on the other hand, is guaranteed to be reliable. I haven't had any problems with IterateChildWindows, but I'm using it as an exploration tool rather than as a way to add functionality to real programs. Use it only when you know that the window hierarchy will not change while it's working.

Recursion makes IterateChildWindows deceptively short, but it's not as simple as it looks:

```
Public Function IterateChildWindows(ByVal iLevel As Integer, _
                                    ByVal hWnd) ' As SysInt
    Static hRet ' As SysInt
    BugAssert hWnd <> hNull
    ' Assume failure for easy exit
    IterateChildWindows = hNull

    ' Handle current window, allowing user to fail
    hRet = DoWindow(iLevel, hWnd)
    If hRet <> hNull Then Exit Function
    ' Get its child (if any)
    hWnd = GetWindow(hWnd, GW_CHILD)
    ' Iterate through each child window
    Do While hWnd <> hNull
        hRet = IterateChildWindows(iLevel + 1, hWnd)
        If hRet <> hNull Then Exit Function
        ' Get next child
        hWnd = GetWindow(hWnd, GW_HWNDNEXT)
        ' Give other processes some cycles
        DoEvents
    Loop
    IterateChildWindows = hRet

End Function
```

IterateChildWindows is located in a separate module named WINITER.BAS. Any project that includes WINITER.BAS must also define a public DoWindow function. Otherwise, IterateChildWindows will cause a *Sub or Function not defined* error, even if you never call it. DoWindow is located in WINWATCH.BAS, not WINWATCH.FRM. Any procedure that is called using the fake-procedure-variable trick must be in a code module.

IterateChildWindows takes two arguments, one indicating the window level and the other the window handle. You must seed each of these values for the first call to IterateWindows, but then it automatically figures out the appropriate arguments for subsequent calls to itself. If you want to start at the desktop, use the GetDesktopWindow API function to get the initial desktop handle, as WinWatch does:

```
Call IterateChildWindows(-1, GetDesktopWindow())
```

WinWatch passes −1 as the starting level to prevent DoWindow from putting the desktop window in the outline control. You could start with some other window handle, such as the handle of the current program:

```
hCurWnd = IterateWindows(0, Me.hWnd)
```

Once you have the initial window handle, you can get the handle of its first child window by calling GetWindow with GW_CHILD. The function returns the child window handle, or hNull if the window has no child. You get the next window at the same level (the next sibling) by calling GetWindow with GW-_HWNDNEXT. The IterateChildWindows function first gets the child of the current window and then loops through all the sibling windows, calling itself to get the children of each sibling. If that sounds confusing, try stepping through the function. You'll soon feel disoriented, if not completely lost. Computers do recursion better than humans.

Just as you provide IterateChildWindows to emulate the EnumChildWindows API function, you can write IterateWindows to emulate the EnumWindows API function. EnumWindows simply processes top-level windows. (See Refresh-TopWindows in code.) Realistically, you'd seldom use IterateWindows. The fake-procedure-variable trick isn't worth the cost for a simple nonrecursive loop through one level of windows; it's simpler to cut and paste the loop code and then insert code to process each window.

Doing windows

IterateWindows first calls DoWindow. The WinWatch version of DoWindow writes information about each window to the outline control or to a log file:

```
Public Function DoWindow(ByVal iLevel As Integer, _
                         ByVal hWnd) As Long
    BugAssert hWnd <> hNull
    If iLevel < 0 Then Exit Function ' Ignore desktop window

    If fLogFile Then
        ' Write data to log file
        Print #hFileCur, GetWndInfo(hWnd, iLevel)
    Else
        ' Add window title; if none, add bracketed window class
        Static s As String, i As Integer
        s = VBGetWindowTextLine(hWnd)
        If s = Empty Then s = "[" & VBGetClassName(hWnd) & "]"
```

(continued)

```
    If IsWindowVisible(hWnd) Or FWatch.chkInvisible.Value Then
        ' Update outline control
        With FWatch.outWin
            .AddItem s                    ' Add title
            i = .ListCount - 1
            .Indent(i) = iLevel + 1       ' Set outline level
            .ItemData(i) = hWnd           ' Store window handle
        End With
    End If
End If
' Always successful
DoWindow = hNull

End Function
```

The WinWatch DoWindow does double duty, creating the log file or updating the outline control, depending on the *fLogFile* flag. It uses *iLevel*—which is

Recursion

A good recursive algorithm looks simple and symmetrical but has a magical complexity when you watch it in action. Code your recursive routines carefully to avoid recursing forever. Recursion works best if you have a limited task with clean exits. Also be sure that you don't recurse too deeply and eat up all your stack space. IterateChildWindows recurses once for each level of child windows, but you're not likely to find more than five levels of child windows. In other words, the algorithm recurses frequently but not deeply. Each level releases its stack resources before going on to the next.

If you use algorithms that recurse deeply (recursive sorting algorithms, for example), try to minimize your stack use. Don't use more parameters than necessary, and declare local variables with Static rather than Dim. Static variables save stack space because they aren't stored on the stack. You'll need to watch out for side effects, however. Static variables retain their values across calls, so you should avoid using Static for any variable that you don't specifically initialize on each entrance.

You must also pay attention to how you declare parameters. Notice that the *iLevel* and *hWnd* parameters of IterateChildWindows are passed by value (using ByVal) rather than by reference. Each level keeps its own local arguments on the stack so that changes to the current level don't affect other levels. If you passed by reference, you'd be affecting the *hWnd* of the higher-level calls each time you set *hWnd* in a recursive call. Everything would be fine as long as you were recursing down, but you'd be lost as soon as you started back up.

incremented for each window level—to set the appropriate number of tabs to the log file or to set the indent level of the outline. Using the *iLevel* parameter gives IterateChildWindows an advantage over the system EnumChildWindows, which offers no clue about the level.

Both IterateChildWindows and DoWindow are functions. This enables you to search for a window with certain features. For example, you could write your own version of FindWindow to search the window hierarchy for a window with a given class, title, or other feature. Your DoWindow function would return the window handle when it found the appropriate window, and it would return hNull in all other cases. Any found handle would bubble up through the levels of recursion, stopping the iteration process and returning the handle via the top-level call to IterateChildWindows. In the WinWatch version of DoWindow, we want to continue as long as any windows are left, so we always return hNull to indicate that DoWindow hasn't found the magic window. In WinWatch, the outer call to IterateChildWindows just throws away the returned handle, using the Call syntax.

> **CHALLENGE** Write FindWindowWild, a function that works just like the FindWindow API function except that you can put wildcard arguments (such as * and ?) in the class and title names. Use IterateChildWindows and the Like operator.

You can use the log file created by WinWatch to get a snapshot of the window state. Want to know the class name of a button or an icon in a particular program? Run WinWatch and click the Log File button. Much of the information about Visual Basic's window hierarchy in Chapter 10 came from studying log files under various conditions.

More window relationships

IterateChildWindows illustrates how to traverse the window tree with Get-Window. Table 5-3 on the following page describes some of the other window relationships.

Except for "owner," all these relationships should be obvious. The owner of a window is the window that is notified when something happens to the first window. You can get a better feel for this by browsing the outline in Win-Watch's Window Hierarchy box. Most windows in the hierarchy don't have an owner, but a dialog box is owned by the window that launched it. The main Visual Basic window containing the menus and the toolbar is the owner of all the other windows—toolbox, project, properties, and code windows.

If you look at the internal data stored for a window (see "Inside CWindow," page 199), you'll see that only three relatives are stored for each window: the parent, the next sibling, and the first child. (The owner isn't a relative, strictly speaking.) You won't see a first, last, or previous sibling, even though Windows provides the GW_HWNDFIRST, GW_HWNDLAST, and GW_HWNDPREV constants. Each of these relationships can be calculated from the given data. For example, the first sibling is actually the first child of the parent. The last sibling is the next's next's next until the next with no next.

Operation	Description
GetWindow with GW_HWNDFIRST	Get the first sibling
GetWindow with GW_HWNDLAST	Get the last sibling
GetWindow with GW_HWNDNEXT	Get the next sibling
GetWindow with GW_HWNDPREV	Get the previous sibling
GetWindow with GW_CHILD	Get the first child
GetWindow with GW_OWNER	Get the owner
GetNextWindow	Get the next or previous sibling
GetTopWindow	Get the top-level window of a specified window
GetDesktopWindow	Get the desktop (the top of the window tree)
GetParent	Get the parent
SetParent	Change the parent of a window
IsChild	Indicate whether two windows are parent and child

Table 5-3. *Window relationships.*

All About Programs

Let's go back and look more closely at major features of Windows monitored by WinWatch. As you saw from comparing Figures 5-1 and 5-2 (pages 194 and 197), a lot of this information differs for 16-bit and 32-bit Windows. When you study the elements closely, you can see why.

Processes

The Processes By Module list box in WinWatch shows all the currently running applications, now known officially as *processes*. This terminology can be confusing. Under MS-DOS, a process was always called a process, but for Windows somebody got the bright idea of calling processes *tasks*. Most of the 16-bit API functions that deal with processes use the word *task*. The terminology has been straightened out, within the constraints of compatibility, in the Win32 API. This book uses the term *process* the way God intended.

A process is a running program, along with all the DLLs it uses. A process usually has one main window, but it can have multiple top windows, no top windows, or invisible top windows. In Visual Basic terms, having one top window means having a startup form, having multiple top windows means starting more than one modal form from Sub Main, having no top windows means doing all processing from Sub Main, and having invisible top windows means setting Visible to False on all top-level forms. In most cases, when you select a process in the Processes By Module list box, a corresponding title is highlighted in the Top Windows list box. Every process has a module, highlighted in the Modules By Exe Name box. In Figure 5-1, CALC appears twice in the processes list, indicating that two instances of it are running.

In 32-bit Windows, a process can have multiple threads of execution, although Visual Basic applications might as well have only one for all you can do about it. If Basic applications use multiple threads, they do so internally—in this version, at least. In 16-bit Windows, you can access a process through its HTASK. In 32-bit Windows, you can access either a process handle or a thread handle, depending on what you want to do. Actually, you can't do much directly with a process, a task, or a thread handle in Basic. Generally, you'll want to access the instance handle, as I'll explain later.

TOOLHELP.DLL (16-bit only) contains a set of functions for iterating through and otherwise manipulating processes (called tasks in the API names). WinWatch uses the TaskFirst and TaskNext functions to build the processes list. Both functions use TTaskEntry:

```
Type TTaskEntry
    dwSize As Long
    hTask As Integer
    hTaskParent As Integer
    hInst As Integer
    hModule As Integer
    wSS As Integer
    wSP As Integer
    wStackTop As Integer
    wStackMinimum As Integer
    wStackBottom As Integer
    wcEvents As Integer
    hQueue As Integer
    szModule As String * 10
    wPSPOffset As Integer
    hNext As Integer
End Type
```

Most of this data is useless in Basic. The only fields WinWatch cares about are *dwSize*, *hInst*, and *szModule*. Here's how the Processes By Module list box is filled:

```
Private Sub RefreshProcessList()
    Dim task As TTaskEntry, iPos As Integer, f As Integer
    task.dwSize = Len(task)
    f = TaskFirst(task)
    Do While f
        ' Add module name to list
        iPos = InStr(task.szModule, sNullChr)
        BugAssert iPos > 0
        lstProcess.AddItem Left$(task.szModule, iPos)
        lstProcess.ItemData(lstProcess.NewIndex) = task.hInst
        ' Get next process
        f = TaskNext(task)
    Loop
End Sub
```

Looping through processes (tasks) follows an iteration pattern that will soon become familiar:

1. Fill in the *dwSize* field to reassure Windows that you really have the right size structure. This step doesn't apply to all iteration APIs, but you'll usually need some initialization.

2. Call TaskFirst (or ModuleFirst or FileFirst or some other First iteration function).

3. Test at the top of the loop to handle the unlikely case of no items in the list.

4. Do whatever the loop does. In this case, put the module name in the list box and store the handle to the instance in the *ItemData* array.

5. Call TaskNext (or some other Next function) until no more items are left.

What is an instance handle, and why did you save it? Let's put that off for a few minutes and talk first about modules and windows.

NOTE   In my first version of this code, I stored the instance handles in a module-level array because I wasn't aware that list boxes had an *ItemData* array. I wanted to set the Sorted property of the list box, but I couldn't because it would have taken a lot of extra work to keep the external array sorted in the same order as the list box. When I finally figured out how to use the *ItemData* array, I got sorting for free. Sometimes it pays to read the documentation.

The Modules List

The Modules By Exe Name list box in WinWatch lists each executable file currently running in the system. The list includes both programs and DLLs in all their forms. You might not have realized that font files (FON), custom controls (VBX or OCX), and device drivers (DRV) are actually DLLs, but there they are in the list. The modules list contains only one copy of each file, even if multiple instances are running, because each instance uses the same executable file.

WinWatch calls the RefreshModuleList sub to create the modules list. This code uses ModuleFirst and ModuleNext to iterate through TModuleEntry variables. You've already been through similar code in RefreshProcessList; the only difference is that you don't have to save anything in the *ItemData* array. The processes list needs an array entry containing an instance handle to uniquely identify each entry because the process name isn't unique. The module name is unique, however, so it can be used to find and mark any entry in the modules list.

The Top Windows List

The Top Windows list box in WinWatch lists each top-level window. Top-level windows are what you probably think of as Windows programs. In fact, the top-level windows list in WinWatch is pretty much the same as the list in the misnamed Task Manager. My bet is that Top Window Manager—excuse me, Task Manager—makes its list with code very similar to this:

```
Private Sub RefreshTopWinList()
    Dim sTitle As String, hWnd, hInst ' As SysInt

    ' Form is top-level, so start with first sibling
    hWnd = GetWindow(Me.hWnd, GW_HWNDFIRST)
    BugAssert hWnd <> hNull
    ' Iterate through each top-level window
    Do While hWnd <> hNull
        sTitle = VBGetWindowTextLine(hWnd)
        ' Display only titled, visible, unowned windows
        If sTitle <> Empty Then
            If IsWindowVisible(hWnd) Then
                If GetWindow(hWnd, GW_OWNER) = hNull Then
                    With lstTopWin
                        .AddItem sTitle
                        hInst = GetWindowData(hWnd, GWD_HINSTANCE)
                        .ItemData(.NewIndex) = hInst
                    End With
                End If
            End If
        End If
```

(continued)

Unique Module Names

How can you be sure that a module name is unique? What if you run one program named CALC.EXE from the Windows directory and a different program that has the same name from another directory? Won't you have two programs with the same module name? No, because Windows won't let you.

To try this out, copy C:\WINDOWS\NOTEPAD.EXE to C:\CALC.EXE. Now use File Manager to run the misnamed CALC.EXE from the root directory. As you might expect, Notepad runs. Now run CALC.EXE from the Windows directory. You might be surprised when a second copy of Notepad runs, not Calculator.

When Windows receives the command to execute CALC.EXE, it first looks in its modules list (the same one accessed by ModuleFirst and ModuleNext) to see whether the module already exists. When it finds the bogus CALC.EXE, Windows decides to save time by reusing the existing CALC code and loading the CALC data from the executable file it previously found, ignoring the directory specified in the execute command.

This little-known behavior can be the source of confusion and crashes when you use beta software, especially DLLs. If you have two versions of a DLL with the same name in different locations on your disk, you might accidentally end up running the wrong one. One program might expect one version while another program expects the other, but only one copy runs at a time. If you try to run both programs, one of them will get the wrong DLL, probably resulting in a fast trip to nowhere.

Fortunately, this is a 16-bit-only problem, and one that you can solve with KILLMOD.BAS, the shortest useful Visual Basic program ever:

```
Sub Main()
    Dim hInst As Integer
    ' Get handle of program passed on command line
    hInst = GetModuleHandle(Command$)
    If hInst = 0 Then Exit Sub
    ' Free modules until none is left
    Do While GetModuleUsage(hInst) > 0
        Call FreeModule(hInst)
    Loop
End Sub
```

Even without a user interface and error checking, KillMod performs the same task as the Windows Process Status (WPS.EXE) program distributed with Visual Basic. Put it in the Tools menu of the 16-bit Visual C++ IDE to kill DLLs that crash during debugging.

```
      ' Get next child
      hWnd = GetWindow(hWnd, GW_HWNDNEXT)
   Loop
End Sub
```

This iteration loop works a lot like the loops for TaskFirst and ModuleFirst, except that you pass the constants GW_HWNDFIRST and GW_HWNDNEXT to GetWindow. You could also say that it's like IterateChildWindows without the recursion. Since ModuleFirst and TaskFirst are in the TOOLHELP DLL, using them is a job for 16-bit Windows only. But iterating through top-level windows with GetWindow works in any environment.

For each found window, you check to ensure that the window meets certain criteria—that it has a title, is visible, and is not owned by another window. Windows that meet all the criteria have their titles and instance handles placed in the list box. You might want to experiment by commenting out the *IsWindow-Visible* or the *GetWindow(hWnd, GW_OWNER)* conditional blocks to change the criteria for identifying top windows. If you comment out the If block that checks for owned windows, you'll get lots of nonmodal dialog boxes. For example, if Visual Basic is running, you'll see the Debug window, each code window, the Project window, and so on in the Top Windows list box. All of these are top-level windows owned by the Visual Basic window.

You'll also want to check out the RefreshAllLists procedure. This procedure calls RefreshTopWinList, RefreshModuleList, RefreshProcessList, and Refresh-FullWinList (more on that later) to update all the window information on the display. It is called when you load WinWatch, when you choose the Refresh button, or when you change the Show Invisible check box.

Now that we've covered top-level windows, modules, and processes, we are ready to talk a little more about handles for windows, modules, tasks, processes, and especially instances.

Instance Handles

Almost everything in Windows has a *handle,* an integer value that uniquely identifies it. Every window has an HWND, every module an HMODULE, every 16-bit task an HTASK. Every 32-bit process has a process HANDLE. (Don't ask me why it isn't called an HPROCESS.) Each process consists of threads, each of which has a thread HANDLE. And so on.

In 16-bit Windows, every instance has an HINSTANCE, but an instance is not like the items mentioned above. Furthermore, although 32-bit Windows has instances and HINSTANCEs, they aren't unique.

In 16-bit Windows, an instance corresponds to an executable image of data in memory. Compare that with a module, which represents the unique code of an executable file. A process represents both the shared code and the unique data of an executable file, plus all shared code and shared data of the DLLs it uses. Note the distinction between shared code and unique data. It would be wasteful for Windows to load multiple copies of the same program's code, since every copy executes the same statements no matter how many other copies are running. But Windows must load a separate copy of the data for each copy of the program. It wouldn't do to change the results in one instance of Calculator, for example, every time you click the equal button in another.

Note, however, that a DLL has only one copy of both its code and its data. That's why DLL code seldom uses global variables. One program using a DLL could change a variable used by another program. (A DLL can have instance data, but that's another story in another book.) A program can have multiple instances, but a DLL has only one.

You can see why 16-bit Windows programmers seldom need handles to modules or processes. The instance handle uniquely identifies whatever you want to work on. A process (or task) handle could uniquely identify a program, but not a DLL. A module handle could identify the shared code, but not which instance is using that code. On the other hand, if you really do need the shared code, the instance handle can identify it indirectly by looking up the module handle in its internal process database. Most Windows API functions use HINSTANCE parameters and return values even when the function really needs an HMODULE. You can always use an HINSTANCE in place of an HMODULE, but it doesn't necessarily work the other way around. You cannot pass an HMODULE when the function needs the instance because Windows won't know which one you mean.

Everything you just learned about instances is wrong in 32-bit Windows. Each instance runs both its code and its data in a completely different address space in order to protect itself from the sins of other instances. Although the instance is in a different virtual memory space, the code might actually reside in the same physical memory space, protected by some miracle of protected-mode architecture that I wouldn't explain here even if I understood it.

Unique instance handles

What can you do with an instance handle? For one thing, you can use it as a unique identifier of each instance. WinWatch stores instance handles in the *ItemData* array of both the Top Windows and the Processes By Module list boxes. If you know the instance handle of the top window, you can use it to look up the same instance in the processes list, and vice versa. Here's the lookup code called when you select an entry in the Top Windows list box:

```
Private Sub lstTopWin_Click()

    ' Flag to prevent recursion
    If fInClick Then Exit Sub
    fInClick = True
    Dim hWnd, hInst ' As SysInt
    Dim i As Integer, sExe As String
    lstResource.Clear

    ' Look up top window (ignore if process has no top window)
    i = lstTopWin.ListIndex
    If i <> -1 Then
        hInst = lstTopWin.ItemData(i)
    Else
        hInst = GetWindowData(hWndCur, GWD_HINSTANCE)
    End If
    ' Get everything you need to know about this window
    FindInstanceInfo hWnd, hInst, sExe
    hTopWndCur = hWnd
    hInstCur = hInst

#If Win32 = 0 Then
    ' Update module list box by looking up Exe name
    lstModule.ListIndex = LookupItem(lstModule, sExe)
    ' Update process list box by looking up instance handle
    lstProcess.ListIndex = LookupItemData(lstProcess, hInst)
#End If
    If hWndCur = 0 Or _
        (GetWindowData(hWndCur, GWD_HINSTANCE) <> hInstCur) Then
        hWndCur = hWnd
        ' Update window outline by looking up instance handle
        outWin.ListIndex = LookupItemData(outWin, hWnd)
        ' Update window display from window handle
        lblWin.Caption = GetWndInfo(hWnd)
    End If

    ClearResource
    UpdateResources
    fInClick = False

End Sub
```

Notice how the *fInClick* flag (declared at the module level) is used to protect the Click procedure against recursion. This procedure sets the ListIndex property of the processes and modules lists, which activates the Click procedures of these two list boxes. Without the flag, the Click procedures of the other list boxes would reactivate this Click procedure, which would reactivate the other Click procedures, which would…you get the point.

The next few lines of the code do some general cleanup, get *hInst* out of the *ItemData* array, and figure out the executable and top-window handle using the multipurpose FindInstanceInfo procedure. The instance handle and the executable name are all you need to look up and set the correct entries in the Modules By Exe Name list box, the Processes By Module list box, and the Window Hierarchy box. You don't update the modules and processes lists under 32-bit Windows because you have no information to put in them. "Looking up list box items," page 239, tells how LookupItem and LookupItemData find values in the list boxes.

For your own information, try examining lstModule_Click, lstProcess_Click, and lstOutWin_Click to see how they compare to lstTopWin_Click.

CHALLENGE Keeping items in sync in the different controls depends on instance handles being unique, but they aren't always unique. If you run 16-bit WinWatch under a 32-bit operating system, 32-bit programs appear in the Top Windows list box, but they won't necessarily synchronize with the window hierarchy outline. If you step through the RefreshTopWinList sub, you can see why: all 32-bit programs have the same instance handle. I'll let you figure out why 32-bit Windows programs think all 16-bit Windows programs are the same program. With enough conditional code, I'm sure someone could figure out how to make WinWatch work the same (or mostly the same) in all environments. Some of the Win32 debugging functions perform the same tasks as the 16-bit functions in TOOLHELP.DLL. Furthermore, Windows 95 (but not Windows NT 3.51) has its own TOOLHELP functions in KERNEL32.DLL. Check out the PView program on the Visual Basic CD (the Tools directory) for proof that it can be done.

The instance executable name

You can use the instance handle to look up important data about a program, such as its executable name and its resources. It's easy enough to get your own instance handle—the new hInstance property of the App object returns it. Getting another program's instance handle is more difficult.

The GetModuleFileName API function takes an instance handle and returns the full pathname of its executable file. Although it has the word *Module* in its name, GetModuleHandle takes an HINSTANCE argument. Feel free to pass either an instance handle or a module handle. Usually, however, you'll have only a window handle, and although you can easily get an instance handle from a window handle, you can't easily get the module handle.

I cover the uglier parts of getting the executable name in several different wrappers, depending on what I start with and what I want to have returned. If I start with an instance handle and want only the name without the path, I call GetInstExeName. If I want the whole works, I call GetInstExePath. If I start with a window handle, I call GetWndExeName or GetWndExePath. I'll show you a couple of these; you can easily figure out the others. Here's the GetWndExeName function:

```
Function GetWndExeName(ByVal hWnd) As String
    BugAssert hWnd <> hNull
    GetWndExeName = GetInstExeName(GetWindowData( _
                              hWnd, GWD_HINSTANCE))
End Function
```

GetWndExeName simply gets the instance handle from the window and passes it down to GetInstExeName. Here's GetInstExeName:

```
Function GetInstExeName(ByVal hInst) As String
    Dim sName As String, cName As Integer
    sName = String$(cMaxPath + 1, 0)
    cName = GetModuleFileName(hInst, sName, cMaxPath + 1)
#If Win32 And afDebug Then
    If cName = 0 Then
        BugMessage "Error: " & Err.LastDllError
    End If
#End If
    GetInstExeName = GetFileBaseExt(Left$(sName, cName))
End Function
```

GetFileBaseExt is a utility function (in UTILITY.BAS) that strips a filename off the end of a full pathname. As you can imagine, GetInstExePath looks just like GetInstExeName except that it doesn't call GetFileBaseExt.

The debugging code illustrates an interesting point. When the WinWatch program calls GetInstExeName under 32-bit Windows, the *cName* variable usually comes back as 0, indicating that GetModuleFileName failed. Err.LastDllError (the Basic equivalent of GetLastError) returns 6, indicating an invalid handle. But you just got that instance handle from a valid window handle. Why is the instance invalid? It's valid enough in its own address space; in fact, if you use this handle when the current window is your own (the Visual Basic environment or the compiled WinWatch program), everything works fine. But a 32-bit instance handle is actually a pointer (address), and trying to use an address from another address space is like trying to explain the legislature to Martians.

That's why 32-bit WinWatch can't get the executable name or any resources other than its own. When you think about it, Windows really shouldn't let WinWatch steal resources out of other people's programs.

NOTE Getting error information has always been a problem under 16-bit Windows. Each function is free to express self-doubt in its own special way. Most functions let you know when something goes wrong, but few of them bother to tell you what it was. The Win32 API is more disciplined. It always returns error information through the GetLastError function. You can't use this function from Basic, however. Instead, you must use the LastDllError property of the Err object. When you call an API function, Basic might call other API functions behind the scenes. The GetLastError value from any function that is called after your function will overwrite the error value from your function. The real GetLastError value for your API call is saved in the LastDllError property. This works whether you use a Declare statement or the Windows API type library.

The name of the module

In 16-bit Windows, the module name is not necessarily the same as the executable name. For example, select an MS-DOS session in WinWatch under 16-bit Windows. The Top Windows list box shows the title (DOS Win 1), the Modules By Exe Name list box shows the name of the executable file (WINOA386.MOD or WINOA286.MOD), and the Processes By Module list box shows the module name (WINOLDAP).

Programmers in other languages can give a module any name they want just by specifying a name in the DEF file. Visual Basic handles this for you, giving every Basic program the same module name as its base executable name. The designers of 32-bit Windows apparently saw the wisdom of this approach and made the module name automatically the same as the base executable name.

Windows doesn't make it particularly easy to get the module name. It's much simpler to use GetInstExeName or GetWndExeName to get the executable filename and use that as the module identifier. But if you do need the module name, the TOOLHELP DLL provides the necessary module functions.

Your homework assignment is to examine the GetInstModule function, which uses the ModuleFindHandle function to get the real module name. For extra credit, you can look up the conversion functions ExeFromModuleName and ModuleFromExeName.

Everything But the Kitchen Sink

When processing an instance, you might need to know the following five pieces of information: the top-level window handle, the instance handle, the module name, the top-level window title, and the top-level window class. FindInstanceInfo takes one of these pieces of information as input and returns all the rest as output. The definition of FindInstanceInfo (in INSTTOOL.BAS) looks like this:

```
Sub FindInstanceInfo(Optional vTopWnd As Variant, _
                     Optional vInst As Variant, _
                     Optional vExe As Variant, _
                     Optional vTitle As Variant, _
                     Optional vClass As Variant)
```

Each parameter either can serve as an input parameter or can return information by reference. All of the parameters are optional, although you'll normally pass at least two of them. A lookup function doesn't make sense unless it has something to look up and someplace to put what it finds. You pass the one known value to use in looking up the others and pass empty variables for all the values you want to look up.

The *vTopWnd* parameter can contain any window handle on entry, but it will always contain the top window handle on exit. Don't pass your only copy of a useful window handle, because it will be overwritten.

If you pass the instance handle or the executable name as the parameter under 16-bit Windows, you might identify a DLL module. A DLL never has a top window, a title, or a class. If *vInst* or *vExe* comes back valid but *vTopWin* comes back empty, you've got a DLL, not an error. Under 32-bit Windows, FindInstanceInfo simply returns empty values for DLLs.

Here is the minimal lookup you can do with FindInstanceInfo:

```
hTopWnd = hWndCur     ' Look up top window from any window
FindInstanceInfo hTopWnd
```

A more common use (see, for instance, any of the list box Click event procedures in WinWatch) is to look up the top window and the executable name from the instance handle:

```
hInst = hInstCur      ' Look up top window and exe name from instance
FindInstanceInfo hTopWnd, hInst, sExe
```

You could also look up all the other elements from the window title:

```
FindInstanceInfo hTopWnd, hInst, sExe, "Calculator", sClass
```

If you want to use named arguments, the possibilities are endless. Here's one that looks up the top window title from the executable name:

```
FindInstanceInfo vTitle:=sTitle, vExe:="CALC.EXE"
```

Implementing FindInstanceInfo is complicated but not difficult, mainly using techniques that we have already discussed. Rather than presenting the complete implementation, here's some pseudocode without error handling and other complications:

```
    ' Find lookup parameter (the one that isn't 0 or empty)
    If vTopWnd <> hNull Then
        ' Make all others 0 or empty
    ElseIf vInst <> hNull Then
        ' Loop through top windows to find corresponding window
    ElseIf vExe <> Empty Then
        ' Loop through top windows to find corresponding window
        ' If none, it's a DLL
    ElseIf vTitle <> Empty Or vClass <> Empty Then
        ' Use FindWindow to get window
    Else
        ' Invalid call--all arguments empty
    End If
    ' Now you have a window handle; use it to get other stuff
    If vInst = hNull Then vInst = GetWindowData(vWnd, GWD_HINSTANCE)
    If vExe = Empty Then vExe = GetInstExeName(hInst)
    vTopWnd = ' Code to get top window
    If vClass = Empty Then vClass = VBGetClassName(hTopWnd)
    If vTitle = Empty Then vTitle = VBGetWindowTextLine(hTopWnd)
End Sub
```

If you try to find a window by its title or its class, you'll have a better chance of finding exactly what you want if you pass both. Different windows can have the same class, the same title, or both. Some top-level windows don't have a title, so an empty title on return isn't necessarily significant. In fact, several aspects of FindInstanceInfo are open to interpretation. If you plan to use this code in your applications, you might want to spend some time studying the implementation.

Handling Multiple Instances

The discussion of Windows so far in this chapter might have enlightened you, but it probably hasn't put much bread on your table. Here's a more practical problem.

What happens if you try to start two copies of the same program? Some programs, such as Calculator, don't mind at all and will keep running copies until you run out of memory. Others, such as previous versions of Visual Basic, quit after displaying a polite message box saying that you can run only one copy. Still others, such as Microsoft Mail, reactivate the current copy every time you try to start a new copy. For every Windows-based program, you need to think about this issue and choose a strategy.

If it's OK to run multiple copies, you don't need to do anything. That's the default. If you want to run only one copy, terminating each additional attempt with an error message, you don't need to do much. Just put the following in Form_Load:

```
If App.PrevInstance Then
    MsgBox "You cannot start more than one copy"
    End
End If
```

This technique has one problem—App.PrevInstance is always False in the Visual Basic environment. You can launch multiple versions of Visual Basic running the same program, but each will think that it's the only one. You'll have difficulty debugging any complicated code that uses the PrevInstance property. You can't test it in the environment because it won't behave the same, but you can't easily test it outside the environment because you don't have a debugger.

A bigger problem with running just one copy is that it's rarely the right thing to do. It's much better to change the focus to the first copy and terminate the second. On the surface, it doesn't seem to be hard to accomplish this in Basic. The following will work for many programs:

```
If App.PrevInstance Then
    MsgBox "Previous Active"
    Dim sTitle As String
    ' Save my title
    sTitle = Me.Caption
    ' Change my title bar so I won't activate myself
    Me.Caption = Hex(Me.hWnd)
    ' Activate other instance
    AppActivate sTitle
    ' Terminate myself
    End
End If
```

Is changing the caption before activating the other instance a neat trick or what? This works great for programs such as WinWatch that always have the same title, but what if the other instance has a different title? Notepad's title contains the name of the current file. So does the Visual Basic environment. In fact, the new Windows 95 standard specifies that any window representing a document should have the document name in the title. But if you don't know the other window title, you can't call AppActivate.

Here's how to handle multiple copies the hard way. You loop through the top-level windows until you find a window that has the same module but a different process. I call the following routine first thing in the Form_Load procedure of Edward, an editor you'll meet in Chapter 8:

```
Sub ActivatePrevInstance(frm As Form)
    ' Comment out next line to debug in environment
    If App.PrevInstance = False Then Exit Sub
    Dim hWndYou ' As SysInt
    Dim sigModYou As Long, sigModMe As Long
    Dim sigProcYou As Long, sigProcMe As Long

    ' Get my own module and process signatures
    sigModMe = GetSigMod(frm.hWnd)
    sigProcMe = GetSigProc(frm.hWnd)
    ' Get first sibling to start iterating top-level windows
    hWndYou = GetWindow(frm.hWnd, GW_HWNDFIRST)
    Do While hWndYou <> hNull
        ' Get module and process signatures of window
        sigModYou = GetSigMod(hWndYou)
        sigProcYou = GetSigProc(hWndYou)
        ' Activate if module same but process different
        If (sigModMe = sigModYou) And (sigProcMe <> sigProcYou) Then
            ' Do something more complicated here if you want
            AppActivate hWndYou
            End
        End If
        ' Get next sibling
        hWndYou = GetWindow(hWndYou, GW_HWNDNEXT)
    Loop
End Sub
```

This code introduces the concept of module and process signatures. A signature is simply a unique value. The Windows API can give you lots of handles, IDs, pointers, and strings for a window. It doesn't matter which one you use as the module signature as long as it's the same for all windows of this module, and different for windows of other modules. Same with the process signature. Different values are unique, depending on whether you're in 16-bit or 32-bit mode:

```
Function GetSigMod(hWnd) As Long
#If Win32 Then
    GetSigMod = GetWindowData(hWnd, GWD_HINSTANCE)
#Else
```

```
    Dim f As Boolean, te As TTaskEntry, hTask ' As SysInt
    hTask = GetWindowTask(hWnd)
    te.dwSize = Len(te)
    f = TaskFindHandle(te, hTask)
    BugAssert f
    GetSigMod = te.hModule
#End If
End Function

Function GetSigProc(hWnd) As Long
#If Win32 Then
    Dim id As Long
    Call GetWindowThreadProcessId(hWnd, id)
    GetSigProc = id
#Else
    GetSigProc = GetWindowTask(hWnd)
#End If
End Function
```

Once you find the appropriate top window, you must activate it by its handle rather than by its window text. The better AppActivate hides the fact that the technique varies for 16-bit and 32-bit code:

```
Sub AppActivate(vTarget As Variant, Optional vWait As Variant)
    If IsNumeric(vTarget) Then
        ' Ignore wait flag with handle
#If Win32 Then
        SetForegroundWindow vTarget
#Else
        SetActiveWindow vTarget
#End If
    Else
        VBA.AppActivate vTarget, vWait
    End If
End Sub
```

CHALLENGE One of Joe Hacker's design rules is "If in doubt, let the user decide." This is often the best way to deal with multiple instances. Put up a dialog box with a list box of existing instances. Let the user decide whether to abort, launch a new instance, or activate an existing one. This is particularly useful in Windows 95 for two reasons. First, one of the recommended models for programs that handle documents is to launch a new instance for each document, possibly communicating shared information between instances. Second, placing shortcut icons on the desktop makes it easy to accidentally launch multiple instances.

Sending and Receiving Messages

Messages make Windows tick, but you wouldn't know it from studying the Visual Basic documentation. Take keyboard events. If you press the B key while a Basic text box has the focus, Windows sends WM_KEYDOWN, WM_CHAR, and WM_KEYUP messages to the text box. But your Basic program sees these messages as the KeyDown, KeyPress, and KeyUp events.

In Visual Basic, most events are caused by Windows messages. Sometimes you'll find a one-to-one mapping, as with the keyboard messages just mentioned. A Form_Load event, however, doesn't correspond directly to a specific message. If you're curious and you happen to have a C or a Pascal compiler, you can use a message filter utility (such as Microsoft's Spy) to see exactly which messages are being sent to which windows. You'll get bored fast watching these C messages. A Visual Basic event spy might be more interesting. You should be qualified to write one by the time you finish this book.

Hardcore Basic programmers can go beyond the events Visual Basic provides and handle their own messages. Sending messages is relatively easy to do with Windows API calls. Receiving messages, however, is a difficult problem that requires some sort of message capture tool. We'll talk about two such tools later in the chapter.

Sending Messages

To understand the point of messages, let's look briefly at how you would write programs for Windows in Basic if you had to write them from scratch the way you do in C. The main routine in every Visual Basic program would look something like this:

```
Dim msg as TMessage
Dim hForm, hControl   ' As SysInt

hForm = CreateWindow("Form", iFormAttr, ...)
hControl = CreateWindow("Control", iCtrlAttr, ...)

' Get next message from Windows queue
Do While GetMessage(msg)
    ' Send message to appropriate window
    TranslateMessage(msg)
    DispatchMessage(msg)
Loop
End
```

Fortunately, Basic creates all the windows it needs—based on the forms you draw and the attributes you set rather than on the code you write—and then keeps reading messages and sending them out to the windows until it gets a WM_QUIT message. WM_QUIT is the only message that causes GetMessage to return False and terminate the loop (and the program). The messages come from the user interface (the keyboard and the mouse, for instance), from messages sent by the system to the windows, from messages sent by the windows to the system, and from messages sent from one window to another.

Meanwhile, the created windows are gobbling up all the messages sent to them and taking the appropriate actions. Each window has a routine (called a *window procedure*) that processes messages. If window procedures were written in Basic, a typical one might look like this:

```
Function WindowProc(hWnd, iMessage, _
                    wParam, lParam as Long) As Long
    ' Set default return value
    WindowProc = 0&
    ' Handle messages
    Select Case iMessage
    Case WM_DOSOMETHING
        DoIt "Whatever it does", wParam, lParam
    Case WM_ASKSOMETHING
        WindowProc = CheckIt("Tell me, please", wParam, lParam)
    Case Else
        ' Call default window procedure
        WindowProc = DefWindowProc(hWnd, iMessage, wParam, lParam)
    End Select
End Function
```

Every form and control in your program (don't confuse me with exceptions) has one of these window procedures. Windows and Visual Basic communicate with them using the SendMessage function, and you can use it too.

The SendMessage function

The Windows API documentation shows the following syntax:

```
LRESULT SendMessage(hWnd, uMsg, wParam, lParam)
HWND hWnd;           // Handle of destination window
UINT uMsg;           // Message to send
WPARAM wParam;       // First message parameter
LPARAM lParam;       // Second message parameter
```

Assuming that untyped parameters are Integers in 16-bit mode and Longs in 32-bit mode, you might translate this to Basic as follows:

```
Function SendMessage(ByVal hWnd, ByVal uMsg, _
                ByVal wParam, ByVal lParam As Long) As Long
```

The *hWnd* parameter is the window to which the message is sent. The *uMsg* parameter is the message number—which is usually a constant such as LB_FINDSTRING or WM_COPY. The *wParam* and *lParam* parameters differ for each message, as does the return value; you must look up the specific message to see what they mean. Often, *wParam* or the return value is ignored.

The *lParam* parameter is particularly interesting. It is a Long, which happens to be the size of a pointer, and this value is often used to pass a pointer to a string or a UDT. In other words, *lParam* is typeless. In Basic, that means that the SendMessage declaration contains the As Any type. Alternatively, you can define several aliased type-safe declarations.

You need two SendMessage Declare statements to cover all your bases:

```
Declare Function SendMessage Lib "User" ( _
    ByVal hWnd As Integer, ByVal wMsg As Integer, _
    ByVal wParam As Integer, ByVal lParam As Any) As Long
Declare Function SendMessageByRef Lib "User" Alias "SendMessage" ( _
    ByVal hWnd As Integer, ByVal wMsg As Integer, _
    ByVal wParam As Long, lParam As Any) As Long
```

The first covers passing Strings and Longs by value. The second covers passing UDTs and anything else by reference. These two Declare statements reside in WINTOOL.BAS. The Windows API type library has additional aliased versions such as SendMessageAsString and SendMessageAsLong.

For example, assume that you have a multiline text control named txtEditor. You can request the selection offset and length with these lines:

```
iPos = txtEditor.SelStart
iLen = txtEditor.SelLength
```

In order to get this information, Basic sends the EM_GETSEL message to the txtEditor window procedure with a call such as the following:

```
iResult = SendMessage(txtEditor.hWnd, EM_GETSEL, 0, 0&)
```

If the window procedure for TextBox controls were written in Basic, it would handle this message in a Select Case block:

```
Case EM_GETSEL
    ' Pack Integer offsets of start and end into Long
    WindowProc = MakeDWord(iStartSel, iEndSel)
```

Basic takes the start of the selection out of the low word and returns it as SelStart. It takes the end of the selection out of the high word and subtracts the start to get the SelLength value. The internal code looks something like this:

```
SelStart = LoWord(iResult)
SelLength = HiWord(iResult) - SelStart
```

If you have time to burn, you can do this yourself by calling SendMessage instead of using the SelStart and SelLength properties. What if you want to undo the last editing change? Simple—just call the Undo method. Unfortunately, the TextBox control doesn't have an Undo method. But you've seen it in Notepad; Windows must have an Undo message. Sure enough, if you check the Windows API documentation, you'll find an EM_UNDO message. You can undo the last editing change with this simple statement:

```
Call SendMessage(txtEditor.hWnd, EM_UNDO, 0, 0&)
```

If you have an Undo menu item, you can check to see whether there is anything to undo with this statement:

```
mnuUndo.Enabled = SendMessage(txtEditor.hWnd, EM_CANUNDO, 0, 0&)
```

You can get the number of lines of text, the current line, or the current column. You can set the indent spacing for tab characters or do a lot of other editing tasks that Basic doesn't support directly. We'll try many of these editing operations with Edward the editor, introduced in Chapter 8.

The same principle holds for other controls such as list boxes and combo boxes: Basic supports the most common operations through methods, events, and properties; you must handle others with SendMessage.

Looking up list box items

One of the more annoying limitations of the Visual Basic ListBox control (and related controls such as FileListBox and Outline) is that you can't look up an item by name. Instead, you have to use the index. Often, however, you don't know the index.

If a list box were a collection (as it should be), you could look up any existing item by name or index through its default Item property:

```
sItem = nlstItems(5)
sItem = nlstItems("Thing")
```

But you can't. You must use the index, and you must do so specifically through a List property rather than using a default Item property:

```
sItem = lstItems.List(5)
```

This limitation is even more annoying if you study the Windows API documentation and learn that the Windows message LB_FINDSTRING finds an item by name. It takes only one line of code to send this message and only three lines to put the whole thing in a neat little wrapper:

```
Function LookupItem(ctl As Control, sItem As String) As Long
    LookupItem = SendMessageAsStr(ctl.hWnd, LB_FINDSTRING, -1, sItem)
End Function
```

The key to this code is the LB_FINDSTRING message constant. The Windows API documentation tells you that the *wParam* value contains either the index of the item where the search should start or −1 to search the entire list. The *lParam* value contains a pointer to the case-insensitive string being sought. You can pass a partial string so that *"BIG"* will find *"BigDeal"* or *"Big Brother"*, whichever comes first. The return value is the index of the found item (or −1 if none is found). Windows also provides an LB_FINDSTRINGEXACT for looking up the full case-sensitive string.

Notice that my LookupItem function uses a Control parameter instead of the more type-safe ListBox parameter. This allows you to use LookupItem on any ListBox-like control; it works, for instance, on the Outline control. Just be sure not to pass a control whose underlying Windows control doesn't support this message. To be safe, this function should use error trapping to trap message failure, but I compromised. Perhaps you shouldn't.

Before I learned about the LB_FINDSTRING message, I looked up items with a linear search. That's still the way you have to look up items in the ItemData array. Basic implements its ItemData feature using the LB_GETITEMDATA and LB_SETITEMDATA messages, but it doesn't provide an LB_FINDITEMDATA message. You have to do it the hard way:

```
Function LookupItemData(ctl As Control, h) As Integer
    BugAssert h <> hNull
    Dim i As Integer
    LookupItemData = -1
    For i = 0 To ctl.ListCount - 1
        If h = ctl.ItemData(i) Then
            LookupItemData = i
            Exit Function
        End If
    Next
End Function
```

Disabling display during updates

Programs such as WinWatch that update many list items at one time need some way to quiet down the display so that the list box isn't redrawn every time an item is added. I know of three ways to do this:

- Set *Visible = False* while adding items, and then restore *Visible = True* when the additions are complete.

- Call the LockWindowUpdate API function when adding items, and turn off the lock when finished.

- Send the WM_SETREDRAW message with the parameter False when adding items; when you've finished, send it again with True.

You can experiment with these three solutions by setting different compile-time constants in the RefreshAllLists sub and observing the difference. If you're willing to take my word for it, here is the code for the winning entry:

```
Sub SetRedraw(ctl As Control, f As Boolean)
    Call SendMessageAsLong(ctl.hWnd, WM_SETREDRAW, f, 0&)
End Sub
```

Look up the WM_SETREDRAW message in the Windows API documentation to see how this works.

Receiving Messages

Visual Basic controls and forms constantly receive messages and translate them into events or set attributes according to instructions in the messages. For example, let's say that you used the Menu Editor to define a File menu named mnuFile with items mnuNew, mnuOpen, and so on. When the user of your application chooses Open, the mnuOpen_Click event occurs, and the code in the mnuOpen_Click event procedure executes.

But what really happens behind the scenes? Windows gets a signal from the mouse port that a click has occurred at a certain screen location (or possibly it discovers that the Alt, F, and O keys have been pressed consecutively). Windows checks its internal information to find out which window owns that location and discovers that the click occurred on the Open item of the File menu. It then sends a slew of messages related to this event, culminating in a WM_COMMAND message with the ID number of the Open item. Meanwhile, the window procedure for the form containing the menu has a Select Case block similar to the one shown on the following page.

```
Select Case iMessage
Case WM_COMMAND
    Select Case wParam
    Case IDM_NEW
        mnuNew_Click
    Case IDM_OPEN
        mnuOpen_Click
    ⋮
    End Select
⋮
End Select
```

This code intercepts the WM_COMMAND message, and the mnuOpen_Click event starts executing. In short, Windows sends messages; Basic turns them into events.

Now consider the system menu. By default, Basic puts the standard system menu on all forms whose ControlBox property is set to True. When a user chooses from a system menu, Windows sends the WM_SYSCOMMAND message to the window (form). The window procedure for a form works this way:

```
' Set default return value
WindowProc = 0&
' Handle messages
Select Case iMessage
Case WM_DOHOPEVENT
    Form.HopEvent_Click
Case WM_GETJUMPDATA
    Form.JumpData = wParam
Case Else
    ' Let default window procedure handle the rest
    WindowProc = DefWindowProc(hWnd, iMessage, wParam, lParam)
End Select
```

Because the WM_SYSCOMMAND message isn't handled by a specific Case statement, it falls through to the Case Else statement to be handled by DefWindowProc. The default window procedure knows how to do the standard operations—move, size, minimize, maximize, close, and switch to—which are the same for any window.

But what if you add an About item to the system menu? Visual Basic won't help you do this, but neither will it stand in your way. It's a simple matter to add an item to the system menu using Windows API calls:

```
Const IDM_ABOUT = 1010

Private Sub Form_Load()
    Dim hSysMenu ' As SysInt
    ' Get handle of system menu
    hSysMenu = GetSystemMenu(Me.hWnd, 0&)
    ' Append separator and menu item with ID IDM_ABOUT
    Call AppendMenu(hSysMenu, MF_SEPARATOR, 0&, 0&)
    Call AppendMenu(hSysMenu, MF_STRING, IDM_ABOUT, "About...")
```

When the user selects this new menu item, Windows sends a WM_SYS-COMMAND message with the IDM_ABOUT value to the window procedure. Having no clue what to do with this message, the window procedure passes it off to DefWindowProc, which also hasn't a clue. Your message rides off into the sunset.

The Message Blaster control

Somehow, you have to get that Windows message translated into a Basic event, where you can handle it, but Basic isn't going to help you. You'll need a message capture utility such as Ed Staffin's Message Blaster, Matt Curland's callback server, or SpyWorks-VB from Desaware. Both Message Blaster and the callback server are provided on this book's companion CD, and I'll talk about them in some detail.

Ed Staffin wrote Message Blaster as a VBX control for previous versions of Visual Basic. He distributed it as shareware, and the control became widely used in the Visual Basic community. Unfortunately, Ed says that a lot of people who used the previous version never paid up. So let me start this discussion with a warning: if you take advantage of the shareware control without paying WareWithAll, Inc., the Egyptian God of the Golden Dune Beetle has a special curse in store for your code. (Yes, I paid.) If common decency and superstition aren't enough incentive to do the right thing, Ed and his partner, Oscar Pearce, have built some time limits into the shareware version of the control.

The new Message Blaster is available only for 32-bit, but you can use the old 16-bit VBX for 16-bit Visual Basic 4. But you can't use both together in the same project. It's easy enough to write conditional code to handle the minor differences between the two versions. The problem is that 32-bit Visual Basic can't handle VBXs; it automatically converts them to picture boxes. Furthermore, 16-bit Visual Basic can't handle 32-bit projects containing OLE controls with no matching 16-bit OLE controls. Again, you get a picture box when you load the wrong version. If you really must have portable code, you might consider a different message capture utility. For now, let's look at how the 32-bit Message Blaster control handles the system menu problem.

To recognize when the user selects your About item on the system menu, you need to capture the WM_SYSCOMMAND message. First put a Message Blaster control (*bstMenu*) on your form and set the message you want to capture. In the real control, you can set the message at design time using the custom property page. I set the messages with run-time code so that you can see how it works. You can check out the code in the TBLAST32.VBP project. Here's how to tell Message Blaster which window and which message to monitor:

```
bstMenu.hWndTarget = Me.hWnd
bstMenu.AddMessage WM_SYSCOMMAND, POSTPROCESS
```

The second parameter of the AddMessage method determines whether Message Blaster generates a WM_SYSCOMMAND event before, after, or instead of sending the normal WM_SYSCOMMAND message.

Message Blaster will automatically create an event procedure in your form. Double-click the Message Blaster control on the form, and type the code to trap your message. The code to trap the selection of the About menu item looks like this:

```
Private Sub bstMenu_Message(ByVal hWnd As Long, ByVal Msg As Long, _
                      wParam As Long, lParam As Long, _
                      nPassage As Integer, _
                      lReturnValue As Long)
    Select Case Msg
    Case WM_SYSCOMMAND
        Select Case wParam
        Case IDM_ABOUT
            MsgBox "Message Blaster Test"
            lReturnValue = 0
        End Select
    End Select
End Sub
```

The Select Case statements are overkill here, since this blaster is trapping only one message (WM_SYSCOMMAND) and one menu item (IDM_ABOUT), but everything is set to add more messages or more menu items.

Trapping messages resembles sending them with SendMessage, except that it works in reverse. Each message uses the *wParam*, *lParam*, and *lReturn* parameters differently. If you look up Windows API help for WM_SYSCOMMAND, you'll see that it handles several kinds of messages in addition to system menu messages. You could trap resizing, moving, maximizing, minimizing, and various other system events by testing for the appropriate *wParam* constants. The tricky part of dealing with messages is handling the *lParam* parameter, which can be stuffed with whatever kind of data a particular message requires. Some messages return data, others return a pointer to data, and others don't return anything. System menus are easy, but for other messages you might need all the skills you learned in Chapter 2 to handle pointers or other data returned in *lParam*.

The TBLAST16.VBP project does exactly the same thing, but the code is slightly different because a few names and arguments of properties, methods, and events differ in the Message Blaster VBX.

So how does Message Blaster work? We'll take the high-level conceptual view without worrying about the details. Message Blaster (like other message capture utilities) subclasses the window that the hWndTarget property specifies. *Subclassing* a window means replacing its window procedure with your window procedure. You save the old window procedure and call it to do normal window processing after (or before) your new window procedure does its own extra operations.

Message Blaster does this behind the scenes. When you set hWndTarget to the handle of the form, Message Blaster saves the address of the form's window procedure and replaces this old procedure with its own window procedure. If the new window procedure were written in Basic, it might look something like this:

```
Function WndProc(ByVal hWnd As Long, ByVal Msg As Long, _
                 ByVal wParam As Long, ByVal lParam As Long) As Long
    Dim iRet As Long
    If hWnd = bstMenu.hWndTarget And Msg = bstMenu.Msg Then
        Select Case bstMenu.nPassage
        Case PREPROCESS
            iRet = bstMenu.OldWindowProc(hWnd, iMsg, wParam, lParam)
            bstMenu.bstMenu_Message hWnd, iMsg, wParam, lParam, _
                                bstMenu.nPassage, iRet
        Case EATMESSAGE
            bstMenu.bstMenu_Message hWnd, iMsg, wParam, lParam, _
                                bstMenu.nPassage, iRet
        Case POSTPROCESS
            bstMenu.bstMenu_Message hWnd, iMsg, wParam, lParam, _
                                bstMenu.nPassage, iRet
            iRet = bstMenu.OldWindowProc(hWnd, iMsg, wParam, lParam)
        End If
    Else
        iRet = bstMenu.OldWindowProc(hWnd, iMsg, wParam, lParam)
    End If
    WndProc = iRet
End Function
```

The new code you write to handle the message is called by the new window procedure for your message, but the old window procedure still gets called for messages you don't handle or for messages you handle only in part (as specified by the passage parameter).

This conceptual picture of how Message Blaster works is quite close to the actual C code for the 16-bit VBX. It's not very close to the C++ code for the 32-bit OLE control, however, because 32-bit mode requires that you jump through a lot of multithreaded hoops to subclass windows that aren't in your process. I won't get into that here.

The callback server

OLE wizard Matt Curland wrote the callback server in his spare time while working as a Visual Basic tester. He has agreed to let me distribute it with my book—with the appropriate warnings and qualifications. (Incidentally, Matt is the source of many other graphics and OLE tricks in this book. Look for his book *Microsoft Guide to Object Programming with Visual Basic 4 and Microsoft Office for Windows 95*, cowritten with Joel Dehlin [Microsoft Press, 1996].)

A few warnings before we begin:

- Subclassing windows is dangerous. You're going behind Visual Basic's back. If you make a mistake, you will crash. Debugging is always difficult and risky. Placing a breakpoint in a message loop for an important window can be fatal. So don't put any bugs in your code.

- This server isn't likely to work with the next version of Visual Basic. Its break-mode feature uses undocumented techniques that will probably fail, and will perhaps be unnecessary in the next version.

- To OLE experts, the concept of the server is not that difficult. It simply takes advantage of the fact that a Visual Basic class is an OLE interface, with the first public property or method in the class located at the first address of the interface. (If that doesn't make sense to you, don't worry. Things will fall into place as we explore polymorphism in Chapter 9 and OLE servers in Chapter 10.)

- The callback server works at a lower level than any Visual Basic programming you've seen so far. You use it to do things up front that Message Blaster does behind the scenes. If you have trouble with the following description, don't feel alone. You don't need to understand the technique completely to use it; just copy the sample class and modify it for your own needs.

You've already heard me rant about Visual Basic's lack of support for procedure variables, function pointers, callbacks, or whatever you want to call them. Well, instead of just complaining, Matt wrote an OLE server to provide them. Subclassing is only one of the tasks you can do with Windows callbacks. For example, I used FindWindow and some ugly name-space hacks to implement the IterateWindows function earlier in this chapter. The callback server lets you use both the EnumWindows and the EnumChildWindows functions in the approved way. (The companion CD has a sample that illustrates this.) You can in theory iterate through fonts, GDI objects, clipboard formats, printer jobs, resources, and who knows what else. But for now, we're interested only in subclassing.

The callback server works by telling Windows how to call a callback function in a class that you provide. Normally, when you deal with the Windows API, you call Windows functions. When you deal with callbacks, Windows calls your functions. Visual Basic doesn't have a way to give Windows the address of your functions, so you must do this indirectly through an OLE server or a control. If you use a control such as Message Blaster, the control creates the event procedure, and you simply fill in the blanks. But OLE servers can't provide event procedures for you. Instead, you must provide the event procedures for them, and you must somehow tell the server how to call your function. You do this by wrapping the function in a class and passing a class object to the server.

Although a server is less convenient and requires more work on your part, it offers several advantages over OLE controls. It's more efficient (which probably won't matter much for handling system menus, though you might see a difference on other messages). The server is also more customizable. Since you don't have to put the callback server on a form, it's easier to use in modular, independent classes.

An OLE server must be registered before you can use it. The Visual Basic CD provides REGSVR.EXE and REGSVR32.EXE for 16-bit and 32-bit servers, respectively. The setup program for this book's companion CD gives you the option of registering the server, but you must register it yourself if you copy the server to another machine. You can build into your setup program the ability to register a server or a control so that the problem of registering servers with REGSVR applies only to you, not to your customers. After you register the server, you must also use the References dialog box to load the server into your project. Both steps are required. If you get OLE errors when you try to use the server, you probably loaded it in the References dialog box but failed to register it.

Let's look at the user code needed to subclass a form window. We'll make the form respond to an About item on its system menu, just as we did with Message

Blaster. The user code (in TCALLME.FRM) is actually simpler than the code in the Message Blaster example:

```
Private sysmenu As New CSysMenu

Private Sub Form_Load()
    Dim hSysMenu As Long, f As Boolean
    ' Get handle of system menu
    hSysMenu = GetSystemMenu(Me.hWnd, 0&)
    ' Append separator and menu item with ID IDM_ABOUT
    Call AppendMenu(hSysMenu, MF_SEPARATOR, 0&, 0&)
    Call AppendMenu(hSysMenu, MF_STRING, IDM_ABOUT, "About...")
    Show
    ' Create system menu object
    If sysmenu.Create(Me.hWnd) = False Then Unload Me
End Sub
```

First, you declare a module-level object of type CSysMenu. Then you add an item to the system menu. Finally, you create the system menu by passing it the handle of the form window. That's all. Obviously, most of the work is going on elsewhere—in the sysmenu object. (Incidentally, the public constant IDM-_ABOUT is defined in a separate Basic module, TCALLME.BAS, so that it can be accessed from either the form or the CSysMenu class.)

The CSysMenu object works a little like Message Blaster, but with one big difference: it's written in Basic. Let's look at the whole works:

```
Private procOld As Long
Private hWnd ' As SysInt
Private cb As CallBack

Function WindowProc(ByVal hWndA, ByVal iMsg, ByVal wParam, _
                    ByVal lParam As Long) As Long
    ' Handle messages
    Select Case iMsg
    Case WM_SYSCOMMAND
        ' Handle menu items
        Select Case wParam
        Case IDM_ABOUT
            MsgBox "Callback Server Test"
            WindowProc = 0
            Exit Function
        End Select
    End Select
    ' Let old window procedure handle other messages
    WindowProc = CallWindowProc(procOld, hWndA, iMsg, wParam, lParam)
End Function
```

```
Public Function Create(ByVal hWndA As Long) As Boolean
    ' Subclass window
    If IsWindowLocal(hWndA) Then
        Destroy
        procOld = SetWindowLong(hWndA, GWL_WNDPROC, cb.ProcAddress)
        ' Required to prevent crashes in break mode
        cb.DebugProc = procOld
        If procOld Then
            hWnd = hWndA
            Create = True
        End If
    End If
End Function

Public Sub Destroy()
    If procOld Then
        ' Unsubclass
        SetWindowLong hWnd, GWL_WNDPROC, procOld
        procOld = 0: hWnd = 0
    End If
End Sub

Private Sub Class_Initialize()
    Set cb = NewCallBack(CBType_WNDPROC, Me, True)
End Sub

Private Sub Class_Terminate()
    Destroy
End Sub
```

Let's start at the bottom with the Class_Initialize event, which is used to set up a Callback object. The CallBack class is defined by the callback server. You create an object of this type by calling the NewCallBack function, passing it the name of the callback type. The NewCallBack function looks like this (as you can see in the Object Browser):

```
Function NewCallBack(Type As VBCallBackType, [VBHandler As Variant], _
                [Contained As Variant]) As CallBack
```

You can see the other available callback types by checking the VBCallBack-Type class in the Object Browser. Use CBType_WNDPROC to subclass windows. This type tells the server what arguments to expect in the WindowProc function. The second parameter is the class containing the message procedure to be called. You can pass it the Me object if you're creating the callback object inside the class. The final argument indicates whether the callback object is being created inside the class. Normally, creating a callback inside the class is a good idea, but be sure to pass False (the default) if you have some reason to create the callback outside the class.

The Create and Destroy methods do the actual subclassing. You subclass a window by calling the SetWindowLong API function (with GWL_WNDPROC) to insert the procedure address of your window procedure. SetWindowLong returns the address of the previous window procedure. Basic doesn't know how to get a procedure address or what to do with it once it has one, but the callback object gets the first address in the class object (which is always the procedure of the first public method or property) and then passes it back in the ProcAddress property. You unsubclass a window by restoring the previous window procedure with SetWindowLong.

The IsWindowLocal function called in the Create method checks to make sure that the handle being subclassed belongs to your program. The problem is that the address of a window procedure in another 32-bit program lives in a completely different address space. It was easy enough to execute foreign code in 16-bit code, but doing so in 32-bit code takes a lot more work than you see here. Message Blaster does that extra work, and so does SpyWorks-VB. You'll need to use one of those controls to subclass foreign windows. Here's the code for IsWindowLocal:

```
Private Function IsWindowLocal(ByVal hWnd As Long) As Boolean
#If Win32 Then
    Dim idWnd As Long
    Call GetWindowThreadProcessId(hWnd, idWnd)
    IsWindowLocal = (idWnd = GetCurrentProcessId())
#Else
    IsWindowLocal = True
#End If
End Function
```

Finally, the WindowProc method does the actual work of handling your messages. If the message coming through is yours, handle it and return. If it isn't yours, call the old window procedure with the CallWindowProc API function to handle other messages. In theory, you could take over all the messages and not bother to call the old window procedure, but you'd have to know an awful lot about the window you're subclassing. Generally, you subclass to enhance, rather than replace, existing message handling.

Look closely at the argument list and return type of the WindowProc function. This function must be the first public member in your class. That's how the callback server figures out the address. If you put another method or property first, Windows will call that other function. Public properties without property procedures are procedures under the surface, so you can't put them before the WindowProc function either (which means you can't have them). If you don't give exactly the size, number, and order of parameters shown, Windows will put the wrong amount of data on the stack, and the program will end up executing data instead of code. Notice that the first three arguments assume the SysInt pseudo-type (described in "Integer Parameters," page 53). This type should be Integer in 16-bit mode and Long in 32-bit mode.

Notice how the design of this class completely hides its operations from the client. In the Message Blaster example, the client knows what message is being trapped and how the message is handled. The callback server is more flexible. Many subclassing operations can be completely hidden within a class. You can add as many properties and methods as you need—as long as the window procedure method comes first. Clients don't need to know that your class subclasses. On the other hand, you could create the class object, then pass it to NewCallBack, and do the subclassing outside the class in client code. The only thing that must be in the class is the window procedure method.

> **NOTE**   If you're writing 16-bit programs under Windows NT, be sure that you run Visual Basic in a separate memory space. (Click the Run In Separate Memory Space check box in the Program Item Properties dialog box in Program Manager.) If your program crashes, you'll have a much better chance of killing it without having to reboot.

Other messages, other events

The same principle applies to lots of other messages. You can trap any event, whether Basic helps you or not. Here are some ideas.

- Intercept menu messages such as WM_MENUINIT and WM_MENU-SELECT so that you can display menu help on a status bar.

- Hit-test with WM_NCHITTEST so that you can display balloon help or perform other operations when the mouse passes certain areas.

- Intercept keyboard or menu events from Windows outside your program. You could implement macros this way.

- Intercept setting changes with WM_WININICHANGE, WM_FONT-CHANGE, or similar change messages.

- Check WM_ENTERIDLE to find a good time to do background processing.

- Use WM_GETMINMAXINFO to control the minimum and maximum sizes of a window.

Visual Basic already handles most important messages, but you can always find others to experiment with. I'll mention ideas for subclassing later in the book.

6

Painting Pictures

There's a Basic Way of painting pictures, and there's a Windows Way. The Basic Way is simple and limited. The Windows Way is complicated and powerful. The trick is to make the unlimited Windows Way look like the easy Basic Way. To do this, you have to understand both ways inside and out. And you have to understand a third way that, for lack of a better term, I call the Real Way of painting pictures.

In real life, people create pictures by daubing paint onto canvas, pushing pencil across paper, scraping chalk on blackboard, scribbling crayons in colorbooks, molding clay into shapes, even gluing other pictures onto cardboard. Computers can't do any of that. The computer world offers only one way to get a picture onto the screen, and that is pixel by pixel.

Georges Seurat constructed his pictures from tiny bits of paint, but you can be sure that even he wouldn't have tried to paint *Bathers* on a computer screen pixel by pixel. Nevertheless, that's how it would have come out on his screen.

Programming graphics is the art of modeling the different ways of creating real pictures so that they come out on the screen or from the printer in the form of pixels. (Don't confuse the issue with exceptions such as plotters.) This chapter discusses both the Windows Way and the Basic Way of drawing and painting pixels and how to mix the two approaches.

Windows to Basic and Back Again

Whether you program graphics with Visual Basic or with some other language, and whether you use the Windows Way or the Basic Way, you'll work in one of two very different modes. The difference is between drawing with a crayon or a pencil and pasting pictures from a magazine. If you're like most of us, you can get nicer results by pasting somebody else's pictures than by creating your own. And you can do it faster.

Creating vector graphics involves drawing dots, lines, rectangles, ellipses, and other geometric shapes. I call this model *drawing*. Basic was good at drawing long before Visual Basic arrived. The Basic Line and Circle statements (now methods) were more flexible than similar routines in many other languages. Technically, you can take drawing as far as you want—even into three dimensions with shading, if your math is better than mine. But some practical limits will affect how much drawing you'll want to do under Windows, and more limits will affect how much you'll want to do with Basic.

Creating raster graphics involves plunking predefined arrays of pixels onto the screen. I call this model *painting*. Ancient Basics gave a passing nod to the concept with the Get and Put graphics statements, but they got lost in the transition to Visual Basic. Visual Basic painting has always been done with the Picture property. Although painting is central to graphics under Windows, support for it through the Picture property was surprisingly weak in previous versions of Visual Basic. The new PaintPicture method goes a long way toward fixing this limitation, although you might still have to back out to Windows to perform some operations.

Here's the quick tour of Windows drawing and painting features, along with the corresponding Visual Basic features.

Device Contexts and Canvas Objects

In Windows, the surface on which you draw is called a *device context*. You access it through a handle called an *HDC*. A device context handle is to graphics what a window handle is to controls and windows.

Once you have the handle to a device context, you can use API calls to put dots, lines, circles, rectangles, text, and existing pictures of various kinds on it. The device context translates your device-independent instructions about what to draw or paint into device-specific instructions for a particular output device. Almost every function in the Graphics Device Interface (GDI) either has an HDC argument or returns an HDC. You simply can't do much graphics work without one.

No official name exists for the corresponding concept in Visual Basic, but some people at Microsoft who ought to know refer to objects that have graphics capabilities as *canvas objects*. I'll use that term to describe the various graphics objects. The Form, PictureBox, and Printer objects are the three standard canvas objects; Screen, Image, Shape, and Line objects also have canvaslike properties and methods.

I like to think of the CCanvas class as forming the top of an inheritance hierarchy such as the one shown in Figure 6-1. My theory is that Visual Basic objects are implemented internally using inheritance and that in a future version, when someone figures out appropriate Basic syntax, we'll get access to the hierarchy.

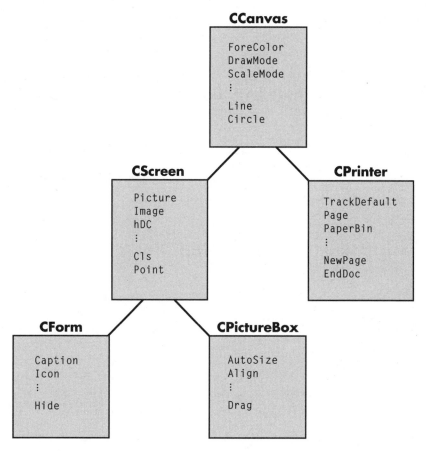

```
                        CCanvas

                      ForeColor
                      DrawMode
                      ScaleMode
                         ⋮
                      Line
                      Circle


        CScreen                        CPrinter

      Picture                        TrackDefault
      Image                          Page
      hDC                            PaperBin
         ⋮                              ⋮
      Cls                            NewPage
      Point                          EndDoc


  CForm              CPictureBox

  Caption            AutoSize
  Icon               Align
     ⋮                  ⋮
  Hide               Drag
```

Figure 6-1. *The CCanvas class hierarchy.*

I have no inside information on this (and would deny it if I did), but thinking hierarchy gives me a useful model of what's going on.

In my theory, the CCanvas class is what C++ programmers would call a virtual base class. It has all the generic properties and methods common to canvas objects, but it isn't visible to users. It's just something to hang your inheritance on. The CPrinter class is inherited from CCanvas and has all its generic properties and methods: ForeColor, DrawMode, DrawStyle, ScaleWidth, ScaleHeight, Line, Circle, and so on. It adds its own printer-specific methods such as New-Page and EndDoc, which are implemented internally using API functions such as StartDoc, EndDoc, StartPage, and EndPage.

The CScreen class is also inherited from CCanvas and is likewise invisible to users. It adds screen-oriented properties and methods such as Picture, Image,

Cls, and Point. The CForm and CPictureBox classes are inherited from CScreen, and each one adds its own unique properties and methods—although most of these have nothing to do with graphics.

I tried to throw the Screen, Image, Shape, and Line classes into this inheritance hierarchy, but they just muddied my nice clean diagram. If you prefer facts to theories, Table 6-1 shows a matrix of some of the more common properties and methods shared by canvas objects.

	Picture-Box	Form	Printer	Image	Shape	Line	Screen
Properties							
hDC	X	X	X				
Picture	X	X		X			
Image	X	X					
MouseIcon, MousePointer	X	X		X			X
Font	X	X	X				
AutoRedraw	X	X					
BackColor	X	X			X		
ForeColor	X	X	X				
FillColor	X	X	X		X		
DrawMode	X	X	X		X	X	
DrawStyle, DrawWidth	X	X	X				
FillStyle	X	X	X		X		
CurrentX, CurrentY	X	X	X				
Width, Height	X	X	X	X	X		X
Left, Top	X	X		X	X		
Scale properties	X	X	X				
TwipsPerPixelX, TwipsPerPixelY			X				X
Methods							
Line, Circle, PSet	X	X	X				
Point	X	X					
Cls	X	X					
Print	X	X	X				
TextWidth, TextHeight	X	X	X				
ScaleX, ScaleY	X	X	X				

Table 6-1. *Properties and methods of canvas objects.*

DC attributes, canvas properties

Every device context has attributes such as color, font, pen, and palette. The
GDI DLL provides access functions for reading and modifying these attributes.
In Visual Basic, canvas objects have properties. Table 6-2 shows how to work
with these attributes via device contexts in Windows and canvas objects in Basic.

Attribute	Windows Way	Basic Way
Background color	GetBkColor and SetBkColor	BackColor
Background mode	GetBkMode and SetBkMode	FontTransparent
Text color	GetTextColor and SetTextColor	ForeColor
Color palette	CreatePalette, SelectPalette, and other palette functions	Picture property with Palette bitmap (such as RAINBOW.DIB)
Brush	Brush creation functions and SelectObject	FillColor and FillStyle (but no way to use bitmap brush)
Pen	Pen creation functions and SelectObject	DrawStyle and DrawWidth
Pen color	Pen definition set by Pen creation functions	Color parameter of Line and Circle methods
Pen position	GetCurrentPosition, LineTo, and MoveTo functions	Line method with Step, CurrentX, CurrentY
Drawing mode	SetROP2	DrawMode
Font	Font creation functions and SelectObject	Font object
Mouse pointer	SelectObject, CreateCursor, and other cursor functions	MousePointer and MouseIcon
Clip and redraw state	Various functions related to repainting, managing regions, and clipping	ClipControls, AutoRedraw, and AutoSize
Scale	SetMapMode	ScaleMode
Window extent and origin	WindowExt and WindowOrg	ScaleLeft, ScaleTop, ScaleWidth, and ScaleHeight
Screen capabilities	GetDeviceCaps	Screen object

Table 6-2. *Graphics properties in Windows and in Basic.*

For the most part, you can stick with the Basic Way for reading and modifying
attributes. Canvas properties don't always match up one to one, but they're
usually more convenient. Basic formerly provided little flexibility for setting the
mouse pointer, but the new MouseIcon property makes custom cursors easy to
implement. In fact, about the only thing I've found that you can't do with Basic

is use a brush (FillStyle) that consists of a bitmap. (After reading "The Windows Way of Painting," page 275, you should be able to figure that out for yourself.)

DC functions, canvas methods

The Windows Way of performing graphics operations is to provide every sort of function you could imagine for every operation, no matter how obscure. The Basic Way is to provide the most important graphics operations through a few methods loaded with optional arguments. The Line method, for example, wraps up the functionality of several API functions. Table 6-3 compares device context functions in Windows with canvas methods in Basic.

Operation	Windows Way	Basic Way
Point drawing	SetPixel	PSet
Point reading	GetPixel	Point
Line drawing	LineTo and MoveTo	Line method or Line control
Circle, pie, and arc drawing	Ellipse, Chord, Arc, and Pie	Circle method or Shape control
Polygon drawing	Polygon, PolyPolygon, and SetPolyFillMode	No way
Blitting	BitBlt, StretchBlt, and PatBlt	PaintPicture method, Image control with Stretch property
Filling shapes	FloodFill and other Fill functions	Basic can create filled shapes but has no way of filling shapes later
Icon painting	LoadIcon, CreateIcon, DestroyIcon, and DrawIcon	Picture object on Image, PictureBox, or Form
Bitmap painting	Various Bitmap functions and SelectObject	Picture object on Image, PictureBox, or Form
Metafile recording	CreateMetaFile and CloseMetaFile	No way
Metafile playing	CopyMetaFile, GetMetafile, and DeleteMetaFile functions	Picture object on Form, Image, or PictureBox
Scrolling	ScrollDC	No way
Managing regions	Various Rgn functions	No way
Printing	Escape and Doc functions	Methods on Print objects
Text output	Many functions including TextOut, ExtTextOut, and GrayString	Print
Text sizing	GetTextExtent	TextWidth and TextHeight
Text alignment	SetTextAlign, SetText-Justification, and SetText-CharacterExtra functions	No way

Table 6-3. *Graphics methods in Windows and in Basic.*

To the hardcore programmer, what Basic doesn't do is more telling than what it does. Some points of interest:

- Visual Basic provides no way to fill a shape. QuickBasic had the Paint statement, but it didn't survive the transition to Visual Basic. You don't usually need to fill shapes as a separate step because you can specify filling when you draw the shape. Nevertheless, "The Windows Way of Drawing," page 267, provides a function for those rare occasions when you need to fill after the fact.

- Another hole in Visual Basic is drawing polygons. You can use the Line method to draw polygons one side at a time, but you might find the Windows Way more convenient.

- Regions are a somewhat obscure part of Windows that you might occasionally need. Basic doesn't do them, and this book doesn't either. But you should be able to apply the general principles described in this chapter to the problem. If you're programming in 32-bit mode, paths make regions easier. (See "Paths," page 582.)

Borrowing Device Context Handles

Basic hides the messy details of maintaining the HDC, but it provides the hDC property with forms, picture boxes, and printer objects for those intrepid souls who like messy details. The hDC property is the bridge between the Windows Way and the Basic Way. You can pass it to any Windows function that takes an HDC parameter.

But you needn't limit yourself to objects that have an hDC property. You can borrow the HDC of anything that has an HWND. *Borrow* is the key word. If a window has an hDC property, it's yours; use it however you want with no concern for what happens when you're done. But if you get the HDC from an HWND, you'd better give it back when you're finished.

The GetDC function grabs the device context of the client area. If you like to live on the edge, you can use the GetWindowDC function to grab the whole window—border, title bar, minimize and maximize buttons, control box, and all. I'm not going to tell you how to draw pictures of Larry, Curly, and Moe to replace the control box and the minimize and maximize buttons of your forms, but neither Windows nor Basic will try to stop you.

Whether you get the DC of the window or the DC of the client area only, you must return it with ReleaseDC when you're done. For example, here's how

WinWatch (from Chapter 5) saves the surface of the current window when you click the Dump button:

```
' Borrow window DC
hDCCur = GetWindowDC(hWndCur)
Call GetWindowRect(hWndCur, rect)
dx = rect.Right - rect.Left + 2: dy = rect.Bottom - rect.Top + 2
' Blit window DC to hidden picture box
With pbDump
    .Width = Screen.TwipsPerPixelX * dx
    .Height = Screen.TwipsPerPixelY * dy
    Call BitBlt(.hDC, 0, 0, dx, dy, hDCCur, 0, 0, vbSrcCopy)
    ' Copy from DC to Picture
    .Picture = .Image
End With
' Give DC back
Call ReleaseDC(hWndCur, hDCCur)
AppActivate hWndOld
' Save Picture property in file
⋮
```

We'll talk about other techniques in this code—BitBlt and assigning the Image property to the Picture property—later in this chapter.

Screen Capability

The Screen object provides some information about the current capabilities of the graphics screen, but it's pitifully short of what you might hope for. The GetDeviceCaps function can tell you anything you need to know about the screen or about any specific device context. This is one of those Swiss-army-knife functions that take 100 different constants as arguments and return a different value depending on which constant you passed.

For example, here's how to determine how many color planes and how many bits per pixel your video supports:

```
cPlanes = GetDeviceCaps(hdcImage, PLANES)
cBitsPerPixel = GetDeviceCaps(hdcImage, BITSPIXEL)
```

You need this information every time you create a bitmap, as you'll see later in this chapter. Although this seems like something the Screen object ought to provide, it doesn't—but the CVideo object does.

The CVideo class is implemented in VIDEO.CLS in the ALLABOUT.VBP project on the companion CD. It's a simple class that wraps the GetDeviceCaps function to tell you everything you ever dreamed of knowing about your video device. Here's enough code to show you how it works:

```
Private hdcScreen As Long

Private Sub Class_Initialize()
    hdcScreen = GetDC(hNull)
End Sub

Private Sub Class_Terminate()
    Call ReleaseDC(hNull, hdcScreen)
End Sub
```

(continued)

Metafiles 2, Visual Basic 1

Metafiles present several interesting problems to the Visual Basic programmer. It's easy enough to assign a metafile to the Picture property from a resource, a file, a clipboard, or a picture. You have to jump through some API hoops to send a metafile to the printer, however, because the printer doesn't have a Picture property. (This chapter doesn't cover that task specifically, but it will give some helpful background.)

Basic also won't help you create or record metafiles. Basic drawing methods such as Line and Circle draw to canvas objects, but they don't know anything about metafiles, and you don't have a way to redirect them to the HDC of a metafile.

What Basic needs is a CMetafile class, inherited from the CCanvas class. CMetafile objects would have all the properties and methods of a PictureBox plus a Play method to replay the metafile and a Save method to write it to disk. You could call the Clear method to wipe out any previous commands and then draw on the CMetafile object using your favorite drawing and painting methods.

In fact, you could design just such a CMetafile class. The API calls to create a metafile are easy enough. The problem is that you would need to reimplement the whole Visual Basic graphics library to give your CMetafile class the Line, Circle, and other methods it needs. Furthermore, you wouldn't be able to do so completely because the syntax of the Line, Circle, and PSet methods isn't a legal procedure syntax that you can emulate in your own methods.

Nevertheless, you could fake it—if you happen to have several months of spare time. It would be a lot easier for Basic to add this class than for you to do it. Maybe in the next version. In the meantime, it's simpler to create metafiles in a drawing program and then play them through the Picture property.

```
Private Function GetCaps(iCode As Long) As Long
    GetCaps = GetDeviceCaps(hdcScreen, iCode)
End Function

Property Get BitsPerPixel() As Long
    BitsPerPixel = GetCaps(BITSPIXEL)
End Property

Property Get ColorPlanes() As Long
    ColorPlanes = GetCaps(PLANES)
End Property
```

In the Test About program, a CVideo object provided the following information about my video card:

```
Technology: Raster Display
Screen size: 1024,768
Bits per pixel: 8  Color Planes: 1  Palette size: 256
Brushes: 2048  Pens: 100  Fonts: 0  Colors: 20
Aspect: X=36, Y=36, XY=51
Raster: BitBlt BigBitmaps FloodFill Palette StretchBlt
Curves: Circles PieChord Ellipses RoundRect
Lines: PolyLine Marker PolyMarker
Polygons: Polygon Rectangle WindPolygon ScanLine
Text: Underline StrikeOut Raster Vector
```

I've found this class to be overkill in most programs; it's usually easier to just call GetDeviceCaps. But once in a while CVideo is just what you need.

Two Ways of Drawing

Basic provides excellent support for vector graphics, but drawing lines, circles, and dots isn't necessarily the best way of doing graphics under Windows. Drawing is one area where Basic p-code can really drag you down. If you want complex images, you can usually get them faster by drawing the shape with a bitmap editor or a drawing program and plunking the result onto the screen.

This is particularly true when you get beyond two-dimensional shapes. If you really know your geometry, you can calculate three-dimensional coordinates and rotate them in space. For a shape of any complexity, the calculation takes seconds for wire-frame images. This might impress your engineer friends, but ordinary users will want shaded images instantly. If it can be done in cartoons and movies, why can't you do it in your program? Well, you can, but you might not be willing to wait.

Recently I looked at a book about animation in Visual Basic that could have been titled *Why You Shouldn't Do Animation in Visual Basic*. The book appeared to be a rather simplistic port of a similar book written for C or some other language. I loaded one of the sample programs and chose a menu item that promised shaded animation. Nothing happened. After a minute or so, I assumed that I had done something wrong and killed the program. After some fruitless experimenting, I finally took the solution of last resort and consulted the documentation. It said that this menu selection might take several hours, depending on your hardware. I thought the Pentium-equipped machine I use at work was pretty hot stuff—but not for this job.

Taking a brief look at the code, I could see why. It looped endlessly through floating-point calculations to create hundreds of bitmaps, which it would then cycle through for the animation. I assume that once all those bitmaps are created and loaded (if you have enough disk space, memory, and patience), cycling through them is reasonably fast. Of course, repainting your screen in the Resize event takes several hours.

The wire-frame versions of the same program took several seconds to calculate, and although it wasn't what you'd need for *Jurassic Park*, the animation seemed fast enough for a demo. I couldn't help thinking that the author would have better served readers by putting the C code in a DLL callable from Visual Basic rather than translating it into Basic. Just because you can do something doesn't mean it's a good idea.

My advice on vector graphics is to keep them short and simple. Remember that whatever you draw must be redrawn any time you resize the window, so think twice before making your graphics forms resizable. Setting the AutoRedraw property simply means that Windows will redraw instead of you.

The Visual Basic Way of Drawing

You probably know more about Basic drawing than I do. It's not that I'm ignorant (though I admit to being weak in math); rather, the simple vector graphics I recommend just aren't that difficult.

The fade trick I'm about to show you, however, is fun and isn't what you might expect. You've no doubt seen the fade from black to blue on the setup screens of many Microsoft products, including 16-bit Visual Basic. Looking at the output, I would have guessed that it was produced with some sort of palette manipulation. It's not.

The Fade procedure simply draws adjacent lines with increasing color intensity. It uses optional arguments to enable defaults. For example, a simple Fade command with no arguments draws a blue fade from top to bottom of the current form. You can draw the fade on any form or picture box. You can specify red, green, or blue fades or any combination of the three. You can specify a horizontal or vertical fade—or both for a diagonal fade. Here are some examples, using named arguments:

```
' Default black to blue vertical fade on current form
Fade Me
' Make it blue to black
Fade Me, vLightToDark:=False
' Red horizontal fade on FBlit
Fade FBlit, vRed:=True, vHoriz:=True
' Violet vertical fade on picture box
Fade pbTest(0), vRed:=True, vBlue:=True
' Black to white diagonal fade on current form
Fade Me, vHoriz:=True, vVert:=True, _
     vRed:=True, vGreen:=True, vBlue:=True
```

Fade draws the background of the Bit Blast program used later in this chapter (BITBLAST.VBP). You'll see it in various figures, starting with Figure 6-4 on page 278, but it's different each time because it is called with random values in the Form_Resize event:

```
Private Sub Form_Resize()
    Fade Me, vRed:=GetRandom(0, 1), vGreen:=GetRandom(0, 1), _
        vBlue:=GetRandom(0, 1), vHoriz:=GetRandom(0, 1), _
        vVert:=GetRandom(0, 1), vLightToDark:=GetRandom(0, 1)
End Sub
```

Hardcore Drawing

Help is coming for all you hardcore programmers who want to draw 3-D shapes in Visual Basic. The OpenGL library is already part of Windows NT. OpenGL supports three-dimensional drawing with shading, lighting, hidden surface removal, texturing, and who knows what else. I was afraid that if I started playing with it, I'd never finish this book, so you're on your own. I don't know whether you can use it effectively from Visual Basic or whether you'll need a control or a server that simplifies access.

OpenGL doesn't exist—and won't ever exist—for 16-bit Windows. One more reason to think 32 bits.

The Fade sub (with other effects in FUN.BAS) is long, but it takes only a few lines to do the real work. Most of the code saves and restores properties and handles defaults based on the optional arguments:

```
Sub Fade(obj As Object, Optional vRed As Variant, _
        Optional vGreen As Variant, Optional vBlue As Variant, _
        Optional vVert As Variant, Optional vHoriz As Variant, _
        Optional vLightToDark As Variant)
    ' Give all optional arguments default values
    If IsMissing(vRed) Then vRed = False
    If IsMissing(vBlue) Then vBlue = False
    If IsMissing(vGreen) Then vGreen = False
    If Not vRed And Not vGreen Then vBlue = True ' Color required
    If IsMissing(vVert) Then vVert = False
    If IsMissing(vHoriz) Then vHoriz = False: vVert = True
    If IsMissing(vLightToDark) Then vLightToDark = True


    ' Trap errors
    On Error Resume Next
    With obj
        ' Save properties
        Dim fAutoRedraw As Boolean, ordDrawStyle As Integer
        Dim ordDrawMode As Integer, iDrawWidth As Integer
        Dim ordScaleMode As Integer
        Dim rScaleWidth As Single, rScaleHeight As Single
        fAutoRedraw = .AutoRedraw: iDrawWidth = .DrawWidth
        ordDrawStyle = .DrawStyle: ordDrawMode = .DrawMode
        rScaleWidth = .ScaleWidth: rScaleHeight = .ScaleHeight
        ordScaleMode = .ScaleMode
        ' Err set if object lacks one of previous properties
        If Err Then Exit Sub
        ' If you get here, object is OK (Printer lacks AutoRedraw)
        On Error GoTo 0
        fAutoRedraw = .AutoRedraw

        ' Set properties required for fade
        .AutoRedraw = True
        .DrawWidth = 2    ' Required for dithering
        .DrawStyle = vbInsideSolid: .DrawMode = vbCopyPen
        .ScaleMode = vbPixels
        .ScaleWidth = 256 * 2: .ScaleHeight = 256 * 2
```

(continued)

```
Dim clr As Long, i As Integer, x As Integer, y As Integer
Dim iRed As Integer, iGreen As Integer, iBlue As Integer
For i = 0 To 255
    ' Set line color
    If vLightToDark Then
        If vRed Then iRed = 255 - i
        If vBlue Then iBlue = 255 - i
        If vGreen Then iGreen = 255 - i
    Else
        If vRed Then iRed = i
        If vBlue Then iBlue = i
        If vGreen Then iGreen = i
    End If
    clr = RGB(iRed, iGreen, iBlue)
    ' Draw each line of fade
    If vVert Then
        obj.Line (0, y)-(.ScaleWidth, y + 2), clr, BF
        y = y + 2
    End If
    If vHoriz Then
        obj.Line (x, 0)-(x + 2, .ScaleHeight), clr, BF
        x = x + 2
    End If
Next
' Put things back the way you found them
.AutoRedraw = fAutoRedraw: .DrawWidth = iDrawWidth
.DrawStyle = ordDrawStyle: .DrawMode = ordDrawMode
.ScaleMode = ordScaleMode
.ScaleWidth = rScaleWidth: .ScaleHeight = rScaleHeight
End With
End Sub
```

The property settings are crucial to making the fade work accurately and efficiently. For example, fading slows to a crawl if you don't set AutoRedraw. The Inside Solid draw style is the only one that works properly, and the Copy Pen draw mode ensures that you will overwrite anything on the background rather than interacting with it. Setting the scale properties makes it easier to draw in multiples of 256 (the number of color intensities) regardless of the size of the target. All these settings must be saved and restored in case someone else wants to draw on your fade with different settings.

Remember, you're drawing the fade only to the current size of the target object. If you allow the object to be resized, you'll need to put Fade in the Resize event. Since Fade is no speed demon, it might be better to make faded forms a fixed size, as the Bit Blast form is.

The Windows Way of Drawing

When you drop the Basic safety net and start drawing with the Windows API, you'll find yourself dealing with issues that didn't concern you before. Scaling becomes a problem. You must figure out what Basic properties mean to Windows, and vice versa. Despite the problems, here are two good reasons why you might want to do this:

- Some operations you might want to perform are not supported in Basic—drawing polygons, managing regions, and filling, for example.

- Some objects on which you might want to draw don't support Basic drawing methods—buttons, menus, list boxes, metafiles, and memory device contexts, for example.

The Fun 'n Games program (FUNNGAME.VBP) shows you how to draw the hard way. Figure 6-2 on the next page shows what might happen when you click the Stars button. The code uses the Polygon API function to draw many random stars and uses the FloodFill function to fill the centers with various colors. The differences between the Basic Way and the Windows Way are hidden by the VBPolygon and VBFloodFill functions.

Let's start with the Star procedure (in FUN.BAS):

```
Sub Star(ByVal x, ByVal y, ByVal dxyRadius, clrBorder As Long, _
        clrOut As Long, clrIn As Long, cvsDst As Object)
With cvsDst
    ' Start is 144 degrees (converted to radians)
    Const radStar As Double = 144 * PI / 180

    ' Calculate each point
    Dim ptPoly(1 To 5) As TPoint, i As Integer
    For i = 1 To 5
        ptPoly(i).x = x + (Cos(i * radStar) * dxyRadius)
        ptPoly(i).y = y + (Sin(i * radStar) * dxyRadius)
    Next

    ' Set colors and style for star
    .ForeColor = clrBorder      ' SetTextColor
    .FillColor = clrOut         ' CreateSolidBrush
    .FillStyle = vbSolid        ' More CreateSolidBrush
    Call VBPolygon(.hDC, ptPoly())

    ' Set color for center
    .FillColor = clrIn          ' CreateSolidBrush
    Call VBFloodFill(.hDC, x, y, .ForeColor)
End With
End Sub
```

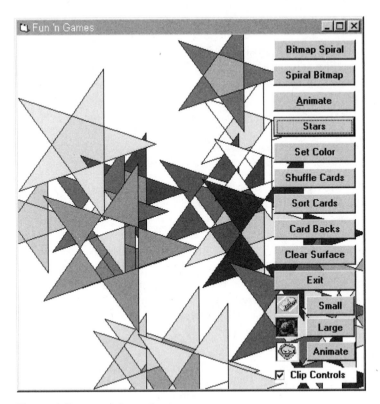

Figure 6-2. *Stars of Windows.*

Star starts with the classic loop for calculating the points of a polygon. You decide how many degrees you want between each point on the circle and then convert degrees to radians (degrees multiplied by *pi* divided by 180). You next loop through each point, using cosine to calculate the *x* points and sine to calculate the *y* points. (Get out your high school geometry book if you want to understand exactly how and why this works.) If you place the points close enough, you'll get a circle, although this isn't a very efficient circle algorithm. If you want a pentagon, use one-fifth of a circle, 72 degrees. If you want a star, use two-fifths of a circle, 144 degrees. You end up going around the circle twice (144 × 5 = 720) to return to the starting point.

As you calculate the points, you put them into an array and then pass the array to VBPolygon, a wrapper for the Polygon API function. (The Polygon function was used in Chapter 2, "Arrays," page 62, as an example of how the API functions expect arrays to be passed.) VBPolygon takes as its argument an array of points measured in twips, uses them to create a duplicate array measured in pixels, and finally passes the new array to the Polygon function by first element and count. It's messy, but not difficult:

```
Function VBPolygon(ByVal hDC, aPoint() As TPoint) As Boolean
    Dim apt() As TPoint, i, iMax, iMin ' As SysInt
    iMax = UBound(aPoint): iMin = LBound(aPoint)
    ' Create array of pixel-adjusted points
    ReDim apt(iMin To iMax) As TPoint
    For i = iMin To iMax
        apt(i).x = aPoint(i).x / Screen.TwipsPerPixelX
        apt(i).y = aPoint(i).y / Screen.TwipsPerPixelY
    Next
    ' Pass first element and count to Polygon
    VBPolygon = Polygon(hDC, apt(iMin), iMax - iMin + 1)
End Function
```

The TPoint type used by VBPolygon and Polygon contains Long x and y values in 32-bit mode and Integer values in 16-bit mode. But the code comes out looking the same in either mode.

VBFloodfill works much the same as VBPolygon does, except that it doesn't worry about array conversion. It simply converts its twips arguments to pixel arguments:

```
Function VBFloodFill(ByVal hDC, ByVal x, ByVal y, _
                     ByVal clr As Long) As Boolean
    VBFloodFill = FloodFill(hDC, x / Screen.TwipsPerPixelX, _
                            y / Screen.TwipsPerPixelY, clr)
End Function
```

FloodFill works by flooding everything around it until it encounters another color with the specified fill color. This allows some interesting effects in the Fun 'n Games program because you can layer different effects on top of each other. The outside of the star (filled by Polygon) is filled with the current FillColor (Brush, in Windows terminology) regardless of the background, but the center of the star (filled by FloodFill) interacts with its background.

Both VBPolygon and VBFloodFill assume that Basic is operating in twips mode and Windows in pixels mode (MM_TEXT). If you change the mode, either in Basic or in Windows, these functions will fail.

What's CPoint?

Polygon, like many GDI functions, uses what Windows calls a POINT structure (and I call a TPoint type). But as you learned in "Type Libraries," page 85, a type library can't define a function that takes a Basic UDT. As a result, I have to provide a Declare statement for Polygon (in GDITOOL.BAS) instead of using the Windows API type library. Because I really hate writing Declare statements, I spent quite a bit of time thinking and experimenting before I finally found a way to use type library definitions for functions that take POINT structures—or their more common cousins RECT structures (which I call TRect types). You can decide for yourself whether this trick is worth the trouble.

All POINT and RECT structures are passed by reference—as LPPOINT and LPRECT, in C SDK jargon. This means that you're passing the address of the first element in the structure. Here's the C definition of GetCurrentPositionEx, for example:

```
BOOL GetCurrentPositionEx(HDC hdc, LPPOINT lpPoint)
```

The Basic Declare statement looks like this:

```
Declare Function GetCurrentPositionEx Lib "GDI" ( _
    ByVal hdc As Long, lpPoint As TPoint) As Boolean
```

(I'm using 16-bit examples here, but the code found in WINGDI.BAS and WINTYPE.BAS also has 32-bit versions.)

Three Ways of Scaling

One of the most confusing issues in GDI programming is setting the scale. Just try to wade through SetMapMode, SetViewPortExt, SetViewPortOrg, and related functions in the Windows API documentation. Visual Basic settles all this nicely for you by doing all calculations in one mode: twips. A twip has an actual size, but it's easier to just think of it as a magical unit. As long as you measure everything with the same kind of units, it doesn't much matter how big the units are. After all, you usually measure controls by eyeballing them against the grid, not by using a ruler.

You can't always use the same kind of units, however. When working with bitmaps, you must usually work in pixel mode (MM_TEXT, in SDK jargon). Visual Basic might convert everything to twips, but when you get down to the API level, you play by API rules, which don't normally use twips. To stir the pot even more, Visual Basic version 4 has a lot of OLE elements. OLE likes to use a mode called HI_METRIC, which you can think of as another kind of magical unit. You use this mode when working with the height and width of picture objects.

A common scenario is that you must work with twips and pixels (and sometimes HI_METRIC units) at the same time. One way to handle mixed modes is to set the ScaleMode property to vbPixels, perform some operations, set the property back to vbTwips, carry out some more operations, and keep changing back and forth as needed. But Basic doesn't recognize HI_METRIC as a ScaleMode value. Besides, changing modes constantly is messy.

If you think about it, though, a TPoint looks a lot like a two-element array. In memory, this code

```
Dim aiCur(0 To 1) ' As SysInt
```

is the same as this code:

```
Type TPoint   ' 16-bit version
    x As Integer
    y As Integer
End Type
Dim ptCur As TPoint
```

What if you wrote the Declare statement this way?

```
Declare Function GetCurrentPositionEx Lib "GDI" ( _
    ByVal hdc As Long, lpPoint As Integer) As Boolean
```

You can also use the TwipsPerPixelX and TwipsPerPixelY properties of the Screen object as a means of converting between pixels and the default mode without changing the default. So you might see lines such as these:

```
dx = Width * Screen.TwipsPerPixelX
dy = Height * Screen.TwipsPerPixelY
```

If you wanted to convert to or from some mode other than pixels in previous versions of Visual Basic, you were out of luck. Version 4 adds a better way of converting between modes: the ScaleX and ScaleY methods, which allow you to convert to and from any mode. For example, the following lines are equivalent to the two preceding lines of code:

```
dx = ScaleX(Width, vbTwips, vbPixels)   ' From twips to pixels
dy = ScaleY(Height, vbTwips, vbPixels)
```

The second and third parameters of ScaleX and ScaleY are optional. The default conversion from HI_METRIC to the current mode betrays the origin of the ScaleX and ScaleY methods, which were intended to make it easy to convert Picture.Width and Picture.Height to twips. The Picture object comes directly from OLE, where HI_METRIC is standard; therefore, any property or any argument that expects a measurement in twips will require the standard conversion *ScaleX(Picture.Width)* or *ScaleY(Picture.Height)*, as shown here:

```
dx = ScaleX(Me.Picture.Width)   ' From HI_METRIC picture to twips
dy = ScaleY(Me.Picture.Height)
```

You pass the first element of the array as shown here:

```
f = GetCurrentPositionEx(hDC, aiCur(0))
```

Review "Arrays," page 62, if you don't remember how this works. The function puts the *x* coordinate in *aiCur(0)* and the *y* coordinate in *aiCur(1)*. In fact, this is how the Windows API type library defines GetCurrentPositionEx, although the type library definition looks somewhat different in WIN.ODL. But it's not defined that way to allow you to pass arrays.

Arrays aren't the only way to define two integers so that they appear next to each other in memory. Imagine a class CPoint that consists only of the following declarations:

```
Public X ' As SysInt
Public Y ' As SysInt
```

Basic documentation doesn't promise that these will appear next to each other in memory, but I figured that they would, and my guess seems to work. I can pass the first element (X) like this:

```
Dim pt As New CPoint
Call GetCurrentPositionEx(hdc, pt.X)
```

What I really want is to make X the default property of the CPoint class. Then I could do this:

```
Call GetCurrentPositionEx(hdc, pt)
```

Unfortunately, Visual Basic doesn't let you define a default property.

The CPoint class in POINT.CLS has a little more to it than just the X and Y members. It also has TwX and TwY properties that convert API pixels to Basic twips. And it has a Point member that you pass to functions that take CPoint arguments. For example:

```
Dim pt As New CPoint
Call GetCurrentPositionEx(hdc, pt.Point)
PSet (pt.TwX, pt.TwY), vbBlue
```

As a practical matter, the CPoint class isn't nearly as useful as the similar CRect class. I haven't found many API functions taking POINT parameters that add much to Basic. GetCurrentPositionEx, for example, is a complicated way to fake Basic's CurrentX and CurrentY properties. Other functions, such as Polygon, take arrays of POINT variables. If you can figure out how to write an NPoints collection class that can be passed to Polygon, let me know. The CRect class, on the other hand, comes in handy, with many useful graphics and window functions. We'll use it with the 32-bit DrawEdge function in Chapter 11.

Basic Windows Painting

You can paint, just as you can draw, the Windows Way, the Basic Way, or both ways at once. The Windows Way of painting is to create GDI objects—bitmaps, icons, and metafiles—and then select them into a device context. The Basic Way of painting is to load bitmaps, icons, and metafiles into a Picture property.

Essentially, you're dropping completed pictures onto a canvas. With previous versions of Visual Basic, it was difficult to go beyond that, and in fact many fine programs have been written without doing so. But we're going to the second level of painting—blitting—after getting acquainted with the Picture class and GDI objects.

Picture Objects

In earlier versions of Visual Basic, Picture was a property whose implementation was undefined to all but the most hardcore custom control writers. Today, Picture is also a class with methods and properties. You can declare Picture objects with Dim, Private, or Public; assign one Picture object to another with Set; and pass Picture objects as arguments. You can even create a Picture object with code, although Basic won't help you, as you'll see later in "Using Icon Resources," page 342. As far as Basic is concerned, you can get Picture objects only indirectly through the LoadPicture function, the LoadResPicture function, or the Load Picture dialog box.

You can use the Object Browser to see what the Picture class looks like. Select *StdType - Standard OLE Types* from the Libraries/Projects list, and then select *Picture* in the Classes/Modules list. You'll see the methods and properties of the class in the Methods/Properties list box, as shown in Figure 6-3 on the next page.

> **NOTE** If you get errors when declaring Picture variables or passing Picture parameters, check to be sure that the Standard OLE Types library hasn't been disabled in the References dialog box. Most of what I say here about Picture objects also applies to Font objects. This book doesn't talk specifically about fonts, but you can see a Font object example in the VBChooseFont common dialog function in COMDLG.BAS.

Picture methods and properties

You might have noticed that the Render method is selected in the Object Browser in Figure 6-3. You won't find Render in Basic documentation, but it is documented somewhere deep in the OLE Control Development Kit as part of the IPicture interface. We'll talk more about the relationship between OLE interfaces and Basic classes in Chapters 7, 10, and 11. For now, just look at the syntax line. If this doesn't look familiar now, it will be by the end of the chapter. The Basic PaintPicture method is just a Basic-friendly wrapper around Render.

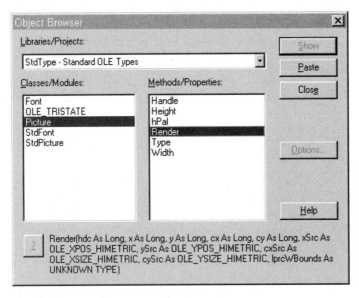

Figure 6-3. *Browsing the Picture object.*

You'll also see the Picture properties listed in the Object Browser—Handle, Height, hPal, Type, and Width—but you'll have to consult Help to see what they are, and even then you might not completely understand what's going on. Let's look at them individually.

The Height and Width properties of a picture are very different from the Height and Width properties of a form or a picture box. The latter properties have values in the current scale mode (which is twips by default), but the Height and Width properties of a picture always have values in the standard OLE mode, HI_METRIC. Use a statement such as *ScaleX(Picture.Width)*, which converts to twips. You can include additional arguments to convert to other modes.

The Type property always returns 0 for empty, 1 for bitmap, 2 for metafile, or 3 for icon. You can use the *vbPicTypeBitmap*, *vbPicTypeMetafile*, or *vbPicType-Icon* constants, but there is no *vbPicTypeNone*. You can also load a cursor into a picture; the Type property will show it as an icon.

The Handle and hPal properties are the link between the Basic Way of pictures and the Windows Way of GDI objects. The hPal property is the handle of the palette for bitmaps. (It's meaningless for icons or metafiles because these don't have palettes.) Unfortunately, palettes are beyond the range of this book, although I think that it must be possible for Basic programmers to manipulate palettes directly in order to get palette fades and other effects. Maybe you can prove it.

The Handle property is the handle of the bitmap, icon, or metafile within the picture. You can have lots of fun with these object handles, as you'll see later. The Handle property is the default member. When you assign a value to a Picture property, you're actually assigning it to the handle. For example, the code

```
imgCur.Picture = LoadPicture("Thing.Ico")
```

actually means the following:

```
imgCur.Picture.Handle = LoadPicture("Thing.Ico")
```

Loading picture objects

Basic provides several ways to load a picture object:

- Use LoadPicture to load from disk. Specifically, you can load a bitmap from a BMP or DIB file. You can load an icon from an ICO file or load a metafile from a WMF file. You can load a cursor from an ICO file or a CUR file.

- Use LoadPicture with no argument to clear a picture file.

- Assign one Picture property from another Picture property or from an Image property.

- Use LoadResPicture to load a picture from a resource file attached to your program. (See Chapter 7.)

- Get a GDI object handle from a Windows API function and assign it to the Picture property. There's more to this than meets the eye, however, as you'll see in Chapter 7.

The Windows Way of Painting

The Windows Way of painting is to beg, borrow, steal, or create a GDI object and then select that object into a device context. GDI objects, like most everything else in Windows, are identified by handle. These handle types include HBITMAP, HPEN, HBRUSH, HFONT, HPALETTE, and HRGN.

I've never found selecting objects into device contexts to be intuitive; I just do it by rote. Let's go through the process with a bitmap. If you can select a bitmap, you can select anything. First you need an HDC to write to, and then you need the handle of a bitmap. How can you get an HBITMAP? Let me count the ways:

■ You can create one with CreateBitmap or CreateCompatibleBitmap. We'll do both in a later section, "Turning a PictureBox Object into a CPictureGlass Object," page 294.

■ You can use the Handle property of a picture object containing a bitmap. Because the Handle is the default member of the picture object, and the picture object is the Picture property, you can think of the Picture property as being the handle. But if you already have a picture containing a bitmap, you probably don't need to select it into anything.

■ You can get a handle to a bitmap out of a bitmap resource. You can get it into a picture with LoadResPicture (but then you don't need it), or you can get it the hard way, as WinWatch does—by digging it out of an EXE file. See "Finding Resources," page 331.

OK. Assuming that you have an HDC and an HBITMAP, you also need a handle to retain the old bitmap. Even if you created an empty DC and didn't think you put a bitmap there, you'd better be prepared to get one out and put it back when you're done. Your code looks something like this:

```
Private hDC, hBitmap, hBitmapOld ' As SysInt
    ⋮
    hBitmapOld = SelectObject(hDC, hBitmap)
```

At this point, if everything goes right, your bitmap appears in the device context. Now you must clean up by selecting the old bitmap (or other object) back into the DC and then deleting your bitmap:

```
Call SelectObject(hDC, hBitmapOld)
Call DeleteObject(hBitmap)
```

I admit that I often ignore the return values. After all, what can you do if your cleanup fails? It's not supposed to. OK, OK; so I should have asserted:

```
f = SelectObject(hDC, hBitmapOld)
BugAssert f
f = DeleteObject(hBitmap)
BugAssert f
```

Is that good enough for you?

Since you don't always know when it's safe to destroy the object, you might find it easier to create a temporary DC, select the bitmap into it, copy your temporary DC to the target DC, and then destroy the temporary:

```
hDCTemp = CreateCompatibleDC(0&)
hBitmapOld = SelectObject(hDCTemp, hBitmap)
' Copy temporary to destination
Call BitBlt(hDCDst, 0, 0, dxDst, dyDst, hDCTemp, 0, 0, vbSrcCopy)
Call SelectObject(hDCTemp, hBitmapOld)
Call DeleteObject(hBitmap)
Call DeleteDC(hDCTemp)
```

Now you're rid of the bitmap and don't need to worry about selecting it out and deleting it later.

The same process applies to pens, brushes, and fonts, although you'll rarely need to use them in Basic. The process is similar for palettes, except that you use the specific SelectPalette function instead of the generic SelectObject.

| NOTE | Technically, HMETAFILE, HCURSOR, and HICON aren't considered GDI objects because you don't select them as you do the others. But they are in the GDI, they work somewhat like objects, and they are part of the Windows Way. Nevertheless, we'll ignore them here. I'll talk about icon and cursor handles in Chapter 7. Other than the sidebar "Metafiles 2, Visual Basic 1," on page 261, you're on your own with metafiles. |

A Word About Blitting

Blitting is such a key part of Windows graphics that it's hard to believe Visual Basic got through three major versions without offering any direct support for it. "Blit" is the common pronunciation for BitBlt, which is a contraction of the term *bit block transfer*. (Many books spell this term *blt*, but I couldn't bring myself to write a word with no vowels.) *Blitting* means combining the pixels of one bitmap with the pixels of another—or, at a lower level, combining the bits of one device context with the bits of another.

You can blit the old-fashioned way, using the Windows API BitBlt function (and its cousins StretchBlt and PatBlt). Or you can blit with the newfangled PaintPicture method. Each way has its strong points. The Bit Blast program (BITBLAST.VBP) shown in Figure 6-4 on the next page illustrates both approaches. The Use BitBlt check box determines which version is used. Both give equivalent results, but the code is quite different, as you'll see.

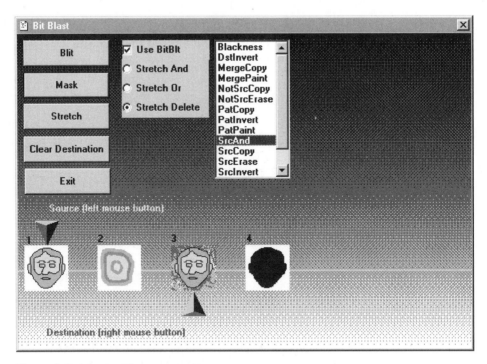

Figure 6-4. *The Bit Blast program.*

To use Bit Blast, select a source picture with the left mouse button and a destination with the right button. Select one of the blit modes in the list box on the right and hit the Blit button (or double-click the selection in the list box). You can get a variety of effects by combining different pictures with different modes.

BitBlt Versus PaintPicture

To blit, you need a source object to blit from and a destination object to blit to. You must specify the size of both objects as well as the blit mode. Figure 6-5 provides a conceptual view of the operation and examples of how each element fits into the syntax of PaintPicture, BitBlt, and StretchBlt.

Here's the Bit Blast code that combines one picture with another. A careful study of this code highlights the differences between the Windows Way and the Basic Way:

```
Private Sub cmdBlit_Click()
    Dim rop As Long
    rop = lstROP.ItemData(lstROP.ListIndex)
```

```
    If chkBitBlt.Value = vbChecked Then
        Call BitBlt(pbDst.hDC, 0, 0, dxBlt, dyBlt, _
                    pbSrc.hDC, 0, 0, rop)
        pbDst.Refresh
    Else
        pbSrc.Picture = pbSrc.Image
        pbDst.PaintPicture pbSrc.Picture, 0, 0, , , , , , , rop
    End If
End Sub
```

The BitBlt method works on the device context of source and destination objects. In Basic, you can blit to the hDC property of forms, picture boxes, and the printer. You can also borrow an HDC from any other window (such as the desktop) using the GetDC and ReleaseDC functions (see "Borrowing Device Context Handles," page 259), or you can create a memory device context, as you'll see later. But you can't use BitBlt on Image controls because they don't have an hDC or hWnd property.

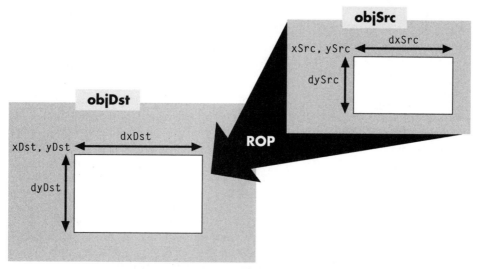

```
objDst.PaintPicture objSrc, xDst, yDst[, dxDst, dyDst, _
                     xSrc, ySrc, dxSrc, dySrc, ROP]
f = BitBlt(objDst.hDC, xDst, yDst, dxDst, dyDst, _
           objSrc.hDC, xSrc, ySrc, ROP)
                ' dxSrc and dySrc understood to be dxDst and dyDst
f = StretchBlt(objDst.hDC, xDst, yDst, dxDst, dyDst, _
               objSrc.hDC, xSrc, ySrc, dxSrc, dySrc, ROP)
```

Figure 6-5. *Three ways to blit.*

BitBlt, like all API functions, lacks optional arguments. You must provide the starting x and y coordinates (0, 0), the height and width of the blit (*dxBlt, dyBlt*), and the starting coordinates of the source (0, 0). Because the sizes of the source and the destination are always the same, you don't need to provide a source size (although you must do so with StretchBlt). For now, we'll skip the last BitBlt argument, which contains the raster operation (ROP) mode; we'll come back to it in "All About ROPS," page 287.

The *dxBlt* and *dyBlt* values are calculated elsewhere with this statement:

```
With pbTest(3)
    dxBlt = ScaleX(.Width, vbTwips, vbPixels)
    dyBlt = ScaleY(.Height, vbTwips, vbPixels)
```

Since all the images being blitted in Bit Blast are the same size, you can use the size of any one; *pbTest(3)* happens to be convenient. BitBlt and its relatives work in pixels by default, so if you're dealing with twips, you must convert. ScaleX and ScaleY usually work best, but the sidebar "Three Ways of Scaling," page 270, discusses other alternatives.

Basic knows nothing about BitBlt and has no idea that you've changed the DC by blitting to it. You must call the Refresh method to make your changes show up on the screen. Refresh is unnecessary when AutoRedraw is set to True on the destination.

If you're familiar with BitBlt (as many Visual Basic programmers are), Paint-Picture could take some getting used to. The argument order and the format are very different. The object to be painted is the destination, and the picture painted from is the first parameter. Notice that PaintPicture works on pictures, whereas BitBlt works on device context handles. That means that you can (and often should) use PaintPicture on Image controls.

The PaintPicture method combines the functionality of BitBlt and StretchBlt. (More on StretchBlt later.) In order to emulate both, PaintPicture needs a lot of arguments. Luckily, most PaintPicture arguments (although not enough to suit me) are optional. After the source picture, the arguments are the starting point of the destination, the size of the destination, the starting point of the source, the size of the source, and finally the ROP.

Since Bit Blast does a simple transfer between picture boxes of the same size, default values are OK for all the location and size arguments. You should be able to write this:

```
pbDst.PaintPicture pbSrc.Picture, , , , , , , , ROP
```

It doesn't work that way, however. PaintPicture requires the arguments for the destination starting point instead of defaulting to 0. So, instead, you need the following:

```
pbDst.PaintPicture pbSrc.Picture, 0, 0, , , , , , ROP
```

Maybe the designer was thinking of blitting from a picture box to a form. A value of 0 doesn't make sense in such a case, but it certainly does in my example and many others.

> **NOTE** The Windows API also provides a PatBlt function to blit a pattern onto a device context. Windows NT goes even further: it provides MaskBlt to create masks and PlgBlt to blit a rectangle onto a parallelogram. Unfortunately, these functions weren't implemented for Windows 95.

StretchBlt Versus PaintPicture

The code for the Stretch button in Bit Blast illuminates more of the differences between the Basic Way and the Windows Way. Figure 6-6 on the next page illustrates what happens when you stretch a bitmap.

The Stretch button performs two blits: one to stretch the image larger while turning it inside out, and one to compress it while turning it backward:

```
Private Sub cmdStretch_Click()
    If chkBitBlt.Value = vbChecked Then
        ' Stretch inside out
        Call StretchBlt(hDC, ScaleX(Width, vbTwips, vbPixels) * 0.97, _
                        ScaleY(Height, vbTwips, vbPixels) * 0.9,_
                        -dxBlt * 3.5, -dyBlt * 6.5, _
                        pbSrc.hDC, 0, 0, dxBlt, dyBlt, vbSrcCopy)
        ' Compress backward
        Call StretchBlt(hDC, ScaleX(Width, vbTwips, vbPixels) * 0.75, _
                        ScaleY(Height, vbTwips, vbPixels) * 0.8, _
                        -dxBlt * 0.9, dyBlt * 0.5, _
                        pbSrc.hDC, 0, 0, dxBlt, dyBlt, vbSrcCopy)
```

(continued)

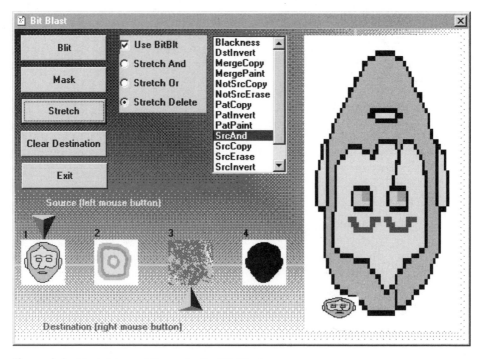

Figure 6-6. *Stretching a bitmap in the Bit Blast program.*

```
         Else
         With pbSrc
             .Picture = .Image
             ' Stretch inside out
             PaintPicture .Picture, Width * 0.97, Height * 0.9, _
                                -.Width * 3.5, -.Height * 6.5
             ' Compress backward
             PaintPicture .Picture, Width * 0.75, Height * 0.8, _
                                -.Width * 0.9, .Height * 0.5
         End With
     End If
End Sub
```

StretchBlt has the same arguments as BitBlt except that it adds arguments for the source size. The whole idea of stretching a bitmap is that the source size and the destination size should differ. Despite its name, StretchBlt can also compress. (Think of it as negative stretching.) You can also stretch pictures backward or inside out by changing the signs of the arguments.

Some differences are obvious. StretchBlt requires that you convert to pixels; PaintPicture uses the default mode (twips, in this case). But the subtle differences are more interesting.

Notice the line that assigns the Image property of the source to the Picture property:

```
With pbSrc
    .Picture = .Image
```

This line ensures that the picture being blitted contains a bitmap. For example, the fourth picture box in Bit Blast contains a blank bitmap with a circle drawn over it using the Circle method. The device context of the picture box contains both the circle and the blank bitmap, but its Picture property contains only the bitmap. If you blit with BitBlt, the entire device context is copied. With Paint-Picture, however, you copy only the picture with its blank bitmap. You would have a similar problem if the picture box's picture contained a metafile or an icon, since PaintPicture can't blit these elements with a ROP mode.

The solution is to copy the image to the picture. When you assign the Image property, Basic takes a snapshot of the device context with all its contents—pictures and drawings—and creates a bitmap, which it hands off as the Image property.

If you comment out the image-to-picture assignment, you'll see another difference in the marble pattern shown in the third box. The size of the picture used by PaintPicture is not the same as the HDC used by StretchBlt. The marble bitmap is much larger than the picture box, but it is clipped because AutoSize is False. PaintPicture stretches the entire picture, including the hidden part. StretchBlt stretches the clipped surface. Assigning the image gives the picture the same clipped snapshot you see on the screen.

When you compress a picture, StretchBlt has to merge many rows of pixels into fewer rows. The SetStretchBltMode function sets one of three modes for dealing with the extra lines. You can combine the extra lines with the remaining lines, using either an AND operation or an OR operation, or you can simply delete the extra lines. Using the SetStretchBltMode function on the destination surface has no effect on how PaintPicture compresses images, however. Visual Basic chooses a default mode (apparently the delete mode), and that's that.

The Bottom Line on PaintPicture

PaintPicture lacks the flexibility for the kinds of masking and blitting operations discussed in the rest of this chapter. It is tied to an unchangeable Picture object, whereas BitBlt and StretchBlt are tied to device contexts that you can change however you want. But you shouldn't throw PaintPicture out of your toolbox. It's certainly the easiest and fastest way to draw a thousand copies of a picture or to draw a picture in a thousand pieces. In other words, you can use it to create great visual effects.

If you're going to be copying a picture around, it's best to use an Image control as the picture container because it has the lowest overhead. You can make it invisible if you don't want to show the source. Simply pass its Picture property to PaintPicture or to any of your procedures that take Picture parameters. For example, this procedure draws a spiral pattern of bitmaps, just as you might use PSet to draw a spiral pattern of dots (think of the pictures as big dots):

```
Sub BmpSpiral(picSrc As Picture, cvsDst As Object)
With cvsDst
    ' Calculate sizes
    Dim dxSrc, dySrc, dxDst, dyDst ' As SysInt
    dxSrc = .ScaleX(picSrc.Width): dySrc = .ScaleY(picSrc.Height)
    dxDst = .ScaleWidth: dyDst = .ScaleHeight
    ' Set defaults (play with these numbers for different effects)
    Dim xInc, yInc, xSize, ySize, x, y ' As SysInt
    xInc = CInt(dxSrc * 0.01): yInc = CInt(dySrc * 0.01)
    xSize = CInt(dxSrc * 0.1): ySize = CInt(dySrc * 0.1)
    Dim radCur As Single, degCur As Integer, angInc As Integer
    degCur = 0: angInc = 55
    ' Start in center
    x = (dxDst \ 2) - (dxSrc \ 2): y = (dyDst \ 2) - (dySrc \ 2)

    ' Spiral until off destination
    Do
        ' Draw at current position
        .PaintPicture picSrc, x, y, , , , , , vbSrcAnd
```

Stretching the Old-Fashioned Way

Although previous versions of Visual Basic didn't provide a built-in way to blit, they did have a built-in way to stretch. The Stretch property of the Image control provided the moral equivalent of StretchBlt with no ROP mode.

If all you want to do with a picture is stretch or compress it, it's hard to beat using the Image control with its Stretch property set to True. That's how the FOpenPicFile dialog box, discussed in "A Better Picture File Dialog Box," page 166, implements its picture. You can check it out in the UpdateFile procedure in OPENPIC.FRM on the companion CD.

So how do you think Visual Basic implements the Stretch and Autosize properties? Your guess is as good—and probably the same—as mine: StretchBlt.

```
' Calculate angle in radians
radCur = (degCur - 90) * (PI / 180)
' Calculate next x and y
x = x + (xSize * Cos(radCur))
y = y + (ySize * Sin(radCur))
' Widen spiral
xSize = xSize + xInc: ySize = ySize + yInc + 1
' Turn angle
degCur = (degCur + angInc) Mod 360
Loop While (x > 0) And (x + dxSrc < dxDst - dxSrc) And _
            (y > 0) And (y + dySrc < dyDst)
End With
End Sub
```

If you have an Image control with a bitmap picture, draw it on the current form with the statement *BmpSpiral imgSmallBmp.Picture, Me.*

Once you get the idea, it's not hard to devise ways to change the algorithm for inward spirals and other patterns. You can also experiment with different ROP codes for combining the images. Figure 6-7 shows one effect.

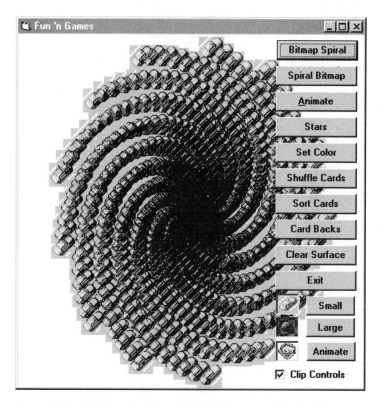

Figure 6-7. *Clicking the Bitmap Spiral button in Fun 'n Games.*

Another PaintPicture trick with many variations is to break a large bitmap into small squares and display the squares in some pattern. For example, you can randomize the position of the squares to form a puzzle and then put them back together. Another variation is to draw the squares in their correct places but create a pattern that makes the picture appear to explode, crush, or spiral onto the surface.

Here's a spiral bitmap effect. To try it, click the Spiral Bitmap button in the Fun 'n Games program. You can load your own digitized pictures or other large bitmaps. Then click the Large button or the picture box adjacent to it.

```
Sub SpiralBmp(picSrc As Picture, cvsDst As Object, _
          ByVal xOff, ByVal yOff)
With cvsDst
    Dim xLeft, xRight, yTop, yBottom ' As SysInt
    Dim dxSrc, dySrc, xSrc, ySrc ' As SysInt
    Dim xDst, yDst, xInc, yInc, x, y ' As SysInt
    ' Initialize
    dxSrc = .ScaleX(picSrc.Width): dySrc = .ScaleY(picSrc.Height)
    xInc = dxSrc / 20: yInc = dySrc / 20
    xLeft = 0: yTop = 0:
    xRight = dxSrc - xInc: yBottom = dySrc - yInc

    ' Draw each side
    Do While (xLeft <= xRight) And (yTop <= yBottom)
        ' Top
        For x = xLeft To xRight Step xInc
            .PaintPicture picSrc, x + xOff, y + yOff, xInc, yInc, _
                x, y, xInc, yInc, vbSrcCopy
        Next
        x = x - xInc: yTop = yTop + yInc
        ' Right
        For y = yTop To yBottom Step yInc
            .PaintPicture picSrc, x + xOff, y + yOff, xInc, yInc, _
                x, y, xInc, yInc, vbSrcCopy
        Next
        y = y - yInc: xRight = x - xInc
        ' Bottom
        For x = xRight To xLeft Step -xInc
            .PaintPicture picSrc, x + xOff, y + yOff, xInc, yInc, _
                x, y, xInc, yInc, vbSrcCopy
        Next
        x = x + xInc: yBottom = y - yInc
        ' Left
        For y = yBottom To yTop Step -yInc
```

```
        .PaintPicture picSrc, x + xOff, y + yOff, xInc, yInc, _
            x, y, xInc, yInc, vbSrcCopy
    Next
    y = y + yInc: xLeft = xLeft + xInc
  Loop
End With
End Sub
```

I can't show you this dynamic effect on the page because the movement is the point; you'll have to try it.

All About ROPs

I have postponed discussing what Basic documentation calls *opcodes* and the Windows API documentation calls *ROPs* (raster operations). I don't know the official pronunciation, but I like to think of them as "ropes," for no good reason. Whatever the name, ROPs are binary encodings that indicate how these three elements will be combined: the source picture, the destination background, and any pattern on the destination background.

Pictures are made up of pixels, and pixels are made up of bits. You combine bits with logical operators: AND, OR, XOR, NOT, and COPY. ROPs specify which logical operators will be used to combine (or not combine) the bits of the source, destination, and pattern. There are 15 named combinations, about 7 more than you'll ever need. This chapter uses only vbSrcCopy, vbSrcAnd, vbSrcPaint, vbNotSrcErase, vbDstInvert, vbSrcInvert, and vbMergePaint. You can see all of them as RasterOp constants in the Visual Basic Objects and Procedures library in the Object Browser.

ROP codes are actually hexadecimal numbers indicating 256 possible combinations of destination, source, and pattern with NOT, AND, OR, XOR, and COPY operators. Most have no practical use. For example, you probably won't need the combination that copies the destination onto itself. You can find the 256 combinations by looking up *Ternary Raster Operations* in the MSDN/VB starter kit on the Visual Basic CD. (Search for *raster*.) Incidentally, PaintPicture accepts all 256 combinations, not just the 15 named ones.

Blitting Images onto Backgrounds

The logical meaning of the various operations probably doesn't give you much idea of their practical use. Here are some step-by-step examples of how to put one image onto another. I can't illustrate the color steps on a black-and-white page, so you'll have to start Bit Blast and follow along. Begin by following the steps listed on the next page.

1. Left-click picture 1 (the face) to make it the source, and right-click picture 4 (the circle) to make it the destination. Now click the Mask button to create a mask of the face in picture 4. The mask consists entirely of black pixels (0 bits) and white pixels (1 bits). Later I'll explain how to create a mask with code.

2. Left-click picture 4, and right-click picture 3 (the marble background). Select MergePaint and click the Blit button (or double-click MergePaint in the list box) to transfer the mask to the marble. The result is a white face on the marble background. MergePaint first changed all the black (masked) bits to white, thus reversing the mask. Then it used an OR operation to combine the source bits with the destination bits. The marble bits that were on, combined with the black outside bits, stay on; and the marble bits that were off, combined with masked black bits, stay off. But all the masked white bits stay on regardless of their status in the marble. MergePaint is a one-step way of doing a DstInvert operation on the mask and then doing a SrcPaint operation from the mask to the marble.

3. Left-click picture 1, and do a SrcAnd from the face to the marble. This puts the face on the marble. That's essentially how we're going to create transparent pictures and animation.

A Short Digression on Patterns

Some ROPs—vbMergeCopy, vbPatCopy, vbPatInvert, and vbPatPaint—work on what SDK documentation calls the *pattern* when it discusses ROPs. When discussing everything else, the document refers to this as the *brush*. Every device context has a brush, and you can change the brush by selecting a new brush into the device context.

In Visual Basic, you change the brush by setting the FillPattern and FillColor properties. Few Basic programmers bother to do this. The transparent black brush provided by default is suitable for most purposes. If you use the default brush, you can ignore all the ROPs that deal with patterns (as I will for the rest of this book).

But first try blitting to and from various boxes with MergeCopy, PatPaint, PatInvert, and PatCopy. You'll see that the leftmost three boxes in Bit Blast have invisible background patterns (set with the FillStyle property) that merge with or overwrite the pictures.

You might expect that a ROP could do all this in one operation. No such luck. The closest you can get is to SrcAnd the face directly onto the marble. This creates a mixture of the face and the marble, which is an interesting effect but isn't how you write video games.

Click Clear Destination to restore the marble, and then try this exercise:

1. Mask the face over the circle (the picture I usually use as a work area).

2. SrcInvert the face onto the marble.

3. SrcAnd the mask onto the marble.

4. SrcInvert the face onto the marble.

Different process, same result—with some bizarre color combinations along the way. Before you try to figure out why, imagine what your screen would look like if you used this technique to move a transparent picture around the screen: you'd see an ugly color change for every update. We'll follow this path no further because it temporarily changes the whole background.

One more example:

1. Mask the face onto the circle.

2. DstInvert the face. It doesn't matter what the source is because it will be ignored.

3. NotSrcErase the mask onto the face. (You can also do this in two steps: SrcPaint the mask onto the face, and then DstInvert the face.) The face now has an inverted background.

4. SrcAnd the mask onto the marble, which masks out the shape of the image on the background.

5. SrcInvert the face onto the marble. Alternatively, you could SrcPaint the face onto the marble.

This might seem strange, but actually it is the same technique used in the CALLDLLS sample program provided with Visual Basic—except that the developers cheated. They created the same inverted image you get from steps 1, 2, and 3 in a bitmap editor. They also created a mask like the one you'll create in the next section with a bitmap editor. Then with steps 4 and 5 they combined these two images on the background. The key difference between this third example and the first example you tried is that the first technique uses the original picture (white background) and a reversed (white) mask, whereas this one uses a reversed picture (black background) and a normal (black) mask.

Windows also uses this technique to display icons. In fact, if you dump the data in an icon (using the memory techniques discussed in Chapter 7), you'll see that the icon image displayed on the screen doesn't even exist internally. An icon consists of a monochrome mask (called the XOR mask) with all the opaque bits black and an image with an inverted background (called the AND mask). If you study the source code of the old IconWorks sample, you can see how it's done. (IconWorks isn't provided with Visual Basic anymore, but this book's companion CD provides a version that is updated to work in 32-bit mode.) We'll do this in the rest of the chapter, defining a class that creates the XOR and AND masks only once when initialized and then using them to put a transparent image on the screen as often as you want. In other words, we'll define icons of any size.

But before you can use any of these techniques, you must create masks.

Creating Masks

You can create masks with a bitmap editor. Just use Save As to copy the image, and then fill with black every pixel you want to be opaque and fill with white every pixel you want to be transparent. This works, but it isn't a particularly good idea. First, it's difficult to change the mask every time you change the image. Second, if you have a color image, you'll end up with a color mask consisting of two colors, although you need only a monochrome mask. Depending on your video system, the color mask can take up a lot more memory than a monochrome mask.

It's also possible to create a mask by looping through every pixel in a picture and setting all the colored pixels to black and all the background bits to white, but I don't recommend it. Instead, you can sneak through the back door and create masks on the fly by copying them. Windows will automatically translate a color bitmap into a monochrome bitmap (and vice versa) when you copy it. Therefore, in order to get a monochrome mask, simply copy a color bitmap to a monochrome bitmap of the same size. All the nonwhite pixels will come out black. The trick is getting a monochrome bitmap. As it turns out, you get one by default when you create a memory DC and a bitmap to go into it.

A memory device context is just like any other device context except that it exists only in memory. You can't see it, but you can copy it to the DC of a visible object such as a form, a picture box, or a printer. In other words, it's like a picture box with Visible set to False—except that it takes up fewer resources. Memory DCs are handy because you can use them to mix masks and images out of sight and then, when everything is ready, copy the invisible DC to the visible one. This reduces the number of visible blits and thus reduces the amount of flicker during animation.

Here's how Bit Blast creates a monochrome memory DC containing a mask:

```
Private Sub cmdMask_Click()
    Dim hdcMono, hbmpMono, hbmpOld ' As SysInt

    ' Create memory device context
    hdcMono = CreateCompatibleDC(0)
    ' Create monochrome bitmap and select it into DC
    hbmpMono = CreateCompatibleBitmap(hdcMono, dxBlt, dyBlt)
    hbmpOld = SelectObject(hdcMono, hbmpMono)
    ' Copy color bitmap to DC to create mono mask
    BitBlt hdcMono, 0, 0, dxBlt, dyBlt, pbSrc.hDC, 0, 0, SRCCOPY
    ' Copy mono memory mask to visible picture box
    BitBlt pbDst.hDC, 0, 0, dxBlt, dyBlt, hdcMono, 0, 0, SRCCOPY
    pbDst.Refresh
    ' Clean up
    Call SelectObject(hdcMono, hbmpOld)
    Call DeleteDC(hdcMono)
    Call DeleteObject(hbmpMono)
End Sub
```

The 0 passed to CreateCompatibleDC tells it to make the new DC compatible with the screen. You could pass it the HDC of something else (a printer, perhaps) to make it compatible with that object. Animation doesn't work too well on printers, so the screen is usually a good choice. CreateCompatibleBitmap creates a bitmap of the given size. At this point, the DC is an imaginary object with no size and no features; you must select something into it with Select-Object to make it real. You might ask (as I did) why a bitmap compatible with a DC compatible with a color screen comes out monochrome. Well, it's just one of those things.

Once you have a monochrome bitmap of the correct size, simply copy and let Windows do the conversion. In Bit Blast, I copy the resulting mask back to a visible picture, but there's usually no need to see the mask, so you can leave it in memory. Finally, you must clean up the mask when you're done. In Bit Blast, you're done as soon as you copy the mask, but in real life you might need to keep the mask around for the life of the image you're animating. You can clean up in Form_Unload or Class_Terminate. Just be sure to do it. I can assure you from hard experience that the consequences of forgetting are unpleasant.

Animating Pictures

Windows doesn't provide much direct support for animation or transparent images. But it does provide everything you need to create your own, including a model: icons. From the outside, an icon looks like an image on a transparent background. Internally, an icon is simply a bitmap with a corresponding mask. Once you understand how the GDI module uses masks to make icons look transparent, you can make your own transparent images, of any size.

When you create an icon with an editor such as IconWorks, you create only the pixel data. The tool automatically creates an AND mask and an XOR mask and puts both (with a header) into an ICO file. Eventually the icon masks are loaded into memory and become accessible through an icon handle (HICON). Programs can then call DrawIcon, which carves a hole in the background surface in the shape of the mask and puts the image into that hole. You must do essentially the same thing to turn any bitmap into an icon. From there, it takes only a few more steps to make your "icon" into a sprite—that is, a moveable image suitable for animation.

CPictureGlass wraps this all up in a class that looks and acts like a picture box, except for one little detail: it's transparent.

> **CHALLENGE** I'm using the term *animate* somewhat loosely. Real animation involves displaying a sequence of transparent images to simulate movement. This chapter does only the simplest form of animation—moving a single image across a background. It's your job to turn the CPictureGlass class into the NMovingPictures collection.

The Glass Picture Box

The CPictureGlass class is simply a PictureBox object in a class. If Visual Basic were a true object-oriented language, CPictureGlass would inherit from PictureBox. Perhaps you would set the InheritsFrom property of CPictureGlass to PictureBox. You won't find out the real syntax until the next version of Visual Basic. At any rate, CPictureGlass would inherit all the properties and methods of PictureBox, but you could add new properties and methods and override existing ones to enhance the capabilities of PictureBox.

Because Visual Basic 4 has no inheritance whatsoever, you have to fake it with *delegation*. Delegation means that CPictureGlass contains a PictureBox control to which it delegates all the tasks that it cannot handle by itself. In this case, PictureBox has the responsibility of providing the picture (since a class has no visible representation) and handling events (since a class can't have events). CPictureGlass takes care of all the blitting and masking necessary to make the picture transparent. The trick is to get the PictureBox control into the class.

Unfortunately, Basic provides no way to initialize an object (or a variable, for that matter) when you create it. Traditionally (a relatively short Basic tradition), you define a Create method to initialize a class. The problem is that an object is invalid between the time it is created with a Dim New statement and the time it is initialized with a Create method. It takes a lot of extra error handling to make sure that users don't abuse the class while it is in a helpless state.

CPictureGlass uses a Create method that takes a PictureBox argument. After initializing, you use a CPictureGlass object in pretty much the same fashion as you use a PictureBox object.

Using CPictureGlass

Let's check out the code in FUN.FRM (project FUNNGAME.VBP) before we talk about the implementation. The CPictureGlass declaration is at the module level so that it can be accessed from various routines:

```
Private pgBitmap As New CPictureGlass
```

The *pgBitmap* variable comes into existence as soon as you load the form, but it has no meaning until you initialize the object in the cmdAnimate_Click sub:

```
Private Sub cmdAnimate_Click()
    If cmdAnimate.Caption = "&Animate" Then
        With pgBitmap
            .Create pbAniBmp
            .Visible = False
            ' Constant controls pace, sign controls direction
            xInc = .Width * 0.05
            yInc = -.Height * 0.05
            ' Start in center
            .Left = (Width / 2) - (.Width / 2)
            .Top = (Height / 2) - (.Height / 2)
            .Visible = True
        End With
        SetTimer ordBitmap
        cmdAnimate.Caption = "Stop &Animate"
    Else
        pgBitmap.Visible = False
        SetTimer ordNone
        cmdAnimate.Caption = "&Animate"
    End If
End Sub
```

The Create method makes *pgBitmap* an object in fact as well as in name. After calling it, you can use CPictureGlass properties such as Visible, Left, Top, Width, and Height just as you would for a PictureBox object.

The SetTimer sub tells the Timer control to handle the animation. (The Fun 'n Games program also uses the same Timer control to animate card backs.) We're not interested in the details of how SetTimer tells the timer which events to handle. All that matters is that the Timer event calls the AnimateBitmap sub every 10 milliseconds when animation is on. Here's the code:

```
Private Sub AnimateBitmap()
    With pgBitmap
        If .Left + .Width > Me.ScaleWidth Then xInc = -xInc
        If .Left < 0 Then xInc = -xInc
        If .Top + .Height > Me.ScaleHeight Then yInc = -yInc
        If .Top < 0 Then yInc = -yInc
        .Move .Left + xInc, .Top + yInc
    End With
End Sub
```

This code simply moves the picture around the form, bouncing back in the other direction when it hits a border. Not very difficult. The hard part is inside.

Turning a PictureBox Object into a CPictureGlass Object

The Create method does most of what CPictureGlass does. This is a long function, so we'll step through it in pieces. But first here are the private variables used by the Create method and other CPictureGlass methods and properties:

```
Private rpb As PictureBox     ' Internal reference to PictureBox
Private hdcImage, hbmpImage, hbmpImageOld ' As SysInt
Private hdcMask, hbmpMask, hbmpMaskOld ' As SysInt
Private hdcBack, hbmpBack, hbmpBackOld ' As SysInt
Private hdcCache, hbmpCache, hbmpCacheOld ' As SysInt
Private fExist As Boolean, fVisible As Boolean
Private xOld, yOld, dxBlt, dyBlt ' As SysInt
Private rop As Long
```

This gives you some idea of the complexity you're going to be dealing with. Let's plunge in.

Create starts out by initializing the internal picture box from the PictureBox argument and setting various defaults and variables:

```
Function Create(rpbA As PictureBox) As Boolean

    ' Clean up any old instance before creating a new one
    If fExist Then Destroy
    On Error GoTo CreateError
    Set rpb = rpbA
    With rpb
        ' Picture must be invisible and borderless with AutoDraw on
        .Visible = False
```

```
        .BorderStyle = vbBSNone: .AutoRedraw = True
        ' Get size of image for copies
        dxBlt = .ScaleX(.Width, .ScaleMode, vbPixels)
        dyBlt = .ScaleY(.Height, .ScaleMode, vbPixels)
    End With
```

By declaring the picture box parameter as PictureBox, you prevent anything else from being passed accidentally. Any object passed as an argument is actually a reference object, so you use the *r* prefix for both the parameter name and the internal picture box variable. After setting the internal picture box, you can use it for all other references to the real object behind the curtain. You'll see the reason for cleaning up any old object before creating a new one as we go through the code.

To work properly, the internal picture box must be invisible and borderless and must have AutoRedraw turned on. You'll usually want to pass a picture box with these properties, but the code ensures that everything is right. It also calculates and saves the pixel dimensions of the picture for later use by GDI functions. The PictureBox object can contain anything—a bitmap, a metafile, an icon, or a drawing created with drawing methods.

Once a CPictureGlass object receives a picture through its Create method, it depends on the fact that nobody is messing with the properties and methods of the original PictureBox object. With real inheritance, you could prevent inappropriate meddling, but with delegation you must trust the user. As a user, you should assume that when you hand over a PictureBox object to a CPictureGlass object, you've given it away and can't access it until the CPictureGlass object is destroyed. If CPictureGlass doesn't give you a property or a method for doing something, it's because you're not supposed to do it. No one will enforce this rule, but you're on your own if you ignore it.

The next step in Create is to build the memory device contexts that will be used to move the image. The first one contains a copy of the image in the picture box:

```
' Create memory DC for image with inverted background (AND mask)
' Create DC compatible with screen
hdcImage = CreateCompatibleDC(0&)
Dim cPlanes, cPixelBits ' As SysInt
cPlanes = GetDeviceCaps(hdcImage, PLANES)
cPixelBits = GetDeviceCaps(hdcImage, BITSPIXEL)
' Create color bitmap same as screen
hbmpImage = CreateBitmap(dxBlt, dyBlt, cPlanes, cPixelBits, 0&)
hbmpImageOld = SelectObject(hdcImage, hbmpImage)
' Copy image (we'll invert its background later)
Call BitBlt(hdcImage, 0, 0, dxBlt, dyBlt, rpb.hDC, 0, 0, vbSrcCopy)
```

This code first creates a DC compatible with the screen. It then creates a bitmap exactly the same size and with the same color attributes as the picture box. Next, it selects the bitmap into the DC. Finally, it blits the image from the HDC of the picture box to the memory DC. The result is an exact replica of the image on the picture box. Since it's faster to blit or perform other operations on a memory DC than it is on a screen DC, we'll use the copy from here on out.

The next step is to create the mask:

```
' Create DC for monochrome mask of image (XOR mask)
' Create device context compatible with screen
hdcMask = CreateCompatibleDC(0&)
' Create bitmap (monochrome by default)
hbmpMask = CreateCompatibleBitmap(hdcMask, dxBlt, dyBlt)
' Select it into DC
hbmpMaskOld = SelectObject(hdcMask, hbmpMask)
' Copy color bitmap to monochrome DC to create mono mask
Call BitBlt(hdcMask, 0, 0, dxBlt, dyBlt, hdcImage, 0, 0, vbSrcCopy)
```

This is the same technique described earlier in "Creating Masks," page 290.

You use the image DC to create the mask DC. Once you've finished, you must return to the image and invert its background by changing its colors and blitting the mask to the image with vbSrcAnd:

```
' Invert background of image to create AND Mask
Call SetBkColor(hdcImage, vbBlack)
Call SetTextColor(hdcImage, vbWhite)
Call BitBlt(hdcImage, 0, 0, dxBlt, dyBlt, hdcMask, 0, 0, vbSrcAnd)
```

"Blitting Images onto Backgrounds," page 287, explained why this inversion is necessary. At this point, the CPictureGlass object contains an XOR mask and an AND mask, just as an icon does—and it will use them in the same way.

Finally, create a DC to save the background and one to draw a temporary picture (but don't blit anything to them yet), and wrap up with some error handling:

```
    ' Create memory DCs for old background and cache
    hdcBack = CreateCompatibleDC(0&)
    hbmpBack = CreateBitmap(dxBlt, dyBlt, cPlanes, cPixelBits, 0&)
    hbmpBackOld = SelectObject(hdcBack, hbmpBack)
    hdcCache = CreateCompatibleDC(0&)
    hbmpCache = CreateBitmap(dxBlt, dyBlt, cPlanes, cPixelBits, 0&)
    hbmpCacheOld = SelectObject(hdcCache, hbmpCache)

    ' Invalid x and y indicate first move hasn't occurred
    xOld = -1: yOld = -1
```

```
    fExist = True: fVisible = True
    Create = True
    Exit Function
CreateError:
    ' Create = False
End Function
```

CPictureGlass Cleanup

All those bitmaps and device contexts in Create have to be cleaned up. The Destroy method (which is called by the Class_Terminate event procedure) provides a place where you can be sure that cleanup happens. Here's the code:

```
Sub Destroy()
    ' Select old mask back to DC
    Call SelectObject(hdcMask, hbmpMaskOld)
    ' Now it's safe to delete DC and bitmask
    Call DeleteDC(hdcMask)
    Call DeleteObject(hbmpMask)
    ' Clean up inverted image DC
    Call SelectObject(hdcImage, hbmpImageOld)
    Call DeleteDC(hdcImage)
    Call DeleteObject(hbmpImage)
    ' Clean up cache DC
    Call SelectObject(hdcCache, hbmpCacheOld)
    Call DeleteDC(hdcCache)
    Call DeleteObject(hbmpCache)
    ' Clean up old background DC
    Call SelectObject(hdcBack, hbmpBackOld)
    Call DeleteDC(hdcBack)
    Call DeleteObject(hbmpBack)
    ' Turn off picture box
    Set rpb = Nothing
    fExist = False
End Sub
```

Moving a CPictureGlass Object

Now you have everything necessary to draw a transparent image anywhere. The Draw method does the work. Users can call the Draw method themselves, but generally they won't. Instead, they'll call the Move method or modify the Left and Top properties, which will in turn call the Draw method.

Conceptually, the Draw method probably works a lot like the GDI DrawIcon function does. The Draw method code appears on the following page.

```vb
Public Sub Draw()
With rpb.Container
    BugAssert fExist
    If fVisible = False Then Exit Sub
    ' Calculate background position on its container
    Dim fAutoRedraw As Boolean, xDst, yDst ' As SysInt
    xDst = .ScaleX(rpb.Left, .ScaleMode, vbPixels)
    yDst = .ScaleY(rpb.Top, .ScaleMode, vbPixels)
    fAutoRedraw = .AutoRedraw
    .AutoRedraw = False
    Dim clrBack As Long, clrFore As Long, hdcDst ' As SysInt
    hdcDst = .hDC

    ' Copy old background to its last location
    If xOld <> -1 Then
        Call BitBlt(hdcDst, xOld, yOld, dxBlt, dyBlt, _
                    hdcBack, 0, 0, vbSrcCopy)
    End If
    ' Save current background and position for next time
    Call BitBlt(hdcBack, 0, 0, dxBlt, dyBlt, _
                hdcDst, xDst, yDst, vbSrcCopy)
    ' Create cache copy of background to work on
    Call BitBlt(hdcCache, 0, 0, dxBlt, dyBlt, _
                hdcDst, xDst, yDst, vbSrcCopy)
    xOld = xDst: yOld = yDst
    ' Save color and set to black and white
    clrBack = GetBkColor(hdcCache)
    clrFore = GetTextColor(hdcCache)
    Call SetBkColor(hdcCache, vbWhite)
    Call SetTextColor(hdcCache, vbBlack)
    ' Mask the background
    Call BitBlt(hdcCache, 0, 0, dxBlt, dyBlt, _
                hdcMask, 0, 0, vbSrcAnd)
    ' Put image in hole created by mask
    Call BitBlt(hdcCache, 0, 0, dxBlt, dyBlt, _
                hdcImage, 0, 0, vbSrcPaint)
    ' Restore color
    Call SetBkColor(hdcCache, clrBack)
    Call SetTextColor(hdcCache, clrFore)
    ' Put finished cache on screen
    Call BitBlt(hdcDst, xDst, yDst, dxBlt, dyBlt, _
                hdcCache, 0, 0, vbSrcCopy)
    .AutoRedraw = fAutoRedraw
End With
End Sub
```

This method, like every other method and property in CPictureGlass, starts out by asserting that the object exists. This assertion will fail if the user declares a CPictureGlass object but then tries to use it before initializing with the Create method. Draw also terminates without doing anything if *fVisible* (controlled by the Visible property) is False.

Draw next restores the previous background (if there is one) and saves two copies of the current background—one to work on and one to restore next time. Without this step, each drawing would work but wouldn't erase itself; you'd see a trail of image "droppings." Finally, you mask out the shape of the image on the background of the temporary copy and plunk the image (with its inverted background) into the hole. Only when the whole image and background have been assembled off-screen do you copy the temporary *hdcCache* to the screen. You could do all this blitting and color changing directly on the container, but you'd end up with a whole lot of shaking.

Other CPictureGlass Properties and Methods

The Create and Draw methods are the heart of the CPictureGlass class, but the class also needs to supply all the other properties and methods that PictureBox users might want at run time. The PictureBox properties and methods fall into several categories.

Transparent Blits

It has been alleged that some video drivers support transparent blits. I have never come across one, and so, being unable to test the feature, I didn't build it into CPictureGlass. However, the Test About program (ALLABOUT.VBP) will tell you whether your system supports transparent blits. If so, you could do faster, smoother animation with the following code:

```
If GetDeviceCaps(hdcImage, DC_CAPS1) And C1_TRANSPARENT Then
    ordModeOld = GetBkMode(hdcImage, NEWTRANSPARENT)
    clrOld = SetBkColor(hdcImage, rpb.BackColor)
    Call BitBlt(rpb.Parent.hdc, xParent, yParent, dxBlt, dyBlt, _
            rpb.hdc, 0, 0, NEWTRANSPARENT)
    Call SetBkMode(hdcImage, ordModeOld)
    Call SetBkColor(hdcImage, clrOld)
End If
```

This is air code because I had nothing to test it with. This feature has been around long enough that hardware vendors ought to support it, and maybe some do. But not for the hardware I use.

Some methods and properties should work the same as they do in PictureBox, so they are simply passed through unchanged. Others enhance a PictureBox feature or replace it with a more appropriate CPictureGlass feature. Some are not implemented specifically because the feature would be inappropriate. And others might be nice, but I didn't get around to them. Figure 6-8 shows a diagram of the CPictureGlass class.

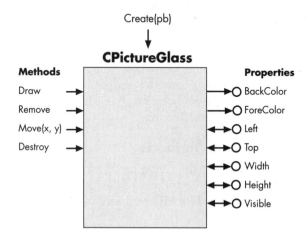

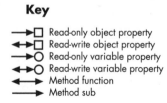

Figure 6-8. *A diagram of CPictureGlass.*

Let's start with the Move method, which is interesting more for how it handles optional arguments than for how it handles the image:

```
Public Sub Move(xLeft As Variant, Optional yTop As Variant)
    BugAssert fExist
    If IsMissing(yTop) Then
        rpb.Move xLeft
    Else
        rpb.Move xLeft, yTop
    End If
    Draw
End Sub
```

When you look at the PictureBox Move method, you'll see that it has two more arguments, Width and Height. But using these arguments changes the size of the object. A CPictureGlass object should never change its size, so these arguments simply aren't implemented. Because the Move method changes the position of the object, it calls the Draw method to erase the last image and redraw the new one.

The Left and Top Property Let procedures are implemented in the same way as Move. The Width and Height Property Let procedures aren't implemented, for the same reason that Move's Width and Height parameters aren't implemented. The Property Get routines for Left, Top, Width, and Height simply pass back the corresponding PictureBox properties:

```
Property Get Left() As Single
    BugAssert fExist
    Left = rpb.Left
End Property
```

The Visible property works in a completely different way. It has nothing to do with the Visible property of the internal picture box. The picture box is set to Invisible in the Create method, and the object is simply never seen again. The CPictureGlass Visible property hooks to an *fVisible* variable that is read by the Draw method to determine whether to redraw the image.

```
Property Get Visible() As Boolean
    BugAssert fExist
    Visible = fVisible
End Property

Property Let Visible(fVisibleA As Boolean)
    BugAssert fExist
    fVisible = fVisibleA
End Property
```

Hardcore Painting

Help is available for all you hardcore programmers who want to do tricks with bitmaps. Microsoft's WinG library is designed to produce professional-quality games under Windows (16-bit or 32-bit). WinG supports off-screen drawing and blitting through a special device context called a *WinGDC*. The sample programs show some impressive animation and dithering techniques. Unfortunately, they're all in C or C++. From my preliminary look, WinG definitely looked usable from Basic, but it might work better if someone wrote an OLE control or server to simplify the C-oriented functions.

You can look through the list of PictureBox properties and methods to see whether you want to implement any others. You could pass through the Tag property or the ZOrder method, but I didn't think it worth the time. Properties and methods related to drawing are inappropriate; if you want to draw something, you should do so before you pass the object to the Create method.

CPictureGlass Events

You might well ask why a CPictureGlass Move method even bothers to move the internal PictureBox object. Why not have the object sitting off-screen somewhere? After all, you're only blitting an image saved at creation time; it doesn't really matter where the original object is. Well, you could do it that way, but then events such as MouseDown, Click, and KeyPress wouldn't work properly.

Remember that classes have no events whatsoever in this version of Visual Basic. In a true object-oriented language, CPictureGlass would inherit the events as well as the properties and methods of PictureBox. As it is, however, all events happen to the internal picture box. If you want to handle them, you must remember that the object you passed in is the same one handling the events. By moving the invisible PictureBox object around underneath the visible CPictureGlass image, you match the events with the location.

Deal Me In

Every Windows programmer has access to one powerful graphics library: CARDS.DLL, the library that is used by Solitaire and other Windows-based card games and comes with all versions of Windows. Figure 6-9 shows CARDS.DLL in action in the Fun 'n Games program.

Using CARDS.DLL is no big secret. Various articles have described the interface, but until now all of them showed examples in C or some other language. The Basic interface is easy for hardcore programmers; it's just a matter of calling the five functions in CARDS.DLL.

Windows 95 and Windows NT both contribute some complications for the 32-bit version, however. Windows NT provides a 32-bit version named CARDS.DLL—the only DLL I have ever encountered that has exactly the same name as a 16-bit DLL. If you install Windows NT over Windows 3.x, you'll have 16-bit CARDS.DLL in your Windows directory and 32-bit CARDS.DLL in your system directory. Windows 95 provides only the 16-bit CARDS.DLL. Apparently, the designers figured that card games were out and action games were in. The Fun 'n Games program can run in either 16-bit or 32-bit mode, but only if it can find an appropriate DLL. I solved this incompatibility problem by getting permission to provide a 32-bit version of the DLL named CARDS32.DLL. The companion CD's setup program can copy this to your disk regardless of your operating system, and you can write and run 32-bit card games even on Windows 95. The

Figure 6-9. *Using CARDS.DLL in the Fun 'n Games program.*

Windows NT card games expect a 32-bit CARDS.DLL, so you'll have to keep this duplicate on your Windows NT disk if you want to play the standard games.

I'll describe the five functions and a few basic game techniques here; check the Fun 'n Games code for details. The hard part is programming the logic of your favorite card game.

Card Functions

The declarations and constants for Cards are located in CARDS.BAS. Here are the five functions of the Cards interface in Basic format.

Function cdtInit

```
Function cdtInit(dx As SysInt, dy As SysInt) As Boolean
```

This function initializes the cards and returns the width and height of a card in pixels through the *dx* and *dy* reference variables.

Function cdtDraw

```
Function cdtDraw(hDC As SysInt, x As SysInt, y As SysInt, _
                ordCard As SysInt, ordDraw As SysInt, _
                clr As Long) As Boolean
```

This function draws a card in its normal size at position *x*, *y* on the device context *hDC*. The *ordDraw* parameter controls whether the front, the back, or the inverted front of the card is drawn (constants *ordFaces*, *ordBacks*, *ordInvert*). The *ordCard* parameter controls which card is drawn. If the faces are shown, use the values 0 through 51 to represent each card. You can use the constants *ordClubs*, *ordDiamonds*, *ordHearts*, and *ordSpades* to represent the first card in each suit, adding numbers 0 through 13 to represent cards from ace to king. For example, *ordDiamonds + 3* is the three of diamonds, *ordHearts + 0* is the ace of hearts, and *ordSpades + 13* is the king of spades.

If the backs are drawn, use the following constants for the different backs: *ordCrossHatch*, *ordPlaid*, *ordWeave*, *ordRobot*, *ordRoses*, *ordIvyBlack*, *ordIvyBlue*, *ordFishCyan*, *ordFishBlue*, *ordShell*, *ordCastle*, *ordBeach*, *ordCardHand*, *ordX*, and *ordO*. The *clr* parameter sets the background color for the *ordCrossHatch* card back, which uses a pattern drawn with lines. All the other backs and fronts are bitmaps, so the color has no effect.

Function cdtDrawExt

```
Function cdtDrawExt(hDC As SysInt, x As SysInt, y As SysInt, _
                    dx As SysInt, dy As SysInt, ordCard As SysInt, _
                    ordDraw As SysInt, clr As Long) As Boolean
```

This function is the same as ctdDraw except that you specify the *dx* and *dy* parameters to indicate the size of the card. The card bitmaps are stretched or compressed, using StretchBlt, to the specified size.

Function cdtAnimate

```
Function cdtAnimate(hDC As SysInt, iCardBack As SysInt, _
                    x As SysInt, y As SysInt, _
                    iState As SysInt) As Boolean
```

This function animates the backs of cards by overlaying part of the card back with an alternative bitmap. It creates effects such as blinking lights on a robot, the sun winking, and a card sliding out of a sleeve. The function works only for cards of normal size drawn with ctdDraw. To draw each state, start with iState set to 0 and increment through until ctdAnimate returns False.

Function cdtTerm

```
Function cdtTerm() As Boolean
```

This function cleans up the card resources. You can call cdtTerm in either Form_Terminate or Form_Unload.

Timer Loops

Animating the card backs illustrates one of the fundamental problems of Windows programming. Before we get to the specifics of making cards wink and flash, however, let's talk about the problem in general.

Let's say that you want to perform some operation (such as animation) in the background forever. This is easy in MS-DOS:

```
Do
    Draw it, x, y
    If x <= xMax Then x = x + 1 Else x = 0
    If y <= yMax Then y = y + 1 Else y = 0
Loop
```

Even in MS-DOS, however, this often doesn't work very well. Your animation might run too fast, or it might run too fast on some machines and too slow on others. To even things out, you can insert a Wait statement:

```
Do
    Draw it, x, y
    If x <= xMax Then x = x + 1 Else x = 0
    If y <= yMax Then y = y + 1 Else y = 0
    Wait 100 ' microseconds
Loop
```

This might work fine for a machine running only MS-DOS, but depending on how Wait was implemented, it might be very rude indeed under Windows. In the bad old days, Wait functions were often written as busy loops:

```
Sub Wait(iDelay As Integer)
    Dim iEnd As Integer
    iEnd = GetTickCount() + iDelay  ' Get microseconds
    Do
    Loop While GetTickCount() < iEnd
End Sub
```

This is the height of bad manners in Windows or in any other non-preemptive multitasking operating system because you are grabbing the processor and throwing away all cycles until you are finished, thus blocking all other programs.

A preemptive multitasking operating system such as Windows NT might be able to jump in and steal control, but you're nevertheless wasting a time slice that could be better used by someone else. Even your MS-DOS programs shouldn't do this because it will cause them to hog the system when running in a Windows MS-DOS session.

One Visual Basic solution is to put DoEvents in the busy loop:

```
Do
    DoEvents
Loop While GetTickCount() < iEnd
```

DoEvents releases your time slice to any other processes that are waiting for their turn to run. If DoEvents were written in Visual Basic, it would look something like this:

```
Do While PeekMessage(msg, pNull, 0, 0, PM_REMOVE)
    TranslateMessage msg
    DispatchMessage msg
Loop
```

In other words, DoEvents handles everyone else's pending messages before returning to deal with your next message. This is better than nothing, but it's not the Windows Way. If other processes use too much time, you'll be way past quitting time when you get control back. In any multitasking system, someone else could want the same time slot you want. Your best chance of getting control at a specific time is to request it politely using a Windows Timer—which in Visual Basic means using the Timer control.

You're probably not accustomed to thinking of the Timer control as just another looping structure comparable to Do/Loop or For/Next. But why not? Consider the following "bad" loop:

```
Dim x As Integer, y As Integer, secStop As Double
Do
    If x <= xMax Then x = x + 1 Else x = 0
    If y <= yMax Then y = y + 1 Else y = 0
    If Draw(it, x, y) = False Then Exit Do
    secStop = Timer + .1   ' Wait one-tenth second
    Do
        DoEvents
    Loop Until Timer > secStop
Loop
```

Notice the following points:

- This loop is an endless Do Loop.

- The loop has an exit in the middle via Exit Do.

- The loop uses the Timer function in a loop to wait one-tenth of a second.

- The loop uses normal local variables, reinitializing them when they exceed a maximum.

Now let's convert to a "good" loop:

```
tmrAnimate.Interval = 100   ' 100 microseconds is one-tenth second
  :
Sub tmrAnimate_Timer()
    Static x As Integer, y As Integer
    If x <= xMax Then x = x + 1 Else x = 0
    If y <= yMax Then y = y + 1 Else y = 0
    If Draw(it, x, y) = False Then tmrAnimate.Enabled = False
End Sub
```

Here's how the code is transformed:

- A Sub statement replaces Do; an End Sub replaces Loop.

- The exit changes from Exit Do to *tmrAnimate.Enabled = False*.

- The time period is set with the Interval property outside the loop.

- The variables must be declared static because you'll leave the loop on every iteration.

Let's see how this technique works in the Fun 'n Games program.

Animating Card Backs

Choosing the Card Backs button draws 13 card backs plus the X and O cards. The program then turns on the timer and animates cards in the background. Try to find the animated card in Figure 6-10, shown on the next page.

Only 4 of the 13 card backs in CARDS.DLL are animated, and another changes color. To keep this animation working smoothly, you must manage variables for the *x* position, the *y* position, the card back, and the animation state. It's not a simple loop.

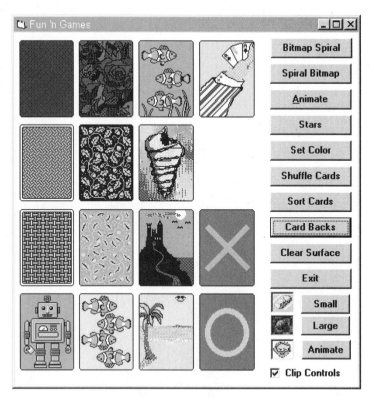

Figure 6-10. *Fun with cards.*

Let's look at the normal loop that draws the cards initially:

```
Private Sub cmdBack_Click()
    ordScale = Me.ScaleMode: Me.ScaleMode = vbPixels
    SetTimer ordBacks
    Me.Cls
    Dim X As Integer, Y As Integer, ordBack As Integer
    ordBack = ordCrossHatch  ' First card back
    ' Draw cards in 4 by 4 grid
    For X = 0 To 3
        For Y = 0 To 3
            Call cdtDraw(Me.hDC, _
                        (dxCard * 0.1) + (X * dxCard * 1.1), _
                        (dyCard * 0.1) + (Y * dyCard * 1.1), _
                        ordBack, ordBacks, QBColor(GetRandom(0, 15)))
            ordBack = ordBack + 1
        Next
    Next
    Me.ScaleMode = ordScale
End Sub
```

The timer loop does essentially the same thing, although its use of static variables makes it look different. Fun 'n Games handles other animation tasks, too; AnimateBacks is one of several subs called by the Timer event procedure:

```
Sub AnimateBacks()
    Static X As Integer, Y As Integer
    Static ordBack As Integer, iState As Integer
    ' Adjust variables
    If ordBack < ordCrossHatch Or ordBack > ord0 Then
        ordBack = ordCrossHatch
        X = 0: Y = 0
    End If
    If X = 4 Then X = 0
    If Y = 4 Then Y = 0: X = X + 1
    ' Save scale mode and change to pixels
    ordScale = Me.ScaleMode: Me.ScaleMode = vbPixels
    Select Case ordBack
    Case ordCrossHatch
        ' Change color of crosshatch
        Call cdtDraw(Me.hDC, _
                    (dxCard * 0.1) + (X * dxCard * 1.1), _
                    (dyCard * 0.1) + (Y * dyCard * 1.1), _
                    ordBack, ordBacks, QBColor(GetRandom(0, 15)))
    Case ordRobot, ordCastle, ordBeach, ordCardHand
        ' Step through animation states
        If cdtAnimate(Me.hDC, ordBack, _
                    (dxCard * 0.1) + (X * dxCard * 1.1), _
                    (dyCard * 0.1) + (Y * dyCard * 1.1),
                    iState) Then
            iState = iState + 1
            Exit Sub     ' Don't move to next card until final state
        End If
        iState = 0
    ' Case Else
        ' Ignore other cards
    End Select
    ' Move to next card
    Me.ScaleMode = ordScale
    ordBack = ordBack + 1
    Y = Y + 1
End Sub
```

Timer loops can be used for a lot more than animation. Think about how to apply them to all your background tasks. Consider doing calculations and file processing while you're handling user input, for instance. In fact, once you become accustomed to thinking in terms of timer loops, you could end up performing tasks in the background that used to be carried out in the foreground.

7

A Handle on Data

Visual Basic is a bit schizophrenic about handling data. It doesn't support the Basic Way of declaring and using data as defined by the developers of early Basics. Instead, it implements its own Visual Basic Way. But the Visual Basic Way has proven inadequate, so now, starting with version 4, Visual Basic also supports the Windows Way. But it supports the Windows Way only sometimes, sort of, and if you have the right tools. Confused? OK, let's look at the three ways one by one.

Three Approaches to Data

The Basic Way of handling data is with the Data and Read statements, which fell by the wayside when QuickBasic became Visual Basic. The Data statement allowed you to define tables of data of mixed types. At design time, you could initialize integers, real numbers, and strings all together in one big table; then, at run time, you could read those statements into variables. It wasn't a great syntax, but it did allow you to initialize simple data types at design time, something that Visual Basic still won't do. In Windows, however, Data and Read are a solution looking for a problem. What you really need in Windows programming is a way to both initialize and read larger, less formatted kinds of data—bitmaps, icons, metafiles, forms, and objects.

The Visual Basic Way of handling data is to allow initialization of properties (including pictures that contain bitmaps, icons, and metafiles) in the Properties window. In early versions of Visual Basic, the actual data was stored directly in the source file and eventually compiled into the executable file. This was easy to do because, historically, Basic source files have been encoded and packed. Because the format wasn't documented, Basic could cram data and code together however it liked, as long as it knew how to decode the resulting files.

But binary source files in an undocumented format caused a lot of problems, especially for source-code control programs. Visual Basic version 2 added a text format for source files. All the simple property data was arranged in the hierarchical table format you're familiar with if you've ever looked at a Visual Basic source file with a text editor. The binary data was crammed into FRX files in some undocumented format. This worked so well that in version 4 all source files are saved in text format (although the environment will read old binary source files). One curious limitation remains: you can initialize the properties of forms and controls at design time, but you can't initialize your own variables.

The Windows Way of storing binary data is very different from the Visual Basic Way. In other programming languages, you maintain binary data for your programs by storing it in resources. Using a visual tool called a *resource editor,* you can create resources such as bitmaps, icons, cursors, menus, and dialog boxes just the way you want them to look in your program. This editor stores the resources in a text file (an RC file) that looks a bit like a simplified Pascal source file. You then use a *resource compiler* to compile RC files into binary RES files, which are in turn inserted directly into executable files so that the resources and the code share the same EXE file. You write code in whatever language you choose to load the resource data at run time.

This seems like a fairly complicated way to do by hand what Visual Basic does automatically. But the Windows Way offers one big advantage over the Visual Basic Way: in Visual Basic, the binary data is tied to the source file. Each FRM file has a matching FRX; if you change the FRM file, you automatically change the FRX. In other words, if you want English, German, and Dutch versions of your program, you must create three versions of each form. In Windows, the resource file is independent of source files. You can create English, German, and Dutch versions of your resource file and combine any one with the executable file without changing a line of source code.

Because many Americans (I'm not without sin) tend to assume that English is the only language worth worrying about, you might not have heard much about this limitation in magazine articles or online forums. But you can bet that Microsoft has heard a lot of complaints about it from foreign programmers as well as from English-language developers who want to sell their software in non-English-speaking countries. As a result, Visual Basic version 4 allows you to use resources in Basic programs. The Windows Way, in the form of RES files, and the Visual Basic Way, in the form of FRX files, can exist side by side in the same program.

The Data Initialization Problem

Before we start looking at new kinds of data such as resources, let's look back at one of the problems confronting programmers in any language: initializing variables. What value does a variable have when you first declare it, and what happens if you try to read it before you initialize it? And how do you get an initial value into a variable? And why bother to initialize variables, anyway?

The last question is easy to answer. Take a look at control and form properties. You initialize them at design time in the Properties window. Think of the extra code if you had to initialize every Caption property of every button at run time. Initialization is so important to control and form properties that new features have been added to support it in Visual Basic version 4. For example, you can now initialize the strings of a ListBox control at design time, a task you had to perform at run time in previous versions. All the good reasons for allowing you to initialize properties are equally good reasons for allowing you to initialize other variables. You often want not only an initial default value but also the ability to change the default.

In some languages, uninitialized variables have a semirandom value. In C, for example, local variables (but not global or static variables) are undefined. If you want an initial value, you must give it. Fortunately for C programmers, this is easy to do. An undefined variable is a disaster waiting to happen, and careful C coders initialize their variables as close to declarations as possible. In contrast, Basic always initializes all variables whenever they are declared. String variables are initialized to an empty string, numeric variables are initialized to 0, and Variants are initialized to Empty.

This difference fits the philosophies of C and Basic. C doesn't initialize variables to a default because local variables must be initialized at run time. This has a cost, and C doesn't do any run-time work unless you ask for it. Undefined variables are dangerous, but that's your problem. Basic is more concerned with safety. If you declare an array of 5000 Integers, Basic will initialize them all to 0 even if it takes extra run-time work to do so.

The problem for Basic programmers is that 0 or Empty might not be the initial value the program needs. In C, you can combine the declaration of a variable with its initialization:

```
int cLastWindow = 20;
```

In Basic, declaration and initialization are different statements:

```
Dim cLastWindow As Integer
cLastWindow = 20
```

This usually works out for local variables, but it's a problem for module-level (private) or global (public) variables. You must declare these in the Declarations section at the top of the module, where executable statements such as variable assignments aren't allowed.

You need to find some other place to put the initialization statement, and that place must be reached only once—either when the module is loaded or the first time the variable is accessed. No matter how you initialize your variables, the initialization statement will be separated from the declaration in your source file, which makes initialization code difficult to maintain. If you change the declaration, you must go to a completely separate location to change the initialization, even though the two parts are logically related.

What you need to initialize variables is a combination declaration and initialization such as this:

```
Dim cLastWindow As Integer = 20
Static fFirstTime As Boolean = True
Private sExeFile As String = "VB.EXE"
Public aiCount(1 To 10) As Long = (1, 2, 3, 4, 5, 6, 7, 8, 9, 10)
Public ai3D(1 To 2, 1 To 3) As Long = ((1, 2), (2, 2), (2, 1))
Private perMe As TPerson = ("McKinney", "Bruce", 21, _
                           ("24 First Ave.", "Andula", _
                            "Basic", "Cathistan", 72948 _
                            ) _
                           )
```

As you know, Basic has no such syntax. It's the only major computer language that doesn't.

Notice that the sample initializations get significantly more complex when you start dealing with arrays, multidimensional arrays, UDTs, and nested UDTs—not to mention initializing collections of arrays of classes. Needless to say, the syntax above is not the only one possible.

Initializing constants is a related problem. Of course, all constants are initialized by definition, but the limited syntax of the Const statement makes it impossible to initialize arrays, UDTs, and strings containing control characters, to mention a few common types. For example, wouldn't it be handy to have the following constants?

```
Const sCrLf = Chr$(13) & Chr$(10)
Const asDays(1 To 7) = ("Sunday", "Monday", "Tuesday", "Wednesday", _
                        "Thursday", "Friday", "Saturday")
```

Neither is a legal syntax. You have to get the equivalent by declaring variables and then initializing them later, even though you have no intention of ever modifying them and would prefer that they were constants.

NOTE You pay a run-time price for initialization in Basic. This was true even in the old days, when the Data statement initialized variables at compile time but you had to call Read at run time. Operating systems are capable of initializing many variables at compile time. The difference is the location of the variable. Stack and heap variables can't be initialized until run time, but you can initialize data variables at compile time. Basic programmers aren't supposed to know or care where their variables are located, so any future initialization system should be consistent regardless of the scope of the variable. It might be OK to require C programmers to know that static variables and local variables have different initial values, but it wouldn't do for Basic.

Initializing Local Variables

Although Basic gives you no direct help, it does give you two roundabout ways to initialize variables. The first technique takes advantage of the default initialization to 0 or Empty.

If you can rule out the empty string as a valid value for a particular string variable, you can assume that the variable is uninitialized when it has this value. The same goes for 0 and numeric variables. For example:

```
Sub InitializeMe()
    Static sNeverEmpty As String, iNeverZero As Integer
    If sNeverEmpty = sEmpty Then sNeverEmpty = "Default"
    If sNeverZero = 0 Then sNeverZero = -1
    ⋮
End Sub
```

Of course, if *sNeverEmpty* can be changed by some other code, and if *sEmpty* is a valid value, this code won't work because *sNeverEmpty* will be randomly changed to "Default" under certain circumstances. It's easy to imagine lots of string variables that should never be empty, but it's harder to think of integer variables that should never be 0.

Notice that the variables in question are static so that they retain the initialized value across calls. You don't need any special initialization code if the variable is reinitialized every time you enter the procedure:

```
Sub InitializeMe()
    Dim sNeverEmpty As String, iNeverZero As Integer
    sNeverEmpty = "Full": sNeverZero = -1
```

If 0 is valid for your numeric values or Empty is valid for your strings, you must create a variable specifically for testing:

```
Sub InitializeMe()
    Static fNotFirstTime As Boolean
    Static sAnyValue As String, iAnyValue As Integer
    If Not fNotFirstTime Then
        fNotFirstTime = True
        sAnyValue = sEmpty: iAnyValue = 0
    End If
    ⋮
```

The double negative makes the code look more complex than it is. Things would be so much clearer if you could initialize the test variable to True:

```
Sub InitializeMe()
    Static fFirstTime As Boolean = True
    Static sAnyValue As String, iAnyValue As Integer
    If fFirstTime Then
        fFirstTime = False
        sAnyValue = sEmpty: iAnyValue = 0
    End If
    ⋮
```

But if you could initialize *fFirstTime* to True, you wouldn't need it because you could initialize *sAnyValue* and *iAnyValue* the same way.

You can use the same principle on global and module-level variables. For example, the IsMissing function works with optional parameters in the same way. I'll show you some related tricks later.

Initializing Form Variables

The second way to initialize variables is to use an initialization event. Most Visual Basic programmers already know this technique because they've used the Form_Load event to initialize form properties and variables. You should also familiarize yourself with two other initialization events: Form_Activate and Form_Initialize.

When a form is loaded, the sequence of events is the following:

1. A form is a class, and all classes have an Initialize event. Form_Initialize is called (or *fired,* as control developers describe calling events) as soon as you touch any variable or property of a control. Use this event to initialize variables private to the form. Normally, you should not touch any form or control properties here because doing so fires the next event.

2. Form_Load fires after Form_Initialize as the visual elements of the form are being created and default values are being assigned to properties. Normally, you should avoid doing anything that will draw something on the form because that causes an automatic firing of the next event. It might be tempting to call Show in Form_Load and then do further processing with the visible form, but you're usually better off doing this in the next event.

3. Form_Activate fires after you have loaded and shown the form. It's possible to load a form without showing it; in this case, Form_Activate isn't fired until you call the Show method. Form_Activate is also called when you switch from one modeless form to another, or when you switch between MDI forms (but not when you return focus from another application). If your application has modeless or MDI forms, don't do anything in Form_Activate that you want to happen only once. Or use a static variable (such as *fNotFirst*) to protect against multiple initializations in Form_Activate.

The interactions between the three initialization events can be confusing. "The Form Dance: Initialize, Load, Unload, Terminate," page 172, discusses some of the issues involved, but sometimes trial and error is the only way to figure out the right initialization sequence for your application.

Initializing Class Objects and Internal Variables

Class modules have a Class_Initialize event that you can use to initialize private variables. But because Class_Initialize is an event, you can't use it to pass data to the class object from its creator. In other words, you can tell a class how to initialize its own variables, but you can't initialize the class object. Yet many classes are completely undefined and unusable until they are initialized.

What you need is a way to combine declaration and initialization:

```
Dim pgStar As New CPictureGlass = (pbStar)
```

Instead, you must initialize by convention. Give your class a Create method, and tell users that they must always call it before using a class object:

```
Dim pgStar As New CPictureGlass
pgStar.Create pbStar
```

"Turning a PictureBox Object into a CPictureGlass Object," page 294, introduced the Create convention. The bottom line is that callers who try to reference an object before initializing it with the Create method get random results.

Convention isn't a very good way to enforce good behavior. Better to leave users no way but the right way.

Most object-oriented languages allow you to initialize objects in their declarations. Unfortunately, initialization syntax can get very complex, especially with objects consisting of other objects. Inheritance adds even more complications. It will be interesting to see how Visual Basic designers resolve this difficulty in future versions that support inheritance.

Initializing Module Variables

Initializing variables in modules is a little trickier. Although there's no Module-_Initialize event in which you can initialize internal values, you can have initialized variables in modules if you're willing to do a little hacking with the static variable technique described earlier.

You might be laboring under the misconception that Basic doesn't support global initialized variables in modules. Not so. Property procedures make it easy, if not obvious. Normally, I think of properties as being attached to forms and classes, but no rule says that a property has to be tied to an object. For example, here's a global variable, *cLastWindow,* initialized to 20:

```
Private fNotFirstTime As Boolean
Private cLastWindowI As Integer
⋮
Public Property Get cLastWindow() As Integer
    If Not fNotFirstTime Then
        fNotFirstTime = True
        cLastWindowI = 20
    End If
    cLastWindow = cLastWindowI
End Property

Property Let cLastWindow(cLastWindowA As Integer)
    fNotFirstTime = True
    cLastWindowI = cLastWindowA
End Property
```

You can use this property from anywhere, just like any other global variable:

```
For i = 1 To cLastWindow
    WipeWindow i
Next
cLastWindow = cLastWindow + 1
```

Users of your module needn't be the wiser about how you wrote it.

If your module contains several variables that need to be initialized, you can write your own Module_Initialize routine. Call it from every procedure that uses one of the variables:

```
If fNotFirstTime = False Then Module_Initialize
```

This might not be as efficient as you'd like. Testing for *fNotFirstTime* all over the place is no fun, but the test is True only once. Don't forget to initialize *fNotFirstTime* along with the other variables.

A property with a Property Get but no Property Let or Property Set acts like a read-only variable—otherwise known as a constant. Let's take my favorite constant, *sCrLf*. It's simply a string consisting of a carriage return and a linefeed. You can't define it with Const because it has two control characters, which must be tied together with the concatenation operator (& or +). Neither Chr$ nor concatenation is allowed in a Const string.

The following solution doesn't really have a problem, because Visual Basic provides *vbCrLf* and the Windows API type library provides *sCrLf*. But if you didn't have a type library with the constant, you could define your own in a module this way:

```
Public Property Get sCrLf() As String
    Static s As String
    If s = sEmpty Then s = Chr$(13) & Chr$(10)
    sCrLf = s
End Property
```

Using Your Own Resources

Resources are the new old way of handling large data chunks in Visual Basic 4. The Test Resources project (TRES.VBP) illustrates some important points about resources. This is an international program, designed for simultaneous release in the United States of America and the Republic of Swinen. The program was written and will be maintained by American programmers in the United States. Nonprogrammers in the United States and Swinen created separate resource files. Strings were translated to Swinish, and visual elements such as bitmaps, cursors, and icons were modified to meet the cultural expectations of Swine. The differences are purely cosmetic, however; the program acts exactly the same for American users and for Swinish users.

On the following page, Figure 7-1 shows the American version of the program; Figure 7-2 shows the Swinish version. To get the full effect, you need to run both versions—sounds and cursors just don't translate to the printed page. I designed the TRES.VBP project file to handle either the American or the Swinish version of the program, but I also provide TRESUS.VBP and TRESSW.VBP, hard-coded to the nationalized versions. You can use these to take an initial look at the program.

Figure 7-1. *The Test Resources program, localized for the United States of America.*

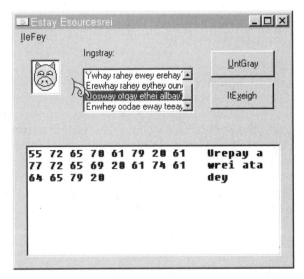

Figure 7-2. *The Test Resources program, localized for the Republic of Swinen.*

Creating a Resource Script

A *resource script* is a text file listing all the data used in a program. It traditionally bears the filename extension RC. After writing your resource script, you compile it into a resource file (RES) and add this file to your Basic project. Visual Basic automatically uses your resources in the environment and compiles them into the EXE file.

The easiest way to understand resource scripts is to look at a sample. Here's the one used by the Test Resources program (TRES.VBP):

```
// TRES.RC - Resource script for Test Resources program

//$ Const ordAppBmp = 101
#if defined(US)
101     BITMAP  "C:\\HARDCORE\\MANHEAD.BMP"
#elif defined(SW)
101     BITMAP  "C:\\HARDCORE\\PIGHEAD.BMP"
#else
#error "No language"
#endif

//$ Const ordAppIcon   = 301
#if defined(US)
301     ICON    "C:\\HARDCORE\\FLGUSA.ICO"
#elif defined(SW)
301     ICON    "C:\\HARDCORE\\FLGSWI.ICO"
#endif

//$ Const ordAppCursor = 401
#if defined(US)
401     CURSOR  "C:\\HARDCORE\\MANHAND.CUR"
#elif defined(SW)
401     CURSOR  "C:\\HARDCORE\\PIGTAIL.CUR"
#endif

//$ Const ordWavGrunt  = 501
#if defined(US)
501     WAVE    "C:\\HARDCORE\\GRUNT.WAV"
#elif defined(SW)
501     WAVE    "C:\\HARDCORE\\OINK.WAV"
#endif
```

(continued)

```
//$ Const ordTxtData   = 601
601      OURDATA
BEGIN
#if defined(US)
       0x7550, 0x6572, 0x7220, 0x7761
       0x6420, 0x7461, 0x2061
#elif defined(SW)
       0x7255, 0x7065, 0x7961, 0x6120
       0x7277, 0x6965, 0x6120, 0x6174
       0x6564, 0x2079
#endif
END

//$ Const ordFrmTitle  = 1001
//$ Const ordMnuFile   = 1101
//$ Const ordMnuGrunt  = 1102
//$ Const ordMnuExit   = 1103
//$ Const ordLstTitle  = 1201
//$ Const ordLstWhat   = 1301
//$ Const ordLstWhy    = 1302
//$ Const ordLstWhere  = 1303
//$ Const ordLstWho    = 1304
//$ Const ordLstWhen   = 1305
STRINGTABLE
BEGIN
#if defined(US)
     1001     "Test Resources"
     1101     "&File"
     1102     "&Grunt"
     1103     "E&xit"
     1201     "Strings:"
     1301     "What's the story?"
     1302     "Why are we here?"
     1303     "Where are they now?"
     1304     "Who's got the ball?"
     1305     "When do we eat?"
#elif defined(SW)
     1001     "Estay Esourcesrei"
     1101     "&IleFey"
     1102     "&UntGray"
     1103     "ItE&xeigh"
     1201     "Ingstray:"
     1301     "At'swhay ethei orystay?"
     1302     "Ywhay rahey ewey erehay?"
     1303     "Erewhay rahey eythey ouney?"
     1304     "Oosway otgay ethei allbay?"
     1305     "Enwhey oodae eway teeay?"
#endif
END
```

Although this script uses conditional code to create American and Swinish resource files from the same script file, you can just as easily create separate scripts for each language. The conditional statements shown here use the C preprocessor language, which looks a lot like the Basic conditional compilation statements except for lowercase characters and a few other minor differences. Also notice that you must double the backslash character because the backslash is an escape character in C. Of course, your resource compiler might use a different syntax.

The resource script contains Basic constants in C-style comments with a unique leading character (//$). This makes it easy to write a wizard program that will search for constant comments and convert them to a Basic module. You can maintain the comments easily next to their data in the resource script, but each time you compile the resource script, you must also update the constant module. You could probably carry this idea further, generating initialization code as well as constants.

NOTE
Many compilers come with resource editors that generate resource scripts; Microsoft Visual C++, for example, comes with a built-in resource editor. The problem with using such tools to generate resource scripts is that they are usually designed for the compiler language. For example, the Visual C++ resource editor creates include files that will be used by both the C++ compiler and the resource compiler. Some of these include files refer to standard C++ include files. For the most part, this is just garbage to the Basic programmer. It is possible to edit the include files to make them usable with Basic, but I find it easier to create my own with a text editor.

Anatomy of a Resource Block

For every resource, you need to supply three pieces of information: the resource type, the resource ID, and the resource data. This gets a little confusing because each can be specified in various ways.

The resource type can be either a predefined type or a type you define. In the sample you just saw, BITMAP, ICON, CURSOR, and STRINGTABLE are predefined resource types. Both Basic and Windows know about these types and include functions and constants to handle them directly. WAVE and OURDATA are custom types for which you must write your own functions.

To access bitmaps, icons, and cursors in Basic, you use the LoadResPicture function. Assume that your resource file has this resource definition:

```
//$ Const ordAppIcon   = 301
#if defined(US)
301    ICON   "C:\\HARDCORE\\FLGUSA.ICO"
#elif defined(SW)
301    ICON   "C:\\HARDCORE\\FLGSWI.ICO"
#endif
```

Your Basic source file should define the following constant:

```
Public Const ordAppIcon = 301
```

You can then load the resource as shown here:

```
Me.Icon = LoadResPicture(ordAppIcon, vbResIcon)
```

Cursors Eat Mouse Icons for Lunch

Basic calls them mouse icons, Windows calls them cursors (not to be confused with carets, the pointers in text boxes), Basic programmers have complained for years about Basic's inability to set them. Finally, Visual Basic version 4 lets you set cursors to your favorite shapes, although this new feature isn't as obvious as it seems.

You can load either cursors or icons into the MouseIcon property, but there's a big difference between them. In fact, their relationship is an artificial one, created by Basic for your convenience. Since icons are so easy to come by and are usually the same size as cursors, Basic provides a shortcut: it automatically converts icons to cursors. But you might not like the price.

Unlike 32-bit Windows, 16-bit Windows does not support color cursors. But most icons in the Visual Basic icon library (or anywhere else) are in color, even if it's only gray. Gray is black in cursors, and dithered colors come out more or less random. You'll rarely be satisfied with the results of loading an ordinary icon. Even in 32-bit mode, where color cursors are supported, you'll soon find that color often isn't appropriate for cursors. Furthermore, most icons are designed as—well, as icons, and they don't really fit as cursors. In addition, you have no control over the cursor hot spot when you use an icon. If your cursor is shaped like a pencil, you'll want the hot spot at the point of the pencil. But if you load a pencil-shaped icon, the hot spot is in the center of the icon. If you click something small, you might not be clicking what you think you're clicking.

The moral: use cursors instead of icons. Although Visual Basic doesn't install any cursors, you can copy them from the \TOOLS\GRAPHICS\CURSORS direc-

To access strings, use LoadResString. Assume that your string table in the resource script looks like this:

```
STRINGTABLE
BEGIN
#if defined(US)
    1001    "Test Resources"
    1101    "&File"
    1102    "&Grunt"
    ⋮
```

You can load a string resource as shown here:

```
mnuFile.Caption = LoadResString(ordMnuFile)
```

To access custom data, use LoadResData. Assume that your custom WAVE resource looks like the code shown at the top of the next page.

---

tory of the Visual Basic CD. You can also create your own cursors with Imag-Edit, the graphics editor provided in the \TOOLS\ImagEdit directory. ImagEdit lets you create color or monochrome cursors and set their hot spots. If you really want to use an icon, load it into ImagEdit, copy it, paste the image into a new cursor, and set the hot spot wherever you want it.

There's only one problem with cursors: Visual Basic doesn't recognize color cursors, even in 32-bit mode. That's the fault of the Picture object, which has been jury-rigged to handle cursors in the MouseIcon property even though it wasn't designed for them. The only way to get a color cursor when running in the environment is to use an icon. You can get color cursors in your 32-bit EXE files, however, if you can live with a little inconvenience during development. Just load your color cursors from resources. They'll come out in black and white (often with ugly dithering) in the environment, but they'll have the right colors when loaded in the EXE. This isn't so bad, since few customers will ever see your program running in the environment.

What's the difference between loading a cursor in the environment and in an EXE? In an EXE, resources are loaded using the standard Windows resource mechanism that we'll examine later in this chapter. Color cursors work fine. Basic can't use this normal mechanism when running in the environment because you aren't really running your program; you're running Visual Basic. Instead, Basic has to dig the resource data directly out of the RES file. This results in the same limitation that you'll encounter with cursors that are placed directly into the MouseIcon property by using the LoadPicture function or the Load Picture dialog box: the colors get lost.

```
//$ Const ordWavGrunt  = 501
#if defined(US)
501     WAVE    "C:\\HARDCORE\\GRUNT.WAV"
#elif defined(SW)
501     WAVE    "C:\\HARDCORE\\OINK.WAV"
#endif
```

You can load this resource into an array of bytes, as shown here:

```
abWavGrunt = LoadResData(ordWavGrunt, "WAVE")
```

Custom data comes back as arrays of bytes, so you'll need a byte function to process it.

For each resource, you need to assign an ID string or number. The sample resource script uses ID numbers with a constant defined for each. You can also define ID strings. In the resource script, you could write the following definition:

```
AppBmp          BITMAP  "C:\\HARDCORE\\MANHEAD.BMP"
```

On the Basic side, you can load it this way:

```
imgMascot.Picture = LoadResPicture("AppBmp", vbResBitMap)
```

This technique works for all resources except strings, which can be identified only by ID number. Because ID strings take more data space than ID numbers, you should avoid overusing ID strings for projects that contain many resources.

You can provide the name of a file containing the data on the same line as the ID and the type, or you can provide the actual data in a BEGIN/END block on subsequent lines. Microsoft's resource script language has its share of quirks, but you get the idea. For resource script arcana, see the MSDN/VB starter kit on the Visual Basic CD.

Compiling Resource Scripts

To compile a resource script, you need a stone-age tool called a resource compiler. Historians tell us that Basic compilers used to be invoked from command lines in a manner not unlike that required for the resource compiler, RC.EXE. Now, don't get me wrong. I'm a command-line kind of guy. I use a Windows command-line session the way most people use Program Manager and File Manager. But resource files are like hamburgers: you don't really want to know where they came from.

Unfortunately, you must handle every step of the resource process by hand, starting with the setup. The Visual Basic CD contains 16-bit and 32-bit resource

Visual Basic Optional

With a 16-bit resource compiler, you can change the resources in an EXE file even if you don't have the source files. This command line replaces whatever resources TRES.EXE has with the U.S. version:

```
rc16 /d US tres
```

This line changes them back to the Swinish version:

```
rc16 /d SW tres
```

Your Swinish translators don't even need Visual Basic. Unfortunately, this technique doesn't work in Microsoft's 32-bit RC.

Changing completed executable files has both obvious benefits and subtle gotchas. On the downside, any version information you enter in the EXE Options dialog box will be overwritten and lost. You can get around this limitation by defining version information in the resource script instead of in Basic.

On the plus side, if you define an icon resource with ID #1 in the resource file and then insert it in the finished executable, you can control the icon used by Program Manager and similar shell programs. This is also the icon displayed when you cycle through running programs by pressing Alt-Tab. Program Manager and similar programs display this icon by grabbing icon #1 out of the executable file with the ExtractIcon API function.

Visual Basic won't let you define an icon #1 in your resource file, however, because it already defines icon resource #1 as the icon you assign to the Icon property of your main form at design time. This is the icon you can describe programmatically as *Forms(0).Icon,* but changing it at run time won't necessarily have the desired effect because your program might not be running when the icon is extracted.

For example, try running the TRES program in different environments. Under Windows 95, you'll see the small U.S. and Swinish flag icons in the Taskbar and in the top left corner of the application, loaded from a resource into the Icon property during Form_Load. But the icon displayed in Windows Explorer, shortcuts, and the Alt-Tab window is the default Visual Basic icon, because the Icon property is uninitialized until run time. Under Windows 3.*x* and Windows NT 3.51, minimized icons show the flag icons, but Program Manager displays the default Basic icon. Although you can get around this as described above in 16-bit mode, you're stuck in 32-bit mode. For icons, this limitation tends to defeat the reason resource support was added to Visual Basic.

The moral: unless you want to change every form icon by hand for every target language, you should probably not use language-specific icons in forms.

compilers, but they're not installed by Setup. You must copy them from the \TOOLS\RESOURCES directory yourself, and you'd better do it carefully. Both versions are named RC.EXE, and both use DLLs with the same imaginative name, RCDLL.DLL. If you copy them both to the same directory, the second overwrites the first. Although this naming convention couldn't be described as smart, it wasn't really a problem for the C compilers that Microsoft resource compilers were designed to work with. Basic programmers who don't use C and want to write portable resource code need to work out a plan to make both resource compilers available in a way that has them using the right DLLs. For example, put the 32-bit version with its DLL in an \RC32 directory and the 16-bit version in an \RC16 directory. Write batch files RC32.BAT and RC16.BAT to run them, or rename the EXEs to RC32.EXE and RC16.EXE.

Your goal in using the resource compiler is to create a separate RES file for each target language. You'll also need separate RES files for the 16-bit and 32-bit environments. A batch file such as the one shown here creates them:

```
@echo off
Rem Make 16-bit US
c:\rc16\rc /v /d US /r /fo tresus.res tres.rc
Rem Make 16-bit Swinish
c:\rc16\rc /v /d SW /r /fo tressw.res tres.rc
Rem Make 32-bit US
c:\rc32\rc /v /d US /r /fo tresus32.res tres.rc
Rem Make 32-bit Swinish
c:\rc32\rc /v /d SW /r /fo tressw32.res tres.rc
If "%1"=="" Goto Done
Rem Make version specific if country (US or SW) given on command line
If exist tres%1.res Copy tres%1.res tres.res
If exist tres%132.res Copy tres%132.res tres32.res
:Done
```

If you change from the U.S. version to the Swinish version from the batch file while TRES.VBP is loaded, your program will change its behavior without changing a character of source code. This feature is nice, but the process of using it can only be described as crude. You can probably think of additional parameters to further define the behavior of the batch file, or, if you have a make utility, you can replace the batch file with a make file. But whatever hacks you use, they shouldn't be necessary.

Visual Basic should simply provide a dialog box that lets you specify your resources and their IDs. Creating a resource script and invoking a resource compiler should take place behind the scenes. Hmmm. You've seen the simple and consistent format of resource scripts. You've seen the mechanical process of compiling them. You have a computer. You know a computer language. You're hardcore. All the elements are present for solving this problem once and for all.

Imagine the Resource Shop, a resource editor created specifically for Visual Basic. You could create new resources by selecting a resource type in a list box and clicking a New Resource button. You'd have a choice of inserting an existing resource from a file or creating a new one. Each resource type would have its own file editor, which you'd define when you create a new resource type. For example, you could run ImagEdit for icons, cursors, and bitmaps, or you could integrate your own more powerful editor. You'd also need editors for metafiles, wave files, strings, and hexadecimal data. You could scroll through existing resources for a project and edit any you wanted to change. Then you'd click a Save button to invoke an invisible resource compiler to compile your invisible resource script and generate a module containing Basic constants for each ID. You could integrate this wonderful tool into the Visual Basic IDE as an add-in. (Details on add-ins in Chapter 10.)

Just hold that thought while we examine resources more carefully, from the inside out.

Using Other People's Resources

The WinWatch program has a feature that we discussed only briefly in Chapter 5: for each program or DLL you select, WinWatch shows all the resources of that program in a list box in the lower right corner of the screen. When you select a resource in the list box, WinWatch displays or otherwise handles the item in the Resource Information area (which is actually a picture box). The display varies, depending on the resource type.

It's an adventure to look at resources in the Windows DLLs, Program Manager, and Visual Basic itself. You can learn a lot about how programmers use resources in other languages. But to understand exactly where resources come from, try looking at TRES.EXE. Although you already know where those resources come from, now you can get the inside view.

> **NOTE**
>
> You could try looking at TRES32.EXE, but you won't find much of interest. As explained in Chapter 5, each 32-bit program runs in its own separate address space. WinWatch can't get resources out of anything other than itself—and it can't do that either, because I didn't write the 32-bit code. So stick with 16-bit for the following exploration.

Stealing Your Own Resources

Figure 7-3 shows WinWatch looking at TRES.EXE. The Resources list box shows the same resource ID numbers and types that are defined in TRES.RC. If you select one of these, you'll see the resource displayed or described in the Resource Information area. WinWatch displays bitmaps and icons, plays sounds, and loads cursors into the Resources list box (and other list boxes). WinWatch simply dumps data (such as OURDATA) that it doesn't know about. You can enhance WinWatch and your own programs to handle new data types correctly.

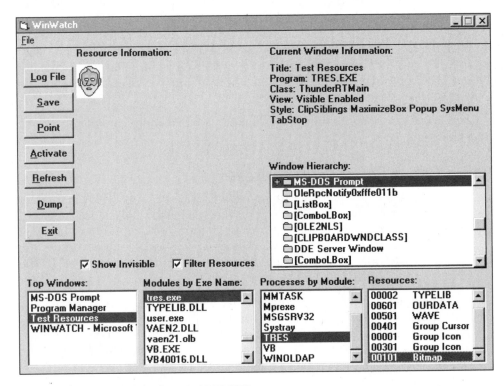

Figure 7-3. *WinWatch looking at TRES.EXE.*

What you don't see in the Resources list box are the strings defined in the string table. Why not? I have to confess ignorance. If you do a hex dump of the EXE file, you can see them there, near the other resources. In general, string resources are a bit of a puzzle; left to its own devices, WinWatch would list numerous string resources that it wouldn't be able to display. We'll talk more about strings later in this chapter; see "Using String Resources," page 349.

TRES.EXE also has a group icon with ID #1. When you select the icon, you'll recognize it as the standard form icon. If you set the Icon property of the main form to a different icon at design time and then recompile, this icon will change. The resource icon is loaded at run time, however. You can also see that TRES.EXE has IID and TYPELIB resources. Chapter 10 will give you an idea of what these are for.

If you browse through the resources in other programs, you'll notice some patterns. Turn off the Filter Resources check box so that you'll see everything, useful or not. Resources with type Group Icon or Group Cursor are usually listed, but those with type Icon or Cursor are not. What's the difference? Windows documentation doesn't say. You'll see other resources such as menus, dialogs, and accelerators in programs written in C or other languages, although you won't see these same features in compiled Visual Basic programs. Basic apparently implements menus, dialogs, and accelerators by creating them at run time rather than creating them with resources.

Finding Resources

If you're wondering how WinWatch finds the resources in executables, the answer is clear: with great difficulty. This is not simple code. In hindsight, the time spent writing it probably wasn't worth the convenience of having it. But since I did write it, let's spend a few minutes talking about it.

Resources are part of the executable file. To get them out, you must figure out where the data is in the file and then read it. WinWatch deals only with running programs and DLLs. It doesn't need to read the resource data out of the file; it just needs to find the ID number (or string) and the type of each chunk of data. Windows provides functions to read any resource for which you know the ID, the type, and the instance handle of the program.

WinWatch could have been written to read the data out of nonrunning executable files on disk, although it would have taken more time and code—for a feature that I consider marginal. You could take it a few steps further yourself, however. If you can read the existing resources out of a file, what's to stop you from writing new ones in their place? In other words, you could write a resource compiler. I'm warning you, though—it's more than a weekend project.

Opening executable files is ugly business. Suffice it to say that the MSDN/VB starter kit provides a road map to the 16-bit Windows executable format. Actually, this road map is more like the directions your Aunt Mazie might scrawl on the back of last month's electric bill when she sends you down Scrub Hollow to find that used washing machine old Ike Scrawnton's son-in-law is trying to sell real cheap. "Turn left at the Hilltop Market, and drive about half a mile to the dirt road just past the Five Mile Creek bridge...."

There's nothing interesting or exciting about this kind of code; simply follow the directions, no matter how complicated and bizarre. To make things even more complex, the executable format for 16-bit programs is completely different from the format for 32-bit programs. Your Aunt Mazie will send you on a different route depending on whether it's Tuesday or Wednesday.

Rather than describe in detail the process of reading executables, I'll just turn you over to Aunt Mazie. In the MSDN/VB starter kit, search for *Executable-File Header Format*. It's all there in twisted black and white. Although the starter kit doesn't contain a similar topic for 32-bit mode, the Win32 executable file format has been described in various documents on the Microsoft Developer Network Development Library CD. The point is, if you steal the code on the pages that follow in this chapter, you won't really need to read the instructions—at least not for 16-bit programs.

CHALLENGE If you'd like to read executables in 32-bit programs, you're on your own. The resource format is similar in some ways, but it's not close enough to allow you to reuse much 16-bit code. So here's the challenge. At the end of the GetResources procedure in WinWatch, you'll find a block of code starting with the comment *'Get Windows NT or Windows 95 resources*. Just replace the current error message code with your own 32-bit resource code. Good luck.

Reading Resources

Reading binary data from specific offsets in a file is not one of Basic's strong points. You can do it in one of two ways: you can read the data into UDTs with fields matching the fields of the file, or you can read the data into a string and hack on specific offsets in the string. I chose the latter method for this particular problem because the fields of an executable are extremely varied and most of them are unimportant here. I won't swear that I made the right choice.

My resource code reads parts of the executable file into arrays of bytes and processes the arrays with the byte functions described in "Reading and Writing Blobs," page 119. You've already seen these functions (in BYTES.BAS), but let's look briefly at the one that reads resource string IDs and string type names. These are stored in the executable in a format that I've never seen elsewhere in any code related to Windows. The first byte of the string is the length, and the remaining bytes contain the string data. This is how Pascal stores strings, so I called the helper function BytesToPStr. Here it is:

```
Function BytesToPStr(ab() As Byte, iOffset As Long) As String
    BugAssert iOffset <= UBound(ab)
    BytesToPStr = MidBytes(ab, iOffset + 1, ab(iOffset))
End Function
```

The sub that actually reads the resources from an executable file into a list box is called GetResources. You can look at the code online to see all the details. Here's a slice to give you the flavor:

```
Private Sub GetResources(hInst, lst As ListBox)

    ' Get full executable path and open file
    Dim sExePath As String, sError As String
    sExePath = GetInstExePath(hInst)
    If GetFileBase(sExePath) = "USER" Then
        sError = "Can't read 32-bit executable"
        GoTo GetResourceError
    End If
    If FileExist(sExePath) = False Then
        sError = "Executable not found": GoTo GetResourceError
    End If

    Dim nFile As Integer
    On Error GoTo GetResourceError
    nFile = FreeFile
    Open sExePath For Binary Access Read Shared As nFile
    Dim abHeader() As Byte
    ReDim abHeader(0 To &H40) As Byte
    Get nFile, 1, abHeader

    ' MS-DOS headers start with magic "MZ" (should never fail)
    BugAssert LeftBytes(abHeader, 2) = "MZ"

    ' In new EXE format, word at offset &H18 is less than 40h
    BugAssert BytesToWord(abHeader, &H18) >= &H40

    ' Get offset of new EXE header
    Dim iNewExe As Integer
    iNewExe = BytesToWord(abHeader, &H3C)
    Get nFile, iNewExe + 1, abHeader

    ' New EXE headers start with magic header "NE"
    Dim sMagic As String
    sMagic = LeftBytes(abHeader, 2)
    ' No OS/2 2.x allowed
    If sMagic = "LE" Then
        sError = "OS/2 2.x file": GoTo GetResourceError
    End If
```

(continued)

```
' Check for Windows or OS/2 format
If sMagic = "NE" Then

    ' Require Windows as operating system
    BugAssert abHeader(&H36) And &H2

    ' Get resources, starting with offset of resource table
    Dim iResTable As Integer, cResTable As Integer
    iResTable = BytesToWord(abHeader, &H24)
```

And so on. The long and the short of it is that random bytes at random locations indicate what type of file an executable file is. You must check some of these and take random actions based on the results. Eventually you get to the resource table. Here, random bits and bytes tell you whether each resource has a name or a number and what type of resource it is. You copy the name or the number and the type name to a string and then add that string to the list box.

Better yet, just trust me, and use this code without looking at it. All you really need to know is that for numbered resources the list box will contain entries such as this:

```
00002    String
```

For named resources, the entries will look like this:

```
CLOCK    Menu
```

When the user clicks an item, the name and the type are parsed directly out of the item string in the list box and passed to the appropriate functions to display the resource. This brings us to a much more interesting question: what can you do with a resource? Well, that depends…

Using Resources the Windows Way

We've already talked about the Visual Basic Way of using resources. The LoadResPicture, LoadResString, and LoadResData functions load resources out of your resource list—but only out of your own list. If you want to load out of someone else's resource list, you have to do it the Windows Way.

You pass Windows the ID name or number and the type of the resource, and it returns a handle to your bitmap, icon, or whatever. And that's not the only way to get a handle to a resource. You can create your own. You can read a handle out of a file. You can get a handle from the clipboard. This section tells you what to do with the various kinds of resource handles you get.

Sorting Out Resources

Windows understands 12 resource types, several of which are of no use to Basic programmers. Rather than fill your list box with useless resource items, GetResources can filter out the ones you don't want, based on the current setting of the Filter Resources check box. I said earlier that the details of GetResources weren't very interesting, but let's look at this block of code anyway:

```
idResType = BytesToWord(abHeader, iPos)
If (idResType And &H8000) <> 0& Then
    ' Use constant resource type
    sResType = sEmpty
    Select Case idResType And &H7FFF
    Case RT_CURSOR
        If Not fFilter Then sResType = "Cursor"
    Case RT_BITMAP
        sResType = "Bitmap"
    Case RT_ICON
        If Not fFilter Then sResType = "Icon"
    Case RT_MENU
        sResType = "Menu"
    Case RT_DIALOG
        If Not fFilter Then sResType = "Dialog"
    Case RT_STRING
         sResType = "String"
    Case RT_FONTDIR
        If Not fFilter Then sResType = "FontDir"
    Case RT_FONT
        If Not fFilter Then sResType = "Font"
    Case RT_ACCELERATOR
        If fFilter Then sResType = "Accelerator"
    Case RT_RCDATA
        sResType = "RCData"
    Case RT_GROUP_CURSOR
        sResType = "Group Cursor"
    Case RT_GROUP_ICON
        sResType = "Group Icon"
    Case Else
        sResType = sEmpty
    End Select
Else
    ' Read resource type name from table
    sResType = BytesToPStr(abHeader, idResType)
End If
```

GetResources reads the type of a resource from a random location and then assigns a type string based on the result. In some cases—specifically for the Cursor, Icon, Dialog, Accelerator, and Font types—*sResType* is left empty if resource filtering is on, which means that type of resource will be ignored. Just turn off filtering if you want to litter your Resources list box with items you won't be able to see.

You can use resources with type Group Cursor or Group Icon, but those with type Cursor or Icon fail for reasons I can't explain. The distinction is vaguely documented, if at all. I assume that nongroup icons and cursors must be private to their own applications. As for Accelerators, I left them out because I couldn't think of any use for them, except perhaps in some sort of macro program. Fonts? Well, what's the point of loading them with the Windows API? If you see a font file loaded in WinWatch (FON files are actually DLLs containing font resources), you can already access that font with the Font object.

Dialog boxes are a different matter. You can display a dialog resource with the CreateDialog (modeless) function or the DialogBox (modal) function. Once you get the resource on the screen, however, you can't get rid of it. The problem is that each dialog box requires its own dialog procedure to handle its various controls. You must pass the address of the dialog procedure when you display the dialog box, but Visual Basic doesn't support procedure variables. You can pass 0 as the dialog procedure argument; the dialog box then sits on your screen, accepting keystrokes and mouse actions and passing all the information back to 0, which doesn't know what to do when you choose the OK button or the Cancel button. The Visual Basic model of forms as dialog boxes works better anyway.

Doing Resources

The GetResources procedure handles getting the resources. The Click event procedure of the Resources list box deconstructs the list box entry and passes it to an appropriate procedure, to do whatever this kind of resource does:

```
Private Sub lstResource_Click()
    Dim sType As String, sResource As String, i As Integer

    sType = lstResource.Text
    BugAssert sType <> sEmpty
    ' Extract resource ID and type
    If Left$(sType, 1) = "0" Then
        sResource = "#" & Left$(sType, 5)
        sType = Mid$(sType, 7)
```

```
Else
    i = InStr(sType, sTab)
    If i = 0 Then i = InStr(sType, " ")
    sResource = Trim$(Left$(sType, i - 1))
    sType = Mid$(sType, i + 1)
End If

' Clear last resource and handle new one
ClearResource
Select Case UCase$(sType)
Case "CURSOR", "GROUP CURSOR"
    ShowCursor hInstCur, sResource
Case "BITMAP"
    ShowBitmap hInstCur, sResource
Case "ICON", "GROUP ICON"
    ShowIcon hInstCur, sResource
Case "MENU"
    ShowMenu hInstCur, sResource
Case "STRING"
    ShowString hInstCur, sResource
Case "RCDATA"
    ShowData hInstCur, sResource
Case "WAVE"
    PlayWave hInstCur, sResource
Case "FONTDIR", "FONT", "DIALOG", "ACCELERATOR"
    pbResource.Print sType & " selected"
Case Else
    ShowData hInstCur, sResource, sType
End Select
pbResource.Refresh

End Sub
```

The first chunk of code parses the ID number or string name of the resource off the left of the item string and the resource type name off the right. If the resource is identified by number, the procedure passes it on as a string containing a pound sign followed by a number (for example, *"#34"*). The API functions that load resources accept that format, and it's easier than passing numbers in some cases and strings in others. The performance cost is negligible in WinWatch.

Notice that ClearResource is called every time you load a new resource. It's also called whenever you select a process, a module, or a top window—anything that causes the program to read a new list of resources. ClearResource removes the representation of the last resource. Sometimes this is as simple as erasing the picture box where the resource was displayed, which can be done reliably for most resources as follows:

```
With pbResource
    .Picture = LoadPicture()
    .Cls
    .Refresh
    ' Resize looks nicer when invisible
    .Visible = False
    .AutoSize = True
    .Width = xPicMax
    .Height = yPicMax
    .Visible = True
End With
```

In other cases, the procedure must take type-specific cleanup actions, such as restoring the original menu or cursor. Let's look at some of the procedures that actually display the resources as well as the cleanup code that clears them. The code will be instructive not only for learning about resources but also for understanding the objects they represent.

> **NOTE**
> WinWatch deals only with 16-bit resources. Most of the code described in the next sections would also work for 32-bit resources, but I didn't have a sample application that provided a framework for systematic testing.

Using Data Resources

Let's start with raw binary data—if you know how that works, you can figure out what to do with other kinds of data. You can cram any binary data you want into a resource file. Use the predefined RT_RCDATA type, or invent your own resource type name. Of course, WinWatch won't know how to handle unknown data types; the best it can do is dump the binary data in hex.

The goal is to turn a resource into an array of bytes, which is the approved way for Basic to handle binary data. You can also handle data as strings, but that's politically incorrect, particularly in a chapter such as this, which deals with multiple languages. Here's how ShowData reads and dumps generic data:

```
Sub ShowData(hInst, sData As String, Optional sDataType As Variant)
    BugAssert hInst <> hNull

    Dim hres As Long, hmemRes As Long, cRes As Long
    Dim pRes As Long, abRes() As Byte
    If IsMissing(sDataType) Then
        hres = FindResourceStrId(hInst, sData, RT_RCDATA)
```

```
    Else
        hres = FindResourceStrStr(hInst, sData, sDataType)
    End If
    If hres = hNull Then
        pbResource.Print "Can't load data"
        Exit Sub
    End If
    ' Allocate memory block and get its size
    hmemRes = LoadResource(hInst, hres)
    cRes = SizeofResource(hInst, hres)
    ' Don't dump more than 500 bytes
    If cRes > 500 Then cRes = 500
    ' Lock it to get pointer
    pRes = LockResource(hmemRes)
    ' Allocate byte array of right size
    ReDim abRes(cRes)
    ' Copy memory block to string
    CopyMemoryLpToByte abRes(0), ByVal pRes, cRes
    ' Unlock and free resource
    Call UnlockResource(hmemRes)
    Call FreeResource(hmemRes)
    pbResource.Print HexDump(abRes, False)

End Sub
```

First you use FindResource to get a handle to the resource. Then you move through the memory-allocation fire drill described in the following section: allocate, lock, process, unlock, free. You'll learn to recognize this pattern.

This code contains a couple of quirky details. First, refer back to the sidebar "CopyMemory: A Strange and Terrible Saga," page 116, to find the story of CopyMemory and its aliased friends CopyMemoryToStr and CopyMemoryRef. Second, UnlockResource doesn't really exist as a separate function. In 16-bit Windows, the C include files implement it as a macro to GlobalUnlock. That's easy to fake with an alias in the Windows API type library. In the 32-bit C include files, UnlockResource is a macro to nothing. It simply returns False. You can't do that with a Declare or type-library statement, so I just aliased it to GlobalUnlock, as in 16-bit mode.

You can probably guess what the HexDump function (or its cousins, HexDumpS and HexDumpB) looks like; check it out in UTILITY.BAS. It dumps in either 8-byte rows (if you pass False as the second argument) or the traditional 16-byte format used by most debuggers. I use the 8-byte form in WinWatch so that the dump will fit in the picture box. Your dumps will look a lot better if you set the font of the output object (label, text box, picture box, printer) to a monospace font.

The Zen of Windows memory management

Normally, the Windows Way of managing memory is the least of your worries. Dim, Redim, Private, Public, and Static do it all for you, for the most part transparently. You don't ordinarily use the Windows memory functions directly because they deal with pointers, and Basic doesn't do pointers. But there are exceptions to every rule.

Secretly, most of the handles you encounter in Windows are simply global memory handles. The Windows memory manager gives you access to the memory blocks you allocate through handles, and Windows itself uses the same mechanism to create memory blocks for everything else. An icon handle is simply the handle of a block of data that Windows allocated and filled with data in icon format. You can use the global memory functions to examine that memory. This undocumented feature isn't guaranteed to work now for any particular type of handle, or in the future for handles that work this way now. The system makes sense, however, and I doubt that it will change.

To make your experimenting less risky—but don't blame me if you have to boot—here's a 30-second introduction to Windows global memory management:

1. Get a handle to a global memory block. You can create a generic one with GlobalAlloc, or you can create a resource block by calling LoadResource on the value returned by FindResource. To be safe, use resource functions instead of global memory functions on resource blocks. You might be able to get a memory block from a function that returns any kind of handle. An HBITMAP or an HICON is a global memory handle at heart, but your HWHATCHAMACALLIT might be something else entirely. You're on your own.

2. Measure the memory with GlobalSize (or remember its size, if you created it with GlobalAlloc). If it's a resource, use SizeofResource. I don't know a way to use a global memory block in Basic if you don't know its size.

3. Lock the memory handle with GlobalLock (or LockResource, if it's a resource handle). This means that you ask the memory manager to let you play with the memory for a while. If your request is granted, you'll be given a pointer to the memory, and other users will be locked out of it.

4. Have your way with the pointer and the stuff it points to. This is the tricky part because, in Basic, a pointer is like a handle—all you can do with it is pass it on to another API function. For example, you can use CopyMemory (an alias to hmemcpy in 16-bit mode) to copy the memory of a pointer to a Basic string. (You must know the size to do this; see step 2.) If you dare, you can modify the string and copy it back to the pointer (again using CopyMemory). If you change the size of the

data, you'll need to call GlobalRealloc to change the size of the original block before copying. You could find other API functions to pass your memory pointers to (such as sndPlaySound, described later).

5. When you're done with the block, use GlobalUnlock (UnlockResource for resources) to release the pointer back to the system. If you read from or write to a pointer after you've unlocked it, you deserve the horrible things that will happen soon if you're lucky or late if you're not—this can be a debugging nightmare.

6. Free the memory if you created it; leave it alone if Windows created it. Use GlobalFree to free memory you created with GlobalAlloc; use FreeResource if you created the handle with LoadResource.

Using Bitmap Resources

WinWatch needs to display the selected bitmap in a picture box, but with certain restrictions. The Picture property of the PictureBox control must contain the entire bitmap, no matter how large, so that you can save the bitmap with the Save button (by calling SavePicture). You might need to clip the actual surface of the picture box so that it won't overwrite the rest of the WinWatch display.

Given those restrictions, you can probably come up with several implementation alternatives. Chapter 6 shows Basic techniques that you can adapt. Here's one way, although I won't claim it's the best:

```
Sub ShowBitmap(hInst, sBitmap As String)
    BugAssert hInst <> hNull

    Dim bmp As TBitmap, f As Integer, hDCMem As Long
    hResourceCur = LoadBitmap(hInst, sBitmap)
    If hResourceCur = hNull Then
        pbResource.Print "Can't load bitmap"
        Exit Sub
    End If

    With pbResource
        ' Create memory DC to hold image and select into it
        hDCMem = CreateCompatibleDC(.hDC)
        f = GetObjectAsBitmap(hResourceCur, Len(bmp), bmp)
        BugAssert f
        hResourceLast = SelectObject(hDCMem, hResourceCur)
        .AutoSize = False
        .Width = bmp.Width * Screen.TwipsPerPixelX
        .Height = bmp.Height * Screen.TwipsPerPixelY
        .Picture = .Image
```

(continued)

```
                ' Hide (until size resolved) and copy image to PictureBox
                .Visible = False
                Call BitBlt(.hDC, 0, 0, bmp.Width, bmp.Height, _
                            hDCMem, 0, 0, SRCCOPY)
                .Refresh
                ' Make picture same as DC contents
                .Picture = .Image
                ' Clean up by reselecting old image and deleting memory DC
                Call SelectObject(hDCMem, hResourceLast)
                f = DeleteObject(hResourceCur)
                BugAssert f
                f = DeleteDC(hDCMem)
                BugAssert f

                ' Clip or resize, depending on size; then make it visible
                If .Width > xPicMax Or .Height > yPicMax Then
                    .AutoSize = False
                    .Width = IIf(.Width > xPicMax, xPicMax, .Width)
                    .Height = IIf(.Height > xPicMax, xPicMax, .Height)
                Else
                    .AutoSize = True
                End If
                .Visible = True
            End With
            ordResourceLast = RT_BITMAP
    End Sub
```

The essence of this code is that you create a memory device context, select the bitmap handle into it, and then blit the DC to the target resource. The rest of the code deals primarily with resizing and clipping the Resources picture box. (You might want to review "The Windows Way of Painting," page 275, if you have trouble following this code.) Since the picture box contains the whole image, even if the image is clipped, a simple SavePicture is all it takes to save the bitmap to disk.

Using Icon Resources

It's a simple matter to show an icon: just load the icon handle with LoadIcon, and then call DrawIcon to display it. When you're done, call DestroyIcon to release the resource. That's how I handled icons in early versions of WinWatch. The ShowIcon sub still shows this code in a conditional block, but eventually I found a better way:

```
Sub ShowIcon(hInst, sIcon As String)
    BugAssert (hInst <> hNull) And (sIcon <> sEmpty)
```

```
        ' Load icon resource
        hResourceCur = LoadIcon(hInst, sIcon)
        With pbResource
            If hResourceCur <> hNull Then
#If fDrawOnly Then
                ' Draw icon
                .Width = Screen.TwipsPerPixelX * 32
                .Height = Screen.TwipsPerPixelY * 32
                Call DrawIcon(.hDC, 0, 0, hResourceCur)
                .Refresh
                ' Make sure picture is a bitmap
                .Picture = .Image
                ' Done, discard handle
                Call DestroyIcon(hResourceCur)
#Else
                ' Convert icon handle to Picture
                .Picture = IconToPicture(hResourceCur)
#End If
                ordResourceLast = RT_ICON
            Else
                pbResource.Print "Can't display icon"
            End If
        End With

End Sub
```

The old version (which is never called unless you create an *fDrawOnly* constant with value True) draws the icon to the hDC of the picture box. DrawIcon works much the same way as the CPictureGlass class described in Chapter 6. The icon consists of a mask and an image, which DrawIcon blits onto the existing background. The result of this operation is not an icon, but a device context containing the previous background and the new icon. The Picture property of the picture box is unchanged. In order to save the image with the SavePicture function, you need to assign the Image property (containing the image on the hDC) to the Picture property.

This technique has two problems. First, notice that the icon size is hard-coded to 32 by 32 pixels. This assumption works under old-fashioned operating systems, but it's not a good idea in Windows 95. "Icons with an Attitude," page 531, discusses the new way to handle icons. The second problem is that you end up with a bitmap instead of an icon. When you try to save it with the WinWatch Save button, you save in the wrong format. Also, if you try to put it into an Image control, it comes out opaque instead of transparent. It looks right in WinWatch, but it isn't.

The IconToPicture function converts an icon handle to a Picture object. If you call SavePicture on the Picture object, you'll get an icon file. Under Windows 95, IconToPicture does a much better job of handling different-sized icons. IconToPicture (in PICTOOL.BAS) works by doing some OLE magic that I won't be able to fully explain here. Nevertheless, let's have a look, starting with some required UDTs and a Declare statement.

Here's the 16-bit version of TPictDesc, the low-level type that actually holds the contents of a Picture object. The 32-bit version is the same except that it has Longs instead of Integers.

```
Type TPictDesc
    cbSizeofStruct As Integer
    picType As Integer
    hImage As Integer            ' hBitmap, hIcon, or hMetafile
    xExt As Integer              ' xExt for metafile, hPal for bitmap
    yExt As Integer              ' yExt for metafile
End Type
```

The Picture class, which describes Picture objects, is actually an OLE interface. Every OLE interface has a unique 128-bit code called a *globally unique ID* (GUID). We'll talk more about OLE and GUIDs in Chapter 10. Here's a UDT to hold a GUID:

```
Type TGuid
    Data1 As Long
    Data2 As Integer
    Data3 As Integer
    Data4(0 To 7) As Byte
End Type
```

Here's the 16-bit Declare statement for the OleCreatePictureIndirect function, which uses both TPictDesc and TGuid. This function is part of the OLE Control Development Kit, the only place you'll find it documented. The 32-bit version is the same except that it uses Longs and is located in OLEPRO32.DLL.

```
Declare Function OleCreatePictureIndirect Lib "oc25.dll" ( _
    lpPictDesc As TPictDesc, riid As TGuid, _
    ByVal fPictureOwnsHandle As Integer, ipic As IPicture) As Integer
```

Finally, you're ready to actually create a picture by initializing the UDT variables and calling the function:

```
Function IconToPicture(hIcon) As Picture
    If hIcon = hNull Then Exit Function
    Dim pic As Picture, picdes As TPictDesc, iidIDispatch As TGuid
    ' Fill picture description
```

ExtractIcon

All that fancy code to extract resources from executable files is wasted on icons. Windows provides the ExtractIcon API to do it all for you (although it lacks corresponding ExtractBitmap and ExtractCursor functions). If you simply need icons, do it the easy way. The following code loops through all the icons in a program specified by its instance handle:

```
iIcon = 0
hIcon = ExtractIcon(hInstMe, sExe, iIcon)
Do While hIcon <> hNull
    ' Do something with icon here
    iIcon = iIcon + 1
    hIcon = ExtractIcon(hInstMe, sExe, iIcon)
Loop
```

```
    picdes.cbSizeofStruct = Len(picdes)
    picdes.picType = vbPicTypeIcon
    picdes.hImage = hIcon
    ' Fill in magic IID number {00020400-0000-0000-C000-000000046}
    iidIDispatch.Data1 = &H20400
    iidIDispatch.Data4(0) = &HC0
    iidIDispatch.Data4(7) = &H46
    ' Create picture from icon handle, ignoring error return
    Call OleCreatePictureIndirect(picdes, iidIDispatch, True, pic)
    ' Result will be valid Picture or Nothing--either way, set it
    Set IconToPicture = pic
End Function
```

If you're wondering how and why this works, join the club. This is a book about Visual Basic, not OLE, so you'll just have to take some of this code on faith. All I can add is a word about the *fPictureOwnsHandle* parameter of the OleCreatePictureIndirect function. This parameter indicates whether the Picture object should own the icon handle and automatically destroy it when the Picture is destroyed. You should always pass True for Visual Basic Picture objects.

Using Cursor Resources

Previous versions of Visual Basic lacked any means of assigning a custom mouse pointer, although this is a common technique in Windows-based programs. Many programmers who tried to get around this limitation turned to the Windows API, but even then solutions proved unexpectedly difficult.

Visual Basic version 4 finally provides a simple and intuitive solution, described in the sidebar "Cursors Eat Mouse Icons for Lunch," on page 324. But

WinWatch can't use the Visual Basic Way because it gets cursors from resources. If you check out the Windows API Help, the solution looks simple: just call SetCursor. When you try this, however, the new cursor flickers on and then disappears. Every time you move the cursor, Visual Basic's original cursor is restored.

Here's how WinWatch works around this limitation:

```
Sub ShowCursor(hInst, sCursor As String)
    BugAssert hInst <> hNull
    ' Get cursor handle
    hResourceCur = LoadCursor(hInst, sCursor)
    If hResourceCur <> hNull Then
        ' Display cursor
        fCustomCursor = True
        hResourceLast = SetClassData(lstResource.hWnd, _
                                GCD_HCURSOR, hResourceCur)
        ordResourceLast = RT_CURSOR
        pbResource.Print "Cursor set"
    Else
        pbResource.Print "Can't set cursor"
    End If
End Sub
```

That's half the operation. You must also restore the cursor when you change resources. Here's the Select Case block in ClearResource that restores the previous cursor. Note that *fCustomCursor*, *ordResourceLast*, and *hResourceLast* are form-level variables so that they can be used from both functions.

```
Case RT_GROUP_CURSOR, RT_CURSOR
    If fCustomCursor Then
        Call SetClassData(lstResource.hWnd, _
                        GCD_HCURSOR, hResourceLast)
        Call DestroyCursor(hResourceCur)
        fCustomCursor = False
    End If
```

ShowCursor uses the Windows LoadCursor function to get the cursor handle and then calls SetClassData to set the list box cursor to the resource cursor. ClearResource uses SetClassData to restore the previous cursor. (Remember that SetClassData is an alias for SetClassWord or SetClassLong, as described in "The Windows Word and the Windows Long," page 206.) Notice that although you pass the handle of one specific list box (*lstResource.hWnd*), the cursor will change over all the list boxes when you run the program. That's because you are changing the setting for the Basic list box class, which has the name

ThunderListBox. Luckily, setting the cursor for list boxes in WinWatch doesn't affect list boxes in other applications.

This is a slimy little hack that happens to work for WinWatch, but in real life you might want to set the cursor for your entire application, or maybe for one particular list box. To do the former, you could iterate through all the controls, setting the cursor for each. (If you try this, don't forget to restore each cursor.) The correct way to set the cursor, however, is to intercept the WM_SETCURSOR message and reinitialize the cursor with the SetCursor function every time you get the message. You can do this with Message Blaster or a similar message control. (See "Receiving Messages," page 241.) But Visual Basic's custom cursor feature makes it unlikely that you'll need this code.

Using Menu Resources

Realistically, you probably won't ever need to use menu resources. But it's so easy to load them that I couldn't resist.

```
Sub ShowMenu(hInst, sMenu As String)
    BugAssert hInst <> hNull

    hResourceCur = LoadMenu(hInst, sMenu)
    If hResourceCur <> 0 Then
        pbResource.Print "Menu set to: "
        pbResource.Print lstTopWin.Text
        hResourceLast = GetMenu(Me.hWnd)
        Call SetMenu(Me.hWnd, hResourceCur)
        ordResourceLast = RT_MENU
#If Win32 = False Then
        bstMenu.hWndTarget = Me.hWnd
        bstMenu.MsgList(0) = WM_COMMAND
        bstMenu.MsgList(1) = WM_INITMENU
#End If
    Else
        pbResource.Print "Can't display menu"
    End If
End Sub
```

First, the code loads the menu, getting back a menu handle. If the handle is valid, you use GetMenu to save the handle of WinWatch's real menu so that you can restore it the next time you change to a new resource or program. Next, you call SetMenu to replace the normal WinWatch menu with the resource menu. Finally, you set up a Message Blaster control to catch the appropriate menu messages. When the user clicks a fake menu or presses the menu selection key, you'll get a WM_INITMENU message; and when the user actually selects an item, you'll get a WM_COMMAND message.

When another resource is selected, the menu must be cleaned up. The following code in the ClearResource procedure resets the previous menu, frees the menu resource, and unhooks the Message Blaster control:

```
Case RT_MENU
    Call SetMenu(Me.hWnd, hResourceLast)
    Call DestroyMenu(hResourceCur)
#If Win32 = False Then
    bstMenu.hWndTarget = hNull
    bstMenu.MsgList(0) = 0
    bstMenu.MsgList(1) = 0
#End If
```

Here's the code that actually handles messages in the Message Blaster event procedure:

```
Private Sub bstMenu_Message(MsgVal As Integer, wParam As Integer, _
                            lParam As Long, ReturnVal As Long)
    If MsgVal = WM_COMMAND Then
        ReturnVal = SendMessageAsLong(hTopWndCur, MsgVal, _
                                      wParam, lParam)
    ElseIf MsgVal = WM_INITMENU Then
        SyncMenu hResourceCur, GetMenu(hTopWndCur)
        ReturnVal = 0&
    End If
End Sub
```

If the message is a WM_COMMAND message, you simply pass it on to the top window of the real application. If it is a WM_INITMENU message, you call a routine named SyncMenu that cycles through each item on the real menu, examines its status (grayed, checked, disabled), and sets the corresponding fake item to the same status. You can look at this procedure in MENUTOOL.BAS, although you should bear in mind that SyncMenu has problems. The fake menu items from the menu resource are not guaranteed to be the same as the real ones in the application because the application is free to call InsertMenu and DeleteMenu to change the menu at any time.

In a way, it's neat that WinWatch allows you to control another application from the WinWatch menu. But if you continue to experiment with it, you'll encounter problems. Some menu items, especially ones that produce dialog boxes, don't work very well. In other cases, the WinWatch menu doesn't match the real menu because the real menu has been changed. Some applications (Microsoft Word, for example) don't even use menu resources, although they certainly have menus.

The fact is that menu resources are not necessarily the best way to handle menus. Visual Basic itself never uses them, as you can tell by examining the

VB.EXE file or any Basic-generated EXE file with WinWatch. We'll discuss the dynamic way of handling menus in "Other People's Menus," page 428.

Another problem with using the Message Blaster control to process menus is that the control will get trashed if you ever try to run WinWatch in 32-bit mode. I warned you in Chapter 5 that WinWatch is only partially functional in 32-bit mode, but having your Message Blaster VBX turned into a PictureBox control is an annoying price to pay just for trying the 32-bit version. If this happens to you, reinstall the Message Blaster control in the 16-bit version and name it bstMenu. WinWatch will be as good as new.

Using String Resources

It's unlikely that you'll need to use string resources from a DLL or a program that you didn't write, but it's so easy that WinWatch implements it. Just pass the ID number of the string to the LoadString API function, along with a string buffer and a maximum length, as shown here:

```
Sub ShowString(hInst, sString As String)
    BugAssert hInst <> hNull
    Dim c As Integer, s As String
    s = Space$(81)
    c = LoadString(hInst, Val(Mid$(sString, 2)), s, 80)
    If c <> 0 Then
        pbResource.Print Left$(s, c)
    Else
        pbResource.Print "Can't display string"
    End If
End Sub
```

Unlike most resource functions, LoadString always takes an ID number instead of a string. In order to accommodate the other kinds of resources more easily, the lstResource_Click event handler passes strings rather than numbers. Therefore, when ShowString gets a string in the format *"#478"*, it must translate the string into the integer 478 before passing the value to LoadString.

Curiously, many strings are invalid. If you read in all the strings from a file, you'll see the *Can't display string* message frequently. I'm not sure why this happens, but so many unreadable strings appeared in my Resources list box that I added some code in GetResources to check the strings there before putting them in the list box. The code is similar to that in ShowString. The Filter Resources check box determines whether invalid strings are filtered out; check it out in the GetResources procedure.

Using Sound Resources

WinWatch is just a demo; in real life, you'll have to do better than a hex dump of your resource data. WinWatch does know about one nonstandard resource, however: sounds in the WAVE format.

Nonstandard formats can be a problem unless everyone who uses the format agrees on the type name. Someone might put a wave file in a program as an RCDATA resource type. If that someone was you, you know what to do. But to WinWatch, it's just data. You could turn the data into a string and search the string for some identifying data instead of producing a hex dump. A hex dump of wave data, for example, looks like this:

```
52 49 46 46 B2 87 00 00  RIFF....
57 41 56 45 66 6D 74 20  WAVEfmt
```

WinWatch could test data blocks to see whether they contain such recognizable formats, but that's up to you. My version recognizes only wave data that has the type name WAVE. This works for TRES. If you see a resource with type WAVE in another program, there's a good chance you'll be able to play it, although you have no guarantee that a particular wave resource won't contain waves for a surfing program.

Assuming that you do have a wave sound resource, here's the code to play it:

```
Sub PlayWave(hInst, sWave As String)
    BugAssert hInst <> hNull
    Dim hWave As Long, hmemWave As Long, pWave As Long
    hWave = FindResourceStrStr(hInst, sWave, "WAVE")
    hmemWave = LoadResource(hInst, hWave)
    pWave = LockResource(hmemWave)
    If sndPlaySoundAsLp(pWave, SND_MEMORY Or SND_NODEFAULT) Then
        pbResource.Print "Sound played"
    Else
        pbResource.Print "Couldn't play sound"
    End If
    Call UnlockResource(hmemWave)
    Call FreeResource(hmemWave)
End Sub
```

If this isn't clear, you might refer to "The Zen of Windows memory management," page 340. The sndPlaySoundAsLP function is a type-safe alias to the multimedia sndPlaySound function. The Windows API type library provides two other aliases. You can use the raw version to play sound files or system alerts. For example, use this statement to play a wave file:

```
f = sndPlaySound("c:\windows\wave\helpme.wav", SND_SYNC)
```

Use this statement to play the sound associated with SystemExclamation in the WIN.INI file:

```
f = sndPlaySound("SystemExclamation", SND_SYNC)
```

When you load a sound with LoadResData, you get back an array of bytes. The Test Resources program (TRES.VBP) uses the sndPlaySoundAsBytes alias to play a wave string:

```
Function PlayWave(ab() As Byte) As Boolean
    PlayWave = sndPlaySoundAsBytes(ab(0), SND_MEMORY Or SND_SYNC)
End Function
```

You can play sounds with the Multimedia MCI control, which is appropriate in the context of other multimedia features. But it's overkill if you're simply playing sounds. Adding a custom control takes up a good chunk of memory resources, whereas using the sndPlaySound function takes up very little.

A bit of advice: if you're tempted to start putting sound resources in your programs left and right, think again. Consider using the existing named sounds in WIN.INI and, if appropriate, adding more named sounds. Then provide an interface that will allow users to install their own sound files for each name. Any sound can get tiresome if the user can't change it. I can tell you for sure that the guy across the hall got pretty sick of the sounds in the Test Resources program before I got it debugged.

CHALLENGE Although it's easy to put metafile resources in your resource scripts, neither Windows nor Basic provides an easy way to play them. In my next book, I just might write a function that loads and plays a metafile from a resource. But if you need this feature now, you'd better do it yourself. Check out the GetMetaFileBits and SetMetaFileBits API functions.

Creating Your Own Resources

It should be obvious from the way sounds are handled that you can put any kind of data into resources. If you use WinWatch to examine an EXE file created by an earlier version of Visual Basic (try the version 3 ICONWRKS.EXE), you'll find a familiar example. Forms used to be resources; you can see them in the file as RCDATA type. Of course, I can't swear that's what they are, but it sure looks like it.

In concept, the steps for creating your own resource types are simple. Let's go through them with the new, previously undocumented TimeTravel resource type, which enables users with appropriate TimeTravel expansion cards and device drivers to experience anything, anyplace, anytime.

1. Define a binary format for your resource. You'll probably want to create an editor that translates user-friendly commands into a tightly compressed binary format. The TimeTravel Editor has a dialog editor that allows you to select the time, place, and conditions of your appearance in easy-to-use dialog boxes. It then compiles these into a TTV file.

2. Put the data into a resource file. The TimeTravel Editor can automatically insert TTV files in an RC file. The line might look like this:

```
1492      TimeTravel    "c:\\ttv\\columbus.ttv"
```

3. Compile the resource script into a RES file, and add the RES file to your Visual Basic project.

4. Write procedures that will process the data. You can write them in Basic if the data is simple enough. Because LoadResData returns an array of bytes, you just need to write code that processes the bytes, converting them to a UDT or another data type if necessary. The TimeTravel resource, however, requires some low-level, high-speed communication between software and device driver. Therefore, the TimeTravel Development Kit (TDK) comes with an OLE server (TTAPI.DLL). Simply register the type library (TTAPI.TLB) in the References dialog box, and you're ready to load the Destination property and call the TravelThruTime method. Here's an example:

```
Dim someday As New CWhenever
someday.Destination = LoadResData(1492, "TimeTravel")
someday.TravelThruTime
```

While it's easy to use TimeTravel resources once you get your hands on them, I didn't have room to put the software on the companion CD. Furthermore, the hardware that is required is difficult to find and prohibitively expensive on this planet. For now, you'll have to play with wave and metafile resources.

8

Don't Write the Same Code Twice

Shortly after I started working at Microsoft, many years ago, I found myself at a party listening to an old-timer reminisce about days past when real programmers wrote programs on punch cards. Well, maybe it wasn't that far back, but the stories were fascinating to a programmer wanna-be. The most startling story went something like this. (I never saw the guy again, so if he reads this, I hope he won't hold me to the quotes or the details.)

"It was my first programming job. I was this green kid working for an old-timer who used to toggle his programs in with switches or something. Still, I thought I was hot stuff. I was smart, I worked long hours, and, most amazing, the things I wrote worked. My boss was short-tempered and generally obnoxious, but I figured that's just the way programmers were. So one day I was coding away, far gone in some hack, when suddenly I felt this really hard blow on the side of the head. I turned around, and there was my boss. He'd been watching me code for who knows how long.

"'Dammit! Don't ever write the same code twice when you're working for me.'"

This event had made a strong impression on the narrator, and his story made a strong impression on me. I would never walk into your office and slap you on the side of the head, but as an author I can get away with outrageous metaphors. So take this chapter as the literary equivalent of a slap upside the head.

"Dammit! Don't ever write the same code twice when you're reading my book."

Of course, everyone gives lip service to modular code, but writing it in Visual Basic isn't as easy as you might hope. Have you ever found yourself reusing code with the cut-and-paste-and-modify method rather than writing a single module and including it in various projects? The temptation is hard to resist.

The message-based Windows architecture makes it difficult to write truly modular code. Visual Basic simplifies the architecture with forms and events, but you still need to share a lot of data among different parts of your code. Making all the parts into independent code entities that you can plug into any project isn't always simple. Version 4 adds a lot of features that make modular code easier, however, and we'll examine many of them in this chapter.

Edward and the CEditor Class

Meet Edward, a text editor with more features than Notepad or, if you use Windows 95, WordPad. Your mission in this chapter is to create Edward with as few lines of code as possible. After you create this text editor, your next mission is to clone Edward and turn the clone into Edward II (EdII for short), a Multiple Document Interface editor with the same features as Edward. For EdII, the challenge is to change as few lines of Edward code as possible—in fact, all the changes should relate to MDI, not to editing. Your third (and ultimate) mission is to put an editor or a file viewer with any or all of Edward's features into any application you want with as much flexibility and as little code as possible.

At this point, you might say, "Why not just buy an editor control that has the extended features I want?" An excellent idea, if you really want a full-featured text editor with features that are not supported by the standard Windows edit control or the RichTextBox control. You will find plenty of fine ones on the market, supporting powerful features such as redefinition of editing keys, extended editing commands, and so on. But this might be overkill if your applications need only simple text editing or viewing features. If the features of Notepad, WordPad, or the Visual Basic editor look adequate, you probably don't need the extra expense and overhead of a third-party editor control.

The CEditor Class

The Visual Basic TextBox control doesn't directly support a lot of the features you need. The new RichTextBox control now available for 32-bit Windows is better, but it's still a text box, not an editor. If you want to find and replace text or load a file using the common dialog, you'll need to write your own code. You can find some sample editing code in the MDINote program supplied as an example with Visual Basic. The problem with this example is that it's designed to illustrate MDI programming, not editing. You could reuse parts of the program by cutting, pasting, and modifying, but you'd soon find yourself doing more modifying than pasting.

What you want is the TextBox control, but with more methods and properties. Wouldn't it be nice, for instance, if the TextBox control had a FileName property? When you set this property to a valid filename, it would load the text of that file into the text box. When you read the property, it would return the name of the file currently in the text box. The RichTextBox control actually has this property. It would also be handy to have a FileOpen method that uses the Open common dialog to load a file into the text box, and you'll need a FileSave method to save the modified contents to a file.

Let's see now—while you have the menu open, you might as well order a few more features. How about SearchFind, SearchFindNext, and SearchReplace methods? Let's have OptionFont and OptionColor methods to set the font and the color of text using the appropriate common dialogs. Why not have an EditUndo method and a FilePrint method? Many editors have a status bar that displays information about file size and current positions, so you'll want to have LineCur, ColumnCur, CharCur, LineCount, ColumnCount, and CharCount

Vendors, Users, and Clients

To avoid confusion in talking about who uses your code, let's define some terms. You, the designer and programmer of the CEditor class, are the *vendor*. The programmers who use CEditor are your *clients*. The people who use programs created with CEditor are *users*. Users are the customers of your clients. Your responsibility to clients is direct; your responsibility to users is indirect.

Forget for the moment that in many cases the vendor, the client, and the user will be the same person—you. You'll write better code if you pretend that thousands of clients will buy your library from computer magazines and software stores and that hundreds of thousands of users will buy programs built with the library. If the users don't like the programs, they won't call you; they'll call your clients. Then the clients will call you.

You have two goals: making it easy for clients to satisfy users, and making clients happy. You make it easy for clients to satisfy users by providing the features users want in their editors and viewers. You make clients happy if they can easily install these editing features. For example, clients will be very happy if they can get standard editing features by simply adding one statement to every edit-related menu, key, or button event. They'll be happier still if they can add unusual or customized editing features with just a little more work.

You need to consider one other factor when writing reusable classes, forms, and code modules for Visual Basic. This book provides the CEditor class as a source module, not a binary module. Vendors of traditional static libraries for other languages as well as vendors of dynamic-link libraries and custom controls for Basic have to decide exactly what they will offer their users—and if the users don't like it, tough. Some library vendors sell or give away source code, but people who modify that source are out of luck when the next update of the library comes along. Because your clients can modify whatever they want, you don't have to worry quite as much about covering every base in your class design.

properties. And of course you'll want an OverWrite property to control insert and overwrite modes.

If you had all these features, creating an editor would simply be a matter of creating the menus, toolbars, buttons, and keystrokes necessary for the editor's user interface and then tying each of these to the appropriate methods and properties. That's what the editor class presented in this chapter does. It packs into one interface just about all the functionality the standard Windows edit controls can possibly have.

The CEditor class is a handy tool that you could use in your projects either as is or with enhancements. More important, however, we'll use it in the following sections to explain and illustrate techniques for writing truly reusable modules.

Edward's Interface

Like many editors, Edward has a dual interface. Figure 8-1 shows Edward in raw-meat mode—that is, nothing but editing space and status bars. (Ignore that menu bar for now.) This editor might have commands, but only for those who memorize them from a book (not supplied). Furthermore, clicking various locations on the status bars produces various actions, but you'll have to figure this out for yourself.

The only thing wimpy about this editor is the menu bar. Those menus are your entry to quiche mode, where friendly dialog boxes hold your hand as they guide you through easy versions of the commands and let you customize colors and fonts. Figure 8-2 on page 358 provides a menu map.

The quiche interface needs no introduction; we all know how menus and dialog boxes work. The raw-meat interface is a little trickier. For example, look at the Line, Column, and Percent items on the bottom status bar, which you would expect to find in any editor. But if you click one of these items, it becomes an entry box in which you can enter a new line, column, or percent value. When you enter a value, the editor moves to the new location.

There's more. When you click the time display, it toggles to a date. When you click the INS item, it grays and switches you to overwrite mode. Click the CAP item, and you toggle the Caps Lock status. The top status bar works the same way, allowing you to enter a new filename or a search string.

Let's briefly look at how the status bars work. The Line item, for instance, is nothing but a 3-D panel that normally displays the current line and the line total. Unknown to the casual viewer, an invisible text box sits on top of the data portion of the panel. When you click this area, the text box becomes visible and

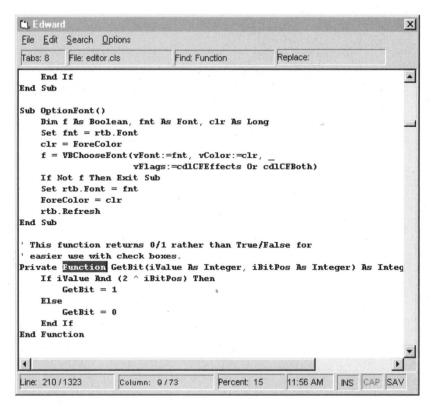

Figure 8-1. *Edward the editor.*

is initialized with the current line number. When you finish editing (by pressing Enter or changing the focus), the text box disappears, and the panel displays the result. More important, the new value is assigned to the Line property of the CEditor object, and the cursor—uh, make that the caret—moves to the new location. You can check out this code in EDWARD.FRM.

Of course, real power editors have a toolbar at the top instead of a status bar. It would be nice to give Edward a toolbar, but toolbars have long been the Achilles' heel of Visual Basic. Plenty of good third-party toolbar controls are available, but I don't know which one you have.

You can create a toolbar by placing button bitmaps on a status bar, but this method is inefficient, hard to implement, and harder to maintain. Visual Basic 4 finally provides a toolbar control, but it's based on COMCTL32.DLL and works for 32-bit mode only. I didn't use it for Edward because I wanted him to run in either 16-bit or 32-bit mode.

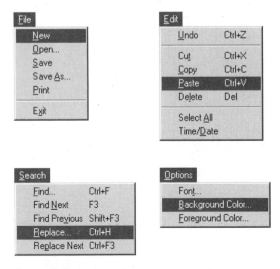

Figure 8-2. *Edward's menu map.*

This brings us to Edward's younger sister, Edwina. You can see her in Figure 8-3. Edwina works only in 32-bit mode, but her RichTextBox control, status bar, and toolbar make her look a lot more stylish. I created Edwina by cloning Edward and replacing his two fake status bars with Toolbar and StatusBar controls. Then I went through and tied some of the more important editing features to the appropriate places in the user interface. I'm not going to say a lot about Edwina except that one of her favorite phrases is "Left as an exercise for the reader." She doesn't know, for example, how to do text entry from a status bar panel, as Edward does. Your work is cut out for you. (Chapter 11 discusses some of the new Windows 95 controls in more detail.) I'll talk about Edwina in this chapter only when the difference affects the CEditor class.

The important point is that Edward and Edwina both use the CEditor class (and the other classes that are discussed in this chapter). All the differences are in EDWARD.FRM and EDWINA.FRM or in conditional code in EDITOR.CLS. In Edwina, you need to set the *fRichText* constant to True on the Advanced tab of the Options dialog box. Although some features are implemented differently for the RichTextBox control, they look the same to the client—except for a few minor cases in which TextBox controls and RichTextBox controls are incompatible. Edward has a slightly more advanced interface because he's older. I wrote him first and had more time to polish. You can give Edwina all the same features and more.

CEditor is designed throughout to work with both the raw-meat and the quiche interfaces (or with any other interface you dream up). A direct interface contains lots of options and alternatives that you can hook up in whatever way you choose. And there's a simple interface that hooks to the typical menu items. The simple interface is less flexible for clients but friendlier for users.

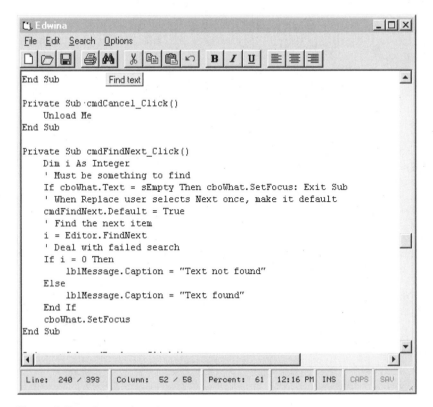

Figure 8-3. *Edwina the editor.*

The Editor Control

The CEditor class works a lot like the CPictureGlass class (described in Chapter 6). Just as CPictureGlass contained a PictureBox control, CEditor contains a TextBox or a RichTextBox control. But while CPictureGlass took its internal picture box apart and rebuilt it as something different, the CEditor class is simply a TextBox control with a few extras. Well, OK, a lot of extras. You might as well call it an editor control rather than an editor class. The class is a mechanism to make CEditor look like a control.

If you look closely at a TextBox control, you'll see that it's actually two controls in one: an entry-field control and an editor control, depending on whether you set the MultiLine property. In entry-field mode, a text box doesn't need properties like ScrollBars and Locked. Similarly, in editor mode, it doesn't need properties like PasswordChar and MaxLength. All the other TextBox properties are shared (although some are clearly more useful in one mode than in the other).

Coding the CEditor class consists of first creating the control and then passing on all the standard editing features of a text box. After that, you can start adding goodies.

Create It

The heart of CEditor is a simple data declaration. Every method and property in the class references the following variable, directly or indirectly:

```
' Internal TextBox
#If fRichText Then
Private rtb As RichTextBox
#Else
Private rtb As TextBox
#End If
```

The *rtb* variable is nothing until you initialize it with the Create method. You pass in a TextBox control, and Create turns it into an editor control:

```
#If fRichText Then
Function Create(rtbA As RichTextBox) As Boolean
#Else
Function Create(rtbA As TextBox) As Boolean
#End If
    Create = True
    On Error GoTo CreateError
    ' Set properties for editing
    If Not rtbA.MultiLine Then GoTo CreateError
    If rtbA.ScrollBars <> vbBoth Then GoTo CreateError
#If fRichText = 0 Then
    rtbA.PasswordChar = sEmpty
#End If
    rtbA.MaxLength = 0
    Set rtb = rtbA
    Exit Function
CreateError:
    Create = False
End Function
```

You aren't likely to pass in a TextBox control intended as an editor with the MultiLine property set to False, but the Create method checks to be sure that you haven't done so. Since MultiLine can't be changed at run time, Create can do nothing except throw you out. For edit-related properties that can be set, it goes ahead and sets the normal edit-mode values.

Edward declares a CEditor object at the form level:

```
Private ed As New CEditor
```

It then initializes the object in Form_Load:

```
Private Sub Form_Load()
    ' Switch to previous instance if available
    ActivatePrevInstance Me

    ' Create editor object
    Dim f As Boolean
    f = ed.Create(txtEdit)
    BugAssert f
    ⋮
```

Pass It On

Once the editor is created, it's a simple (but tedious) matter to pass all the TextBox properties and methods on to editor users. Here's an example:

```
Property Get BackColor() As Long
    BackColor = rtb.BackColor
End Property

Property Let BackColor(iBackColorA As Long)
    rtb.BackColor = iBackColorA
End Property
```

That's easy. Now you just have to write about 30 properties and 10 methods. This isn't my idea of fun, but fortunately you have a wizard to handle the details. The Property Shop was introduced in Chapter 4. At the time, you might have seen this application as overkill and wondered whether it wouldn't be just as easy to write properties with a text editor. Well, the Property Shop saves a lot of typing for classes such as CEditor, which simply pass on properties from an internal control. Figure 8-4 on the next page shows the Property Shop in action.

You do have to change a few defaults. First, clear the Make Internal check box. You don't want to create a separate internal variable for each property; they'll all use the same text box object. Next, check the Sticky Internal check box and enter *rtb*, followed by a period, in the Internal Prefix box. This tells the Property Shop not to change the prefix every time you change the type.

Now you can churn out properties as fast as you can type the names. Look up the properties in Help if you're not sure what type to use. Variant always works, but String, Integer, or Long might be more efficient for some properties. Keep hitting the Append button to add more properties to the property list in the text box at the bottom of the form. You can send the whole batch at once.

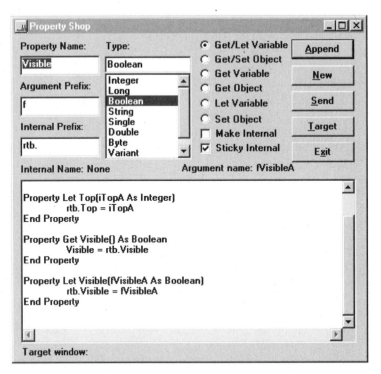

Figure 8-4. *The Property Shop does editor properties.*

You'll encounter a couple of special issues. Several properties—Alignment, BorderStyle, HideSelection, hWnd, and Parent—are read-only, and you can't define a Property Let or Property Set procedure for them. The Parent and Container properties don't work as you might expect because they reference objects, so you must use Set in the Property Get and Property Set procedures:

```
Property Get Parent() As Object
    Set Parent = rtb.Parent
End Property

Property Set Parent(vParentA As Object)
    Set rtb.Parent = vParentA
End Property
```

The Property Shop won't help you pass through methods. But there are only a few of them, and most are one-liners:

```
Public Sub Refresh()
    rtb.Refresh
End Sub
```

The only tricky part of methods involves optional arguments. The Move method has three of them, handled as follows:

```
Sub Move(X As Variant, Optional Y As Variant, _
        Optional dx As Variant, Optional dy As Variant)
    If IsMissing(Y) Then
        rtb.Move X
    ElseIf IsMissing(dx) Then
        rtb.Move X, Y
    ElseIf IsMissing(dy) Then
        rtb.Move X, Y, dx
    Else
        rtb.Move X, Y, dx, dy
    End If
End Sub
```

Edward uses these standard CEditor properties and methods the same way it would use the TextBox versions.

The Dirty Bit

When you try to quit a file, any civilized editor will warn you if your file has changed and will ask whether you want to save it. To do this, the editor saves the dirty or clean status in a flag (often called a bit, even if it isn't). The first time the user changes the file, the editor sets the dirty bit. When the user saves the file, the editor clears the dirty bit. If the user wants to change files or quit, the editor checks the dirty bit and posts a warning if it is set.

In the TextBox control, the DataChanged property controls the dirty bit. You won't discover this in any Visual Basic documentation. All references to the DataChanged property claim that DataChanged is for bound controls. Nevertheless, it also works fine for unbound text boxes. Unfortunately, this "bug" has been fixed in the RichTextBox control. No matter. The dirty bit of a text box or a rich text box is actually controlled by the EM_GETMODIFY and the EM_SETMODIFY messages. It's easy to implement a DirtyBit property using SendMessage. This design separates testing for unbound data changes from testing for bound changes. Here's the code for DirtyBit:

```
Property Get DirtyBit() As Boolean
    DirtyBit = SendMessageAsLong(rtb.hWnd, EM_GETMODIFY, 0, 0)
End Property

Property Let DirtyBit(fDirtyBitA As Boolean)
    Call SendMessageAsLong(rtb.hWnd, EM_SETMODIFY, fDirtyBitA, 0)
End Property
```

Edward uses the DirtyBit property to identify when a file needs to be saved before the user quits or transfers. It also displays the current save status at the bottom of the screen. Here's how Edward updates the save status:

```
panSave.ForeColor = IIf(ed.DirtyBit, vbGrayText, vbWindowText)
```

Rich or Poor

We're going to make clients decide at design time whether they want a rich text box or a poor one. Of course, users of 16-bit Windows have no choice because Windows 3.*x* has no official RichTextBox control. I expect that a control vendor will soon provide a 16-bit control named RichTextBox that just happens to have exactly the same methods and properties as Microsoft's 32-bit version. If that happens, users of CEditor will be ready. In the meantime, you can get a rich editor in Windows 95 or Windows NT by defining *fRichText = 1* in the Options dialog box of the 32-bit Visual Basic environment. Make sure that the text box you pass in the Create method is really a RichTextBox control.

Handling the difference between rich and poor at design time is a choice. You could design the class to handle either kind of text box at run time. The *rtb* variable would be declared without conditionals or type:

```
Private rtb As Object
```

The Create method would work as shown here:

```
Function Create(rtbA As Object) As Boolean
    If TypeName(rtbA) = "TextBox" Then
        ' Do TextBox stuff
    ElseIf TypeName(rtbA) = "RichTextBox"
        ' Do RichTextBox stuff
    Else
        ' Anything else is invalid
        Assert True
    End If
```

This strategy would let you use both kinds of objects in the same project, but, realistically, most developers know at design time what kind of editor they want. The conditional strategy has better type checking and creates smaller programs because each CEditor object has only the code it needs.

With careful coding, you can write your editor so that it builds either way, just by changing one compile-time constant. You can use compile-time or run-time testing to allow your editor to take advantage of the more powerful features of the RichTextBox control, which are passed through the CEditor class.

You can also change the status by clicking the status bar. For example, to throw away your latest changes, click the SAV item before you exit; Edward won't prompt you to resave. The Click event procedure (*panSave_Click*) toggles the status as shown here:

```
ed.DirtyBit = Not ed.DirtyBit
```

It then updates the color (as shown earlier) to indicate the new status.

The dirty bit is managed at several different levels by different players. Edward and any other editors you create with CEditor should normally save and open all files through calls to methods of the editor class. That way, you can ensure that the class will clear the DirtyBit property every time it saves a file or opens a new one. If you subvert this system (and CEditor provides low-level methods and properties to let you do this), you'd better clear the DirtyBit property yourself when appropriate. You normally don't set the DirtyBit property because the TextBox control does this whenever the data changes.

When a client editor such as Edward takes an action that might destroy a dirty file, it has two choices: it can test the DirtyBit property itself and take appropriate action; or it can call the DirtyDialog method to test DirtyBit and, if necessary, query the user about the appropriate action to take. DirtyDialog is so named because it tests the dirty bit and also because it is a quick-and-dirty hack based on the MsgBox function. You might want to call a real form-based dialog box in a real editor, but DirtyDialog gives you an easy model of how such a form might work:

```
Public Function DirtyDialog() As Integer
    Dim s As String
    DirtyDialog = True ' Assume success
    ' Done if no dirty file to save
    If Not DirtyBit Then Exit Function
    ' Prompt for action if dirty file
    s = "File not saved: " & FileName & ". Save now?"
    Select Case MsgBox(s, vbYesNoCancel)
    Case vbYes
        ' Save old file
        FileSave
    Case vbCancel
        ' User wants to terminate file change
        DirtyDialog = False
    Case vbNo
        ' Do nothing if user wants to throw away changes
    End Select
End Function
```

Edward calls the DirtyDialog method from the mnuFileNew, mnuFileOpen, and QueryUnload event procedures. It doesn't need to call mnuFileExit because QueryUnload will catch that case. Here are two examples, a positive test and a negative one:

```
Private Sub mnuFileNew_Click()
    If ed.DirtyDialog Then ed.FileNew
End Sub
Private Sub Form_QueryUnload(Cancel As Integer, _
                            UnloadMode As Integer)
    If Not ed.DirtyDialog Then Cancel = True
End Sub
```

Extending the CEditor Class

The editing area in Notepad has the look and feel of a standard Windows text box, and Notepad has an Undo command. The Basic TextBox control is also based on the standard Windows text box, but it doesn't have an Undo method. If Windows can have one, why can't we?

Well, we can. You just have to roll your own by sending the appropriate messages. You can tell exactly what properties a text box can have by looking up messages that start with *EM_* in the Windows API Help file. You'll recognize a lot of them: EM_LIMITTEXT is the MaxLength property, EM_GETPASSWORD-CHAR and EM_SETPASSWORDCHAR are the PasswordChar property, and so on. But you'll also notice some interesting messages that don't correspond to TextBox properties. Why not?

Basic controls provide methods and properties for only the most popular features—or, to be more specific, for the favorite features of the Basic designers. The designers seem to like a few more features in each new version. For example, the TextBox control now has a Locked property; you no longer have to fake it with the EM_SETREADONLY message. But for now, let's talk about how you can add some of the methods and properties Basic forgot.

> **NOTE** The RichTextBox control supports the EM_ messages of the TextBox control plus a few of its own. The Undo messages, for example, work the same in Edwina as they do in Edward.

Undo Methods and Properties

Windows maintains an undo buffer on text boxes and provides three edit messages to control the buffer: EM_UNDO, EM_CANUNDO, and EM_EMPTYUN-DOBUFFER. It's easy enough to wrap these up as features of the CEditor class:

```
Sub EditUndo()
    Call SendMessageAsLong(rtb.hWnd, EM_UNDO, 0, 0&)
End Sub

Sub ClearUndo()
    Call SendMessageAsLong(rtb.hWnd, EM_EMPTYUNDOBUFFER, 0, 0&)
End Sub

Property Get CanUndo() As Boolean
    CanUndo = SendMessageAsLong(rtb.hWnd, EM_CANUNDO, 0, 0&)
End Property
```

Because the last parameter of SendMessage (*lParam*) can take String, Long, or other arguments, the Windows API type library provides aliases (such as Send-MessageAsLong) for each. This is about as simple as SendMessage gets. You pass the handle, the message constant, and zeros for the *wParam* and *lParam* parameters because these particular messages don't need them. (For a review of SendMessage, see "Sending Messages," page 236.)

Edward has an Edit menu with an Undo item. Here's the menu event:

```
Private Sub mnuEditUndo_Click()
    ed.EditUndo
End Sub
```

Edward doesn't use the ClearUndo method, but it does use the CanUndo property to disable the Undo menu item when there's nothing to undo (an enhancement over Notepad, which always enables Undo). The main Edit menu event procedure handles the update:

```
Private Sub mnuEdit_Click()
    mnuEditUndo.Enabled = ed.CanUndo
End Sub
```

You usually don't attach code to the event procedure for the top menu items, but it's handy for updating the disabled or checked state of items that might be changed by events outside the menu.

Edward's undo feature isn't as powerful as the undo feature in more powerful editors. It won't undo nonediting commands, and it might not undo other commands the way you think it should. But it's easy to implement and better than nothing.

Notice the naming convention in the menu code. Where appropriate, I create method names from the name of the menu (Edit) and the item (Undo) where you would normally put the method names. Of course, nothing prevents you from tying this method to a button or a keystroke or even from putting it on some other menu with some other name. I copy the Notepad interface here because most developers are familiar with Notepad even if they (like me) prefer something (anything) different.

Status Methods and Properties

Whoever heard of an editor that doesn't display status such as the current line and column? If Edward didn't have a status bar, we'd have to admit to being as weak as—well, can you think of any programmer's editor you're intimately familiar with that lacks a status bar?

Let's move on from this sensitive topic without naming names.

Edward, unlike Notepad and other such weaklings, displays its status, getting the information from CEditor, which in turn gets it by sending messages to the internal text box. The TextBox control knows a lot about its current status, but the way you get at the status is far from straightforward, as you'll see from studying the CEditor properties and methods.

The CEditor class can supply status information through properties. The Lines, Columns, and Characters properties provide the total number of lines, columns, and characters. Similarly, the Line, Column, and Character properties provide the current line, column, and character. The Percent property supplies the current position as a percentage of the total file length.

You could use these properties to build a status bar, but it's more efficient to call the GetEditStatus function. To get the information from separate properties, you'd end up sending more messages, since several pieces of the information depend on others. To use GetEditStatus, you pass variables by reference to receive various pieces of data. Of course, this could be overkill if you need only part of the information, which is why CEditor also provides each piece as a separate property.

Before looking at the implementation of GetEditStatus, let's carefully consider how it will be used. The client (Edward, in this case) will display the status however it wants; CEditor merely provides the information. Edward updates the position (and any other status information) in its display with its own RefreshStatus sub. RefreshStatus needs to be called any time the status might have changed—in other words, every time the editing caret moves (whenever someone presses a key or clicks a mouse button). So let's work backward, starting with a Click event procedure:

```
Private Sub txtEdit_Click()
    RefreshStatus
End Sub
```

RefreshStatus is also called initially in Form_Load and in the KeyUp event procedure. (Notice that this is the KeyUp procedure, rather than KeyPress, because KeyPress isn't called for cursor keys.)

RefreshStatus gets the status information from the CEditor object and displays it on the 3-D panels at the bottom of the form:

```
Private Sub RefreshStatus()
    Dim iLine As Long, cLine As Long, iCol As Long
    Dim cCol As Long, iChar As Long, cChar As Long
    ed.GetEditStatus iLine, cLine, iCol, cCol, iChar, cChar

    panLine.Caption = "Line: " & FmtInt(iLine, 4) & _
                      " / " & FmtInt(cLine, 4, True)
    panCol.Caption = "Column: " & FmtInt(iCol, 3) & _
                      " / " & FmtInt(cCol, 3, True)
    panPercent.Caption = "Percent: " & _
                      FmtInt((iChar / (cChar + 1)) * 100, 3)
    panSave.ForeColor = IIf(ed.DirtyBit, vbGrayText, vbWindowText)
    panWhat.Caption = Left(panWhat.Caption, 6) & ed.FindWhat
    panWith.Caption = Left(panWith.Caption, 9) & ed.ReplaceWith
    panFile.Caption = Left(panFile.Caption, 6) & ed.FileTitle
    panTabs.Caption = Left(panTabs.Caption, 6) & ed.Tabs
End Sub
```

FLAME

Basic must be the only computer language ever invented whose formatting features don't allow you to right-justify integers—that is, to generate a simple list of numbers that looks like this:

```
 345
  62
   9
1053
```

Just try doing that with the Format function or the Print statement. A Basic program manager once told me that the ability to right-justify numbers wasn't worth adding because spaces don't have the same width as digits in proportional fonts. Well, yes, but...Fortunately, this quirk is more an annoyance than a limitation. The FmtInt function (UTILITY.BAS) allows you to left-justify or right-justify an integer in a field of a given width. The heart of this function consists of the following expression:

```
Right$(Space$(iWidth) & Trim$(Str$(iVal)), iWidth)
```

You prepend the maximum number of spaces and trim off the extra. Not difficult, but it shouldn't be necessary.

Now let's return to the GetEditStatus method, which sends messages to check on the current caret position:

```
Sub GetEditStatus(iLine As Long, cLine As Long, _
                  iCol As Long, cCol As Long, _
                  iChar As Long, cChar As Long)
    Dim i As Long
    ' Count of lines
    cLine = SendMessageAsLong(rtb.hWnd, EM_GETLINECOUNT, 0, 0&)
    ' Current line (zero adjusted)
    iLine = 1 + SendMessageAsLong(rtb.hWnd, EM_LINEFROMCHAR, _
                                  Lo(rtb.SelStart), 0&)
    ' Current character
    iChar = rtb.SelStart + 1
    ' Length is position of last line plus length of last line
    cChar = SendMessageAsLong(rtb.hWnd, EM_LINEINDEX, _
                              Lo(cLine - 1), 0&)
    i = SendMessageAsLong(rtb.hWnd, EM_LINELENGTH, Lo(cChar - 1), 0&)
    cChar = cChar + i
    ' Column count is current line length
    cCol = SendMessageAsLong(rtb.hWnd, EM_LINELENGTH, _
                             Lo(iChar - 1), 0&)
    ' Column is current position minus position of line start
    i = SendMessageAsLong(rtb.hWnd, EM_LINEINDEX, Lo(iLine - 1), 0&)
    iCol = iChar - i
End Sub
```

What Windows has isn't exactly what you need, but it is what you need to get what you need. Everything comes from SendMessage calls except the current character position, which is simply the zero-adjusted SelStart property. Notice that I defined Columns as the length of the current line; you might prefer to define it as the width of the longest line in the text box or as the current screen width of the text box based on the average character width of the current font.

The tricky part of this code is the call to the Lo function. I didn't include this in my original code, and I used Edward for a long time before I finally tried it on a file large enough to reveal my bug, which this hack fixes. The Lo function looks like this:

```
#If Win32 Then
Private Function Lo(ByVal i As Long) As Long
    Lo = i
End Function
#Else
Private Function Lo(ByVal i As Long) As Integer
    Lo = LoWord(i)
End Function
#End If
```

It does nothing in 32-bit mode, but in 16-bit mode it calls the LoWord function (from VBUTIL) to convert a Long to an Integer. Imagine, for example, that you are on character 35,000 of a file that is 40,000 bytes. GetEditStatus sends the EM_LINEFROMCHAR message to the text box to convert this character to a line, putting 35,000 in the SendMessage *wParam* argument. Beep! Overflow! You can't pass 35,000 in a Basic Integer parameter. But Windows can receive 35,000 because it's looking for an unsigned integer. If you pass −30,636, Windows will receive it as 35,000. I don't even want to think about the math for this conversion, but the Lo function does it automatically. Technically, the 32-bit version of the Lo function ought to call a LoDWord function in case somebody wants to use Edwina to edit a file larger than 2,147,483,647 bytes. I'll worry about that when one of my clients' users reports running into it in real life.

The CEditor class also has LineText, LinePosition, and LineLength methods returning the text, the character position, and the length of either the current line or a selected line. Here's the code for LineLength:

```
Public Function LineLength(Optional iLine As Variant) As Long
    If IsMissing(iLine) Then iLine = Line
    LineLength = SendMessageAsLong(rtb.hWnd, EM_LINELENGTH, _
                                   Lo(LinePosition(iLine)), 0&)
End Function
```

Notice that the LineLength method can access the Line property without qualification. Within the CEditor class module, public properties and methods are procedures that can be accessed like any others. The call to Line is treated like a call to Me.Line.

> **NOTE**
>
> LineLength is defined as a function method rather than as a Property Get procedure. What's the difference? To a user, they can look the same. For example, if you look at the following lines individually, you can't tell whether LineLength is a property or a function:
>
> ```
> c = LineLength          ' Get length of current line
> c = LineLength(5)       ' Get length of line 5
> ```
>
> But when you read the two lines together, you can tell that LineLength is a function because it has an optional argument, which properties aren't permitted to have (at least not in this version). You can fake Property Get procedures with functions, but there's no workaround if you want to give a Property Let procedure an optional argument.

Summary of CEditor Features

The CEditor class combines the best of the TextBox and RichTextBox controls and then adds its own features. Table 8-1 lists the most important properties and methods of the RichTextBox and Textbox controls and the CEditor class.

	RichTextBox	TextBox	CEditor
Property			
Alignment		X	X
Appearance	X	X	X
BackColor	X	X	X
BorderStyle	X	X	
BulletIndent	X		X *
Character, Characters			X
Column, Columns			X
Container, Parent	X	X	X
DataChanged, DataField, DataSource	X	X	X
DirtyBit			X
DisableNoScroll	X		X *
DragIcon, DragMode	X	X	X
Enabled, Visible	X	X	X
FileName	X		X
FileOpenFilter, FileTitle			X
FindWhat, ReplaceWith			X
FindWhatList, ReplaceWithList			X
Font	X	X	X
ForeColor		X	X
HelpContextID	X	X	X
HideSelection	X	X	X
hWnd	X	X	X
Index	X	X	
LastError			X
Left, Top, Width, Height	X	X	X
Line, Lines			X
LineText			X
LinkItem, LinkMode, LinkTimeOut, LinkTopic		X	X **
LoadMode			X

Table 8-1. *Editor properties and methods.* *(continued)*

Table 8-1. *continued*

	RichTextBox	*TextBox*	*CEditor*
Locked	X	X	X
MaxLength	X	X	
MouseIcon, MousePointer	X	X	X
MultiLine	X	X	
Name	X	X	
Object	X		
OverWrite			X
PasswordChar	X	X	
Percent			X
ScrollBars	X	X	
SearchOptionCase, SearchOptionDirection			X
SearchOptionWord			X
SelAlignment, SelCharOffset	X		X *
SelIndent, SelHangingIndent, SelRightIndent	X		X *
SelBold, SelItalic, SelStrikethru, SelUnderline	X		X *
SelColor	X		X *
SelFontName, SelFontSize	X		X *
SelLength, SelStart, SelText	X	X	X
SelRTF, TextRTF	X		X *
SelTabs, SelTabCount	X		X *
TabIndex	X	X	
TabStop	X	X	X
Tabs			X
Tag	X	X	X
Text	X	X	X
WhatsThisHelpID	X	X	X
Method			
Create			X
DirtyDialog			X
Drag	X	X	X
EditCopy, EditCut, EditDelete, EditPaste			X
EditUndo, ClearUndo, CanUndo			X
EditSelectAll			X
FileOpen, FileNew, FileSave, FileSaveAs			X

(continued)

Table 8-1. *continued*

	RichTextBox	TextBox	CEditor
Find	X		X *
FindNew, ReplaceNext			X
GetEditStatus			X
GetLineFromChar	X		X
LinePosition, LineLength			X
LinkExecute, LinkPoke, LinkRequest		X	X **
LoadFile, SaveFile	X		X
Move	X	X	X
OptionColor, OptionFont			X
Refresh	X	X	X
Scroll			X
SearchFind, SearchFindNext, SearchReplace	X		X
SelPrint	X		X *
SetFocus	X	X	X
ShowWhatsThis	X	X	X
Span, UpTo	X		X *
ZOrder	X	X	X

* Only when CEditor contains a RichTextBox control
** Only when CEditor contains a TextBox control

As for events, TextBox and RichTextBox are the same, with one big exception. RichTextBox has a SelChange event—something TextBox could certainly use. Also, TextBox has DDE events (LinkClose, LinkError, and so on), but like most new OLE controls, RichTextBox expects you to use OLE rather than DDE. Finally, the CEditor class has a KeyPress event even though classes aren't supposed to have events. We'll talk about it later in this chapter; see "Handling the Insert State," page 400.

CHALLENGE There's work to do. You could start by implementing the RichTextBox control's Find, Span, and UpTo methods for the TextBox control. The Whole Word option for text searches doesn't work for either environment. SelPrint works only with RichTextBox, but it could be implemented for TextBox. In fact, CEditor is notoriously ignorant of printing. It's up to you to add the Print Setup, Page Setup, and Print Preview dialog boxes. Once you implement all these features, you can integrate them into Edward and Edwina.

Common Dialog Extensions

CEditor obviously needs some way to open and save programs. It should also be able to change the printer setup, the font, and the background or text color. Luckily, the CommonDialog control provides all this functionality in a neat package. There's only one problem: where will you put the control?

Like all controls, CommonDialog must reside on a form, whether it needs one or not. In this case, you'd like to tie the Open dialog box to the CEditor class, not to the Edward form, but you can't put a control on a class. This is annoying, since the CommonDialog control has no visual representation. What are the possible workarounds? You could require clients of CEditor to provide a CommonDialog control and pass it as an argument in the Create function just as a TextBox control is passed. I don't much care for that solution, but I suppose it could work.

Consider some other unusual aspects of the CommonDialog control. First, it has no events. So what is it doing on a form if it has no events? The biggest difference between an OLE server and an OLE control is that the control has events. Also, a server doesn't have to reside on a form. If CommonDialog were an OLE server, you could write the line

```
Private dlg As New CommonDialog
```

in CEditor and then start calling methods and properties.

But it isn't an OLE server, and you can't. This raises another question. Why aren't the common dialogs implemented as Basic statements and functions? They're functions in Windows, so why does Visual Basic provide them as an object? Probably because they have too many arguments. Imagine trying to pass the title, the filter, the starting directory, and all the other common dialog properties as arguments under Visual Basic version 3, with no named arguments and no line-continuation character. A simple call to open a file would be hundreds of characters long.

But in version 4—control? What CommonDialog control? We don't need no stinkin' CommonDialog control!

You can implement common dialogs the old-fashioned way, as a library of routines. In the process, you can get rid of all the overhead of the control. Instead, you'll have a lean and mean layer of Windows and Basic code, while also using named and optional arguments to give your solution the look and feel (but not the cost) of object-oriented programming.

The Windows/Basic Way of Implementing Common Dialogs

You've already seen one alternative to the CommonDialog control: "A Better Picture File Dialog Box," page 166, introduced FOpenPicFile, which replaces the Open dialog box for picture files. You can turn back to that section to compare the draw-your-own-dialog-box approach to the CommonDialog control approach. Now I'll introduce a third alternative: the Windows-API-in-a-Basic-wrapper approach.

The Windows API file open function is named GetOpenFileName, so naturally our version is VBGetOpenFileName. In the Windows version, you put all your input and output data into a UDT and pass the UDT variable as an argument. GetOpenFileName reads the input data out of the structure variable (Windows sees UDTs as structures), displays the dialog box, and writes any resulting output data to the structure variable. This is relatively easy in C, but it's messy in Basic because you must fill in all the fields of the UDT variable, whether or not you need them. A wrapper interface hides the ugly details. The named optional arguments of VBGetOpenFileName not only simplify access but also make calling the function look unexpectedly like using the CommonDialog control.

As usual, let's look at the calling code before the implementation. For easy comparison with both the form method and the control method you saw in "Using the Picture File dialog box," page 167, this example opens pictures instead of text files, but CEditor uses the same technique.

```
Dim sFile As String, f As Boolean
f = VBGetOpenFileName( _
    vFileName:=sFile, _
    vInitDir:="c:\windows", _
    vFlags:=cdlOFNFileMustExist Or cdlOFNHideReadOnly, _
    vFilter:=sFilter) ' *.bmp;*.dib;*.ico;*.wmf;*.cur
If f And sFile <> sEmpty Then pbBitmap.Picture = LoadPicture(sFile)
```

Compare this to the CommonDialog control version:

```
With dlgOpenPic
    .InitDir = "c:\windows"
    .Flags = cdlOFNFileMustExist Or cdlOFNHideReadOnly
    .Filter = sFilter ' *.bmp;*.dib;*.ico;*.wmf;*.cur
    .ShowOpen
    If .FileName <> sEmpty Then
        pbBitmap.Picture = LoadPicture(.FileName)
    End If
End With
```

In the control version, you put input data into properties and read output data out of properties. In the function version, you pass input data as arguments. For output data, you pass variables by reference and read the data out of the variables after the call. In the control version, you get constants such as *cdlOFNFileMustExist* from the type library associated with the control. In the function version, you use the Windows API constants defined in my common dialog module (COMDLG.BAS). Although Windows API constants are documented with long, uppercased names such as OFN_FILEMUSTEXIST, CEditor uses the friendlier names of the CommonDialog control.

Using Common Dialogs

CEditor uses four of the common dialogs, and it would use more if possible. But the Find and Replace dialog boxes don't work in Basic, which is probably why the CommonDialog control doesn't provide them either. We'll talk more

---

PERFORMANCE

Problem: Compare the size cost of drawing your own common dialog forms, using the CommonDialog control, or calling the Windows API common dialog functions inside a thin wrapper.

Problem	16-Bit Mode	32-Bit Mode
Draw your own	28 KB	32 KB
Use CommonDialog control	18 KB + 81 KB	22 KB + 93 KB
Call API functions	25 KB	29 KB

Conclusion: This comparison isn't exact because the draw-your-own option is based on FOpenPicFile, which does a little more work than the real common dialog. But it's clear (and predictable) that drawing your own forms takes more code than using common dialogs. Loading Basic forms is also likely to be slower than loading common dialogs, although I didn't specifically test this. Calling API functions has a smaller size cost and is probably faster. Using the CommonDialog control creates the smallest EXE file, but that's because the real code is in the control. Of course, the control code is shared by other programs that use the control. What matters more than disk space is how much memory the program uses at run time, which is not an easy thing to test. The size of the CommonDialog control isn't necessarily a good indication of how much memory it will use, since a good portion of its code deals with controlling properties at design time.

---

about this problem later. For now, let's look at the common dialogs implemented in the COMDLG.BAS module and called by CEditor in EDITOR.CLS:

- The FileOpen method calls VBGetOpenFileName, which calls Windows GetOpenFileName.

- The FileSaveAs method calls VBGetSaveFileName, which calls Windows GetSaveFileName.

- The OptionFont method calls VBChooseFont, which calls Windows ChooseFont.

- The OptionColor method calls VBChooseColor, which calls Windows ChooseColor.

If you've seen one common dialog function, you've seen them all, so let's go through the process for the most common and most complicated—the Open dialog box. The Save As dialog box is almost identical, and the Font and Color dialog boxes are simple by comparison.

It all starts with the mnuFileOpen_Click event:

```
Private Sub mnuFileOpen_Click()
    If ed.DirtyDialog Then ed.FileOpen
    RefreshStatus
End Sub
```

After checking to make sure that the current file is saved, you call the FileOpen method of the CEditor object.

FileOpen in turn calls VBGetOpenFileName:

```
Function FileOpen() As Boolean
    FileOpen = False
    Dim f As Boolean, sFile As String, sFileTitle As String
    f = VBGetOpenFileName( _
        vFileName:=sFile, _
        vFileTitle:=sFileTitle, _
        vInitDir:=sDirLast, _
        vFlags:=cdlOFNFileMustExist Or cdlOFNHideReadOnly, _
        vFilter:=sFilter)
    If f And sFile <> sEmpty Then
        On Error Resume Next
        sDirLast = CurDir$
```

```
            LoadFile sFile, ordLoadMode
            FileName = sFile

            BugAssert Err = 0
            FileOpen = True
        End If
End Function
```

You've already seen how to call the Open dialog box. The purpose of this exercise is to get the filename. (I reluctantly chose *vFileTitle* as the name, for compatibility with the bizarre common dialog naming scheme.) Remember that the file title is what many people call the filename (FILE.EXT), and the filename is what many people call the full path (D:\DIR\FILE.EXT). It doesn't matter which you use because the common dialog always changes to the current directory before selecting. In any case, you pass whatever you get to the Load-File method:

```
Sub LoadFile(sFileName As String, Optional vFileType As Variant)
With rtb
    If IsMissing(vFileType) Then vFileType = 0
#If fRichText Then
    ' Pass through RichTextBox method
    .LoadFile sFileName, vFileType
#Else
    ' Ignore optional argument
    Dim s As String
    s = GetFileText(sFileName, errLast)
    If errLast = 0 Then
        If Len(s) <> FileLen(sFileName) Then
            ' Use this to mean file too long
            errLast = 62 ' Input past end of file
        Else
            rtb.Text = s
            sFileCur = sFileName
        End If
    End If
#End If
    DirtyBit = False
End With
End Sub
```

That's the end of the line if you have a RichTextBox control; it already has a LoadFile method that you can simply pass through. LoadFile has an optional file type argument that determines whether to load the file as a rich text file

(RTF) or a text file (TXT). Since the Open dialog box has no setting for this, the CEditor class allows you to control it through the LoadMode property, which maintains the setting in an *ordLoadMode* variable. The LoadMode property has no effect on text boxes. You can load a file either by passing its name to the LoadFile method or by assigning to the FileName property. The only difference in CEditor is that LoadFile allows you to set the load mode.

If you have a TextBox control, you need only one more step. LoadFile calls GetFileText (a general utility in UTILITY.BAS) to do the actual work:

```
Function GetFileText(sFileName As String, _
                     Optional vErr As Variant) As String
    Dim nFile As Integer, cFile As Long, sText As String
    On Error GoTo GetFileTextError
    nFile = FreeFile
    'Open sFileName For Input As nFile ' Don't do this!!!
    ' Let others read but not write
    Open sFileName For Input Access Read Lock Write As nFile
    sText = Input$(LOF(nFile), nFile)
    Close nFile
    GetFileText = sText
    Exit Function

GetFileTextError:
    vErr = Err
End Function
```

LoadFile translates the results of GetFileText to a format that is handy for CEditor. It passes back a failure for clients who want to know only whether an error occurred, and it sets an error number (accessed through a LastError property) for clients who want to know why. LoadFile also generates a fake error for files that are too large to fit in a text box.

This can happen very easily under Windows 3.*x* and Windows 95 with the TextBox control. The underlying Windows text box suffers from a 64-KB limit in these environments, but you'll probably run out of space even with files a little smaller than that. With the TextBox control under Windows NT or with the RichTextBox control in any supporting environment, you can theoretically handle files as large as 8 gigabytes, but you'll probably run out of memory long before that.

Implementing VBGetOpenFileName

Finally we get to the hard part—implementing a Basic wrapper for Get-OpenFileName. The trick is to use the UDT that's expected by the Windows GetOpenFileName function internally, but to hide it behind named arguments. From the earlier call example, VBGetOpenFileName might look object-oriented,

A Lesson in Etiquette: Share Your Files

Warning: There will be a test at the end of this sidebar.

In a previous life, I worked on some low-level code that—for reasons that don't concern us here—opened the MS-DOS console device. Like all MS-DOS devices, this one can be opened like a file by using an open function on the filename CON. But my code failed sometimes on some machines with some configurations. After many hours of frustration, I discovered the problem.

The Mode program distributed with certain versions of MS-DOS opened the console device when you changed the number of screen lines with a command such as *mode CO80,43*. The Mode program changes line height by writing an ANSI command to the console, thus instructing the ANSI.SYS device driver to make the change. I wouldn't have cared about any of this except for one thing: the dastardly Mode programmer opened the file with default sharing and left the device open forever. Had this code been written in Basic instead of C or assembler, it would have looked something like this:

```
Open "CON" For Output As #nFile
```

I never saw the offending code except in a debugger, but I can guess that the dirty hacker used defaults for the Access attribute, and certainly for the Lock attribute. If you don't set the Lock attribute under MS-DOS (and Windows 3.*x*), you get compatibility share mode, which means that no one else can open your file until you close it. As a result, any time anyone who had set line height with the Mode command ran my program, it failed. And there was nothing I could do to fix it.

The specific moral to this story: always set the Lock attribute when you use the Open statement. Think carefully about how your programs will interact with files opened by other programs, whether those other programs are on your own machine or on remote machines. Then choose a setting: Shared, Lock Read, Lock Write, or Lock Read Write. You can't control what other people do, but you can ensure that your programs never end up as the object of ridicule in a sidebar about programming etiquette.

The general moral to this story: never use a default you don't understand.

Now for the test. What happens if Edward opens a text file with the following statement and the Visual Basic editor tries to open the same file at about the same time?

```
Open sFileName For Input As hFile
```

Hint: The behavior under Windows 3.*x* will differ from that under Windows 95 or Windows NT.

but it's really just a function in a Basic code module. COMDLG.BAS contains all of the private types and declarations used by the public functions VBGet-OpenFileName, VBGetSaveFileName, VBChooseColor, and VBChooseFont.

The TOpenFileName UDT

In "Variable-Length Strings in UDTs," page 82, we discussed part of TOpen-FileName (called OPENFILENAME in Windows documentation). Let's take a look at the whole works (32-bit this time):

```
Private Type TOpenFileName
    lStructSize As Long              ' Filled with UDT size
    hwndOwner As Long                ' Tied to vOwner
    hInstance As Long                ' Ignored (used only by templates)
    lpstrFilter As String            ' Tied to vFilter
    lpstrCustomFilter As String      ' Ignored (exercise for reader)
    nMaxCustFilter As Long           ' Ignored (exercise for reader)
    nFilterIndex As Long             ' Tied to vFilterIndex
    lpstrFile As String              ' Tied to vFileName
    nMaxFile As Long                 ' Handled internally
    lpstrFileTitle As String         ' Tied to vFileTitle
    nMaxFileTitle As Long            ' Handled internally
    lpstrInitialDir As String        ' Tied to vInitDir
    lpstrTitle As String             ' Tied to vTitle
    Flags As Long                    ' Tied to vFlags
    nFileOffset As Integer           ' Ignored (exercise for reader)
    nFileExtension As Integer        ' Ignored (exercise for reader)
    lpstrDefExt As String            ' Tied to vDefExt
    lCustData As Long                ' Ignored (needed for hooks)
    lpfnHook As Long                 ' Ignored (no hooks in Basic)
    lpTemplateName As Long           ' Ignored (no templates in Basic)
End Type
```

That's a pretty big UDT, but you don't need all the fields. I ignored some parts because they're frills. For example, you don't need to return the positions of the filename and the extension in the resulting full pathname because, if you really need them, you can parse them out yourself or call GetFullPathName. You could use hooks and templates in C to customize the standard dialog boxes, but Basic lacks the procedure variables you need to make them work. The fields I do handle are adequate to provide the required features 98 percent of the time.

Fields of the UDT are used for both input and output. You put data in before the call; you get other data out afterward. Some fields (*Flags*, for instance) work for both. Our function can receive output information through variables that are passed by reference. Of course, you don't have to pass variables because all but one of the arguments are optional. For example, you could ignore the *vFlags* parameter or pass it as a constant. If you ignore or pass a constant, the function won't know the difference and will write the results back to the temporary variable created by Basic. No harm done, but you won't see any results.

Handling optional parameters

The first part of the VBGetOpenFileName function handles optional arguments, giving defaults for any missing values:

```
Function VBGetOpenFileName(vFileName As Variant, _
                          Optional vFileTitle As Variant, _
                          Optional vFlags As Variant, _
                          Optional vOwner As Variant, _
                          Optional vFilter As Variant, _
                          Optional vFilterIndex As Variant, _
                          Optional vInitDir As Variant, _
                          Optional vTitle As Variant, _
                          Optional vDefExt As Variant) As Boolean

    Dim opfile As TOpenFileName, s As String
With opfile
    .lStructSize = Len(opfile)

    ' vFileName must get reference variable to receive result
    ' vFileTitle can get reference variable to receive title
    If IsMissing(vFileTitle) Then vFileTitle = sEmpty
    ' vFlags can get reference variable or constant with bit flags
    If IsMissing(vFlags) Then vFlags = 0
    ' vFilter can take list of filter strings separated by |
    If IsMissing(vFilter) Then vFilter = "All (*.*)| *.*"
    ' vFilterIndex can take initial filter index (one-based)
    If IsMissing(vFilterIndex) Then vFilterIndex = 1
    ' vOwner can take handle of owning window
    If Not IsMissing(vOwner) Then .hwndOwner = vOwner
    ' vInitDir can take initial directory string
    If Not IsMissing(vInitDir) Then .lpstrInitialDir = vInitDir
    ' vDefExt can take default extension
    If Not IsMissing(vDefExt) Then .lpstrDefExt = vDefExt
    ' vTitle can take dialog box title
    If Not IsMissing(vTitle) Then .lpstrTitle = vTitle
```

The only parameter that isn't optional is *vFileName*, since you must pass it a variable in order to get the filename back. Everything else can have defaults, but you must set them. A parameter that will be used later must be initialized so that the missing values won't create errors when used later in the function. The *vFileTitle* and *vFlags* parameters can take variables to receive output values, but if nothing is passed in, defaults are set. The last four parameters—*vOwner*, *vInitDir*, *vDefExt*, and *vTitle*—are simply initialized in the UDT variable. If you don't pass these parameters, you don't need to initialize the UDT variable be-cause it already has the appropriate default value of 0. Incidentally, each UDT field you ignore gets 0.

Handling filters, filenames, and flags

Like the CommonDialog control, VBGetOpenFileName expects filter strings to be separated by a pipe character (|); but Windows expects to find a null char-acter separating filter strings, with a double null at the end. You must do the conversion and put the modified string in the field. Here's the code:

```
' To make Windows-style filter, replace pipes with nulls
Dim ch As String, i As Integer
For i = 1 To Len(vFilter)
    ch = Mid$(vFilter, i, 1)
    If ch = "|" Then
        s = s & sNullChr
    Else
        s = s & ch
    End If
Next
' Put double null at end
s = s & sNullChr & sNullChr
.lpstrFilter = s
.nFilterIndex = vFilterIndex
```

After the new filter string is created, you simply assign it to the pointer field in the UDT variable. See "Variable-Length Strings in UDTs," page 82, for an expla-nation of why this works.

The *lpstrFile* and *lpstrFileTitle* fields must point to string buffers that are long enough to hold any potential value. That maximum length is given in the *nMaxFile* and *nMaxFileTitle* fields. You simply set this length with the con-stants *cMaxPath* and *cMaxFile* (from the Windows API type library) and pad each string out to this maximum. In C, you can fail because of a small buffer, but here you can ensure that that won't happen. You'll convert the resulting strings back to a Basic format later.

```
' Pad file and file title buffers to maximum path
s = vFileName & String$(cMaxPath - Len(vFileName), 0)
.lpstrFile = s
.nMaxFile = cMaxPath
s = vFileTitle & String$(cMaxFile - Len(vFileTitle), 0)
.lpstrFileTitle = s
.nMaxFileTitle = cMaxFile
```

Finally, you strip out any inappropriate flags passed by the user, and then you stuff what's left into the *Flags* field:

```
' Pass in flags, stripping out non-VB flags
.Flags = vFlags And &H1FF1F
```

The flags you might pass here are the same ones you would pass to the CommonDialog control; check out the CommonDialog documentation for a list. You can see the same constants in Windows API Help in a less friendly format (OFN_READONLY rather than cdlOFNReadOnly).

Let Windows do the rest

At this point, you've provided all the necessary input data in the UDT variable, which is ready to pass to the Windows GetOpenFileName function. The data that is provided by the dialog box comes back in the Windows format as null-terminated strings. You must do a little translation to get it back to the Basic caller in a suitable format:

```
If GetOpenFileName(opfile) Then
    VBGetOpenFileName = True
    vFileName = StrZToStr(.lpstrFile)
    vFileTitle = StrZToStr(.lpstrFileTitle)
    vFlags = .Flags
Else
    VBGetOpenFileName = False
    vFileName = sEmpty
    vFileTitle = sEmpty
    vFlags = 0
End If
```

The strings in the UDT variable are actually buffers padded to the maximum length. Windows will write the output string into the variable, but it won't change the padding. You must strip the padding yourself and pass it back to the reference variable the user passed to receive it. If the user didn't pass a variable for the *vFileTitle* or *vFlags* parameter, Basic creates temporary variables for them. You can write the output string or integer to the temporary, which is then thrown away.

VBOpenFileName serves as a model for other Basic common dialog functions. Check out the VBGetSaveFileName, VBChooseColor, and VBChooseFont functions in COMDLG.BAS. You can see them in action in the FileSaveAs, OptionFont, and OptionColor methods of the CEditor class.

Find and Replace Extensions

If you look in the Windows API documentation, you'll find that the common dialog DLL (COMMDLG.DLL or COMDLG32.DLL) contains Find and Replace dialog boxes, which are called with the FindText and ReplaceText functions.

These dialog boxes look a lot like those you see in Notepad and Write. But you won't see hide nor hair of these functions in the CommonDialog control.

Is this a conspiracy to make you write your own dialog forms instead of using the ones Windows provides? As a hardcore programmer, you don't have to take this lying down. What's to stop you from implementing VBFindText and VBReplaceText functions the same way you implemented the others? Well, I wasted three or four days trying to prove that nothing could stop me, and I'm not one to give up easily. But eventually I did stop. Here's why.

The Find and Replace dialog boxes are different from all the other common dialogs in one important way: they're modeless. Once you pop them up on the screen, you can go back to your editor and keep working. The dialog box sticks around until you specifically close it. For a modeless dialog box to communicate with the editor window, the application must handle keyboard messages in its main window loop. In "Sending and Receiving Messages," page 236, I talked about message loops and why Visual Basic programmers don't usually have to worry about them. But in the case of the Find and Replace dialog boxes, you do want to get into the main message loop and handle certain keyboard events such as those involving the Tab and Enter keys.

You don't need to hear the details of how I wasted time trying to capture keyboard events in a DLL hook procedure or with a message control. Suffice it to say that I pulled out every trick in this book, and none of them worked. I could display the dialog boxes on the screen. I could read text and settings from them. The mouse worked fine. But I couldn't get the Tab and Enter keys to work.

If you want to try this out yourself, you'll probably suffer some of the same frustrations I encountered, and maybe some new ones. Or maybe you'll find the solution. But before you start down that road, consider the alternatives.

If you try 20 different editors and word processors, you're likely to encounter 20 different kinds of Find and Replace dialog boxes. The standard Find and Replace dialog boxes aren't very popular with Windows programmers. Everyone seems to have a different idea about how to find strings. Some applications have modal dialog boxes (Visual Basic 3); others have modeless dialog boxes (Visual Basic 4). There's something to be said for both approaches. You'll also see a lot of variations in button names, available features, and the way certain features work. If you roll your own, you choose the features; if you use the standard dialog boxes, Windows chooses.

Remember that in this chapter you're writing a library module for others. Your goal is to make it easy for your clients to offer their users whatever the clients think is most appropriate. But of course you must also try to judge the needs of the end users. In designing a library, as in designing an application, you have to make compromises. Ideally, you'd like to offer clients the ability to pass arguments that would specify whatever kind of Find and Replace dialog boxes they want to use. Realistically, if you try to offer every variation ever seen in a text editor, you'll never finish.

A reasonable compromise is to design Find and Replace dialog boxes that you like, while also allowing the class users to specify a different form if they want. CEditor will expect Find and Replace dialog boxes to have certain standard properties, but it won't care what the dialog boxes look like or how they work.

Designing Find and Replace Dialog Boxes

Because I like the design of Visual Basic's Find and Replace dialog boxes, I used them as the model for Edward's (although I sometimes wish that the Find dialog box was modal instead of modeless).

The obvious design is to create a Find form and a Replace form, on the premise that these are separate operations. But if you study Figure 8-5 carefully, you'll notice a lot of shared features. In fact, the Find dialog box morphs into the Replace dialog box with a simple mouse click. I'd argue that the most efficient way to implement them in Basic is to create one form that can appear in Find or Replace format, depending on how you set the properties.

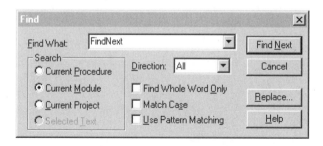

Figure 8-5. *Visual Basic's Find and Replace dialog boxes.*

The trade-off here is code versus data. If you create two dialog boxes, you get two forms plus doubles of all the controls that appear in both. You also duplicate the code that handles common features. If you create one dialog box, you get only one form, one copy of each control, and one copy of all the code that handles the controls—although you need to add morphing code to hide unnecessary controls in the Find dialog box, to move controls around, to change button names, and so on.

As you can see in Figure 8-6, Edward's Find and Replace dialog boxes differ a little from those in Visual Basic. The framed Search options in the Visual Basic dialog boxes—which allow you to choose the current procedure, module, project, or selected text—don't apply to a general text editor, so you can use that area for messages instead.

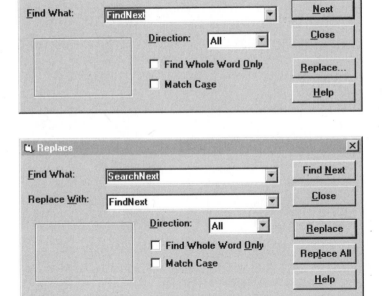

Figure 8-6. *CEditor Find and Replace dialog boxes.*

The Use Pattern Matching check box is also missing. Although the Visual Basic library has the power to help you provide pattern matching, it doesn't make that power easily available. The Basic Like operator supplies a powerful pattern-matching language for comparing strings, but you need an InStrLike for finding them. I've seen code that does clever hacks with the Like operator for kludge pattern searching, but I don't have an extra chapter to explain something that works only part of the time. Besides, this kind of speed-critical operation works best in a compiled language. Maybe we'll see the equivalent of InStrLike in the next version. Recognizing whole words is a much simpler problem, which you should have no trouble solving.

Implementing the FSearch Form

CEditor can use a Find and Replace form, but your form needn't be the one this book provides as a model. In fact, your editor might not use a dialog box at all if you prefer a status-bar or keyboard-only interface for finding and replacing.

For maximum flexibility, all the raw power of finding and replacing is built into CEditor. The FSearch form doesn't know a thing about how to find or modify text within a text box; it only knows how to handle the buttons and other controls on the form.

Programs that use CEditor can perform find and replace operations at three levels:

- Call Find and Replace functions in response to keystrokes or another nondialog interface. Edward uses the quick-and-dirty Find and Replace fields on the top status bar to access a simple subset of the Find and Replace functions.

- Call SearchFind and SearchReplace functions, usually in response to Find and Replace items on a Search menu. These functions produce Find and Replace dialog boxes. By default, you'll get the ones shown in this chapter.

- Replace the default Find and Replace dialog boxes with your own. You can use the ones provided as a model or branch off on your own. Any dialog box that you create must have several standard properties that we'll discuss later, but the interface is up to you.

If your program uses only the first level, you must take two additional steps. First, add the constant *fNoSearchForm = 1* to the Conditional Compilation Arguments field on the Advanced tab of the Options dialog box. This removes references to FSearch that would cause errors at compile time. Second, remove the FSearch module. If you don't use it, don't pay for it.

Loading the FSearch form

Let's take a high-speed look at how the default FSearch form is loaded for finding text. (Replacing works the same way, so we'll look only at the simpler case of finding.) In the normal sequence (followed by Edward), the client program provides a Find item on a Search menu. The menu event procedure calls the SearchFind method of the CEditor class. CEditor implements SearchFind by creating a new search form and initializing key properties of the form, particularly an Editor property. The Editor property enables the form to call methods of the CEditor class that actually do the work of finding text in the text box.

Now let's examine this process a little more slowly. Here is Edward's menu event procedure:

```
Private Sub mnuSearchFind_Click()
    ed.SearchFind
End Sub
```

And here's how SearchFind loads the FSearch form:

```
Sub SearchFind()
    Dim fnd As New FSearch
    ' Set properties on the FSearch form
    fnd.ReplaceMode = False
    Set fnd.Editor = Me
    ' Load, but don't show yet
    Load fnd
    ' Local form destroys automatically
End Sub
```

SearchFind creates a new FSearch object, sets two key properties (ReplaceMode and Editor), and then loads the form. If you prefer to write your own FSearch module, you can do so with only two limitations: your form module must be named FSearch, and it must have ReplaceMode and Editor properties.

Since these properties normally don't need any validation, it's easy to define them as public variables:

```
' Public properties required for any FSearch
Public ReplaceMode As Boolean
Public Editor As CEditor
```

ReplaceMode determines whether the form will be used as a Find form or a Replace form in a particular instance. In fact, you can see that the implementation of SearchReplace looks a lot like the implementation of SearchFind except that the ReplaceMode property is set to True.

The Editor property provides nothing less than the whole CEditor class. Notice that this property is set to Me, thus giving the form access to the current class object. This gets a bit tricky. Edward has only one instantiation of the CEditor class, a module-level object variable named *ed*, declared in the Edward form module. The object named *ed* gets all its features from the CEditor template. One of these features allows the object to loan itself to an FSearch form. The

FSearch form calls its copy of the object *Editor*, but this is just a reference to Edward's *ed* object.

The FSearch form is a temporary object that disappears into the ozone as soon as a user clicks Close. Notice that the form is loaded but not shown. The Load statement turns over control to the Form_Load procedure of the form, which will show itself when it's good and ready.

Resizing forms and moving controls

The FSearch form first resizes and redraws itself based on the information passed to it in the ReplaceMode property. The drawing code is isolated in a private sub named DrawForm. Form_Load calls this sub, and so does the Replace button, which morphs the Find dialog box into the Replace dialog box.

You might expect that moving controls around would be easy and that resizing the form to fit the new control positions would be even easier. But you might be wrong. To make everything come out right, you have to pay close attention to the difference between the Top and Height properties on the one hand and the closely related ScaleTop and ScaleHeight properties on the other. (The FSearch form moves vertically only, so you can ignore similar potential problems with Left and Width.)

Part of the confusion results from the dual purpose of the Scale properties of forms. You set the ScaleTop and ScaleHeight properties to change the form's coordinate system. You read ScaleTop and ScaleHeight to get the size of the form's client area, perhaps when you're doing graphics work or when you're resizing. There's not much relationship between reading and setting these properties, and there probably should be separate properties for each purpose. In any case, I find it helpful to think of the Scale properties as read-only when moving and resizing. If you start modifying the coordinate system by changing the ScaleTop and ScaleLeft settings, you've made the coordinate system for Height and Width completely different from the system for ScaleHeight and ScaleWidth, and all bets are off for moving and resizing.

When you move controls around on the form, their positions are in the client area, which is determined by the ScaleTop and ScaleHeight properties. When you resize the form, you are working with the entire form, whose area is determined by the Top and Height properties. This makes for messy calculations. To resize, for example, you calculate the desired height of the client area and then add the height of the title bar and any form border, which can be calculated as Height minus ScaleHeight. Figure 8-7 on the next page illustrates.

I avoid complex calculations of control positions by saving the original positions of the controls (set at design time) and then moving controls into relative

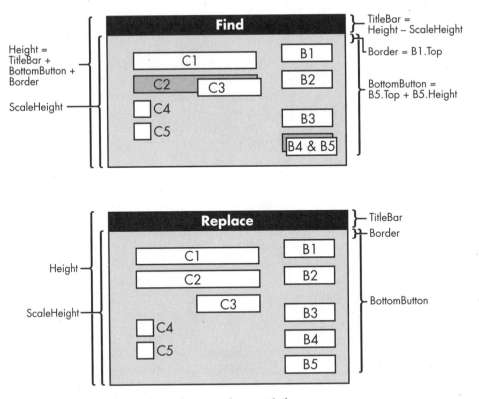

Figure 8-7. *Calculations for redrawing the search form.*

positions. This approach assumes that all controls have the same height, which they do on the FSearch form. You might not have this luxury on your own forms. Here's the code that saves the original control and button positions:

```
' Get initial button and control positions for later placement
If fNotFirst = False Then
    fNotFirst = True
    yControl2 = cboWith.Top
    yControl3 = cboDirection.Top
    yControl4 = chkWord.Top
    yControl5 = chkCase.Top
    yButton5 = cmdHelp.Top
End If
```

Once you have the positions, you can place the controls properly. Here's the Replace portion of the code; you can see the Find section in SEARCH.FRM.

```
' Modify buttons and controls for current mode
If ReplaceMode Then
    cmdCancel.Caption = "&Close"
    cmdReplace.Default = True
    cmdFindNext.Caption = "Find &Next"
    cmdReplace.Caption = "&Replace"
    Caption = "Replace"
    cmdAll.Visible = True
    lblWith.Visible = True
    cboWith.Visible = True
    cmdHelp.Top = yButton5
    frmMessage.Top = yControl3
    cboDirection.Top = yControl3
    lblDirection.Top = yControl3
    chkWord.Top = yControl4
    chkCase.Top = yControl5
Else ' Find
    ⋮
```

When the controls are in the correct position, you must calculate the new form height, as shown here:

```
Dim dyTitleBar As Double, dyBtnLow As Double, dyBorder As Double
' Calculate height of title bar
dyTitleBar = Height - ScaleHeight
' Add height of lowest element (help button moves up and down)
dyBtnLow = cmdHelp.Top + cmdHelp.Height
' Add border around closest element (top button)
dyBorder = cmdFindNext.Top
' Set height
Height = dyTitleBar + dyBtnLow + dyBorder
```

Initializing controls on the FSearch form

The FSearch form must initialize all the properties of its controls based on the information passed in the Editor property. It does this in the Form_Load procedure (SEARCH.FRM). The information must be reloaded every time the form is loaded because, like all polite forms, this one goes away when not in use. It is possible to hide a form instead of unloading it, which might seem like an attractive way to retain form data. But a form retained in memory when not in use steals memory from other programs. The form data might not be very expensive, but the form representation is.

For that reason, the settings of all the FSearch controls are stored in the form's copy of the CEditor object and accessed through properties. You need to load all these properties into the form at load time and then update them in the

CEditor object any time a user changes them in the FSearch form controls. Incidentally, this makes it possible for any client program to control the same settings from an interface that doesn't use an FSearch form. Here's the first part of the code that initializes the FSearch controls:

```
' Initialize all the control values from editor
With Editor
    chkWord.Value = -.SearchOptionWord
    chkCase.Value = -.SearchOptionCase
    cboDirection.ListIndex = -.SearchOptionDirection
```

Consider the case-sensitivity setting. SearchOptionCase is a Boolean property of the CEditor class that stores the setting. The chkCase control is a check box that has the same setting. This code initializes the check box to the values of the CEditor object. Notice the negation sign that changes the Boolean property setting (0 or −1) to the format expected by a CheckBox control (0 or 1). Of course, when the user changes the setting on the form, the Editor setting must also change. Here's the event procedure that does it:

```
Private Sub chkCase_Click()
    Editor.SearchOptionCase = Not Editor.SearchOptionCase
End Sub
```

> **WARNING** There's a small hole in the mechanism that keeps CEditor properties in sync with form controls. If a user changes a property from a client program while a modeless form is active, the search form property will be out of sync with the editor property. You could solve the problem with a timer on the form to update the controls periodically, just in case. But this seems unlikely (and is in fact impossible in Edward), so I'll leave the fix to you.

Working with search string lists

It's easy to load and keep in sync the settings for case, whole word, and direction, but managing the Find and Replace boxes is more difficult because these are lists of the most recently used strings. We'll specifically discuss the Find list (called Find What on the form); the Replace list (Replace With) works the same way.

In CEditor, the Find list is stored in a collection, but it is presented to the world as the FindWhat property. The property looks like a simple string variable (and can be used as such), but it actually represents the last string in the collection. On the FSearch form, the Find strings are stored in the drop-down combo box named cboWhat. A combo box, like other kinds of list boxes, is simply a collection with a user interface, despite the difference in syntax. Figure 8-8 shows what the data looks like in both formats.

FindWhatList collection

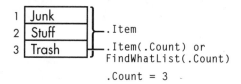

cboWhat combo box

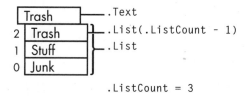

Figure 8-8. *A Find list in a collection and in a combo box.*

Here's the second part of the Form_Load initialization code (you saw the first part in the previous section) that initializes the FSearch form controls:

```
Dim v As Variant
For Each v In .FindWhatList
    cboWhat.AddItem v
Next
cboWhat.Text = .FindWhat
For Each v In .ReplaceWithList
    cboWith.AddItem v
Next
cboWith.Text = .ReplaceWith
```

This code reads items from a collection property (FindWhatList in the CEditor class) into the Find What drop-down combo box and initializes the combo text to the last element in the collection. You can see that the collection can be accessed in two ways: the FindWhatList collection property is used for iteration; and the FindWhat string property is used to access the current (last) item in the collection.

You can perform a limited number of operations on a Find list, whether it is stored in a collection or in a combo box:

■ You can read the top of the list. In the combo box, you do this by reading the Text property. In the CEditor class, you read from the FindWhat property.

■ You can assign a string to the list. In the combo box, the user does this by typing text into the text field or by selecting a string from the drop-down list. In CEditor, you assign a string to the FindWhat property. Note that if the string you assign already exists, it moves to the top of the list but isn't duplicated; the list contains only one copy of each string.

■ You can iterate through the strings in the list. In the combo box, the user can do this by clicking the drop-down arrow and inspecting the list, scrolling if necessary. In CEditor, you use For Each to iterate through the FindWhatList collection.

None of this happens automatically. Most of the work occurs when a string is assigned. Here's the Property Let code that handles adding a new string to the collection:

```
Property Let FindWhat(sWhatA As String)
    Dim v As Variant, i As Integer ' i = 0
    For i = 1 To FindWhatList.Count
        ' If item is in list, move to end of list
        If FindWhatList(i) = sWhatA Then
            FindWhatList.Remove i
            FindWhatList.Add sWhatA
            Exit Property
        End If
    Next
    ' If item isn't in list, add it
    FindWhatList.Add sWhatA
End Property
```

You must carry out a similar operation every time the user types a new string into the combo box. Check it out in cboWhat_LostFocus in SEARCH.FRM.

> **NOTE** Why use an indexed For loop instead of a For Each loop to iterate through this collection? Because the Remove method requires an index for simple unkeyed collections. For examples of keyed and unkeyed collections, see "Collecting Objects," page 174. Also notice the inefficient linear search. This approach works for small collections such as these search string lists, but you wouldn't want to use it on a large collection or list box.

Reading a string from the collection is much easier. Here's the Property Get:

```
Property Get FindWhat() As String
    If FindWhatList.Count Then
        FindWhat = FindWhatList(FindWhatList.Count)
```

```
    Else
        FindWhat = sEmpty
    End If
End Property
```

It simply returns the last item in the collection or an empty string if the collection is empty. The Text property of a drop-down combo box serves the same purpose.

Your next assignment is to save the Find and Replace lists with the SaveSetting function at termination and restore them with GetSetting at startup. While you're at it, you should save the user's favorite font and colors. And, of course, any respectable editor should provide a list of the most recently edited files and reopen the last one with the cursor position restored.

Finding and replacing text

Once you've set up the form in the proper format, managed all the controls, and coordinated communications with CEditor, only one minor detail is left: finding and replacing the text. You must provide both general functions that you can call from any interface and a specific form implementation to find and replace in response to clicking buttons on the FSearch form.

The task of finding and replacing text is especially susceptible to bugs because it is so boring. Handling all the options and variations can deaden the mind and give you an unjustified sense of confidence. Most of us write this kind of code every day, but we don't want to pay for pages and pages of it in a programming book, so I'll leave you to find any "boredom" bugs by yourself. But I will offer you a small highlight map for your self-guided tour.

Your first tour stop should be FindNext, the workhorse of CEditor. Even the ReplaceNext method leans heavily on FindNext. Most of the work in FindNext consists of handling the case and direction options. (The actual searching is done by the InStr and InStrR functions.)

Next, look at ReplaceNext. Again, most of the code deals with finding the next match, handling options, and ensuring that the matching text is selected. Once that's done, replacing is as simple as assigning the SearchWith text to the Sel-Text property.

You will probably also want to stop at some of the places in EDWARD.FRM where user-interface code calls FindNext and ReplaceNext. For example, the mnuSearchFindNext_Click event calls ed.SearchFindNext. If the FindWhat property has text, SearchFindNext calls FindNext. Otherwise, SearchFindNext calls SearchFind to get something to search. You can also see FindNext called from the txtWhat_LostFocus event of the Find panel.

Finally, look at the way FindNext and ReplaceNext are called from the cmd-FindNext_Click and cmdReplace_Click events of the FSearch form. The code is more complex than you might expect, but it deals with coordinating buttons and other controls, not with the actual searching. Notice that, unlike the Visual Basic Find and Replace dialog boxes, the FSearch form doesn't detect when you've wrapped all the way around; it just keeps wrapping forever. That's the way I like it, but you could easily add code to detect a complete wrap.

NOTE   Don't look too hard at my InStrR implementation. This is the type of function that should be recoded in C using an efficient string search algorithm so that searching backward will be as fast as searching forward with InStr. I thought at first that this problem would be at least partially solved by the Find method of the RichTextBox control, which duplicates most of the functionality of the CEditor FindNext method. The only problem is that the Find function won't search backward. You might expect that if you passed a starting position greater than the ending position, Find would search backward. But a backward search always fails, and it's not Visual Basic's fault. The Find method obviously is implemented using the EM_FINDTEXT message, but when I try to search with SendMessage and EM_FINDTEXT, I get the same result. You could speed up RichTextBox searches a little by reimplementing FindNext using the Find method instead of InStr, but you'd still have to use InStrR for backward searches.

The CKeyState Class

Visual Basic comes with a handy Key State control for displaying or changing the state of control keys such as Caps Lock, Num Lock, and Insert. But unless you're really attached to the fonts used on the key status buttons, you should delete KEYSTA*.* from your hard disk right now. Those predefined key buttons have a heavy cost in disk space and Windows resources. Why should you ship KEYSTA16.OCX or KEYSTA32.OCX to every customer at a cost of more than 100 KB when you can roll your own in Basic for almost nothing?

The font and colors of the Key State control are a little garish for my taste anyway. Edward achieves a more subtle look (similar to that of the status bar in Microsoft Word for Windows) by displaying the key state in gray or black on 3-D panels. You could use an invisible Key State control to achieve this effect, but the code required to do the same thing in Windows is so simple that the control isn't worth the trouble. Instead, let's wrap up everything in the CKeyState class.

Using the CKeyState Class

From a user's perspective, the CKeyState class represents the entire keyboard. It has properties that allow you to read or modify the state of any key on the keyboard.

Of course, most users are interested only in the state of the toggle keys Caps Lock, Insert, Num Lock, and Scroll Lock. Therefore, CKeyState provides properties that offer easy access to these keys: CapsState, InsState, NumState, and ScrollState.

Let's look at how Edward handles the Caps Lock key with the CapsState property. The letters *CAP* are displayed on a 3-D panel in black if Caps Lock is on or in gray if it's off. You can toggle the state of the key not only by pressing the key on your keyboard but also by clicking the panel.

Edward's main form maintains a private *kbd* variable to represent the keyboard as known to Edward:

```
Private kbd As New CKeyState
```

This variable is used in the event sub that toggles the Caps Lock state when you click the CAP panel:

```
Private Sub panCaps_Click()
    kbd.CapsState = Not kbd.CapsState
    panCaps.ForeColor = IIf(kbd.CapsState, vbWindowText, vbGrayText)
    ed.SetFocus
End Sub
```

The critical line is the first one, which simply toggles the state by setting the property to its opposite. After that, you set the color according to the new keyboard state.

Because the user can change the Caps Lock state at any time by pressing the key, you need to check periodically to see whether the panel color needs to change. The place to check such things is in a timer. In theory, the need to use a timer with CKeyState is a disadvantage, compared to the Key State control. The control has a built-in timer, so you don't need to add one. In practice, most applications that maintain a key state display need a timer anyway. Edward, for example, needs one to periodically update its time display, as you can see in the timer sub:

```
Private Sub tmr_Timer()
    panCaps.ForeColor = IIf(kbd.CapsState, vbWindowText, vbGrayText)
    ed.OverWrite = Not kbd.InsState
    panIns.ForeColor = IIf(ed.OverWrite, vbGrayText, vbWindowText)
    If fDate Then
        panTime.Caption = Format$(Date$, "General Date")
    Else
        panTime.Caption = Format$(Time$, "Medium Time")
    End If
End Sub
```

Edward's timer interval is 500 (half a second), which seems to be adequate for keeping the display accurate without slowing down the editor. Actually, editors are among the least demanding of applications. Not many people can type fast enough to keep the keyboard handler from waiting.

Edward handles the Caps Lock key and the Insert key the same way, but it ignores Num Lock and Scroll Lock. CKeyState provides other handy features not used by Edward. For instance, the KeyPressed property lets you check to see whether a given key is pressed. You specify the key by its virtual key code. (Virtual key codes are in the Visual Basic Objects and Procedures type library under KeyCodeConstants. You can also find them with Windows-style names, such as VK_DELETE, in the Windows API type library under UserConst.)

```
fShift = kbd.KeyPressed(VK_CONTROL) ' Is Ctrl key down?
```

You can also press a key programmatically:

```
kbd.KeyPressed(VK_F1) = True     ' Press F1
DoEvents
kbd.KeyPressed(VK_F1) = False    ' Release F1
```

Handling the Insert State

Although Edward handles the Insert key as a toggle, like the Caps Lock key, toggling Insert off doesn't automatically switch a text box to overwrite mode. In fact, there isn't any overwrite mode. Notepad and Write must be the only text editors in history without an overwrite mode. But just because a feature isn't built in doesn't mean you can't add it.

It's easy to add overwrite mode by inserting code in the KeyPress event procedure, but this presents a design problem. You can't add event procedures to classes. The only way you can handle specific keystrokes is in the KeyPress event procedure of Edward's text box. But that means you'd have to cut and paste the same code to every other program that needed an overwrite mode. You want the overwrite code to be in the editor class, not in the edit code that uses Edward.

The solution is to give the editor class a KeyPress method, even though this method won't automatically be called as an event procedure. You can then call the KeyPress method from the real event procedure:

```
Private Sub txtEdit_KeyPress(KeyAscii As Integer)
    ed.KeyPress KeyAscii
End Sub
```

You'll need to add the same code to the KeyPress sub of any TextBox or RichTextBox control tied to the editor class, but that's really no different from adding the FileOpen method to the FileOpen menu event.

The code to handle overwrite mode is relatively simple:

```
Public Sub KeyPress(KeyAscii As Integer)
    If KeyAscii > 31 Then
        If OverWrite Then
            rtb.SelLength = rtb.SelLength + 1
            ' Don't overwrite LF in CR/LF sequence
            If Right$(rtb.SelText, 1) = sCr Then
                rtb.SelLength = rtb.SelLength - 1
            End If
        End If
    End If
End Sub
```

Every time a key is pressed, you extend the selection one character so that you overwrite the next character with the new character. The KeyPress sub tests the OverWrite property. Unlike most properties, this one needs no validation or other action. You can simply define it as a public variable:

```
Public OverWrite As Boolean
```

Of course, Edward has to manage the OverWrite property so that the KeyPress sub in the editor class will do the right thing. Edward ties the OverWrite property to the state of the Insert key:

```
ed.OverWrite = Not kbd.InsState
panIns.ForeColor = IIf(ed.OverWrite, vbGrayText, vbWindowText)
```

That's not the only way to handle it. You could simply treat the Insert key as a normal key, toggling OverWrite each time it's pressed and ignoring the toggle state of the key. This approach points out an important distinction: Edward uses both the CEditor class and the CKeyState class, but no other connection exists between the two. CEditor doesn't use the CKeyState class and vice versa. The classes are two separate tools that make Edward more modular.

CHALLENGE The KeyPress event in CEditor is the perfect place to add new command keys or to change the editing behavior of the class in other ways. Feel free to add macro handling or key reassignment. You might need to add a KeyUp event if you want to handle function keys or control keys that aren't seen by the KeyPress event procedure.

Implementing the CKeyState Class

To a programmer, CKeyState is a simple wrapper for the Windows functions GetKeyboardState and SetKeyboardState. These two functions work on an array of 256 bytes representing the 256 keys on the keyboard. What? Your keyboard doesn't have 256 keys? Well, if it did, you could put them in this array. Windows is just leaving room for expansion.

The new Byte type in Visual Basic makes key handling easy. In previous versions, you had to treat the 256-byte array as a 256-character string, strip out the appropriate character, and convert to an integer. An array of bytes is much simpler. CKeyState property procedures share the following private array:

```
Private abKeys(0 To 255) As Byte
```

To read the state of a key, you get all the key states and then read the one you want, using the virtual key code as an index into the key array:

```
Property Get CapsState() As Boolean
    ' Get toggle and pressed state of all keys
    GetKeyboardState abKeys(0)
    ' Check low bit for state
    CapsState = abKeys(VK_CAPITAL) And 1
End Property
```

The low bit of each toggle key indicates whether the toggle is on or off. Notice how we pass the array to GetKeyboardState by passing the first element. "Arrays," page 62, explains how this works.

To change the state of a key, you must read in the current key states, modify the key in the array, and write the result back with SetKeyboardState:

```
Property Let CapsState(fCapsStateA As Boolean)
    ' Get toggle and pressed state of all keys
    GetKeyboardState abKeys(0)
    ' Set low bit to new pressed state
    If fCapsStateA Then
        abKeys(VK_CAPITAL) = abKeys(VK_CAPITAL) Or 1
    Else
        abKeys(VK_CAPITAL) = abKeys(VK_CAPITAL) And &HFE
    End If
    ' Store changed array
    SetKeyboardState abKeys(0)
End Property
```

The KeyPressed property works the same way, except that the pressed state of a key is stored in the high bit and you must provide the virtual key code of the key. Here's the Property Get procedure:

```
Property Get KeyPressed(iKey As Integer) As Boolean
    ' Get toggle and pressed state of all keys
    GetKeyboardState abKeys(0)
    ' Check high bit for state
    KeyPressed = abKeys(iKey) And &H80
End Property
```

A Property Get with an argument makes the property look like an array element, as described in the sidebar "Property Arrays," page 190. Check out the KeyPressed Property Let in KEYSTATE.CLS.

9

Stir-Fry

"What's for dinner?"

"Stir-fry."

"Oh, no."

"I thought you liked my stir-fry."

"Well, sometimes. But...Hey, what is that? You're not going to put rhubarb in there, are you?"

"I'll have you know that rhubarb is the definitive ingredient in the matchless stir-fries of the Basic tribe of northeastern Cathistan."

"Oh, sure. Now you're a master of authentic ethnic cooking. But tell me—do those folks use picante sauce in their stir-fries?"

"Who said anything about picante sauce?"

"I tasted it in one of your concoctions, just last week."

"Yeah, and you went back for seconds. It was good, wasn't it?"

"Well, not as bad as I expected. But it wasn't really stir-fry. Not with corn and avocados. Hey! Put that Worcestershire back where you got it."

"Who's doing the cooking here?"

"I don't get it. You've got three brands of Chinese stir-fry sauce and one of Korean, two kinds of soy sauce, three kinds of teriyaki, Thai peanut and fish sauces, God knows what else from the Philippines and Malaysia, and that's not even mentioning your Indian spices. You've got enough without visiting other continents."

"I just don't want my cooking to get predictable."

"I wouldn't worry about that."

You shouldn't worry about this chapter being predictable, either. It's just your Basic, everyday stir-fry. I've thrown in all the vegetables, sauces, and algorithms that don't fit anywhere else. It's not as bad as you think; quite tasty, actually.

Everything You Always Wanted to Know About...

These days, almost every application you see puts system information in its About dialog box. There's no official ABAPI standard, but everyone seems to be doing it. In early Windows-based programs, the About dialog box simply named the application, but over the years About boxes have come to serve serious (and not so serious) roles.

Some About dialog boxes contain secret commands that activate an animation or a list of developers. Others provide system information such as available memory and other resources. You'll also find stern copyright warnings, serial numbers, jokes, and copy protection schemes.

The latest addition to About dialog boxes in Microsoft applications (including Visual Basic itself) is a System Info button that brings up Microsoft's information application, MSINFO.EXE or MSINFO32.EXE. Microsoft provides this program with many of its applications so that you can display, print, or write to a disk every piece of information about your system that an internal or external support person might need. Any of your customers who have recent Microsoft applications (including Visual Basic) will have the information program.

You can add the About dialog box presented here to your applications with very little work: just set any application-specific About properties, and load the About form. The dialog box displays some general system information and provides a button to activate an information application. Of course, like any self-respecting About dialog box, this one has an undocumented command that starts an animation sequence.

The All About program (ALLABOUT.VBP) demonstrates the About dialog box, along with tabs containing other information. Figure 9-1 shows the All About program in action. We'll discuss the Version and System tabs in this chapter. The Video tab exercises the CVideo class, discussed in Chapter 6. The Drives tab exercises the CDrive class and the NDrives collection, both of which were discussed in Chapter 4.

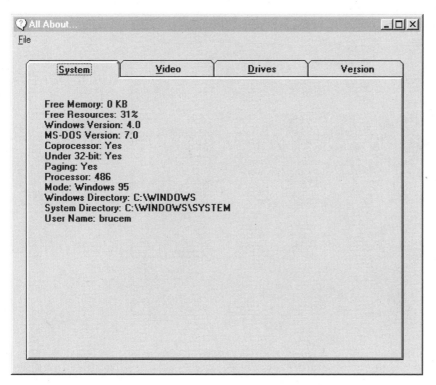

Figure 9-1. *The All About program.*

The About Form

All you need to create your own About dialog box is to write some code such as the following in the event procedure of an About menu item. You can set the About properties that are unique to your company or application, but everything else comes from the system.

```
Private Sub mnuAbout_Click()
    Dim about As New FAbout
    about.UserInfo(2) = "Don't even think " & _
                        "about stealing this program"
    Load about
    If about.Error Then MsgBox "I don't know nuttin'"
    Unload about
End Sub
```

That code comes from the About menu of the All About program. Figure 9-2 on the following page shows the results.

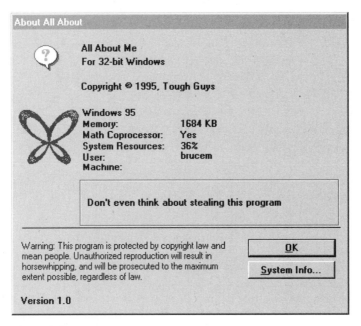

Figure 9-2. *About All About.*

The About form gets its information from several sources. The title and other information about the program come from the App object. System information comes from a System object. The form gets its undocumented animation command from...well, if I told you, it wouldn't be undocumented.

The About form provides several properties that allow you to enter program-specific information. The UserInfo array property lets you enter general information; and the InfoProg, Copyright, and Comments properties allow you to override information that the form ordinarily figures out for itself. After you set the properties you want (the form also works if you don't set anything), you simply show the form and let the Form_Load procedure take over:

```
Sub Form_Load()
    Dim sRoot As String, sInfo As String
    Me.Caption = "About " & App.ProductName
    lblApp.Caption = App.Title
#If Win32 Then
    sRoot = "c:\Program Files\Common Files\Microsoft Shared"
    sInfo = "\msinfo\msinfo32.exe"
    If ExistFile(sRoot & sInfo) = False Then
        sRoot = System.WindowsDir & "\msapps"  ' Windows NT
    End If
    lblEnviron.Caption = "For 32-bit Windows"
#Else
```

```
        sRoot = System.WindowsDir & "\msapps"
        sInfo = "\msinfo\msinfo.exe"
        lblEnviron.Caption = "For 16-bit Windows"
#End If
        ' Allow override because some customers might not have MSINFO
        If InfoProg = sEmpty Then InfoProg = sRoot & sInfo
        If ExistFile(InfoProg) = False Then cmdInfo.Visible = False
        ' Icon from first form is application icon
        Me.Icon = Forms(0).Icon
        imgIcon.Picture = Forms(0).Icon
        lblMode.Caption = System.Mode
        lblMemory.Caption = System.FreeMemory & " KB"
        lblCoprocessor.Caption = IIf(System.HasCoprocessor, "Yes", "No")
        lblResources.Caption = System.FreeResources & "%"
        lblUser.Caption = System.USER
        lblMachine.Caption = System.Machine
        If UserInfo(1) = sEmpty And UserInfo(2) = sEmpty And _
                                    UserInfo(3) = sEmpty Then
            fmUserInfo.Visible = False
        Else
            fmUserInfo.Visible = True
            lblUserInfo(0).Caption = UserInfo(1)
            lblUserInfo(1).Caption = UserInfo(2)
            lblUserInfo(2).Caption = UserInfo(3)
        End If
        If Copyright = sEmpty Then Copyright = App.LegalCopyright
        lblRights.Caption = Copyright
        If Comments = sEmpty Then Comments = App.Comments
        lblComment.Caption = Comments
        lblVersion.Caption = "Version " & App.Major & "." & App.Minor
        Show vbModal
End Sub
```

Most of the information for the About box comes from the App and System objects. We'll focus on the System object later, but first a word about the new version properties in the App object. In Visual Basic version 4, you can (and should) specify version resources for your programs in the EXE Options dialog box (accessed from the Make EXE File dialog box). "The CVersion Class," page 415, discusses what version resources are and why you should use them. For now, simply note that the About form gets program information from the ProductName, LegalCopyright, Comment, Major, and Minor properties, which are tied to the version resources entered in the EXE Options dialog box.

This sounds simple, but when I wrote the About form, early in the beta period of Visual Basic 4, those properties didn't exist, and the version information wasn't available to Basic programs. I originally wrote the CVersion class to read version resources directly from the EXE file so that I could fill in the information on the About form. But since version resources are stored in the EXE file, and the EXE file isn't really running when you run in the environment, my About form looked strangely naked during development in the IDE. I had to debug the compiled EXE program from log files produced by debug procedures. Mercifully, the final version uses an easier feature that works both in the environment and in EXE files.

The CSystem Class and the System Object

Visual Basic provides some useful global objects—App, Printer, and Screen—but it lacks a System object to tell you everything you need to know about your environment. Well, now it has one—mine.

The CSystem class (in SYSTEM.CLS) groups a lot of useful system information and makes it available through an easy-to-use, object-oriented interface. But what you really want is a system object rather than a system class. Sure, you could declare multiple system objects with different names, but they'd all have the same information because your program is running on only one system.

Forms support implicit variable declaration, as described in "Form Classes Versus Form Objects," page 164. It would be nice if classes had the same feature (under user control rather than being automatic). I'd like to be able to set an Implicit property for a class named CSystem and automatically create one (and only one) variable with the name *System*. (Incidentally, I'd also like to be able to clear an Implicit property for forms to eliminate implicit variable declaration when I don't want it. Maybe next version.) In the meantime, I make do by declaring my own system object.

The declaration looks like this:

```
Public System As New CSystem
```

You must add a module, SYSTEM.BAS, containing only this declaration. Users must add both SYSTEM.CLS and SYSTEM.BAS to their projects. Unfortunately, they can also declare as many additional local, static, and module-level CSystem objects as they want. You could implement a reference-counting scheme to ensure that there is only one system object, but I didn't bother.

Properties of the CSystem class fall into one of two categories. Some pieces of information—the Windows and MS-DOS versions, and whether your machine has a coprocessor—never change, at least not while a program is running. For this kind of information, CSystem gets all the data it needs in Class_Initialize and stores it in private variables. You can then access the data through Property Get procedures. Other pieces of information—the amount of memory available, for instance—change all the time and must be calculated on request in Property Get procedures.

Unchanging system information

Because system information in 16-bit mode tends to differ from that in 32-bit mode, the Class_Initialize sub ends up with a lot of conditional code:

```
Private Sub Class_Initialize()
    Dim dw As Long, c As Integer

#If Win32 Then
    dw = GetVersion()
    iWinMajor = dw And &HFF&
    iWinMinor = (dw And &HFF00&) / &H100&
    fUnder32 = True
    If dw And &H80000000 Then
        ' Windows 95 is 7.0
        iDosMinor = 0
        iDosMajor = 7
        sMode = "Windows 95"
    Else
        ' NT is 5.10
        iDosMinor = 10
        iDosMajor = 5
        sMode = "Windows NT"
    End If

    ' Emulator is integrated so that 32-bit always has coprocessor
    fCoprocessor = True
    ' 32-bit always has paging
    fPaging = True
    GetSystemInfo sys
    Select Case sys.ordProcessorType
    Case 386
        sProcessor = "386"
    Case 486
        sProcessor = "486"
    Case 586
        sProcessor = "586"
    Case 2000
        sProcessor = "R2000"
    Case 3000
        sProcessor = "R3000"
    Case 4000
        sProcessor = "R4000"
    Case 21064
        sProcessor = "A21064"
    Case Else
        sProcessor = "Unknown"
    End Select
```

(continued)

```
#Else
    dw = GetVersion()
    iWinMajor = dw And &HFF&
    iWinMinor = (dw And &HFF00&) / &H100&
    iDosMinor = (dw And &HFF0000) / &H10000
    iDosMajor = (dw And &HF000000) / &H1000000
    dw = GetWinFlags()
    If dw And WF_STANDARD Then
        sMode = "Standard"
    Else
        sMode = "386 Enhanced"
    End If
    fCoprocessor = IIf(dw And WF_80x87, True, False)
    fPaging = IIf(dw And WF_PAGING, True, False)
    fUnder32 = False
    If dw And WF_WINNT Then
        fUnder32 = True
        sMode = "WOW " & sMode
    ElseIf iWinMajor = 3 And iWinMinor = 95 Then
        fUnder32 = True
        sMode = "WOW " & sMode
    End If
    If dw And WF_CPU286 Then
        sProcessor = "286"
    ElseIf dw And WF_CPU386 Then
        sProcessor = "386"
    ElseIf dw And WF_CPU486 Then
        sProcessor = "486"
    Else
        sProcessor = "Unknown"
    End If

#End If

    sWinDir = String$(cMaxPath, 0)
    c = GetWindowsDirectory(sWinDir, cMaxPath)
    sWinDir = Left(sWinDir, c)
    sSysDir = String$(cMaxPath, 0)
    c = GetSystemDirectory(sSysDir, cMaxPath)
    sSysDir = Left(sSysDir, c)

End Sub
```

You can see most of this information displayed on the System tab of All About in Figure 9-1, on page 407.

I won't offer a lengthy explanation of the Win16 GetWinFlags function, the Win32 GetSystemInfo function, or the GetVersion function (which is common to all versions of Windows but returns a different format for each). The code demonstrates most of their workings, and you can also look up the strange details in the MSDN/VB starter kit.

Once you have the information, it's easy to provide access through properties such as this one:

```
Property Get WinMajor() As Integer
    WinMajor = iWinMajor
End Property
```

At one point during the development of CSystem, I decided to improve efficiency by changing my Property Get procedures to public variables. Why store the Windows version in variables accessed through Property Get procedures when you can put it in public variables? As it turns out, there's a reason: to prevent users of the System object from changing the Windows version. The System object should be read-only, and the only way to make it so is to provide all information through Property Gets with no corresponding Property Lets.

Dynamic system information

Information about system resources is the most common (and useful) information provided by most About dialog boxes. The Windows 3.1 Program Manager showed the way (choose About Program Manager from the Help menu), and other programs have followed. Under 16-bit systems, information about remaining resources can predict your success in launching one more application or tell you why an application that usually works is going haywire today.

The System object returns three different flavors of resource information: FreeUserResources, FreeGdiResources, and plain old FreeResources. Under Windows NT, all three always return a reassuring 100 percent. Windows 95 isn't that generous, but you won't see the same problems that were common under Windows 3.x.

What are resources, anyway? Maybe not what you think. Free resources are not free memory, which CSystem also returns. Under 16-bit Windows, memory must be allocated in 64-KB segments. Windows uses one of these segments to store all the miscellaneous data needed by the User DLL (controlling Windows and related elements) and uses another segment for data needed by the GDI DLL (controlling display graphics). When either segment gets filled up, things start going wrong, and not always in very polite ways. Buttons and picture boxes might refuse to paint, your system can slow to a crawl, and weird events can occur. This can happen even when you have megabytes of system memory left.

Windows 3.1 (but not version 3.0) provides the GetFreeSystemResources function, which returns your remaining system resources as a percentage. You can find the GDI, user, or system resources by passing different constants to the function. The system resources number is simply the lower of the GDI or user percentages. For instance, if you have 25 percent of GDI free and 50 percent of user free, Windows says that 25 percent of the system resources are free. Here's how CSystem provides the information:

```
Property Get FreeResources() As Long
#If Win32 Then
    mem.iLength = Len(mem)
    GlobalMemoryStatus mem
    FreeResources = 100 - mem.iMemoryLoad
#Else
    FreeResources = GetFreeSystemResources(GFSR_SYSTEMRESOURCES)
#End If
End Property
```

FreeGdiResources and FreeUserResources are the same except for the constant passed to GetFreeSystemResources. The 32-bit code is the same for all three because both GDI and user memory come from the same place in 32-bit Windows. The Win32 GlobalMemoryStatus function provides one source for all the memory information you could ever want (and a lot that you don't care about). For example, here's how it is used in the FreeMemory property:

```
Property Get FreeMemory() As Long
#If Win32 Then
    mem.iLength = Len(mem)
    GlobalMemoryStatus mem
    FreeMemory = mem.iAvailPhys \ 1024
#Else
    FreeMemory = GetFreeSpace(0) \ 1024
#End If
End Property
```

Realistically, you seldom need to worry about free memory. Under Windows 3.*x*, you'll normally run out of resources long before you run out of memory; and under various versions of 32-bit Windows, free memory is subject to interpretation. You're not likely to run out of memory, because you have available not only the physical memory on your machine but also as much virtual memory as Windows can swap to your disk. Having plenty of virtual memory left is no guarantee that you won't slow to a thrashing, grinding crawl, of course. GlobalMemoryStatus purports to give you the information you need to evaluate remaining virtual and physical memory, but realistically it's a moving limit that you're unlikely to hit.

The CSystem class also has properties to return a network user name and a machine name, but the implementation is uninteresting. You can see output from all the System properties by clicking the System tab in All About.

CHALLENGE Windows 3.x won't warn you about low system resources, but you can warn yourself by writing a little application that displays your current GDI and user resources (numerically if you're lazy, or with meters if you're not). This application needs a timer that updates the numbers periodically—say, once a minute. During the update, if either number is less than a specified threshold—say, 20 percent—a dialog box tells you to close down some windows or restart your system. Launch this program on startup, and you'll never run out of resources again. Just be sure to write your application tight and small so that it doesn't take up too many resources. Or better yet, do what I do: switch to 32-bit Windows, where your chances of running out of resources are nil.

The CVersion Class

I was once foolish enough to write what must have been the most complicated batch file ever to ship with a commercial product. I speak of the disastrous MASM 5.0 SETUP.BAT, powered by the infamous batch utility WHAT.EXE. I won't lead you through that sad history (except to note that writing polite batch files is harder than programming in assembler). But I would like to mention the batch file versioning problems I experienced with early versions of MS-DOS, since they relate to version problems we still suffer with Visual Basic.

In those days, a new MS-DOS version (and operating systems that emulated it) seemed to come out every few months, each with a different undocumented trick for displaying a blank line. In some versions, two spaces following the ECHO command did the job. In others, you had to use a text editor that let you insert the ASCII character 0 or 255 after ECHO. The current method (ECHO followed immediately by a dot) didn't work in early versions.

You might have hoped to escape such problems in Windows and Visual Basic, but version differences remain the bane of all those who program for Windows. You'll still find controls and DLLs that change their interface in a fashion that seems as random as the MS-DOS batch language. If your system seems to crash in unexpected ways, chances are good that somehow you're running an outdated version of a DLL or a control you didn't even know you had.

Fortunately, Windows 3.1 added resources for embedding version data in your programs and an API for finding version information in other programs. The CVersion class wraps this functionality in one handy package.

Version resources

The Version tab in the All About program is a good place to start examining version resources. The New button brings up an Open dialog box in which you can select a program, a DLL, a control, a font file, or another executable file. If the file has version resources, they are displayed as shown in Figure 9-3, which displays the resources of Visual Basic itself.

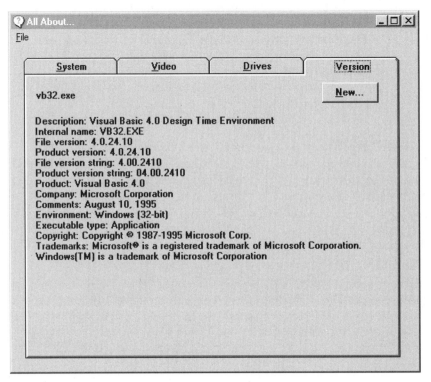

Figure 9-3. *The version resources of Visual Basic.*

You can learn a lot about resources by experimenting on various programs and DLLs, including compiled Visual Basic programs. Compare programs created with versions 3 and 4 of Visual Basic. Compare system DLLs to programs, or compare programs created with other languages to Basic programs. Some programs don't have version resources, but most polite Windows executables do.

Normally, version data comes from a resource script (an RC file). Resource data has a special format similar to (but more complicated than) the resource formats described in "Anatomy of a Resource Block," page 323. You can see an example in VBUTIL.RC, the resource script for the VBUTIL DLL. It's possible to enter resource data in a resource script and compile it into your Visual Basic program as described in Chapter 7, but Visual Basic provides an easier way: you can use the EXE Options dialog box, accessed by choosing the Options button in the Make EXE File dialog box. Figure 9-4 shows the EXE Options dialog box entries for the All About program. In Figure 9-5 on the next page, you can see how these entries are displayed in the All About program.

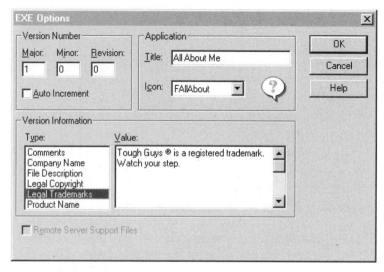

Figure 9-4. *The EXE Options dialog box.*

NOTE The WinWatch program (WINWATCH.VBP) also displays version resources when you select a file in WinWatch's Modules By Exe Name list box.

Testing version numbers

You can use the Windows API version functions to display version information (as WinWatch and All About do), but more likely you'll want to read the version numbers of DLLs (or controls) used by your program. If the DLL version is incompatible, you can terminate with a polite request to update the DLL rather than with a rude command to boot the system.

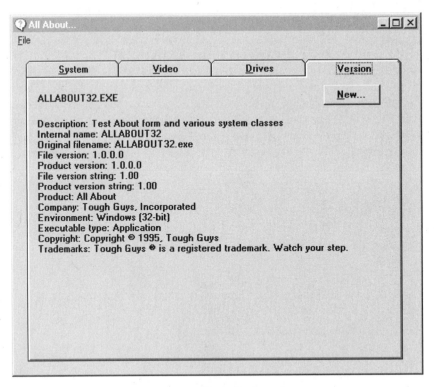

Figure 9-5. *The version resources of the All About program.*

For example, here's how All About checks to be sure that you haven't overwritten my Visual Basic Utility DLL with the Vermont Business University Tools for Industrial Liquidity DLL:

```
Sub ValidateVBUtil()
    Dim verUtil As New CVersion, f As Boolean
    Const sUtil = "C Utility Functions for Visual Basic"
#If Win32 Then
    f = verUtil.Create("VBUTIL32.DLL")
#Else
    f = verUtil.Create("VBUTIL16.DLL")
#End If
    If Not f Or _
        verUtil.FileVersionString <> "1.00" Or _
        verUtil.Company <> "MS-PRESS" Or _
        verUtil.Description <> sUtil Then
        MsgBox "Invalid DLL"
        End
    End If
End Sub
```

What's in a Name?

How do you name a program?

- You can assign a name as the caption of your main form. WinWatch displays this name as the title of the form window.

- You can assign a name to the Title property of the App object by assigning a string to the property at run time. You also can assign App.Title at design time by filling in the Title field of the EXE Options dialog box. By studying a Visual Basic program in WinWatch, you can see that this name then becomes the title given to a second window, which seems to mirror the main form. This second window is marked as being visible, but you can't see it. Maybe it's hiding behind the main form. The App.Title name, not the caption of the main form, appears in the Windows Task List.

- You can enter a name as a Product Name value in the EXE Options dialog box. The name you enter (if any) is embedded in the EXE file as a version resource.

- You can enter a name in the Project Name field on the Project tab of the Options dialog box. The name you enter appears as the first word in the Libraries/Projects field of the Object Browser. It will be used as the OLE server name if you make your project a server. (See Chapter 10.)

- And of course you have the project filename, ending with VBP, and the program filenames, ending with EXE. The name you give the 16-bit version of your program need not be the same as the name of the 32-bit version. In fact, they'd better be different if you want them to reside in the same directory. I always append the digits *32* to the 32-bit version (ALLABOUT.EXE and ALLABOUT32.EXE). It's not a problem if adding *32* makes the name longer than eight characters; all the 32-bit operating systems recognized by Visual Basic 4 accept long filenames.

CVersion class implementation

Once somebody (me, in this case) writes a version class, the rest of us (you, in this case) can simply use it without understanding how it works. The code of CVersion is somewhat complex, but it doesn't introduce any new programming techniques, so I'll just give a "Cliffs Notes" summary here and encourage you to look up the details in VERSION.CLS.

Version functions are located in separate Windows DLLs—VER.DLL for 16-bit mode or VERSION.DLL for 32-bit mode. Rather than incorporate the version functions into the Windows API type library, as I've done for most of the API functions in this book, I put private Declare statements, constants, and UDTs in VERSION.CLS. You shouldn't need to use these version functions in any other context anyway.

Version data comes in two parts. The first part is a block of numeric data in a UDT. This comes out the same in any language: version 1.0 in Japanese or Urdu is still version 1.0. The second part consists of language-specific string data. One block of strings—the only one currently recognized by CVersion—is in a translated form meant to be usable from any version of the program.

The Create method starts by calling GetFileVersionInfoSize. You pass this function the name of the executable file, and it returns the size of the version data and a handle to the data. You then pass the size, the handle, the executable name, and a buffer (of the given size) to GetFileVersionInfo, which fills the buffer.

You now have a block of version data in an unreadable format. You must call VerQueryValue to read it. You pass some semirandom strings to VerQueryValue to first get the fixed UDT portion of the data and later get a hexadecimal key (case-sensitive and with leading zeros) that identifies the translated version of the data. You could then call VerLanguageName to get language-specific data, but I don't. The Create method of CVersion saves the key, the UDT for fixed data, and the data block (as a string) in private variables of the class.

Class properties based on fixed data simply return fields of the internal UDT variable. Class properties based on the language-specific string data call VerQueryValue, passing it the saved key and data string.

Got all that? There will be a quiz. Actually, the Windows API documentation on this subject is not very clear, and programming the class was not easy. It's much easier to follow my completed code.

CHALLENGE CVersion implements only the most common part of version resources, so there's plenty of room to enhance it. For example, you can embed language-specific version information in a file and then use version resource functions to extract different version data for different languages.

Animating the About Dialog Box

I can't tell you much about the secret animation features of the About form because they're secret. You'll just have to click every possible location and press every possible key combination to figure them out. Or you could look at the source code.

One hint: you can replace my crude animation with your own sophisticated version by giving your animation function the same name and parameters as mine and making it respond to arguments in the same way.

The CSortedListBox Class

Who needs a sorted list box class when list boxes have a Sorted property? Well, how about people who want to sort some way other than in descending, case-insensitive, alphabetical order? How about people who want to change the sort order at run time?

We talked about sorting and searching in "Sorting, Shuffling, and Searching," page 128; now it's time to put those algorithms to work. The Test Sort program (TSORT.VBP) also appeared in Chapter 3, but at that time we were interested in sorting arrays. Now we're interested in the list box part of the program. Check it out in Figure 9-6.

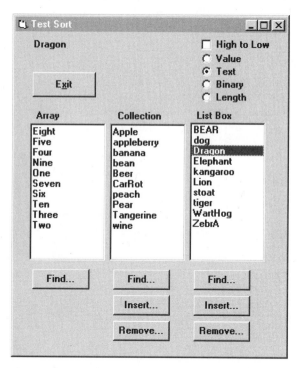

Figure 9-6. *Sorting arrays, collections, and list boxes.*

CSortedListBox is another containment class. You should have containment down by now, based on the CPictureGlass and CEditor classes. In this case, you pass an ordinary ListBox control (or a close relative) to the Create method of the CSortedListBox class. The Create method stores the real list box internally, sorts its items, and then translates all commands (through methods and properties) so that the list box always remains properly sorted. Like other containment classes, CSortedListBox requires disciplined use. You can't use it until you create it, and once you pass a list box to it, you had better not mess with the real list box. If you violate this rule, you can get things back in sync by calling the CSortedListBox Refresh method.

Creating a Sorted List Box

CSortedListBox requires three internal variables for its own functionality, plus all the properties borrowed from the original list box. Here are the real guts of the class:

```
Private lst As Control
Private ordMode As Integer
Private fHiToLo As Boolean
```

The Create method initializes these variables, and the rest of the class maintains and uses them.

```
Function Create(lstA As Control, Optional vHiToLo As Variant, _
              Optional vMode As Variant) As Boolean

    ' Must have ListCount, List, ListIndex, AddItem, and RemoveItem
    On Error GoTo CreateFail
    Dim v As Variant
    LastError = errNotListBox
    v = lstA.ListCount
    lstA.AddItem v, 0
    v = lstA.List(0)
    lstA.List(0) = v
    v = lstA.ListIndex
    lstA.RemoveItem 0
    ' Make sure list isn't already sorted
    LastError = errAlreadySorted
    If lstA.Sorted Then GoTo CreateFail

    ' Initialize internal data
    LastError = errUnknown
    fHiToLo = False
    ordMode = ordSortVal
    If Not IsMissing(vHiToLo) Then fHiToLo = vHiToLo
    If Not IsMissing(vMode) Then ordMode = vMode
    Set lst = lstA
    ' Sort it
    Sort 0, lst.ListCount - 1
    Create = True
    LastError = errNone
    Exit Function
```

```
CreateFail:
    Create = False
End Function
```

Have you noticed that up to now I've mostly referred to list boxes rather than to ListBox controls? I do that for the same reason that Create takes a *Control* parameter rather than a *ListBox* parameter. Essentially, you can pass any control that looks, acts, talks, and smells like a list box. The first few lines of code do nothing but verify that the control really has the properties and methods necessary to sort it. If any one of these is missing, the error trap throws you out.

You should be able to pass most combo boxes and any third-party controls that have listlike methods. Incidentally, the Outline control meets most of the requirements but fails because it doesn't have a Sorted property. That's OK—you don't really want to sort outlines anyway. You could probably enhance this class to sort the rows or columns of a grid, but that's up to you.

If everything goes well, the Create method sets the internal lst object to the external *lstA* parameter, sorts it—and you're in business.

CHALLENGE FileListBox and friends fail in the Create method because you can't add or remove items. Technically, you don't need to add or remove items to sort a list box, but you do need to exchange items, and you can't do that with a FileListBox control because you can't assign anything to the List property. You could, however, design a class that makes an internal list box look and act like a FileListBox control except that it can be sorted by date, name, extension, or attributes. You just use the Dir function to reload the list box in the current sort order at appropriate times. I've always wanted a file list box like that, and the only reason I didn't create one for this book is that I can do most of what I want with the new 32-bit ListView control. But if you can't, you can use the CSortedListBox class as a model for your own CSortedFileListBox class.

Collection Methods and Properties

My biggest beef with list boxes is that although they look and act like collections, they're not quite collections. For one thing, they're zero-based instead of one-based. For another, they have the wrong property and method names—ListCount, List, AddItem, and RemoveItem instead of Count, Item, Add, and Remove.

You can curse the darkness, or you can light a candle. I did both. The CSorted-ListBox class has one-based collection methods and properties. It looks and works like a collection, with the exception of the limitations on iteration and default properties described in "The NDrives Collection," page 185. For compatibility, it also has zero-based methods and properties with the ListBox names. This class represents my idea of how list boxes ought to work. If you like this interface, nothing (except time and performance concerns) prevents you from writing a similar wrapper class for unsorted list boxes.

The design of CSortedListBox is more interesting than its code. This class tries to combine the best features of list boxes and collections, keeping in mind that list boxes can't work quite the same way as collections. The biggest difference is that list boxes have a selected item, but collections don't. Other differences are simply limitations of list boxes, limitations that CSortedListBox attempts to eliminate. Table 9-1 compares what you can do with a list box, a collection, and a sorted list box (represented by *lst*, *n*, and *srt*, respectively).

Operation	With a List Box	With a Collection	With a Sorted List Box
Get item 3	s = lst.List(2)	s = n.Item(3)	s = srt.Item(3)
Get index of "Pig"	Can't do it	Can't do it	i = srt.Item("Pig")
Change item 3	lst.List(2) = "Dog"	Can't do it	srt.Item(3) = "Dog"
Change item "Pig"	Can't do it	Can't do it	srt.Item("Dog") = "Cat"
Select item 3	lst.ListIndex = 2	Can't do it	srt.Index = 3
Select item "Cat"	Can't do it	Can't do it	srt.Index = "Cat"
Get selected index	i = lst.ListIndex	Can't do it	i = srt.Index
Get selected item	s = lst.List(lst.ListIndex)	Can't do it	s = srt.IndexItem
Add item "Cat"	lst.AddItem "Cat"	n.Add "Cat"	srt.Add "Cat"
Remove item 3	lst.RemoveItem 2	n.Remove 3	srt.Remove 3
Remove item "Pig"	Can't do it	Can't do it	srt.Remove "Pig"
Iterate by item	Can't do it	For Each v in n	Tough luck
Iterate by index	For i = 0 To lst.ListCount - 1	For i = 1 To n.Count	For i = 1 To srt.Count

Table 9-1. *List box and collection operations.*

Most of these operations are clear once you understand list boxes and collections, but a few bear further study. For example, you can index a CSortedList-Box object by number or by string value. You can also index collections by string value, but

```
obj = n.Item("Pig")
```

and

```
i = srt.Item("Pig")
```

don't mean exactly the same thing. Indexed collections return objects, as explained in "Collections 201 (Objects)," page 183, but sorted list boxes contain strings, not objects. Indexing has to mean something different.

I made the Item property return a numeric index if you pass a string, or a string if you pass an index. Purists might object to a property returning different types for different arguments, but it works in this case.

Here are some additional features of the CSortedListBox class:

- You can have only one copy of each item. I could have designed the class to allow duplicate entries, but that doesn't make much sense for sorted items.

- Items with different case are considered different. You could add another sort mode that ignores case and allows one of each item regardless of case.

- To get the selected item, you can use *s = srt.Item(srt.Index)* as you would for a list box, but I also provide the less awkward shortcut *s = srt.ListItem*.

- List boxes and collections require you to remove an item by its index, which usually means that you must iterate through the list to find the index. CSortedListBox lets you remove by string value.

- CSortedListBox has a built-in error system that allows you to get the most recent error by number with the LastError property or by string with the LastErrorStr property. If there's no error, LastError returns 0, and LastErrorStr returns an empty string. Check it out in the sample.

- When no item is selected, the Index property is 0 rather than −1. This makes for easier conditional testing. You can also set Index to 0 to select nothing.

Finding Items

Rather than examining all of the code, let's just look at the most interesting property. The Item property illustrates indexing by number or string, and its Property Get procedure has a quirky return value that changes depending on the argument.

Remember that the Item property can be used for reading items:

```
Debug.Print .Item(3)
Debug.Print .Item("Lion")
```

The first syntax works just like the ListBox List property except that it is one-based. Here's the code that makes it happen:

```
Property Get Item(vIndex As Variant) As Variant
    LastError = errNone
    If IsNumeric(vIndex) Then
        ' For numeric index, return string value
        Item = lst.List(vIndex - 1)
    Else
        ' For string index, return matching index or 0 for none
        Item = Match(vIndex)
        If Item = 0 Then LastError = errItemNotFound
    End If
End Property
```

The Variant type comes in handy here and throughout the implementation of CSortedListBox. In this procedure, *IsNumeric* tests whether an entry is a number or a string. You could probably pass something other than those two with unexpected results, but testing with *TypeName("String")* wouldn't do any better. Let it stand.

Using the Item property for assignment looks like this:

```
.Item(3) = "Deer"
.Item("Lion") = "Big Cat"
```

It works this way:

```
Property Let Item(vIndex As Variant, vItemA As Variant)
    LastError = errNone
    ' For string index, look up matching index
    If Not IsNumeric(vIndex) Then
        vIndex = Match(vIndex)
        ' Quit if old item isn't found or if new item is found
        If vIndex = 0 Then
            LastError = errItemNotFound
            Exit Property
        End If
        If Match(vItemA) Then
            LastError = errDuplicateNotAllowed
            Exit Property
        End If
    End If
```

```
        ' Assign value by removing old and inserting new
        Remove vIndex
        Add vItemA
End Property
```

This code converts a string index to a numeric index and then uses the Remove and Add methods to assign it in the proper sort order. You can't assign to the Item property of the ListBox control because that usually puts the replacement in the wrong place—as I learned the hard way in early versions of the code.

Both procedures call the Match function to look up an item name in the list box. How do you suppose Match works? If you remember Chapter 5 ("Looking up list box items," page 239), you might want to use the SendMessage API function with the LB_FINDSTRINGEXACT message, as I did in an early version. But this message is case-insensitive, and that's not what you need. Furthermore, Windows doesn't know that the internal list box is sorted; the only way it can find an item is with a linear search. But you know that it's sorted. The most efficient way to find a sorted item is with a binary search, and I just happen to have one handy:

```
Private Function Match(ByVal sItem As String) As Long
    Dim iPos As Integer
    If BSearch(sItem, iPos) Then Match = iPos + 1 Else Match = 0
End Function
```

I could have used the BSearchArray function in SORT.BAS (refer back to "Binary Search," page 138) for CSortedListBox, but to keep the class more modular, I cloned it, made a few modifications, and stuck it in SLISTBOX.CLS. I did the same with the Sort algorithm, also discussed in Chapter 3.

Sorted Collections

A list box is just a collection with a different syntax. If you have a sorted list box class, you're not very far from having a sorted collection class. So have at it. Clone CSortedListBox. Delete the properties and methods unique to list boxes (those dealing with selected items and the list box interface). Change some names here and there, and you've got it.

Whoa! Not so fast. Collections can be either indexed or unindexed. Collections contain objects, not strings. You'll need to deal with those differences. You could create an NSortedStrings class by cloning because a collection of strings is unindexed by definition. But a collection of objects sorted by a specified field is a different matter.

I've supplied you with code to sort collections in a procedural style. Check out SortCollection and BSearchCollection in SORT.BAS, and then look at how they are used to sort a collection of strings in TSORT.VBP. This should help get you started writing your own CSortedCollection class.

PERFORMANCE

Problem: Compare filling, shuffling, searching, and sorting arrays to performing the same operations on collections.

Problem	16-Bit Mode	32-Bit Mode
Fill an array	2 ms	1 ms
Fill a collection	9 ms	6 ms
Shuffle an array	22 ms	35 ms
Shuffle a collection	271 ms	116 ms
Sort an array	2743 ms	3906 ms
Sort a collection	8844 ms	6636 ms
Search an array 50 times	36 ms	60 ms
Search a collection 50 times	95 ms	86 ms

Conclusion: Collection operations are always expensive, but the big factor here is the cost of swapping collection items. Swapping array items is a simple matter of assignment through a temporary variable. Swapping collection items requires removing both items and reinserting them in each other's position. Study the CollectionSwap procedure in SORT.BAS to see how this works. To see more differences, run the Time It application and try operating on different sizes of arrays and collections. The length of some operations increases arithmetically when you increase the number of elements. In other operations, the performance can vary greatly depending on the number of elements and on random factors about the data on which you operate. In particular, collection operations seem to slow down dramatically as you add more elements.

Other People's Menus

Maybe you've noticed from the samples in this book that I don't care for menus. I much prefer toolbars, hot keys, buttons, dialog boxes, and controls. Although I don't use menus much in my own programs, I like them in other people's programs. That's because menus are subversive. An application that has a menu item for each of its commands has given you the key to execute those commands from outside the application.

This section explains how to execute other people's menus indirectly with the Run Menu program or directly with CMenuList and CMenuItem objects.

The Run Menu Program

Run Menu is one of those rare beasts, a Visual Basic program with no user interface. You pass it a command line, and it takes some silent, invisible action, just like...well, like certain old MS-DOS–based programs. There's no law saying that programs written for Windows have to have windows.

The Run Menu manual consists of one page with the following command-line syntax at the top:

RUNMENU {/c"*winclass*" | /t"*wintitle*"} /i"*item*[.*item*[.*item*]...]"

According to the manual, you must pass Run Menu a class, a title, or both. The title can have wildcards (the same ones recognized in Visual Basic's Find and Replace dialog boxes). For example, *Clock** matches a window with the title *Clock - 12/25/95*. You can have multiple levels of menu items, such as Edit.Find or simply Find. Of course, the more specific you are, the better chance you'll have of finding the right item (if two or more items have the same name). Each item can have wildcards. For example, *Search.Find** matches *Search.Find* or *Search.Find Next*, whichever comes first.

You can call the Run Menu program (RUNMENU.EXE or RUNMENU32.EXE) from Basic with the Shell function or from any other language with a similar function. You can call it from the macro languages of many applications and from the customizable tool menus of others. From a character-mode session of Windows NT or Windows 95, you can simply type the command.

Try the following under Windows 3.*x*. Create a new item in Program Manager. Name it Exit Windows, and give it this command line:

```
C:\HARDCORE\RUNMENU.EXE /t"Program Manager*" /i"Exit Windows*"
```

If you don't like the default Visual Basic icon, you'll need to select an icon file in Program Manager. You can't change the icon of Run Menu because the program has no startup form for the icon.

CHALLENGE To be honest, the author of the Run Menu manual got a little ahead of the developer of the Run Menu program. The code for three levels of menu items separated by periods doesn't actually exist. Not yet, anyway. For now, you must give the name of the menu item you want and hope that the menu tree doesn't contain any duplicates. You can save the imaginative manual writer's reputation by enhancing the Find method of the CMenuList class to match the documentation.

To create the program, all you need is a Sub Main in RUNMENU.BAS. Use the Project tab of the Options dialog box from the Tools menu to set the startup form to Sub Main. Here's the code:

```
Sub Main()
    ' Convert command line to strings
    Dim sItem As String, sClass As String, sTitle As String
    ParseMenuCmd Command$, sClass, sTitle, sItem

    ' Find window handle
    Dim hWnd As Long
    hWnd = VBFindTopWindow(sClass, sTitle)
    If hWnd = hNull Then ErrorExit

    ' Find menu item
    Dim menu As New CMenuList, ritem As CMenuItem
    If Not menu.Create(hWnd) Then ErrorExit
    If Not menu.Find(sItem, ritem) Then ErrorExit
    If Not ritem.Execute Then ErrorExit
End Sub
```

In the first part, ParseMenuCmd parses the command line into strings for the class, title, and item. ("Code Review," page 91, discusses parsing.) VBFind-TopWindow works much as the Windows FindWindow function does except that VBFindTopWindow searches only top-level windows—the only ones that normally have menus—and recognizes wildcards, using the Like operator, for window titles. ("Iterating Through Windows," on page 214, describes looping through top-level windows.) VBFindTopWindow lives in WINTOOL.BAS.

The bottom line is that you come up with a window handle and pass it to some kind of menu object that returns results through some other kind of menu object. These two menu classes—CMenuList and CMenuItem—form a twisted web of recursive data exchanges.

CMenuList and CMenuItem Objects

Menus work the same way as other tree structures, such as file directories, the system Registry, or the internal window list described in Chapter 5. Like most trees, a menu tree consists of a list of items. Some items contain data only; others are lists of more items. Lists of lists are best navigated through recursion. Each list knows how to traverse itself, but when it encounters a child list, it must turn over control and let the child traverse itself.

Figure 9-7 presents one view of how menu lists can contain other menu lists. This containment view differs from the usual tree view, for good reason. The nesting levels get smaller and smaller until you can't see them. This view works for menu trees because they rarely contain more than three nested levels.

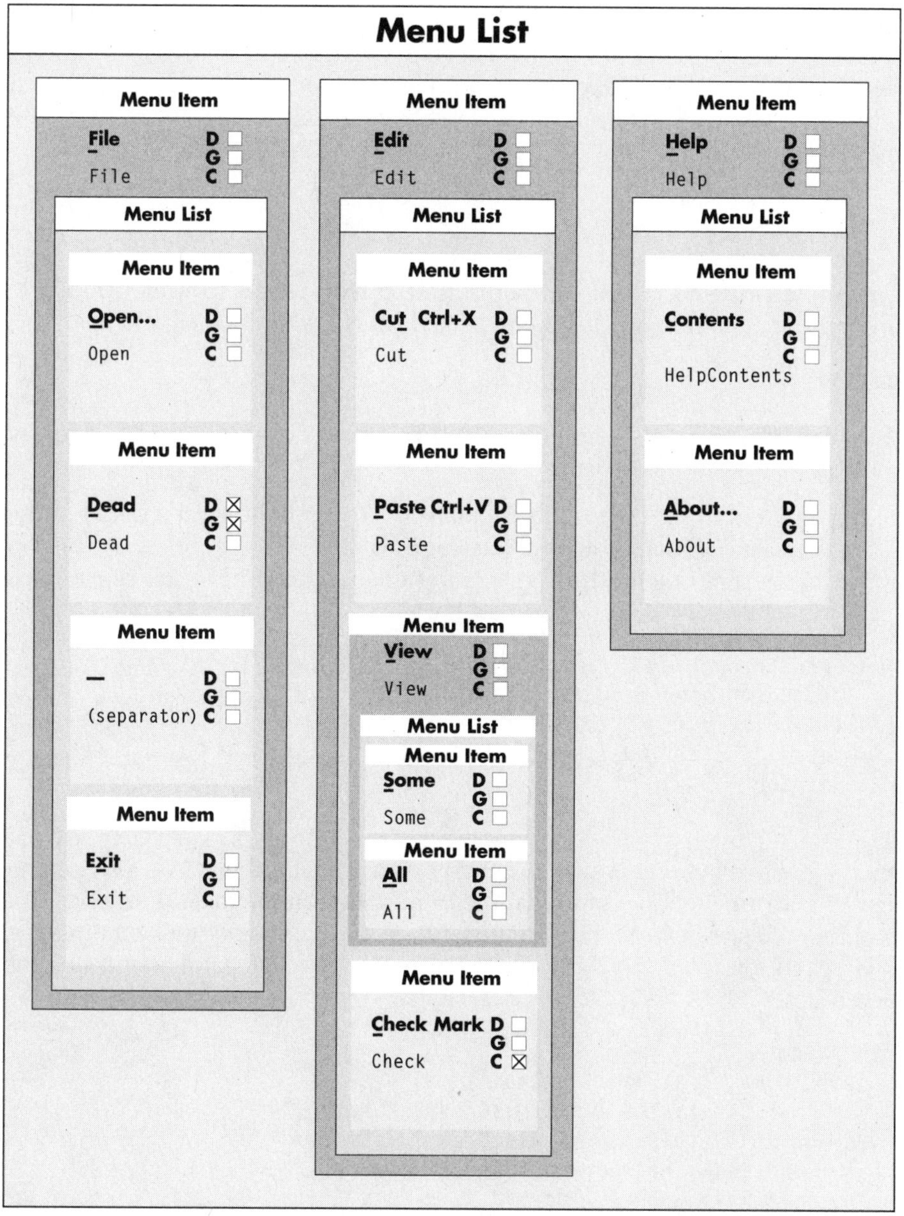

Figure 9-7. *Containment view of a menu tree.*

The object-oriented way of encapsulating a tree is to provide separate classes for lists and items. In this system, you need to create only the top list of the tree. The top list automatically creates its child lists, which in turn create their own children, and so on. Here's an example of creating a menu list from the cmdMenus_Click sub in HARDCORE.FRM (see HARDCORE.VBP):

```
Dim menu As New CMenuList, ritem As CMenuItem
Call menu.Create(Me.hWnd)
```

The simplest operation you can perform on a menu list is to walk through it, carrying out an action on each item. Here's what a walk looks like:

```
menu.Walk
```

Of course, you must also define what you want to do to each item—a messy problem that we'll discuss later.

Finding an item in the tree works recursively. You call the Find method of the top list, passing an empty item object for it to set if it finds a match. The top Find calls the Find methods of any lists it encounters. The result filters back down the tree:

```
Dim s As String
s = InputBox("Enter menu item to find: ")
If Not menu.Find(s, ritem) Then
    MsgBox "Can't find item: " & s
    Exit Sub
End If
```

Once you have an item, you can get any data contained in a Windows menu item or perform any operation that the Windows menu item can carry out. For example, the state of a menu item consists of the menu text and settings such as checked, disabled, and grayed. You can get the state of a found item as shown here:

```
With ritem
    s = "Name: " & .Name & sCrLf
    s = s & "Text: " & .Text & sCrLf & "State: "
    s = s & IIf(.Disabled, "Disabled ", sEmpty)
    s = s & IIf(.Checked, "Checked ", sEmpty)
    s = s & IIf(.Grayed, "Grayed ", sEmpty)
    s = s & IIf(.Popup, "Popup ", sEmpty) & sCrLf
    txtTest.Text = s
End With
```

You can perform operations on a menu item, such as changing its state or highlighting it. But what you really want to do to a menu item is execute it. Here's how:

```
Call ritem.Execute
```

It might look easy, but recursion is usually simpler in theory than in practice. The rest of this explanation concentrates on the organization and interaction of the two classes. But first a word about the API calls that make menus work.

Menus in the Windows API

Windows provides a rich set of functions to manipulate what it calls menus (what I call menu lists) and menu items. Users can think of the whole tree as one menu, but to Windows each submenu is a separate menu with its own menu handle. Windows usually doesn't distinguish between the top menu list with all its children (the menu tree) and a lower-level menu list.

Each menu item has an identification number (ID) and a position. The ID has the advantage of never changing. But it also has the disadvantage of not necessarily being unique, because all items consisting of other lists have the same ID, −1. The position is always unique, but it can change if someone inserts or deletes a menu item. Most API functions that you call to operate on an item require that you pass the item's menu handle and either the position or the ID, along with a flag indicating which one you are passing.

I save both the position and the ID as private members of the CMenuItem class, but I use the position in API calls whenever possible because of its uniqueness. This means that the representation of the menu in CMenuList and CMenuItem objects can get out of sync with the actual menu. Keep in mind that the menu can change at any moment, as its owning window responds to menu selections or other commands. Items can be disabled, deleted, or inserted, thus invalidating your carefully constructed tree. To get things back in sync, you can call the Refresh method on the top-level menu.

The creation process, part one

All the real work of the CMenuList and CMenuItem classes happens when you call the Create method. Once a CMenuList object is created, it's easy to traverse it with the Walk method or the Find method. Once a CMenuItem object is created, it's easy to execute the item or to get and modify its state. But the creation process itself is no easy matter.

Let's start where the caller starts—with CMenuList. Or, better yet, let's start with the private members, since the primary mission of the Create method is to initialize internal data:

```
Private nItems As New Collection
Private hMenu As Long, idMax As Long
' Warning! These members should be static--that is, one variable
' available to all objects of the given type. The entire menu tree
' has only one window handle. But Basic doesn't have static
' variables, so you must fake them.
Private hWnd As Long, fSys As Boolean
' Warning! Violation of encapsulation standards! This property
' should not be public, but its partner class won't work otherwise.
' Don't use this property directly.
Public Parent As CMenuList
```

Uh-oh. You're running into trouble before you even get started. You'll need to look at Create to see why. Here's the first part of the Create method:

```
Function Create(hA As Long, Optional vSys As Variant) As Boolean
    If IsMissing(vSys) Then fSys = False Else fSys = CBool(vSys)
    If IsWindow(hA) Then
        ' Create system or normal menu from hWnd
        If fSys Then
            hMenu = GetSystemMenu(hA, False)
        Else
            hMenu = GetMenu(hA)
        End If
        hWnd = hA
    Else
        ' Don't accept menu handle from top node
        If IsMenu(hA) And Parent Is Nothing Then Exit Function
        hMenu = hA: hWnd = WinHandle
    End If
```

This code deals with overloaded parameters. The first parameter takes a window handle when you call the Create method from the top-level list, but it needs a menu handle when the top-level list calls it to create submenu lists. Windows provides the GetMenu and GetSystemMenu functions to convert a window handle to a menu handle, but it doesn't provide any way to get a window handle from a menu handle. This makes things messy, as you'll see when we look at item creation. In summary, you need both a window handle and a menu handle for each level, but all you get is a window handle for the top-level list.

The same problem occurs with the second parameter, which specifies creating a normal menu or a system menu. You'll need that system flag when you try to execute a deeply nested menu item, but you can get it only at the top level.

Here's the WinHandle property, which makes it possible to get the one and only internal hWnd:

```
Property Get WinHandle() As Long
    If Parent Is Nothing Then
        WinHandle = hWnd
    Else
        WinHandle = Parent.WinHandle
    End If
End Property
```

Only the top list (the one without a parent) knows its window handle. Every other level must get the handle from its parent, which might need to turn to its parent, and so on. This simple procedure might call itself several times before it finally gets the handle. The SysMenu property returns the *fSys* flag in the same way.

On to CMenuItem creation. Once you have both a valid menu and a window handle, the second part of the creation process goes like this:

```
    ' Create each item in list and add to collection
    Dim ritem As CMenuItem, i As Long, f As Boolean
    DestroyMenus
    For i = 0 To Count - 1
        Set ritem = New CMenuItem
        ' Create will also create new submenus
        f = ritem.Create(i, hMenu, Me)
        BugAssert f        ' Should never fail
        nItems.Add ritem
        ' Needed by InsertNew method
        If ritem.ID > idMax Then idMax = ritem.ID
    Next
    Create = True
End Function
```

This code simply creates each item in the list and adds it to an internal collection of items. In other words, it hands over control to the Create method of CMenuItem, passing through all the information the item object will need to create itself. Notice that one of the things passed through is Me—the CMenuList object itself. Users should never create CMenuItem objects directly, and the requirement that they create with an existing CMenuList object makes it difficult for them to do so.

The creation process, part two

Let's look at the internal variables that are initialized by the CMenuItem Create method:

```
Private hWnd As Long, hMenu As Long
Private idID As Long, iPos As Long, fSys As Boolean
Private rmenuChild As CMenuList
```

There's not much to initialize. Most properties of the class are calculated on request, based on the saved ID or position.

The actual creation works as shown here:

```
Function Create(iPosA As Long, hMenuA As Long, _
                rmenuA As CMenuList) As Boolean
    ' Store properties
    BugAssert IsMenu(hMenuA)
    hMenu = hMenuA: iPos = iPosA
    hWnd = rmenuA.WinHandle: fSys = rmenuA.SysMenu
    idID = GetMenuItemID(hMenu, iPos)

    ' Create new menu list for any submenu
    If idID = -1 Then
        Dim menu As New CMenuList, f As Boolean
        ' Must set parent before creating--yuck!
        Set menu.Parent = rmenuA
        f = menu.Create(GetSubMenu(hMenu, iPos))
        BugAssert f      ' Should never fail
        Set rmenuChild = menu
    End If
    Create = True
End Function
```

The interesting part is how the CMenuItem Create method calls the CMenuList Create method to create submenus. You can see part of the interaction between the two classes in Figure 9-8.

The convention I've used in classes throughout this book is that you should call Create before using any other property or method. An object is invalid until it's created. But the CMenuItem class sets the Parent property of the CMenuList object before creating it. Furthermore, if you look back at the Parent property, you'll see that it's public even though the user should never change it. This violation of class decency is a hack to avoid a "catch-22." The Create method of the CMenuList object must know its parent so that it can use the parent's Win-Handle property. But the Create method of the CMenuItem object is the only place where the parent is known and can be set. You'll probably need to read the code several times to be clear on this, although I doubt you'll have as much trouble as I had writing and debugging it.

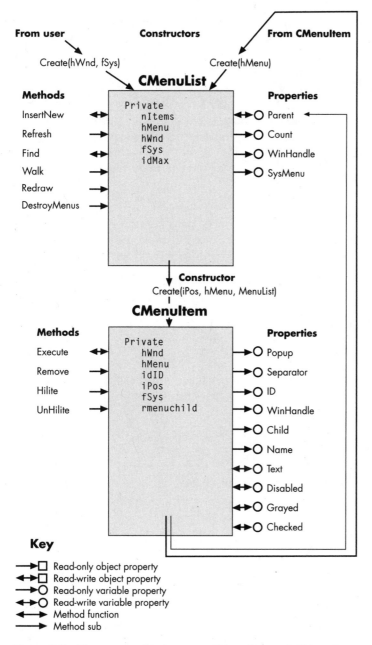

Figure 9-8. *The partnership between CMenuList and CMenuItem.*

You C++ hackers could prevent unauthorized access if CMenu-List were declared a friend of CMenuItem. As a trusted friend, CMenuList could change a private *rmenuParent* member of CMenuList, but no one else could access the member except through a read-only Parent property. Basic doesn't have friend classes, however, and probably never will because they create so many side issues that many experienced C++ programmers consider *friend* their enemy. Basic programmers must be content with secret members—that is, public members that can't be accessed because you don't tell anyone about them.

CMenuItem properties and methods

The properties of the CMenuItem class simply pass internal data to Windows API functions to read or modify the menu data. I'll show you a few examples, and you can check out others in the code in MENUITEM.CLS.

The Text property calls GetMenuString to get the text of a menu item or ModifyMenu to change the text:

```
Property Get Text() As String
    Dim s As String, c As Integer
    Const cMaxStr = 80
    s = String$(cMaxStr, 0)
    c = GetMenuString(hMenu, iPos, s, cMaxStr, MF_BYPOSITION)
    Text = Left$(s, c)
End Property

Property Let Text(sTextA As String)
    Dim afState As Long
    afState = GetMenuState(hMenu, iPos, MF_BYPOSITION)
    afState = afState Or MF_BYPOSITION Or MF_STRING
    Call ModifyMenu(hMenu, iPos, afState, idID, sTextA)
End Property
```

You should assign values to the Text property with care. You're changing the actual menu text, not an internal representation of it. Be sure that you include an ampersand in the menu item text to indicate the access character. Check the Windows documentation for information on other effects such as right-justified items and accelerator keys.

Generally, you access menu items via the Name property rather than the Text property. The name is simply a version of the text with all extraneous stuff removed. For example, if the text is *Find...   Ctrl+F*, the name is *Find*. You can check out this code in the Property Get Name procedure.

The Checked, Grayed, and Disabled properties are similar, except that you use the GetMenuState API function to get the state and either EnableMenuItem or CheckMenuItem to change it. Enabling a menu item doesn't necessarily mean that you can execute it. The window owning the menu might keep track of the state in its own variable that you can't modify.

The Execute method uses the SendMessage function to execute the menu item:

```
Function Execute() As Boolean
    Dim iMsg As Long
    iMsg = IIf(fSys, WM_SYSCOMMAND, WM_COMMAND)
    Execute = (SendMessageAsLong(hWnd, iMsg, idID, 0&) = 0)
End Function
```

Notice how Execute uses the *fSys* member to decide which message to send. The system menu flag was obtained in the top-level CMenuList Create method and passed down through as many levels of recursion as necessary to reach the current item. Don't take the return value for the Execute function too seriously. It indicates only whether someone received and handled the message, not whether the action the message requested was successfully completed.

Walking the menu tree

The primary action you carry out on a CMenuItem object is to use properties and methods that control its state. The primary action you carry out on a CMenuList object is to walk the menu tree. This isn't necessarily obvious from the names of some of the CMenuList methods, but walking the menu tree is what happens behind the scenes in the Walk, Find, and Refresh methods.

Let's start with Walk because it is the simplest (although Find is the most common). The Walk method simply traverses the menu tree, calling a function named MenuWalker for each item:

```
Sub Walk(Optional vLevel As Variant)
    If IsMissing(vLevel) Then vLevel = 0
    Dim ritem As CMenuItem
    For Each ritem In nItems
        ' Walk through current list until user says stop
        If Not MenuWalker(ritem, CInt(vLevel)) Then Exit Sub
        ' Recurse through submenus
        If ritem.Popup Then ritem.Child.Walk vLevel + 1
    Next
End Sub
```

MenuWalker is a function you define. It works a lot like the DoWindow function described in "Iterating the hard way," page 215. A default MenuWalker is defined in the class, mainly because MenuWalker must exist to prevent a *Sub or*

Function not defined error. MenuWalker simply displays basic item information to the Debug window. It appears within a conditional compilation block:

```
#If fMenuWalker = 0 Then
Function MenuWalker(ritem As CMenuItem, iLevel As Integer) As Boolean
    Dim s As String
    s = "Name: " & ritem.Name & " ( "
    s = s & IIf(ritem.Disabled, "Disabled ", "")
    s = s & IIf(ritem.Checked, "Checked ", "")
    s = s & IIf(ritem.Grayed, "Grayed ", "")
    s = s & IIf(ritem.Popup, "Popup ", "") & ")"
    Debug.Print String$(iLevel, sTab) & s
    ' Your MenuWalker can return False to stop walk
    MenuWalker = True
End Function
#End If
```

To replace the default MenuWalker with your own, define a MenuWalker function (with the same parameters and parameter types) in a separate code module. (You can't use a form module or a class module.) You'll need to define *fMenuWalker = 1* in the Conditional Compilation Arguments field on the Advanced tab of the Options dialog box. This uses the same ugly name-space hack described in "Jury-Rigged Procedure Variables," page 134.

The Find method looks very much like the Walk method. It iterates through the menu tree in the same way, but it looks for a matching string rather than calling MenuWalker. Finding a matching string in either the form *Item* or the form *Item1.Item2.Item3* introduces some complications that you can study online, but the iteration problem is essentially the same. In fact, you can think of Find as simply another MenuWalker function.

When you call the Refresh method, the top-level node and all the subnodes are re-created. But first the existing version must be cleaned out. This is done in the Create method and in the Class_Terminate sub by calling the private function DestroyMenus. DestroyMenus walks the menu tree (exactly as Walk does), destroying items by setting them to Nothing and removing them from the internal item collection.

CHALLENGE The cooperating class model shown here for menu trees can be applied to any tree-structured data. For example, you could replace the IterateChildWindows function described in Chapter 5 with CWindowList and CWindowItem classes. As an even more interesting challenge, you could create cooperating directory (CFileList) and file (CFileItem) classes to model a file directory tree.

Grid Boxes

Visual Basic's Properties window offers a convenient color dialog box that pops up when you click the down arrow for BackColor, ForeColor, or any other color property. (This is in addition to the more sophisticated Color Palette dialog box available from the View menu.) Wouldn't it be nice to include a similar dialog box in your own programs?

In fact, you might have noticed one when testing the Fun 'n Games program (FUNNGAME.VBP) discussed in Chapter 6. I skipped the Color dialog box in that chapter, but now I'm ready to talk about it and about how you could expand on the idea. You can also see this dialog box in HARDCORE.FRM (in HARDCORE.VBP).

The FGetColor Form

FGetColor is a simple little form. The following code demonstrates how easy it is to use an FGetColor form to change the background color:

```
Private Sub cmdColor_Click()
    Dim getclr As New FGetColor
    Static clrLast As Long
    ' Load last color used
    If clrLast <> 0& Then getclr.Color = clrLast
    getclr.Show vbModal
    ' Save chosen color for next time
    clrLast = getclr.Color
    Me.BackColor = clrLast
End Sub
```

Figure 9-9 on the next page shows the results. This color palette contains three rows of default colors, but, unlike the color palette that pops up in the Properties window, it does not include a fourth row of custom colors. The fourth row wouldn't be hard to add, but you would need to provide a way to define custom colors.

Here's a quick summary of the implementation:

■ The form has its MinButton, MaxButton, and ControlBox properties set to False and its Caption property left empty so that the form won't have a title bar. The BorderStyle property is set to Fixed Single to prevent the user from resizing. The ScaleMode property is set to Pixel so that everything can be measured exactly in pixels. AutoDraw is set to False, which means that you must handle the Paint event.

■ Form_Initialize initializes a three-dimensional array corresponding to three rows of 16 color boxes.

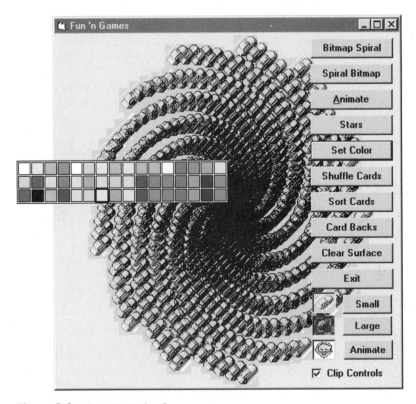

Figure 9-9. *The FGetColor form.*

- Form_Load sets the exact width and height so that you don't need to size the form at the pixel level at design time.

- Form_Paint draws the color boxes and fills them with the colors from the array.

- Form_MouseDown calculates which color box is under the mouse pointer and draws a selection box around the color.

- Form_MouseUp undraws the selection box and sets an internal variable with the selected color.

- The Color Property Get procedure returns the selected color from its internal variable. The Color Property Let procedure searches for the box that matches a given color and makes it the default. This allows you to initialize so that the form remembers the color that was selected the last time you loaded the form. (Review the code at the start of this section to see how this works.)

I won't explain the code in detail, but the Form_Paint sub will give you the flavor:

```
Private Sub Form_Paint()
    Dim x As Long, y As Long, ix As Long, iy As Long
    ' Draw colors in their boxes
    x = 1
    FillStyle = vbSolid
    For ix = 1 To 16
        y = 1
        For iy = 1 To 3
            FillColor = aColor(ix, iy)
            Line (((ix - 1) * 17) + 1, _
                ((iy - 1) * 17) + 1)-Step(15, 15), , B
            y = y + 17
        Next
        x = x + 17
    Next
End Sub
```

You can see more of the code in GETCOLOR.FRM.

The CGetColor Class

The FGetColor form is great as far as it goes, but in some applications you might want to have a color palette always available on the form instead of one that pops up in response to a button. I created the CGetColor class by copying all the FGetColor code into a class and then changing a few key names and code sections.

Much like the CPictureGlass class described in Chapter 6, CGetColor contains a picture box. To use it, you must declare an object, usually at the module level:

```
Private pal As New CGetColor
```

Then you must create the object by passing it a picture box to work on. Normally you'll create the object in the Form_Activate event after the form has been displayed:

```
Private Sub Form_Activate()
    If fCreated = False Then fCreated = pal.Create(pbColor)
End Sub
```

Notice how the *fCreated* variable is used to ensure that the object is created only once even though Form_Activate can be called multiple times.

Since a class does not have MouseDown, MouseUp, and Paint events, you'll have to write your own events and call them from within the corresponding

PictureBox events. For example, here's how a picture box MouseDown event calls a GetColor_MouseDown event:

```
Private Sub pbColor_MouseDown(Button As Integer, Shift As Integer, _
                             x As Single, y As Single)
    If fCreated Then pal.GetColor_MouseDown Button, Shift, x, y
End Sub
```

You can read the Color property from within the picture box Click event:

```
Private Sub pbColor_Click()
    BackColor = pal.Color
End Sub
```

The CGetColor class module resembles the FGetColor form module except that the Create method takes the place of Form_Load. Of course, Create also has additional code to set an internal PictureBox object to the PictureBox argument. All the graphics methods must use the internal picture box instead of the default form surface. Other than a few name changes (GetColor_MouseDown instead of Form_MouseDown), everything else looks and works much as it does in the FGetColor form. You can see the details in GETCOLOR.CLS.

Bit Editors

The FGetColor form and the CGetColor class are handy, but the real point of this section is to talk about one of the many projects I didn't get around to as I wrote this book. I'd planned to show you a complete bit editor that would create or edit bitmaps (any size), icons (large or small), cursors (hot spot included), toolbar buttons (showing up and down states), or any other kind of bit picture. It would do automatic conversions—bitmap to icon, large icon to small icon, icon to cursor, color to mono—and would have all kinds of cool drawing tools. For now, however, this program exists only in my imagination. I'll have to describe it in a very high-level pseudocode—English.

First, let's look at CGetColor again. What is a CGetColor class? It's a grid of cells that knows when you click it and takes an action based on the chosen cell. What is a bit editor? It's a grid of cells that knows when you click it and takes an action based on the chosen cell. The only difference is the action. Most bit editors have a big-bits mode in which bits are shown larger than life—much like the color cells in CGetColor. But even in actual size, it's still just a grid of one-pixel cells.

CGetColor is hard-coded to a 16 by 3 grid. The CBitEdit class must be dynamic, to accommodate any size grid. It should also have bit-picture modes. In icon mode, the grid has submodes for the common sizes—16 by 16 and 32 by 32—but it can create icons of any size for hardcore Windows 95 programmers. Icon mode must also know about masks and transparency. Cursor mode creates a 32 by 32 grid and handles transparency as well as hot spots. Bitmaps are always a custom size; in fact, you should be able to resize by dragging. The CBitEdit class needs properties to set the mode and resize the grid, subject to conversion rules. It also needs both big-bit and life-size modes, and it should be able to display both modes at once on separate canvases.

CGetColor is hard-coded to give each cell a specific color. CBitEdit must be able to read different colors into its grid from a file. It must also be able to save its grid to a file with the appropriate extension—BMP, ICO, CUR, and so on. The file format to save is determined by the bit-picture mode.

CGetColor is hard-coded to set its Color property to the color of the cell you click. CBitEdit needs various methods to determine what happens for each click and drag. A Draw method sets the cell to the current color. A Spray method colors the surrounding cells in a diminishing pattern. A Fill method starts at the current cell and fills all the surrounding cells up to the closest border. A Line method starts a stretch operation that determines the end points of a line. And so on.

Filtering the Polymorphic Way

The Debug Wizard program was introduced in Chapter 1, but only as a tool. Now it's time to look at the code. Debug Wizard is the Windows equivalent of an MS-DOS filter such as SORT or MORE. Like all filters, its role is to convert a file from one form to another by applying a set of rules. In this case, the filter transforms assertion and profile statements by analyzing each line and modifying it if appropriate.

A filter consists of two parts. It must iterate through the lines of a file, reading them from a source and writing them to a target. This code works the same regardless of what the filter does. The filter must also apply the transformation to each line. This code is different for every kind of filter. It's a familiar problem. One part of the code is generic; one part is specific. You want to reuse the generic part but provide different implementations of the specific part.

The traditional way to combine generic and specific code is with procedure variables, but Basic doesn't have them. "Jury-Rigged Procedure Variables," page 134, described a way to get around this limitation. You can take advantage of Basic visibility rules to define different implementations of the same procedure for different programs. This ugly hack has significant limitations, but it performs well if you can live with them. We've seen the technique with sorting and with recursive iteration through windows. (See "Iterating Through Windows," page 214.)

This section will introduce another, more flexible (although less efficient) technique, using polymorphic classes.

The Object Hack for Procedure Variables

I introduced the concept of polymorphism in Chapter 4 but haven't said much about it since, although we've used it from time to time. For example, the CEditor class in Chapter 8 works for either TextBox controls or RichTextBox controls, and the CSortedListBox class (discussed earlier in this chapter) works on any ListBox-like control. These classes can contain different control objects, but as long as the object methods and properties the class uses have the same names and the same parameter types, the class doesn't care about the object types. That's polymorphism.

That's also a solution to the problem of combining generic and specific code. You write different classes with different implementations, but you give them the same standard interface so that generic code can use specific objects without knowing or caring what those objects do or how they do it.

This technique turns object-oriented programming on its head, as shown in Figure 9-10 on page 448. So far, I've talked about classes whose primary purpose is encapsulation. All implementation details of a particular operation are hidden within the class, and many different users call the same class with different methods and properties to get different results. With polymorphism, you implement multiple versions of a class with the same interface. One user calls the standard interface of any of the class implementations to get different results.

In our filter problem, the generic part is the FilterText function. It takes care of the details of opening a file, reading each line, writing each transformed line, and finally closing the file. The specific part is the filter class, which is any class that has a standard filter interface, consisting of SourceFile and TargetFile properties, and a DoFilter method. Let's look at both parts in turn.

The FilterText Function

FilterText is located in UTILITY.BAS so that it can be called easily from any project. There's nothing special about the code:

```
Function FilterText(rfilt As Object) As Integer
    ' FilterText = 0 (assume success)

    ' Target can be another file or replacement of current file
    Dim sTarget As String, fReplace As Boolean
    sTarget = rfilt.TargetFile
    If sTarget = sEmpty Or sTarget = rfilt.SourceFile Then
        sTarget = GetTempFile(".", "FLT")
        fReplace = True
    End If
```

```
    ' Open input file
    On Error GoTo FilterTextError1
    Dim nIn As Integer, nOut As Integer
    nIn = FreeFile
    Open rfilt.SourceFile For Input Access Read Lock Write As #nIn

    ' Open target output file
    Dim sLine As String, iLine As Long
    On Error GoTo FilterTextError2
    nOut = FreeFile
    Open sTarget For Output Access Write Lock Read Write As #nOut

    ' Filter each line
    On Error GoTo FilterTextError3
    Do Until EOF(nIn)
        Line Input #nIn, sLine
        iLine = iLine + 1
        If Not rfilt.DoFilter(sLine, iLine) Then Exit Function
        Print #nOut, sLine
    Loop

    ' Close files
    On Error GoTo FilterTextError1
    Close nIn
    Close nOut
    If fReplace Then
        ' Destroy old file and replace it with new one
        Kill rfilt.SourceFile
        On Error Resume Next    ' No more errors allowed
        Name sTarget As rfilt.SourceFile
        ' If this fails, you're in trouble
        BugAssert Err = 0
    End If
    Exit Function

FilterTextError3:
    Close nOut
FilterTextError2:
    Close nIn
FilterTextError1:
    FilterText = Err
End Function
```

Encapsulation

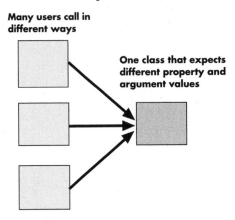

Polymorphism

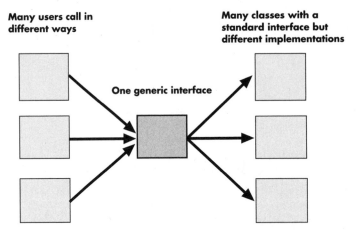

Figure 9-10. *Encapsulation and polymorphism.*

Notice that FilterText takes an *Object* parameter, which should actually be a filter object. In a more perfect language, this parameter would have a type more specific than Object. The sidebar "No Inheritance," page 452, describes how it would work. For the current version, you are responsible for passing the right kind of object.

The code for opening and processing the file is just what you'd predict except for the use of the SourceFile and TargetFile properties and the DoFilter method. These are the standard interface of any filter class. You can see why. FilterText will fail rudely if the object passed to it doesn't have the expected members, or if the members have incompatible types, or if they don't do what FilterText expects them to do.

A two-way communication path exists between the parts. FilterText receives the source file and possibly a target file from the filter object. It passes the current line text and number to the filter object. It then receives the modified source line back through a reference parameter. Someone outside has to set the SourceFile property before calling FilterText. (TargetFile can be blank, indicating that the source file should be modified.)

Now let's look at the other side of the transaction.

> **NOTE** The error trap in FilterText doesn't have anything to do with polymorphic classes, but it does illustrate a stair-stepped error trap. Often when something goes wrong while you're building something with a series of Basic statements, you need to unbuild it in the opposite order, undoing only the parts you have finished. A carefully designed series of error traps can take you back to the initial state.

CFilter Classes

A CFilter class is any class with a standard filter interface. In Basic, CFilter is an imaginary class—a standard that you must follow but one that the language doesn't enforce. Here's what a class that follows the CFilter standard should look like:

```
'' Standard CFilter interface starts here

Public SourceFile As String, TargetFile As String

Function DoFilter(sLine As String, ByVal iLine As Long) As Boolean

'' Standard CFilter interface ends here
```

There's not much room for creativity here. The SourceFile and TargetFile properties could be defined with Property Get and Property Let procedures if you wanted some file validation beyond that already provided by FilterText. But that's about it.

The creativity comes in with the implementation of DoFilter and with any other properties and methods you want to add to the class. The purpose of DoFilter is to modify the line text passed to it, but the specific transformation is determined by the designer of the class. Notice that *sLine* is passed by reference so that the modified version will be returned to the caller, but *iLine* is passed by value so that the caller's copy can't be changed.

Here's how the CBugFilter class implements its DoFilter method:

```
Function DoFilter(sLine As String, ByVal iLine As Long) As Boolean

'' Standard CFilter interface ends here
    DoFilter = True     ' Always finish this filter

    Select Case ordFilterType
    Case ordDisableBug
        CommentOut sLine, sBug
    Case ordEnableBug
        CommentIn sLine, sBug
    Case ordDisableProfile
        CommentOut sLine, sProfile
    Case ordEnableProfile
        CommentIn sLine, sProfile
    Case ordExpandAsserts
        ExpandAsserts sLine, iLine
    Case ordTrimAsserts
        TrimAsserts sLine
    End Select
End Function
```

This DoFilter method simply selects one of several internal procedures based on the internal *ordFilterType* variable. This variable is validated by Property Get and Property Let procedures:

```
Property Get FilterType() As Integer
    FilterType = ordFilterType
End Property

Property Let FilterType(ordFilterTypeA As Integer)
    If ordFilterTypeA > ordInvalid And _
        ordFilterTypeA <= ordMaxFilter Then
        ordFilterType = ordFilterTypeA
    Else
        ordFilterType = ordInvalid
    End If
End Property
```

You can see the filter type constants in BUGFILT.BAS. If you've used the Debug Wizard program or if you remember its description from Chapter 1, you can probably guess the implementation of the internal functions CommentIn, CommentOut, ExpandAsserts, and TrimAsserts. They're in BUGFILT.CLS if you want to check.

Using Filters

To use a filter, you first create a filter object and then set its properties. Your filter will always have SourceFile and TargetFile properties because that's part of the definition of a filter class. You must set the SourceFile property, and you can set TargetFile if you want to write the results of the filter to a separate file.

You might also need to set other filter-specific properties. The CBugFilter class used by Debug Wizard has a FilterType property that you use to indicate what kind of filtering operation you want. A filter class can have as many other properties and methods as its designer wants to give it.

After you've set up the filter object, you pass it to FilterText. The Debug Wizard program uses a BugFilter procedure to set up everything correctly:

```
Sub BugFilter(sFileCur As String, ordAction As Integer)
    Dim filter As New CBugFilter
    filter.SourceFile = sFileCur
    filter.FilterType = ordAction
    If FilterText(filter) Then
        MsgBox "Can't process " & sFileCur & ": " & Err.Description
    End If
End Sub
```

This procedure is located in a separate module, BUGWIZ.BAS, so that any project that wants bug filtering can call it without including the interface in the Debug Wizard form.

The Debug Wizard form has a button for each kind of filtering. For example, the Enable Bug Procedures button is implemented with the following code:

```
Private Sub cmdEnableBug_Click()
    HourGlass Me
    BugFilter sFileCur, ordEnableBug
    HourGlass Me
End Sub
```

> **NOTE** The HourGlass sub is a useful little procedure that displays an hourglass cursor during an operation and then removes it. Check it out in UTILITY.BAS. Always use a pair of HourGlass procedures—the first to display the cursor and the second to remove it.

No Inheritance

In Visual Basic, you make up polymorphic classes out of thin air. Your internal conventions and your self-discipline in following them are all that keep your classes compatible. This is bad. As Joe Hacker says, "Don't trust users to do right. Make them do right by providing no alternative."

In most object-oriented languages, polymorphism is enforced through inheritance and virtual procedures. You don't ask users to follow a convention. You give them a virtual base class to inherit from.

In the example, you would define a virtual CFilter class with a virtual DoFilter method and nonvirtual SourceFile and TargetFile properties. A virtual class exists only to inherit from, and a virtual method or property does nothing in the virtual base class but is implemented by each inherited class. You would define CBugFilter as being inherited from CFilter using some Basic syntax that hasn't been invented yet. By inheriting, you would get the SourceFile and TargetFile properties without doing anything extra. You'd have to implement your own DoFilter method, but it would automatically have the same parameters as the virtual DoFilter in CFilter.

What's the point? Type safety and early binding. In the current implementation, the FilterText function takes an *Object* parameter. In other words, you can pass anything to it—a form, a control, or any unrelated class object. With our imaginary class, the *FilterText* parameter would be type CFilter. If you passed anything other than a filter object based on a class inherited from CFilter, you'd get a specific compile-time error rather than a vague run-time error. You'd also get much better performance, for reasons I'll discuss in Chapter 10.

Polymorphic Sorting

The Test Polymorphic Sort program illustrates an object-oriented way of sorting. It works much the same way as the filter sample.

The sort routines in SORTPOLY.BAS take a helper argument of type Object. The helper object should belong to a polymorphic class that has Compare, Swap, and CollectionSwap methods. Check out the methods in CSortHelper (SORTHELP.CLS) for one way of implementing them. When the sort, search, and shuffle procedures in SORTPOLY.BAS need to compare or swap, they call the helper methods. I've already described the technique for filters, so I'll let you explore the code on your own.

You can examine the modules of Test Sort (TSORT.VBP) and those of Test Polymorphic Sort (TSRTPOLY.VBP) for a side-by-side comparison of the namespace technique described in "Jury-Rigged Procedure Variables" (page 134)

PERFORMANCE

Problem: Compare sort procedures that depend on compare and swap procedures using a name-space hack to those that use compare and swap methods from a polymorphic helper class.

Problem	16-Bit Mode	32-Bit Mode
Shuffle using the name-space hack	15 ms	11 ms
Shuffle using the polymorphic class hack	135 ms	115 ms
Sort using the name-space hack	1251 ms	1761 ms
Sort using the polymorphic class hack	9190 ms	8701 ms
Search using the name-space hack	41 ms	60 ms
Search using the polymorphic class hack	2851 ms	259 ms

Conclusion: Whoa! Polymorphism might be cool, but it's not free. You'll see why when we talk about late versus early binding in Chapter 10 ("Behind the Scenes at the OLE Factory," page 479).

and the polymorphic class technique. The polymorphic technique allows you to sort more than one kind of data in the same project. You can provide as many sort helper classes as you want and pass different ones to the sort procedures depending on the circumstances. But what's the cost?

Other People's Programs

One of the best ways to leverage your application's power is to get other people's programs to do part of the work. The Shell command makes this easy at the first level, but hardcore programmers must do more than simply call Shell. They have to hack around problems such as these:

- Shell assumes that you are sending a child program off to perform some independent task and that you no longer care what it does. If your program depends on results from the child program, you'll need to do extra work to determine when the program has finished.

- Shell assumes that you are running a Windows-based program. If you are running an MS-DOS–based program or a 32-bit console application, you might want to take extra steps to run it politely.

- Shell assumes that you are willing to let Windows decide where and how your Windows-based program will appear on the desktop. You'll have more work to do if you don't like the default behavior.

- Shell assumes that you know which program you want to run, but it's also possible to specify a document file and let Windows decide which program should work on the document.

- It's easy to keep track of 16-bit programs in 16-bit mode or 32-bit programs in 32-bit mode, but keeping track of 16-bit programs in 32-bit mode can be a problem.

Launching programs is probably the one area in which 16-bit Windows and 32-bit Windows differ the most. Any time you go beyond the Basic Shell function, you must use conditional code.

The Test Execute program shown in Figure 9-11 illustrates some of the more interesting ways you can launch other people's programs. You can use this program to experiment with different arguments to the various shell functions. When you've determined what works best for your situation, hard-code the appropriate settings.

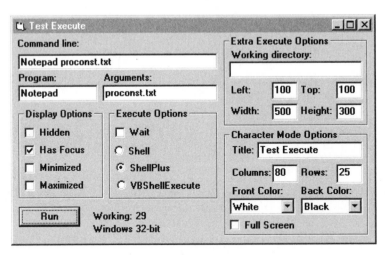

Figure 9-11. *The Test Execute program.*

Using Shell

The first thing you have to decide when running some else's program is whether to run synchronously or asynchronously. Generally, programs written for Windows want to run asynchronously. You send your children off to play and forget about them. Or you keep in touch by phone—OLE, DDE, or the clipboard, in Windows' terms. Character-based programs (at least those that have survived the Windows onslaught) will usually prefer to operate synchronously. You send your children to the store to get some flour and eggs, but you can't finish baking until they get back with the goods—usually a modified file. Of course, nothing prevents character-based programs from working independently or Windows-based programs from modifying data for their parents.

By default, the Shell function assumes that you want to run programs asynchronously. Running programs synchronously requires an extra effort. Most hardcore Basic programmers know how to use the GetModuleUsage API function to wait for a program to terminate in 16-bit Windows; it's one of the first tricks you learn from programming magazines, books, and online forums. Basic documentation says that Shell returns the task ID of the started program— and the returned identifier is indeed a unique identifier, but it's not a task or process ID. It's an instance handle. The GetModuleInstance API takes a module handle or an instance handle and returns the reference count of the number of programs using the module. When the reference count reaches 0, the program is no longer running. The code looks something like this:

```
hInst = Shell("calc.exe", vbNormalFocus)
Do While GetModuleUsage(hInst)
    DoEvents
Loop
```

This code assumes, however, that your instance of the program is the only one running. If there are multiple instances, you'll have to wait until they all close down. This makes sense for a function named GetModuleUsage, which deals with modules, not instances. It just happens (as Chapter 5 explains) that most module functions accept instance handles. What you really want is a task identifier, not an instance handle. The TaskFromInst function in INSTTOOL.BAS solves the problem by returning a unique task handle if the program is still running or 0 if it's finished. You saw similar code in "Instance Handles," page 225.

What hardcore programmers really want to know is how to do this in 32-bit mode. The 32-bit Shell function really does return a process ID. Processes have both handles and IDs, and the two differ as much from each other as they do from instance handles. Every 32-bit process has a single ID, but every program that needs access to a process must open a separate handle to it. You'll have to get a handle from the ID with the Win32 OpenProcess function in order to determine whether the process has terminated.

If you want to wait for a shelled program to finish, here's the code:

```
hProg = Shell(txtCmd.Text, GetDisplay)
If fWait Then WaitOnProgram hProg
```

And here's the conditional code that implements the wait:

```
Sub WaitOnProgram(idProg) ' SysInt parameter
#If Win32 Then
    ' Get process handle
    Dim hProc As Long, iRet As Long
    hProc = OpenProcess(PROCESS_ALL_ACCESS, False, idProg)
    ' Wait until process terminates
    If hProc <> hNull Then
        iRet = WaitForSingleObject(hProc, INFINITE)
        CloseHandle hProc
    End If
#Else
    Do While TaskFromInst(idProg)
        DoEvents
    Loop
#End If
End Sub
```

The tricky part of using this procedure is that *idProg* is an instance handle in 16-bit mode but a process ID in 32-bit mode.

The 16-bit code simply loops, wasting time until the program finishes. The DoEvents statement in the loop lets other programs run, but it also lets your program respond to other events such as keystrokes and button clicks. You can start another copy of your program while waiting for the first to finish.

In 32-bit mode, it's a completely different story. The WaitForSingleObject API function stops the Test Execute program dead in its tracks. You can click away as much as you want, but nothing fazes the Test Execute program until the child terminates. This is very efficient for other programs in the system because you're not using any resources while you wait, but be careful. Your program won't even be repainted. In fact, if you do this in the environment, the whole Visual Basic IDE will be dead, since it's the real program waiting for the shelled program to finish. "Threads and Synchronization," page 590, has more to say about threads and the mechanism used to temporarily shut them down.

Often, you don't want to wait idly for that other program, but you do want to know when it's finished. The IsRunning function can tell you:

```
Function IsRunning(idProg) As Boolean ' SysInt parameter
#If Win32 Then
    Dim hProc As Long, iRet As Long
    ' Get process handle
    hProc = OpenProcess(PROCESS_QUERY_INFORMATION, False, idProg)
    ' Check status of process
    If hProc <> hNull Then GetExitCodeProcess hProc, iRet
    IsRunning = (iRet = STILL_ACTIVE)
```

```
    CloseHandle hProc
#Else
    IsRunning = TaskFromInst(idProg)
#End If
End Function
```

In this case, the 32-bit code calls GetExitCodeProcess to check on whether the program is over. The 16-bit code calls TaskFromInst to check the same thing. The Test Execute program calls IsRunning from a timer control until the shelled program finishes. Your programs can do the same with a more useful background task. You can also put IsRunning in a loop if the sudden impact of WaitForSingleObject seems too extreme for your 32-bit programs:

```
Do While IsRunning(idProg)
    DoEvents
Loop
```

Using ShellPlus

The Shell function is fine for normal use, but in 32-bit mode you can get better control of your programs with the ShellPlus function. It does directly what the Shell function does behind the scenes, but instead of providing convenient defaults whether or not you want them, it puts you in control through oodles of optional arguments.

The base functionality of ShellPlus is the same as Shell. I could have put it in BETTER32.BAS as a replacement for Shell, but I thought that a function with this many optional arguments deserved its own name. The first and probably most useful additional argument is *vWait*. If you pass True for this parameter, ShellPlus handles the wait using the techniques shown earlier:

```
hProg = ShellPlus("Notepad", vbNormalFocus, True)
```

Your document will be ready when you return. Perhaps you don't care about waiting, but you'd like to ensure that Notepad starts with C:\HARDCORE as its working directory. No problem.

```
hProg = ShellPlus("Notepad", vbNormalFocus, , "C:\HARDCORE")
```

The next step is to specify how big the Notepad window should be and where it should appear. At this point, you're about maxed out on positional arguments and need to switch into named-argument mode:

```
hProg = ShellPlus("Notepad colors.txt", _
                  vInitDir:="C:\HARDCORE", _
                  vx:=100, vy:=100, _
                  vdx:=500, vdy:=400)
```

Of course, in real life you'd probably want to calculate the position and size arguments as percentages of the total screen size rather than as hard-coded pixel numbers. Also, note that the size arguments *vdx* and *vdy* won't have any effect on a program that calculates its own size (such as Calculator).

Some of the other optional arguments have no effect on Windows-based programs, but they do control how character-based applications (called *console applications,* in Win32 jargon) appear on the screen. You can specify the title, the number of rows and columns, and the color:

```
hProg = ShellPlus(Environ$("COMSPEC"), _
                  vTitle:="The Meaning of Life", _
                  vx:=90, vy:=90, _
                  vCols:=90, vRows:=40, _
                  vColor:=&H2E)
```

The color argument puts yellow text on a hideous green background. Does that take you back or what? Some of us remember when we had only 16 colors and specified them in the high and low nybbles of a byte. But we don't remember being able to make our screens 90 columns by 40 rows. Back in those days, you could have 80 or 40 columns and 25, 43, or 50 rows—take it or leave it. You still have those limitations with MS-DOS programs, but programs in 32-bit character mode and command-line sessions are more flexible.

You won't find many 32-bit console applications under Windows 95. The command processor, COMMAND.COM, is an MS-DOS program and won't respond to ShellPlus settings. Things are much better under Windows NT. CMD.EXE is a 32-bit console application, and so are most of the command-line tools such as FIND, SORT, and XCOPY. You'll get much better control if you define program information files (PIFs) for your MS-DOS–based programs and execute them with Shell or ShellPlus.

ShellPlus calls what must be one of the three most complicated Win32 functions, CreateProcess. Actually, CreateProcess isn't quite as bad as it looks— once you figure out that most of its many argument variations don't apply to you. ShellPlus has a lot of code to process optional arguments, but it all boils down to this:

```
' Create the process and run it
If CreateProcess(sNullStr, sPathName, pNull, pNull, False, _
                 0&, pNull, vInitDir, start, proc) Then
    ShellPlus = proc.dwProcessID
    If fWait Then WaitOnProgram (proc.dwProcessID)
    CloseHandle proc.hProcess
    CloseHandle proc.hThread
End If
```

The *start* variable is a UDT of type TStartupInfo containing all the size and position data for starting the window. The *proc* variable is a UDT of type TProcessInformation that returns handles and ID numbers for the process and main thread. You can find the details in INSTTOOL.BAS.

> **NOTE** The Shell function takes the same constants known to Create-Process, ShellExecute, and their obsolete API ancestor WinExec. These are the same constants used by ShowWindow to modify the appearance of an existing window, and, frankly, many of them don't make sense in the context of starting a new program. The Display Options settings in the Test Execute program—Hidden, Has Focus, Minimized, and Maximized—work better for me. Take a look at the logic in the check box event procedures and the GetDisplay function (TEXECUTE.FRM), which translate these sensible settings into the arbitrary constants required by Windows.

Using ShellExecute

Use CreateProcess or Shell to run other people's programs when you know what you're doing. But you might find ShellExecute more convenient when only the user knows what you're doing. For example, if you want to let Windows decide how to process a document, you can pass the document name to ShellExecute. In the Test Execute program, you can try this by setting the mode to ShellExecute, typing a document filename in the Arguments field, and leaving the Program field blank.

ShellExecute has a lot of arguments, most of which have defaults. Sounds like a case for optional arguments. Check out VBShellExecute in INSTTOOL.BAS. You pay a performance price for the extra convenience of ShellExecute, so don't call it when writing execution scripts that are similar to batch files. We'll talk more about ShellExecute and its ability to work with the Registry in "Registry Blues," page 539.

Unlike Shell and ShellPlus, ShellExecute doesn't search the PATH environment variable for your program. If you're passing it an executable file, you need to search the path yourself by calling SearchForExe (in UTILITY.BAS). It calls the SearchDirs function described in "SearchPath," page 108.

ShellExecute returns what it claims is an instance handle. It is, in 16-bit mode. You can test the return value the same way you would test the return value from Shell. But the 32-bit version doesn't look or work like an instance handle, and you can't use it to tell when a process has terminated. Windows 95 has a ShellExecuteEx function that can return a process handle, but it's hardly worth the trouble because you usually call ShellExecute in response to a user select-ing a document. If you don't even know which program will process the docu-ment, you're probably not going to depend on the results. Therefore, the Wait option is disabled in the Test Execute program when the VBShellExecute mode is active.

When All Else Fails, Hit It with a Hammer

If the techniques described in this section seem too complex, try this low-tech batch file solution. Your calling program can create a batch file. The batch file creates a temporary file, calls your program, and then deletes the temporary file. You write the batch file to disk, run it, and then periodically check to see whether the temporary file still exists. When the temporary file disappears, your program is finished. You can delete the batch file.

10

The OLE Gospel

Step right up, there. Take your seats, folks. Fasten your seatbelts. This ride is perfectly safe, but you wouldn't want to tempt gravity, would you? You will be upside down, backward, and inside out, but that's just part of the fun. Our specially designed OLE carts with the virtual windows on the sides, top, and bottom give you a complete view of the scenery, while also protecting you from crashes and bugs.

Now, folks, let me remind you that everything you see is live. This is not a movie or an illusion. What you see over there on your left really is the Visual Basic Integrated Development Environment. It's being driven by a live programmer, and we don't have any idea what crazy stunts this person may be up to. You're perfectly safe, but nothing is scripted.

Keep your eyes peeled on the right. That's where the add-in will appear. When we start the tour, I don't know whether to expect a tame add-in or a wild one. A tame add-in is a compiled executable program. They tend to be fast but predictable. A wild add-in runs in another copy of the IDE, and it's...well, it's wild.

I see some movement there on the right. Oh, boy, looks like we've got a wild one. That's another 32-bit IDE starting up now. Wow, look at those menus hum! Talk about hardcore. Hey! I know that guy. That's our author! Let's see whether he's creating a new add-in or debugging the one in this chapter. He's loading the add-in. Whoa! Just count those menu items! That file controller must know how to handle every event the IDE can send. OK, here we go.

He's running the add-in. The first thing it does is check the VB.INI file to see if it's already listed in the Add-Ins32 section. It isn't, so he puts it there. You can see the name, BasicTools.CAddInManager. Yes! That's us!

Now if you'll turn back to the left, I expect some action in the other IDE soon. OK, he's going over to the Add-In Manager dialog box on the Add-Ins menu. You can see the IDE opening up VB.INI and putting everything it finds in the Add-Ins32 section into the dialog box. There's the add-in he put in a minute ago from the other IDE. He's clicking it, and...Yahoooooo! Hang on to your hats!

On the left, coming up fast. The IDE checks the system Registry for any OLE server named BasicTools with a class named CAddInManager. Yes! Now it creates a CAddInManager object and calls its ConnectAddIn method. The IDE is passing itself to the add-in as an Application object. Talk about late-bound polymorphism!

Now the action switches back to the right. The ConnectAddIn method on the IDE side has become a ConnectAddIn event on the add-in side. The CAddIn-Manager object takes the IDE instance passed to it and starts creating an add-in hierarchy of its own. It's hooking up file and menu events in their own classes. See how each object in the hierarchy passes itself to its member objects so that they're all interconnected through Parent properties?

Whew! Are we having fun yet? Well, nothing to do now except wait for a file or menu event. Watch out! Here comes one now! Oh, no!

Talk about sudden stops. I told you those seatbelts would come in handy. Well, it looks like we're stuck in the debugger. Nothing's happening at the keyboard. Our developer is probably heading off to lunch. Or maybe he's just thinking. Happens all the time. Well, we have a little technical lecture to keep you amused until he gets back.

Visual Basic Spreads the OLE Gospel

That little adventure gives you a preview of the exciting world of OLE. (We'll get back to add-ins later.) Some historians allege that OLE was once an acronym meaning "object linking and embedding," but according to knowledge-able Microsoft insiders, the word actually was taken from the Basic dialect of northeastern Cathistan, where it means "the thing that interfaces with all."

These days, OLE simply means...OLE, and it represents Microsoft's vision of the future. I use the word *vision* in its religious sense, which is how Microsoft's public relations department thinks of it. Even the titles of the practitioners are religious. Go to any conference where programmers gather, and you'll find at least one seminar taught by a person whose official title is OLE Evangelist. Figure 10-1 is a doctored version of one of the mystic images these zealots show on their overhead projectors. It illustrates the little-known fact that Visual Basic version 4 is the leader of an insidious conspiracy to take over the world for OLE. Let's look at some of the ways Visual Basic preaches and practices the OLE doctrine.

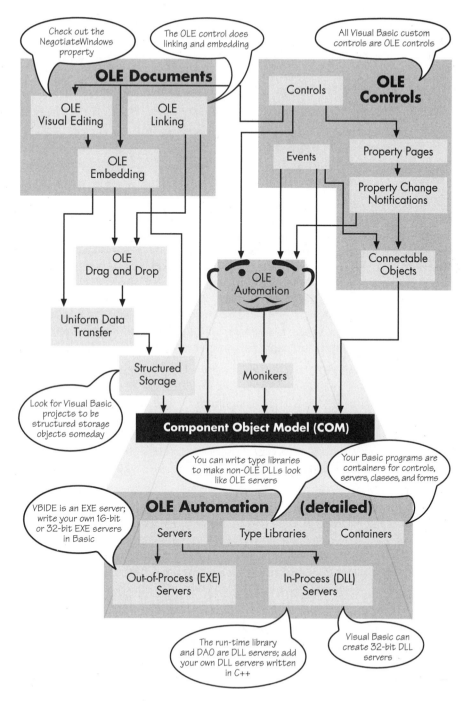

Figure 10-1. *Visual Basic in an OLE icon.*

- The Visual Basic run-time library is simply an OLE DLL. You can also enhance the language by adding your own OLE DLLs. Although there's no official term, I think of them as OLE libraries. You'll usually write them in C++ or another low-level language. (You can write OLE DLLs with the 32-bit version of Visual Basic, but these have a different purpose, as you'll see in a minute.)

- Visual Basic supports OLE linking and embedding through the OLE control. Version 4 adds support for visual editing. Linking and embedding are too easy for a hardcore book, and this is the last you'll hear of these topics.

- Visual Basic allows you to program OLE Automation applications. I see a lot of requests for assistance with this, but most are concerned with the application side of the problem. I'm not going to talk about programming OLE applications such as Microsoft Word for Windows, Microsoft Excel, and Visio because I don't know which ones you have. Besides, other books cover this topic. Microsoft Press publishes two good ones: *Developing Applications with Microsoft Office for Windows 95,* by Christine Solomon (1996); and *Microsoft Guide to Object Programming with Visual Basic 4 and Microsoft Office for Windows 95,* by Joel P. Dehlin and Matthew J. Curland (real soon now).

- Visual Basic supports OLE type libraries (which you install with the References dialog box and see in the Object Browser). Most well-behaved OLE servers, including the Visual Basic libraries and controls and any servers you create, have type libraries. Another kind of type library makes a non-OLE DLL (such as the Windows system DLLs) look like an OLE object. The Windows API type library supplied with this book is such a library. See Chapter 2 for details about how to load it in the References dialog box and how to use the functions in it.

- All the controls supplied with Visual Basic and by other vendors are (or should be) OLE servers, in a special format known as OLE controls. (The non-OLE VBX controls from previous versions are recognized in 16-bit only and might not be recognized at all in future versions.) For the most part, it doesn't matter that OLE is what makes these controls tick, but it does illustrate one more way in which Visual Basic is an OLE pioneer.

- Visual Basic supports creating OLE Automation servers. I'll talk a lot in this chapter about this new feature of version 4. I'll explain briefly how to create a simple OLE server and how to program that server from another application.

■ The Visual Basic environment is itself an OLE server. You can customize it by creating your own OLE servers in a specific format known as an *add-in*. Add-ins must program the environment's VBIDE object and must provide objects that the VBIDE object knows how to talk to. Most of this chapter describes how to make your add-in objects understand what VBIDE tells them and how to make add-ins tell the VBIDE what to do in a format it understands.

The Prime Number Server

If you skipped Chapter 4 in order to go directly to the OLE chapter, do not pass Go, do not collect $200. Under Visual Basic, OLE applications must be object-oriented. You can't implement them without implementing classes. You can look at this as a hoop to jump through, and simply turn your functions into methods of a do-nothing class. Or you can take it as an opportunity to rethink your application. As a sample, let's implement the Sieve of Eratosthenes OLE server.

The Sieve of Eratosthenes has traditionally been used as a benchmark program for measuring the performance of different machines, operating systems, programming languages, and compilers and interpreters. Here we'll expand it to measure the difference between different kinds of OLE servers. In the process, we'll look at OLE servers and clients in "slow motion." You don't really need to know every detail in order to create or use OLE servers, but since you're hardcore, you might as well know the inside story.

I'll show you both client and server written in Visual Basic because OLE communication is easier to understand if you control both parts. But keep in mind that OLE doesn't know or care what language is used. When you purchase a server, you often won't know what language it was written in. Similarly, if you create a server in Basic, your clients need not know what language you used.

> **NOTE** In real life, you'll always need to create a test client to make sure that your server works. Visual Basic is the ideal language in which to write your test client, even if the server is written in C++ or some other language.

A Functional Way of Prime Numbers

The first task in converting an existing program to an OLE server is to change the model from functional to object-oriented. Of course, if you're starting from scratch, you can start out object-oriented, but you still need to put yourself in an object state of mind. Most of us still program in functional mode. Here's how I changed my way of thinking about the Sieve of Eratosthenes.

First, look at the sieve in functional form. The algorithm shown here is pretty much the same as the one presented in *Byte* magazine in 1983 and used by hundreds of reviewers in many languages ever since. Variable names have been changed to protect the guilty. The only logical change is that nonprime numbers are marked with True rather than False to take advantage of Basic's automatic initialization to 0.

```
Function Sieve(iMaxPrime As Integer, fDisplay As Boolean, _
               lstOutput As ListBox) As Integer
    Dim iCur As Integer, i As Integer, s As String, cPrime As Integer
    Dim af() As Boolean
    ReDim af(0 To iMaxPrime + 1) As Boolean

    If fDisplay Then lstOutput.Clear
    For iCur = 2 To iMaxPrime
        If Not af(iCur) Then      ' Found a prime
            If fDisplay Then lstOutput.AddItem iCur
            For i = iCur + iCur To iMaxPrime Step iCur
                af(i) = True      ' Cancel its multiples
            Next
            cPrime = cPrime + 1
        End If
    Next
    Sieve = cPrime
End Function
```

You'll usually want to calculate all primes up to a given number several times to get useful timings. The Sieve program in Figure 10-2 shows a user interface for doing this. If you're simply testing speed, you can throw away the results, but you do need a display mode to prove that the numbers you're calculating are really primes. The timing is useless with the display on, however, because you're timing more display than calculation. The program has options for early-bound versus late-bound, Basic versus C++, and getting all versus getting one at a time.

In most sieve applications, you don't really care about prime numbers, only about how long it takes to calculate them in different environments. This model doesn't make much sense for testing an OLE server. A server has to serve something, so you should at least pretend that the user of your class really needs the data. So let's say that prime numbers are very useful in calculating proportional radial intensity vectors of the newly discovered subatomic particles called quinks. To properly serve the powerful programs searching the universe for quinks, you need an OLE server that hands over prime numbers.

You can start by implementing the object-oriented way in the same program that uses the functional way. If you can access the object from your own program, you can do the same thing through OLE from another program.

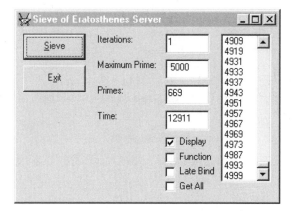

Figure 10-2. *The Sieve of Eratosthenes server.*

An Object-Oriented Way of Prime Numbers

One way to make the program object-oriented is to turn the Sieve function into a method that fills an array of prime numbers passed by reference. The CSieve class does this through the AllPrimes method. The code is very similar to the code used for the Sieve function. The problem with this kind of method is that you must calculate all the prime numbers before you can get the first one. But some clients can't wait. They want a steady stream of numbers fed to them one at a time.

The trick in getting numbers one at a time is to break the Sieve function—which seems like an integrated whole—into its parts. Here's what Sieve really does:

- Keeps its state (number of primes, current number) in local variables

- Initializes an array to False by redimensioning it

- Loops through each potential prime number

- Marks out all multiples of primes

- Counts the primes as it finds them

You can break these tasks into the following members, methods, and properties:

- The state is kept in private variables shared by all the methods and properties rather than in local variables. This includes the array of flags for each potential prime (*af*), the number currently being tested (*iCur*), the maximum prime (*iMaxPrime*), and the count of primes (*cPrime*).

- A ReInitialize method resets all the internal variables and starts counting again from 0.

- A MaxPrime property sets the maximum number of primes. From a user's viewpoint, it would be better not to have a maximum and instead to simply calculate whether each number is a prime without reference to later primes. But you'd have to turn to someone other than Eratosthenes for an algorithm. So let's stick with the sieve. When you change the maximum, you break the algorithm. Therefore, the MaxPrime Property Let procedure must call ReInitialize to start counting from 0.

- A NextPrime property calculates and returns the next prime.

- A Primes (read-only) property tells you how many prime numbers have been encountered so far.

Here's the code to implement these methods and properties:

```
Private af() As Boolean, iCur As Integer
Private iMaxPrime As Integer, cPrime As Integer

Private Sub Class_Initialize()
    ' Default size is largest integer
    iMaxPrime = 32766
    ReInitialize
End Sub

Sub ReInitialize()
    ReDim af(0 To iMaxPrime)
    iCur = 1: cPrime = 0
End Sub

Property Get NextPrime() As Integer
    NextPrime = 0
    ' Loop until you find a prime or overflow array
    iCur = iCur + 1
    On Error GoTo OverMaxPrime
    Do While af(iCur)
        iCur = iCur + 1
    Loop
    ' Cancel multiples of this prime
    Dim i As Long
    For i = iCur + iCur To iMaxPrime Step iCur
        af(i) = True
    Next
```

```
    ' Count and return it
    cPrime = cPrime + 1
    NextPrime = iCur
OverMaxPrime:        ' Array overflow comes here
End Property

Property Get MaxPrime() As Integer
    MaxPrime = iMaxPrime
End Property

Property Let MaxPrime(iMaxPrimeA As Integer)
    iMaxPrime = iMaxPrimeA
    ReInitialize
End Property

Property Get Primes() As Integer
    Primes = cPrime
End Property
```

As you can see, the NextPrime property does most of the work. It looks quite different from the Sieve function, but it does essentially the same thing. You might need to study both the Sieve function and the NextPrime property for a minute to see the connection.

The code that calls the class methods also doesn't look much like the code that calls the function. (Ignore early binding versus late binding, and focus for now only on functional versus object-oriented.)

```
If chkFunction = vbChecked Then
    ' Functional version
    ms = timeGetTime()
    For i = 1 To cIter
        txtPrimes.Text = Sieve(iMaxPrime, fDisplay, lstOutput)
    Next
    txtTime.Text = timeGetTime() - ms
ElseIf chkLate <> vbChecked Then
    ' Object-oriented version, early bind
    Dim siv As New CSieve
    If chkAll <> vbChecked Then
        ' Get one at a time
        siv.MaxPrime = txtMaxPrime.Text
        ms = timeGetTime()
        For i = 1 To cIter
            siv.ReInitialize
```

(continued)

```
        Do
            iPrime = siv.NextPrime
            If fDisplay And iPrime Then
                lstOutput.AddItem iPrime
                lstOutput.TopIndex = lstOutput.ListCount - 1
                lstOutput.Refresh
            End If
        Loop Until iPrime = 0
    Next
    txtTime.Text = timeGetTime() - ms
    txtPrimes.Text = siv.Primes
Else
    ' Get all at once
```

Notice that writing the prime numbers moves outside the class, where it belongs. The class allows you to do whatever you want with the results, whereas the function handles only writing to a list box. Check the AllPrimes method in SIEVE.CLS to see how you could make the function return an array rather than modify a list box.

The OLE Way of Prime Numbers

Once you have an object-oriented solution, you're just a few clicks away from an OLE server. Here's all you have to do to turn the CSieve class and the FSieve form into the Sieve server. None of the steps require writing code. Figure 10-3 illustrates the steps and settings.

1. Set the Public property of the class to True, as shown in Figure 10-3.

2. Set the Instancing property to Not Creatable, Creatable SingleUse, or Createable MultiUse. The CSieve class setting is Creatable MultiUse so that more than one client at a time can read prime numbers. Top-level classes should be creatable, but if you create a public object hierarchy, you might want to make higher-level classes Not Creatable. When a user creates the base of the hierarchy, the base creates all its children, but users can create children only through the base. We'll talk about hierarchies later in the chapter.

3. Make your class into a program by providing it with a startup form or module. The Sieve server uses Sub Main in SIEVESRV.BAS as its startup form. "Debugging Servers," page 481, explains more about this. Actually, a server doesn't even need a user interface, but it does need a startup form. Yes, it's a contradiction that the startup form needn't be a form, but the important thing is that it can't be a class. Once a server program starts, it can sit idly, waiting for a client to create objects of its class.

4. Give your server a project name. Because every program must have a project name, Visual Basic by default fills this field in the Options dialog box with the base name of the project file. Accepting the default is usually a bad idea. For example, your project name can't be the same as a class name. That's OK, because naming your class George, your startup module George, and your project George isn't such a great idea anyway.

5. Set the StartMode field to Standalone or OLE Server. This setting doesn't control whether or not your program is an OLE server; it simply specifies whether the program will come up in Standalone mode or in Server mode in the Visual Basic environment. If your server has a user interface, you should normally choose Standalone mode. (The Sieve EXE server described later has this setting.) If your server has no user interface, choose OLE Server. (The Sieve DLL server has this setting.)

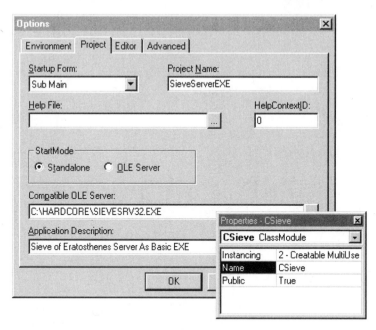

Figure 10-3. *Settings for OLE servers.*

6. Give your server an application description. The description is optional, but you'll have a rude server indeed if you fail to provide it. Any client that wants to register and use your services will have to guess your purpose from the project name. When you write a server, you don't know who will use it. It might be called from Excel, from Word, or from a program you've never heard of. Visual Basic itself is a typical client. It offers a References dialog box for loading and registering the types of servers, and it has an Object Browser for displaying those types. Both use the application description to identify the server.

7. Write a help file for your server, and provide the filename and context ID of the server help topic in the Help File and HelpContextID fields. Why doesn't SieveServer have a help file? Well, uh…it has a virtual help file.

8. Build an EXE or a DLL for the server, and load it in the Compatible OLE Server field. If you want to debug the server from a client that uses early binding (and most clients should), you'll need to provide a compatible server. After you've released your server to the world, you'll probably want to fill in this field with the released version while you're working on version 2, to help keep your server's methods and properties in sync with the clients that depend on it.

9. Register the server. If you try to use a server that isn't in the Registry database, you'll get an OLE Automation error. Although registering an EXE server is so simple that you'll usually do it without even realizing it, registering a DLL server can be a messy business. Either way, you need to understand exactly what's happening, and I'll tell you in "Registering servers," page 473.

EXE servers versus DLL servers

If you are working in 32-bit mode, you must choose whether you want to build a DLL server or an EXE server. DLL servers are much faster, as you'll see in the "Performance" sidebar on page 482, because they are in the same process as the client program. Sending data from a DLL to a program is very efficient, even though OLE adds some overhead. An EXE server, on the other hand, is a completely different program, and the overhead of sending data across process boundaries is high.

That doesn't mean you always want DLL servers. Microsoft Excel isn't a DLL, for example, although clearly its automation clients would run faster if it were. If your server does nothing but serve, build the DLL server. If your program is primarily a program and secondarily a server, build the EXE server. A few other unusual features (such as a server that must have modeless dialog boxes) also require EXE servers. The server described in "The server side of file notification," page 595, for example, is an EXE server so that its operation won't affect the performance of its clients. And 16-bit Basic servers must always be EXEs, although they can be designed to work like DLLs.

In order to time DLL servers, I created a separate DLL server using the CSieve class. This is an artificial situation. Normally, a client won't use a DLL server and an EXE server that expose the same class, but I did it to prove a point. The classes in the two servers must have different names, so I renamed the class in the DLL server to CDSieve and renamed its file to SIEVED.CLS. (It's actually just a copy of SIEVE.CLS created with the Save File As command.)

The DLL server project (SIEVEDLL.VBP) consists of SIEVED.CLS and the startup "form" SIEVEDLL.BAS. Here's all the code in the startup module:

```
Sub Main()

End Sub
```

You can't get much simpler than that.

You could also build a 16-bit "DLL" server using the same project. Give it the name SIEVEDLL.DLL. (Windows doesn't care if you call an EXE file a DLL.) But of course the 16-bit IDE has no Make DLL File menu item, so what comes out is really an EXE regardless of the name. Since it has no interface, the 16-bit version never shows up on your screen. It looks and acts like a slow DLL.

You'll find important differences between EXE and DLL servers. First, you can't actually debug a DLL server. When you run the server in the Visual Basic environment, it's not really a DLL, regardless of what you name it or what plans you have for it. If you're designing your server to be a DLL, you should check the Use OLE DLL Restrictions check box on the Advanced tab of the Options dialog box. This will enforce DLL restrictions such as the one against modal dialogs. Without this setting, you could be in for some ugly surprises when you finally decide to make a DLL from your completely debugged server.

The second difference is in how you register DLL and EXE servers. Let's check behind the curtain.

Registering servers

You register an EXE server by running it. You can check this out with the Sieve-ServerEXE program. Open the Registry Editor, and then find the SieveServer-EXE.CSieve class using the Find menu item (on the Search, View, or Edit menu, depending on your operating system). Delete the entry. The Sieve is gone. Now run the SieveServerEXE program. Restart or refresh the Registry Editor. The Sieve is back.

By using the command-line options */regserver* and */unregserver,* you can register or unregister any OLE EXE server without invoking the program's normal user interface. If you want to register SIEVESRV32.EXE without taking over the user's screen, you can do it from your setup program with this statement:

```
Shell "SIEVESRV32.EXE /regserver"
```

If it seems a little strange that all your OLE servers are able to recognize these command-line options without any programming by you, check it out with the Registry Editor.

This is essentially what the setup programs created with the Setup Toolkit will do. As a practical matter, this issue affects you, not your customers. Chances are you'll run your EXE server program from the IDE sometime during development of the program. It will be registered automatically, and you'll have no trouble. Then you'll put the client and server programs on a disk for a fellow programmer who also runs Visual Basic (thus bypassing setup). Your client program will fail rudely because the server isn't registered on your colleague's disk. The workaround is easy: just tell your colleague to run the server program once before running the client.

Now try running a DLL server with the */regserver* command-line option:

```
Shell "SIEVEDLL32.DLL /regserver"
```

Ha! You know better than to run a DLL. There is a solution. Hidden away on your Visual Basic distribution CD (not copied to your disk during setup) are the programs REGSVR.EXE and REGSVR32.EXE. The command-line REGSVR is the 16-bit version that registers 16-bit DLLs written in languages that support 16-bit DLLs. REGSVR32 registers your 32-bit Basic DLLs. So here's the correct command line:

```
Shell "regsvr32 SIEVEDLL32.DLL"
```

Both REGSVR programs have a */u* option to unregister a server and a */s* (silent) option to register without displaying a success dialog box. The setup programs created by the Setup Toolkit can handle this registration for your customers. When you choose the Make DLL File menu item, Visual Basic automatically registers the DLL. In other words, you usually won't need to call REGSVR32, but it's there if you really need it.

The C++ Sieve Server

Any server that you can write in Basic you can also write in C++. But is it worth the trouble? Judge for yourself by comparing the CSieve class written in Basic to the CCSieve class written in C++. CCSieve (in the SIEVE directory on the companion CD) gives you an idea of what Visual Basic does behind the scenes.

It's difficult and not very meaningful to compare Basic and C++ code, but we can do it anyway. The SIEVE.CLS file contains about 80 lines of code. The SIEVE.CPP and SIEVE.H files provide the same functionality in about 300 lines, but this is misleading. The project contains about 800 additional lines of code that set up the OLE framework. If you count only the executable lines that calculate prime numbers, the two versions are roughly the same—with maybe slightly fewer lines in C++ because the language syntax is more compact. In either case, the code you see is the tip of the iceberg. A lot more C++ code lurks within the OLE DLLs. With the Basic version, you see even less of the iceberg, but mostly it's the same iceberg. The Visual Basic library code that connects Basic servers to the OLE DLLs is written in C++, and it must perform essentially the same tasks as the framework code surrounding the CCSieve class.

I heard a speaker at a recent C++ seminar claim that OLE servers created with Visual Basic would never be fast enough for real use. Phooey! Visual Basic isn't written in Visual Basic. What your server serves might indeed be slower if it were written in Visual Basic; it's true that p-code can't match C++ native code. But if your program is disk-bound or user-interface intensive, you won't be able to tell the difference—except in the amount of code you need to write and the amount of time it takes to debug it.

Comments in the code explain how I wrote the C++ server and why I made certain implementation choices. It was a long, tedious process, with many iterations of the compile and debug cycle so familiar to C and C++ programmers. And what did I get for that extra work? Check the "Performance" sidebar on page 482.

Using a Server

Figure 10-4 on the next page shows an application that reads prime numbers from the prime number server described earlier. The SieveClient program looks a lot like the SieveServer program, but it doesn't know a prime number from a lottery number. I created SieveClient by cloning SieveServer and removing features. The code for using a class in your own program isn't any different from the code for using a class in an outside server program.

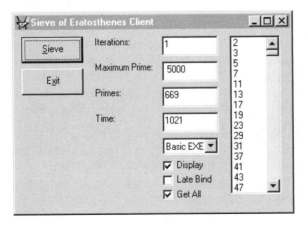

Figure 10-4. *The Sieve of Eratosthenes client.*

The big question clients must decide is whether they can use a type library. The SieveClient program illustrates both possibilities, referred to as *early binding* and *late binding*. The "Performance" sidebar on page 482 shows why you should use a type library for early binding if you can get your hands on one.

CHALLENGE If you have Visual Basic Enterprise Edition, you can enhance the Sieve server and client programs to work through Remote OLE Automation. I haven't tried this, but in theory the Sieve server should work without any code changes. It would be interesting to compare the speed with the numbers presented in the "Performance" sidebar on page 482.

If you have a type library for the server, load it in the References dialog box, shown in Figure 10-5. Use the Browse button to find the type library. Some type libraries (such as the Windows API type library introduced in Chapter 2) come in a separate file with a TLB or an OLB extension. Others are embedded as resources in EXE or DLL files. Servers created with Visual Basic always have a type library embedded in the EXE or DLL file. You can load SieveServer into SieveClient by browsing for the appropriate executable file. Looking at 32-bit only, the file will be SIEVESRV32.EXE (Basic EXE), SIEVEDLL32.DLL (Basic DLL), or SIEVE32.DLL (C++ DLL).

Once the type library is loaded, you can examine it with the Object Browser. Figure 10-6 shows SieveServer in SieveClient's Object Browser. You would see the same thing in SieveServer's Object Browser.

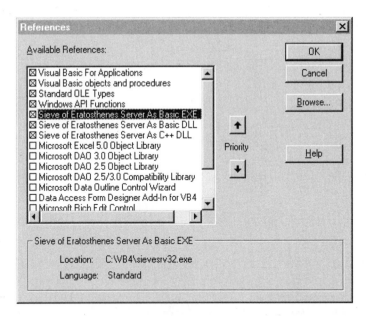

Figure 10-5. *Sieve servers in the References dialog box.*

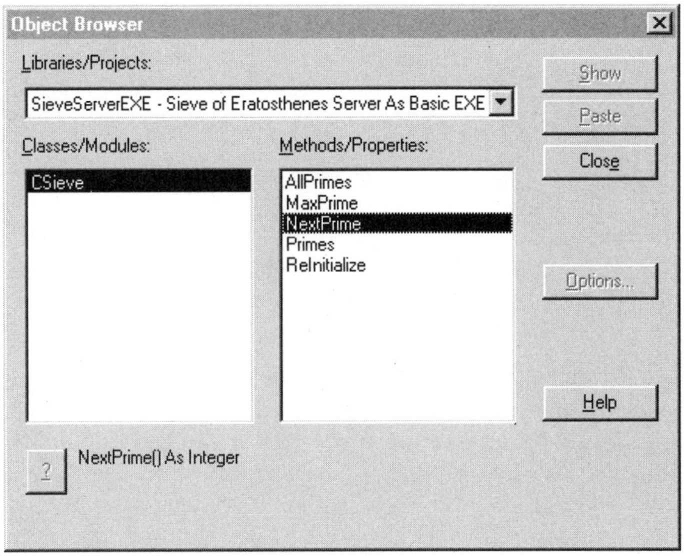

Figure 10-6. *Browsing a type library.*

The code to use the server with early binding declares an object with the New keyword:

```
Dim siv As New CSieve
siv.MaxPrime = txtMaxPrime.Text
⋮
```

You can't always use a type library, however. When OLE Automation first came out, no client languages used type libraries. Visual Basic version 3, for example, didn't know a type library from the public library. Many early servers didn't come with type libraries because there were no clients to use them. If you're using an old server, you might need to use late binding. But check around before you settle for the old way. Some old servers such as Word 6 for Windows didn't come with type libraries, but you can get libraries for them now through product support.

Another reason for not using a type library is that you might not know the name of the server until run time. You'll see an example of this later when we talk about add-ins.

If you must use late binding, you at least need to know the exact name of the server so that you can load it with the CreateObject function. The code looks like this:

```
Dim rsiv As Object
Select Case cboServer.ListIndex
Case ordBasicEXE
    Set rsiv = CreateObject("SieveServerEXE.CSieve")
⋮
```

The SieveServer program does late binding a little differently:

```
Dim rsiv As Object
Set rsiv = New CSieve
rsiv.MaxPrime = txtMaxPrime.Text
```

This code uses the early-bound name CSieve for late binding to the rsiv object. SieveServer has no reason to do late binding except to prove that it can be done. Neither does SieveClient, for that matter, since it's hooked up to a type library. But the late-binding code branches in SieveClient would work even if you disconnected the type library. Normally, late binding is about as good an idea as writing temporary files to floppy disks—avoid it.

Behind the Scenes at the OLE Factory

One way or another, the Sieve client program is going to need all the information it can get about the Sieve server. The client needs the settings and the information that you saw in Figure 10-3 on page 471.

How can the server share the information, and how can the client find it? Part of the information is shared through the system Registry. Figure 10-7 on the next page shows all the data in the Registry related to the SieveServerEXE program. This is the God's-eye view; you can't really see all these entries at one time in the Registry Editor. If you haven't used the Registry Editor (REGEDIT.EXE under Windows 3.*x* and Windows 95 or REGEDT32.EXE under Windows NT), you'd better load it up and follow along. In theory, your programming tools should automatically take care of both registering and unregistering servers and other Registry entries, but if you ever deal with beta software, you should get used to the idea of sometimes fixing Registry entries by hand.

Some Registry entries are named, and some are numbered. Named entries have numbered subentries, and numbered entries contain data such as the title and location of the server. The numbers are globally unique IDs. A GUID, you'll remember, is a unique 128-bit number that distinguishes a class and its data from all other OLE classes that ever have been or will be created. You'll have to trust that GUIDs are unique. The OLE documentation has some interesting statistics about the infinitesimal chance of two programs that follow the rules in assigning GUIDs just happening to come up with the same 128-bit number.

If you check all the cross-links in Figure 10-7, you'll start to get an idea of what's going on. The server writes its name, number, and data to the Registry. A client can look up the server it needs by name. The name entry contains the number, which the client can use to look up data. OLE has functions that take care of the details of registering servers, handling class IDs, and looking up data in the Registry. Visual Basic has functions that take care of calling those OLE functions. You simply fill in dialog boxes, declare objects, and call properties and methods.

If you use late binding, information about the class comes from the Registry and from the EXE file of the server. CreateObject uses the name passed in its argument to look up the server's class ID. The ID number is used to look up other data, including the filename of the server. If the server isn't already running, it is launched. Through magic that need not concern us, the addresses of all the properties and methods are looked up. This is called *binding* because it binds the names of the class, methods, and properties used in the client program to the code for those items in the server program. Late binding works fine, except that looking up the data takes time when time is in short supply—at run time.

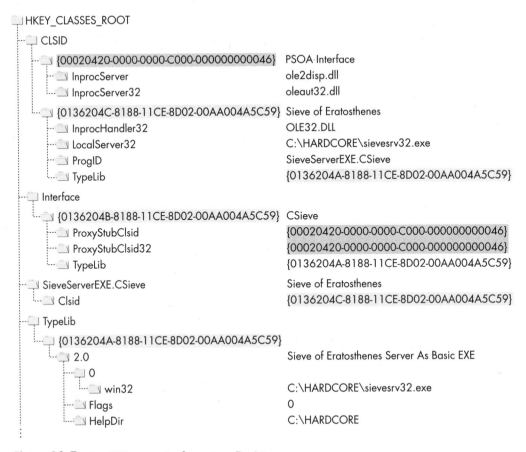

Figure 10-7. *An OLE server in the system Registry.*

OLE also provides a faster, more complicated system based on type libraries. When you compile a server program, your compiler knows a lot about your program that the client would like to know later. If you save all that information in a file, clients who know the name, location, and format of the file can read the data at design time. If the client already knows the names, parameters, and types of all the methods and properties in the class, and if it has a map for finding the corresponding code addresses in the server, it has a lot less work to do at run time.

Of course, the client's idea of what's in the server program must match what's actually in the server, even if the current version of the server was written after the client was written. The client can use only the properties and methods that it knows about. You can see how easily this could get out of sync. Imagine that the Actualize method returned a Long in version 1. Now that you're designing version 2, you decide that it would be better to return a Variant. Your old clients are not going to appreciate the improvement. Rather than changing an existing method, you should add a new one. For example, you can add a new Actualizationize method that returns a Variant. Old clients can Actualize, new clients can Actualizationize, and you won't be doing anything actionable.

That's where the Compatible OLE Server field on the Project tab of the Options dialog box comes in. If you install the EXE or DLL file for your existing server in this field, Visual Basic reads in that server's type library. Every time you change the server code, Visual Basic compares the type library of the server in memory to the embedded type library of the executable file. If your change causes a conflict for existing clients, you'll get a warning. You can decide whether your bright idea is bright enough to justify breaking old clients.

Debugging Servers

In previous versions of Visual Basic, you got an error if you tried to run two copies of the Visual Basic environment. With OLE servers, however, you usually need to debug the client and the server at the same time. Therefore, in version 4 you can run as many copies as memory allows (although two is usually enough).

If you're debugging a client that uses late binding, the process is simple. Load the server into one IDE, set breakpoints at key points in the server, and run it. Now load the client into another IDE and debug it normally.

This takes a little getting used to. You have to constantly switch back and forth between IDEs as you hit breakpoints or step through one or the other. Don't stop the server while the client is using it. Visual Basic is pretty sophisticated about this and will warn you if you try to do anything questionable.

NOTE   The sample programs run 32-bit servers from 32-bit clients and 16-bit servers from 16-bit clients, but OLE has no such limitation. You can use late-bound 16-bit servers from 32-bit clients or, under Windows NT or Windows 95, use late-bound 32-bit servers from 16-bit clients. For example, it's hard for a 16-bit program to read from or write to the 32-bit Registry, but it's easy to call a 32-bit OLE server that reads from and writes to the Registry. Of course, if you can write a 32-bit OLE server, you should also be able to write a 32-bit client. But if you can do that, you can write to the Registry without calling a server to do it for you.

Debugging a client that uses early binding is a little more complex. You have to make the EXE or DLL file of the server so that the client will have a type library to load. After making the executable file, enter it in the Compatible OLE Server field on the Project tab of the Options dialog box. Start the client IDE, and load the executable file in the References dialog box. Run the server first, and then

PERFORMANCE

Problem: Compare calculating prime numbers functionally, with objects, locally, externally, and with early or late binding.

Problem	16-Bit Mode	32-Bit Mode
Sieve function in current program	272 ms	257 ms
Early-bound object with NextPrime in current program	420 ms	334 ms
Late-bound object with NextPrime in current program	2247 ms	1922 ms
Early-bound object with AllPrimes in current program	329 ms	282 ms
Late-bound object with AllPrimes in current program	322 ms	288 ms
Early-bound object with NextPrime in Basic EXE server	25802 ms	15008 ms
Late-bound object with NextPrime in Basic EXE server	54971 ms	31995 ms
Early-bound object with AllPrimes in Basic EXE server	407 ms	342 ms
Late-bound object with AllPrimes in Basic EXE server	443 ms	373 ms
Early-bound object with NextPrime in Basic DLL server	n/a	131 ms
Late-bound object with NextPrime in Basic DLL server	n/a	737 ms
Early-bound object with AllPrimes in Basic DLL server	n/a	113 ms
Late-bound object with AllPrimes in Basic DLL server	n/a	115 ms
Early-bound object with NextPrime in C++ DLL server	131 ms	24 ms
Late-bound object with NextPrime in C++ DLL server	2037 ms	610 ms
Early-bound object with AllPrimes in C++ DLL server	96 ms	17 ms
Late-bound object with AllPrimes in C++ DLL server	96 ms	18 ms

Conclusion: Switching from a functional approach to an object-oriented approach doesn't have a significant cost in itself. In fact, as long as you stay in the same program, these variations of the Sieve algorithm don't differ much. You do need to worry about late binding, however. Use type libraries and declare your objects with the New keyword when possible. Passing data across an OLE boundary has a significant cost, but you can reduce it by using early binding and transferring data in large chunks. Of course, total performance might not be an important goal; some clients could prefer an even flow of data instead of big chunks that take a long time to process.

the client. If you forget to set the executable as the compatible OLE server, the client IDE will ignore the server in the second IDE and instead will run the server in the executable file. You'll never hit any breakpoints in the server, no matter what you do.

Debugging servers can be messy at best. That's why you should debug your classes internally before you make them public. That's how I debugged the CSieve class. You aren't likely to encounter problems in the server class that haven't already shown up first in the local class.

CSieve has absolutely no need for the user interface that you see in the SieveServerEXE program. In fact, the user interface is displayed only when you load the program directly. When a client tries to use the CSieve class when SieveServerEXE isn't running, OLE loads the program for you. If you load the EXE program, the App.StartMode property will be *vbSModeStandalone*. If OLE starts the program, App.StartMode will be *vbSModeAutomation*. You can check this property to determine whether to display a user interface. Here's how SieveServerEXE does it in the Sub Main of SIEVESVR.BAS:

```
Sub Main()
    If App.StartMode = vbSModeStandalone Then
        Dim frm As New FSieveServer
        Load frm
    End If
End Sub
```

If OLE loaded the program for you, it will automatically unload the program when all clients that are using the program have terminated. This works only if the server has no forms loaded, which is one reason the Sieve server loads its form only in Standalone mode. If you want the user interface to appear when you debug the program, you should set StartMode to Standalone on the Project tab of the Options dialog box.

Server Strategies

OLE servers create some interesting new possibilities. The experience of Tough Guys Incorporated illustrates some of the extreme ones; you might prefer something a little less drastic.

When Visual Basic 4 hit the streets, Biff Bummer, vice-president of software development, laid down the law: "Don't write the same code twice while you're working for me. I want every program that comes out of this shop from here on out to be an OLE server. You're writing a calculator? Don't let me see anybody calculating the square root in the cmdSquare_Click handler of the Square Root button. No, you had better call the Square method of a CCalc object. We're not paying ten different people to write ten different calculators. We write one public calculator class for everybody, and everybody better use it."

This ultimatum was met with skepticism at first. But the policy was not without its supporters and successes. The official Calculator server was indeed written, and it was indeed used by all, despite some quiet grumbling about the pointlessness of using the Subtract method instead of the subtraction operator. Young Joe Hacker Jr. won praise for his complex Widgician application with its ten-level object hierarchy, starting with CWidget as the base class and working its way up to the NWonkers collection. No one denied that the hierarchy was far superior to calling the old Widgiterium program with its 50 command-line options.

But many programmers felt that the OLE server thing was going a little too far. There might just be some program somewhere that didn't need to share its functionality with the world. Sally Clockstein was leader of the opposition, and everyone knew she was a dangerous opponent. No one was surprised when Biff came to work one morning and found his empty office locked and his personal effects in boxes in the hall. Sally moved in the next day, and Biff's protégés started shopping their résumés.

A week later, Sally laid down the law: "Drawing forms isn't real programming, and we're not going to pay real programmers to do it. Components are the wave of the future. I want every Basic class you write to be a separate DLL server. If that means we dump 16-bit clients, so be it. We're sending ten of you to C++ boot camp next week to learn how to write controls, and the rest of you can forget you ever wrote a function that wasn't a method or a variable that wasn't a property. It's classes and servers from here on out. We've hired some high school students to come in after school and string your components together into applications."

This edict was met with the wild enthusiasm reserved for all such cultural revolutions. But gradually hard disks began to fill up with OLE servers, exposing classes such as CPlus, CMinus, and CEnthusiasm.

Every parable has its limits, and this one passed them some time ago. So let's cut to the moral: use OLE servers and object-oriented programming, but don't let them use you.

Redesigning Visual Basic

The add-in adventure ride at the beginning of this chapter was more exciting than enlightening. Let's take a slower look at add-ins. But let me warn you. The Visual Basic extensibility system is not simple, and the documentation and samples provided for it are...well, they're OK for the people they're designed for, but that's probably not you. Nevertheless, look at the payoff.

You can rewrite the Visual Basic environment. Does some feature of the IDE drive you crazy? Do you encounter it at least 100 times during a typical workday? Well, fix it. I'm not claiming that you can fix everything or add every imaginable feature. Some of the information you might need isn't easily available, but a determined programmer who understands low-level Windows programming can usually get around the limitations.

We'll start by looking at the VBIDE hierarchy and what it takes to hook it up to your add-in.

The VBIDE Hierarchy

Add-ins provide an example of something we haven't talked about much: an object hierarchy. The closest we've come are the interrelated menu classes described in "Other People's Menus," page 428. If you program an OLE server for Microsoft Excel, Microsoft Project, or most other large programs, you'll be dealing with an object hierarchy. (Microsoft Word 6 for Windows is an exception—it has a single WordBasic object with no hierarchy.) After you've written a few add-ins for Visual Basic, programming most other OLE hierarchies should be a snap.

The VBIDE hierarchy isn't really all that large compared to some others—Microsoft Excel's, for instance. But it is complicated, with many interactions between its classes and your classes. If I had to describe it in one word, I'd say *quirky*. That would be all right if the complications paid off with power. Unfortunately, the Visual Basic extensibility system is strangely limited by its original design goals. We'll talk a lot about those limitations and how to get around them. For now, however, take an initial look at the hierarchy, shown in Figure 10-8 on the following two pages.

If you study Figure 10-8 for a few moments, patterns begin to emerge. For example, every object in the hierarchy has a Parent property and an Application property. This lets you traverse the hierarchy easily. For example, if you are working on a form Property object far down the ActiveProject branch of the hierarchy and you find that you need to uncheck a MenuLine object, how do you get over to the AddInMenu branch? Well, you can traverse up your branch to the top with the Parent property:

```
Parent.Parent.Parent.Parent.AddInMenu.MenuItems.Checked = False
```

But you're more likely to use the Application property to start at the top and go down:

```
Application.AddInMenu.MenuItems.Checked = False
```

Keep this in mind when you start building an add-in hierarchy to communicate with the VBIDE hierarchy.

Application As Application

- LoadProject
- FullName
- LastUsedPath
- ReadOnlyMode
- Version
- Name
- Application
- Parent
- FileControl
- ActiveProject
- AddInMenu

ActiveProject as ProjectTemplate

- AddFile
- AddFormTemplate
- AddMDIFormTemplate
- AddReference
- AddToolboxProgID
- AddToolboxTypelib
- AddToolboxVBX
- RemoveComponent
- ConnectEvents
- DisconnectEvents
- ReadProperty
- WriteProperty
- FileName
- IsDirty
- Application
- Parent
- ActiveForm
- Components
- SelectedComponents

AddInMenu As SubMenu

- Enabled
- Caption
- Application
- Parent
- MenuItems

MenuItems Collection

- Add
- AddMenu
- Remove
- Count
- Application
- Parent
- Item

SelectedComponents Collection

- Count
- Application
- Parent
- Item

Item As SubMenu

- Enabled
- Caption
- Application
- Parent
- MenuItems

Item As MenuLine

- Enabled
- Checked
- Caption
- ConnectEvents
- DisconnectEvents
- HelpContextID
- HelpFile
- Application
- Parent

Item As Component

- Reload
- InsertFile
- SaveAs
- FileNames
- FileCount
- Name
- IsDirty
- IconState
- Application
- Parent

Key

- Read-only object property
- Read-write object property
- Read-only variable property
- Read-write variable property
- Method function
- Method sub

486

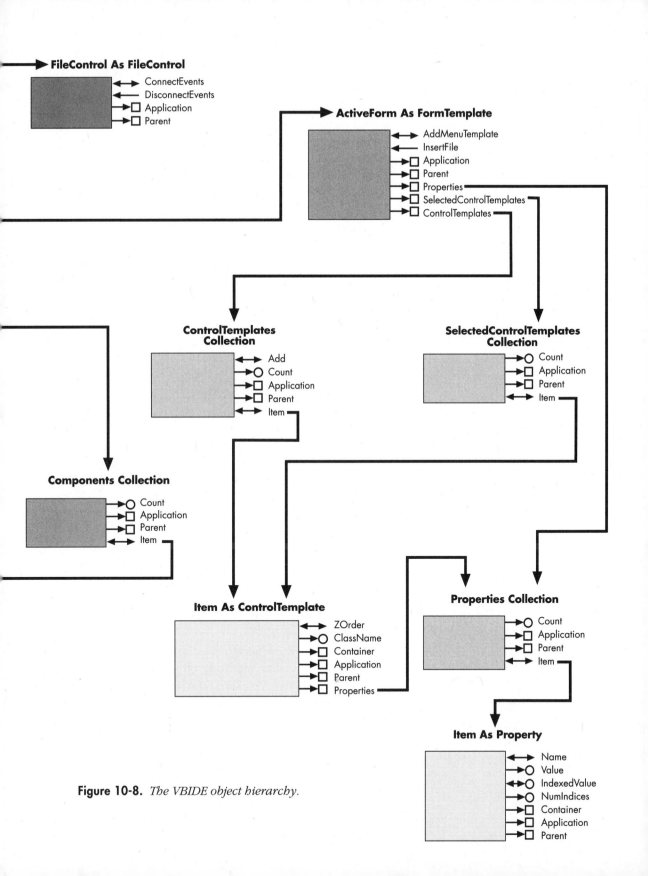

Figure 10-8. *The VBIDE object hierarchy.*

You will also notice lots of collections: the MenuItems collection, the Components and SelectedComponents collections, the ControlTemplates and SelectedControlTemplates collections, and the Properties collection. Each collection has a Count property and an Item method (always the default). If it makes sense to add items to the collection, it has an Add method. If it makes sense to remove items, it has a Remove method. Again, keep these lessons in mind for your own hierarchy.

Some objects in the hierarchy are associated with events. The MenuLine class is associated with menu events on the Add-Ins menu, the FileControl class is associated with file events, and the ProjectTemplate class is associated with the grayed-out source-control menu events on the Tools menu. These classes have ConnectEvents and DisconnectEvents methods that create a connection between user actions in the IDE (such as menu and toolbar button clicks) and event subs in add-in classes that you provide.

The VBIDE hierarchy presents an abstract picture that doesn't match up exactly with a real Visual Basic IDE. The hierarchy has add-in menus but lacks the rest of the menu structure, not to mention the toolbar or keyboard commands. It has projects and the various files that make up projects, but some of these files are better supported than others. For example, you can easily manipulate the controls and properties of forms through the hierarchy, but you can't get at class properties. File events such as loading and saving files are represented by the methods of the FileControl class, but other user events, such as compiling programs or clicking in the Properties window, don't have corresponding features in the hierarchy. Of course, just because something isn't directly represented in the hierarchy doesn't mean that you can't do it.

The BTOOLS Hierarchy

Once you figure out the VBIDE hierarchy, you need to design your own add-in hierarchy. The VBIDE hierarchy is "theirs." It exists in a program that is completely different from your add-in's program or DLL. If you don't like their hierarchy, tough. But you can make your own hierarchy that "fixes" some of the problems in theirs and provides logical access to the services you need on your side of the interaction.

The BTOOLS hierarchy is my version of an add-in hierarchy. Its command-based design separates commands from the methods of invoking them. It comes with a Customize dialog box that makes it easy to reassign internal and external commands to different menu items, toolbar buttons, or keystrokes.

Figure 10-9 shows the Commands tab of the Customize dialog box, where you define external commands to enhance the environment. Does this look familiar? A bit like the customization feature of every substantial MS-DOS program

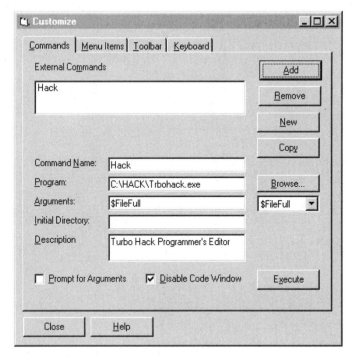

Figure 10-9. *The Commands tab of the Customize dialog box.*

that has appeared on the market for the past 10 years? Is this feature built into every programmer's editor you've ever seen, except one? Are you one of those with limited customization needs who would gladly trade the whole complex add-in model for this dialog box? Well, now you have it. But don't skip the rest of the chapter, because you still have some work to do in order to make the dialog box fully customizable.

Figure 10-10 on the next page shows the Menu Items tab, where you assign commands to menu items on the Add-Ins menu. You can assign the external commands defined on the Commands tab or internal commands defined (and properly registered) in code. You can guess what the Toolbar and Keyboard tabs are for, but don't get excited. If you click them, you'll see the words most dreaded by readers of programming books: "Left as an exercise for the reader..."

Behind the Customize dialog box lurks the somewhat complex BTOOLS hierarchy, shown in Figure 10-11 on pages 492 and 493. At the top is the Add-In Manager. Just as every node in the VBIDE hierarchy has an Application property and a Parent property, the nodes of BTOOLS have a Manager property and a Parent property. In addition, BTOOLS nodes have an Application property for easy sideways access to the other hierarchy.

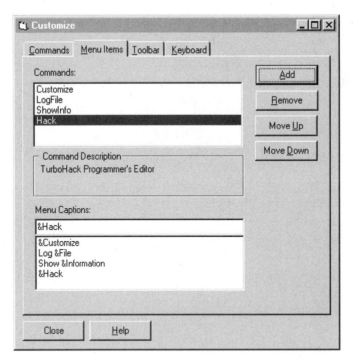

Figure 10-10. *The Menu Items tab of the Customize dialog box.*

The Commands node is the most important node below the Manager in the BTOOLS hierarchy. It is a collection of internal and external commands. You place the commands you define in code either directly in this module or in child nodes of the Commands module. The Commands node also manages external commands defined by the Commands tab of the Customize form. Although external and internal commands are defined differently, they can be executed or assigned to menu items in the same way. You can call a command from anywhere in the hierarchy by looking up its name in the Commands collection and calling the Commands.Execute method.

The other second-level nodes manage the events that can call commands. The FileHandler object manages all the file events supported by the VBIDE. By default, the file event handlers simply log information about the event, but you can add code for other actions. The MenuItems collection contains the items you have added to the Add-Ins menu. Each item is an object that contains all the properties needed to look up the associated commands. The SourceItems, Keys, and ToolButtons collections, should you decide to implement them, would work in much the same way as the MenuItems collection. SourceItems would be tied to the grayed Get, Check Out, Check In, and Undo Check Out items on the Tools menu. The ToolButtons and Keys collections would be tied to your toolbar and keystroke implementations. You'll find out how this works when we discuss the MenuItems collection.

Of course, the BTOOLS hierarchy is not the only way to write add-ins. The sample add-ins that come with Visual Basic assume a model of many small add-ins with limited functionality, installed separately. My hierarchy assumes a more complex system of multiple commands within a single add-in. But even if you prefer the model of multiple small add-ins, the BTOOLS hierarchy can teach you many important techniques that you can use on a smaller scale.

Anatomy of an Add-In

Every add-in you write must make a two-way connection between the external VBIDE hierarchy and its internal object hierarchy. The add-in passes information about its objects and classes to VBIDE, and VBIDE passes the base of its hierarchy to the add-in. There's not much room for creativity in making this connection, but you have to wade through the boring details before you can start having fun.

Here are the elements that an add-in uses to make its connections:

- An initial startup code module to register the classes of the add-in so that they can be used by any VBIDE that happens along.

- An add-in manager class that knows how to respond to IDE requests for add-in services. An object of this class receives information from the IDE and uses it to connect event handler objects so that they will be activated when events happen in the IDE. It also disconnects the same event handlers when the IDE terminates or closes the add-in. In other words, the add-in manager is a bit like AUTOEXEC.BAT. Anything that needs to be done only once should be put here. I also use the Manager object as the base of my hierarchy.

- Event handler classes to respond to menu and file events in the IDE. Not every add-in needs every type of event handler. An add-in might have no menu items, or it might ignore file events. VBIDE recognizes three kinds of events: Add-In Menu events, Tool Menu events (only for the normally grayed source-control items), and file events caused by certain commands that modify files. You could add other event classes that handle other events, such as toolbar or key events. Somehow or other, directly or indirectly, your add-in needs to respond to user actions.

- Work modules to massage forms, modules, classes, and various other IDE elements.

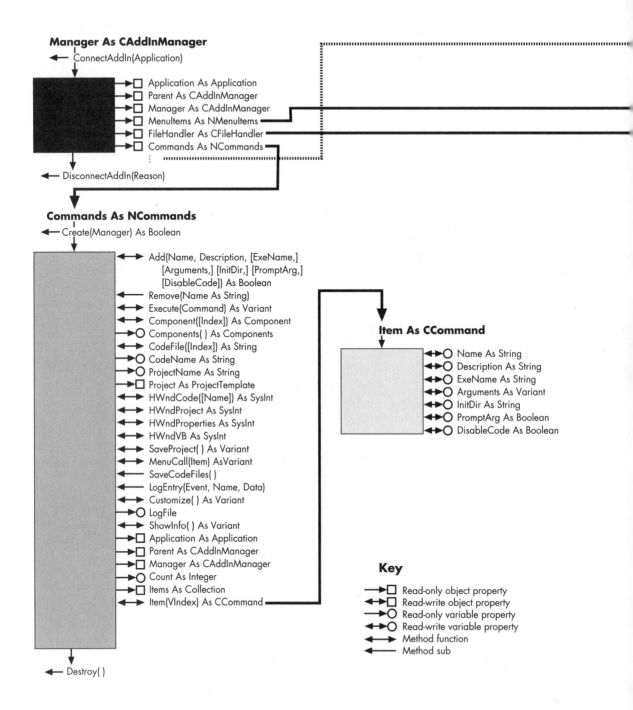

Manager As CAddInManager

← ConnectAddIn(Application)

→☐ Application As Application
→☐ Parent As CAddInManager
→☐ Manager As CAddInManager
→☐ MenuItems As NMenuItems
→☐ FileHandler As CFileHandler
→☐ Commands As NCommands

← DisconnectAddIn(Reason)

Commands As NCommands

← Create(Manager) As Boolean

↔ Add(Name, Description, [ExeName,]
    [Arguments,] [InitDir,] [PromptArg,]
    [DisableCode]) As Boolean
← Remove(Name As String)
↔ Execute(Command) As Variant
↔ Component([Index]) As Component
→O Components( ) As Components
↔ CodeFile([Index]) As String
→O CodeName As String
→O ProjectName As String
→☐ Project As ProjectTemplate
↔ HWndCode([Name]) As SysInt
↔ HWndProject As SysInt
↔ HWndProperties As SysInt
↔ HWndVB As SysInt
↔ SaveProject( ) As Variant
↔ MenuCall(Item) AsVariant
← SaveCodeFiles( )
← LogEntry(Event, Name, Data)
↔ Customize( ) As Variant
→O LogFile
↔ ShowInfo( ) As Variant
→☐ Application As Application
→☐ Parent As CAddInManager
→☐ Manager As CAddInManager
→O Count As Integer
→☐ Items As Collection
↔ Item(VIndex) As CCommand

← Destroy( )

Item As CCommand

↔O Name As String
↔O Description As String
↔O ExeName As String
↔O Arguments As Variant
↔O InitDir As String
↔O PromptArg As Boolean
↔O DisableCode As Boolean

Key

→☐ Read-only object property
↔☐ Read-write object property
→O Read-only variable property
↔O Read-write variable property
↔ Method function
← Method sub

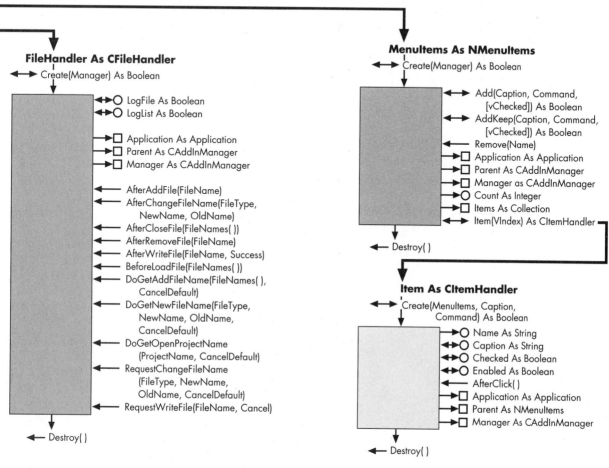

Add your SourceItems, Keys, and ToolButtons objects here

FileHandler As CFileHandler

Create(Manager) As Boolean

- LogFile As Boolean
- LogList As Boolean

- Application As Application
- Parent As CAddInManager
- Manager As CAddInManager

- AfterAddFile(FileName)
- AfterChangeFileName(FileType, NewName, OldName)
- AfterCloseFile(FileNames( ))
- AfterRemoveFile(FileName)
- AfterWriteFile(FileName, Success)
- BeforeLoadFile(FileNames( ))
- DoGetAddFileName(FileNames( ), CancelDefault)
- DoGetNewFileName(FileType, NewName, OldName, CancelDefault)
- DoGetOpenProjectName (ProjectName, CancelDefault)
- RequestChangeFileName (FileType, NewName, OldName, CancelDefault)
- RequestWriteFile(FileName, Cancel)

- Destroy( )

MenuItems As NMenuItems

Create(Manager) As Boolean

- Add(Caption, Command, [vChecked]) As Boolean
- AddKeep(Caption, Command, [vChecked]) As Boolean
- Remove(Name)
- Application As Application
- Parent As CAddInManager
- Manager as CAddInManager
- Count As Integer
- Items As Collection
- Item(VIndex) As CItemHandler

- Destroy( )

Item As CItemHandler

Create(MenuItems, Caption, Command) As Boolean

- Name As String
- Caption As String
- Checked As Boolean
- Enabled As Boolean
- AfterClick( )
- Application As Application
- Parent As NMenuItems
- Manager As CAddInManager

- Destroy( )

Figure 10-11. *The BTOOLS object hierarchy.*

The add-in startup module

Every program, OLE server or not, must have a startup module, and add-ins are no exception. Normally, the startup module for an add-in should be a code module with a Sub Main. I give mine the same base name as the project (for example, BTOOLS.BAS). Perhaps you can think of a reason to use a startup form, but generally the startup module has a very specific and limited task. When it finishes, it steps aside to wait for an IDE startup event.

Here's the code I put in my startup module:

```
Sub Main()
    If Not RegisterAddIn("BasicTools.CAddInManager") Then
        MsgBox "Can't register Add-In"
    End If
End Sub
```

The add-in must register itself by writing the name of its project and its add-in manager class to VB.INI. Visual Basic should provide the RegisterAddIn function, but it doesn't. All programmers must write the same code to register their add-ins. I place RegisterAddIn in a separate module called ADINTOOL.BAS, along with other general procedures useful in any add-in. Here's the code:

```
Function RegisterAddIn(sAddIn As String) As Boolean
    Dim s As String, f As Boolean
#If Win32 Then
    Const sSection = "Add-Ins32"
#Else
    Const sSection = "Add-Ins16"
#End If
    Const sIni = "VB.INI": Const cMax = 80

    ' Register add-in in VB.INI if it's not already registered
    s = String$(cMax + 1, 0)
    f = GetPrivateProfileString(sSection, sAddIn, _
                                sEmpty, s, cMax, sIni)
    If Not f Then
        f = WritePrivateProfileString(sSection, sAddIn, "0", sIni)
    End If
    RegisterAddIn = f
End Function
```

Technically, this function is capable of failing, but I can't think of a scenario in which it would.

That leaves the question of why you're writing to VB.INI. Well, you have to write the data someplace, and in a format known both to the add-in and to the IDE. Both parties know about VB.INI, so by convention the add-in writes the data there, and the IDE reads it from there. The project name must be the one entered in the Project Name field on the Project tab of the Options dialog box. The class must be the one you create to connect the add-in to the IDE. In my convention, this is the Manager object I put at the top of my hierarchy.

I also use the startup module for global definitions that are needed throughout the add-in. Most important, I assign a string constant to each internal command and menu item:

```
Public Const sItemCustomize = "&Customize"
Public Const sItemLogFile = "Log &File"
Public Const sItemShowInfo = "Show &Information"

Public Const sCmdCustomize = "Customize"
Public Const sCmdLogFile = "LogFile"
Public Const sCmdShowInfo = "ShowInfo"
```

If I had toolbar or keyboard handlers, I'd also put a string name for each internal entry here. (I'm talking about internal commands only. User-defined commands and menu items are entered in the Customize dialog box and saved in settings between invocations of the add-in.)

You might be tempted to put some global variables in this module. Don't do it. If you load more than one copy of the IDE, the global variables of the first copy will overwrite the variables of the second. You have only one add-in, no matter how many copies of the IDE you run. That's why every node in the hierarchy needs its own Application property; they might not all point to the same IDE. Of course, you don't need to worry about one instance stepping on another's constants, so put as many constants here as you like.

The startup module can also contain any functional procedures that are used only by this particular add-in. Notice the difference between BTOOLS.BAS, which can be used for anything that is shared by any of the modules of the BTOOLS project, and ADINTOOL.BAS, which contains routines that might be of value to any add-in.

The add-in manager class

The startup module connects the add-in to any instance of the IDE by writing its project and class names to VB.INI. The IDE reads VB.INI to get the names and adds them to its list in the Add-In Manager dialog box. When a user selects the add-in in the dialog box, the IDE must connect itself to the add-in. The communication is two-way. The add-in connects to any IDE, but the IDE must pass instance-specific information back to the add-in.

The add-in establishes this communication by creating an object of the class it gets from VB.INI. If the IDE were written in Basic, the code might look like this:

```
' Create add-in reference object
Dim raddin As Object
Set raddin = CreateObject(sClass)   ' Project.Class from VB.INI
' Call its ConnectAddIn method
raddin.ConnectAddIn Me
```

But what exactly is this connector class that the add-in creates and the IDE uses? Very simply, it's any class that

- has a ConnectAddIn sub with an Application argument

- has a DisconnectAddIn sub with an Integer argument

- is registered by name in VB.INI, as shown earlier in the RegisterAddIn function

In order to be useful, the add-in manager class should define ConnectAddIn and DisconnectAddIn to perform certain tasks that we'll talk about in a minute. But the IDE doesn't really care. All it knows is that it will call ConnectAddIn and pass it an Application object argument when the user tells it to start. When the user tells it to quit, it will call DisconnectAddIn with an ordinal code indicating the reason. In other words, you've got a case of late-bound polymorphism. It's late-bound because the IDE doesn't know the name of the class it needs to create until it reads the name from VB.INI.

Polymorphic or not, if the ConnectAddIn method you provide in your manager class doesn't do certain things, your add-in won't be very useful. My manager class is a little different from the ones in the sample add-ins provided with Visual Basic because it doesn't do the necessary work itself. Instead, it creates the hierarchy discussed earlier and delegates the event connections to member classes.

Here are the properties of the CAddInManager class:

```
' IDE instance
Private rap As Application

' All commands known to add-in
Public Commands As New NCommands
' File event handler and handle
Public FileHandler As New CFileHandler
' Collections relating commands to ways of invoking commands
Public MenuItems As New NMenuItems
' Add KeystrokeItems and ToolbarItems here
```

The public members just happen to be the same properties shown in the hierarchy map in Figure 10-11, on pages 492 and 493. The private member *rap* is actually the Application property, but since it's supposed to be read-only, a Property Get statement protects it from being modified.

The ConnectAddIn method simply initializes all these properties:

```
Public Sub ConnectAddIn(rapA As Application)
    Set rap = rapA

    ' Create initializes internal commands
    If Not Commands.Create(Me) Then GoTo Fail

    ' Inform IDE of file event handler, and get receipt
    If Not FileHandler.Create(Me) Then GoTo Fail

    ' Initialize MenuItems collection
    If Not MenuItems.Create(Me) Then GoTo Fail

    ' Initialize hard-coded menu items (ignore fail)
    Call MenuItems.Add(sItemCustomize, sCmdCustomize)
    Call MenuItems.Add(sItemLogFile, sCmdLogFile, Commands.LogFile)
    Call MenuItems.Add(sItemShowInfo, sCmdShowInfo)

    ' Do same with keys and toolbars

    ' Report connection as event
    Commands.LogEntry "Connect: ", "Program", rap.FullName
    Exit Sub
Fail:
    On Error Resume Next
    DisconnectAddIn vbextAddInRemoveFail
    MsgBox "Could not connect add-in"
End Sub
```

The key part of this sub is the first line, which assigns the application instance object *rapA*, passed from the IDE, to an internal variable *rap*. This variable will be passed down to every other object in the hierarchy. It's available in the Manager object through the following Property Get procedure:

```
Property Get Application() As Application
    Set Application = rap
End Property
```

The rest of the class initializes the first-level objects of the property using Create methods. These Create methods do the actual work of building the hierarchy and connecting the IDE events to the hierarchy. You'll see just how they work in a moment. First, let's look briefly at DisconnectAddIn, which is essentially ConnectAddIn, only backward:

```
Public Sub DisconnectAddIn(ordReason As Integer)

    ' Log disconnect
    Commands.LogEntry "Disconnect: ", "Reason", _
        Switch(ordReason = vbextAddInRemoveExit, _
            "Visual Basic IDE closing", _
            ordReason = vbextAddInRemoveUser, _
            "Unchecked in AddIn Manager", _
            ordReason = vbextAddInRemoveFail, "Connect failed")

    ' Clean up hierarchy objects
    MenuItems.Destroy
    FileHandler.Destroy
    Commands.Destroy

End Sub
```

Debugging Add-Ins

Debugging add-ins is so obvious that no one tells you how to do it. But you can't complain because...well, why'd you put those bugs in there anyway?

Actually, it's a lot like debugging any other OLE server except that you have direct access to only one side of a two-way transfer. Sometimes you're the client; sometimes you're the server. Here's what you do, step by step:

1. Load your add-in project into Visual Basic. We'll call this IDE the sister IDE.

2. Run it. Nothing happens. That's because nothing's connected to the add-in.

3. Run another copy of Visual Basic. We'll call this IDE the brother. (It's not a parent-child relationship, but definitely closer than just friends.)

4. In the brother IDE, choose Add-In Manager from the Add-Ins menu. If you remembered step 2, you'll see your add-in listed. Select its check box, and close the dialog box. If you forgot to run your add-in, you'll see zip. Your add-in won't be registered in VB.INI, and you'll have to shut down the brother IDE and start over.

5. Now you can play with any commands your add-in put on the menus or installed in file event handlers of the brother IDE.

To the IDE calling them, ConnectAddIn and DisconnectAddIn are methods; but to the CAddInManager class object that receives them, they are events. An event is simply a method that you define but somebody else calls. This is how a control works. The control calls methods, but the form owning the control sees events. In fact, you can think of the Visual Basic IDE as one big control designed specifically for add-ins.

Although you've seen the manager class, you still don't know much about how add-ins work, because everything is hidden in the Create, Add, and Destroy methods of the second-level objects. Let's examine some of those.

The FileHandler object

The CFileHandler class, like many hierarchy classes, has only one object: File-Handler. Its primary role is to manage standard file events. The BTOOLS version of FileHandler just logs these events in a handsome format and writes the text to a log file or the Debug window. FileHandler's secondary purpose is to let other objects in the hierarchy log events to the same destination. Its tertiary purpose is to be a standard member of the hierarchy and provide the standard properties you'll come to know well—Application, Parent, and Manager.

---

6. Go back to the sister IDE and pause by clicking Break on the Run menu or the Break toolbar button. (Don't choose End, whatever you do.) Set breakpoints in your add-in at key places that you want to examine. Run again.

7. Go back to the brother IDE and take an action that will cause the execution to hit a breakpoint. For example, select an item from the Add-In menu or save a file.

8. Go back to the sister IDE and step through your code. Remove all bugs. This might take a few iterations of steps 2 through 7. You should also periodically shut down both IDEs and save changes. It's tempting to fix bugs while the code is running, but keep in mind that a lot can go wrong in an interaction this complex.

9. Terminate the brother IDE, or disable your add-in in the Add-In Manager dialog box.

10. Terminate the add-in in the sister IDE. If you made changes while executing the add-in, be sure to save them now.

The process of debugging an add-in won't always go so smoothly. You can't debug add-in classes locally before connecting them, as you can with most server classes. You'll also get tired of the exact sequence of starting the two IDEs. The whole process, in fact, can be tedious.

It all starts with the Create method. Let's review how Create was called:

```
If Not FileHandler.Create(Me) Then GoTo Fail
```

The parent class passes itself to the child, which receives it as shown here:

```
Function Create(rmanA As CAddInManager) As Boolean
    On Error GoTo CreateFail
    Set rman = rmanA
    Set rap = rman.Application
    hConnect = rap.Application.FileControl.ConnectEvents(Me)
    If hConnect Then Create = True
CreateFail:
End Function
```

Create sets its internal copies of the Manager and Application objects, which look like this:

```
Private hConnect As Long
Private rman As CAddInManager
Private rap As Application
```

The standard linking objects are made available (read-only) to other parts of the hierarchy by the following properties:

```
Property Get Application() As Application
    Set Application = rap
End Property

Property Get Parent() As CAddInManager
    Set Parent = rman
End Property

Property Get Manager() As CAddInManager
    Set Manager = rman
End Property
```

Every object in the hierarchy has the same properties, which always work the same way (except that each object has a different parent).

The important task is connecting this class to the IDE so that when a file event happens on that other side, the IDE knows where to send the corresponding method. More polymorphism. The FileHandler object passes itself to the IDE's FileControl object via the ConnectEvents method:

```
hConnect = rap.Application.FileControl.ConnectEvents(Me)
```

The ConnectEvents method passes back a receipt in the form of a handle, which you save internally for disconnection. Now that the IDE has the File-Handler object, it can call the standard file event methods. It's your job to see that the FileControl object actually has those methods and that they have the arguments expected by the IDE.

For example, here's a BeforeLoadFile event handler:

```
Public Sub BeforeLoadFile(FileNames() As String)
    Dim iLo As Integer, iHi As Integer, i As Integer
    iLo = LBound(FileNames): iHi = UBound(FileNames)
    LogEntry "BeforeLoadFile:", "FileNames(" & iLo & ")", _
            FileNames(iLo)
    For i = iLo + 1 To iHi
        LogEntry sEmpty, "FileNames(" & i & ")", FileNames(i)
    Next
    ' Put your event code here
End Sub
```

If you've seen one file event, you've seen them all. Check out the others in FILEHAND.CLS.

The IDE keeps sending events down the pike whenever the user does something to a file. The add-in can check what has already happened with some events and can preview and possibly cancel what is about to happen with others.

The LogEntry method formats three string arguments and writes them to the destination that seems appropriate, based on log settings. You can look it up in FILEHAND.CLS. The log output from BeforeLoadFile might look like this:

```
BeforeLoadFile:            FileNames(0)    = UTILITY.BAS
                           FileNames(1)    = DOMENU.BAS
                           FileNames(2)    = RUNMENU.BAS
                           FileNames(3)    = DEBUG.BAS
                           FileNames(4)    = WINTOOL.BAS
                           FileNames(5)    = PARSE.BAS
```

This method is public so that any other object can log an event to the same destination in the same format. You might have noticed that the ConnectAddIn and DisconnectAddIn methods announce themselves using this mechanism.

For the FileHandler object, everything ends with the Destroy method:

```
Sub Destroy()
    On Error Resume Next
    rap.Application.FileControl.DisconnectEvents hConnect
End Sub
```

It simply calls the IDE's DisconnectEvents function, passing it the handle saved by the Create method. Destroy turns off error handling because if the parent is destroying itself as the result of an error, DisconnectEvents might fail, but you don't want it to fail with an error message box. Destroy must always succeed, even if it fails.

To make your file event handlers do additional work besides logging, you have several alternatives:

■ Hard-code the additional behavior into the appropriate file handler method in FILEHAND.CLS.

■ Define a new command for the Commands collection, and call Commands.Execute from the event handler to do the work. I'll explain how later. This is a more flexible approach because the new command can also be called from a menu, a toolbar button, or any other event.

■ Add a collection of commands for each file control event. When an event is called, iterate through its collection, calling each command. You can implement a tab on the Customize form to add commands for each file event. Rather then modifying FILEHAND.CLS, you are simply adding commands to one location, the Commands collection.

> **NOTE** In most object-oriented languages, you wouldn't make up file event methods out of thin air. You would inherit them from a provided FileControl class, which ensures that the methods have the correct names and arguments. You would still have to implement the behavior of the file event methods.

The MenuItems collection

In addition to file events, add-ins know about menu events of two varieties: the dynamic menu items you add to the Add-Ins menu, and the static items on the Tools menu (normally grayed), to which you can attach source-control events. If you understand the dynamic ones, the static ones should be easy, so I'll deal with dynamic menus only.

Menu items are added and handled through the AddInMenu branch of the VBIDE hierarchy. (See Figure 10-8 on pages 486 and 487.) You tell the IDE the captions of the menu items to put on the Add-Ins menu. You also tell the IDE what to do when a user clicks a menu item. You do this by connecting a menu handler class to deal with menu events (just as you connect a file handler class to deal with file events). When a user clicks a dynamic menu item, the IDE sends an AfterClick method to the class that has been connected to receive event menus. So make sure that your connected class has an AfterClick method.

The BTOOLS add-in provides a MenuItems collection that hides a lot of the messy details of adding and handling menus. We'll look at these details now, but if you reuse the BTOOLS architecture, you can work at a higher level. The MenuItems object works like a collection, but its type NMenuItems is just a class that stores menu items in an internal collection. Like any self-respecting collection class, NMenuItems has Add, Remove, and Item methods as well as a Count property. These members protect access to the internal collection. "The NDrives Collection," page 185, describes the collection class technique and its limitations: Item can't be defined as the default member, and you can't use For Each to iterate through the collection unless you're willing to expose your supposedly hidden collection through an Items method. You'll have to put up with these limitations because NMenuItems needs to intercept and modify calls to the Add and Remove methods before passing them to the internal collection.

The code path for adding, executing, and removing a menu item is long and somewhat torturous. Let's take a brief tour of a simple hard-coded command, starting in the ConnectAddIn sub (ADDINMAN.CLS). We'll skip over Menu-Items.Create, which just sets up the standard hierarchy properties, and go directly to the Add method:

```
Call MenuItems.Add(sItemCustomize, sCmdCustomize)
```

The Add method of MenuItems can pass three pieces of information: the name of the command to be executed by the menu, the caption of the menu, and, optionally, the checked state of the menu (omitted here). The string constants defined in BTOOLS.BAS give the menu caption "&Customize" and the command name "Customize". Although the Customize menu item is added in the ConnectAddIn sub, you could add a menu item from anywhere. Most other menu items are added through the Menu Items tab of the Customize dialog box, but if you want to add a menu item in a file event, who's to stop you?

The next step is the Add method of the MenuItems collection:

```
Function Add(sCaption As String, sCmd As String, _
            Optional vChecked As Variant) As Boolean
    Dim ritem As CItemHandler, f As Boolean
    On Error GoTo AddFail
    ' Create menu handler object
    Set ritem = New CItemHandler
    If IsMissing(vChecked) Then vChecked = False
    f = ritem.Create(Me, sCaption, sCmd, vChecked)
    If f = False Then GoTo AddFail
    ' Put in collection indexed by command name
    menus.Add ritem, sCmd
    Add = True
AddFail:
End Function
```

You first create a new CItemHandler object and then add it to the internal *menus* collection. The collection is indexed not by the menu caption, as you might expect, but by the name of the command associated with it. Later you'll use this indexing to look up and execute the commands. The MenuItems collection also has an AddKeep method that calls the Add method and then stores the item with the SaveSetting statement. You can call Add to add internal menu commands, and you can call AddKeep to add dynamic menu commands requested by the user.

Now let's see how item handlers are created. Here are the internal members of CItemHandler (ITEMHAND.CLS), followed by its Create method:

```
Private ritems As NMenuItems
Private rman As CAddInManager
Private rap As Application
Private rline As MenuLine
Private sName As String
Private hConnect As Long

Function Create(ritemsA As NMenuItems, _
                sCaption As String, sCmd As String, _
                Optional vChecked As Variant) As Boolean
    On Error GoTo CreateFail
    Set ritems = ritemsA
    Set rman = ritems.Manager
    Set rap = ritems.Application
    ' Add menu text to VBIDE Add-Ins menu
    Set rline = rap.AddInMenu.MenuItems.Add(sCaption)
    ' Connect menu line
    hConnect = rline.ConnectEvents(Me)
    sName = sCmd
    Caption = sCaption
    If Not IsMissing(vChecked) Then Checked = vChecked
    Create = True
CreateFail:
End Function
```

You already know how the standard properties work, so let's skip to the line that adds the menu caption to the MenuItems collection of the AddInMenu object of the Application object. The Add method returns a MenuLine object. Refer back to Figure 10-8, pages 486 and 487, to see where MenuLine fits in the VBIDE hierarchy. You call the ConnectEvents method of this object to connect the current CItemHandler class to the menu line. This tells the IDE where to send menu events when it receives them from the user. The IDE returns a handle as a receipt, and you save it for later disconnection. You also save the name and the caption for easy access through a read-only Name property and a read-write Caption property.

Now when a user clicks the menu line, the IDE calls an AfterClick method on the registered class. You see it here as an AfterClick event, which looks like this:

```
Public Sub AfterClick()
    With rman.Commands
        .Execute .Item(sName)
    End With
End Sub
```

This code looks up the command name of the menu item in the Commands collection and passes it to an Execute method. (This will make more sense after we discuss the Commands collection.)

Let's briefly go through the destruction process, starting with DisconnectAddIn (ADDINMAN.CLS). It removes all the menu items with the following code:

```
MenuItems.Destroy
```

The Destroy method looks like this:

```
Sub Destroy()
    On Error Resume Next
    Dim v As Variant
    For Each v In menus
        ' Remove from menu collection
        Remove v.Name, vKeep:=True
    Next
End Sub
```

Of course, you can also remove a specific menu item from anywhere—such as the Menu Items tab of the Customize dialog box—as long as you know its name. Notice that the Destroy method passes True to the *vKeep* parameter to indicate that dynamic menu items should not be removed from the permanent settings. When the user requests removal of a dynamic menu item, you pass False so that the item will be permanently removed. You can see how this works in the Remove method of the MenuItems collection:

```
Sub Remove(sName As String, Optional vKeep As Variant)
    ' Disconnect and remove from IDE menu
    menus.Item(sName).Destroy
    ' Remove from internal collection
    menus.Remove sName
    If IsMissing(vKeep) Then vKeep = False
    ' Unregister
    If Not vKeep Then
        DeleteSetting App.ExeName, sMenuSection, sName
    End If
End Sub
```

Just one more step: the Destroy method of the menu item.

```
Sub Destroy()
    On Error Resume Next
    ' Disconnect event
    rline.DisconnectEvents hConnect
    ' Remove from parent menu
    rline.Parent.Remove rline
End Sub
```

This code finally disconnects the menu item from the IDE and removes it from the IDE Add-Ins menu.

If your head is spinning, keep in mind that add-in menus need not be so complicated. Check out the ALIGN sample that comes with Visual Basic. It provides a simple class that installs each menu item. The complication in the BTOOLS add-in comes from allowing a single item handler class to handle multiple items that might not be fully defined until run time. The advantage of this more complicated system is that once you write it, you never have to mess with it again. You can add new menu items whenever you want by calling the Add method of the MenuItems collection. The dynamic Commands collection is what makes all this possible.

CHALLENGE   My MenuItems collection doesn't deal with nested menus. The VBIDE hierarchy supports submenus, and you might want to use them if the Add-Ins menu starts filling up. It's simply a matter of adding a ParentMenu property to CItemHandler and teaching the Create method how to add submenus with items on them.

The Commands collection

The heart of my add-in strategy is the Commands collection. Unlike the MenuItems collection and the FileHandler object, the Commands collection has no connection to VBIDE. It's simply my way of making commands dynamic and assignable to any user event.

Let's start at the bottom and work our way up as we did for the MenuItems collection. The Commands collection can contain two kinds of commands: internal commands such as Customize and Show Information, which you define in code; and external commands, which call external programs to do the work.

Internal commands are initialized by the Create method. You call Create in the CAddInManager class as shown here:

```
If Not Commands.Create(Me) Then GoTo Fail
```

Like all Create methods in my hierarchy, it passes the current object so that the child will have a way to refer back to its parent.

The Create method looks like this:

```
Function Create(rmanA As CAddInManager) As Boolean
    On Error GoTo CreateFail
    Set rman = rmanA
    Set rap = rman.Application

    ' Initialize internal commands here
    If Not Add(sCmdCustomize, _
          "Display Customize dialog box") Then GoTo CreateFail
    If Not Add(sCmdLogFile, _
          "Write IDE events to a log file") Then GoTo CreateFail
    If Not Add(sCmdShowInfo, _
          "Display current state of the IDE") Then GoTo CreateFail

    ' Initialize commands from settings
    If Not AddSettings Then GoTo CreateFail

    ' Restore last LogFile setting
    fLogFile = GetSetting(App.ExeName, sCmdLogFile, sValue, False)

    Create = True
CreateFail:
End Function
```

Create starts by initializing the standard hierarchy properties. Then it initializes internal commands by setting their properties and adding them to an internal commands collection with an Add method. Finally, it initializes commands by calling the AddSettings function and restores the state of the LogFile property (which controls whether the Log File menu item is checked).

NOTE   The new settings statements (SaveSetting, DeleteSetting, GetSetting, and GetAllSettings) get a workout in the BTOOLS project. Check them out in CMDS.CLS and MNUITEMS.CLS. These might not be the most intuitive statements in Basic (particularly the unique syntax of GetAllSettings), but they sure beat the API alternative of using profile functions in 16-bit mode and Registry functions in 32-bit mode.

Every time you write a new internal command, you need to add it to the Create method. This points out a major difference between the NCommands class and other classes in the hierarchy: NCommands is designed to be modified, to continue growing as you think up new add-in commands. Other classes can be modified if you want to improve or fix the hierarchy, but they are designed to be used as they are.

The Add method allows you to add a command from anywhere, not only from inside the Create method. The code looks like this:

```
Function Add(sName As String, _
             sDescription As String, _
             Optional vExeName As Variant, _
             Optional vArguments As Variant, _
             Optional vInitDir As Variant, _
             Optional vPromptArg As Variant, _
             Optional vDisableCode As Variant) As Boolean

    Dim rcmd As CCommand
    On Error GoTo AddFail
    Set rcmd = New CCommand
    With rcmd
        .Name = sName
        .Description = sDescription
        If Not IsMissing(vExeName) Then .ExeName = vExeName
        If Not IsMissing(vArguments) Then .Arguments = vArguments
        If Not IsMissing(vInitDir) Then .InitDir = vInitDir
        If Not IsMissing(vPromptArg) Then .PromptArg = vPromptArg
        If Not IsMissing(vExeName) Then .DisableCode = vDisableCode
        cmds.Add rcmd, sName
        If .ExeName <> sEmpty Then
            ' Save external commands to Registry or INI file
            Serialize rcmd
        End If
    End With
    Add = True
AddFail:
End Function
```

The code creates a CCommand object, initializes its properties (if you passed the corresponding optional arguments), and adds it to the internal *cmds* collection. The CCommand class is a dumb class consisting of data only—no methods or property procedures. Here's the whole class:

```
Public Name As String
Public Description As String
Public ExeName As String
Public Arguments As Variant
```

```
Public InitDir As String
Public PromptArg As Boolean
Public DisableCode As Boolean
```

The key property is Name, which serves as the string index for the *cmds* collection. Commands should also have a description, which shows up on the Commands tab of the Customize dialog box. The ExeName property, which is used to test whether a given command is internal or external, must be empty for internal commands. The Arguments property is a Variant so that you can pass any data you like to an internal command. Most internal commands ignore this property; external commands always expect it to be a command-line string. The rest of the properties apply only to external commands.

Briefly, the Destroy and Remove methods clean out each command in the collection. If you define a new internal command that needs cleanup, you should put the destruction code in the Destroy method.

When you're ready to execute a command—either internal or external—call the Execute method, passing it a CCommand object. The object contains everything known by the caller and needed by the callee. Here's the half of Execute that handles internal commands:

```
Function Execute(rcmd As CCommand) As Variant
    If rcmd.ExeName = sEmpty Then
        ' Handle internal commands
        Select Case rcmd.Name
        Case sCmdCustomize
            Execute = Customize
        Case sCmdLogFile
            LogFile = Not LogFile
            Execute = True
        Case sCmdShowInfo
            Execute = ShowInfo
        Case Else
            BugAssert False
        End Select
    Else
        ' Handle external commands
    ⋮
```

The ExeName property identifies whether the command is internal or external. The Name property identifies the specific command. The sample commands don't use arguments, but the Arguments property could provide any information you wanted to pass. Since the return value is a Variant, it can pass back anything the callee wants to tell the caller.

Each branch of the Select Case block calls the method associated with the command. Here's an example of a command method:

```
Function ShowInfo() As Variant
    Dim info As New fInfo
    Static fLog As Boolean
    If info.Create(Me) = False Then Exit Function
    info.LogMode = fLog
    info.Show vbModal
    fLog = info.LogMode
    Unload info
    ShowInfo = True
End Function
```

This code shows a modal form that can display status information about the IDE object or a log of IDE file events. There's a lot of interesting code behind this dialog box. In particular, look at the GetInfo function (in ADINTOOL.BAS), which traverses the whole VBIDE hierarchy, writing out all the information it can find about the project. A command function can return anything that fits in a Variant (just about anything), but this one simply returns True or False.

So how is a command called? If it is an internal command and if the name is known at compile time, you can call its method by name:

```
Manager.Commands.ShowInfo
```

You could do this, for example, if you wanted to call a command from a file event handler method. Usually you won't know the method name until run time, but you'll be able to find it. Remember how a menu item calls a command:

```
Public Sub AfterClick()
    With rman.Commands
        .Execute .Item(sName)
    End With
End Sub
```

The menu item contains a copy of the command name, which it uses to look up the corresponding item in the Commands collection. You can call commands the same way from your ToolButtons and Keys classes once you write them.

Let's review the steps needed to add a new internal command:

1. Assign a unique name to the command, and make the constant globally available in BTOOLS.BAS.

2. Add the command name and description to the Commands class by calling the Add method from within the Create method of CMDS.CLS.

3. Direct the command to its command method from the Select Case block in the Execute method of CMDS.CLS.

4. Define the Command method next to the other internal methods at the bottom of CMDS.CLS.

Command helpers

The Commands collection is home to a herd of helper methods and properties designed to make it easier to define new commands. The helpers are not the kind of elements you would want to attach to a menu or a keystroke; many are shortcuts for methods and properties of the VBIDE hierarchy. You could type

```
Application.ActiveProject.SelectedComponents(0).FileNames(0)
```

but it's easier to type this shortcut:

```
CodeFile
```

Other helpers do real work, such as returning various IDE window handles and saving files.

The helpers are public so that you can access them from anywhere in the hierarchy through Manager.Commands, but generally you will use them from the Commands collection. Table 10-1 on the next page presents a summary.

As you work with add-ins, you'll probably want to add your own helper functions. Let's look briefly at one, the HWndCode helper. This function—which would be a read-only property if properties could use optional arguments—returns the window handle of an IDE code editing window. Once you have a window handle, you can do just about anything; the discussion in Chapter 5 only scratches the surface. That chapter also describes how to use FindWindow to find the handle of a window from its title and class name. Using the Win-Watch program from Chapter 5, you can see that IDE code windows have the class name VBCodeWin. Their title is always the name of the current module. Since the module name is stored in the IDE component object, it's a simple matter to convert to a handle:

```
Function HWndCode(Optional vName As Variant) As Long
    If IsMissing(vName) Then vName = CodeName
    HWndCode = FindWindow("VBCodeWin", vName)
End Function
```

Finding the names of the IDE Project, Properties, and main windows is almost as easy.

Helper	Description
Project	Shortcut for Applications.ActiveProject
Component([*index*])	A component indexed by class name, if *index* is given; otherwise, the current component
Components	The Components collection
CodeFile([*index*])	The current code file indexed by class name, if *index* is given; otherwise, the current code file
CodeName	The class name of the current code file
ProjectName	The project name
HWndCode([*index*])	The window handle of the indexed or current code window
HWndProject	The window handle of the Project window
HWndProperties	The window handle of the Properties window, if one is associated with a component
HWndVB	The window handle of the main Visual Basic window containing menus and toolbars
SaveCodeFiles	Saves each component file that has been modified since the last save
ExpandArgs	Expands a command line containing macros ($FileFull, $ProjectFull, and so on) into the associated filenames
LogEntry	Formats and writes event, name, and data strings to the current log file or the Debug window

Table 10-1. *The helper methods and properties of the Commands collection.*

External commands

External commands work the same way as internal commands, but with more properties. It could take a whole chapter to explain them, so for now we'll pick up coverage of this subject at the drive-through window. You can follow the action in Figure 10-9 on page 489.

Joe Hacker has just purchased TurboHack, the ultimate programmer's editor. It features thought macros that create bug-free, object-oriented, super-efficient Basic code at the click of a button. Joe loads Visual Basic and selects Customize from the Add-Ins menu. From the Commands tab, he clicks Browse and uses a common dialog to find TRBOHACK.EXE as his program.

To build a command-line argument, he clicks the combo box to the right of Arguments and selects $FileFull as the macro that represents the current code file. This macro will be expanded to the full pathname of the current CLS, FRM, or BAS file when the command is called at run time. Joe types *Hack* in the Command Name field but leaves the description blank—he knows what the command is without any stupid description. He clicks the Disable Code Window check box so that he can't accidentally edit the same file in Visual Basic and TurboHack at the same time. Finally he hits the Add button.

The Add button gathers all the information (see CUSTOM.FRM for details) and adds the new command to the Commands collection with this code:

```
Private Sub cmdToolAdd_Click()
    ' Improve validation here
    If Not Manager.Commands.Add(sName:=txtToolCommand, _
                                sDescription:=txtToolDescribe, _
                                vExeName:=txtToolProg, _
                                vArguments:=txtToolArgs, _
                                vInitDir:=txtToolInitDir, _
                                vPromptArg:=chkToolPrompt, _
                                vDisableCode:=chkToolDisable) Then
        MsgBox "Can't add command"
    Else
        lstToolCommand.AddItem txtToolCommand
    End If
    lblToolError = sEmpty
End Sub
```

The Add method serializes the settings for the new command so that they will be reinstalled the next time the add-in is loaded.

Joe skips over the Menu Items tab (he doesn't like menus) to the Keyboard tab (which he implemented the day after he bought this book) and assigns the Hack command to Ctrl+K. He hesitates for a minute but then moves to the Toolbar tab, where he adds a toolbar button and gives it a meat cleaver icon. Again, both the keyboard and toolbar settings are serialized for later use.

Ready to hack! Joe loads this very project (he's been implementing add-in commands to integrate a resource editor and resource compiler into Visual Basic), but instead of editing source in Visual Basic, he clicks the Hack button. His Toolbar control looks up the Hack command corresponding to the Hack button and then calls the Execute method of the Commands collection. You have already seen the internal commands branch of Execute. The external branch is somewhat more complex:

```
Else
    ' Handle external commands
    ' Execute won't work for "new" project with no filenames
    If GetFileExt(CodeFile) = sEmpty Then Exit Function
```

(continued)

```
' Resembles Save Project menu item, but doesn't save project file
SaveCodeFiles
Dim s As String, sName As String, sFile As String
' Handle arguments
If rcmd.PromptArg Then
    s = InputBox("Enter command-line arguments: ")
Else
    s = rcmd.Arguments
End If
s = ExpandArgs(s)

' Set properties
If rcmd.DisableCode Then EnableWindow HWndCode, False
Dim hProg ' As SysInt
hProg = Shell(rcmd.ExeName & sSpace & s, vbNormalFocus)
If rcmd.DisableCode Then
    Do While IsRunning(hProg)
        DoEvents
    Loop
    EnableWindow HWndCode, True
    Component.Reload
End If
End If
```

The code first saves all the dirty code files so that the file Joe edits will be in sync with the code in the IDE. It then gets the arguments, either from a dialog box or from a command line entered on the Commands tab. A command line can contain macros representing the files that are current at the time Execute is called. We won't look at ExpandArgs, but I will note that it uses the parsing procedures from Chapter 3.

If the DisableCode option was given (as it normally should be for any command that modifies code files), the Windows API EnableWindow function disables the code windows. (It will enable them again when the command has finished.) This prevents modifying both files at the same time, which would knock them out of sync.

After expanding the arguments, the code passes the executable name and arguments to the Shell function and waits until the program finishes. You could no doubt enhance this code further based on the techniques described in "Other People's Programs," page 453. After the external program returns, you enable the code windows again and then call the Reload method to get the modified file from disk.

The Add-In Challenge

I've spent a lot of time talking about how to connect and disconnect add-ins and how to set up an add-in hierarchy. That's fine as far as it goes, but at some point your add-in has to do something. Before I start tossing out ideas, let's talk about some of the limitations of the VBIDE system.

The hierarchy tree betrays the origin of Visual Basic IDE extensibility. The designers planned the extensibility system to be used for two purposes: form wizards and source-control systems.

The ActiveForm branch of ActiveProjects was designed for modifying forms and controls. This branch of the tree has a rich set of properties and methods but no events. You can modify forms and controls yourself, but you can't react to user actions that modify them. Form wizards don't need events, and so the ActiveForm branch doesn't provide them. The sample ALIGN wizard provided with Visual Basic is a classic example of an add-in that modifies a form. Form wizards are a very nice feature, and those who want to create them will be generally happy with the VBIDE hierarchy.

The FileControl branch was designed specifically for source-control systems, which need to react to file actions by automatically checking files in and out every time a file is opened or saved. This branch provides plenty of events but no properties or methods. You can react to file events, but you can't create them. The sample program SPY shows you how to monitor file events, but the actual work you might do in response to events is left to your imagination. Source-control systems are great, but most programmers will purchase one (or use the one provided with Visual Basic Enterprise Edition) rather than write their own. Most programmers will be more interested in how they can adapt this system to other purposes.

Of course, there's more to extensibility than form wizards and source-control systems. Many hardcore programmers might be more interested in code wizards. The ActiveProject branch and its SelectedComponents and Components branches provide some help in modifying code events, but these branches seem to be an afterthought. You have to hack to do obvious things such as saving a project file or disabling code windows while you're editing files. It's clear from the design (or lack of it) that code wizards weren't a primary goal.

The AddInMenu branch of the hierarchy allows you to add menus for controlling the actions allowed by the other branches. But here again, important elements are strangely lacking. Why can you define and handle menu events but not toolbar or keyboard events? Why can you put events on the Add-Ins menu but not on the Tools menu (except for the mysterious source-control items that are normally grayed in Visual Basic Standard and Professional Editions)? Why can't you define accelerator keys for the menu items you add to the Add-Ins menu?

The bottom line is that we just have to do what we can with the tools we're given. As hardcore programmers, we're more interested in the unintended uses of add-ins and in ways to get around the built-in limitations. No hardcore programmer worthy of the name is stopped for long by the claim that form management can't have events or that file management can only react to events.

Keep in mind that Visual Basic add-ins existed in previous versions of Visual Basic. VBAssist from Sheridan Software Systems implemented form wizards for Visual Basic 3, and several companies figured out ways to add source-control systems. If they could do it with no help, you can do it with some help, even if the new extensibility system isn't all you might hope for.

If hack we must, then hack we will. Here are some ideas.

Macro Editor and Recorder

Visual Basic's code editor might be better than a poke in the eye with a sharp stick, but not by much, when compared to real programmer's editors such as Visual Slick Edit, CodeWright, MultiEdit, or RimStar. Think of the productivity if you could map the keyboard for your editing commands, record common key sequences as macros, and write your own powerful editing commands. If Basic is such a great macro language for applications like Microsoft Word for Windows and Microsoft Excel, why shouldn't it be a great macro language for programming tools?

Alas, the extensibility system provides no help. You could attach an interface for your macro editor to an add-in menu, but you'd have to hook it up to the code window yourself. The HWndCode method of the Commands collection provides the window handle. All you need to do is subclass it with a Message Blaster control. Intercept all WM_CHAR messages headed for code windows, and translate them to the appropriate commands and macros. Chapter 5 describes or hints at most everything you need to know.

Call Your Own Editor

OK, so writing your own macro editor for Visual Basic is a major project that most of us don't have time to take on. If you can't make Visual Basic's editor into a real editor, why not call a real editor from an add-in command? Refer back to "External commands," page 512, for one way to do it.

Hook Up Debug Wizard

Debug Wizard, discussed in Chapter 1 and again in Chapter 9, automatically enables or disables assert and profile procedures. The wizard works on one file at a time, specified in a dialog box. It wouldn't be difficult to hook up this wizard as an add-in. Instead of loading the wizard as a separate program and specifying each file it processes, you could hook it up to an add-in menu command. From that point, you could either apply the wizard to the current component or iterate through the Components collection and call the wizard on every class, form, and code module.

Hook Up the Property Shop

Chapter 4 introduced the Property Shop. As designed, it's a stand-alone program that interacts with the IDE by putting the text of the properties on the clipboard and then using SendKeys to paste them. What could an add-in do to make this behavior more integrated? Not very much. You could tie the Property Shop form to an add-in menu item instead of a separate program. But the extensibility model doesn't help you connect the code window to the wizard. The HWndCode property of the Commands collection gives you the handle of the current code window. From this, you can figure out the window title and call AppActivate on it.

A Metacommand Processor

One of my favorite features of modern Pascals (borrowed from Modula 2) is the *uses* statement. At the top of each module, you specify with a *uses* statement all the other modules on which the current module depends. The language then ensures that all these modules are present. This would be a handy feature to have in Basic, and you could use add-ins to provide it.

As an example, consider the SORT.BAS module. If you add this module to a project, you'll get errors because SORT.BAS uses the GetRandom function from UTILITY.BAS. If you add UTILITY.BAS to the project, you'll still get errors because UTILITY.BAS uses several procedures from DEBUG.BAS. If SORT.BAS had a *Uses UTILITY.BAS* statement, and UTILITY.BAS had a *Uses DEBUG.BAS* statement, you wouldn't get any errors because adding SORT.BAS would automatically add UTILITY.BAS, which would add DEBUG.BAS. But how can you add a statement to the language?

You can do it by adding what QuickBasic called a *metacommand*. The statement must be a comment in a particular format that is recognized by the add-in. In the QuickBasic tradition, let's say that a metacommand is specified by a comment character followed by a dollar sign. Thus a USES metacommand looks like this:

```
'$ Uses UTILITY.BAS
```

The advantage of this system is that if the add-in which processes the *Uses* metacommand isn't hooked up, no harm's done (except that it doesn't work). Basic considers it just another comment.

A ProcessUses procedure automatically adds any used modules to the project. ProcessUses is called when a new module is added to the project (the After-AddFile event). It searches through the new module for USES metacommands and, if it finds any, adds the used modules to the project. You will also want a ProcessAllUses procedure that iterates through the Components collection and applies the USES processor to all files. You'll call this procedure when you add a USES metacommand to a file that is already in the project.

Define Your Own Option Statements

The Option Explicit command is a great safety feature, but it's not hard to think of other Option statements. How about Option SysInt? This option inserts the following lines into any module you add:

```
#If Win32 Then
DefLng A-Z
#Else
DefInt A-Z
#End If
```

"Writing Portable Code," page 40, discusses these statements and explains what they're for. You can probably think of other Option statements. Perhaps you could add an Options tab to the Customize dialog box for setting and controlling these options.

Restore Windows

Every time you open a project, you need to restore the positions of the code windows to your own preferences. I always want my code windows to contain about 80 characters per line, but Visual Basic always opens them with some measly, inadequate size that varies depending on screen resolution. Furthermore, Basic won't tell me the width of the window in characters, the number of lines, or the current position of the caret. Most programmer's editors will at least restore the last project you were working on, but not Visual Basic's IDE.

Quit your whining! When I was your age, we had 64-KB machines with 5-megabyte hard disks, and we liked it. So get off your butt and write an add-in. You've got the handle of the code windows, don't you? What more do you need?

Process Resources

As Chapter 7 noted, Visual Basic supports resources, but it doesn't do much to integrate them into the IDE. Wouldn't it be nice if your RC file was automatically recompiled as needed? The extensibility system can't help because the IDE knows nothing about RC files, only about RES files. You have to use another editor to edit the RC file.

Nevertheless, there is something an add-in could do. It could detect when a file is being run or an EXE created in the BeforeCompileProject event. It could then check the dates of the RC and RES files and recompile the RC file if it is later. Only one problem: there is no BeforeCompileProject event. You have to create your own with Message Blaster.

While you're messing with resources, go ahead and write the tool described in "Compiling Resource Scripts," page 326, and hook it up as an add-in.

Enforce Coding Conventions

I don't think I pulled any punches in giving my opinion of Visual Basic's default naming convention (see "Naming Conventions," page 14). It's one thing to tell you not to use the read-only Command1 convention, but what I really want to do is change the default. When I create a new button, I want the IDE to give the name as *cmd* (without a number), change the focus to the Properties window, and put the cursor immediately after the prefix so that I can type in the qualifier.

Implementing this is simple enough. Just intercept the AfterClick event of the Properties window. Look up the control type name in a collection containing all your prefixes indexed by type name, and insert the correct prefix. But the Properties window has no AfterClick event, much less one that passes the control type name as an argument. You'll have to do this yourself by finding the Properties window and intercepting clicks with Message Blaster—another difficult challenge for the hardcore programmer.

You can take coding convention enforcement as far as you want. Read in each module, and validate its naming and other conventions. Parse the entire file to spot coding techniques that violate your standards of programming decency. Check for unused variables and procedures. Calculate metrics such as the number and the average length of functions. You could even try some optimizations. Your add-in could become a combination pretty printer, syntax checker (lint to you C programmers), and optimizer. But why stop with the difficult when you can attempt the impossible? Go ahead and write a compiler. P-code is nice during development, but nothing beats native code for speed. Why, if you had a native code compiler, Basic might even be fast enough to write your compiler in Basic.

Obviously, you won't accomplish any of these jobs in a day. But programs that analyze Basic code in this way exist today, and once you've got one, it's relatively easy to integrate it as an add-in.

11

The New Frontier

Visual Basic: Good evening, hardcore programmers. I'm your host, and to-night we're going to meet some very special guests. I'm sure you've heard a lot of talk lately about the operating systems that you and I will be working with in the next few years. Well, tonight you'll meet those systems—and I don't mean experts talking about the systems. No, you are going to hear the operating-system story straight from the horse's mouth. So without further ado, I'll intro-duce our first guest, who needs no introduction: Windowwwwsssss Threeeeee Onnnnne!

Audience: Boo! Get down! Hisssssss!

Visual Basic: Now, come on! Is that any way to treat a guest? Show some gratitude! Think of the good times.

Windows 3.1: Hey, it's cool. I know how you feel. I'm no spring chicken. In fact, I'm tired, and I'm going to be retiring real soon now. But just keep this in mind while you flirt with my young friends: they may have the features, but I've got one thing they haven't got.

Heckler: Oh, yeah? You're about 16 bits short of a load.

Windows 3.1: Yeah, sure. I've heard it all before. But if you can't give me a little respect, I'll just take my users and go home.

Silence falls.

Visual Basic: Well, with that sobering thought, let's move along to our next guest, Windows NT.

Scattered applause.

Windows NT: Hey, a tough audience tonight. You folks wouldn't give a cheer for Charles Babbage or Lady Lovelace.

Voice from the crowd: We're not in a very patient mood.

Windows NT: Well, don't blame me. Some of my friends here might have kept you waiting, but I've been around for years.

Voice: But what good's a 32-bit operating system without a 32-bit programming language?

Visual Basic: OK, OK, I apologize. Take your shots, but then let's get down to business. And speaking of business, I think a lot of you will be doing business with my next guest, Windows 95.

Mixed reaction. Some enthusiastic cheering mixed with a few catcalls and one loud wolf whistle.

Windows 95:   Thank you, folks. Thank you very much. I'm just thrilled to be here and show you a few tricks. Here's a property sheet—is that beautiful or what? And watch this. See how I can move my Taskbar to any side of the screen? Nice, huh? Look at my cute little icons. And here's Explorer. Beats the heck out of File Manager, doesn't it? Look at these shortcuts...

Second Windows 95:   And we can do all these tricks from multiple threads.

Third Windows 95:   Watch me change screen resolution at run time.

Fourth Windows 95:   I'm just going to plug in this new modem and keep on running.

Oohs and ahs from the audience.

Windows NT: Oh, come on! I've been doing preemptive multitasking for years, and nobody cared. She comes in with a few gadgets, and everybody's rolling in the aisles. You want a show? Well, check out my 3-D graphics.

Windows 95:   You want graphics? Here's Doom running in a window.

Windows NT: But that's just blitting! Even our old-fashioned friend can do WinG. Let's see you do this world transform. Sure, you look 32-bit, but tell me: how many bits are significant in your coordinate system?

Windows 95:   Well, if you're going to get snippy about technical details, what about image color matching? Let's see you do that!

Visual Basic: Hold on! We're on the same team here. There's no point in arguing about details.

Voice: Hey! What about us? All these features are fine for users, but can we program this stuff in Basic?

Visual Basic: That's what we're here to find out.

Going to Chicago

Large portions of this book were written and tested during a time when Windows 95 was no more than a gleam in Bill Gates's eye. During most of that time, this mythical operating system bore the name of a real city, and writers like me had a field day with the name. Chicago was a state of mind. We lived in Chicago. We created pseudowords—*Chicago-like, pre-Chicago, Chicagoable.*

But Windows 95? What can you do with that? This chapter is about a subject too big to fit under a commonplace name such as Windows 95, Windows NT, or even Win32. Rather than invent a new word, I'm going to borrow the old one and expand it to include all of what it takes to create new programs for the new Windows interface. The Chicago state of mind is something Carl Sandburg might have described this way:

> *Code Hacker for the World,*
> *Tool Maker, Stacker of Silicon,*
> *Player with Networks and the Nation's Baud Handler;*
> *Stormy, husky, brawling,*
> *City of the Big Chips.*

In contrast to this bold new attitude, you'll also see Chicago resistance. When deadlines get tight, you'll see it in Visual Basic, in Visual C++, in Microsoft Office, and even in Windows 95 itself. You'll feel it, too. Change is hard. There's never enough time, the tools aren't good enough—but most of all, it's difficult to change the way we think about programming. But change we must if we want our programs to be competitive in the marketplace.

Chicago-wise, every program written from here on out will fit somewhere on a rating scale whose broadest categories include the following:

- Chicago-friendly

- Chicago-polite

- Chicago-indifferent

- Chicago-rude

The higher up this scale you place your applications, the better the users who run Windows 95 and Windows NT will like them. Naturally, you want to create applications at the top of the scale, but...

What's It Gonna Cost Me This Time?

Everyone wants their programs to be Chicago-friendly—as long as it doesn't cost much. Most programmers live in the real world. We don't believe in free updates or full backward compatibility. Such skepticism is well founded. Yes,

Windows 95 will run "any" Windows 3.*x* application. But no, not all old applications will look and feel "right." Yes, you can compile and run any (well, almost any) Visual Basic 3 program under Visual Basic 4. But no, not every program will qualify for the 32-bit Windows logo. Here's a quick rundown of what it will cost you to make your applications look as good and work as well as possible under Windows 95 and Windows NT with Visual Basic 4.

Chicago-friendly means writing your applications to take full advantage of 32-bit features. To really be Chicago-friendly, a program needs to use threads, memory-mapped files, interprocess synchronization and communication, and all sorts of other goodies. Frankly, doing this with Visual Basic is somewhere between difficult and impossible.

I'm not saying that you won't figure out how to use these features; it's just that Visual Basic 4 won't help you and will often stand in your way. You'll need to call API functions directly to do some jobs; you'll have to write support DLLs in another language for others; and, in a few cases, you won't be able to do what you want, period. Still, this is the new frontier for hardcore programmers. I'll give some hints and throw out some ideas in this chapter, but it would take another book this long to thoroughly explore the possibilities.

Making your applications Chicago-polite is a different matter. By *polite*, I mean programs that follow the new user-interface standards. Visual Basic will help you use many of these new features. Others will take a little extra effort. The broad category of Chicago-polite includes many subcategories. Whatever the cost, this work will be important. In the early days after the release of Windows 95 (and the next version of Windows NT, which supports a similar user interface), your programs will get extra points for being Chicago-polite. But within a short time, polite will be the standard, and you'll lose points for not meeting it.

The cost of being Chicago-polite isn't very high. In most cases, you can achieve this in ways that work for both 16-bit and 32-bit versions of your programs and that look OK whether you are running Windows 95 or Windows NT. In fact, many Chicago-polite programs will also end up looking better under 16-bit versions of Windows.

If you simply compile your old Visual Basic 3 programs under Visual Basic 4, most of them will work, sometimes with a few minor changes, but they'll be Chicago-indifferent. Your icons will be squashed into small icons like roadkill. Your colors might come out wrong if users customize their systems. Important system events will be ignored. In short, your programs will look like they were ported from another operating system.

Finally, some of the techniques commonly used today are Chicago-rude. For example, Windows 95 and Windows NT users will curse your product if it assumes that all filenames are limited to 11 characters.

Handling Different Environments

Some techniques work only in Windows 95, some work only in Windows NT, some work only in 16-bit versions of Windows. You can test your environment and take the appropriate action. For every environment test, you need to decide whether to test at run time or at compile time.

In a previous life, I converted the Microsoft FORTRAN run-time library from 16 bits to 32 bits. If the library I started with had been written in Visual Basic (maybe not such a bad idea), it might have looked something like this:

```
' Check environment at run time
ordOS = GetOsEnvironment()
#If fDebug = False Then
    #If fDOS Then
        ' Do stuff that is the same for MS-DOS and Windows
        If ordOS = ordWindows Then
            ' Optimize some stuff for Windows at run time...
        Else
            ' Do safe MS-DOS stuff...
        End If
    #Else If fOS2 Then
        ' 16-bit OS/2...
    #Else
        ' Other stuff...
    #End If
#Else
    #If fDOS Then
        ' Do stuff that is the same for MS-DOS and Windows
    #Else
        ' Other stuff
    #End If
#End If
```

That's the way I found the 16-bit code. I could have added another layer of environment tests for 32-bit code. But we decided that 16-bit mode was on the way out and that we would never update that source tree. So we just cloned the 16-bit code and removed irrelevant dependencies. Notice that I had several levels of testing before I even started any work. Some tests were done at compile time, some at run time. This is the kind of maintenance nightmare nobody needs.

On the following page, you'll find my rules of thumb for keeping environment testing under control in Visual Basic programs.

■ Do all testing for 16-bit or 32-bit environments at compile time, using conditional compilation. You need to have two EXE files anyway. (I'll destroy exceptions to this rule in a minute.) Visual Basic provides predefined *Win32* and *Win16* constants to make it easy. In the long run, you'll be able to let the 16-bit branches die of attrition (or write a wizard to kill them). It's theoretically possible to create separate EXE files for Windows 95, Windows NT, Windows 3.1, Windows for Workgroups, Windows in standard mode, and Windows emulated under OS/2, but I wouldn't test at compile time for anything other than 16-bit and 32-bit Windows.

■ Do error testing whenever possible to handle features that are available only in Windows 95 or Windows NT. Most features unique to one system degrade gracefully. For example, if you call Windows NT APIs under Windows 95, they'll fail with an error indicating that the feature isn't implemented. Most Visual Basic features that enable parts of the Windows 95 interface work acceptably under Windows NT and, in many cases, under Windows 3.*x*. You needn't do anything special.

■ If you really need to handle a feature differently under Windows 95 and Windows NT, test the system at run time. "The CSystem Class and the System Object," page 410, explains how to check your current environment. You could also test at run time for different versions and modes of 16-bit Windows, but one is usually enough.

■ Don't thunk. If you don't know what *thunk* means, skip this item, and consider yourself lucky. Thunking layers are available to call 32-bit APIs from 16-bit Basic programs. This was a temporary hack for those who had no 32-bit language, but if you're reading this, you have 32-bit Visual Basic. There are thunking layers in 32-bit Windows that call 16-bit APIs from 32-bit code (that's how old programs run), but if I knew how to call such layers from Visual Basic, I wouldn't confess it.

NOTE | What about Macintosh? What about MIPS? What about PowerPC? If you'd like to write Visual Basic code for these environments, your day may come. The Visual Basic for Applications engine used in Visual Basic is the same one used in Microsoft Excel, Project, and Access (and someday in Word for Windows). This engine already works in Microsoft Excel for the Macintosh. As for non-Intel systems that run Windows NT, porting the 32-bit version of Visual Basic should be easy—although perhaps not as easily done as said. The powers that be will decide whether and when the benefit is worth the effort. If this step is ever taken, you'll have a lot more environment testing to worry about and another set of hardcore hacks to learn.

System-Dependent Features

Here's a brief preview of features that are dependent on Windows NT or Windows 95. I list them now so that most of you can avoid them; I'll note exceptions as we go. For those brave pioneers who want to explore these areas, you have my encouragement, but not my help.

Windows 95 has the following features not handled by Windows NT:

Plug and Play The Windows 95 system sends messages when Plug and Play events happen. Windows NT doesn't. There's no portability problem here. You simply handle the events with the System Events control. You won't get any system events from Windows NT, but when Plug and Play is implemented in some future version, your code will be ready to handle it.

Pen input Windows 95 has APIs to handle pen input. If you need it, you need Windows 95. This topic is too specific to cover here, but it's just another API. All you need is a third-party custom control. Failing that, you can call the API directly. Windows NT will be able to handle pen input eventually.

Telephony and Unimodem These new communications APIs are another powerful feature that Windows 95 gets first.

Image color matching This technology, which allows professional-quality color matching, is very powerful and useful for art professionals who need complete control over how colors appear on screens and other output devices. I would expect this technology to be more useful under Windows NT, but Windows 95 is the lucky winner.

Windows NT is the older brother, so it's not surprising to find that it has some advanced features that the initial version of Windows 95 lacks:

Unicode Internally, every Windows NT string is a Unicode string. This caused numerous problems for the developers of Visual Basic, and it will cause numerous problems for you if you write DLLs in C or some other language. Unicode is to Win32 what segments were to Win16. Generally, however, you shouldn't have too much trouble if you stick to Basic. "Unicode Versus Basic," page 72, discusses your choices.

Security Windows NT supports security attributes that let you protect all your application's data from prying eyes. You will see security attributes in many Win32 API functions as parameters with type LPSECURITY_ATTRIBUTES. If you want your code to be usable on Windows 95, you must pass a null (0) to these parameters. You should give the parameter ByVal Long type in Declare statements so that you can pass 0. (That's how they're declared in the Windows API type library.) If you want to actually use security attributes in your Windows NT programs, you're on your own.

32-bit coordinates All the parameters and structure fields containing coordinates have type Long in Win32 API functions. This is true for many of the functions in GDI and USER. Although the functions look the same under Windows NT and Windows 95, the contents can differ at run time. Windows 95 coordinate values are actually 16-bit values in a 32-bit holder. The high word will always be 0. This means that if you purchase a screen that covers your whole wall with a resolution of 70,000 by 70,000 pixels, you'll have no trouble setting ScaleMode to *vbPixels* under Windows NT, but it won't work under Windows 95.

World transforms I dropped out of math in high school and wouldn't be able to code a transform if my career depended on it. I can't even understand the documentation, except to see that this is a very cool feature for those who want to scale, rotate, shear, or translate graphics output.

Asynchronous file I/O If you use Visual Basic's FileCopy statement to copy a 5-megabyte file to a remote network drive, your screen might not be repainted for a long, long time. One solution is to write your own FileCopy that calls DoEvents between chunks. Another solution is to do asynchronous file I/O by using the ReadFile and WriteFile API functions with the OVERLAPPED structure to copy in the background. The system lets you know when the copy is completed, and you can test the results with GetOverlappedResult. You can check into this, but it looks tough in Basic because the system uses multithreading to implement this feature and a Win32 event (different from a Visual Basic event) to notify you when the copy is finished. This feature will be more attractive when it works in Windows 95.

> **NOTE** At the time I wrote this, the biggest difference between Windows NT and Windows 95 was the user interface. I didn't include the interface in the preceding lists because Microsoft has already announced a forthcoming version of Windows NT that will have the Windows 95 user interface. It will be available by the time many of you see this book. I wouldn't waste time writing code that assumes a different interface for Windows NT and Windows 95. Most of this chapter deals with the user interface as though it exists on both platforms.

The New Look and Feel

The biggest challenge you face in adapting applications to 32-bit mode is handling the new Windows 95 user interface. Visual Basic gives you some of these features free, but others require additional work. A few demand serious hacking with the Windows API or even with DLLs in another language.

Before you can figure out what you have to do, you need to know the results you want. That's where the *Windows Interface Guidelines for Software Design* comes in. You can find an online version in the MSDN/VB starter kit demo on the CD-ROM provided with Visual Basic Professional Edition. The book is published by Microsoft Press (1995). If you want to get the true Chicago spirit, you should get to know this book. It's like a tourist brochure that tells you what Chicago looks like and why you should go there. This chapter is a preliminary Basic street map that tells you exactly how to get to some of the more interesting places in Chicago.

The 3-D Feel

Windows 95 has a 3-D feel throughout. Its square buttons and windows give a more sharply defined effect than the rounded borders of previous versions.

The three-dimensional effect is easy to achieve in Visual Basic 4. Instead of using THREED.VBX, you set the Appearance property to 3D (the default). This works in either 16-bit or 32-bit mode. You can provide the same feel at a lower level using new Win32 draw functions. We'll talk briefly about two of these, DrawEdge and DrawFrameControl.

DrawEdge creates the low-level 3-D effects the system uses to draw 3-D buttons and other controls. You can also use it to draw your own controls. Imagine writing your own Button class that does everything CommandButton does, and more. The Test Edges program (in TEDGE.VBP) demonstrates the techniques you might use in such a class. You can play with the check boxes to see which flags give different effects. Some combinations aren't meaningful, but you can experiment until you find the ones you like. Figure 11-1 on the following page shows some of the more common effects. For an uncommon and surprising effect, click the Adjust check box repeatedly.

The code to actually draw the button looks like this:

```
DrawEdge hDC, edge.Rect, afBorder, afStyle
```

The *edge* object variable is CRect type. CRect works the same way as the CPoint class described in "What's CPoint?" on page 269. When passing a CRect object to an API function, you must always pass the Rect property so that the first element of the object is passed by reference. Refer to Chapter 6 to see how this works.

Here's the definition of the *edge* variable:

```
Private edge As New CRect
```

The initialization is shown on the next page.

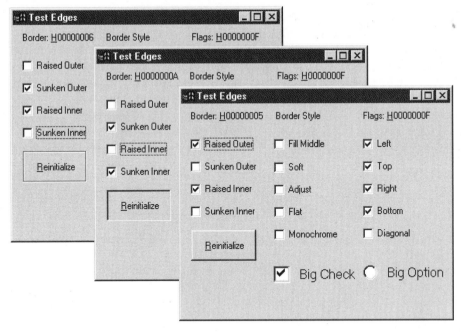

Figure 11-1. *Drawing edges and controls.*

```
With lblButton
    edge.Left = .Left
    edge.Top = .Top
    edge.Right = .Left + .Width
    edge.Bottom = .Top + .Height
    UpdateEdges
End With
```

The CRect object is drawn over a transparent label containing the button text. This makes it easy to size the rectangle and to respond to clicks on the label as if they were on the button. The CRect class has Tw properties that automatically convert between twips on your form and the pixels used by API functions, but they aren't needed here because label coordinates are already in pixels. The rest of the code deals with maintaining the *afBorder* and *afStyle* bit flag variables that will be passed to DrawEdge.

NOTE You could use the TRect type instead of the CRect class. You'd have to write your own Declare statement for DrawEdge instead of using the DrawEdge definition from the Windows API type library. You would be able to pass a TRect variable directly instead of passing the Rect property.

The DrawFrameControl function works at a higher level than DrawEdge. This function can draw different kinds of predefined buttons and other controls such as the CheckBox control and the OptionButton control shown in Figure 11-1. You pass flags that describe the type and the state of the control. Like the button control shown earlier, the fake button is drawn on top of a transparent label so that the label can respond to mouse events. Here's how the Click event of the label calls DrawFrameControl to toggle the check box:

```
Private Sub lblBigCheck_Click()
    If afChk <> (DFCS_BUTTONCHECK Or DFCS_CHECKED) Then
        afChk = DFCS_BUTTONCHECK Or DFCS_CHECKED
    Else
        afChk = DFCS_BUTTONCHECK
    End If
    DrawFrameControl hDC, chk.Rect, DFC_BUTTON, afChk
End Sub
```

DrawEdge and DrawFrameControl are rarely worth the extra trouble; it's much simpler to use the predefined controls. But if you occasionally need to create your own controls (such as the large CheckBox and OptionButton controls in the sample), it's sometimes easier to fake it in Basic than it is to write a new control in C++.

If you like these functions, check out the other new draw functions added for Windows 95: DrawAnimatedRects, DrawCaption, DrawState, DrawStatusText, and DrawTextEx.

Icons with an Attitude

Iconically speaking, Windows 95 is a whole new metaphor. You'll see icons everywhere—big ones and little ones, in list views, tree views, title bars, and taskbars. The Picture property has always made standard icons easy to use with Visual Basic, so you might expect that small icons would be a simple extension of an existing feature. Not so. Let's take a closer look at what icons really are and how the Picture object handles (or fails to handle) them.

The icons we're used to are always 32 by 32 pixels, in as many as 16 colors. They consist of a color bitmap of the icon image and a monochrome mask with the outline of the image. They work very much like the CPictureGlass class (described in Chapter 6) except that they have a fixed size and built-in API calls to handle them (DrawIcon, CreateIcon, LoadIcon, and so on). Although icons were generally 32 by 32 bits in previous versions of Windows, the detailed specification allowed any size—a possibility that was rarely tapped. Windows 95 supports four specific icon sizes: small (16 by 16), large (32 by 32, with most video adapters), huge (48 by 48), and shell size (determined by the user on the Appearance tab of the Display Properties dialog box). In addition, you can define icons of arbitrary sizes, although Windows leaves you on your own to manage them.

The ICO file format supports multiple images. You can and should put small icons and large icons in the same file. Unfortunately, the icon tool of choice, IconWorks, doesn't know a small icon from smallpox. You have to use the ImagEdit tool provided in the TOOLS directory on the Visual Basic CD to create icons with multiple images. Technically, you could put images of any size in ICO files, but ImagEdit supports only 32 by 32, 16 by 16, and—for that one last CGA monitor left on earth—32 by 16. The icons supplied with Visual Basic 4 contain large and small images, although most parts of Visual Basic can't do much with the small image, at least not without a little help.

Visual Basic has always supported the concept of a Picture object that can contain an icon, a metafile, or a bitmap. The Picture object (like the Font object) is one of the features OLE took from Visual Basic. You can see the class properties and methods under Standard OLE Types in the Visual Basic Object Browser. OLE hasn't fixed one big problem with the Picture object, however: it can contain only one icon image. So if you call LoadPicture on an icon file that contains multiple images, which image is loaded? The same questions apply to LoadResPicture and the Load Picture dialog box. You could handle this problem in several ways, but all of them require redesigning the Picture architecture, a redesign that didn't take place for this version of Visual Basic.

Let's compare the Windows 95 way of icons to the Basic way of icons and try to figure out some hacks to bring Basic around to the Windows 95 point of view.

Windows 95 icons versus Basic icons

In Windows 95, the size of shell icons is determined by the user. Try it. Right-click on the desktop and choose Properties to bring up the Display Properties dialog box. Select the Appearance tab, click the Item combo box, and select Icon. Chances are you'll see the default icon size, 32. Change it to 37 or 24. All the icons on your desktop will change to the new size. If you move to Windows Explorer and set Large Icons mode, you'll see the same size. This feature is part of the new philosophy of allowing users to customize more parts of the desktop. Users with visual disabilities can make their icons as large as they want. Those who want to cram as much stuff as they can onto their screens, visibility be damned, can have small icons everywhere.

So what happens when you perform similar operations in Basic? You can see what I see in the Test Icons program (TICON.VBP), shown in Figure 11-2, but this isn't necessarily what you'll see if you run the program yourself. Part of the code that controls how icons are displayed resides in the Picture object, which is not part of Visual Basic. The DLL files containing Picture object code are actually part of the Control Development Kit (CDK), which is part of Microsoft

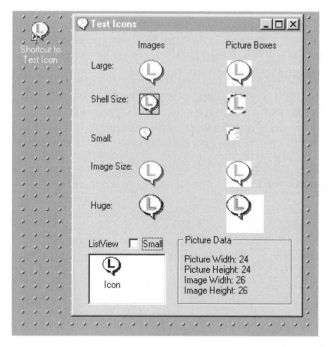

Figure 11-2. *Icons for every occasion.*

Visual C++. These files will be updated with bug fixes during the life of Visual Basic 4. If you purchase a new copy of Microsoft Visual C++ or a program developed in C++ that uses the DLLs containing the Picture object, you'll get the same fixes in Visual Basic.

In the meantime, let's examine how icons work in the DLLs released with Visual Basic 4. In order to make image differences more visual, I used a modified dual-image icon (I.ICO) that has a blue *L* in the large icon image and a pink *S* in the small image. (Don't try this at home.) When I captured the screen shot, my desktop icon size was 24 by 24, the size that showed up in a shortcut to the Test Icons program (also shown in Figure 11-2 for comparison). You won't get these five icon images from Basic's LoadPicture, but before talking about my better LoadPicture, let's look at what Basic controls do with icons of different sizes.

- The large icon comes out at 32 by 32, which is, alas, the system icon size (from GetSystemMetrics) of my monitor. My boss turned down my request for a 48-inch monitor with a 4096 by 4096 display and 48 by 48 icons. In fact, I've never seen a display adapter with a system icon size other than 32, so I'm not sure what Visual Basic would do with one.

- The shell size icon comes out right in the Image control and in the ListView control. It's the same size as the shortcut icon (24 by 24). If you look closely, you'll see some jaggies on the icon edge, indicating that this image has been compressed from its real image size (32 by 32). The PictureBox control gets the frame size right, but it seems to stretch the 24 by 24 image to 32 by 32 and then clip the edges.

■ The small icon comes out right in the Image control, but the PictureBox control makes the same mistake it made for the shell size icon. Of course, PictureBox controls can't handle icon transparency, so getting the size wrong is the least of the PictureBox problems.

■ The image size icon comes out right in both controls—32 by 32—but how did the program decide to get the large image instead of the small one? We'll get to that.

■ The huge icon is all wrong in both controls. It's being displayed in a 48 by 48 frame, but the image is 32 by 32. And look at those jaggies. My guess is that the image has been stretched to 48 by 48 and then crammed back down to 32 by 32.

Visual Basic and the Picture object just don't have a Chicago state of mind about icons. Programs written for Windows 95 are supposed to display large icons with code like this:

```
cx = GetSystemMetrics(CX_ICON)
cy = GetSystemMetrics(CY_ICON)
f = DrawIconEx(hdc, x, y, hIcon, cx, cy, 0, NULL, DI_NORMAL)
```

I imagine that under the surface DrawIconEx calls StretchBlt to stretch the image and mask bitmaps of the icon from their actual size to the desired icon size. Small icons work the same way except that they must stretch the actual icon bitmaps down to the hard-coded size of 16 by 16. Shell size icons get the user-selected size using a technique similar to that found in my GetShellIconSize function. You can see the code in FILEINFO.BAS.

When Windows 95 uses multiple-image icon files or resources, it often doesn't need to do any stretching. It can simply blast a 16 by 16 image onto a small icon, or a 32 by 32 image onto a large icon with the default size. If the target icon size doesn't match any of the images in the file or resource, Windows probably has an algorithm for deciding which image will best stretch into the target size.

This works out pretty well for C programmers because they load icons from resources or files, which can contain multiple images. Basic programmers load icons from Picture objects, which can contain only a single image. Worse yet, none of the ways to load an icon into a picture gives you any choice about which image to load. For example, the Basic LoadPicture function always loads the system metrics size. If the user keeps the default icon size (usually 32 by 32), LoadPicture always loads a 32 by 32 icon. If the icon file being loaded contains a single 16 by 16 image, LoadPicture stretches it to 32 by 32 before storing it in the Picture object. A small icon puffed into a large icon container looks just as bad as a large icon crammed into a small icon container.

You can get around the problem in Basic by stretching that large small icon back down to a small icon. In an Image control, set the Stretch property to True and the width and height to 16 pixels. The ImageList control does this automatically when you request small icons. If you load dual-image icons into an ImageList, however, you'll always get large icons stretched down to small icons rather than small icons at their normal size. In fact, the only thing Visual Basic does right with dual-image icons is display them correctly in the Icon property. Small icons come out right in the Taskbar and in the left corner of the application's title bar. Large icons come out right if placed on the desktop. This is the most pervasive use of large and small icons, so it's good that it works. But you can do lots of other things with icons—things that hardcore programmers won't give up on easily just because Basic doesn't help them.

A better LoadPicture

As you know from Chapter 7 ("Using Icon Resources," page 342), you can load any icon into a picture if you have a handle for the icon. The IconToPicture function (PICTOOL.BAS) turns an icon handle into a Picture object. So if you could get the handle of a small icon image out of a multi-image icon file, you then could load it into a picture.

It so happens that the Win32 API has a new LoadImage function that delivers icons, cursors, and bitmaps. I don't need it for bitmaps, and I haven't figured out a good way to use it for cursors, but it works fine for icons. You tell it what size icon you want, and it gives you a handle to that icon. As an added benefit, LoadImage can load either from an ICO file or from an icon resource. In other words, it does most of the work of the Basic LoadPicture and LoadResPicture functions. I use LoadImage to create a better LoadPicture that takes an additional optional argument specifying what kind of icon to load. Here's how the Test Icons program calls my new LoadPicture:

```
' Load icon with Basic's LoadPicture (system metrics size)
img(ordDefault).Picture = LoadPicture("i.ico")
pb(ordDefault).Picture = LoadPicture("i.ico")
' Load icon stretched to system metrics size
img(ordShell).Picture = LoadPicture("i.ico", vbIconShell)
pb(ordShell).Picture = LoadPicture("i.ico", vbIconShell)
' Load small (16 by 16) icon, squashing if necessary
```

(continued)

```
img(ordSmall).Picture = LoadPicture("i.ico", vbIconSmall)
pb(ordSmall).Picture = LoadPicture("i.ico", vbIconSmall)
' Load first icon image in file with its real size
img(ordReal).Picture = LoadPicture("i.ico", vbIconRealSize)
pb(ordReal).Picture = LoadPicture("i.ico", vbIconRealSize)
' Load icon stretched to 48 by 48
img(ordHuge).Picture = LoadPicture("i.ico", 48)
pb(ordHuge).Picture = LoadPicture("i.ico", 48)
```

Notice the fourth set of commands. This is how you load small icons and others of unusual size from single-image icon files. Basic normally stretches these icons to the system metrics size, but if you give the *vbIconRealSize* constant, you should get the real size of the image. Normally, you should let Windows decide which image to use and when. But if you had an icon editor that let you define icons of any size, you could use them to get transparent images in animation. I wonder what it would take to enhance IconWorks...

Here's the code for the better LoadPicture from BETTER32.BAS:

```
#If Win32 Then
Function LoadPicture(Optional vPicture As Variant, _
                     Optional vIconType As Variant) As Picture
    Dim hIcon As Long, sExt As String, xy As Long, af As Long
    ' If no picture, return Nothing (clears picture)
    If IsMissing(vPicture) Then Exit Function
    ' Use default LoadPicture for all except icons with argument
    sExt = GetFileExt(CStr(vPicture))
    If UCase$(sExt) <> ".ICO" Or IsMissing(vIconType) Then
        Set LoadPicture = VB.LoadPicture(vPicture)
        Exit Function
    End If

    Select Case vIconType
    Case vbIconRealSize
        xy = 0: af = LR_LOADFROMFILE Or LR_LOADREALSIZE
    Case vbIconSmall
        xy = 16: af = LR_LOADFROMFILE
    Case vbIconShell
        Static dxyShell As Long
        If dxyShell = 0 Then dxyShell = GetShellIconSize()
        xy = dxyShell: af = LR_LOADFROMFILE
    Case Is > 0
        xy = vIconType: af = LR_LOADFROMFILE
    Case Else ' Includes vbIconDefault
        xy = 0: af = LR_LOADFROMFILE Or LR_DEFAULTSIZE
    End Select
```

```
        hIcon = LoadImage(0&, CStr(vPicture), IMAGE_ICON, xy, xy, af)
        ' If this fails, use original load
        If hIcon <> hNull Then
            Set LoadPicture = IconToPicture(hIcon)
        Else
            Set LoadPicture = VB.LoadPicture(vPicture)
        End If
End Function
```

This function deals only with icons. The first section of code checks for other types or for a command line without an optional argument and then calls the normal LoadPicture to do the work. If an optional argument is provided, the code sets up the appropriate size and flags and calls LoadImage. Finally, it checks to see whether LoadImage worked, and, if not, it again falls back on the original LoadPicture. The LoadImage function is implemented as a stub under Windows NT 3.51, so you'll always fall through to the old LoadPicture. That's OK because all icons are the same size in that environment.

A little better LoadResPicture

Since LoadImage can load from resources as well as from files, it's relatively easy to enhance LoadResPicture in the same way we enhanced LoadPicture. The code to do this is in BETTER32.BAS. It's a little more complicated because you have to deal with resources specified by string name or by integer index, but most of the code is the same.

There is one big difference, however. LoadImage can read icons from resources in an EXE file, but it hasn't a clue about how to read them in the Visual Basic environment. When you run in the environment, you're not really running your own program; you're running VB32.EXE. If you try to load icon resource 25 using the Windows API, you'll get Visual Basic's resource 25 or, more likely, you'll get an error. The real LoadResPicture knows how to dig your resource out of some internal format known only to Madame Basic's crystal ball. The best I can do is detect the environment with a function called IsExe and then call the real LoadResPicture.

You might think that having icons be one size in the environment and another in an EXE would be unworkable. Actually, it's not so bad. For example, assume that you put multi-image icons in a resource file and then load them into an ImageList control as small icons at run time. You'll end up with large icons squished to small icons in the environment, but your small icons will come out as small icons in the EXE. You can do the same thing for Image controls by playing with the image size and the Stretch property. It's an annoying problem for you, but your customers will never be the wiser.

If you read Chapter 5 carefully, you can guess the implementation of IsExe (in UTILITY.BAS). Hint: it uses GetModuleFileName. This function should be unnecessary. Basic knows full well at compile time whether your program is an EXE or whether you're running in the environment. It should provide this information in a predefined #Const used like this:

```
#If IsExe Then
    ' Call original LoadResPicture
#Else
    ' Call LoadImage
#End If
```

Maybe next time.

Use System Colors and Sizes

What was the first difference that jumped out at you the first time you loaded Visual Basic 4 under Windows 95 (assuming for the moment that you were experienced with Visual Basic 3)? Chances are you said something like, "Holy Hypotenuse, Batman! They've changed the default color of forms. Windows has adopted bat colors—yellow with a black title bar." Or perhaps not. Actually, most people saw gray forms with a blue title bar. But whatever color you saw, you didn't really see it, because by default forms don't have a color.

The default BackColor property of forms is *vb3DFace*, a constant that evaluates to &H8000000F. (Look it up under SystemColorConstants in the Visual Basic Objects and Procedures library in the Object Browser.) Color values are made up of red, green, and blue elements in the first 3 bytes of a Long, but this number has &H80 in the fourth byte. In other words, it's not a valid color. It's a constant that represents a system color. In cruder languages such as C++, you must call an API function:

```
BackColor = GetSysColor(COLOR_3DFACE)
```

Visual Basic does this for you when you write this:

```
BackColor = vb3DFace
```

It's your responsibility to use the system constants faithfully rather than hardcoding specific colors. If your user creates a Batman color scheme with the Display Properties dialog box, who are you to argue? Obviously, there are exceptions. If you're writing a hospital application and decide that it's important to make your forms a sickly green, you might decide to consciously override a user's color choices with your own.

The user can change a lot besides colors under Windows 95. On the Appearance tab of the Display Properties dialog box, for instance, you can change not only colors but also sizes for many elements. So if you're a hardcore programmer whose programs use the size of window elements, such as the height of the title bar or the width of a scroll bar, make sure that you get the true size of these elements. The same goes for fonts. The user can change almost any font used in menus, windows, or other standard elements. Information about your system is available from one of two places. You can get system colors and many other system parameters by using GetSystemMetrics. Values specific to the user interface are located in the Registry, in the Control Panel\Desktop\WindowMetrics key of HKEY_CURRENT_USER. It's better not to read them directly if you can find an alternative, however, because the Registry isn't guaranteed to always be in sync with the shell. The GetShellIconSize function, for example, gets icon sizes indirectly, through system image lists.

Registry Blues

The Registry has been around for quite a while, but you could usually ignore it under 16-bit Windows. The fatal flaw of the 16-bit Registry was its 64-KB capacity. Certain programs filled up a good chunk of that all by themselves, leaving you with little idea of how much Registry space was left or what would happen if it overflowed. Furthermore, you couldn't assign multiple values to a Registry key. For all practical purposes, the 16-bit Registry was left for OLE applications, which used it transparently.

It's a different story in Win32. You now have all the space you need. Microsoft strongly recommends that you stop using INI files and similar techniques and instead make the Registry your one-stop data storage mechanism. (I'm resisting the temptation to take cheap shots at Visual Basic's use of VB.INI.) This is more easily said than done. The problem isn't manipulating the Registry (although the Registry functions aren't among the most intuitive in the Windows API). Rather, it's figuring out what to write where. Take a look at one fine, upstanding citizen, and see whether you can learn anything about Registry duties.

Duties of a good citizen

If any program ought to be well behaved under Windows 95, it's WordPad. Figure 11-3 on the next page shows an abbreviated version of WordPad's Registry entries on my machine, and the following list provides some explanation.

■ The DOC extension is registered as the official extension for several document types, including Microsoft Word for Windows and WordPad. DOC is a popular extension, and your machine might have other document entries.

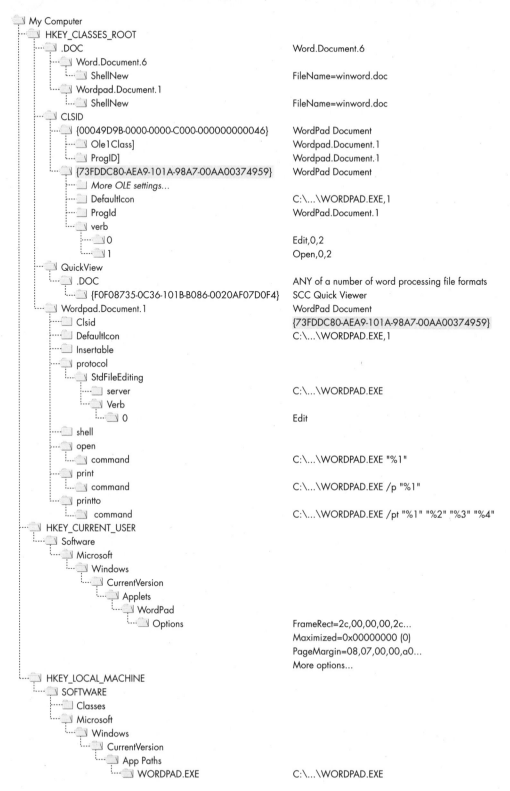

My Computer
- HKEY_CLASSES_ROOT
  - .DOC — Word.Document.6
    - Word.Document.6
      - ShellNew — FileName=winword.doc
    - Wordpad.Document.1
      - ShellNew — FileName=winword.doc
  - CLSID
    - {00049D9B-0000-0000-C000-000000000046} — WordPad Document
      - Ole1Class] — Wordpad.Document.1
      - ProgID] — Wordpad.Document.1
    - {73FDDC80-AEA9-101A-98A7-00AA00374959} — WordPad Document
      - More OLE settings...
      - DefaultIcon — C:\...\WORDPAD.EXE,1
      - ProgId — WordPad.Document.1
      - verb
        - 0 — Edit,0,2
        - 1 — Open,0,2
  - QuickView
    - .DOC — ANY of a number of word processing file formats
      - {F0F08735-0C36-101B-B086-0020AF07D0F4} — SCC Quick Viewer
  - Wordpad.Document.1 — WordPad Document
    - Clsid — {73FDDC80-AEA9-101A-98A7-00AA00374959}
    - DefaultIcon — C:\...\WORDPAD.EXE,1
    - Insertable
    - protocol
      - StdFileEditing
        - server — C:\...\WORDPAD.EXE
        - Verb
          - 0 — Edit
    - shell
    - open
      - command — C:\...\WORDPAD.EXE "%1"
    - print
      - command — C:\...\WORDPAD.EXE /p "%1"
    - printto
      - command — C:\...\WORDPAD.EXE /pt "%1" "%2" "%3" "%4"
- HKEY_CURRENT_USER
  - Software
    - Microsoft
      - Windows
        - CurrentVersion
          - Applets
            - WordPad
              - Options — FrameRect=2c,00,00,00,2c...
                Maximized=0x00000000 (0)
                PageMargin=08,07,00,00,a0...
                More options...
- HKEY_LOCAL_MACHINE
  - SOFTWARE
    - Classes
    - Microsoft
      - Windows
        - CurrentVersion
          - App Paths
            - WORDPAD.EXE — C:\...\WORDPAD.EXE

Figure 11-3. *WordPad Registry entries.*

- WordPad is OLE-enabled so that you can embed or link WordPad documents. This is the purpose of the next two entries in the CLSID branch. We're not particularly interested in this capability right now, but you can see the general idea.

- The DOC extension is registered under QuickView so that WordPad files can be browsed when you select Quick View from a document's context menu. It would be nice if you could enable a QuickView viewer for document types that your programs create. We'll talk about that briefly later.

- The document type Wordpad.Document.1 has several entries. Notice that the Clsid entry has a GUID pointing to the OLE CLSID entries. (See the second item in this bulleted list.) The DefaultIcon entry provides the location of the WordPad document icon, which is embedded as resource 1 in WORDPAD.EXE. The command entries for *open*, *print*, and *printto* give the command line that is invoked if you choose Open or Print from the document context menu or if you drag the document to a Printer object. If you thought command lines were out of fashion under Windows 95, think again. It's a good idea to add similar command-line options and command entries to any program that creates and manages documents.

- All the permanent WordPad settings from dialog boxes and toolbars are saved in the Registry rather than in INI files. If you use the new Settings functions, all your 32-bit settings are saved in the same place.

- WordPad stores its location in the App Paths branch of HKEY_LOCAL-_MACHINE. This allows Windows 95 to find and run WordPad even if it isn't in the PATH environment variable. For example, you can type *WordPad* from the Run item of the Start menu or use the Start command in a command-line session. Under MS-DOS first and later under Windows, it seemed that every setup program tried to insinuate its startup directory into the PATH environment, resulting in endless paths of long-forgotten directories. The App Paths entry allows programs to stop this rudeness, although I wouldn't bet much that they will. By default, setup programs created with the Setup Wizard or the Setup Toolkit will register the App Paths for your 32-bit programs. You don't need to worry about it. Of course, you don't necessarily want to run setup on your own programs during development, which is why I created the AppPath program, discussed in the next section.

You have two types of Registry settings: document and application. None of the sample programs in this book create their own document types, but most programs in real life do. About document types, I'll say only that you should study the Windows interface guidelines and do the right thing. If you can write one thing to the Registry, you can write anything. Let's concentrate on the application settings. The most common ones—those holding permanent program settings—are handled for you by GetSetting, GetAllSettings, SaveSetting, and DeleteSetting.

You'll find a small difference between the recommended settings location (followed by WordPad) and the location that is used by Visual Basic programs. The Windows interface guidelines recommend that the settings be placed under a CompanyName branch in the Software branch of HKEY_CURRENT_USER. Visual Basic settings are placed in a branch called VB and VBA Program Settings. So if your application name is the same as someone else's Visual Basic program name, your settings could conflict with theirs. Another possibility is that multiple users might log on to the same machine. If you want settings to apply to all users of a machine rather than to the current user only, you should save the settings in HKEY_LOCAL_MACHINE. Ideally, another settings function would allow you to set the Registry location where settings are to be stored. Of course, nothing prevents you from replacing the current settings functions with your own better versions.

The AppPath program

Visual Basic takes care of most of your Registry problems, but the hardcore programmer can always find one more thing to register. That doesn't mean you know where to register it, but that's a different story.

The AppPath program (APPPATH.VBP) is handy for making your programs available from any directory. You could easily adapt it to perform any standard Registry task. For hardcore command-line users, AppPath takes a command line specifying the path of the program to be registered. But if it doesn't get a command line, it puts up a wimpy common dialog and a message box. Of course, the first thing you'll want to do with AppPath after you build it is register its path so that you can call it from anywhere. In a command-line session or from the Run item of the Start menu, type this line:

```
apppath /o /p c:\hardcore\apppath.exe
```

The /o indicates that you want to override any existing setting, and /p indicates that you also want to register a working directory. (AppPath doesn't really need a working directory, but for this discussion let's pretend that it does.)

You can examine the code that parses the command line and displays the common dialog in APPPATH.BAS. Here we'll focus on SetAppPath and the other functions in REGISTRY.BAS. Look first at a call to SetAppPath:

```
SetAppPath sExeSpec, fSetPath
```

The *fSetPath* variable specifies whether to create a path indicating the program's working directory.

My Registry functions work at three levels. REGISTRY.BAS contains high-level functions such as GetAppPath, SetAppPath, and RemoveAppPath. These specific functions call more general wrapper functions: GetRegValue, SetRegValue, GetRegNameStr, SetRegNameStr, and DeleteRegKey. Finally, the generic functions call API functions such as RegOpenKey, RegCreateKey, RegQueryValue, RegSetValue, RegQueryValueEx, RegSetValueEx, and RegDeleteKey. Some of the API functions have aliases for type-safe handling of different types—for example, RegQueryValueExStr, RegQueryValueExInt, and RegQueryValueEx-Bytes. The API functions are designed for C, so it's handier to call my wrappers. If you use the Registry a lot, you'll probably want to fill out this library with wrappers and high-level functions for other Registry tasks.

The goal of the SetAppPath function is to create a Registry entry that looks conceptually like this:

```
HKEY_...\App Paths\AppPath.Exe  (Default)  C:\HARDCORE\APPPATH.EXE
                                Path       C:\HARDCORE;
```

The code to achieve this depends on the following constant:

```
Const sAppPath = "SOFTWARE\Microsoft\Windows\CurrentVersion\App Paths"
```

It also needs the root path constant HKEY_LOCAL_MACHINE, defined in the Windows API type library. Here's the implementation:

```
Function SetAppPath(sExeSpec As String, _
                    fSetPath As Boolean) As Boolean
    Dim sExeName As String
    sExeName = GetFileBaseExt(sExeSpec)
    If SetRegValue(HKEY_LOCAL_MACHINE, _
                sAppPath, sExeName, sExeSpec) Then
        ' Success if name set regardless of path success
        SetAppPath = True
    End If

    ' Set path subkey if requested
    If fSetPath Then
        Dim sExePath As String
        sExePath = GetFileDir(sExeSpec)
        sExePath = Left(sExePath, Len(sExePath) - 1) & ";"
        SetRegNameStr HKEY_LOCAL_MACHINE, _
                    sAppPath & "\" & sExeName, "Path", sExePath
    End If
End Function
```

The first part of the code splits off the filename with GetFileBaseExt (from the family of path functions in UTILITY.BAS) and then calls SetRegValue to set the default value. SetRegValue sets the default value for a given key to a given string. This default is the only value you can set in 16-bit mode, and it must always be a string. SetRegValue is a portable function that can set values in either 16-bit or 32-bit mode.

The second part of the code calls another path function to strip the path out of the full path specification. It then sets the Path value to this directory. In the 32-bit Registry, you can set named Registry values (such as Path) to numeric or string values. I provide the 32-bit SetRegNameStr, SetRegNameInt, and SetReg-NameBytes functions.

The implementation of SetRegNameStr hides some of the more unpleasant details of calling the RegSetValueExStr function (a string alias for RegSetValueEx):

```
#If Win32 Then
Function SetRegNameStr(hKeyRoot As Long, sKey As String, _
                       sName As String, sVal As String) As Boolean
    Dim hKey As Long
    If RegCreateKey(hKeyRoot, sKey, hKey) <> 0 Then Exit Function
    SetRegNameStr = (RegSetValueExStr(hKey, sName, 0&, REG_SZ, _
                                      sVal, Len(sVal)) = 0)
    RegCloseKey hKey
End Function
```

This code follows a pattern that you'll see in all the other Registry functions. You open or create a Registry key, getting back a handle to the key through a reference parameter. Use RegOpenKey when reading data; use RegCreateKey when writing data (because it will create the key and any required parent keys if they don't exist). You then call the appropriate Registry function on the open key. Finally, you close the key.

Once you register a program's path with AppPath, you might notice that the path is recognized in some cases and not in others. For example, assume that you've registered C:\HARDCORE\APPPATH.EXE but that C:\HARDCORE isn't in your normal path. Basic's Shell command and the ShellPlus function (discussed in "Other People's Programs," page 453) fail. Running a program from Windows Explorer or from the Run item of the Windows 95 Start menu works. Entering *apppath* in a command-line session fails, but typing *start apppath* works. Calling *apppath* from a batch file fails. What's the difference? All the variations that work are calling the ShellExecute function behind the scenes. ShellExecute also performs various other handy tasks, such as automatically calling the application associated with a document type. When it's called, it checks the AppPath Registry key. The performance cost for using ShellExecute is insignificant for launching a single program, but if you plan to launch a series of programs (as batch files often do), you might consider another alternative. For example, you could look up the AppPath value in the Registry the first time and store it for later calls to Shell or ShellPlus.

CHALLENGE   For some reason, Registry editors tend to be crude and ugly. The Windows 95 editor is a step in the right direction, but it lacks the AutoRefresh feature that is the only redeeming quality of the Windows NT version. As for the Windows 3.x version, the less said the better. None of the Registry editors provide a good way to switch between related entries. So what's the problem? All you need is a tree view on the left, a list view on the right, a toolbar, a status bar, and a few menu items. No problem.

Faking Quick View

If you look up Quick View in the MSDN/VB starter kit, you'll find several articles about Windows 95's new file viewer technology. The more you read, the more you'll see that Visual Basic programmers are in for a difficult time. First, file viewers must be written as in-process (DLL) OLE servers. Basic DLL servers fit that description, so it's not out of the question. Second, shell extensions must implement OLE interfaces—IShellExtInit and specific interfaces such as IContextMenu and IShellPropSheetExt. (We'll use an IMalloc interface from the Windows API type library later in this chapter.) Implementing interfaces for Basic is a difficult problem, but not out of the question, although it is mostly beyond the scope of this book. I suspect, however, that someone will have to write a file viewer OLE server in C++ before any but the hardest of hardcore programmers will be able to write Basic file viewers. (Go ahead. Prove me wrong.)

In the meantime, here's a quick hack to fake file viewers by modifying the Registry. This exercise sets up a file viewer for the Debug Log document type. Debug Logs are the files (with extension DBG) created by BugMessage and other debugging procedures, as described in "Assert Yourself," page 29. The first step in viewing these files is to create a file viewer application. Edwina, the editor introduced in Chapter 8, has a file viewer (read-only) mode that you can invoke by passing a command line in the format *edwina /v file.ext*.

The easiest way to install Edwina as the file viewer for Debug Log is with Windows Explorer. Choose Options from the View menu. On the File Types tab of the dialog box, click the New Types button. Fill in all the fields of the subsequent dialog box for your document type, giving Quick View as an action and assigning *c:\hardcore\edwina /v* as the program to be invoked. (Don't click the Enable Quick View check box—this is the normal viewer mechanism that you're trying to circumvent.) Now when you right-click a Debug Log document in Windows Explorer, the menu contains a Quick View item. When you click this item, Edwina opens your debug document.

This is fine for you, but it doesn't do much for your customers. You need to install your viewer directly into the Registry in your setup program. If you study what Windows Explorer did to the Registry, you can figure out how to do the same without Explorer. Here are the steps:

1. Install a .dbg key in HKEY_CLASSES_ROOT, and give it the value *dbgfile*.

2. Install a dbgfile key in HKEY_CLASSES_ROOT, and give it the value *Debug Log*.

3. Install a DefaultIcon key in dbgfile, and point it to the icon for your document type.

4. Install a Shell key in dbgfile.

5. In the Shell key, install action keys for any actions you want. Normally, a document type should have Open and Print keys, but we'll add an additional Quick_View key with the value *&Quick View* as the title to be displayed on the context menu.

6. Add a command key with the value *c:\hardcore\edwina /v %1*.

Try this, step by step, in the Registry Editor before you program it.

The other side of this problem is using the Debug Log document type in your programs. If you have a program that displays documents (such as the Columbus program described later in this chapter), you must be able to run that program's Quick View command or any other commands it has. Let's start with the file extension:

1. In HKEY_CLASSES_ROOT, look up the Registry entry for the extension, and read its value (the document type).

2. Open the value in HKEY_CLASSES_ROOT.

3. Open the Shell key of the document type key.

4. Iterate through the command keys in the Shell key, using RegEnumKey. This isn't too different from using Dir$ or other enumeration procedures.

5. For each command, create a context menu item.

6. Add the other standard context menu commands—Cut, Delete, Properties, and so on. The Properties command poses a particularly interesting problem, as you'll see later in the chapter.

7. Respond to user selection of commands on the context menu by calling the ShellExecute function. For example, if the user clicks the Quick View menu item, you give the following command:

```
h = ShellExecute(hWnd, "Quick_View", sFileName, _
                 sNullStr, sEmpty, 0)
```

This is the high-altitude aerial view. Don't be surprised if the road looks a little rougher when you start driving on it. You should also be aware that this isn't the approved method. You're supposed to use the IContextMenu interface, but you'll find this difficult—though perhaps not impossible—from Visual Basic.

Context Menus

For years, too many applications written for Windows pretended that all mice had only one button, in clear defiance of reality. Of late, software vendors have rejected this self-amputation theory, but they still haven't been able to agree on the purpose of the right mouse button. Some prefer using it for Help, some for an application-specific verb, and some to generate a popup menu of possible actions. The third choice seems to have gained ascendancy recently, and it should get a big boost because Windows 95 makes this behavior the new standard. Once people get used to Windows 95, they'll expect a popup menu any time they right-click the screen. If your application doesn't provide one, they'll be annoyed.

Visual Basic makes popup, or context, menus easy. I wasted considerable time and energy thinking about ways to use the Windows API to create context menus. You can indeed use the TrackPopupMenu API, but you'll need a message tool such as the Message Blaster control to catch the resulting menu events. It's a hard way to go. The Menu Design window and the PopupMenu statement provide a simple alternative.

The real problem with context menus is design, not implementation. For each control on each form (and for the form background), you must design a menu with the appropriate verbs. This can get complicated if your application has menu items that need to be grayed or removed in certain modes. I create my design in the Menu Design window, making each context menu a separate menu at the top level. I make these menus visible at design time so that I can easily edit the menu events. I hide them in Form_Load:

```
cmnuContext.Visible = False
```

Implementation of context menus is complicated by the differences between Windows 95 and Windows NT with the Windows 95 shell (still forthcoming at publication time) on the one hand, and Windows 3.*x* and Windows NT 3.51 without the shell on the other hand. Here's the way to handle the difference:

```
Private Sub txtEdit_MouseDown(Button As Integer, Shift As Integer, _
                             X As Single, Y As Single)
    ' Mouse down on Win3 and WinNT without shell
    If Not HasShell And Button = 2 Then
        PopupMenu cmnuContext, , , , cmnuCut
    End If
End Sub

Private Sub txtEdit_MouseUp(Button As Integer, Shift As Integer, _
                           X As Single, Y As Single)
    ' Mouse up on Win95 and WinNT with shell
    If HasShell And Button = 2 Then
        PopupMenu cmnuContext, vbPopupMenuRightButton, , , cmnuCut
    End If
End Sub
```

The HasShell function looks like this:

```
Function HasShell() As Boolean
#If Win32 Then
    Dim dw As Long
    dw = GetVersion()
    If (dw And &HFF&) >= 4 Then
        HasShell = True
        ' Proves that operating system has shell, but not
        ' necessarily that it is installed. Some might argue
        ' that this function should check Registry under WinNT
        ' or SYSTEM.INI Shell= under Win95
    End If
#Else
    HasShell = False
#End If
End Function
```

Although this code works fine with the RichTextBox control in Edwina, the TextBox control in Edward supplies another twist. The Windows 95 shell provides its own context menus for the TextBox control (although not for the RichTextBox control). If you try to put your own context menu over a TextBox control, you'll see both conflicting context menus appear seemingly at random. There's no easy way to turn off the shell's menus, so it's best to turn off yours by keeping the MouseDown event shown in the preceding code but omitting the MouseUp event.

The real complication in designing context menus comes in handling your program's modes and controls. I can't help you with that except to urge you to handle all modes correctly and call common functions from menu events rather than duplicating code.

What Is a File?

The concept of a file used to be simple, but no more. Under 32-bit Windows, files are complicated and getting more so. OLE introduces the concept of structured files that look more like directory trees than the simple files we're used to. But that's getting ahead of the story. This version of Visual Basic doesn't handle structured OLE files. Ordinary files have enough new features anyway. Here are some of them:

- Filenames are long—up to 256 characters. Filenames are case-sensitive (sort of) and can have *"Embedded Spaces and.multiple.extensions"* as this one does.

- Files have new dates and times. Under Windows 3.*x* and MS-DOS, the date of the last file modification was stored with the file. Under Win32, three dates are stored with each file: creation, last modification, and last access. These dates can differ depending on the file system; more on this later.

- Files have new attributes: compressed and temporary. You won't have much reason to deliberately manipulate these attributes under Visual Basic, but you should be aware that documentation for the Basic GetAttr function and SetAttr statement isn't exactly telling the truth when it lists six file attributes instead of eight.

- Full file paths can be specified in the UNC format (*server**share*). This isn't new, but it has become more pervasive. You can always use UNC directory names to access network resources without saving a connection to them.

- Each file has a document type that controls how it is handled by Windows Explorer and Open dialog boxes. Some of the information that can be associated with a document type includes large and small icons, an OLE verb, a file viewer, and commands for printing and performing drag-and-drop operations. The most common way to define a document type is to associate it with a filename extension.

- You can perform new operations on files: delete, copy, move, and rename. You don't consider those operations new? We'll see.

File dates, times, and attributes

The official Basic FileDateTime function still believes that the last file modification time is the only time available, even in 32-bit mode. The new and improved FileDateTime function in BETTER32.BAS knows not only about the last modification time but also about the creation time and the last access time. What it doesn't know is which file system you have. Some file systems save only part of the file times, and you can't get more than the system provides.

Windows 95 directly supports only one file system, called VFAT. The VFAT system is an enhancement of the FAT (file allocation table) system, known and despised by MS-DOS and Windows 3.*x* programmers. Windows NT supports VFAT and any other installable file system you choose to install. The default Windows NT file system is referred to as NTFS; it supports all three file times. VFAT supports two and a half file times: it maintains the time and date of creation and last modification, but for last file access it maintains only the date. Windows 95 can access NTFS files (including all three file times) through the network, but local drives must use the VFAT system.

Under MS-DOS, file times were accurate to the nearest two seconds since 1980. Under Win32, they're accurate to the nearest micromillisecond (or some such) back to sometime just after Columbus logged onto America with his Z80 computer (or whatever they had back then). OK, the truth: they're accurate to the number of 100-nanosecond intervals since January 1, 1601.

My better FileDateTime works like the old version except that it takes additional optional arguments for the last access and creation times. The function returns the modification time directly and the other two times by reference:

```
Dim vModified as Variant, vAccessed As Variant, vCreated As Variant
vModified = FileDateTime(sFile, vAccessed, vCreated)
Print "Last modified: " & vModified
Print "Last accessed: " & vAccessed
Print "Created: " & vCreated
```

Under NTFS, the output looks like this:

```
Last modified: 7/12/95 12:48:52 PM
Last accessed: 7/9/95 1:31:36 PM
Created: 7/6/95 3:49:24 PM
```

Under VFAT, the output looks like this:

```
Last modified: 7/12/95 12:48:52 PM
Last accessed: 7/9/95 1:31:36 PM
Created: 7/6/95
```

Even if you don't care about FileDateTime, you might want to examine the code in BETTER32.BAS, since it illustrates how to convert a Win32 API time to a Basic time. In summary, you call FindFirstFile, FindClose, FileTimeToLocal-FileTime, FileTimeToSystemTime, DateSerial, and TimeSerial; and you use the Basic TimeSerial and DateSerial functions to convert the result to a Basic-style time in a Variant.

Getting file interface information

Open up Windows Explorer and set the display mode to Details. You'll see some information that we all know how to get as well as some you probably haven't seen before and don't know how to deal with in Visual Basic.

Notice that Windows Explorer lists some filenames with extensions and some without. Actually, Explorer isn't showing filenames at all. You are seeing display names, which you can get by calling the SHGetFileInfo API function. Windows 95 uses the display name that is registered for the file document type. If a file doesn't have a registered document type, the shell will report the full filename, including the extension, as the display name. Generally, Windows uses the extension to determine the document type. In some cases, the system can use a binary pattern in the first part of the file to distinguish documents that have the same extension. OLE structured files have a file type unrelated to any extension.

When you get the display name, you can also get other information from SHGetFileInfo, including the file type string, the file attributes, the executable type, and various forms of large and small icons. All this comes from the Registry entry for the document type. (Windows has defaults for files with no document file type.) SHGetFileInfo will also work on directories, disk drives, and special folder locations such as My Computer, Network Neighborhood, Desktop, and Recycle Bin.

Wrapping up file information

The SHGetFileInfo function is complicated, in the typical API style—in other words, it's un-Basic and needs some wrappers. I wrote my wrappers as a class named CFileInfo. As usual, let's watch this class in action before we start to examine how it works.

The Windows 95 Interface application (TWIN95.VBP) demonstrates the information you can get and the operations you can perform on files. If you turn ahead to page 554, you can see a frozen shot of the program (Figure 11-4). But to really get a feel for what you can do, you'll have to try out the program. A lot is going on in this application; you'll need to study the Win32 API help to fully understand the functions.

Busted

The Visual Basic environment provides a good example of how not to program files under 32-bit Windows. Try comparing the modification and creation times of a Basic source file. Now modify the source in the IDE, save, and compare again. The creation time and the modification time are always the same. In other words, the IDE isn't modifying the file when you hit the Save button. Instead, it's re-creating the file, probably in the same way most 16-bit programs modify a file: copy to a temporary file, make the changes on the copy, and, if all goes well, close the temporary, delete the old version, and rename the temporary to the old name.

Uh-oh. What's that flashing red light in the mirror?

"OK, buddy. You know what you did wrong?"

"I didn't do anything, officer. I've been saving files that way for years, and nobody ever complained before."

"Yeah, that's because you were driving on 16-bit roads. We couldn't recognize you guys there, but I can spot an old MS-DOS programmer a mile off on this new 32-bit superhighway."

"Hey, how did you know?"

"Look at that file creation time. When I see one that's the same as the write time, 95 times out of 100 it's one of you old programmers replacing a file without copying the time and attributes."

"What's wrong with that?"

"I bet this file is actually three months, maybe a year old. You're falsifying data. It might be an innocent mistake, but you're hurting yourself. The file taxes are higher on newer files. And it also screws up our maintenance equipment. Tell you what—I'll give you a break. Just take this warning ticket into the station within three days and pick up our ReplaceFile function from BETTER32.BAS. Use it from now on, and we'll cancel the 4-MB disk fine."

```
Function ReplaceFile(sOld As String, sTmp As String) As Boolean
    Dim fnd As TFindData, hFind As Long, hOld As Long, f As Boolean
    ' Get file time and attributes of old file
    If FindFirstFile(sOld, fnd) = -1 Then GoTo ReplaceFail
    ' Replace by deleting old and renaming new to old
    On Error GoTo ReplaceFail
    VBA.Kill sOld
    Name sTmp As sOld
    On Error GoTo 0
```

The following code from the program shows how to get the information displayed for the source file, including large and small icons in Image controls:

```
Dim fi As New CFileInfo, s As String, sTmp As String
If fi.Create(txtSrc.Text) = False Then Exit Sub
s = s & "Display name: " & fi.DisplayName & sCrLf
s = s & "Type name: " & fi.TypeName & sCrLf
sTmp = fi.ExeType
If sTmp <> sEmpty Then
    s = s & "Executable type: " & sTmp & sCrLf
End If
s = s & "Attributes: &H" & Hex(fi.Attributes, 8) & sCrLf
s = s & "Length: " & fi.Length & " bytes" & sCrLf
s = s & "Created: " & fi.Created & sCrLf
s = s & "Last modified: " & fi.Modified & sCrLf
s = s & "Last accessed: " & fi.Accessed & sCrLf
lblSrc.Caption = s
imgLIcon.Picture = fi.LargeIcon()
imgSIcon.Picture = fi.SmallIcon()
imgLIconSel.Picture = fi.LargeIcon(fiSelected)
imgSIconSel.Picture = fi.SmallIcon(fiSelected)
imgLIconLink.Picture = fi.LargeIcon(fiLinkOverlay)
imgSIconLink.Picture = fi.SmallIcon(fiLinkOverlay)
```

A spin box (see the upper right corner of the screen in Figure 11-4 on the next page) lets you select a special folder location. You can use a CFileInfo object to get information on these locations, too; you pass a special folder constant instead of a filename. The most interesting are CSIDL_BITBUCKET (Recycle Bin),

```
    ' Assign old attributes and time to new file
    hOld = lopen(sOld, OF_WRITE Or OF_SHARE_DENY_WRITE)
    f = SetFileTime(hOld, fnd.ftCreationTime, _
                    fnd.ftLastAccessTime, fnd.ftLastWriteTime)
    lclose hOld
    If f = False Then GoTo ReplaceFail
    f = SetFileAttributes(sOld, fnd.dwFileAttributes)
    If f Then ReplaceFile = True
ReplaceFail:
End Function
```

"Now why didn't I think of that? Hey, thanks."

"No problem, buddy. But if I catch you overwriting file times again, I'm going to throw the disk at you."

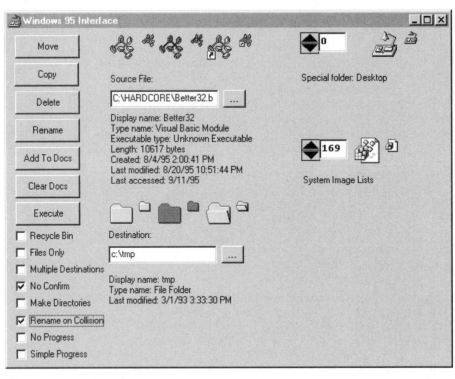

Figure 11-4. *File information and operations.*

CSIDL_DESKTOP (Desktop), and CSIDL_DRIVES (My Computer). You can see the others in the Windows 95 Interface application or in the Windows API type library. This user code displays the data for one of these constants:

```
Sub DrawSpecialFolder(iFolder As Integer)
    fiFolder.Create iFolder    ' Create module-level folder object
    lblSpecLoc.Caption = "Special folder: " & fiFolder.DisplayName
    imgLSpecLoc = fiFolder.LargeIcon
    imgSSpecLoc = fiFolder.SmallIcon
End Sub
```

Whether you're getting information for a file, a directory, a disk, or a special folder, you start by creating a CFileInfo object (defined in FILEINFO.CLS) and calling the Create method. Then you call any property you need. A lot is going on behind the scenes in the Create method:

```
Function Create(vFileItemA As Variant) As Boolean
    Dim f As Boolean, h As Long
    Destroy      ' Assume fail
```

```
        If VarType(vFileItemA) = vbString Then
            If Len(vFileItem) <= 3 And Mid$(vFileItemA, 2, 1) = ":" Then
                ' Must be drive, get attributes
                afAttr = 0: afOption = 0
            Else
                ' For file, get information in advance
                h = FindFirstFile(vFileItemA, fd)
                If h = -1 Then Exit Function
                FindClose h
                afAttr = fd.dwFileAttributes
                afOption = SHGFI_USEFILEATTRIBUTES
            End If
            f = GetFileInfo(CStr(vFileItemA), fi, afOption Or _
                        SHGFI_DISPLAYNAME Or SHGFI_TYPENAME, afAttr)
        Else
            ' For special folders, everything comes from system
            afAttr = 0: afOption = 0
            f = GetItemInfo(CLng(vFileItemA), fi, _
                        SHGFI_DISPLAYNAME Or SHGFI_TYPENAME)
        End If
        If f Then
            vFileItem = vFileItemA
            fCreated = True
        End If
        Create = fCreated
End Function
```

The Create method starts by calling Destroy to reset defaults for private variables that might have unwanted values left over from previous calls. The key private variables are the TFileInfo variable *fi* filled by SHGetFileInfo and the TFindData variable *fd* filled by FindFirstFile. Various other information is saved in private variables so that property procedures can access it later.

The Create method's main job is to determine whether the caller passed a special folder constant or a string containing a file, directory, or drive name. Based on the results, Create calls either GetFileInfo or GetItemInfo, which in turn passes options to SHGetFileInfo. GetFileInfo and GetItemInfo are located in FILEINFO.BAS so that those who prefer a functional style can call them directly rather than going through CFileInfo.

SHGetFileInfo doesn't return complete file information, so you must call FindFirstFile to get part of the data. You could get the file length with Basic's FileLen, get the attributes with GetAttr, and get the file time with FileDateTime, but you would be hitting the disk three times. FindFirstFile, the API function behind the Basic Dir$ function, gets all the file data with only one disk access. FindFirstFile doesn't work on drives, so the Create method has special code to handle that possibility.

One of the most important pieces of data retrieved is the option flag SHGFI-_USEFILEATTRIBUTES. One way or another, SHGetFileInfo must have the file attributes of the data it analyzes. If you already have the file attributes from a call to FindFirstFile, you pass them and use this flag to signal that SHGetFile-Info need not check them again. You can't get the attributes for disks or special folders, however, and SHGetFileInfo will fail if you claim you have them.

Once you have lined up everything for a file, a directory, or a drive, you call GetFileInfo:

```
Function GetFileInfo(sFile As String, fi As TFileInfo, _
                     ByVal afOption As Long, _
                     Optional vAttr As Variant) As Long
    If IsMissing(vAttr) Then vAttr = 0
    afOption = afOption And (Not SHGFI_PIDL)
    GetFileInfo = SHGetFileInfo(sFile, vAttr, fi, Len(fi), afOption)
End Function
```

If you're getting a special folder location, the code looks quite different:

```
Function GetItemInfo(iItem As Long, fi As TFileInfo, _
                     ByVal afOpt As Long) As Long
    ' Get item ID pointer, but don't use attributes
    afOpt = afOpt Or SHGFI_PIDL And (Not SHGFI_USEFILEATTRIBUTES)
    Dim objMalloc As IMalloc, pItemID As Long
    SHGetMalloc objMalloc
    ' Getting special folder can fail, causing a Basic error
    On Error Resume Next
    SHGetSpecialFolderLocation 0, iItem, pItemID
    If Err Then Exit Function
    GetItemInfo = SHGetItemInfo(pItemID, 0, fi, Len(fi), afOpt)
    objMalloc.Free pItemID
    Set objMalloc = Nothing
End Function
```

This short function does a stunning piece of OLE magic that would take another book almost this long to fully explain. If you're not an OLE wizard, you'll have to take part of the following explanation of OLE memory allocation on faith. The SHGetSpecialFolderLocation function allocates a chunk of data called an ITEMIDLIST and then returns a pointer to it. You can pass this pointer to SHGetItemInfo (which is simply SHGetFileInfo aliased to take a pointer variable instead of a string). The problem is that SHGetSpecialFolderLocation allocates the data with an OLE IMalloc interface but then neither frees it nor provides a function to free it. You must free it yourself, using an IMalloc object.

What is an IMalloc object, and where would you get one? To answer the first question, read Kraig Brockschmidt's twelve-hundred-page tome *Inside OLE*, 2d edition (Microsoft Press, 1995). To answer the second question, check the IMalloc interface in the Windows API type library source file WIN.ODL. The SHGetMalloc function returns an IMalloc interface pointer that you can use as a class object to allocate, free, and check data. Of course, all you really want to do with it is free the data passed by SHGetSpecialFolderLocation.

If you can figure out the IMalloc interface definition in WIN.ODL, you might be able to figure out how to write interface definitions for other standard OLE and Windows 95 interfaces. You can then use the objects from Visual Basic. If you had ITypeLib and ITypeInfo objects, you could create your own object browser. If you had an IShellFolder object, you could iterate through the Windows 95 shell namespace, hitting the Desktop, My Computer (with all your drives, directories, and files), Control Panel, Recycle Bin, and the rest. If you had an IShellLink object, you could create your own shortcuts on the desktop. And so on...

Once you've created a CFileInfo object, getting the properties is a simple matter of returning the data stored by the Create method. Here, for example, is the SmallIcon property:

```
Function SmallIcon(Optional vOverlay As Variant) As Picture
    Dim fiT As TFileInfo
    If fCreated = False Then Exit Function
    If IsMissing(vOverlay) Then vOverlay = 0&
    ' Filter out any invalid flags -- only overlays allowed
    vOverlay = vOverlay And (SHGFI_LINKOVERLAY Or SHGFI_SELECTED _
                        Or SHGFI_OPENICON)
    ' Add in standard and small icon flags
    vOverlay = vOverlay Or afOption Or SHGFI_ICON Or SHGFI_SMALLICON
    GetFileItemInfo vFileItem, fiT, vOverlay, afAttr
    Set SmallIcon = IconToPicture(fiT.hIcon)
End Function
```

The vOverlay property allows you to optionally specify whether the standard icon will appear selected, as a shortcut, or open. The open overlay isn't really an overlay; it's a completely different icon indicating that a folder is open. The open flag is ignored for files, which don't have a separate icon for the open state.

You can probably guess the implementation of the Length, Created, Modified, and Accessed properties, which use data received from the call to FindFirstFile. The ExeType property uses SHGetFileInfo with the SHGFI_EXETYPE flag to return the same information you could get from my ExeType function (found in EXETYPE.BAS). Incidentally, Windows NT (but not Windows 95) has a Get-BinaryType function that provides similar information.

NOTE SHGetFileInfo retrieves additional data not used in the CFileInfo class. For example, large and small icons used by the system are maintained in two internal ImageLists. Unfortunately, the Visual Basic ImageList control doesn't give you a way to use them. It's possible to iterate through the system ImageList control directly by using ImageList API functions with SHGetFileInfo, a technique illustrated in the Windows 95 Interface application. It turned out to be a dead end, however; I couldn't find anything useful to do with system ImageLists in Basic that couldn't be done more easily without them.

Iterating through files

Sometime during your programming career, you've probably known the frustration of working with the Dir$ function. It's very easy to use for simple operations, but it runs out of power quickly.

The worst limitation of Dir$ is documented right up front: you can't call it recursively. This is a severe limitation for a function that ought to be able to iterate through your entire hard disk, finding files that match a given description or displaying directory trees. Workarounds exist, but the performance is unacceptable; see the "Performance" sidebar on the facing page. The other problem with Dir$ is that it returns only the filename. If you're building a file display with attributes, file length, and file time, you have to hit the disk once for each item for each file.

But nothing prevents you from calling the Win32 FindFirstFile, FindNextFile, and FindCloseFile functions to iterate through files yourself. You can recurse as much as you like and grab all the file data you need in one fell swoop. That's what Dir$ is doing under the surface, anyway—but it's throwing away all the information it finds except the filename. The Win16 API doesn't have FindFirstFile and friends. I planned to write them for the VBUTIL DLL, but this somewhat difficult task requires memory tricks not used by the Microsoft C run-time function _dos_findfirst. I never got around to it.

My Basic function to iterate through files is called Files. It works a lot like Dir$ except that it returns all the file information you could ever want through a CFileInfo object. Here's a typical iteration loop, from the Columbus application:

```
Dim hFind As Long, fi As New CFileInfo
sFile = Files(hFind, fi, "*.*", vbDirectory)
Do While sFile <> sEmpty
    If sFile <> "." And sFile <> ".." Then
        AddIconImages imlstLIcon, imlstSIcon, fi, fi.TypeName
        Set nod = tvwFiles.Nodes.Add(iCur, tvwChild, , _
                                    fi.DisplayName, fi.TypeName)
        nod.Tag = sFile
        ' Add dummy node
        If DirHasDir(sFile) Then
            tvwFiles.Nodes.Add nod.Index, tvwChild, , ":"
        End If
    End If
    sFile = Files(hFind, fi, "*.*", vbDirectory)
Loop
```

PERFORMANCE

Problem: Compare the speed of finding files with the Dir$ function to equivalent techniques such as using FindFileFirst in 32-bit mode and using the operating system's *dir /s* command.

Problem	16-Bit Mode	32-Bit Mode
Use the Basic Dir$ function	46 sec	61 sec
Use the Win32 FindFirstFile function	n/a	8 sec
Use Shell to call the *dir /s* command	29 sec	9 sec
Use the Windows 95 Find command	n/a	5 sec

Conclusion: The Dir$ function is clearly a loser, whereas FindFirstFile performs quite well. Your results will vary widely depending on the host operating system, the size of the disk, and how many levels of nested directories it has. For example, FindFirstFile was faster than *dir /s* on Windows 95, but the opposite was true on Windows NT. The times in the table were recorded under Windows 95 on a machine with a 512-MB hard disk. Try it for yourself with the Time It program. You could probably write a C++ DLL version of the Basic FindFiles function (in FINDFILE.BAS) that would match the results of the speedy Windows 95 Find command.

The iteration loop from Columbus looks like a Dir$ loop, but with several important differences. First, each call to the Files function must pass a handle variable. In the first call, which usually occurs just before the loop, the handle value must be 0. In this case, *hFind*, a local variable, is automatically initialized to 0. After the first call, the handle will contain a real handle, returned by reference, which you must maintain until the loop finishes. The handle enables the Find function to do recursion. The function DirHasDir in COLUMBUS.FRM, for example, also calls the Files function to determine whether the current directory has a child directory, but that's OK because the inner function has its own handle. You couldn't do that with Dir$.

Each call to the Files function looks exactly the same. You always pass the same CFileInfo object by reference (*fi*, in this case) and the same wildcard specification and attributes—with one exception. If you need to get out of a loop early, you pass the special attribute *vbStopFind*:

```
sFile = Files(hFind, fi, "*.*", vbStopFind)
```

If you abandon a Files loop without stopping, you will end up with dangling memory chunks.

The Files function is straightforward API programming:

```
Function Files(hFiles As Long, fi As CFileInfo, _
               ByVal sSpec As String, _
               Optional vInAttr As Variant) As String
    Dim fd As TFindData, sName As String, f As Boolean
    Dim sPath As String, afAttr As Long
    If Not IsMissing(vInAttr) Then afAttr = vInAttr ' Else 0

    ' Stop finding and close handle early
    If afAttr = vbStopFind Then
        f = FindClose(hFiles)
        hFiles = 0: Exit Function
    End If
    f = True
    Do
        ' Get first or next file
        If hFiles = 0 Then
            hFiles = FindFirstFile(sSpec, fd)
        Else
            f = FindNextFile(hFiles, fd)
        End If
```

```
        If (f = False Or hFiles = INVALID_HANDLE_VALUE) Then
            If Err.LastDllError = ERROR_NO_MORE_FILES Then
                f = FindClose(hFiles)
            End If
            hFiles = 0: Exit Function
        End If
        ' Keep looping until something matches attributes
    Loop While (afAttr <> vbNormal) And _
                ((afAttr And fd.dwFileAttributes) = 0)
    ' Get file data and return through reference
    sPath = GetFileDir(sSpec)
    sName = StrZToStr(fd.cFileName)
    fi.CreateFile sPath & sName, _
                fd.dwFileAttributes, fd.nFileSizeLow, _
                SysToVBTime(fd.ftLastWriteTime), _
                SysToVBTime(fd.ftLastAccessTime), _
                SysToVBTime(fd.ftCreationTime)
    Files = sName
End Function
```

OK, so it's not so straightforward. First, you handle the optional *vInAttr* argument and the possible request to terminate early. Easy enough. Then you call FindFirstFile the first time (signaled by a 0 handle). The handle from FindFirst-File is returned through a reference and used by FindNextFile on each subsequent call. You can see why you'd better not mess with that handle.

The tricky part is looping until you match the attributes. If the user asks for directories only, you might need a lot of iterations to find the first match. The only problem is that *vbNormal* is 0, in defiance of logic. Zero isn't a bit flag—it's the absence of a bit flag—so you must handle it specially. Technically, you could change the attribute for each call, but your results would be unpredictable.

Finally, the function gets the data. It reuses the file specification each time to find the path, which you use to initialize a new CFileInfo object. This means that you must either pass the same full path specification to the Files function for each call or, if you use relative paths, make sure that the path never changes between calls. This can get a little tricky for recursive calls that change the directory, but everything works out if each level of recursion puts things back the way it found them.

Notice that the Files function calls the CreateFile method of CFileInfo rather than the Create method discussed earlier. The CreateFile method works almost like the Create method. But instead of calling FindFirstFile to get file data, it takes arguments that just happen to match all the fields of the UDT returned by FindFirstFile.

CHALLENGE A more elegant solution to the problem of iterating through files would be to have an NFilesInfo collection that iterates through CFileInfo objects. Each directory would be represented by a collection, and you could recursively iterate through collections of collections. But the NFilesInfo collection needs to be written in C++. If you're going to go that far, you might as well rewrite the CFileInfo object in the same language. Your collection should be based on iterating through the shell namespace using the IShellFolder interface rather than iterating through the file system with FindFirstFile and FindNextFile.

Politically correct file operations

Deleting, copying, renaming, and moving files should be simple, right? Basic provides the Kill, FileCopy, and Name statements for the first three operations, and it's easy to write a FileMove using the other three. In fact, you don't even need to do that in 32-bit mode because, contrary to documentation, the Name statement can move files across disks. Who could be offended by such simple features?

Well, you might be offended if the FileCopy statement overwrote an important file without asking for confirmation. I might be ticked off if your Kill statement accidentally killed all the files in the DeleteMe.Not folder, with no way to recover them. Our customers might be frustrated and confused if our FileCopy brought the whole system to a halt while copying a 1-MB file from a remote drive to a floppy disk with no visual clue of why the keyboard and the mouse weren't responding.

The SHFileOperation function provides the means to delete, rename, copy, and move files with all the protections, warnings, and status reports you could ever imagine, and some that you never dreamed of. I use SHFileOperation to fix FileCopy in BETTER32.BAS and to add FileDelete, FileRename, and File-Move functions. I could have replaced Kill, but the name doesn't imply much politeness or flexibility, so I put the new functionality on FileDelete. (Besides, I fixed the Kill function in a different and incompatible way by allowing it to take multiple file specifications on its command line.) The Name statement can't be fixed because it isn't a legal Basic function. You can't write your own procedure that uses the *As* syntax, as Name does.

Before examining the better FileCopy, let's glance at the UDT that is used by SHFileOperation:

```
Type TFileOperation
    hWnd                     As Long    ' Parent window for dialog
    wFunc                    As Long    ' Copy, move, rename, delete
```

```
    pFrom                       As String ' Source
    pTo                         As String ' Destination (delete ignores)
    fFlags                      As Long   ' Options
    fAnyOperationsAborted       As Long   ' Indicates partial failure
    hNameMappings               As Long   ' Completed operations
    lpszProgressTitle           As String ' Title for dialog
End Type
```

I ignore the *fAnyOperationsAborted* and *hNameMappings* fields, which supply more complete information about the completed operation. But you can feel free to enhance with them. The *hWnd* and *lpszProgressTitle* fields control features of the "flying files" dialog box that appears when an operation takes more than a second or so. I provide optional arguments for these. You can get a feel for the rest from the implementation of FileCopy:

```
Function FileCopy(sSrc As String, sDst As String, _
                  Optional vOptions As Variant, _
                  Optional vTitle As Variant, _
                  Optional vOwner As Variant) As Boolean
    If HasShell Then
        Dim fo As TFileOperation, f As Long
        fo.wFunc = FO_COPY
        fo.pFrom = sSrc
        fo.pTo = sDst
        If Not IsMissing(vOptions) Then fo.fFlags = vOptions
        If Not IsMissing(vTitle) Then fo.lpszProgressTitle = vTitle
        If Not IsMissing(vOwner) Then fo.hWnd = vOwner
        ' Mask out invalid flags
        fo.fFlags = fo.fFlags And FOF_COPYFLAGS
        f = SHFileOperation(fo)
        FileCopy = (f = 0)
    Else
        ' For Windows NT 3.51
        On Error Resume Next
        ' FileCopy expects full name of destination file
        VBA.FileCopy sSrc, sDst
        If Err Then
            Err = 0
            ' Better FileCopy can handle destination directory
            sDst = NormalizePath(sDst) & GetFileBaseExt(sSrc)
            VBA.FileCopy sSrc, sDst
        End If
        ' Enhance further to emulate SHFileOperation options
        ' such as validation and wildcards
        FileCopy = (Err = 0)
    End If
End Function
```

The rudest thing about the SHFileOperation function and other Windows 95–only functions is that they aren't correctly unimplemented on Windows NT 3.51. Unimplemented API functions are supposed to fail and set GetLastError (Err.LastDllError in Basic) to ERROR_CALL_NOT_IMPLEMENTED (120), but these actually set the error to ERROR_PATH_NOT_FOUND (3). If you need to write functions that work on Windows 95, Windows NT 3.51 without the shell, and a future version of Windows NT with the shell, don't depend on the behavior of function failure as you do with most Win32 functions. Instead, use the HasShell function described earlier in "Context Menus," page 547.

The trick in calling FileCopy, FileMove, FileRename, and FileDelete is to pass the correct flags. Table 11-1 offers a brief summary of the flags with Visual Basic–style names. The default behavior is to produce a confirmation dialog box if anything is to be deleted or overwritten and to put up a progress dialog box if the operation lasts long enough to make a user wonder what's going on. You can test other operations with the Windows 95 Interface application, shown in Figure 11-4 on page 554.

Flag	Purpose
vbFileOpNoConfirm	Overwrite or delete files without confirmation
vbFileOpRecycleBin	Put deleted files (except those from floppy disks) in Recycle Bin
vbFileOpNoProgress	Prevent display of a progress dialog box for slow operations
vbFileOpSimpleProgress	Simplify the progress dialog box by not showing filenames
vbFileOpRenameOnCollision	Create new numbered files (*Copy #1 of....*) if copied or moved files conflict with existing files
vbFileOpMultiDestFiles	Copy or move a wildcard source to multiple target files rather than to a single destination directory
vbFileOpFilesOnly	Interpret a wildcard source to mean files only, not directories
vbFileOpNoConfirmMkDir	Create any needed destination directories without confirmation

Table 11-1. *Option flags for file operation functions.*

More Interface Stuff

If I had planned this book better, I would've had two or three chapters on programming the Windows 95 shell. Here are some of the other issues I would have covered in detail:

- Wouldn't it be nice to have a drop-down list for selecting drives and directories, like the one in Windows Explorer and the Open common dialog? Well, tough luck. Windows 95 provides no way to reuse the standard control. Not in Basic or in any language. You can create your own by iterating through the shell namespace with the IShellFolder interface in some languages. Good luck doing it in Basic. You can, however, produce a similar effect with the Browse For Folder dialog box. I wrap the SHBrowseForFolder API function in the Basic function BrowseForFolder (in FILEINFO.BAS). You pass in arguments to set the initial state of the dialog box, and then get the results from the return value. To see it in action, click the button next to the Destination field in the Windows 95 Interface application shown in Figure 11-4.

- You can add files to the Documents list on the Start menu by calling the AddToRecentDocs procedure (in FILEINFO.BAS), which in turn calls SHAddToRecentDocs. You can clear the list with ClearRecentDocs. The Windows 95 Interface application (Figure 11-4) has buttons that use these functions.

- If your application needs to put a status icon on the Taskbar, you can call Shell_NotifyIcon to install or remove the icon. I wrap the Shell-_NotifyIcon function in the CTrayIcon class; you can see it in action in the Windows 95 Interface application. I use a Message Blaster control to monitor double-clicks on the icon and display a message box. (Be careful when testing this application. If you interrupt the program with the End button or the End menu item, you'll never hit the Unload event where CTrayIcon objects are destroyed. You'll end up with orphaned icons on your Taskbar.)

- You can write shell extensions for your document types. Shell extensions enable your documents, and the icons associated with them, to respond to events in the Windows 95 shell. You can create context menus, drag-and-drop handlers, and property sheet handlers for your document types. These features are not the same as similar features in your application because they affect your documents, not your program. In fact, your program might not be running when the shell extension goes into action. Or the shell extension might need to load your application. Unfortunately, you'll have a difficult time writing shell extensions in Basic for the same reason you'll have trouble with file viewers: they must be written as in-process OLE servers that implement OLE interfaces—the general IShellExtInit interface and a specific extension interface such as IContextMenu or IShellPropSheetExt. I'm not saying it can't be done in Basic—just that it won't be easy.

- You can make good use of new help features such as the What's This? help button. There's a programming element to this, but most of the work lies in creating the help files. (I confess to not writing a single help file for the samples provided with this book. You're on your own.)

- To support Plug and Play, you can install the System Information control. Unlike other controls, this one isn't installed on your disk, but it's on the Visual Basic CD with its own help file. You can monitor various events, particularly those that change the screen size.

- Use property sheets everywhere you can. Create a property sheet form for your document types, using either the TabStrip or SSTab control. Put a Properties item on your toolbars and context menus whenever appropriate.

Common Controls

I remember my amazement, back in the dark ages of Windows 1 and 2, when I learned that every programmer who wanted an Open dialog box had to write the code to fill the list box by reading the files out of the directory. The common dialog functions introduced in Windows 3 solved the problem for dialog boxes, but everyone still had to write their own toolbars, outlines, status bars, and what have you.

Somewhere during the time frame of Windows for Workgroups, the common controls DLL was created and was used to implement the toolbars of File Manager. The source code for this DLL appeared as a sample in the Windows for Workgroups Software Development Kit, and it later became available on the Microsoft Developer Network. COMMCTRL.DLL became a kind of standard, though not official or well documented. It was one of three toolbar implementations used by different groups at Microsoft. (You can see the differences if you study old Microsoft applications carefully.)

Microsoft didn't necessarily start the industry trend toward toolbars, status bars, and property sheets, but it jumped on the bandwagon and eventually standardized most common controls by expanding the 16-bit COMMCTRL.DLL into COMCTL32.DLL. Visual Basic wrapped this C-specific DLL into the Microsoft Windows common controls. Standard common controls were implemented only for 32-bit mode, however, and, as a result, Visual Basic provides only 32-bit versions of the controls. Because the 32-bit common controls grew out of the 16-bit versions, it's theoretically possible to write portable code that uses the common subset by programming the DLL directly rather than using controls. But it's not something you'd want to do in Basic. I speak here from experience; writing portable common controls is one of the dead ends I discovered early in the development of this book.

Let's look at the most important new controls. The product documents normal use, so we'll focus on some problems and workarounds you won't find in the manuals. But first a comment on one aspect of all the new controls: they use collections to the max. If you don't fully understand collections, you might want to review "Collecting Objects," page 174, in Chapter 4.

ImageList Controls

ImageList controls work behind the scenes in the Toolbar, ListView, TreeView, StatusBar, and TabStrip controls. The Visual Basic control that implements the ImageList concept is specifically designed to work with its partner controls. But if you look closely at ImageLists, you'll see that they also have a wider potential. Unfortunately, the control doesn't provide built-in features for some of the things you might like to do with it. Fortunately, it does provide one undocumented feature that allows hardcore programmers to do whatever they want.

An ImageList is a collection of images of the same size and type, but they're more than just images. When you insert an image into the list, the control gives it a mask. If the image is an icon, its internal mask is reused. If it is a bitmap or a metafile, a mask is created, probably using a technique similar to the one used for CPictureGlass ("Creating Masks," page 290). The end result is a collection of icons of the same size. When you attach an ImageList to another control, you don't need to worry about what gets drawn and how, but you'll understand the process better if you experiment with the methods of an unattached ImageList.

The Test ImageList program (TIMAGE.VBP), shown in Figure 11-5 on the following page, illustrates operations you can perform directly with ImageList controls. The images on the right side of the screen represent the images in lists of icons and bitmaps, respectively. The bitmap on the left provides a background to demonstrate how images can be drawn in different ways. To see how the different operations work on a solid background, use the Picture check box to turn the picture off. You can experiment with this program to understand the fundamental difference between icons and bitmaps and how you can handle each correctly in ImageLists.

Figure 11-6, page 569, shows a map of ImageList methods and properties. ImageLists provide four ways of placing images on a surface: the Picture property, the ExtractIcon method, the Overlay method, and the Draw method. Two properties, BackColor and MaskColor, affect the operations of the four drawing mechanisms.

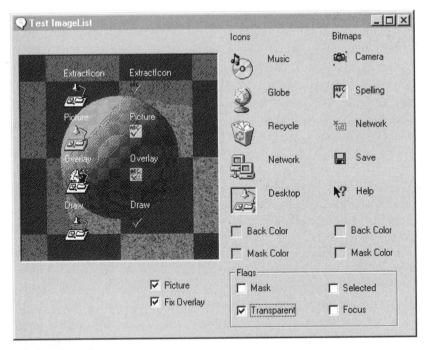

Figure 11-5. *Drawing with ImageLists.*

The Picture property and the ExtractIcon method

The Picture property of the ListImage object simply returns the picture you put into the ImageList. If you put in an icon, you get back an icon; if you put in a bitmap, you get back a bitmap. This works for icons no matter where you place the picture, but bitmaps don't look good unless they contain a solid image or unless the background of the image is the same as the background of the target picture. This makes the Picture property somewhat inflexible for general use, but of course you can use PaintPicture to do anything you want with it.

Don't try to use the Picture property to replace an image. This property is read-only, so you might as well think of it as the Picture method. To replace an image (this is true for any collection element), you must remove the old item and add a new one at its position.

The ExtractIcon method converts an image to an icon. If the image is already an icon, ExtractIcon is the equivalent of the Picture property. With a bitmap,

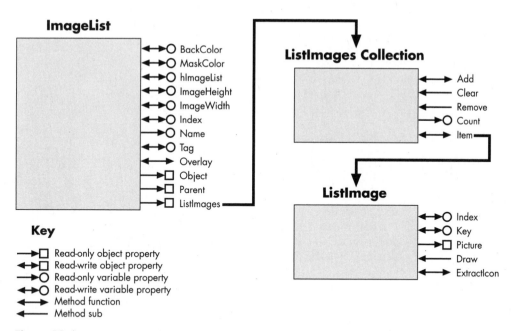

ImageList

←→O	BackColor
←→O	MaskColor
←→O	hImageList
←→O	ImageHeight
←→O	ImageWidth
←→O	Index
→O	Name
←→O	Tag
←→	Overlay
→□	Object
→□	Parent
→□	ListImages

ListImages Collection

←→	Add
←	Clear
←	Remove
→O	Count
←→	Item

ListImage

←→O	Index
←→O	Key
→□	Picture
←	Draw
←→	ExtractIcon

Key

→□	Read-only object property
←→□	Read-write object property
→O	Read-only variable property
←→O	Read-write variable property
←→	Method function
←	Method sub

Figure 11-6. *An ImageList map.*

ExtractIcon stretches or compresses it to the standard icon size, as determined by GetSystemMetrics, and uses the MaskColor property of the ImageList to make the image transparent. You can save the result to a file with SavePicture. Just make sure that you set the MaskColor property to the color of the bitmap background. To see how this works, use the Mask Color check box to set different colors that appear in the bitmap. This is a roundabout way to convert a bitmap to an icon. It's much easier to use ImagEdit, although most bitmaps look terrible when converted to icons. The mechanism would be a lot more flexible if you could convert to an icon of any size (the size of the bitmap, for example). What you really want from ExtractIcon is its transparency, not a standard icon size. More on that later.

The Overlay method

You can use the Overlay method to combine any two ListImage objects in an ImageList. This works fine on a solid background, but, as Figure 11-5 illustrates, icons don't come out right. The top image is placed on the bottom image transparently, but the bottom image is placed on the background opaquely. In other words, the Overlay method converts an icon to a bitmap. You can get around this bug by inserting the overlaid image back into the ImageList and then using ExtractIcon to remove it as an icon. Here's the code to use Overlay normally and the code to fix the problem:

```
With imlstIcons
    If chkOverlay.Value <> vbChecked Then
        ' Overlay without bug fix
        imgIconOverlay.Picture = .Overlay(iIconsLast, iIcons)
    Else
        ' Save old background and mask color
        Dim clrBack As Long, clrMask As Long
        clrBack = .BackColor: clrMask = .MaskColor
        ' Set color that does not occur in image
        .BackColor = vbMagenta: .MaskColor = vbMagenta
        ' Insert overlay, extract as icon, remove, and restore color
        .ListImages.Add 1, , .Overlay(iIconsLast, iIcons)
        imgIconOverlay.Picture = .ListImages(1).ExtractIcon
        .ListImages.Remove 1
        .BackColor = clrBack: .MaskColor = clrMask
    End If
End With
```

This technique works in the sample because I found a temporary background and mask color, *vbMagenta*, that didn't occur in any of the sample icons. But what if you were loading the icons at run time? I suppose you could check every pixel in the icon with the Point method, but it's easier to simply draw the images on top of each other using the techniques shown in the next section.

The Draw method and the DrawImage function

The Draw method allows you to draw an image from an ImageList directly onto a form, a picture box, or anything else that has an hDC property. This method does, however, illustrate a flaw in the ImageList design, one that belies the purpose of the underlying ImageList API functions.

You call the Draw method as shown here:

```
imlstBmps.ListImages(iBmps).Draw pb.hDC, x, y, imlNormal
```

The final style argument can be *imlNormal*, *imlTransparent*, *imlSelected*, or *imlFocus*. The latter two specify an image dithered to different degrees, to give it a shaded effect. The values of these constants are 0 through 3. They are what C programmers call an enumeration. You select one and only one. But what if you want to draw a transparent selected image? In fact, transparent is the only way I'd ever want to draw a selected or focus image.

Let's look at the API functions behind the Draw method. An image list is created with the ImageList_ family of API functions. The Draw method uses either the ImageList_Draw function or its enhanced cousin, ImageList_DrawEx. To keep things simple, we'll use ImageList_Draw, which is called this way:

```
f = ImageList_Draw(hImageList, i, hdc, x, y, _
                   ILD_TRANSPARENT Or ILD_SELECTED)
```

Notice the final style argument. It's obviously a bitfield, not an enumeration. The values of the ILD_ constants confirm this: &H0, &H1, &H2, &H4, &H10—not 0, 1, 2, 3. Furthermore, there are five of them, not four. ILD_MASK draws a monochrome mask of the image, but you won't find a parallel *imlMask* constant. Perhaps the designer of the ImageList control didn't know why a Basic programmer would want a mask. But you do (if you read Chapter 6). The constant ILD_NORMAL has the value 0, which indicates the absence of any modifying bits rather than a separate kind of image.

Hardcore programmers have to forget the ImageList Draw method and go down to the API to get what they need. To do that, you'll need an ImageList handle. If you look in the ImageList documentation, you won't find a handle property. But if you look in the Object Browser, there it is: hImageList. This is all you need to fix the Draw method or any other ImageList limitations. Keep in mind that the default scale mode of the API is pixels, not twips, and that API indexes are zero-based, not one-based. Here's a DrawImage function that replaces the Draw method:

```
Sub DrawImage(imlst As ImageList, vIndex As Variant, hDC As Long, _
              x As Long, y As Long, Optional vDraw As Variant)
    If IsMissing(vDraw) Then vDraw = ILD_TRANSPARENT
    ImageList_Draw imlst.hImageList, _
                   imlst.ListImages(vIndex).Index - 1, hDC, _
                   x / Screen.TwipsPerPixelX, _
                   y / Screen.TwipsPerPixelY, vDraw
End Sub
```

This version is hard-coded to assume twips. Notice that it adjusts the one-based ImageList index. By default, it draws transparent images.

I would rather have designed this function to take a ListImage object instead of an ImageList control and an index, calling it like this:

```
DrawImage imlstIcons.ListImage(iIcons), hDC, x, y
```

But the hImageList property is on ImageList, and ListImage has no Parent property to refer back to the ImageList. I must supply an extra argument:

```
DrawImage imlstIcons, iIcons, hDC, x, y
```

ImageList Challenge

The ImageList API functions have other features that aren't passed through in the ImageList control. Here are some ideas you might try, using the declarations, constants, and functions in COMCTL.BAS and the Windows API type library. Look at the extra arguments of ImageList_DrawEx. You can stretch an image to any size and control its background and foreground colors. Unfortunately, you can't use ROP arguments to blit images as you can with the PaintPicture method or the BitBlt function. The ImageList_ExtractIcon and ImageList_GetIcon functions give you a handle to an icon. If you carefully study the earlier section on icons, you can come up with a way to get the transparency of an icon without stretching it to the standard icon size (even if you have inserted a bitmap). Use the handle with the IconToPicture function (PICTOOL.BAS), or draw directly with the DrawIconEx API function.

It wouldn't be difficult to write a class wrapper that fixes many of the ImageList control's limitations. For that matter, you could totally replace the ImageList with your own implementation using the API. Since ImageList doesn't have events, there's a good case for making it a server rather than a control anyway. Of course, you wouldn't be able to initialize the images of an ImageList server at design time, but many programs could live with that limitation.

Normally, you use an ImageList like a roll of snapshots that you can access by name or by number. But if you arrange these snapshots in sequential order, like movie frames, you could generate a moving picture just by playing them in sequence. It wouldn't be too difficult to build an animation class based on an ImageList control.

You can use similar techniques to get around limitations of other common controls. ImageList is invisible and has its own special handle and API functions. Other controls have an hWnd property that you can use to send messages to their windows.

TreeView and ListView Controls

On the surface, TreeView and ListView controls seem to offer an easy way to create applications that look like Windows Explorer. Personally, I like the idea of Windows Explorer more than its actual implementation. I was looking forward to creating my own better exploration program. My plan was to clone the real Explorer and then start adding my own features. You can see how far this plan progressed, with the Columbus application shown in Figure 11-7.

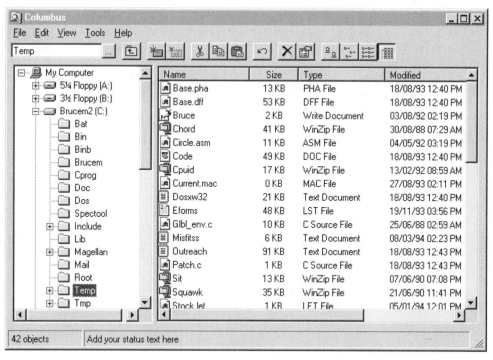

Figure 11-7. *Columbus sails west.*

Yes, it looks sort of like Windows Explorer (although it starts at My Computer rather than at the desktop). Yes, it performs the basic operations of Windows Explorer. Yes, you could enhance it to add more Explorer features, and you could add other features that Windows Explorer lacks. But the performance of this application is awful. Perhaps someone more hardcore than I am could optimize it slightly, but I'm afraid the optimizations you really need must be done in a compiled language. I named early versions of this program Meriwether after one of my favorite explorers, Meriwether Lewis, but eventually I renamed it Columbus, after the man who never did reach the East by sailing west.

CHALLENGE Although the Columbus program is unfinished, check out its splitter bar. The CHSplitter (HSPLIT.VBP) and CVSplitter (VSPLIT.VBP) classes provide horizontal and vertical splitter bars that separate and automatically resize two controls passed to their Create methods. You can find lots of ways to use them. You could start by giving Edwina or Edward two resizable editing windows (like those in the Visual Basic editor).

Although TreeView and ListView controls turned out to be a dead end for managing files, I learned a lot in the effort. Both controls are too large and complicated for anyone with a normal memory to keep their structure in mind. I found working with them easier after I created the maps shown in Figures 11-8 and 11-9. I'll share a few high-level pointers that you can use in other applications that display Registry entries, the window hierarchy, or any other tree-structured data.

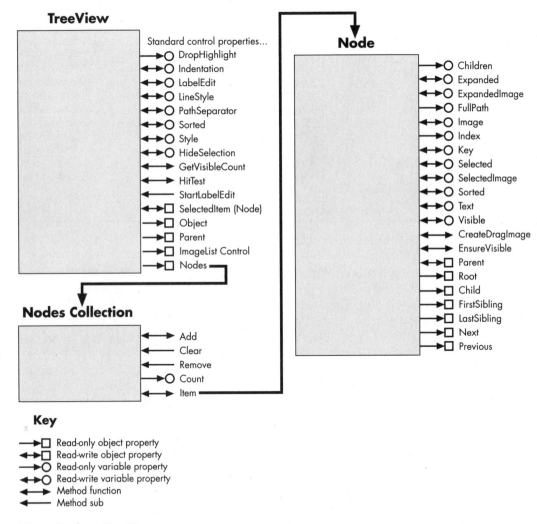

Figure 11-8. *A TreeView map.*

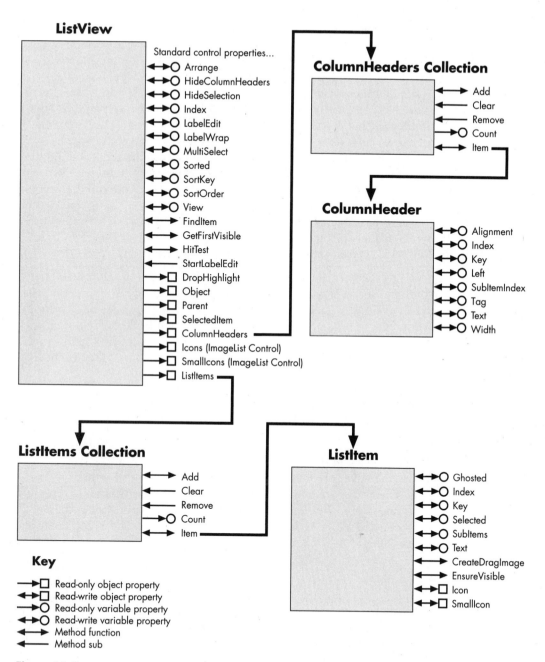

Figure 11-9. *A ListView map.*

■ Although the TreeView control seems to be designed to be completely filled at initialization, this strategy doesn't work for many kinds of data. It would take a very long time to fill an Explorer-style program with all the files on a large network disk. Furthermore, the levels could get out of sync if other programs deleted or created files after the control was initialized. A better strategy is to fill each level as it is expanded. The problem is that if you don't fill in the next branch of a TreeView, that branch won't have a plus button, and you won't have any way to expand it. The solution is to determine whether the branch has children and, if it does, to fill it with a single fake child rather than with its real children. When the user takes an action that would expand the branch, you delete the fake child and fill in the real children (filling any of their children that have children with fakes). You must choose a value for the fakes that is illegal for real children. In Columbus, I used ":" in the Tag field, where I store the filename in valid children.

■ You must be careful to destroy collapsed trees (filling them with fake children if necessary) so that they don't eat up all your memory. I failed to clear out dead TreeView nodes during the early stages of developing Columbus, instead creating a new copy of each node every time it was expanded. The results weren't pretty. If you see paint problems in other applications while developing a TreeView application, take another look at your cleanup code.

■ You might need to store data that isn't shown in the TreeView or ListView control. Columbus shows the shell display name, but it also needs to store the real file, directory, or disk name of each TreeView node so that you can use it to find your place in the real file hierarchy from any place in the TreeView hierarchy. TreeView and ListView controls don't have the *ItemData* array common to other ListBox-type controls. This is a serious limitation for some applications, and you might even find cases where an old-fashioned Outline works better than a newfangled TreeView. ListViews and TreeViews do allow you to store string data in the Tag property.

■ The obvious place to store unseen data that you're going to search for later is in the Key property. This works for ListViews, but you'll have trouble using the key for TreeViews. The problem is that every key must be unique. What are your chances of finding a disk with no duplicate directory names? In fact, what are the chances of finding any tree-structured data without duplicates? The whole point of a tree is that each node can be independent. A TreeView control would be much easier to manage if it were organized as a collection of node collections, somewhat like the CMenuList and CMenuItem classes described in "Other People's Menus," page 428. That's not to say you can't use keys with TreeViews, but you'll need to come up with a scheme to handle duplicate keys.

- Images in the ImageList for TreeView and ListView images should be keyed, but you must be careful how you insert the keys. Each file type must have one and only one image with the file type name as the key. For every file, I use error trapping to identify whether the file type image is already in the ImageList. If the key doesn't exist, I insert it. This can't be doing much for performance, but I couldn't figure out another way. TreeView and ListView applications written in other languages can use the internal system ImageLists, but the Visual Basic controls don't support them.

- ListViews don't have an ItemDblClick event, but you need to identify double-clicks on ListView items to know when to open them. ListViews do have a DblClick event, but it won't tell you which item was clicked. You can work around this limitation by saving the x and y coordinates in the Mouse_Down event. In the DblClick event, use the coordinates with the HitTest method to identify which item was double-clicked.

Toolbar and StatusBar Controls

Check out the toolbar and the status bar in Edwina or Columbus. I won't get into the code but will simply say that I had to implement these features the same way everyone else does—with sweat and blood and experimentation. Ask my office neighbors about my expertise in profanity.

To use a Toolbar control efficiently, you must understand ImageLists and collections inside out. Plan the buttons in detail, and get your ImageList right the first time because every time you change a button image, you're in trouble. You must unhook the ImageList from the Toolbar control to modify, insert, or delete an image, even though unhooking means that all your button indexes are destroyed and that you must reinitialize them one by one. You might even consider attaching the ImageList with code at run time rather than trying to manage it at design time.

Most of the work involved in creating a toolbar is directed toward managing the Buttons collection and coordinating it with the ListImages collection of the ListImage. The Panels collection of the StatusBar control is a little easier because you don't have to worry about ImageLists.

The first step in getting any Toolbar control to work properly is to set the MaskColor property of the ImageList used for button images to the same color as the background of the buttons. The toolbar buttons that ship with Visual Basic have a gray background (&HC0C0C0&), and you should normally use this color. The default MaskColor (black) washes out the black outlines on toolbar buttons. (Incidentally, the original Visual Basic 4 shipped with wrong versions of the Open and Delete toolbar buttons, but the correct versions are available on the companion CD.)

Figure 11-10 shows a map of the Toolbar methods and properties.

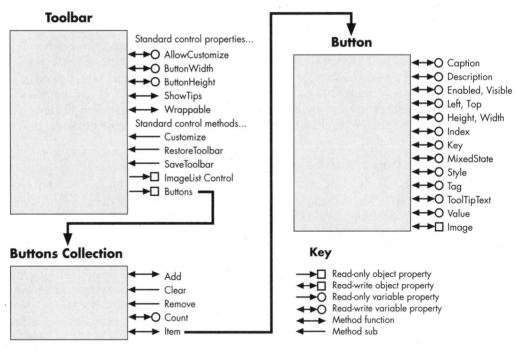

Figure 11-10. *A Toolbar map.*

I don't mind that toolbars are based on the ImageList control, but I shouldn't have to worry about it. When I set up toolbar buttons, I want to just click a button that brings up the Picture dialog box and lets me install the button image. If the dialog box adds the image to an ImageList behind the scenes and ties the image index to a button index, that's OK with me. But as a user, I don't care about this implementation detail. I just want to put images on buttons. Any add-in vendor who gives me a tool that hides the connection between toolbars and ImageLists will get my business. In fact, I don't even care that a toolbar is a control. The Toolbar editor should be on the main Visual Basic toolbar right next to the Menu editor. Toolbars aren't an extra feature—they're the standard. Every program should have one. And that includes 16-bit programs! But enough of this ranting. At least now I can put a Flame button on my 32-bit toolbars.

The Quest for the 32-Bit Grail

The Win32 API offers many new features untapped by Visual Basic. The difficult part is deciding which of these features are

- time wasters—challenging and fun to play with, but nothing your customers will want to pay for

- frustrating dead ends that won't really deliver for Visual Basic until they are integrated into the language

- useful features at a reasonable development price

I'll try to give you a brief outline of areas of interest, but in the end you'll have to decide for yourself.

New Graphics Features

Win32 raises the graphics standards in many ways. The OpenGL and WinG APIs mentioned in Chapter 6 can take your graphics to a new level, but you'll also find more modest improvements.

Bezier curves

Drawing curves with software is a difficult problem for the math-impaired. You can plot each separate point on a curve defined by a formula, but first you have to figure out the formula. The only variation is what you plot with—points, line segments, arcs, or even bitmaps. The addition of PolyBezier and PolyBezierTo in Win32 makes it easy to draw graceful curves. Making them fit your desired shape is a different matter.

Pierre Bezier invented the technique that bears his name back when the cars he designed were smaller and cost less than the computers he designed with. (Well, maybe cars weren't really smaller than computers in the 1960s, but they did cost less.) Anyway, the simplest Bezier curve is defined by four points. The outside points are the start and the end of the curve. The middle two points control the curve—that is, they pull and push it, they exert a magnetic attraction on it, they whip it into shape, they stretch it...the only way you're going to understand what they do is to try them out.

Figure 11-11 shows the Bezier Curves program (TBEZIER.VBP). You can see the curve here, but you'll have to run the program to see how it works. Drag with the left mouse button to control the top of the curve; drag with the right button to control the bottom.

The code starts with an array of four points:

```
Private apt(0 To 3) As TPoint
```

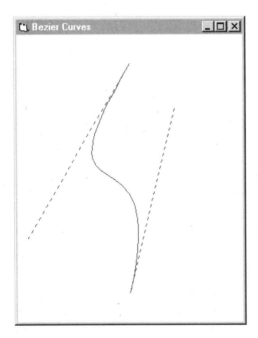

Figure 11-11. *Bezier curves.*

InitBezier fills these points with initial values:

```
Sub InitBezier(cxClient As Long, cyClient As Long)
    apt(0).x = ScaleX(cxClient / 2, vbTwips, vbPixels)
    apt(0).y = ScaleY(cyClient / 4, vbTwips, vbPixels)
    apt(1).x = ScaleX(cxClient / 4, vbTwips, vbPixels)
    apt(1).y = ScaleY(cyClient / 2, vbTwips, vbPixels)
    apt(2).x = ScaleX(3 * cxClient / 4, vbTwips, vbPixels)
    apt(2).y = ScaleY(cyClient / 2, vbTwips, vbPixels)
    apt(3).x = ScaleX(cxClient / 2, vbTwips, vbPixels)
    apt(3).y = ScaleY(3 * cyClient / 4, vbTwips, vbPixels)
    ForeColor = vbRed
End Sub
```

The points are scaled because PolyBezier, like most GDI functions, expects pixels by default. Points 0 and 3 are the start and the end of the curve. To draw the curve, call DrawBezier:

```
Sub DrawBezier()
    DrawStyle = vbSolid
    PolyBezier hdc, apt(0), 4
    DrawStyle = vbDot
    MoveTo hdc, apt(0).x, apt(0).y
    LineTo hdc, apt(1).x, apt(1).y
    MoveTo hdc, apt(2).x, apt(2).y
    LineTo hdc, apt(3).x, apt(3).y
End Sub
```

The curve is drawn with a solid line style, and lines connecting the control points are drawn with a dotted line style, so that you can see how the control points work. In a real-life program, you wouldn't show the control points. Notice that you use the MoveTo and LineTo functions instead of the Basic Line statements. The points are already in pixels, so it's easier to stick with API functions. (Actually, MoveTo isn't an API function; see the sidebar "MoveTo Comes Full Circle," page 582.)

After you run the program for a few minutes, you can probably guess the code for the MouseMove and MouseDown events. They set the color to the background color and call DrawBezier to erase the current curve and control lines. Then they calculate new positions for the control points. Finally they reset the draw color and redraw with DrawBezier.

MoveTo Comes Full Circle

The Win16 API has a MoveTo function, which returns a DWord containing the packed x and y coordinates of the previous current position:

```
dw = MoveTo(hDC, x, y)
```

The returned DWord is the equivalent of a TPoint variable. Some languages (but not Basic) allow you to typecast a DWord to a TPoint. Of course, most users don't care about the return value and simply call it like this:

```
MoveTo hDC, x, y
```

It apparently never occurred to the designers of MoveTo that Windows might someday have 32 bits. There's no good way to pack two 32-bit variables into a return value. For that reason, MoveTo was marked obsolete several versions ago and replaced with MoveToEx, although MoveTo was still supported for compatibility in 16-bit Windows.

The Win32 API has no MoveTo, only MoveToEx. The new function has a fourth parameter that returns the previous position through a reference variable of TPoint type. It also returns a Boolean value to indicate success:

```
f = MoveToEx(hDC, x, y, ptJunk)
```

This is very convenient for the 1 percent of the time when you need to save the last position. The rest of the time, you can pass a null. The type-library syntax makes it impossible to define a single function that can take either a TPoint or a null pointer, but the Windows API type library provides an aliased Move-ToNull function:

```
f = MoveToNull(hDC, x, y, pNull)
```

The GDI tool module, GDITOOL.BAS, provides a MoveTo wrapper (32-bit only) that gets rid of that last worthless parameter:

```
f = MoveTo(hDC, x, y)
```

If you ignore the return value (usually there's no reason not to), you end up with this:

```
MoveTo hDC, x, y
```

Look familiar?

CHALLENGE You can draw more than one Bezier curve by adding more elements to the array. Each curve needs three points in the array. The end point of the last curve serves as the starting point of the next curve. The next two points are control points. The last point is the end point of the curve. Your challenge is to enhance the Bezier sample to demonstrate multiple curves. You could also add a Bezier curve drawing tool to the IconWorks sample. Use the tool in Windows Paintbrush as a model.

Paths

Paths are recorded sequences of deferred line drawing commands. The idea is that you can draw an irregular, invisible shape using various commands and then perform an operation on the whole shape at once. Let's try it:

```
' Start recording path
BeginPath hDC
' Do some draw operations
ForeColor = vbYellow
FillColor = vbRed
FillStyle = vbSolid
Line (ScaleWidth * 0.2, ScaleHeight * 0.3)- _
    (ScaleWidth * 0.8, ScaleHeight * 0.7)
Circle (ScaleWidth * 0.5, ScaleHeight * 0.5), _
       ScaleHeight * 0.3
' Stop recording path
EndPath hDC
' Do something to finished path
StrokeAndFillPath hDC
' Update device context
Refresh
```

If you step through this code, nothing happens when you step over the Line and Circle statements. The figures aren't drawn until you reach the Stroke-AndFillPath procedure, and they usually won't be visible until you call the Refresh method. Both figures are filled (except in the intersection) with the current FillColor and FillStyle, even though the Line statement doesn't have the *F* argument that specifies filling.

We're mixing Basic statements and Windows API statements, but that's OK because the Basic statements are calling API functions under the surface. The Line statement probably calls Rectangle, Circle probably calls Ellipse, and they're both working on the same device context that was passed to the path procedures. The API documentation has a long list of line drawing functions that you can use in paths, but the only Basic statements are Line, Circle, and Print.

Since when did Print get to be a line drawing statement? Well, since Windows got TrueType fonts. Try this:

```
' Set a large, TrueType font
With Font
    .Name = "Lucida Console"
    .Bold = True
    .Italic = True
    .Size = 48
End With
ForeColor = vbGreen
FillColor = vbMagenta
FillStyle = vbDiagonalCross
' Make Print statement into a path, and then fill
BeginPath hDC
Print "Hello"
EndPath hDC
StrokeAndFillPath hDC
Refresh
```

This code draws outlined green text filled with magenta cross-hatches. I was going to include a screen shot of this, but it was just too hideous.

Besides drawing and filling a path, you can also draw it (StrokePath), fill it (FillPath), turn it into a region (PathToRgn), or turn it into a clipping region (SetClipPath). I don't have much to say about regions and clipping regions, except that paths make them easier to manage. In fact, I'm not going to discuss path-related functions such as FlattenPath, WidenPath, SetMiterLimit, Close-Figure, and ExtCreatePen. You can explore these on your own.

> **NOTE** You must set AutoRedraw to True to use paths. I also found that some path features behaved differently under Windows 95 than under Windows NT.

Interprocess Communication

Windows has always had a variety of ways for programs to communicate with each other. Fashions change. Here's what's in and what's out in Visual Basic interprocess communications:

- OLE servers are hot. They are the most convenient way to share data and code inside your own process, across processes, and—if you have the right tool (Visual Basic Enterprise Edition)—across machines. But the overhead for using EXE servers is high. You can use DLL servers in 32-bit mode, but then you can't write portable code.

■ DDE is out of fashion. It is still supported for compatibility, and Visual Basic still supports it as fully as in previous versions. But this technology has reached a dead end and will never be enhanced.

■ A Remote Procedure Call API exists for calling procedures on different machines. I've never used this API, and I have no idea whether it would be useful directly from Visual Basic. I do know that the proxy programs that make remote OLE possible in the Visual Basic Enterprise Edition employ remote procedure calls below the surface.

■ OLE hasn't done anything to invalidate the clipboard, which is still an effective way to make data from your program available to other programs and to use data made public by other programs. If you're supplying the data, the problem is letting other programs know it's there. If you're receiving the data, the problem is knowing when useful information is available.

■ AppActivate and SendKeys provide a convenient way to activate another program and send it keystrokes. For example, you can send keystrokes to the program to paste from the clipboard (as the Property Shop does; see Chapter 4). SendKeys is a Basic implementation of the more general technique mentioned in the following list item.

■ You can easily send Windows messages to another program with SendMessage or PostMessage, but receiving them is a little more difficult. You'll need a message tool such as Message Blaster or the callback server, both described in Chapter 5.

■ Win32 adds an important new message, WM_COPYDATA, that allows you to send chunks of data from one program to another. Copying data is more complicated than you might expect. All data resides at addresses in memory, but each program has a different address space and can't understand anything about data in another program's address space. The WM_COPYDATA message hides the details of getting data from your address space to the address space of another process. Internally, the WM_COPYDATA message uses memory-mapped files.

■ Under Win16, you can share data by allocating it with the GlobalAlloc function and the GMEM_SHARE flag. That doesn't work in Win32, where the only way to share data between processes is with memory-mapped files, as you'll see.

■ The Win32 file notification APIs allow you to monitor file events in other processes (or in your own process). I'll show you this one, too.

Let's examine two of the more interesting techniques for interprocess communications.

Shared memory through memory-mapped files

Memory-mapped files provide a way to look at a file as a chunk of memory. This feature is very useful in languages that support examining memory at arbitrary addresses. You map the file and get back a pointer to the mapped memory. You can simply read or write to memory from any location in the file mapping, just as you would from an array. When you've processed the file and closed the file mapping, the file is automatically updated. In other words, the operating system takes care of all the details of file I/O.

The API calls to create a file mapping are relatively simple, and you could easily call them from Visual Basic. There's only one problem. See if you can spot it:

```
' Open file
hFile = CreateFile(sFileName, GENERIC_READ Or GENERIC_WRITE, 0, _
                   pNull, OPEN_ALWAYS, FILE_ATTRIBUTE_NORMAL, _
                   pNull)
' Open file mapping of it called MySharedMapping
hFileMap = CreateFileMapping(hFile, pNull, PAGE_READWRITE, 0, 0, _
                             "MySharedMapping")
' Get pointer to memory representing file
pFileMap = MapViewOfFile(hFileMap, FILE_MAP_WRITE, 0, 0, 0)
```

At this point, *pFileMap* is the address of a block of memory containing the file contents. Now, what can you do in Visual Basic with a pointer you receive from an API function? Repeat after me: "Pass it to another API function." In other words, you're stuck.

In C, you can treat a pointer like an array:

```
pFileMap[0] = 'A'
bTest = pFileMap[1]
```

But Basic provides no similar capability. You can use CopyMemory to copy the file mapping to some other location in memory, but that usually defeats the purpose. The fact is that memory-mapped files won't be much use to Basic programmers until they're integrated into the language. Imagine this code:

```
Dim abFileMap() As Integer
hFileMap = FreeFile
Open sFileName For FileMap With abFileMap As #hFileMap
For i = 0 to UBound(abFileMap)
    abFileMap(i) = CalculateMagicNumber(abFileMap(i))
Next
Close hFileMap
```

This might not be the best syntax. In fact, the next version of Visual Basic might implement file mapping behind the scenes with the existing syntax.

Although Basic does not support using memory-mapped files for file I/O, it doesn't stand in your way if you want to use them for shared memory. You can create a file mapping that isn't mapped to a file by passing a magic number (you guessed it, −1) instead of a handle to the CreateFileMapping function. This gives you a pointer to a named chunk of memory. Any program that knows the name can also get a pointer to the memory. You still can't access the memory at that location directly in Basic, but any program can use CopyMemory to read or write to the memory.

The process is a little complicated, so I encapsulated it in the CSharedString class. You can see how it works in Figure 11-12 (TSHARE.VBP). You'll need to run more than one instance of the program to see the point. Change the text in one copy, and click the Set Data button. Go to another instance of the program, and click the Get Data button to read the current value.

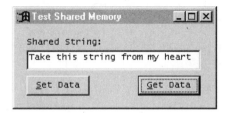

Figure 11-12. *Sharing strings.*

Here's the code to use a shared object:

```
Private share As New CSharedString
    ⋮
Private Sub Form_Load()
    If share.Create("MyShare") Then
        If share.Data = sEmpty Then
            share.Data = "Hello from the Creator"
        End If
        txtShare.Text = share.Data
    End If
End Sub
Private Sub cmdSet_Click()
    share.Data = txtShare.Text
End Sub

Private Sub cmdGet_Click()
    txtShare.Text = share.Data
End Sub
```

When the first program creates a CSharedString object, the value is an empty string, so the first program initializes to a string of its choice. When subsequent programs create objects, the value is whatever the previous program set. You can specifically destroy a shared string object by setting it to Nothing, but that's usually unnecessary. The object is destroyed automatically when it goes out of scope during program destruction.

The Data property of CSharedString is one more case in which a default member would be handy. If Visual Basic classes allowed me to specify the Data property as the default property, I could use a CSharedString just as I use any other string:

```
Private sShared As New CSharedString
sShared = "Why can't I do this?"
```

Most of the implementation work is done in the Create method, where the internal variables—*h* for handle, *p* for pointer, and *e* for error—are initialized:

```
Function Create(sName As String) As Boolean
    ' Create = False
    If sName = sEmpty Then Exit Function
    ' Try to create file mapping of 65535 (only used pages matter)
    h = CreateFileMapping(MEM_HANDLE, pNull, PAGE_READWRITE, _
                          0, 65535, sName)
    e = Err.LastDllError
    ' Unknown error, bail out
    If h = hNull Then Destroy: Exit Function

    ' Get pointer to mapping
    p = MapViewOfFile(h, FILE_MAP_WRITE, 0, 0, 0)
    If p = pNull Then e = Err.LastDllError: Exit Function
    If e <> ERROR_ALREADY_EXISTS Then
        ' Set size of new file mapping to 0 by copying first 4 bytes
        Dim c As Long ' = 0
        CopyMemory ByVal p, c, 4
    ' Else
        ' Existing file mapping
    End If
    e = 0
    Create = True
End Function
```

Here's a summary of what's going on. First the code calls CreateFileMapping to create a read-write memory mapping that is 65,535 bytes in length, with the name passed in the Create method. Wait a minute! You don't want 65,535 bytes of memory just to share a 20-byte string. Don't worry. Through the wonders of memory paging, you'll use only the pages you touch. In other words, you'll use one page of memory (4 KB) for that 20-byte string. That's enough to make you a little careful about how many shared memory objects you create, but it's not the same as throwing away 64 KB.

After you create a file mapping (memory mapping would be a more accurate term in this context), you need to call MapViewOfFile to get a pointer to it. You'll get the same return (a pointer) whether you're opening an existing mapping or creating a new one. You need to distinguish these two cases, and the only way to do so is to check the error value for ERROR_ALREADY_EXISTS, which isn't really an error. If it's a new mapping, you need to initialize it.

You can do this however you want as long as everyone who uses the data knows the convention. I save a shared string as a Long containing the string length, followed by the bytes of the string. I thought about extending this format to allow other types of data—such as arrays—but finally decided to leave that to you. If you have multiple data formats, you'll need to save additional information indicating the type as well as the length. Here is my code to read and write the data:

```
Property Get Data() As String
    If h = hNull Then e = ERROR_INVALID_DATA: Exit Property
    BugAssert p <> pNull

    ' Copy length out of first 4 bytes of data
    Dim c As Long, sData As String
    CopyMemory c, ByVal p, 4
    ' Copy rest of memory into string
    If c = 0 Then Exit Property ' Data = sEmpty
    sData = String$(c, 0)
    CopyMemory ByVal sData, ByVal (p + 4), c
    Data = sData
End Property

Property Let Data(s As String)
    If h = hNull Then e = ERROR_INVALID_DATA: Exit Property
    BugAssert p <> pNull

    Dim c As Long
    c = Len(s)
    ' Copy length to first 4 bytes and string to remainder
    CopyMemory ByVal p, c, 4
    CopyMemory ByVal (p + 4), ByVal s, c
End Property
```

Finally, you need to unmap the data. Here's the private Destroy method, which is called from Class_Terminate:

```
Private Sub Destroy()
    UnmapViewOfFile p
    CloseHandle h
    h = hNull
    p = pNull
End Sub

Private Sub Class_Terminate()
    If h <> hNull Then Destroy
End Sub
```

WARNING When you test shared string objects, don't terminate by using the End toolbar button, the End item on the Run menu, or the End statement. Instead, unload your forms. This is good practice in general, but it's particularly important with the shared string class. Ending a program short-circuits the normal destruction mechanism, and you'll "End" up with dangling copies of the shared memory. A shared memory mapping is destroyed only when all its clients have unmapped it. If a program dies without unmapping, its mapping handle dies with it. The only way to get rid of the shared data is to log off.

Threads and Synchronization

Perhaps the most interesting new capability of Win32 is its ability to create new threads of execution and to synchronize operations among them. In the long run, this will be the way to make operations run independently and interact smoothly. But not yet.

Visual Basic itself doesn't use threads in critical areas, and neither can you. For example, the next time you print a Visual Basic project, notice how the Print dialog box works in the 32-bit Visual Basic IDE. You specify what you want to print, click OK, and then watch a print message box until the print job is finished. You can't edit or do anything else in the IDE until your document has been shipped off to the printer. In a multithreaded print implementation (ideally, all 32-bit print commands would be multithreaded), you wouldn't have to wait. The print thread would be launched independently, and you could do other chores while it worked in the background.

Of course, background operations can be implemented in other ways. Many 16-bit programs have had background printing for years, but it isn't always smooth and clean. Although I haven't tried it, I imagine that you could implement background printing by launching a modeless form that handles the printing. The form would have a timer that periodically calls timer events to do chunks of the print job. But this technique depends on your ability to break the background task into chunks. A multithreaded implementation lets the operating system break the job into chunks.

Some hardcore programmers are undoubtedly saying, "If there's an API to launch threads, I'm sure I could call it." Indeed there is a CreateThread function, but you'll have some difficulty calling it from Basic.

The first problem is that one of CreateThread's parameters is the address of a procedure that will implement the thread. You could write a Basic function or sub to implement the thread, but Basic provides no way to pass the address of that procedure to CreateThread. For the sake of argument, however, let's assume that you're really hardcore and have figured out how to get the address of your procedure by using a callback utility.

Now that you've started a thread, you hit the second problem. If you call any Basic library procedure, load a form, or use an OLE control, you'll die hard and fast. The reason is that none of the internal Basic code is thread-safe. *Thread-safe* means that the code has been written so that it can be safely reentered at any time by any thread. When multiple threads are running, the operating system automatically switches between them. One thread might be in the middle of the Basic Print code when it loses control. Another independent thread then gets control and calls the Basic Print code. But the first thread has modified a global variable used by Print. The second thread comes in and modifies the same variable. The first thread gets control back, but the variable it was depending on to have the same value it had just a few microseconds ago has been mysteriously modified. Crash!

Thread-safe code must be written very carefully to ensure that each thread has independent data or, if data is shared, that different threads cooperate in accessing it. Perhaps the Visual Basic library will be rewritten to be thread-safe in the next version. If that happens, you'll probably see some new statements and attributes that will make it easy to create and manage threads written in Basic. Multithreading is such a low-level feature that it won't work as an add-on to the language; it must be built in.

The only way to use threads now is to write them in another language. It is possible to write a thread procedure in a DLL and then call CreateThread to launch that procedure from another procedure in the DLL. I know some hardcore programmers who are experimenting with this. But here you'll hit the third problem with threads: they need to communicate with each other. When you send a thread off to do some work, you'll want to know when it has finished or when it has completed milestone tasks. The Win32 API provides many ways for threads to both communicate and synchronize their activities—semaphores, events, mutexes, critical sections. For now, let's just say that using threads requires a whole new way of thinking.

For example, assume that you have a PrintDialog form in Basic, which allows the user to set some options. When the user clicks the OK button, the form calls the LaunchPrintThread function from your PRINT.DLL. LaunchPrintThread calls CreateThread, passing it the address of a PrintIt function, also located in the DLL. PrintIt prints your data. The PrintDialog form has a thread (all executing code is actually a thread under Win32), but it's a dumb thread that believes it is the only thread in the operating system. You also have the PrintIt thread, which is as smart as you made it. In particular, it must be smart enough not to call any Basic code. How can your smart thread notify your dumb thread when it finishes printing?

This reminds me of a Mark Twain story that lampooned a certain type of ridiculous adventure story common in his day. After taking his heroes through a series of increasingly harrowing situations, he ended the story with the comment that he had created an impossible predicament and had no idea how to resolve it. That's where I'm tempted to leave you with multithreading, but I have found one case in which you can use multithreading indirectly in Basic.

The File Notification Server
In the example I'm thinking of, the DLL that you send to do a task knows about threads. Your code (and the Visual Basic environment, if you're using it) stops dead and waits for the thread in that DLL to perform a task. When the thread returns, your Basic code wakes up and continues on its way—back to wait on the servant again. The thread-smart servant here is KERNEL32.DLL, whose assigned task is checking to determine whether anyone has changed any files or directories.

Try this experiment. Run Windows Explorer in one window. Then go to a command-line session or another instance of Windows Explorer, and delete a file in the directory shown by the original Explorer. Watch what happens to the Explorer window. How does Windows Explorer know that a file has changed? The same way your programs can know: by using FindFirstChangeNotification, FindNextChangeNotification, and FindCloseChangeNotification.

The client side of file notification
The File Notification Server (NOTIFY.VBP) encapsulates the file change notification in an OLE server that you can use from any 32-bit program. You can see how it works in the Browse Picture Files program (BROWSE.VBP), which acts as a client of the File Notification Server. Browse Picture Files is an enhanced version of the Picture File dialog box described in Chapter 4; you can see it in Figure 11-13. It not only displays icons, cursors, bitmaps, and metafiles but also

copies, deletes, renames, and moves them. And it updates its display when other processes remove, create, or modify picture files or directories.

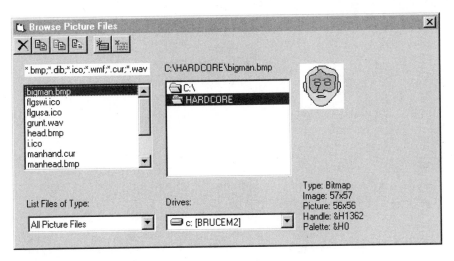

Figure 11-13. *Browsing pictures.*

The Browse Picture Files program uses the following code to request file notifications from the File Notification Server:

```
Private Sub dirPic_Change()
With notify
    filPic.Path = dirPic.Path
    If filPic.ListCount > 0 Then
        filPic.ListIndex = 0
    End If

    ' Watch whole drive for directory changes
    If hNotifyDir <> -1 Then .Disconnect hNotifyDir
    hNotifyDir = .Connect(Me, dirPic.Path, _
                    FILE_NOTIFY_CHANGE_DIR_NAME, False)
    ' Watch only current directory for file changes
    If hNotifyFile <> -1 Then .Disconnect hNotifyFile
    hNotifyFile = .Connect(Me, dirPic.Path, _
                    FILE_NOTIFY_CHANGE_FILE_NAME, False)
    ' Watch only current directory for file modifications
    If hNotifyChange <> -1 Then notify.Disconnect hNotifyChange
    hNotifyChange = .Connect(Me, dirPic.Path, _
                    FILE_NOTIFY_CHANGE_LAST_WRITE, False)

End With
End Sub
```

Skip the first few lines that handle normal directory changes, and concentrate on the code that connects the FBrowsePictures form to the server. First you disconnect any previous connection, and then you connect the server to the new directory. The first connection tells the server to report any changes to the current directory. The last Boolean parameter indicates whether to check child directories. Windows 95 doesn't support True, so you should normally supply False. Changes include any directories that have been created, removed, or renamed. The next connection looks for any files whose names have changed in the current directory. Deleting a file or creating a new file obviously changes the filename. The third connection looks for files that have been modified. If you change the current image file with ImagEdit or some other tool, the change appears in the Browse Picture Files program as soon as you save the file.

Notice that each call to Connect passes the Form object in the first parameter. This tells the notification server which class to call when it needs to send the client a change notification. A form is a superset of a class. It's all the same to the server. Another program might prefer to send a class object. The server sends messages to the class by calling a FileChange method. Any form or class object you pass to the server must have a method with the exact name, parameters, and return type expected by the server. Here's what the method looks like in FBrowsePictures:

```
Public Sub FileChange(sDir As String, ordType As Long, _
                      fSubDir As Boolean)
    BugMessage "Directory: " & sDir & sCrLf
    BugMessage " (" & ordType & ":" & fSubDir & ")" & sCrLf
    Select Case ordType
    Case FILE_NOTIFY_CHANGE_DIR_NAME, FILE_NOTIFY_CHANGE_FILE_NAME
        Dim i As Integer
        ' Refresh drive, directory, and file lists
        i = filPic.ListIndex
        filPic.Refresh
        filPic.ListIndex = IIf(i, i - 1, i)
        dirPic.Refresh
        drvPic.Refresh
    Case FILE_NOTIFY_CHANGE_LAST_WRITE
        ' Refresh current picture in case it changed
        filPic_Click
    End Select
End Sub
```

This code is a little sloppy, although there's no harm done in this case. It refreshes everything in sight rather than trying to figure out exactly what changed. You might be able to be more exact in your code. Now let's look at where those notification calls come from.

The server side of file notification

The File Notification Server is an EXE server, not a DLL server. DLL servers work only in 32-bit mode, but file notification is 32-bit-only technology. So why not use a more efficient DLL server? Because it's too efficient. You want the server code to run in a separate thread, and putting it in a separate EXE is the only way to be certain of that in Basic. Performance isn't really an issue with file notification. The more important issue is making sure notifications don't slow down normal operation of the client.

The Connect method is what launches each file notification thread, but before we examine it, let's look at some of the data it uses. The server maintains an array of notification handles. In addition, it must keep a parallel array of the data associated with each handle. Later you'll see why the handles need to be in a separate array. For each notification, the server maintains four pieces of information: the directory to be watched, the type of event, a flag indicating whether to check subdirectories, and the target object to be called when a file event occurs (the FBrowsePictures object, in the example). The data structures look like this:

```
Public Type TConnection
    sDir As String
    ordType As Long
    fSubTree As Boolean
    objTarget As Object
End Type

' Actually cLastNotify + 1 allowed
Public Const cLastNotify = 28
' One extra blank item in each array for easy compacting
Public ahNotify(0 To cLastNotify + 1) As Long
Public aconNotify(0 To cLastNotify + 1) As TConnection
Public aerr(errFirst To errLast) As String
' Count of connected objects managed by class
Public cObject As Long
```

I use an array with a fixed size because it's easier, but you could probably remove the size limit by using a collection. You'd still need an array of handles, but you could build it dynamically whenever a notification was added or deleted. The other interesting thing about this data is that it's public data residing in NOTIFY.BAS, not in NOTIFY.CLS. Every client using the server can share this same array, and every created object uses the same array of notifications. For you C++ gurus, public data in a module used by a server is similar to static variables in C++.

On the following page, you can see how the Connect method initializes this data for each notification request.

```
Function Connect(objTarget As Object, sDir As String, _
                 ordType As Long, fSubTree As Boolean) As Long
    Connect = INVALID_HANDLE_VALUE ' Assume fail
    Dim i As Long, h As Long
    ' Find blank handle space
    For i = 0 To cLastNotify
        If ahNotify(i) = INVALID_HANDLE_VALUE Then
            ' Set up notification
            h = FindFirstChangeNotification(sDir, fSubTree, ordType)
            Connect = h
            If h = INVALID_HANDLE_VALUE Then
                ' Change notification unsupported on remote disks
                If Err.LastDllError <> ERROR_NOT_SUPPORTED Then
                    RaiseError errInvalidArgument
                End If
                Exit Function
            End If
            ' Store information
            ahNotify(i) = h
            With aconNotify(i)
                Set .objTarget = objTarget
                .sDir = sDir
                .ordType = ordType
                .fSubTree = fSubTree
            End With
            Exit Function
        End If
    Next
    RaiseError errTooManyNotifications
End Function
```

Connect looks for a blank slot in the array. When it finds one, it initializes the slot with a file notification handle obtained by calling the FindFirstChange-Notification API function. You can see what happens to the parameters passed by the client. If everything goes well, Connect stores the handle and other data in the appropriate arrays. You can look through the code to see the details of how RaiseError handles errors and Disconnect undoes the work done by Connect. The important point about this code is that FindFirstChangeNotification requests that the kernel send off a thread to watch for file events. All you need to do is wait for the event to happen. But wait where? Who will the kernel notify when it gets a file event? It can't wait in the Connect event (which must return to the client), but where else can it go?

The only other place is Sub Main in the server module, and that is indeed where we wait for server events. The code looks like this:

```
Sub Main()
    Dim iStatus As Long, f As Boolean, objTarget As Object
    ' Keep waiting for file change events until no more objects
    Do
        ' Wait 100 milliseconds for notification
        iStatus = WaitForMultipleObjects(Count, ahNotify(0), _
                                         False, 100)
        Select Case iStatus
        Case WAIT_TIMEOUT
            ' Nothing happened
            DoEvents
        Case 0 To Count
            ' Call client object with information
            On Error Resume Next
            With aconNotify(iStatus)
                .objTarget.FileChange .sDir, .ordType, .fSubTree
            End With
            If Err <> 0 Then RaiseError errNoFileChangeMethod
            On Error GoTo 0
            ' Wait for next notification
            f = FindNextChangeNotification(ahNotify(iStatus))
        Case WAIT_FAILED
            ' Indicates no notification requests
            DoEvents
        Case Else
            Debug.Print "Can't happen"
        End Select
    ' Class Initialize and Terminate events keep reference count
    Loop Until cObject = -1
End Sub
```

The Win32 WaitForMultipleObjects function waits for what Windows calls an object. An object can be a process, a thread, a mutex, an event, a semaphore, console input, or a change notification. I'm not even going to define these things, much less explain why or how you would want to wait on one. The point here is that you must put the handles of those objects in a contiguous array and pass the number of objects, followed by the address of the first object. You must also indicate whether you want to wait until all objects have returned or wait only for the first one. In this case, you pass False to wait for any file notification object. Finally, you pass the timeout period, 100 milliseconds.

When I say that WaitForMultipleObjects waits, I mean that literally. As soon as the thread executing this Basic server code hits WaitForMultipleObjects, it stops dead. The server is no longer running. All the other programs in the system get all the cycles, and you get nothing. That's what you asked for. If you doubt it, change the timeout period to the constant INFINITE (–1) with the server running in the IDE. The server locks tight, and absolutely nothing happens in it (or in the IDE if it's running the server) except responses to file events. The client keeps running and responding to file change notifications, but when the client tries to call the server's Disconnect method, no one's home. A timeout period is desperately needed so that the server can get control (in the WAIT_TIMEOUT case) and respond to other Connect and Disconnect requests.

When a file notification object does come through, WaitForMultipleObjects returns its index into the handle array. The *Case 0 to Count* block handles the notifications by using the stored client object to call the client's FileChange event procedure. It must then call FindNextChangeNotification to wait for the next event. Incidentally, Count is simply a Property Get procedure that counts the handles in the array.

One Last Challenge

All the tools are now in place to create the Hardcore Hacker's Object Chop Shop. Let's take a little tour through this not-so-Basic development factory. It's built right into the Visual Basic environment as an add-in, but once you open it, things are very different. It looks like Windows Explorer, but the tree view contains a code resource library with forms, classes, and code modules. When you click a form or class module, it displays a graphical view of properties and methods. Naturally, this view shows connections and dependencies between related modules, and you can open your favorite programmer's editor to edit any module with a mouse click.

You can also browse through graphical elements such as icons, bitmaps, cursors, and metafiles. Click any of them to open a graphical editor that makes ImagEdit and IconWorks look like finger paints. You can drag graphical elements and drop them into resource files, which are automatically compiled. In fact, you can drag just about anything. Drag that form to the Visual Basic Project window to add it to your project. But since that form depends on two code modules and a class module, you automatically get those, too. And talk about wizards—the Chop Shop is packed with them. Sure, it has enhanced versions of Debug Wizard from Chapter 1 and the Property Shop from Chapter 4, but that's only the beginning. As just one example, a combination Code and Form Wizard takes the grunt work out of generating toolbars.

Sound good? Well, there's nothing between you and that dream environment but a few weekends—OK, some week nights too—of Hardcore Visual Basic.

INDEX

Bruce McKinney was a factory assembly worker, a logger, a newspaper reporter, a PR flunkie, and an unpublished fiction writer before he discovered computers and lost all interest in the real world. During his 10 years at Microsoft, he has written programming manuals and online help for assembler, Basic, and C. Bruce also served for a time as czar of sample programs, writing or revising many of the samples known to long-time Microsoft language customers. He was a software developer on Microsoft C 7 and FORTRAN Power Station 1. He holds a journalism degree from the University of Washington and a computer science degree from the University of Hard Knocks. Bruce is also a coauthor of *Running Windows NT* (Microsoft Press, 1994). He can be reached at brucem_MS@msn.com.

The manuscript for this book was prepared using Microsoft Word 6.0 for Windows and submitted to Microsoft Press in electronic form. Galleys were prepared using Microsoft Word 6.0 for Windows. Pages were composed by VersaTech Associates using Aldus PageMaker 5.0 for Windows, with text type in Garamond and display type in Futura Medium Bold. Composed pages were delivered to the printer as electronic prepress files.

Cover Graphic Designer
Glen Mitsui, Studio MD

Interior Graphic Designer
Kim Eggleston

Principal Artist
David Holter

Principal Compositor
VersaTech Associates

Principal Proofreader
Jennifer Harris

Indexer
Shane-Armstrong Information Systems

Discover how easy software development for Windows® can be with Microsoft® Visual Basic®!

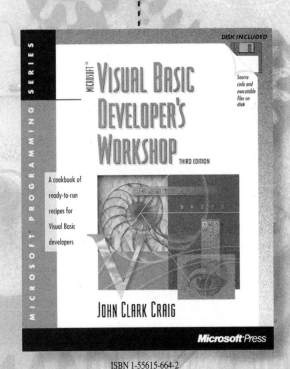

ISBN 1-55615-664-2
496 pages, one 3.5" disk
$39.95 ($53.95 Canada)

*M*ICROSOFT VISUAL BASIC DEVELOPER'S WORKSHOP

THIRD EDITION

You'll find this book-and-disk package, which takes a cookbook approach to Visual Basic programming, appealing whether you're an intermediate or advanced Visual Basic programmer. The disk contains an excellent collection of more than 50 ready-to-run programs, or "mini-applications," and the text provides tried-and-true recipes for successful Visual Basic applications. The programs in MICROSOFT VISUAL BASIC DEVELOPER'S WORKSHOP can be customized or incorporated directly into your programming projects. Information on programming concepts and techniques runs throughout. Let MICROSOFT VISUAL BASIC DEVELOPER'S WORKSHOP help you realize the powerful capabilities of Visual Basic.

Available December 1995!

Microsoft Press

IMPORTANT—READ CAREFULLY BEFORE OPENING SOFTWARE PACKET(S). By opening the sealed packet(s) containing the software, you indicate your acceptance of the following Microsoft License Agreement.

MICROSOFT LICENSE AGREEMENT

(Book Companion Disks)

This is a legal agreement between you (either an individual or an entity) and Microsoft Corporation. By opening the sealed software packet(s) you are agreeing to be bound by the terms of this agreement. If you do not agree to the terms of this agreement, promptly return the unopened software packet(s) and any accompanying written materials to the place you obtained them for a full refund.

MICROSOFT SOFTWARE LICENSE

1. GRANT OF LICENSE. Microsoft grants to you the right to use one copy of the Microsoft software program included with this book (the "SOFTWARE") on a single terminal connected to a single computer. The SOFTWARE is in "use" on a computer when it is loaded into the temporary memory (i.e., RAM) or installed into the permanent memory (e.g., hard disk, CD-ROM, or other storage device) of that computer. You may not network the SOFTWARE or otherwise use it on more than one computer or computer terminal at the same time.

2. COPYRIGHT. The SOFTWARE is owned by Microsoft or its suppliers and is protected by United States copyright laws and international treaty provisions. Therefore, you must treat the SOFTWARE like any other copyrighted material (e.g., a book or musical recording) except that you may either (a) make one copy of the SOFTWARE solely for backup or archival purposes, or (b) transfer the SOFTWARE to a single hard disk provided you keep the original solely for backup or archival purposes. You may not copy the written materials accompanying the SOFTWARE.

3. OTHER RESTRICTIONS. You may not rent or lease the SOFTWARE, but you may transfer the SOFTWARE and accompanying written materials on a permanent basis provided you retain no copies and the recipient agrees to the terms of this Agreement. You may not reverse engineer, decompile, or disassemble the SOFTWARE. If the SOFTWARE is an update or has been updated, any transfer must include the most recent update and all prior versions.

4. DUAL MEDIA SOFTWARE. If the SOFTWARE package contains both 3.5" and 5.25" disks, then you may use only the disks appropriate for your single-user computer. You may not use the other disks on another computer or loan, rent, lease, or transfer them to another user except as part of the permanent transfer (as provided above) of all SOFTWARE and written materials.

5. SAMPLE CODE. If the SOFTWARE includes Sample Code, then Microsoft grants you a royalty-free right to reproduce and distribute the sample code of the SOFTWARE provided that you: (a) distribute the sample code only in conjunction with and as a part of your software product; (b) do not use Microsoft's or its authors' names, logos, or trademarks to market your software product; (c) include the copyright notice that appears on the SOFTWARE on your product label and as a part of the sign-on message for your software product; and (d) agree to indemnify, hold harmless, and defend Microsoft and its authors from and against any claims or lawsuits, including attorneys' fees, that arise or result from the use or distribution of your software product.

DISCLAIMER OF WARRANTY

The SOFTWARE (including instructions for its use) is provided "AS IS" WITHOUT WARRANTY OF ANY KIND. MICROSOFT FURTHER DISCLAIMS ALL IMPLIED WARRANTIES INCLUDING WITHOUT LIMITATION ANY IMPLIED WARRANTIES OF MERCHANTABILITY OR OF FITNESS FOR A PARTICULAR PURPOSE. THE ENTIRE RISK ARISING OUT OF THE USE OR PERFORMANCE OF THE SOFTWARE AND DOCUMENTATION REMAINS WITH YOU.

IN NO EVENT SHALL MICROSOFT, ITS AUTHORS, OR ANYONE ELSE INVOLVED IN THE CREATION, PRODUCTION, OR DELIVERY OF THE SOFTWARE BE LIABLE FOR ANY DAMAGES WHATSOEVER (INCLUDING, WITHOUT LIMITATION, DAMAGES FOR LOSS OF BUSINESS PROFITS, BUSINESS INTERRUPTION, LOSS OF BUSINESS INFORMATION, OR OTHER PECUNIARY LOSS) ARISING OUT OF THE USE OF OR INABILITY TO USE THE SOFTWARE OR DOCUMENTATION, EVEN IF MICROSOFT HAS BEEN ADVISED OF THE POSSIBILITY OF SUCH DAMAGES. BECAUSE SOME STATES/COUNTRIES DO NOT ALLOW THE EXCLUSION OR LIMITATION OF LIABILITY FOR CONSEQUENTIAL OR INCIDENTAL DAMAGES, THE ABOVE LIMITATION MAY NOT APPLY TO YOU.

U.S. GOVERNMENT RESTRICTED RIGHTS

The SOFTWARE and documentation are provided with RESTRICTED RIGHTS. Use, duplication, or disclosure by the Government is subject to restrictions as set forth in subparagraph (c)(1)(ii) of The Rights in Technical Data and Computer Software clause at DFARS 252.227-7013 or subparagraphs (c)(1) and (2) of the Commercial Computer Software — Restricted Rights 48 CFR 52.227-19, as applicable. Manufacturer is Microsoft Corporation, One Microsoft Way, Redmond, WA 98052-6399.

If you acquired this product in the United States, this Agreement is governed by the laws of the State of Washington.

Should you have any questions concerning this Agreement, or if you desire to contact Microsoft Press for any reason, please write: Microsoft Press, One Microsoft Way, Redmond, WA 98052-6399.

097-000-680